NINETEENTH CENTURY EUROPE

EUROPE

Sources and Perspectives

from History

MICHAEL S. MELANCON
Auburn University

JOHN C. SWANSON
Utica College of Syracuse University

PEARSON
Longman

New York   San Francisco   Boston
London   Toronto   Sydney   Tokyo   Singapore   Madrid
Mexico City   Munich   Paris   Cape Town   Hong Kong   Montreal

Senior Acquisitions Editor: Janet Lanphier
Executive Marketing Manager: Sue Westmoreland
Project Coordination, Text Design, and Electronic Page Makeup: WestWords, Inc.
Senior Cover Design Manager: Nancy Danahy
Cover Designer: Nancy Sacks
Cover Illustration/Photo: Claude Monet, French, 1840–1926, *Arrival of the Normandy Train, Gare Saint-Lazare*, 1877, oil on canvas, 59.6 x 80.2 cm, Mr. and Mrs. Martin A. Ryerson Collection, 1933.1158, The Art Institute of Chicago. Photography © The Art Institute of Chicago.
Photo Researcher: Jody Potter
Senior Manufacturing Buyer: Alfred C. Dorsey
Printer and Binder: Courier Corporation
Cover Printer: Courier Corporation

For permission to use copyrighted material, grateful acknowledgment is made to the copyright holders on pp. 395–397, which are hereby made part of this copyright page.

Library of Congress Cataloging-in-Publication Data

Nineteenth century Europe : sources and perspectives from history / [edited by] Michael S. Melancon, John C. Swanson.
    p. cm.
  ISBN 0-321-17210-8
  1. Europe—History—1789-1900—Sources. 2. Europe—History—19th century—Sources. I. Melancon, Michael S., II. Swanson, John C. (John Charles)
D299.N57 2006
940.2'8—dc22

2006013735

Please visit us at www.ablongman.com

ISBN 0-321-17210-8

1 2 3 4 5 6 7 8 9 10—CRS—09 08 07 06

—CONTENTS—

—THEMATIC CONTENTS—

Individual-State Relations

Politics

Liberalism

Nationalism

Modernization

Industrialization & Technology

Scientific Change

Urbanization (Rural Life) and Education

Society and Culture

Gender

Class

Cultural Uncertainty

Europe: the Continent and the World

—PREFACE—
for Instructors and Interested Students

This reader provides students with direct images of European history from 1789 to 1914, that is, the so-called long nineteenth century that many commentators see as stretching from the French Revolution to World War I. In the selections, certain themes that reflect significant developments in Europe during the late eighteenth, nineteenth, and early twentieth centuries stand out quite sharply. These themes are of various type and importance. Some are overtly political, others bear on society, culture, or individual life. All of them helped shape European nations, the experiences of people living in them, and, indirectly, the ways of life of much of the global population.

Individual-State Relations

Perhaps the single most important underlying theme in these selections is the relationship between the individual and the state. Throughout the period covered by this text and beyond, this relationship remained in dynamic flux. In earlier eras, the individual occupied a quite passive position in state and society, with the exception, of course, of great leaders. During the late eighteenth and nineteenth centuries, a series of developments—broader political participation, the rise of the nation-state, the expansion of mass education, a shift from rural to urban life, and technological transformations—sharply altered the relationship between individuals and the societies and states they inhabited. As democratic constitutional government with legally protected rights became more common, individuals asserted themselves more clearly, while at the same time state and society, which in some ways gained in power and uniformity, yielded somewhat in their direct control over people's lives. A principal question remains: What is the proper role of the state and society in human life? The selections from this reader and the sequel that covers the following century remind us of a range of possibilities. Presumably, there is no final answer.

Politics: Liberalism, Nationalism, and Modernization

Liberalism, nationalism, and modernization are a second set of themes in these selections. If the individual's relationship to the state and society was an "underlying" theme of Europe's history during the nineteenth century, liberalism, nationalism, and modernization were the "overlying" themes, that is, the ones that dominated people's concerns and actions in an overt fashion.

- The reader's principal political theme is an uneven, often interrupted but definite progress of constitutional democracy. The political movement that underlies constitutional democracy and its corollary, representative government, is known as *classical liberalism*. Especially after 1848, liberal government in its pure republican form or as constitutional monarchy gradually became the norm in Europe.
- At the same time, *nationalism* provided a kind of subtext for much of Europe's post–1789 political history. Unfortunately, the early gentle vision of national equality and self-determination gave way by the end of the nineteenth century to a rampant chauvinism that led directly to imperialism and the first all-European war, as well as to many subsequent problems.

■ *Modernization* signifies the more or less unceasing industrialization, urbanization, education, and technological transformation that occurred throughout Europe between 1789 to 1900. Technological development created new modes of production, transportation, and communication. The growth of cities, at a time of overall demographic expansion, altered the balance between city and countryside. New scientific outlooks on the origins of life and on human psychology also profoundly changed how people thought about life itself. The end result was a different way of life in a different environment for millions of Europe's inhabitants.

Taken together liberalism, nationalism, and modernization constituted the primary spheres of political action and ideology during the nineteenth century. In fact, they continue to do so today.

Society and Culture: Gender, Class, Cultural Uncertainty, and Violence

Along with the principal historical themes mentioned above, several subthemes of great significance thread their way through the various sections. Among these are the women's question, class conflict, and the breakdown of traditional values or, to put the matter another way, cultural uncertainty. This last became associated with a certain tendency to solve problems by one or another form of overt violence.

■ The question of *women's status* arises in the first chapter with Olympe de Gouges's complaint about the French Revolution's lack of recognition of women's rights and reappears in various guises throughout much of the reader. Selections from Tolstoy's *Anna Karenina* and Ibsen's *A Doll's House* portray the stark limitations placed upon even upper- and middle-class women, whereas the writings of Tristan, Gaskell, and others in this reader portray the far worse plight of women from humble backgrounds. Only during the twentieth century did women eventually win the right to have property, to vote, and to work under roughly equal conditions as men.

■ Class issues rose to special prominence during and after the French Revolution. The initial struggle between nobilities and middle classes soon gave way to tension between working classes and the wealthy middle class. The perception by educated people of the *class conflict* between the proletariat and the bourgeoisie lay at the basis of the socialist movement. By the 1820s and 1830s, socialists had already leveled a strong critique of classical liberalism before liberalism had become fully entrenched on the European scene. By mid-century, the Marxist version of socialism raised class struggle to the status of the principal moving element in history and predicted a universal victory for workers.

■ Political, social, and economic changes inevitably found their reflection in a merciless reexamination of European ideological, cultural, and religious beliefs. This scrutiny did not so much lead to new values as to a questioning of and a falling away of belief in the old ones. Many of the problems of the late nineteenth and early twentieth centuries reflected *cultural uncertainty* and even despair.

■ A tragic consequence of this spiritual malaise was a rise in what one might call routinized violence as a mode of achieving various goals. One aspect of this development concerned the means used by an array of European powers to conquer global empires. These same nations then turned the identical destructive military technologies against one another when World War I broke out. Long before the world war, however, terrorist assassinations and bombings had made their debut on the European scene, bringing the nineteenth century to a close on a note of *political violence* that continued unabated as the new century opened.

Europe: the Continent and the World

Another significant subtheme that requires separate discussion concerns relations among European nations and European relations with the outside world. Regarding European inter-relations, the French Revolution introduced a quarter of a century of wars and strife among European nations, after which European leaders and populations, exhausted by seemingly endless turmoil, strove to create the conditions for a lasting peace. The relative success of their efforts is suggested by the fact that from the time of the 1814–1815 Vienna Congress, no major or lengthy wars threatened overall peace on the continent. Toward the end of the nineteenth century the Vienna arrangements were clearly floundering on the shoals of extreme nationalism, arms buildups, and the race for global empires. Regarding Europe's relations with the rest of the world, global European commercial networks and technological advances signified a kind of European international hegemony. After 1880, this culminated in the division of much of the world into European empires. Although European wars of the first half of the twentieth century weakened Europe's influence and relative strength in the rest of the world, as of 1900 nothing seemed to challenge European global hegemony.

—PREFACE—
for Students and Interested Instructors

The Reader's Approach to Historical Understanding

The reader utilizes five types of selections: the writings of influential historical actors and theorists (Napoleon, de Staël, Marx, Nightingale, Darwin, Freud, and Nietzsche); important historical documents (declarations, constitutions, and treaties); memoirs of persons who witnessed great historical events (St. John and Leighton); important visual images (situated at the beginning of each section); and excerpts from fiction (novels, poetry, or plays of Eliot, Hardy, Balzac, and Ibsen) selected to illustrate important events or developments. Through these prisms, each revealing in a special way, students both comprehend and experience the past.

- ■ The value of the first four—writings of great historical figures, important documents, memoirs, and images—are clear enough. They are what practicing historians call the *primary sources* of history. They testify directly to what happened, although, students should be aware, primary sources reflect subjectivity and are open to interpretation. Regardless, they form a major part of the historical record, subject to collection, analysis, and evaluation, used by historians to characterize the historical past. They represent a *first* kind of historical memory.
- ■ The value of *fiction*—the final of our four types of selections—for understanding real past events is of a different and less obvious nature. The fiction carefully chosen here is itself a form of memoir. The fictional excerpts come from works of authors who themselves witnessed the things they wrote about (Hugo's vivid portrayal of the French Revolution is the exception that proves the rule). These pieces add a new perspective to regular memoirs in that they reflect the efforts of talented writers who not only knew firsthand the eras they described but who, by nature of their special literary talents, captured intuitively how historical events influence the lives of living, albeit fictional, human beings. The authors of fiction employ made up characters and situations to illustrate real life experience at the human level. In these cases, they do so against the backdrop of vast historical events such as wars, revolutions, or profound social, economic and technological transformations. One might characterize these fictional writings as a *second* kind of historical memory.

The reader's compilers believe that all these selections will deeply enhance students' awareness of the historical events recounted and analyzed in course lectures and textbooks.

- ■ The lectures and texts are the foundations of the course.
- ■ The readings and images illustrate thoughts, motivations, memory, and emotions or, put another way, the structures erected upon the foundations.

Taken all together, these various sources of historical knowledge and understanding create for students an historical recollection as rich in emotional and intellectual content as in facts and structure. The student will take away from the course a permanent, usable sense of the past, a *third* kind of historical memory. The readings, chosen for their centrality or insightfulness rather than for ease, will provide special rewards for the engaged and interested student.

Most of the persons whose writings (and images) comprise this reader are very well known. Students should turn to their history texts for further data about them. The section introductions contain historical sketches and biographical data for each author of contributions to the section. Additional sketches accompany each individual selection and image, which will further aid in orienting students. In some cases lecturers may wish to offer supplemental biographical information. At appropriate places in the reader, the editors have provided orientation sketches for fiction pieces and bibliographical data and original publication dates for each selection utilized.

How to Read and Understand Texts as Sources

Students using this reader face a rewarding and challenging experience. The reward comes from careful reading and active class discussion. Students who become familiar with these texts will be better informed about the world we live in. A first challenge arises from the inherent difficulty of some of the texts, all of which are present in the reader not because of their simplicity but because of their significance and centrality. A second challenge reflects the reality that, as noted above, users will find several types of sources in the various sections. What should students make of these various types of sources? A handy guide for approaching each text, whatever its nature, are the basic questions *who, what, where, when,* and *why?* Who wrote the document? What is the nature of the document? Where and under what circumstances was it written? When was it written? Perhaps most importantly, why and for whom was it written? In other words, students should actively search for evidence about each selection's *perspective,* that is, its point of view. Clues for answering these questions can be found in class lectures, the course textbook, in material accompanying the texts in this reader, and in the texts themselves. This kind of approach is called critical reading. Students who take pains to read these texts critically, in part by answering the questions noted above, will already know much of what they need to know about the readings.

What about differences among the types of sources? As noted above, *primary sources* testify directly to historical events and constitute a first type of historical memory. Of the various types of primary sources, a reader can approach *documents* such as treaties, declarations, and constitutions with a sense that the texts mean what they say in the most direct fashion. Matters such as dating, circumstances, and authorship are easily addressed. Even so, questions about the motivations of the persons drafting the documents need to be answered. The consequences, intended and unintended, of the documents as they are deployed in real life also remain open for discussion. These are rewarding areas for persons who wish to increase their understanding of the past.

The *theoretical or programmatic writings* of great historical figures—Mill, Tristan, Marx, Darwin, and Freud—also offer much in terms of understanding of the past but require a greater degree of caution than documents. On the one hand, these writings, like documents, have real historical status since they reflect the thinking of persons directly involved in making or influencing history. On the other, these authors also advocate causes, both good and bad. Persons who later consult such writings need to supply objectivity where it may have been lacking. As was the case in respect to documents, the consequences of the writings of great figures can be a revealing area of investigation and thought. Some of these writings, students should note, are consulted now only to help understand the past, whereas others continue to influence people and make history even today. Students might ask themselves which is the case for each such selection and why that is the case.

Memoirs (and diaries) of persons who experienced historical events require the greatest caution of all. Memories of events, even for eye witnesses, change over time. Readers also have to measure the memoirists' objectivity. Does the memoirist have an axe to grind or not? If so, is this obvious or is it hidden? Recollections of events, however, usually do not occupy the same status as documents and theoretical and programmatic writings in that memoirs do not make history and normally have few direct consequences, except in the realm of influencing how past historical events are portrayed. None of this negates the value of memoirs as real sources. They offer much in terms of directness that secondary sources (histories written later on the basis of primary sources) can never approach.

Fiction, a second and altogether different type of historical memory, raises other questions entirely. The fiction pieces do not represent historical fact, nor do they have the goal of recreating history in any direct sense. The very name fiction suggests the imaginary nature of the author's goals. Regardless, the fiction selections chosen for this reader, whether novels or poetry, do reflect real experience in the sense that the persons writing the fiction actually experienced the events under discussion. Whether or not the authors attempted to make their writings historically accurate in the factual sense is beside the point for this collection (for the users' information no selections that seriously distort the past appear here). The point is that for us their value is in their psychological and emotional rather than factual truth. In this sense, they are similar to memoirs, with this great exception—memoirists usually strive to maintain factual and psychological truth, whereas fiction writers strive mainly for the latter. The fiction rounds out but never contributes directly to the data and analysis obtained from the historical primary sources. Although students can and should pose some of the same questions about fiction as about non-fiction, in the case of fiction they need not be so concerned about answers that pertain to facts.

As students grapple with the readings offered in this collection, they can further enrich their experience by actively seeking out the historical themes represented by the various selections. A guide to the principal themes can be found in this preface, in the introductions to each section, and in the introductions to each piece. Lectures and textbooks also aid in this task. On reading each selection, students should pose themselves the questions noted above (why? when? and so forth) and at the same time pose several other basic questions: What is this selection about? Why is it present in this reader? Which historical theme or themes does it shed light upon? The lists of questions that accompany each section will help launch this investigation by leading students to the principal themes and discussion points raised by the sections and specific readings. The thematic table of contents that follows the book's table of contents will also be of help in identifying themes raised by specific readings. The ultimate result of utilizing these tools will be a deep understanding of the historical events under discussion. A final word of advice: never read these texts simply to obtain facts. Always consider authors' outlooks and motivations, essential elements in critical reading and understanding.

Understanding Visual Images as Historical Sources

As historical sources, *visual images* differ somewhat from written texts. The images presented here are primary sources in that they represent actual persons, events, or situations. Even the paintings and prints are primary sources since the artists, direct contemporaries of the subjects portrayed, intended to record actual situations or events, albeit in ways that deepen our understanding. As with written texts, some viewers may not agree with or appreciate the composers' interpretations. The visual images are also texts, although not ones expressed in words. As with a written text, all types of visual images have authors, subject matter, and composition. Texts, written or visual, similarly create impressions and thoughts in our minds. Consequently, we must question the visual text just as we do the written one: who, what, when, where, and why. Photos present a new problem: photographers are usually anonymous. Appropriate questions concern why the photographer happened to be on the spot or chose to go there, what is and is not included in the image, what does it emphasize and deemphasize, what mood does it portray, is it intended as a critique or to promote something or merely to record. Paintings, especially by famous artists, are easier to decipher in the sense that we know or can find out the artist's characteristics and views. A picture may be worth a thousand words but a picture, like writing, can deceive or simply influence viewers one way or another. Interpreting visual images requires at least as much care as written texts, although potential rewards are great.

Acknowledgments

We would like to thank several individuals for useful suggestions about readings. We are grateful to Professor Louise Katainen of Auburn University for bringing to our attention Grazia Deledda's *Reeds in the Wind* and to Professor Stephan Gerson of New York University for suggesting Emile Zola's *The Ladies' Paradise*. A great debt is also owed to our students, who shared with us their opinions about the reader and its selections, as did, most generously and effectively, the editors at Longman and the numerous readers consulted from the European history field.

—PART ONE—

Print of the Storming of the Bastille

In France, the Storming of the Bastille, ancient prison of the French monarchy, has become the symbol of the French Republic. Its yearly anniversary is the equivalent of the United States's 4th of July. In this image, the grim stone towers loom threateningly over the streets filled with the people of Paris who attack the fortress's armed guards. Less clear from this image is the actual lack of a significant defense of the Bastille and its virtual emptiness of political prisoners in an era when the French monarchy was much less bloody-minded than in the past.

The French Revolution

A watershed in European history, the French Revolution (1789–1815) demarcated the old regime from the modern period. For the first time, Enlightenment ideals underlay a European society. Politics, economics, and even culture came to reflect the desires of the people, no longer subjects of the monarch but citizens of the state. Yet, when hostile powers attacked France in 1792, the revolution spun out of control and, under the Jacobins, became a reign of terror. In 1794 moderates imposed order by arresting and guillotining the Jacobins and creating the Directory, a dull dictatorship. In 1799 the military hero Napoleon Bonaparte overthrew the Directory and took the title First Consul. In 1804 he named himself Emperor of France, although he still saw himself as the "son" of the revolution. Napoleon's limitless ambition dealt a heavy blow to the revolution's legacy and his wars of conquest helped give rise to modern nationalism when other peoples responded to the French threat.

As one of its first acts in August 1789, the month after the storming of the Bastille so graphically portrayed in the print, the new Assembly of France promulgated the "Declaration of the Rights of Man and Citizen." The document's Enlightenment language ringingly proclaimed equal rights for all men. Although the Declaration later served as the foundation of many liberationist movements, the authors had excluded women. Seeking to right this omission, Olympe de Gouges (1745–1793), wrote the "Declaration of the Rights of Woman" in 1791 and addressed it to the queen. In a 1794 speech to the Convention, the Jacobin leader Maximilien Robespierre (1758–1794) explained that in order to achieve liberty the democratic "republic of virtue" must employ terror against enemies and entrenched custom.

Domestic turmoil plagued France throughout the revolutionary era. In his novel *Ninety-Three* (1881), Victor Hugo (1802–1885), born after the revolution, brought to life the revolutionary conflict between aristocrats and Republican forces. As the revolution deepened, Louis XVI joined a chorus of conservative voices to warn in his 1791 Declaration that it could bring no benefit to the nation or, by inference, to the world. Others had different views. In his letters, collected in *The Mind of Napoleon*, Bonaparte (1768–1821) argued that he was true heir to the revolution. His actions, he insisted, had carried to the rest of Europe the ideals of "liberty, equality, and fraternity."

Study Questions

1. Why did Olympe de Gouges write the "Declaration of the Rights of Woman"?
2. How did Louis XVI, Robespierre, and Napoleon differ in their views of the French Revolution?
3. Did Louis XVI's criticisms of democracy have any validity?
4. Why did Napoleon consider himself to be the son of the French Revolution?
5. What role does class play in the conflicts described by Victor Hugo?
6. Image: How does this image of the Storming of the Bastille foreshadow later events of the French Revolution?

Declaration of the Rights of Man and Citizen

When members of the third estate, people of the educated middle class, refused to be dismissed by the king and instead insisted on launching France in the direction of parliamentary rule, they needed a document that summarized their goals. Leaders of the American Revolution had similarly written the famous Declaration of Independence, which to a certain degree served as a model for the French document. The French Assembly's Declaration outlined basic human rights (freedom of speech, association, and so forth) and, by adding Citizens, emphasized that the government in France would be participatory. They hoped, in vain as it turned out, that the political development of France would follow the outline they had provided.

The representatives of the French people, organized in National Assembly, considering that ignorance, forgetfulness, or contempt of the rights of man are the sole causes of public misfortunes and of the corruption of governments, have resolved to set forth in a solemn declaration the natural, inalienable, and sacred rights of man, in order that such declaration, continually before all members of the social body, may be a perpetual reminder of their rights and duties; in order that the acts of the legislative power and those of the executive power may constantly be compared with the aim of every political institution and may accordingly be more respected; in order that the demands of the citizens, founded henceforth upon simple and incontestable principles, may always be directed towards the maintenance of the Constitution and the welfare of all.

Accordingly, the National Assembly recognizes and proclaims, in the presence and under the auspices of the Supreme Being, the following rights of man and citizen.

1. Men are born and remain free and equal in rights; social distinctions may be based only upon general usefulness.

2. The aim of every political association is the preservation of the natural and inalienable rights of man; these rights are liberty, property, security, and resistance to oppression.

3. The source of all sovereignty resides essentially in the nation; no group, no individual may exercise authority not emanating expressly therefrom.

4. Liberty consists of the power to do whatever is not injurious to others; thus the enjoyment of the natural rights of every man has for its limits only those that assure other members of society the enjoyment of those same rights; such limits may be determined only by law.

5. The law has the right to forbid only actions which are injurious to society. Whatever is not forbidden by law may not be prevented, and no one may be constrained to do what it does not prescribe.

6. Law is the expression of the general will; all citizens have the right to concur personally, or through their representatives, in its formation; it must be the same for all, whether it protects or punishes. All citizens, being equal before it, are equally admissible to all public offices, positions, and employments, according to their capacity, and without other distinction than that of virtues and talents.

7. No man may be accused, arrested, or detained except in the cases determined by law, and according to the forms prescribed thereby. Whoever solicit, expedite, or execute arbitrary orders, or have them executed, must be punished; but every citizen summoned or apprehended in pursuance of the law

From: *A Documentary Survey of the French Revolution*, ed. John Hall Stewart (New York: Macmillan Company, 1951), pp. 113–115.

must obey immediately; he renders himself culpable by resistance.

8. The law is to establish only penalties that are absolutely and obviously necessary; and no one may be punished except by virtue of a law established and promulgated prior to the offence and legally applied.

9. Since every man is presumed innocent until declared guilty, if arrest be deemed indispensable, all unnecessary severity for securing the person of the accused must be severely repressed by law.

10. No one is to be disquieted because of his opinions, even religious, provided their manifestation does not disturb the public order established by law.

11. Free communication of ideas and opinions is one of the most precious of the rights of man. Consequently, every citizen may speak, write, and print freely, subject to responsibility for the abuse of such liberty in the cases determined by law.

12. The guarantee of the rights of man and citizen necessitates a public force; such a force, therefore, is instituted for the advantage of all and not for the particular benefit of those to whom it is entrusted.

13. For the maintenance of the public force and for the expenses of administration a common tax is indispensable; it must be assessed equally on all citizens in proportion to their means.

14. Citizens have the right to ascertain, by themselves or through their representatives, the necessity of the public tax, to consent to it freely, to supervise its use, and to determine its quota, assessment, payment, and duration.

15. Society has the right to require of every public agent an accounting of his administration.

16. Every society in which the guarantee of rights is not assured or the separation of powers not determined has no constitution at all.

17. Since property is a sacred and inviolable right, no one may be deprived thereof unless a legally established public necessity obviously requires it, and upon condition of a just and previous indemnity.

Declaration of the Rights of Woman
Olympe de Gouges

The French Assembly, consisting entirely of males, many with legal training, had used accustomed male-oriented language. Olympe de Gouges, an outspoken young woman of humble birth who had married an older man of some wealth, resented the exclusion of women from the formulations of equality and citizenship. Her Declaration, which condemned the oppression of women, eventually became one of the cornerstones of the feminist movement. During the radical phase of the French Revolution, however, her opposition to violence and to the guillotining of the royal couple transformed her into a suspect figure and she herself suffered execution by the guillotine. Possibly, even the radical revolutionaries did not want to deal with her advocacy of the women's cause.

To be decreed by the National Assembly in its last sessions or by the next legislature.

Preamble

Mothers, daughters, sisters, female representatives of the nation ask to be constituted as a national assembly. Considering that ignorance, neglect, or contempt for the rights of woman are the sole causes of public misfortunes and governmental corruption, they have resolved to set forth in a solemn declaration the natural, inalienable, and sacred rights of woman: so that by being constantly present to all the members of the social body this declaration may always remind them of their rights and duties; so that by being liable at every moment to comparison with the aim of any and all political institutions the acts of women's and men's powers may be the more fully respected; and so that by being founded henceforward on simple and incontestable principles the demands of the citizenesses may always tend toward maintaining the constitution, good morals, and the general welfare.

In consequence, the sex that is superior in beauty as in courage, needed in maternal sufferings, recog-

From: *The French Revolution and Human Rights: A Brief Documentary History*, ed. Lynn Hunt (New York: Bedford Books, 1996), pp. 124–129.

nizes and declares, in the presence and under the auspices of the Supreme Being, the following rights of woman and the citizeness.

1. Woman is born free and remains equal to man in rights. Social distinctions may be based only on common utility.

2. The purpose of all political association is the preservation of the natural and imprescriptible rights of woman and man. These rights are liberty, property, security, and especially resistance to oppression.

3. The principle of all sovereignty rests essentially in the nation, which is but the reuniting of woman and man. No body and no individual may exercise authority which does not emanate expressly from the nation.

4. Liberty and justice consist in restoring all that belongs to another; hence the exercise of the natural rights of woman has no other limits than those that the perpetual tyranny of man opposes to them; these limits must be reformed according to the laws of nature and reason.

5. The laws of nature and reason prohibit all actions which are injurious to society. No hindrance should be put in the way of anything not prohibited by these wise and divine laws, nor may anyone be forced to do what they do not require.

6. The law should be the expression of the general will. All citizenesses and citizens should take part, in

person or by their representatives, in its formation. It must be the same for everyone. All citizenesses and citizers, being equal in its eyes, should be equally admissible to all public dignities, offices, and employments, according to their ability, and with no other distinction than that of their virtues and talents.

7. No woman is exempted; she is indicted, arrested, and detained in the cases determined by the law. Women like men obey this rigorous law.

8. Only strictly and obviously necessary punishments should be established by the law, and no one may be punished except by virtue of a law established and promulgated before the time of the offense, and legally applied to women.

9. Any woman being declared guilty, all rigor is exercised by the law.

10. No one should be disturbed for his fundamental opinions; woman has the right to mount the scaffold, so she should have the right equally to mount the tribune, provided that these manifestations do not trouble public order as established by law.

11. The free communication of thoughts and opinions is one of the most precious of the rights of woman, since this liberty assures the recognition of children by their fathers. Every citizeness may therefore say freely, I am the mother of your child; a barbarous prejudice [against unmarried women having children] should not force her to hide the truth, so long as responsibility is accepted for any abuse of this liberty in cases determined by the law [women are not allowed to lie about the paternity of their children].

12. The safeguard of the rights of woman and citizeness requires public powers. These powers are instituted for the advantage of all and not for the private benefit of those to whom they are entrusted.

13. For maintenance of public authority and for expenses of administration, taxation of women and men is equal; she takes part in all forced labor service, in all painful tasks; she must therefore have the same proportion in the distribution of places, employments, offices, dignities, and in industry.

14. The citizenesses and citizens have the right, by themselves or through their representatives, to have demonstrated to them the necessity of public taxes. The citizenesses can only agree to them upon admission of an equal division, not only in wealth,

but also in the public administration, and to determine the means of apportionment, assessment, and collection, and the duration of the taxes.

15. The mass of women, joining with men in paying taxes, have the right to hold accountable every public agent of the administration.

16. Any society in which the guarantee of rights is not assured or the separation of powers not settled has no constitution. The constitution is null and void if the majority of individuals composing the nation has not cooperated in its drafting.

17. Property belongs to both sexes whether united or separated; it is for each of them an inviolable and sacred right, and no one may be deprived of it as a true patrimony of nature, except when public necessity, certified by law, obviously requires it, and then on condition of a just compensation in advance.

Postscript

Women, wake up; the tocsin of reason sounds throughout the universe; recognize your rights. The powerful empire of nature is no longer surrounded by prejudice, fanaticism, superstition, and lies. The torch of truth has dispersed all the clouds of folly and usurpation. Enslaved man has multiplied his force and needs yours to break his chains. Having become free, he has become unjust toward his companion. Oh women! Women, when will you cease to be blind? What advantages have you gathered in the revolution? A scorn more marked, a disdain more conspicuous. During the centuries of corruption you only reigned over the weakness of men. Your empire is destroyed; what is left to you then? Firm belief in the injustices of men. The reclaiming of your patrimony founded on the wise decrees of nature; why should you fear such a beautiful enterprise? . . . Whatever the barriers set up against you, it is in your power to overcome them; you only have to want it. Let us pass now to the appalling account of what you have been in society; and since national education is an issue at this moment, let us see if our wise legislators will think sanely about the education of women.

Women have done more harm than good. Constraint and dissimulation have been their lot. What force has taken from them, ruse returned to them; they have had recourse to all the resources of their charms, and the most irreproachable man has not resisted them. Poison, the sword, women controlled everything; they ordered up crimes as much as virtues. For centuries, the French government, especially, depended on the nocturnal administration of women; officials kept no secrets from their indiscretion; ambassadorial posts, military commands, the ministry, the presidency [of a court], the papacy, the college of cardinals, in short everything that characterizes the folly of men, profane and sacred, has been submitted to the cupidity and ambition of this sex formerly considered despicable and respected, and since the revolution, respectable and despised. . . .

Under the former regime, everyone was vicious, everyone guilty. . . . A woman only had to be beautiful and amiable; when she possessed these two advantages, she saw a hundred fortunes at her feet. . . . The most indecent woman could make herself respectable with gold; the commerce in women was a kind of industry amongst the highest classes, which henceforth will enjoy no more credit. If it still did, the revolution would be lost, and in the new situation we would still be corrupted. Can reason hide the fact that every other road to fortune is closed to a woman bought by a man, bought like a slave from the coasts of Africa? The difference between them is great; this is known. The slave [that is, the woman] commands her master, but if the master gives her her freedom without compensation and at an age when the slave has lost all her charms, what does this unfortunate woman become? The plaything of disdain; even the doors of charity are closed to her; she is poor and old, they say: why did she not know how to make her fortune?

Other examples even more touching can be provided to reason. A young woman without experience, seduced by the man she loves, abandons her parents to follow him; the ingrate leaves her after a few years and the older she will have grown with him, the more his inconstancy will be inhuman. If she has children, he will still abandon her. If he is rich, he will believe himself excused from sharing his fortune with his noble victims. If some

engagement ties him to his duties, he will violate it while counting on support from the law. If he is married, every other obligation loses its force. What laws then remain to be passed that would eradicate vice down to its roots? That of equally dividing [family] fortunes between men and women and of public administration of their goods. It is easy to imagine that a woman born of a rich family would gain much from the equal division of property [between children]. But what about the woman born in a poor family with merit and virtues; what is her lot? Poverty and opprobrium. If she does not excel in music or painting, she cannot be admitted to any public function, even if she is fully qualified. . . .

Marriage is the tomb of confidence and love. A married woman can give bastards to her husband with impunity, and even the family fortune which does not belong to them. An unmarried woman has only a feeble right: ancient and inhuman laws refuse her the right to the name and goods of her children's father; no new laws have been made in this matter. If giving my sex an honorable and just consistency is considered to be at this time paradoxical on my part and an attempt at the impossible, I leave to future men the glory of dealing with this matter; but while waiting, we can prepare the way with national education, with the restoration of morals and with conjugal agreements.

Form for a Social Contract between Man and Woman

We, _____ and _____, moved by our own will, unite for the length of our lives and for the duration of our mutual inclinations under the following conditions: We intend and wish to make our wealth communal property, while reserving the right to divide it in favor of our children and of those for whom we might have a special inclination, mutually recognizing that our goods belong directly to our children, from whatever bed they come [ligitimate or not], and that all of them without distinction have the right to bear the name of the fathers and mothers who have acknowledged them, and we impose on ourselves the obligation of subscribing to the law that punishes any rejection of one's own blood [refusing to acknowledge an illegitimate child]. We likewise obligate ourselves, in the case of a separation, to divide our fortune equally and to set aside the portion the law designates for our children. In the case of a perfect union, the one who dies first will give up half his property in favor of the children; and if there are no children, the survivor will inherit by right, unless the dying person has disposed of his half of the common property in favor of someone he judges appropriate. [She then goes on to defend her contract against the inevitable objections of "hypocrites, prudes, the clergy, and all the hellish gang."]

The King's Declaration
Louis XVI

Although it did not staunch the revolutionary tide running so strong in his country, the King's Declaration outlined some of the problems he and other defenders of the old order saw if traditional hierarchical structures and established institutions were replaced by democratic ones. His dark vision seems to have been fulfilled as the original revolution in France became increasingly radical and eventually lapsed into violence.

As long as the King could hope to see order and the welfare of the kingdom regenerated by the means employed by the National Assembly, and by his residence near that assembly in the capital of the kingdom, no sacrifice mattered to him; ... but today, when his sole recompense for so many sacrifices consists of seeing the monarchy destroyed, all powers disregarded, property violated, personal security everywhere endangered, crimes unpunished, and total anarchy taking the place of law, while the semblance of authority provided by the new Constitution is insufficient to repair a single one of the ills afflicting the kingdom, the King, having solemnly protested against all the acts issued during his captivity, deems it his duty to place before Frenchmen and the entire universe the picture of his conduct and that of the government which has established itself in the kingdom. ...

But the more sacrifices the King made for the welfare of his people, the more the rebels labored to disparage the value thereof, and to present the monarchy under the most false and odious colors.

The convocation of the Estates General, the doubling of the deputies of the third estate, the King's efforts to eliminate all difficulties which might delay the meeting of the Estates General and those which arose after its opening, all the retrenchments which the King made in his personal expenses, all the sacrifices which he made for his people in the session of 23 June, finally, the union of the orders, effected by

From: *A Documentary Survey of the French Revolution,* ed. John Hall Stewart (New York: Macmillan Company, 1951), pp. 205–210.

the King's wish, a measure which His Majesty then deemed indispensable for the functioning of the Estates General, all his anxiety, all his efforts, all his generosity, all his devotion to his people—all have been misjudged, all have been misrepresented.

The time when the Estate General, assuming the name of National Assembly, began to occupy itself with the constitution of the kingdom, calls to mind the memoirs which the rebels were cunning enough to have sent from several provinces, and the movements of Paris to have the deputies disregard one of the principal clauses contained in their *cahiers,* namely that providing that *the making of the laws should be done in concert with the King.* In defiance of that clause, the assembly placed the King entirely outside the constitution by refusing him the right to grant or to withhold his sanction to articles which it regarded as constitutional, reserving to itself the right to include in that category those which it deemed suitable; and for those regarded as purely legislative, reducing the royal prerogative to a right of suspension until the third legislature, a purely illusory right as so many examples prove only too well.

What remains to the King other than a vain semblance of monarchy? ...

Let us, then, examine the several branches of the government.

Justice. The King has no share in making the laws; he has only the right to obstruct, until the third legislature, matters which are not regarded as constitutional, and to request the National Assembly to apply itself to such and such matters, without possessing the right to make a formal proposal thereon. Justice is rendered in the name of the King . . . ; but it is only a matter of form . . . One of the most recent decrees of the Assembly deprived the King of one of the finest prerogatives everywhere associated with monarchy, that of pardoning and commuting penalties. . . . Morever, this provision lessens royal majesty in the eyes of the people, so long accustomed to having recourse to the King in their needs and difficulties, and to seeing in him the common father who can relieve their afflictions!

Internal Administration. There is entirely too much authority in the hands of the departments, districts, and municipalities, which impede the working of the machine, and may often thwart one another. All these bodies are elected by the people, and are not under the jurisdiction of the government, according to law, except for the execution of decrees or for those special orders which are the consequence thereof. . . . Moreover, these bodies have acquired little influence and esteem. The Societies of the Friends of the Constitution . . . are often more powerful, and, consequently, the action of the government is of no effect. . . .

According to decrees, the disposition of military forces is in the hands of the King. He has been declared the supreme head of the army and navy; but all the work of constituting these two forces has been done by committees of the assembly without the participation of the King; everything, even the slightest regulation of discipline, has been effected by them; . . . What becomes of an army when it no longer has leaders or discipline? Instead of being the power and safeguard of a state, it becomes the terror and scourge thereof. . . .

Foreign Affairs. Appointment to ministerial posts at foreign courts and the conduct of negotiations have been reserved to the King; but the King's liberty in such appointments is as void as for those of officers in the army; . . . The revision and confirmation of treaties, which is reserved to the National Assembly, and the nomination of a diplomatic committee absolutely nullify the second provision. . . .

Finances. The King declared, even before the convocation of the Estates General, that he recognized the right of the assemblies of the nation to grant subsidies, and that he no longer wished to tax the people without their consent. All the *cahiers* of the deputies to the Estates General were agreed in placing the re-establishment of the finances foremost among matters to be dealt with by that assembly; some imposed restrictions in favor of articles to be given priority. The King eliminated the difficulties which such restrictions might have occasioned, by taking the matter in his own hands and granting, in the session of 23 June, everything that was desired. On 4 February, 1790, the King urged the assembly to take effective action on such an important matter; it has done so only recently . . . There is still no exact statement of receipts and expenditures . . . The ordinary taxes are at present greatly in arrears, and the extraordinary expedient of the first one billion, two hundred millions in *assignats* is almost exhausted. . . . The regulation of funds, the collection of taxes, the assessment among the departments, the rewards for services rendered, all have been removed from the King's supervision. . . .

Finally, decrees have pronounced the King supreme head of administration of the kingdom; other subsequent enactments have regulated the organization of the ministry so that the King . . . may change nothing therein without new decisions of the assembly. . . .

This form of government, so vicious in itself, is becoming still more so for several reasons. 1st, The assembly, through its committees, constantly exceeds the limits it has prescribed for itself; it devotes itself to matters dealing only with the internal administration of the kingdom and with that of justice, and thus it acquires all authority; through its Committee on Investigations it even exercises a veritable despotism, more barbarous and insufferable than any ever known to history. 2nd, There exist in almost all the cities, and even in some towns and villages, of the kingdom associations known under the name of Friends of the Constitution. Contrary to the tenor of the law, they do not tolerate any others not affiliated with them; they constitute an immense corporation, more dangerous than any that formerly existed. Without being authorized thereto, and even in defiance of all decrees, they deliberate upon all questions of government, correspond among themselves upon all matters, make and receive declarations, post decrees, and have acquired such a preponderance that all the administrative and judicial bodies, not even excepting the National Assembly itself, usually obey their orders.

The King does not think it possible to govern a kingdom of such great extent and importance as France through the means established by the National Assembly, as they exist at present. His Majesty, in granting to all decrees, without distinction, a sanction which he well knew could not be refused, was influenced by a desire to avoid all discussion, which experience has shown to be useless to say the least; he feared, moreover, that he would be suspected of wishing to retard or to bring about the failure of the efforts of the National Assembly, in the success of which the nation took so great an interest; he placed his confidence in the wise men of that assembly ...

But the closer the Assembly draws to the end of its labors, the more we see the wise men losing their influence, the more we see measures which only render difficult or even impossible the carrying on of government, and daily engender increasing mistrust and disfavor toward it. Other regulations, instead of applying healing balm to the wounds which still bleed in several provinces, only aggravate the discontent and embitter the malcontents. The spirit of the clubs dominates and pervades everything; thousands of calumniating and incendiary newspapers and pamphlets, distributed daily, are simply their echoes, and prepare men to think as they wish them to. The National Assembly has never dared remedy that licence, so far removed from true liberty; it has lost its influence and even the force which it would need to retrace its steps and to change whatever it would seem desirable to correct. We judge from the spirit which prevails in the clubs, and from the manner in which they make themselves masters of the new primary assemblies, what is to be expected from them; and if they show any inclination to revise anything, it is in order to destroy the remainder of the monarchy and to establish a metaphysical and philosophical government which would be impossible to operate.

Frenchmen, is that why you sent your representatives to the National Assembly? Would you want the anarchy and despotism of the clubs to supplant the monarchical government under which the nation has prospered for fourteen hundred years? Would you want to see your King overwhelmed with insults and deprived of his liberty, while he devotes himself entirely to the establishment of yours?

Love for their kings is one of the virtues of Frenchmen, and His Majesty has personally received too many touching proofs thereof ever to be able to forget them. The rebels are well aware that, so long as this love abides, their work can never succeed; they know, likewise, that in order to enfeeble it, it is necessary, if possible, to destroy the respect which has always accompanied it; and that is the source of the outrages which the King has experienced during the past two years, and of all the ills which he has suffered. His Majesty would not here delineate the distressing picture of these if he did not wish to make known to his faithful subjects the spirit of these rebels who would rend the bosom of their *Patrie,* while feigning to desire its regeneration. ...

In view of all these facts and the King's present inability to effect the good and prevent the evil that is perpetrated, is it astonishing that the King has sought to recover his liberty and to place himself and his family in safety?

Frenchmen, and especially you Parisians, you inhabitants of a city which the ancestors of His Majesty were pleased to call the good city of Paris, distrust the suggestions and lies of your false friends. Return to your king; he will always be your father, your best friend. What pleasure will he not take in forgetting all his personal injuries, and in beholding himself again in your midst, when a constitution, freely accepted by him, shall cause our holy religion to be respected, the government to be established upon a firm foundation and made useful by its functioning, the property and position of every person no longer to be disturbed, the laws no longer to be violated with impunity, and, finally, liberty to be established on firm and immovable foundations.

Signed, LOUIS

The King forbids his Ministers to sign any order in his name until they have received further instructions; he enjoins the Keeper of the Seal of State to send the Seal to him when required so to do.

Signed, LOUIS

Paris, 20 June, 1791.

Speech on Terror

Maximilien Robespierre

In the starkest contrast to the king, Robespierre at the height of his power wished to push forward the agenda of the revolution at all costs. In his view, the republic and its supporters monopolized all virtue. They in fact were obliged to use the most extreme means to defeat the revolution's enemies. Terror in the hands of the friends of democracy itself became a virtue, an argument used by all despots and tyrants before and after Robespierre.

It is time to state clearly the goal of the revolution and the ends we want to attain; it is time for us to become aware ourselves both of the obstacles which still keep us from reaching that goal and of the means which we must adopt to achieve it.

*　　*　　*

What is the aim we want to achieve? The peaceful enjoyment of liberty and equality, the reign of that eternal justice whose laws have been engraved, not in stone and marble, but in the hearts of all men, even in the heart of the slave who forgets them or of the tyrant who denies them.

We want a state of affairs where all despicable and cruel passions are unknown and all kind and generous passions are aroused by the laws; where ambition is the desire to deserve glory and to serve the fatherland; where distinctions arise only from equality itself; where the citizen submits to the magistrate, the magistrate to the people and the people to justice; where the fatherland guarantees the well-being of each individual, and where each individual enjoys with pride the prosperity and the glory of the fatherland; where all souls elevate themselves through constant communication of republican sentiments and through the need to deserve the esteem of a great people; where the arts are the decorations of liberty that ennobles them,

where commerce is the source of public wealth and not only of the monstrous opulence of a few houses.

In our country we want to substitute morality for egoism, honesty for honor, principles for customs, duties for decorum, the rate of reason for the tyranny of custom, the contempt of vice for the contempt of misfortune, pride for insolence, magnanimity for vanity, love of glory for love of money, good people for well-bred people, merit for intrigue, genius for wit, truth for pompous action, warmth of happiness for boredom of sensuality, greatness of man for pettiness of the great; a magnanimous, powerful, happy people for the polite, frivolous, despicable people— that is to say, all the virtues and all the miracles of the Republic for all the vices and all the absurdities of the monarchy.

In one word, we want to fulfill the wishes of nature, accomplish the destiny of humanity, keep the promises of philosophy, absolve Providence from the long reign of crime and tyranny.

*　　*　　*

What kind of government can realize these marvels? Only a democratic or republican government.

*　　*　　*

But what is the fundamental principle of the democratic or popular government, that is to say, the essential strength that sustains it and make it move. It is virtue: I am speaking of the public virtue which brought about so many marvels in Greece and Rome and which must bring about much more

From: *Major Crises in Western Civilization*, vol. II *1745 to the Nuclear Age*, eds. Richard W. Lyman & Lewis W. Spitz (New York: Harcourt, Brace & World, Inc. 1965), pp. 71–72.

astonishing ones yet in republican France; of that virtue which is nothing more than love of fatherland and of its laws.

*   *   *

If the strength of popular government in peacetime is virtue, the strength of popular government in revolution is both virtue and terror: terror without virtue is disastrous, virtue without terror is powerless. Terror is nothing without prompt, severe, and inflexible justice; it is thus an emanation of virtue; but is less a particular principle than a consequence of the general principle of democracy applied to the most urgent needs of the fatherland. It is said that terror is the strength of despotic government. Does ours then resemble despotism? Yes, as the sword that shines in the hands of the heroes of liberty resemble the one with which the satellites of tyranny are armed. Let the despot govern his brutalized subjects through terror; he is right as a despot. Subdue the enemies of liberty through terror and you will be right as founders of the Republic. The government of revolution is the despotism of liberty against tyranny.

Ninety-Three

Victor Hugo

The protagonist in this novel is revolutionary France itself. The various characters, some based upon historical figures and others entirely fictional, are not as important as the country they aided or injured. Throughout the novel, again and again Hugo poses the fateful question: can an action at one and the same time be good and bad? Although Hugo was born after the events about which he wrote, his imaginative faculty was so strong and the style he used so clearly evoked reality that the passages chosen seem to reflect eye witness reportage.

The Convention

We approach the grand summit.

Behold the Convention!

The gaze grows steady in presence of this height.

Never has a more lofty spectacle appeared on the horizon of mankind.

There is one Himalaya, and there is one Convention.

The Convention is perhaps the culminating point of History.

During its lifetime—for it lived—men did not quite understand what it was. It was precisely the grandeur which escaped its contemporaries; they were too much scared to be dazzled. Everything grand possesses a sacred horror. It is easy to admire mediocrities and hills; but whatever is too lofty, whether it be a genius or a mountain,—an assembly as well as a masterpiece,—alarms when seen too near. An immense height appears an exaggeration. It is fatiguing to climb. One loses breath upon acclivities, one slips down declivities; one is hurt by sharp, rugged heights which are in themselves beautiful; torrents in their foaming reveal the precipices; clouds hide the mountain-tops; a sudden ascent terrifies as much as a fall. Hence there is a greater sensation of fright than admiration. What one feels is fantastic enough,—an aversion to the grand. One sees the abyss and loses sight of the sublimity; one sees the monster and does not perceive the marvel. Thus the Convention was at first judged. It was measured by the purblind,—it, which needed to be looked at by eagles.

To-day we see it in perspective, and it throws across the deep and distant heavens, against a background at once serene and tragic, the immense profile of the French Revolution.

* * *

The 14th of July delivered.

The 10th of August blasted.

The 21st of September founded.

The 21st of September was the Equinox; was Equilibrium,—*Libra*, the balance. It was, according to the remark of Romme, under this sign of Equality and Justice that the Republic was proclaimed. A constellation heralded it.

The Convention is the first avatar of the peoples. It was by the Convention that the grand new page opened and the future of to-day commenced.

Every idea must have a visible enfolding; a habitation is necessary to any principle; a church is God between four walls; every dogma must have a temple. When the Convention became a fact, the first problem to be solved was how to lodge the Convention.

At first the Riding-school, then the Tuileries, was taken. A platform was raised, scenery arranged,—a great grey painting by David imitating bas-reliefs; benches were placed in order; there was a square tribune, parallel pilasters with plinths like blocks

From: Victor Hugo, *Ninety-Three*, in *Works of Victor Hugo*, Volume VII (New York: Chesterfield Society n.d.), pp. 142–144, 162–163, 166–167, 226–232.

and long rectilinear stems; square enclosures, into which the spectators crowded, and which were called the public tribunes; a Roman velarium, Grecian draperies; and in these right-angles and these straight lines the Convention was installed,—the tempest confined within this geometrical plan. On the tribune the Red Cap was painted in grey. The royalists began by laughing at this grey red cap, this theatrical hall, this monument of pasteboard, this sanctuary of papier-maché, this Pantheon of mud and spittle. How quickly it would disappear! The columns were made of the staves from hogsheads, the arches were of deal boards, the bas-reliefs of mastic, the entablatures were of pine, the statues of plaster; the marbles were paint, the walls canvas; and of this provisional shelter France has made an eternal dwelling.

When the Convention began to hold its sessions in the Riding-school, the walls were covered with the placards which sprouted over Paris at the period of the return from Varennes.

On one might be read: "The king returns. Any person who cheers him shall be beaten; any person who insults him shall be hanged." On another: "Peace! Hats on! He is about to pass before his judges." On another: "The king has aimed at the nation. He has hung fire; it is now the nation's turn." On another: "The Law! The Law!" It was within those walls that the Convention sat in judgment on Louis XVI.

At the Tuileries, where the Convention began to sit on the 10th of May, 1793, and which was called the Palais-National, the assembly-hall occupied the whole space between the Pavillon de l'Horloge, called the Pavilion of Unity, and the Pavilion Marsan, then named Pavilion of Liberty. The Pavilion of Flora was called Pavillon Egalité. The hall was reached by the grand staircase of Jean Bullant. The whole ground-floor of the palace, beneath the story occupied by the Assembly, was a kind of long guard-room, littered with bundles and camp-beds of the troops of all arms, who kept watch about the Convention. The Assembly had a guard of honour styled "the Grenadiers of the Convention."

A tricoloured ribbon separated the palace where the Assembly sat from the garden in which the people came and went.

*   *   *

At the same time that it threw off revolution, this Assembly produced civilization. Furnace, but forge too.

In this caldron, where terror bubbled, progress fermented. Out of this chaos of shadow, this tumultuous flight of clouds, spread immense rays of light parallel to the eternal laws,—rays that have remained on the horizon, visible forever in the heaven of the peoples, and which are, one, Justice; another, Tolerance; another, Goodness; another, Right; another, Truth; another, Love.

The Convention promulgated this grand axiom: "The liberty of each citizen ends where the liberty of another citizen commences,"—which comprises in two lines all human social law. It declared indigence sacred; it declared infirmity sacred in the blind and the deaf and dumb, who became wards of the State; maternity sacred in the girl-mother, whom it consoled and lifted up; infancy sacred in the orphan, whom it caused to be adopted by the country; innocence sacred in the accused who was acquitted, whom it indemnified. It branded the slave-trade; it abolished slavery. It proclaimed civic joint responsiblity. It decreed gratuitous instruction. It organized national education by the normal school of Paris; central schools in the chief towns; primary schools in the communes. It created the academies of music and the museums. It decreed the unity of the Code, the unity of weights and measures, and the unity of calculation by the decimal system. It established the finances of France, and caused public credit to succeed to the long monarchical bankruptcy. It put the telegraph in operation. To old age it gave endowed almshouses; to sickness, purified hospitals; to instruction, the Polytechnic School; to science, the Bureau of Longitudes; to human intellect, the Institute. At the same time that it was national it was cosmopolitan. Of the eleven thousand two hundred and ten decrees which emanated from the Convention, a third had a political aim; two thirds, a human aim. It declared universal morality the basis of society, and universal conscience the basis of law. And all that servitude abolished, fraternity proclaimed, humanity protected, human conscience rectified, the law of work transformed into right, and from onerous made honourable,—national riches consolidated, childhood instructed and raised up, letters and sciences propagated, light illuminating all heights, aid to all sufferings, promulgation of all principle,—the Convention accomplished, having in its bowels that hydra, the Vendée; and upon its sholders that heap of tigers, the kings.

*   *   *

Spirits which were a prey of the wind. But this was a miracle-working wind. To be a member of the Convention was to be a wave of the ocean. This was true even of the greatest there. The force of impulsion came from on high. There was a Will in the Convention which was that of all, and yet not that of any one person. This Will was an Idea,—an idea indomitable and immeasurable, which swept from the summit of heaven into the darkness below. We call this Revolution. When that Idea passed, it beat down one and raised up another; it scattered this man into foam and dashed that one upon the reefs. This Idea knew whither it was going, and drove the whirlpool before it. To ascribe the Revolution to men is to ascribe the tide to the waves.

The Revolution is a work of the Unknown. Call it good or bad, according as you yearn toward the future or the past, but leave it to the power which caused it. It seems the joint work of grand events and grand individualities mingled, but it is in reality the result of events. Events dispense, men suffer; events dictate, men sigh. The 14th of July is signed Camille Desmoulins; the 10th of August is signed Danton; the 2d of September is signed Marat; the 21st of September is signed Grégoire; the 21st of January is signed Robespierre; but Desmoulins, Danton, Marat, Grégoire, and Robespierre are mere scribes. The great and mysterious writer of these grand pages has a name,—God; and a mask, Destiny. Robespierre believed in God: yea, verily!

The Revolution is a form of the eternal phenomenon which presses upon us from every quarter, and which we call Necessity. Before this mysterious complication of benefits and sufferings arises the Wherefore of history. *Because:* this answer of him who knows nothing is equally the response of him who knows all.

In presence of these climacteric catastrophes which devastate and revivify civilization, one hesitates to judge their details. To blame or praise men on account of the result is almost like praising or blaming ciphers on account of the total. That which ought to happen happens; the blast which ought to blow blows. The

Eternal Serenity does not suffer from these north winds. Above revolutions Truth and Justice remain as the starry sky lies above and beyond tempests.

*   *   *

The Two Poles of the Truth

At the end of a few weeks, which had been filled with the vicissitudes of civil war, the district of Fougères could talk of nothing but the two men who were opposed to each other, and yet were occupied in the same work; that is, fighting side by side the great revolutionary combat.

The savage Vendean duel continued, but the Vendée was losing ground. In Ille-et-Vilaine in particular, thanks to the young commander who had at Dol so opportunely replied to the audacity of six thousand royalists by the audacity of fifteen hundred patriots, the insurrection, if not quelled, was at least greatly weakened and circumscribed. Several lucky hits had followed that one, and out of these successes had grown a new position of affairs. Matters had changed their face, but a singular complication had arisen.

In all this portion of the Vendée the Republic had the upper hand,—that was beyond a doubt. But which republic? In the triumph which was opening out, two forms of republic made themselves felt,—the republic of terror, and the republic of clemency; the one desirous to conquer by rigour, and the other by mildness. Which would prevail? These two forms—the conciliating and the implacable—were represented by two men, each of whom possessed his special influence and authority: the one a military commander, the other a civil delegate. Which of them would prevail?

One of the two, the delegate, had a formidable basis of support; he had arrived bearing the threatening watchword of the Paris Commune to the battalions of Santerre: "No mercy; no quarter!" He had, in order to put everything under his control, the decree of the Convention, ordaining "death to whomsoever should set at liberty and help a captive rebel chief to escape." He had full powers, emanating from the Committee of Public Safety, and an injunction commanding obedience to him as delegate, signed ROBESPIERRE, DANTON, MARAT. The other, the soldier, had on his side only, this strength,—pity. He had only his own arm, which chastised the enemy; and his heart, which pardoned them. A conqueror, he believed that he had the right to spare the conquered.

Hence arose a conflict, hidden but deep, between these two men. The two stood in different atmospheres; both combating the rebellion, and each having his own thunderbolt,—that of the one, victory; that of the other, terror.

Throughout all the Bocage nothing was talked of but them; and what added to the anxiety of those who watched them from every quarter was the fact that these two men so diametrically opposed were at the same time closely united. These two antagonists were friends. Never sympathy loftier and more profound joined two hearts; the stern had saved the life of the clement, and bore on his face the wound received in the effort. These two men were the incarnation,—the one of life, the other of death; the one was the principle of destruction, the other of peace, and they loved each other. Strange problem! Imagine Orestes merciful and Pylades pitiless. Picture Arimanes the brother of Ormus!

Let us add that the one of the pair who was called "the ferocious" was, at the same time, the most brotherly of men. He dressed the wounded, cared for the sick, passed his days and nights in the ambulance and hospitals, was touched by the sight of barefooted children, had nothing for himself, gave all to the poor. He was present at all the battles; he marched at the head of the columns and in the thickest of the fight, armed,—for he had in his belt a sabre and two pistols,—yet disarmed, because no one had ever seen him draw his sabre or touch his pistols. He faced blows, and did not return them. It was said that he had been a priest.

One of these men was Gauvain; the other was Cimourdain. There was friendship between the two men, but hatred between the two principles; this hidden war could not fail to burst forth. One morning the battle began.

Cimourdain said to Gauvain: "What have we accomplished?"

Gauvain replied: "You know as well as I. I have dispersed Lantenac's bands. He has only a few men left. Then he is driven back to the forest of Fougères. In eight days he will be surrounded."

"And in fifteen days?"

"He will be taken."

"And then?"

"You have read my notice?"

"Yes. Well?"

"He will be shot."

"More clemency! He must be guillotined."

"As for me," said Gauvain, "I am for a military death."

"And I," replied Cimourdain, "for a revolutionary death." He looked Gauvain in the face, and added: "Why did you set at liberty those nuns of the convent of Saint Marc-le-Blanc?"

"I do not make war on women," answered Gauvain.

"Those women hate the people; and where hate is concerned, one woman outweighs ten men. Why did you refuse to send to the revolutionary tribunal all that herd of old fanatical priests who were taken at Louvigné?"

"I do not make war on old men."

"An old priest is worse than a young one. Rebellion is more dangerous preached by white hairs. Men have faith in wrinkles. No false pity, Gauvain! The regicides are liberators. Keep your eye fixed on the tower of the Temple."

"The Temple tower! I would bring the Dauphin out of it. I do not make war on children."

Cimourdain's eyes grew stern. "Gauvain, learn that it is necessary to make war on a woman when she calls herself Marie Antoinette, on an old man when he is named Pius VI. and Pope, and upon a child when he is named Louis Capet."

"My master, I am not a politician."

"Try not to be a dangerous man. Why, at the attack on the post of Cossé, when the rebel Jean Treton, driven back and lost, flung himself alone, sabre in hand, against the whole column, didst thou cry, 'Open the ranks! Let him pass?'"

"Because one does not set fifteen hundred to kill a single man."

"Why, at the Cailleterie d'Astillé, when you saw your soldiers about to kill the Vendean Joseph Bézier, who was wounded and dragging himself along, did you exclaim, 'Go on before! This is my affair!' and then fire your pistol in the air?"

"Because one does not kill a man on the ground."

"And you were wrong. Both are to-day chiefs of bands. Joseph Bézier is Mustache, and Jean Treton is Jambe d'Argent. In saving those two men you gave two enemies to the Republic."

"Certainly I could wish to give her friends, and not enemies."

"Why, after the victory of Landéan, did you not shoot your three hundred peasant prisoners?"

"Because Bonchamp had shown mercy to the republican prisoners, and I wanted it said that the Republic showed mercy to the royalist prisoners."

"But, then, if you take Lantenac you will pardon him?"

"No."

"Why? Since you showed mercy to the three hundred peasants?"

"The peasants are ignorant men; Lantenac knows what he does."

"But Lantenac is your kinsman."

"France is the nearest."

"Lantenac is an old man."

"Lantenac is a stranger. Lantenac has no age. Lantenac summons the English. Lantenac is invasion. Lantenac is the enemy of the country. The duel between him and me can only finish by his death or mine."

"Gauvain, remember this vow."

"It is sworn."

There was silence, and the two looked at each other.

Then Gauvain resumed: "It will be a bloody date, this year '93 in which we live."

"Take care!" cried Cimourdain. "Terrible duties exist. Do not accuse that which is not accusable. Since when is it that the illness is the fault of the physician? Yes, the characteristic of this tremendous year is its pitilessness. Why? Because it is the grand revolutionary year. This year in which we live is the incarnation of the Revolution. The Revolution has an enemy,—the old world,—and it is without pity for it; just as the surgeon has an enemy,—gangrene,— and is without pity for it. The Revolution extirpates royalty in the king, aristocracy in the noble, despotism in the soldier, superstition in the priest, barbarism in the judge; in a word, everything which is tyranny, in all which is the tyrant. The operation is fearful; the Revolution performs it with a sure hand. As to the amount of sound flesh which it sacrifices, demand of Boerhaave what he thinks in regard to that. What tumour does not cause a loss

of blood in its cutting away? Does not the extinguishing of a conflagration demand an energy as fierce as that of the fire itself? These formidable necessities are the very condition of success. A surgeon resembles a butcher; a healer may have the appearance of an executioner. The Revolution devotes itself to its fatal work. It mutilates, but it saves. What! you demand pity for the virus? You wish it to be merciful to that which is poisonous? It will not listen. It holds the post,—it will exterminate it. It makes a deep wound in civilization, from whence will spring health to the human race. You suffer? Without doubt. How long will it last? The time necessary for the operation. After that you will live. The Revolution amputates the world. Hence this hemorrhage,—'93."

"The surgeon is calm," said Gauvain, "and the men that I see are violent."

"The Revolution," replied Cimourdain, "needs savage workmen to aid it! It pushes aside every hand that trembles. It has only faith in the inexorables. Danton is the terrible, Robespierre is the inflexible; Saint-Just is the immovable, Marat is the implacable. Take care, Gauvain! these names are necessary. They are worth as much as armies to us; they will terrify Europe."

"And perhaps the future also," said Gauvain. He checked himself, and resumed: "For that matter, my master, you err. I accuse no one. According to me, the true point of view of the Revolution is its irresponsibility. Nobody is innocent, nobody is guilty. Louis XVI. is a sheep thrown among lions: he wishes to escape, he tries to flee, he seeks to defend himself; he would bite if he could. But one is not a lion at will; his craze to be one passes for crime. This enraged sheep shows his teeth: 'The traitor!' cry the lions; and they eat him. That done, they fight among themselves."

"The sheep is a brute."

"And the lions, what are they?"

This retort set Cimourdain thinking. He raised his head, and answered: "These lions are consciences. These lions are ideas. These lions are principles."

"They produce the reign of Terror."

"One day, the Revolution will be the justification of this Terror."

"Beware lest the Terror become the calumny of the Revolution." Gauvain continued: "Liberty,

Equality, Fraternity,—these are the dogmas of peace and harmony. Why give them an alarming aspect? What is it we want? To bring the peoples to a universal republic. Well, do not let us make them afraid. What can intimidation serve? The people can no more be attracted by a scarecrow than birds can. One must not do evil to bring about good; one does not overturn the throne in order to leave the gibbet standing. Death to kings, and life to nations! Strike off the crowns; spare the heads! The Revolution is concord, not fright. Clement ideas are ill served by cruel men. Amnesty is to me the most beautiful word in human language. I will only shed blood in risking my own. Besides, I simply know how to fight; I am nothing but a soldier. But if I may not pardon, victory is not worth the trouble it costs. During battle let us be the enemies of our enemies, and after the victory their brothers."

"Take care!" repeated Cimourdain, for the third time. "Gauvain, you are more to me than a son; take care!" Then he added thoughtfully: "In a period like ours, pity may become one of the forms of treason."

Any one listening to the talk of these two men might have fancied he heard a dialogue between the sword and the axe. . . .

— READING 6 —

Writings and Sayings

Napoleon Bonaparte

Although he ultimately ruled as an emperor and had wished to pass power hereditarily to his son, Napoleon argued that his wars across Europe and his introduction of the Napoleonic Law Code to all areas that came under his rule constituted the spread of the revolution's ideals. In his view, humans did not desire complete freedom but relative freedom, equality, and security under the law. The Napoleonic state, in his view, accomplished these real goals of the revolution.

The Revolution Consolidated

[Proclamation, December 15, 1799] Citizens, the Revolution has been made fast to the principles that started it. The Revolution is ended.

[Stenographic transcript, Conseil d'Etat, 1805; subject under discussion: a proposal to maintain feudal rights in the annexed provinces of Piedmont] I say: we have had a jubilee. The social order has been overthrown; the king, who was the apex of all legislation, has been guillotined. . . . Everything has been uprooted. . . .

You cannot undo the past. The annexed territories must be just like France, and if you went on annexing everything as far as Gibraltar and Kamchatka the laws of France would have to spread there, too. I am pleading the cause of the humble folk; the others never lack good dinners and brilliant drawing rooms that will plead for them.

[Conversation, 1816] In this gigantic struggle between the present and the past, I am the natural arbiter and mediator. I tried to be its supreme judge. My whole internal administration, my whole foreign policy were determined by that great aim.

From: *The Mind of Napoleon: A Selection from His Written and Spoken Words*, ed. and trans. J. Christopher Herold (New York: Columbia University Press, 1955), pp. 72–75, 84–85, 245, 251–256.

Liberty, Equality, Vanity

[Conversation, 1803] I have come to realize that men are not born to be free.

[Conversation, 1804] Liberty means a good civil code. The only thing modern nations care for is property.

[Conversation, 1800s] Liberty is a need felt by a small class of people whom nature has endowed with nobler minds than the mass of men. Consequently, it may be repressed with impunity. Equality, on the other hand, pleases the masses.

[Conversation, 1800s] In Paris—and Paris means France—people are unable to take an interest in things unless they also take an interest in persons. The old monarchic way of life has accustomed us to personify everything. This would be a bad state of affairs for a people that seriously desires liberty. But the French are unable to desire anything seriously except, perhaps, equality. Even so, they would gladly renounce it if everyone could entertain the hope of rising to the top. Equality in the sense that everyone will be master—there you have the secret of all your vanities. What must be done, then, is to give everybody the hope of being able to rise.

[Conversation, 1815] My motto has always been: A career open to all talents, without distinctions of birth.

[Conversation, 1816] Democracy, if it is reasonable, limits itself to giving everyone an equal opportunity to compete and to obtain.

[Conversation, 1816, related by Las Cases] Concerning the Legion of Honor, the Emperor said, among other things, that the variety and the specialization of the old orders of chivalry tended to strengthen caste divisions, whereas the single decoration of the Legion of Honor and the universality of its application was the symbol of equality. The old orders kept the classes divided, while the new decoration ought to bring about the cohesion of the citizen body. Its influence, its effects within the national family might become incalculable: it was the common center, the universal incentive of all the diverse ambitions.

[Conversation, early 1800s] It is very easy to govern the French through vanity.

[Conversation, 1800] When a Frenchman is torn between fear of a policeman and fear of the devil, he will side with the devil. But when he is caught between the devil and fashion, he will obey fashion.

[Letter to his brother Jérôme, then king of Westphalia, 1807] What the peoples of Germany desire most impatiently is that talented commoners should have the same right to your esteem and to public employments as the nobles, that any trace of serfdom and of an intermediate hierarchy between the sovereign and the lowest class of the people should be completely abolished. The benefits of the Code Napoléon, the publicity of judicial procedure, the creation of juries must be so many distinguishing marks of your monarchy. And, if I may give you my whole opinion, I count more firmly on their effects for the enlargement and consolidation of your kingdom than on the results of even the greatest military victories. Your people must enjoy a degree of freedom, equality, and prosperity unknown to the people of the Germanies, and this liberal regime must produce, in one way or another, the most salutary changes affecting the politics of the Confederation of the Rhine and the power of your monarchy. This manner of governing will give you a more powerful shield against Prussia than the Elbe, fortifications, and French protection. What nation would wish to return under the arbitrary Prussian government once it had tasted the benefits of a wise and liberal administration? The peoples of Germany, the peoples of France, of Italy, of Spain all desire equality and liberal ideas. I have guided the affairs of Europe for many years now, and I have had occasion to convince myself that the buzzing of the privileged classes is contrary to the general opinion. Be a constitutional king.

*   *   *

"A Single Party and a Single Will"

[Newspaper editorial, 1801, on the "ideologist" opposition in the Tribunate] They are a dozen or fifteen men and think they are a party. Their endless ravings they call oratory. . . . Infernal machines have been set against the First Consul, knives have been sharpened, impotent plots have been fomented. Add to this, if you will, the sarcasms and the insane notions of twelve or fifteen befogged metaphysicians. Against this handful of enemies he will pit the people of France.

[Conseil d'Etat, 1802] The opposition in England is completely harmless. Its members are not partisans. They do not long for either feudalism or Jacobinism. Their influence is legitimately owed to their talents, and they merely try to sell themselves to the Crown. With us, it is quite different. Here the opposition consists of the Jacobins and of the ex-privileged classes. Those people do not merely compete for positions or money: the former want their clubs back, the latter the old regime. There is a great difference between free discussion in a country whose institutions are long established and the opposition in a country that is still unsettled.

[Conversation, 1803] *The First Consul* (in his bathtub): An opposition, as in England, is that it? I haven't been able to understand yet what good there is in an opposition. Whatever it may be, its only result is to diminish the prestige of authority in the eyes of the people.

Joseph Bonaparte: It's easy to see that you don't like it; you have taken good care of it.

The First Consul: Let another govern in my place, and if he doesn't, like me, make an effort to silence the talkers, he'll see what will happen to him. As for me, let me tell you that in order to govern well one needs absolute unity of power. I won't shout this from the roof tops, since I mustn't frighten a lot of people who would raise loud cries of despotism, if they were allowed to talk, and who would write about it, if they were allowed to write. But I have begun to put good order into all this.

[Proclamation, 19 Brumaire, Year VIII/November 10, 1799] I have refused to be the man of any party.

[Repeated saying, 1799] I have opened up a vast road. He who marches straight ahead shall be safe. He who strays to the right or to the left shall be punished.

[Instructions to an ambassador, 1803] In France there is but a single party and a single will.

[Conversation, 1816] Who ever heard me ask, throughout the years I was in power, to what party anyone belonged, or ever had belonged to, or what he had said, done, or written? Let them imitate me! I always was known to have but one question, one aim: 'Do you want to be Frenchmen with me?' And if they said yes, I pushed everyone into a defile of granite rock, closed off to the right and to the left, where he was forced to march on to the other end—and there I stood, pointing to the honor, glory, and splendor of the fatherland.

*　　*　　*

France as the Master Nation

[Conseil d'Etat, 1800s] I want the title of French citizen to become the finest and most desirable on earth. I want every Frenchman traveling anywhere in Europe to be able to believe himself at home.

[Letter to Joseph, 1806] I believe I have already told you that I intend to place the kingdom of Naples in my family. Together with Italy, Switzerland, Holland, and the three kingdoms of Germany, it will constitute my federated states, or the true French Empire.

[Conversation, c.1810] The French Empire shall become the metropolis of all other sovereignties. I want to force every king in Europe to build a large Palace for his use in Paris. When an Emperor of the French is crowned, these kings shall come to Paris, and they shall adorn that imposing ceremony with their presence and salute it with their homages.

[Conversation, 1816] It was a part of my ceaseless dreams to make Paris the true capital of Europe. At times, for instance, I wanted it to become a city of two, three, or four million inhabitants—in a word, something fabulous, something colossal and unprecedented, with public establishments commensurate with its population.

*　　*　　*

A Political Testament

[Deathbed statement, recorded by Montholon on April 17, 1821] The Emperor spent a quiet night, although he perspired abundantly. About three o'clock, he had me called. When I arrived, he was sitting up, and the brilliance of his eyes made me fear that this fever had increased. Noticing my concern, he said to me in a kindly voice:

"I am not worse, but I have become preoccupied, while talking with Bertrand, about what the executors of my will are to say to my son when they see him. Bertrand doesn't understand me. He and Lafayette are still exactly as they were in 1791, with their utopias, their English notions, their bills of grievances and States-General. All they see in the Revolution of 1789 is a mere reform of abuses, and they refuse to admit that it constituted, all in itself, a complete social rebirth.

*　　*　　*

"There is nothing worse than decent people in a political crisis when their consciences are under the spell of false ideas. You will understand me: all you need do is remember the things I have dictated to you on the aims of my reign. But all this may be scattered here and there in your memory when the time comes for you to speak of it. I had better sum up in a few words the advice I leave to my son, so that you can explain my thought to him in detail. Write:

"'My son must have no thought of avenging my death: he must take advantage of it. Let him never forget my accomplishments; let him forever remain, as I have been, French to the finger tips. All his efforts must tend to a reign of peace. If, merely to imitate me and without an absolute necessity, he wants to resume my wars, he would be a mere ape. To do my labors over again would mean that I have accomplished nothing. To complete my work, on the other hand, would be to demonstrate the firmness of its foundations and to make intelligible the ground plan of the edifice that I had merely sketched. One cannot do the same thing twice in a century. I have been obliged to subdue Europe by force; today, Europe must be persuaded. I have saved the Revolution, which was on the point of death; I have washed off its crimes, I have held it up to the eyes of Europe resplendent with glory. I have implanted new ideas in the soil of France and Europe: their march cannot be reversed. Let my son reap the fruit of my seed. Let him develop all the elements of prosperity contained in the soil of France—at that price, he may yet become a great ruler.

"'The Bourbons will not last. When I am dead, there will be a universal reaction in my Favor, even in England. That is a fine inheritance for my son. It is possible that, in order to wipe out the memory of their persecutions, the English will favor the return of my son to France. But in order to live on good terms with England, it is necessary at all costs to favor her commercial interests. This necessity entails two consequences: either fight England or share the world with her. The second alternative is the only possible one in our day.

*   *   *

"'France is the one country in which the leaders exercise the least influence; to lean on them is to build on quicksand. Nothing great can be accomplished in France except by leaning on the masses. Besides, a government must look for support where it can find it. There are moral laws that are as inflexible and imperious as physical laws. The Bourbons cannot find support except in the nobles and the priests, no matter what constitution they may be forced to adopt, just as water must find its level despite the pump that has temporarily lifted it. As for me, I always leaned on everybody without exception; I gave the first example of a government favoring the interests of all. I did not govern for or through the nobles, the priests, the bourgeoisie, or the workers. I have governed for the entire community, for the whole great French family. To keep a nation's interests divided is a disservice to all classes and gives rise to civil war. What nature has made one cannot be divided but only mutilated.

*   *   *

"'In my youth, I had illusions. I got rid of them fast. The great orators who dominate political

assemblies by the glitter of their words are generally the most mediocre statesmen. You must not fight them with words—they usually command a still more sonorous vocabulary than your own—you must counter their fluency with closely reasoned logic. Their strength consists in vagueness; you must lead them back to the reality of facts. Practice kills them. In the Conseil d'Etat there were men far more eloquent than I, but I regularly defeated them with this simple argument: Two and two is four.

"'France is swarming with highly capable and practical-minded men. The difficulty lies merely in finding them and giving them a chance to pursue their careers. There are men behind ploughs who should be in the Conseil d'Etat, and there are ministers who ought to be behind a plough.

*   *   *

"'My son should never be surprised at seeing the most reasonable-looking men suggest the most absurd plans, from agrarian reform to Oriental despotism. All systems have their apologists in France. Let him listen to everything, but also let him evaluate everything according to its true merit, and let him surround himself with all the true talents produced by the nation. The French people has two equally powerful passions which seem opposed to each other but which in fact derive from the same sentiment—love of equality and love of distinctions. A government cannot satisfy those two needs except by being exceedingly just. In its laws and its actions, the government must be the same for all; honors and rewards must be given to those men who, in the eyes of the government, are most worthy of them.

*   *   *

"'My son will have to reign with a free press. In our day, this is a necessity. In order to govern, the question is not to follow out a more or less valid theory but to build with whatever materials are at hand. The inevitable must be accepted and turned to advantage.

"'In the hands of the government, a free press may become a powerful ally by carrying sound principles and doctrines to the remotest corners of the Empire. To leave it to its own devices is to sleep next to a powder keg.

*   *   *

"'. . . Our enemies are the enemies of mankind. They want to put chains around the people, whom they regard as a herd. They want to oppress France and to make the river flow back to its source: let them beware lest it overflow! Under my son the conflicting interests can coexist in peace, and the new ideas can spread and grow in strength without hurt and without victims. Humanity would be spared incalculable misfortunes. But if the blind hatred of the kings pursues my blood after my death, I shall be avenged nonetheless—but cruelly avenged.

"'Civilization will be the loser in any case. If the people break their chains, Europe will be flooded with blood; civilization will disappear amid civil and foreign wars. It will take more than three hundred years to destroy, in Europe, that royal authority which only yesterday still represented the common interest but which required several centuries to emerge from the grip of the Middle Ages. If, on the other hand, the North [i.e., Russia] should march against civilization, the struggle will be less long but the blows will be more fatal. The welfare of the people, all the achievements of so many years, will be lost, and no one can foresee what may be the disastrous consequences.

"'The restoration of my son is in the interest of the people as well as of the kings. Outside the ideas and principles for which we have fought and which I made triumph I see nothing but slavery or confusion for France and Europe alike.

*   *   *

"'Europe is marching toward an inevitable change. To retard her march is to waste strength in a futile struggle. To favor it is to strengthen the hopes and aspirations of all.

"'There are national aspirations that must be satisfied sooner or later, and toward this aim we must march. . . . The serious questions will no longer be resolved in the North but in the Mediterranean: there is enough on its shores to satisfy the ambitions of all the powers, and with the shreds of uncivilized countries the happiness of the civilized nations can be bought. If only the kings would see the light, there would no longer be in Europe any cause for hatred among nations.

*   *   *

"'In order to know whether his administration is good or bad, whether his laws are in harmony with custom, my son should ask for a yearly report on the number of sentences passed by the tribunals, together with their motivations. If crimes and misdemeanors increase, this is proof that misery is on the rise and that society is badly governed. Their decrease is proof of the contrary.

"'Religious ideas have a more powerful influence than is thought by certain shortsighted philosophers; they can render great service to humanity. By being on good terms with the pope, it is possible even today to dominate the consciences of a hundred million men.

*   *   *

"'My son should read much history and meditate upon it: it is the only true philosophy. Let him read and meditate upon the wars of the great captains: it is the only way to learn the art of war.

"'Yet no matter what you say to him, no matter what he learns, he will profit little from it if in his innermost heart he lacks that sacred flame, that love of the good which alone inspires great deeds.'"

—PART TWO—

Image of a Wealthy Middle-Class Family
This image portrays a very wealthy family. The walls are filled with ornately framed art works and servants hover everywhere, as the richly dressed young ladies of the family join their parents in afternoon tea. The impression is one of the new rich, as portrayed in the writings of Balzac and William Thackeray, imitating, with a touch of vulgarity, their perceptions of gentry life.

Restoration and Bourgeois Culture, 1815-1848

After decades of post-1789 tumult, many Europeans yearned for stability. At the Congress of Vienna (1814–1815), European leaders sought to create peace and avoid future political challenges. By setting up a system to enforce the collective will, the Vienna Congress established a mechanism that prevented great wars for the next hundred years and hinted at future international bodies. Simultaneously, Europe's leaders restored the old dynasties and tried to prevent social and political change. The hopelessness of this last task is suggested by the contradictory titles historians use for the 1815–1848 era: the Age of Metternich (symbol of conservatism) and the Age of Revolutions.

Emperor Alexander I of Russia (1777–1825) wrote the document, "Holy Alliance," during the Vienna Congress to outline and extend the conservative program. Even so, more than anyone else Prince Clement von Metternich (1773–1859) of Austria stamped his personality on the restored *ancien régime*. His "Carlsbad Decrees" (1819) brought restoration ideas to life with stern limitations on freedom of speech and association in the German Confederation. His "Confession" (1820) expressed certitude in established values, yearning for an old way of life, and foreboding for the future. Meanwhile, the French political writer, Joseph de Maistre (1753–1821), provided a theoretical basis for continuing the old regime in his essay, "The Authority of Custom" (1814). The conservative writers closely intertwined their political views with religion, which enjoyed a resurgence during the early decades of the nineteenth century. Regardless, Metternich's fears of the future were well-founded. The old dynasties now ruled over profoundly altered societies. The French and American revolutions had captured imaginations even as the Napoleonic Code annulled ancient rights and privileges wherever French armies went. Economically active persons of whatever class now carved out places for their endeavors. In his novel *Harlot High and Low* (1839–1847), Honore de Balzac (1799–1850) unsparingly describes the upwardly mobile bourgeoisie. This same wealthy middle class is the subject of the print of a well-provided English family at tea, surrounded by servants and every luxury.

Study Questions

1. What role does religion play in the political views of Alexander I, Metternich, and de Maistre?
2. Why do they object to constitutions?
3. How does Balzac portray class?
4. What were the defining aspects of Restoration Europe?
5. What new ideas challenged the old world during the early nineteenth century?
6. Image: What does this portrayal tell us about the newly rich during the nineteenth century?

Holy Alliance

Alexander I

At the Congress of Vienna, the Great Powers attempted to restore the order of prerevolutionary Europe. Through a balance of power and the concert of Europe, they hoped to maintain the status quo and prevent further revolutions. Alexander I of Russia went one step further in his document, Holy Alliance, which aimed at preventing change within European societies. Acceded to by all European monarchs except the King of England, it came to symbolize the restoration.

In the Name of the very Holy and Indivisible Trinity.

Their majesties, the Emperor of Austria, the King of Prussia and the Emperor of Russia, in view of the great events which the last three years have brought to pass in Europe and in view especially of the benefits which it has pleased Divine Providence to confer upon those states whose governments have placed their confidence and their hope in Him alone, having reached the profound conviction that the policy of the powers in their mutual relations, ought to be guided by the sublime truths taught by the eternal religion of God our Saviour, solemnly declare that the present act has no other aim than to manifest to the world their unchangeable determination to adopt no other rule of conduct, either in the government of their respective countries or in their holy religion, than the precepts of justice, charity and peace. These, far from being applicable exclusively to private life, ought on the contrary directly to control the resolutions of princes and to guide their steps as the sole means of establishing human institutions and of remedying their imperfections. Hence their majesties have agreed upon the following articles:

Article I. Conformably to the words of Holy Scripture which command all men to look upon each other as brothers, the three contracting monarchs will continue united by the bonds of a true and indissoluble fraternity, and regarding themselves as compatriots, they will lend aid and assistance to each other on all occasions and in all places; viewing themselves, in their relations to their subjects and to their armies, as fathers of families, they will direct them in that spirit of fraternity by which they are animated, for the protection of religion, peace and justice.

Article II. Hence the sole principle of conduct, be it between the said governments or their subjects, shall be that of rendering mutual service, and testifying by unceasing good-will, the mutual affection with which they should be animated. Considering themselves all as members of one great Christian nation, the three allied princes look upon themselves as delegates of Providence called upon to govern three branches of the same family, viz: Austria, Russia and Prussia. They thus confess that the Christian nation, of which they and their people form a part, has in reality no other sovereign than He alone to whom belongs by right the power, for in Him alone are to be found all the treasures of love, of knowledge and of infinite wisdom, that is to say God, our Divine Saviour, Jesus Christ, the word of the most High, the word of life. Their majesties recommend, therefore, to their peoples, as the sole means of enjoying that peace which springs from a good conscience and is alone enduring, to fortify themselves each day in the principles and practice of those duties which the Divine Saviour has taught to men.

From: *The Western Tradition: A Book of Readings from the Ancient World to the Atomic Age,* ed. Eugen Weber (Boston: D.C. Heath & Co., 1965), pp. 582–583.

Article III. All those powers who wish solemnly to make avowal of the sacred principles which have dictated the present act, and who would recognize how important it is to the happiness of nations, too long agitated, that these truths should hereafter exercise upon human destiny all the influence belonging to them, shall be received into this Holy Alliance with as much cordiality as affection.

Engrossed in three copies and signed at Paris, year of grace 1815, September $\frac{14}{26}$.

Signed: Francis
Frederick
William
Alexander

The Carlsbad Decrees

Prince Metternich

While a student at Strasbourg, Metternich, son of a noble family, witnessed first hand the revolutionary activity of the late eighteenth century. Because of this experience, he became an extreme conservative and spent his life fighting against political unrest. Metternich masterminded the Congress of Vienna, and his Carlsbad Decrees (1819) spelled out the strict limitations on freedom of speech and association in Central Europe. His Confessions of Faith (1820) suggest his yearning for a stable, conservative world as opposed to the changes that threatened the stability of early-nineteenth-century Europe.

1. A special representative of the ruler of each state shall be appointed for each university, with appropriate instructions and extended powers, and shall reside in the place where the university is situated. This office may devolve upon the existing curator or upon any other individual whom the government may deem qualified.

The function of this agent shall be to see to the strictest enforcement of existing laws and disciplinary regulations; to observe carefully the spirit which is shown by the instructors in the university in their public lectures and regular courses, and, without directly interfering in scientific matters or in the methods of teaching to give a salutary direction to the instruction, having in view the future attitude of the students. Lastly, he shall devote unceasing attention to everything that may promote morality, good order, and outward propriety among the students. . . .

2. The confederated governments mutually pledge themselves to remove from the universities or other public educational institutions all teachers who, by obvious deviation from their duty, or by exceeding the limits of their functions, or by the abuse of their legitimate influence over the youthful minds, or by propagating harmful doctrines hostile to public order or subversive of existing governmental institutions, shall have unmistakably proved their unfitness for the important office intrusted to them. . . .

No teacher who shall have been removed in this manner shall be again appointed to a position in any public institution of learning in another state of the union.

3. Those laws which have for a long period been directed against secret and unauthorized societies in the universities shall be strictly enforced. These laws apply especially to that association established some years since under the name Universal Students' Union (*Allgemeine Burschenschaft*), since the very conception of the society implies the utterly unallowable plan of permanent fellowship and constant communication between the various universities. The duty of especial watchfulness in this matter should be impressed upon the special agents of the government.

The governments mutually agree that such persons as shall hereafter be shown to have remained in secret or unauthorized associations, or shall have entered such associations, shall not be admitted to any public office.

4. No student who shall be expelled from a university by a decision of the university senate which was ratified or prompted by the agent of the government, or who shall have left the institution in order to escape expulsion, shall be received in any other university.

From: *Readings in European History,* ed. James Harvey Robinson (Boston: Ginn & Company, 1906), pp. 547–550.

*   *   *

1. So long as this decree shall remain in force no publication which appears in the form of daily issues, or as a serial not exceeding twenty sheets of printed matter, shall go to press in any state of the union without the previous knowledge and approval of the state officials.

Writings which do not belong to one of the above-mentioned classes shall be treated according to the laws now in force, or which may be enacted, in the individual states of the union. . . .

2. Each state of the union is responsible, not only to the state against which the offense is directly committed, but to the whole Confederation, for every publication appearing under its supervision in which the honor or security of other states is infringed or their constitution or administration attacked. . . .

4. The Diet shall have the right, moreover, to suppress on its own authority, without being petitioned, such writings included in Article I, in whatever German state they may appear, as, in the opinion of a commission appointed by it, are inimical to the honor of the union, the safety of individual states, or the maintenance of peace and quiet in Germany. There shall be no appeal from such decisions, and the governments involved are bound to see that they are put into execution. . . .

7. When a newspaper or periodical is suppressed by a decision of the Diet, the editor thereof may not within a period of five years edit a similar publication in any state of the union.

*　　*　　*

1. Within a fortnight, reckoned from the passage of this decree, there shall convene, under the auspices of the Confederation, in the city and federal fortress of Mayence, an extraordinary commission of investigation to consist of seven members, including the chairman.

2. The object of the commission shall be a joint investigation, as thorough and extensive as possible, of the facts relating to the origin and manifold ramifications of the revolutionary plots and demagogical associations directed against the existing constitution and the internal peace both of the union and of the individual states; of the existence of which plots more or less clear evidence is to be had already, or may be produced in the course of the investigation. . . .

3. The central investigating commission is to furnish the Diet from time to time with a report of the results of the investigation, which is to be carried out as speedily as possible. . . .

Confession of Faith

Prince Metternich

Confession of Faith: Metternich's Secret Memorandum to the Emperor Alexander

'L'Europe,' a celebrated writer has recently said, *'fait aujourd'hui pitié à l'homme d'esprit et horreur à l'homme vertueux.'*

It would be difficult to comprise in a few words a more exact picture of the situation at the time we are writing these lines!

Kings have to calculate the chances of their very existence in the immediate future; passions are let loose, and league together to overthrow everything which society respects as the basis of its existence; religion, public morality, laws, customs, rights, and duties, all are attacked, confounded, overthrown, or called in question. The great mass of the people are tranquil spectators of these attacks and revolutions, and of the absolute want of all means of defence. A few are carried off by the torrent, but the wishes of the immense majority are to maintain a repose which exists no longer, and of which even the first elements seem to be lost.

What is the cause of all these evils? By what methods has this evil established itself, and how is it that it penetrates into every vein of the social body?

Do remedies still exist to arrest the progress of this evil, and what are they?

These are doubtless questions worthy of the solicitude of every good man who is a true friend to order and public peace—two elements inseparable in principle, and which are at once the first needs and the first blessings of humanity.

Has there never been offered to the world an institution really worthy of the name? Has truth

From: *Memoirs of Prince Metternich, 1815–1829,* ed. Prince Richard Metternich, trans. Mrs. Alexander Napier (London: Richard Bentley & Son, 1881), vol. 3, pp. 454–476.

been always confounded with error ever since society has believed itself able to distinguish one from the other? Have the experiences bought at the price of so many sacrifices, and repeated at intervals, and in so many different places, been all in error? Will a flood of light be shed upon society at one stroke? Will knowledge come by inspiration? If one could believe in such phenomena it would not be the less necessary, first of all, to assure oneself of their reality. Of all things, nothing is so fatal as error; and it is neither our wish nor our intention ever to give ourselves up to it. Let us examine the matter!

The Source of the Evil

Man's nature is immutable. The first needs of society are and remain the same, and the differences which they seem to offer find their explanation in the diversity of influences, acting on the different races by natural causes, such as the diversity of climate, barrenness or richness of soil, insular or continental position, &c. &c. These local differences no doubt produce effects which extend far beyond purely physical necessities; they create and determine particular needs in a more elevated sphere; finally, they determine the laws, and exercise an influence even on religions.

It is, on the other hand, with institutions as with everything else. Vague in their origin, they pass through periods of development and perfection, to arrive in time at their decadence; and, conforming to the laws of man's nature, they have, like him, their infancy, their youth, their age of strength and reason, and their age of decay.

Two elements alone remain in all their strength, and never cease to exercise their indestructible influence with equal power. These are the precepts of morality, religions as well as social, and the necessities created by locality. From the time that men attempt to swerve from these bases, to become rebels against these sovereign arbiters of their destinies, society suffers from a *malaise* which sooner or later will lead to a state of convulsion. The history of every country, in relating the consequences of such errors, contains many pages stained with blood; but we dare to say, without fear of contradiction, one seeks in vain for an epoch when an evil of this nature has extended its ravages over such a vast area as it has done at the present time. The causes are natural.

History embraces but a very limited space of time. It did not begin to deserve the name of history until long after the fall of great empires. There, where it seems to conduct us to the cradle of civilisation, it really conducts us to ruins. We see republics arise and prosper, struggle, and then submit to the rule of one fortunate soldier. We see one of these republics pass through all the phases common to society, and end in an almost universal monarchy—that is to say, subjugating the scattered portions of the then civilised world. We see this monarchy suffer the fate of all political bodies: we see its first springs become enfeebled, and finally decay.

Centuries of darkness followed the irruption of the barbarians. The world, however, could not return to barbarism. The Christian religion had appeared; imperishable in its essence, its very existence was sufficient to disperse the darkness and establish civilisation on new foundations, applicable to all times and all places, satisfying all needs, and establishing the most important of all on the basis of a pure and eternal law! To the formation of new Christian States succeeded the Crusades, a curious mixture of good and evil.

A decisive influence was shortly exercised on the progress of civilisation by three discoveries—the invention of printing, that of gunpowder, and the discovery of the New World. Still later came the Reformation—another event which had incalculable effects, on account of its influence on the moral world. From that time the face of the world was changed.

The facilitation of the communication of thoughts by printing; the total change in the means of attack and defence brought about by the invention of gunpowder; the difference suddenly produced in the value of property by the quantity of metals which the discovery of America put in circulation; the spirit of adventure provoked by the chances of fortune opened in a new hemisphere; the modifications in the relations of society caused by so many and such important changes, all became more developed, and were in some sort crowned by the revolution which the Reformation worked in the moral world.

The progress of the human mind has been extremely rapid in the course of the last three centuries. This progress having been accelerated more rapidly than the growth of wisdom (the only counterpoise to passions and to error); a revolution prepared by the false systems, the fatal errors into which many of the most illustrious sovereigns of the last half of the eighteenth century fell, has at last broken out in a country advanced in knowledge, and enervated by pleasure, in a country inhabited by a people whom one can only regard as frivolous, from the facility with which they comprehend and the difficulty they experience in judging calmly.

Having now thrown a rapid glance over the first causes of the present state of society, it is necessary to point out in a more particular manner the evil which threatens to deprive it, at one blow, of the real blessings, the fruits of genuine civilisation, and to disturb it in the midst of its enjoyments. This evil may be described in one word—presumption; the natural effect of the rapid progression of the human mind towards the perfecting of so many things. This it is which at the present day leads so many individuals astray, for it has become an almost universal sentiment.

Religion, morality, legislation, economy, politics, administration, all have become common and accessible to everyone. Knowledge seems to come by inspiration; experience has no value for the presumptuous man; faith is nothing to him; he substitutes for it a pretended individual conviction, and to arrive at this conviction dispenses with all inquiry and with all study; for these means appear too trivial to a mind which believes itself strong enough to embrace at one glance all questions and all facts. Laws have no value for him, because he has not contributed to make them, and it would be beneath a man of his parts to recognise the limits traced by rude and ignorant generations. Power resides in himself; why should he submit himself to that which was only useful for the man deprived of light and knowledge? That which, according to him, was required in an age of weakness cannot be suitable in an age of reason and vigour, amounting to universal perfection, which the German innovators designate by the idea, absurd in itself, of the Emancipation of the People! Morality itself he does not attack openly, for without it he could not be sure for a single instant of his own existence; but he interprets its essence after his own fashion, and allows every other person to do so likewise, provided that other person neither kills nor robs him.

In thus tracing the character of the presumptuous man, we believe we have traced that of the society of the day, composed of like elements, if the denomination of society is applicable to an order of things which only tends in principle towards individualising all the elements of which society is composed. Presumption makes every man the guide of his own belief, the arbiter of laws according to which he is pleased to govern himself, or to allow some one else to govern him and his neighbours; it makes him, in short, the sole judge of his own faith, his own actions, and the principles according to which he guides them.

Is it necessary to give a proof of this last fact? We think we have furnished it in remarking that one of the sentiments most natural to man, that of nationality, is erased from the Liberal catechism, and that where the word is still employed, it is used by the heads of the party as a pretext to enchain Governments, or as a lever to bring about destruction. The real aim of the idealists of the party is religious and political fusion, and this being analysed is nothing else but creating in favour of each individual an existence entirely independent of all authority, or of any other will than his own, an idea absurd and contrary to the nature of man, and incompatible with the needs of human society.

The Course Which the Evil Has Followed and Still Follows

The causes of the deplorable intensity with which this evil weighs on society appear to us to be of two kinds. The first are so connected with the nature of things that no human foresight could have prevented them. The second should be subdivided into two classes, however similar they may appear in their effects.

Of these causes, the first are negative, the others positive. We will place among the first the feebleness and the inertia of Governments.

It is sufficient to cast a glance on the course which the Governments followed during the eighteenth century, to be convinced that not one among them was ignorant of the evil or of the crisis towards which the social body was tending. There were, however, some men, unhappily endowed with great talents, who felt their own strength, and were not slow to appraise the progressive course of their influence, taking into account the weakness or the inertia of their adversaries; and who had the art to prepare and conduct men's minds to the triumph of their detestable enterprise—an enterprise all the more odious as it was pursued without regard to results, simply abandoning themselves to the one feeling of hatred of God and of His immutable moral laws.

France had the misfortune to produce the greatest number of these men. It is in her midst that religion and all that she holds sacred, that morality and authority, and all connected with them, have been attacked with a steady and systematic animosity, and it is there that the weapon of ridicule has been used with the most ease and success.

Drag through the mud the name of God and the powers instituted by His divine decrees, and the revolution will be prepared! Speak of a social contract, and the revolution is accomplished! The revolution was already completed in the palaces of Kings, in the drawing-rooms and boudoirs of certain cities, while among the great mass of the people it was still only in a state of preparation.

It would be difficult not to pause here to consider the influence which the example of England had for a long time exercised on France. England is herself placed in such a peculiar situation that we believe we may safely say that not one of the forms possible to that State, not one of its customs or institutions, would suit any Continental State, and that where we might wish to take them for models, we should only obtain inconvenience and danger, without securing a single one of the advantages which accompany them.

According to the bent of minds in France, at the time of the convocation of the *notables,* and in consequence of the direction which public opinion had received for more than fifty years—a direction which, latterly, had been strengthened and in some sort adapted to France by the imprudent help which her Government had given to the American revolution—all reform in France touching the very foundations of the monarchy was soon transformed into a revolution. What might have been foreseen, and what had been foretold by everybody, the Government alone excepted, was realised but too soon. The French Revolution broke out, and has gone through a complete revolutionary cycle in a very short period, which could only have appeared long to its victims and to its contemporaries.

The scenes of horror which accompanied the first phases of the French Revolution prevented the rapid propagation of its subversive principles beyond the frontiers of France, and the wars of conquest which succeeded them gave to the public mind a direction little favourable to revolutionary principles. Thus the Jacobin propaganda failed entirely to realise criminal hopes.

Nevertheless the revolutionary seed had penetrated into every country and spread more or less. It was greatly developed under the *régime* of the military despotism of Bonaparte. His conquests displaced a number of laws, institutions, and customs; broke through bonds sacred among all nations, strong enough to resist time itself; which is more than can be said of certain benefits conferred by these innovators. From these perturbations it followed that the revolutionary spirit could in Germany, Italy, and later on in Spain, easily hide itself under the veil of patriotism.

Prussia committed a grave fault in calling to her aid such dangerous weapons as secret associations always will be: a fault which could not be justified even by the deplorable situation in which that Power then found itself. This it was that first gave a strong impulse to the revolutionary spirit in her States, and this spirit made rapid progress, supported as it was in the rest of Germany by the system of foreign despotism which since 1806 has been there developed. Many Princes of the Rhenish Confederation were secretly auxiliaries and accomplices of this system, to which they sacrificed the institutions which in their country from time immemorial had served as a protection against despotism and democracy.

The war of the Allies, by putting bounds to the predominance of France, was vigorously supported in Germany by the same men whose hatred of France was in reality nothing but hatred of the military despotism of Bonaparte, and also of the legitimate power of their own masters. With wisdom in the Governments and firmness in principles, the end of the war in 1814 might nevertheless have insured to the world the most peaceful and happy future. Great experiences had been gained and great lessons, which might have been usefully applied. But fate had decided otherwise.

The return of the usurper to France, and the completely false steps taken by the French Government from 1815 to 1820, accumulated a mass of new dangers and great calamities for the whole civilised world. It is to the first of these misfortunes that is partly due the critical state in which France and the whole social body is placed. Bonaparte destroyed in a hundred days the work of the fourteen years during which he had exercised his authority. He set free the revolution which he came to France to subdue; he brought back men's minds, not to the epoch of the 18th Brumaire, but to the principles which the National Assembly had adopted in its deplorable blindness.

What Bonaparte had thus done to the detriment of France and Europe, the grave errors which the French Government have since committed, and to which other Governments have yielded—all these unhappy influences weigh heavily on the world of to-day; they threaten with total ruin the work of restoration, the fruit of so many glorious efforts, and of a harmony between the greatest monarchs unparalleled in the records of history, and they give rise to fears of indescribable calamities to society.

In this memoir we have not yet touched on one of the most active and at the same time most dangerous instruments used by the revolutionists of all countries, with a success which is no longer doubtful. I refer to the secret societies, a real power, all the more dangerous as it works in the dark, undermining all parts of the social body, and depositing everywhere the seeds of a moral gangrene which is not slow to develop and increase. This plague is one of the worst which those Governments who are lovers of peace and of their people have to watch and fight against.

Do Remedies for This Evil Exist, and What Are They?

We look upon it as a fundamental truth, that for every disease there is a remedy, and that the knowledge of the real nature of the one should lead to the discovery of the other. Few men, however, stop thoroughly to examine a disease which they intend to combat. There are hardly any who are not subject to the influence of passion, or held under the yoke of prejudice; there are a great many who err in a way more perilous still, on account of its flattering and often brilliant appearance: we speak of *l'esprit de système;* that spirit always false, but indefatigable, audacious and irrepressible, is satisfactory to men imbued with it (for they live in and govern a world created by themselves), but it is so much the more dangerous for the inhabitants of the real world, so different from that created by *l'esprit de système.*

There is another class of men who, judging of a disease by its outward appearance, confound the accessory manifestations with the root of the disease, and, instead of directing their efforts to the source of the evil, content themselves with subduing some passing symptoms.

It is our duty to try and avoid both of these dangers.

The evil exists and it is enormous. We do not think we can better define it and its cause at all times and in all places than we have already done by the word 'presumption,' that inseparable companion of the half-educated, that spring of an unmeasured ambition, and yet easy to satisfy in times of trouble and confusion.

It is principally the middle classes of society which this moral gangrene has affected, and it is only among them that the real heads of the party are found.

For the great mass of the people it has no attraction and can have none. The labours to which this class—the real people—are obliged to devote them-

selves, are too continuous and too positive to allow them to throw themselves into vague abstractions and ambitions. The people know what is the happiest thing for them: namely, to be able to count on the morrow, for it is the morrow which will repay them for the cares and sorrows of to-day. The laws which afford a just protection to individuals, to families, and to property, are quite simple in their essence. The people dread any movement which injures industry and brings new burdens in its train.

Men in the higher classes of society who join the revolution are either falsely ambitious men or, in the widest acceptation of the word, lost spirits. Their career, moreover, is generally short! They are the first victims of political reforms, and the part played by the small number among them who survive is mostly that of courtiers despised by upstarts, their inferiors, promoted to the first dignities of the State; and of this France, Germany, Italy, and Spain furnish a number of living examples.

We do not believe that fresh disorders with a directly revolutionary end—not even revolutions in the palace and the highest places in the Government—are to be feared at present in France, because of the decided aversion of the people to anything which might disturb the peace they are now enjoying after so many troubles and disasters.

In Germany, as in Spain and Italy, the people ask only for peace and quiet.

In all four countries the agitated classes are principally composed of wealthy men—real cosmopolitans, securing their personal advantage at the expense of any order of things whatever—paid State officials, men of letters, lawyers, and the individuals charged with the public education.

To these classes may be added that of the falsely ambitious, whose number is never considerable among the lower orders, but is larger in the higher ranks of society.

There is besides scarcely any epoch which does not offer a rallying cry to some particular faction. This cry, since 1815, has been *Constitution.* But do not let us deceive ourselves: this word, susceptible of great latitude of interpretation, would be but imperfectly understood if we supposed that the factions attached quite the same meaning to it under the different *régimes.* Such is certainly not the case. In pure monarchies it is qualified by the name of 'national representation.' In countries which have lately been brought under the representative *régime* it is called 'development,' and promises charters and fundamental laws. In the only State which possesses an ancient national representation it takes 'reform' as its object. Everywhere it means change and trouble.

In pure monarchies it may be paraphrased thus:—'The level of equality shall pass over your heads; your fortunes shall pass into other hands; your ambitions, which have been satisfied for centuries, shall now give place to our ambitions, which have been hitherto repressed.'

In the States under a new *régime* they say:—'The ambitions satisfied yesterday must give place to those of the morrow, and this is the morrow for us.'

Lastly, in England, the only place in the third class, the rallying cry—that of Reform—combines the two meanings.

Europe thus presents itself to the impartial observer under an aspect at the same time deplorable and peculiar. We find everywhere the people praying for the maintenance of peace and tranquillity, faithful to God and their Princes, remaining proof against the efforts and seductions of the factious who call themselves friends of the people and wish to lead them to an agitation which the people themselves do not desire!

The Governments, having lost their balance, are frightened, intimidated, and thrown into confusion by the cries of the intermediary class of society, which, placed between the Kings and their subjects, breaks the sceptre of the monarch, and usurps the cry of the people—that class so often disowned by the people, and nevertheless too much listened to, caressed and feared by those who could with one word reduce it again to nothingness.

We see this intermediary class abandon itself with a blind fury and animosity which proves much more its own fears than any confidence in the success of its enterprises, to all the means which seem proper to assuage its thirst for power, applying itself to the task of persuading Kings that their rights are confined to sitting upon a throne, while those of the people are to govern, and to attack all that centuries have bequeathed as holy and worthy of man's respect—denying, in fact, the

value of the past, and declaring themselves the masters of the future. We see this class take all sorts of disguises, uniting and subdividing as occasion offers, helping each other in the hour of danger, and the next day depriving each other of all their conquests. It takes possession of the press, and employs it to promote impiety, disobedience to the laws of religion and the State, and goes so far as to preach murder as a duty for those who desire what is good.

One of its leaders in Germany defined public opinion as 'the will of the strong man in the spirit of the party'—a maxim too often put in practice, and too seldom understood by those whose right and duty it is to save society from its own errors, its own weaknesses, and the crimes which the factious commit while pretending to act in its interests.

The evil is plain; the means used by the faction which causes these disorders are so blameable in principle, so criminal in their application, and expose the faction itself to so many dangers, that what men of narrow views (whose head and heart are broken by circumstances stronger than their calculations or their courage) regard as the end of society may become the first step towards a better order of things. These weak men would be right unless men stronger than they are come forward to close their ranks and determine the victory.

We are convinced that society can no longer be saved without strong and vigorous resolutions on the part of the Goverments still free in their opinions and actions.

We are also convinced that this may yet be, if the Governments face the truth, if they free themselves from all illusion, if they join their ranks and take their stand on a line of correct, unambiguous, and frankly announced principles.

By this course the monarchs will fulfil the duties imposed upon them by Him who, by entrusting them with power, has charged them to watch over the maintenance of justice, and the rights of all, to avoid the paths of error, and tread firmly in the way of truth. Placed beyond the passions which agitate society, it is in days of trial chiefly that they are called upon to despoil realities of their false appearances, and to show themselves as they are, fathers invested with the authority belonging by right to the heads of families, to prove that, in days of mourning, they know how to be just, wise, and therefore strong, and that they will not abandon the people whom they ought to govern to be the sport of factions, to error and its consequences, which must involve the loss of society. The moment in which we are putting our thoughts on paper is one of these critical moments. The crisis is great; it will be decisive according to the part we take or do not take.

There is a rule of conduct common to individuals and to States, established by the experience of centuries as by that of everyday life. This rule declares 'that one must not dream of reformation while agitated by passion; wisdom directs that at such moments we should limit ourselves to maintaining.'

Let the monarchs vigorously adopt this principle; let all their resolutions bear the impression of it. Let their actions, their measures, and even their words announce and prove to the world this determination—they will find allies everywhere. The Governments, in establishing the principle of *stability*, will in no wise exclude the development of what is good, for stability is not immobility. But it is for those who are burdened with the heavy task of government to augment the well-being of their people! It is for Governments to regulate it according to necessity and to suit the times. It is not by concessions, which the factious strive to force from legitimate power, and which they have neither the right to claim nor the faculty of keeping within just bounds, that wise reforms can be carried out. That all the good possible should be done is our most ardent wish; but that which is not good must never be confounded with that which is, and even real good should be done only by those who unite to the right of authority the means of enforcing it. Such should be also the sincere wish of the people, who know by sad experience the value of certain phrases and the nature of certain caresses.

Respect for all that is; liberty for every Government to watch over the well-being of its own people; a league between all Governments against factions in all States; contempt for the meaningless words which have become the rallying cry of the factious; respect for the progressive development of institutions in lawful ways; refusal on the part of every monarch to aid or succour partisans under any mask whatever—such are happily the ideas of the great monarchs: the world will be saved if they bring them into action—it is lost if they do not.

Union between the monarchs is the basis of the policy which must now be followed to save society from total ruin.

What is the particular object towards which this policy should be directed? The more important this question is, the more necessary it is to solve it. A principle is something, but it acquires real value only in its application.

The first sources of the evil which is crushing the world have been indicated by us in a paper which has no pretension to be anything more than a mere sketch. Its further causes have also there been pointed out: if, with respect to individuals, it may be defined by the word *presumption*, in applying it to society, taken as a whole, we believe we can best describe the existing evil as the *confusion of ideas*, to which too much generalisation constantly leads. This is what now troubles society. Everything which up to this time has been considered as fixed in principle is attacked and overthrown.

In religious matters criticism and inquiry are to take the place of faith, Christian morality is to replace the Law of Christ as it is interpreted by Christian authorities.

In the Catholic Church, the Jansenists and a number of isolated sectarians, who wish for a religion without a Church, have devoted themselves to this enterprise with ardent zeal: among the Protestant sects, the Methodists, sub-divided into almost as many sects as there are individuals; then the enlightened promoters of the Bible Societies and the Unitarians—the promoters of the fusion of Lutherans and Calvinists in one Evangelical community—all pursue the same end.

The object which these men have in common, to whatever religion they may ostensibly belong, is simply to overthrow all authority. Put on moral grounds, they wish *to enfranchise souls* in the same way as some of the political revolutionists who were not actuated by motives of personal ambition wished to *enfranchise the people*.

If the same elements of destruction which are now throwing society into convulsion have existed in all ages—for every age has seen immoral and ambitious men, hypocrites, men of heated imaginations, wrong motives, and wild projects—yet ours, by the single fact of the liberty of the press, possesses more than any preceding age the means of contact, seduction, and attraction Whereby to act on these different classes of men.

We are certainly not alone in questioning if society can exist with the liberty of the press, a scourge unknown to the world before the latter half of the seventeenth century, and restrained until the end of the eighteenth, with scarcely any exceptions but England—a part of Europe separated from the continent by the sea, as well as by her language and by her peculiar manners.

The first principle to be followed by the monarchs, united as they are by the coincidence of their desires and opinions, should be that of maintaining the stability of political institutions against the disorganised excitement which has taken possession of men's minds; the immutability of principles against the madness of their interpretation; and respect for laws actually in force against a desire for their destruction.

The hostile faction is divided into two very distinct parties. One is that of the Levellers; the other, that of the Doctrinaires. United in times of confusion, these men are divided in times of inaction. It is for the Governments to understand and estimate them at their just value.

In the class of Levellers there are found men of strong will and determination. The Doctrinaires can count none such among their ranks. If the first are more to be feared in action, the second are more dangerous in that time of deceitful calm which precedes it; as with physical storms, so with those of social order. Given up to abstract ideas inapplicable to real wants, and generally in contradiction to those very wants, men of this class unceasingly agitate the people by their imaginary or simulated fears, and disturb Governments in order to make them deviate from the right path. The world desires to be governed by facts and according to justice, not by phrases and theories; the first need of society is to be maintained by strong authority (no authority without real strength deserves the name) and not to govern itself. In comparing the number of contests between parties in mixed Governments, and that of just complaints caused by aberrations of power in a Christian State, the comparison would not be in favour of the new doctrines. The first and greatest concern for the immense majority of every nation is the stability of the laws, and their uninterrupted action—never their change. Therefore let the Governments govern, let them maintain the groundwork of their institutions, both ancient and modern; for if it is at all times dangerous to touch them, it certainly would not now, in the general confusion, be wise to do so.

Let them announce this determination to their people, and demonstrate it by facts. Let them reduce the Doctrinaires to silence within their States, and show their contempt for them abroad. Let them not encourage by their attitude or actions the suspicion of being favourable or indifferent to error: let them not allow it to be believed that experience has lost all its rights to make way for experiments which at the least are dangerous. Let them be precise and clear in all their words, and not seek by concessions to gain over those parties who aim at the destruction of all power but their own, whom concessions will never gain over, but only further embolden in their pretensions to power.

Let them in these troublous times be more than usually cautious in attempting real ameliorations, not imperatively claimed by the needs of the moment, to the end that good itself may not turn against them—which is the case whenever a Government measure seems to be inspired by fear.

Let them not confound concessions made to parties with the good they ought to do for their people, in modifying, according to their recognised needs, such branches of the administration as require it.

Let them give minute attention to the financial state of their kingdoms, so that their people may enjoy, by the reduction of public burdens, the real, not imaginary, benefits of a state of peace.

Let them be just, but strong; beneficent, but strict.

Let them maintain religious principles in all their purity, and not allow the faith to be attacked and morality interpreted according to the *social contract* or the visions of foolish sectarians.

Let them suppress Secret Societies, that gangrene of society.

In short, let the great monarchs strengthen their union, and prove to the world that if it exists, it is beneficent, and ensures the political peace of Europe: that it is powerful only for the maintenance of tranquillity at a time when so many attacks are directed against it; that the principles which they profess are paternal and protective, menacing only the disturbers of public tranquillity.

The Governments of the second order will see in such a union the anchor of their salvation, and they will be anxious to connect themselves with it. The people will take confidence and courage, and the most profound and salutary peace which the history of any time can show will have been effected. This peace will first act on countries still in a good state, but will not be without a very decided influence on the fate of those threatened with destruction, and even assist the restoration of those which have already passed under the scourge of revolution.

To every great State determined to survive the storm there still remain many chances of salvation, and a strong union between the States on the principles we have announced will overcome the storm itself.

The Authority of Custom

Joseph de Maistre

In the post-Napoleonic order, the Catholic thinker Joseph de Maistre became the chief theorist of those who wanted a return to a prerevolutionary mentality. If the modern world witnessed the progress of liberal ideas and civil society, de Maistre represented its opposite. He argued that civil liberties were dependent on religious fidelity. In response to the revolutionary cry for "liberty, equality, and fraternity," he answered with "throne and altar." His view of monarchy was intensely religious.

The Fallacy of the Written Constitution

One of the grand errors of an age, which professed them all, was, to believe that a political constitution could be written and created *à priori;* whilst reason and experience unite in establishing that a constitution is a Divine work, and that that which is most fundamental, and most essentially constitutional, in the laws of a nation, is precisely what cannot be written.

It has often been supposed to be an excellent piece of pleasantry upon Frenchmen, to ask them *in what book the Salic law was written?* But Jérôme Bignon answered, very apropos, and probably without knowing the full truth of what he said, *that it was written* IN *the hearts of Frenchmen.* Let us suppose, in effect, that a law of so much importance existed only because it was written; it is certain that any authority whatsoever which may have written it, will have the right of annulling it; the law will not then have that character of sacredness and immutability which distinguishes laws truly constitutional. The essence of a fundamental law is, that no one has the right to abolish it: now, how can it be above *all,* if *any one* has made it? The agreement of the people is impossible; and even if it should be otherwise, a compact is not a law, and binds

From: *The Conservative Tradition in European Thought,* ed. Robert L. Schuettinger (New York: G.P. Putnam & Sons, 1970), pp. 272–283.

nobody, unless there is a superior authority by which it is guarantied.

Hence it is that the good sense of antiquity, happily anterior to sophisms, has sought, on every side, the sanction of laws, in a power above man, either in recognizing that sovereignty comes from God, or in revering certain unwritten laws as proceeding from him.

Ask Roman history what was precisely the power of the Senate: she is silent, at least as to the exact limits of that power. We see, indeed, in general, that the power of the people and that of the Senate mutually balanced each other, and that the opposition was unceasing; we observe also that patriotism or weariness, weakness or violence, terminated these dangerous struggles: but we know no more about it.

The English Constitution is an example nearer to us, and, therefore, more striking. Whoever examines it with attention, will see *that it goes only in not going* (if this play upon words is permissible). It is maintained only by the exceptions. The *habeas corpus,* for example, has been so often and for so long time suspended, that it is doubted whether the exception has not become the rule. Suppose for a moment that the authors of this famous act had undertaken to fix the cases in which it should be suspended; they would *ipso facto* have annihilated it.

At the sitting of the House of Commons, June 26, 1807, a lord cited the authority of a great statesman to show that the King had no right to dissolve Parliament during the session; but this opinion was contradicted: Where is the law? Attempt to make a law, and to fix exclusively *by writing* the case where the King has this right, and you will produce a revolution. *The King*, said one of the members, *has this right when the occasion is important;* but what is an *important* occasion? Try to decide this too by writing.

Towards the end of the last century, a great outcry was made against a Minister, who had conceived the project of introducing this same English Constitution (or what was called by that name) into a kingdom which was convulsed, and which demanded a constitution of some kind, with a sort of frenzy. He was wrong, if you please, so far at least as one can be wrong when he acts in good faith. But who at that time had the right of condemning him? If the principle is granted, *that man can create a constitution*, this Minister had the same right to make his own as well as another. Were the doctrines on this point doubted? Was it not believed, on all sides, that a constitution was the work of intelligence, like an ode or tragedy? Had not *Thomas Paine* declared, with a profoundness that charmed the Universities, *that a constitution does not exist, so long as one cannot put it into his pocket?* The eighteenth century, which distrusted itself in nothing, hesitated at nothing.

The more we examine the influence of human agency in the formation of political constitutions, the greater will be our conviction that it enters there only in a manner infinitely subordinate, or as a simple instrument; and I do not believe there remains the least doubt of the incontestable truth of the following propositions:—

1. That the fundamental principles of political constitutions exist before all written law.

2. That a constitutional law is, and can only be, the development or sanction of an unwritten pre-existing right.

3. That which is most essential, most intrinsically constitutional, and truly fundamental, is never written, and could not be, without endangering the state.

4. That the weakness and fragility of a constitution are actually in direct proportion to the multiplicity of written constitutional articles.

We are deceived on this point by a sophism so natural, that it entirely escapes our attention. Because

man acts, he thinks he acts alone; and because he has the consciousness of his liberty, he forgets his dependence. In the physical order, he listens to reason; for although he can, for example, plant an acorn, water it, etc., he is convinced that he does not make the oaks, because he witnesses their growth and perfection without the aid of human power; and moreover, that he does not make the acorn; but in the social order, where he is present, and acts, he fully believes that he is really the sole author of all that is done by himself. This is, in a sense, as if the trowel should believe itself the architect. Man is a free, intelligent, and noble being: without doubt; but he is not less an *instrument of God.* . . .

Let us now consider some one political constitution, that of England, for example. It certainly was not made *à priori*. Her Statesmen never assembled themselves together and said, *Let us create three powers, balancing them in such a manner, etc.* No one of them ever thought of such a thing. The Constitution is the work of circumstances, and the number of these is infinite. Roman laws, ecclesiastical laws, feudal laws; Saxon, Norman, and Danish customs; the privileges, prejudices, and claims of all orders; wars, revolts, revolutions, the Conquest, Crusades; virtues of every kind, and all vices; knowledge of every sort, and all errors and passions;—all these elements, in short, acting together, and forming, by their admixture and reciprocal action, combinations multiplied by myriads of millions, have produced at length, after many centuries, the most complex unity, and happy equilibrium of political powers that the world has ever seen.

Now since these elements, thus projected into space, have arranged themselves in such beautiful order, without a single man, among the innumerable multitude who have acted in this vast field, having ever known what he had done relatively to the whole, nor foreseen what would happen, it follows, inevitably, that these elements were guided in their fall by an infallible hand, superior to man. The greatest folly, perhaps, in an age of follies, was in believing that fundamental laws could be written *à priori*, whilst they are evidently the work of a power above man; and whilst the very committing them to writing, long after, is the most certain sign of their nullity. . . .

These ideas (taken in their general sense) were not unknown to the ancient philosophers: they keenly felt the impotency, I had almost said the nothingness, of writing, in great institutions; but no one of them has seen this truth more clearly, or expressed it more happily, than Plato, whom we always find the first upon the track of all great truths. According to him, "the man who is wholly indebted to writing for his instruction, *will only possess the appearance of wisdom.* The word is to writing, what the man is to his portrait. The productions of the pencil present themselves to our eyes as living things; but *if we interrogate them, they maintain a dignified silence.* It is the same with writing, *which knows not what to say to one man, nor what to conceal from another.* If you attack it or insult it without a cause, it cannot defend itself; *for its author is never present to sustain it.* So that he who imagines himself capable of establishing, clearly and permanently, one single doctrine, by writing alone, IS A GREAT BLOCK-HEAD. If he really possessed the true germs of truth, he would not indulge the thought, that *with a little black liquid and a pen* he could cause them to germinate in the world, defend them from the inclemency of the season, and communicate to them the necessary efficacy. As for the man who undertakes to write *laws or civil constitutions,* and who fancies that, because he has written them, he is able to give them adequate evidence and stability, whoever he may be, a private man or legislator, he disgraces himself, whether we say it or not; for he has proved thereby that he is equally ignorant of the nature of inspiration and delirium, right and wrong, good and evil. Now, this ignorance is a reproach, though the entire mass of the vulgar should unite in its praise."

After having heard the *wisdom of the Gentiles,* it will not be useless to listen further to Christian Philosophy.

"It were indeed desirable for us," says one of the most eloquent of the Greek fathers [St. Chrysostom], "never to have required the aid of the written word, but to have had the Divine precepts written only in our hearts, by grace, as they are written with ink in our books; but since we have lost this grace by our own fault, let us then, as it is necessary, seize *a plank instead of the vessel,* without however forgetting the pre-eminence of the first state. God never revealed any thing in writing to the elect of the old Testament: He always spoke to them directly, because He saw the purity of their hearts; but the Hebrew people having fallen into the very abyss of wickedness, books and laws became necessary. The same proceeding is repeated under the empire of the New Revelation; for Christ did not leave a single writing to his Apostles. Instead of books, he promised to them the Holy Spirit: *It is He,* saith our Lord to them, *who shall teach you what you shall speak.* But because, in process of time, sinful men rebelled against the faith and against morality, it was necessary to have recourse to books."

The Necessity for Reliance upon God

If the desires of a mere mortal were worthy of obtaining of Divine Providence one of those memorable decrees which constitute the grand epochs of history, I would ask Him to inspire some powerful nation, which had grievously offended Him, with the proud thought of constituting itself politically, beginning at the foundations. I would say, "Grant to this people every thing! Give to her genius, knowledge, riches, consideration, especially an unbounded confidence in herself, and that temper, at once pliant and enterprising, which nothing can embarrass, nothing intimidate. Extinguish her old government; take away from her memory; destroy her affections; spread terror around her; blind or paralyze her enemies; give victory charge to watch at once over all her frontiers, so that none of her neighbors could meddle in her affairs, or disturb her in her operations. Let this nation be illustrious in science, rich in philosophy, intoxicated with human power, free from all prejudice, from every tie, and from all superior influence; bestow upon her every thing she shall desire, lest at some time she might say, *this was wanting* or *that restrained me;* let her, in short, act freely with this immensity of means, that at length she may become, under Thy inexorable protection, an eternal lesson to the human race."

We cannot, it is true, expect a combination of circumstances which would constitute literally a miracle; but events of the same order, though less remarkable, have manifested themselves here and there in history, even in the history of our days; and, though they may not possess, for the purpose of example, that ideal force which I desired just now, they contain not less of memorable instruction.

We have been witnesses, within the last twenty-five years, of a solemn attempt made for the regeneration of a great nation mortally sick. It was the first experiment in the great work, and the *preface*, if I may be allowed to express myself thus, of the frightful book which we have been since called upon to read.

But, it will be said, *we know the causes which prevented the success of that enterprise.* How then? Do you wish that God should send angels under human guises commissioned to destroy a constitution? It will always be necessary to employ second causes; this or that, what does it signify? Every instrument is good in the hands of the great Artificer: but such is the blindness of men, that if, to-morrow, some constitution-monger should come to organize a people, and to give them a constitution made *with a little black liquid*, the multitude would again hasten to believe in the miracle announced. It would be said, again, *nothing is wanting; all is foreseen; all is written*; whilst, precisely because all could be foreseen, discussed, and written, it would be demonstrated, that the constitution is a nullity, and presents to the eye merely an ephemeral appearance.

I believe I have read, somewhere, *that there are few sovereignties in a condition to vindicate the legitimacy of their origin.* Admitting the reasonableness of the assertion, there will not result from it the least stain to the successors of a chief, whose acts might be liable to some objections. If it were otherwise, it would follow, that the sovereign could not reign legitimately, except by virtue of a deliberation of all the people, that is to say, *by the grace of the people*; which will never happen: for there is nothing so true, as that which was said by the author of the *Considerations on France—that the people will always accept their masters, and will never choose them.* It is necessary that the origin of sovereignty should manifest itself from beyond the sphere of human power; so that men, who may appear to have a direct hand in it, may be, nevertheless, only the circumstances. As to legitimacy, if it should seem in its origin to be obscure, God explains Himself, by His prime-minister in the department of this world,—TIME.

But, since every constitution is divine in its principle, it follows, that man can do nothing in this way, unless he reposes himself upon God, whose instrument he then becomes. Now, this is a truth, to which the whole human race in a body have ever rendered the most signal testimony. Examine history, which is experimental politics, and we shall there invariably find the cradle of nations surrounded by priests, and the Divinity constantly invoked to the aid of human weakness. Fable, much more true than ancient history, for eyes prepared, comes in to strengthen the demonstration. It is always an oracle, which founds cities; it is always an oracle, which announces the Divine protection, and successes of the heroic founder.

The most famous nations of antiquity, especially the most serious and wise, such as the Egyptians, Etruscans, Lacedaemonians, and Romans, had precisely the most religious constitutions; and the duration of empires has always been proportioned to the degree of influence which the religious principle had acquired in the political constitution: *the cities and nations most addicted to Divine worship, have always been the most durable, and the most wise; as the most religious ages have also ever been most distinguished for genius.*

Not only does it not belong to man to create institutions, but it does not appear that his power, *unassisted*, extends even to change for the better institutions already established. The word *reform*, in itself, and previous to all examination, will be always suspected by wisdom, and the experience of every age justifies this sort of instinct. We know too well what has been the fruit of the most beautiful speculations of this kind.

To apply these general maxims to a particular case, it is from the single consideration of the extreme danger of innovations founded upon simple human theories, that, upon the great question of parliamentary reform, which has agitated minds in England so powerfully, and for so long a time, I find myself constrained to believe, that this idea is pernicious, and that if the English yield themselves too readily to it, they will have occasion to repent. *But,* say the partizans of reform, (for it is the grand argument,) *the abuses are striking and incontestable: now can a formal abuse, a defect, be constitutional?* Yes, undoubtedly, it can be; for every political constitution has its essential faults, which belong to its nature, and which it is impossible to separate from it; and, that which should make all reformers tremble, is that these faults may be changed by circumstances; so that in showing that they are new, we cannot prove that they are not necessary. What prudent man, then, will not shudder in putting his hand to the work? Social harmony, like musical concord, is subject to the law of *temperament in the general key*. Adjust the *fifths* accurately, and the *octaves* will jar, and conversely. The dissonance being then inevitable, instead of excluding it, which is impossible, it must be *qualified* by distribution. Thus, on both sides, *imperfection is an element of possible perfection*. In this proposition there is only the form of a paradox.

Voltaire, who spoke of every thing, during an age, without having so much as penetrated below the surface, has reasoned very humourously on the sale of the offices of the magistracy which occurred in France: and no instance, perhaps, could be more apposite to make us sensible of the truth of the theory which I am setting forth. *That this sale is an abuse*, says he, *is proved by the fact, that it originated in another abuse*. Voltaire does not mistake here as every man is liable to mistake. He shamefully mistakes. It is a total eclipse of common sense. *Everything which springs from an abuse, an abuse!* On the contrary; one of the most general and evident laws of this power, at once secret and striking, which acts and makes itself to be felt on every side, is, that the remedy of an abuse springs from an abuse, and that the evil, having reached a certain point, destroys itself.

The error of this great writer proceeds from the fact, that, *divided between twenty sciences*, as he himself somewhere confesses, and constantly occupied in communicating instruction to the world, he rarely gave himself time to think. "A dissipated and voluptuous court, reduced to the greatest want by its foolish expenses, devises the sale of the offices of the magistracy, and thus creates" (what it never could have done freely, and with a knowledge of the cause,) "it creates," I say, "a rich magistracy, irremovable and independent; so that the infinite power *playing in the world* makes use of corruption for creating incorruptible tribunals" (as far as human weakness permits). There is nothing, indeed, so plausible to the eye of a true philosopher; nothing more conformable to great analogies, and to that incontestable law, which wills that the most important institutions should be the results not of deliberation, but of circumstances.

Here is the problem almost solved when it is stated, as is the case with all problems. *Could such a country as France be better judged than by hereditary magistrates?* If it is decided in the affirmative, which I suppose, it will be necessary for me at once to propose a second problem which is this: *the magistracy being necessarily hereditary, is there, in order to constitute it at first, and afterwards to recruit it, a mode more advantageous than that which fills the coffers of the sovereign with millions at the lowest price, and which assures, at the same time, the opulence, independence, and even the nobility* (of a certain sort) *of the supreme judges?* If we only consider venality as a means to the right of inheritance, every just mind is impressed with this, which is the true point of view. This is not the place to enter fully into this question; but enough has been said to prove that Voltaire has not so much as perceived it.

Let us now suppose a man like him at the head of affairs: he will not fail to act in accordance with his foolish theories of laws and of abuses. He will borrow at six and two thirds per cent to reimburse his nominal incumbents, creditors at two per cent: he will prepare minds by a multitude of paid writings, which will insult the magistracy and destroy public confidence in it. Soon Patronage, a thousand times more foolish than Chance, will open the long list of his blunders: the distinguished man, no longer perceiving in the right of inheritance a counterpoise to oppressive labours, will withdraw himself, never to return; and the great tribunals will be abandoned to adventurers without name, without fortune, and without consideration.

Such is the natural picture of most reforms. Man in relation with his Creator is sublime, and his action is creative: on the contrary, so soon as he separates himself from God, and acts alone, he does not cease to be powerful, for this is a privilege of his nature; but his action is negative, and tends only to destroy.

Withdrawn, by his vain sciences, from the single science which truly concerns him, man has believed himself endowed with power *to create*. . . . He has believed, that it was himself who invented languages; while, again, it belongs to him only to see that every human language is *learned* and never invented. He has believed that he could constitute nations; that is to say, in other terms, *that he could create that national unity, by virtue of which one nation is not another.* Finally, he has believed that, since he had the power of creating institutions, he had, with greater reason, that of borrowing them from other nations, and transferring them to his own country, all complete to his hand, with the name which they bore among the people from whom they were taken, in order, like those people, to enjoy them with the same advantages.

If the formation of all empires, the progress of civilization, and the unanimous agreement of all history and tradition do not suffice still to convince us, the death of empires will complete the demonstration commenced by their birth. As it is the religious principle which has created every thing, so it is the absence of this same principle which has destroyed every thing. The sect of Epicurus, which might be called *ancient incredulity*, corrupted at first, and soon after destroyed every government which was so unfortunate as to give it admission. Every where *Lucretius* announced *Cesar*.

But all past experience disappears before the frightful example afforded by the last century. Still intoxicated with its fumes, men are very far from being, at least in general, sufficiently composed, to contemplate this example in its true light, and especially to draw from it the necessary conclusions. It is then very important to direct our whole attention to this terrible scene.

It was only in the first part of the eighteenth century, that impiety became really a power. We see it at first extending itself on every side with inconceivable activity. From the palace to the cabin, it insinuates itself every where, and infests every thing. Soon a simple system becomes a formal association, which, by a rapid gradation, changes into a confederacy, and at length into a grand conspiracy which covers Europe.

Then that character of impiety which belongs only to the eighteenth century, manifests itself for the first time. It is no longer the cold tone of indifference, or at most the malignant irony of skepticism; it is a mortal hatred; it is the tone of anger, and often of rage. The writers of that period, at least the most distinguished of them, no longer treat Christianity as an immaterial human error; they pursue it as a capital enemy; they oppose it to the last extreme; it is a war to the death.

However entire Europe having been civilized by Christianity, the civil and religious institutions were blended, and, as it were, amalgamated in a surprising manner. It was then inevitable that the philosophy of the age should unhesitatingly hate the social institutions, from which it was impossible to separate the religious principle. This has taken place: every government, and all the establishments of Europe, were offensive to it, *because* they were Christian; and *in proportion* as they were Christian, an inquietude of opinion, an universal dissatisfaction, seized all minds. In France, especially, the philosophic rage knew no bounds; soon a single formidable voice, forming itself from many voices united, is heard to cry, in the midst of guilty Europe. "Depart from us! Shall we then forever tremble before the priests, and receive from them such instruction as it pleases them to give us? TRUTH throughout Europe, is concealed by the fumes of the censer; it is high time that she come out of this noxious cloud. We shall speak no more of Thee to our children; it is for them to know, when they shall arrive at manhood, whether there is such a Being as Thyself, and what Thou art, and what Thou requirest of them. Every thing which now exists, displeases us, because Thy name is written upon every thing that exists. We wish to destroy all, and to reconstruct the whole without Thee. Leave our councils, leave our schools, leave our houses: we would act alone: REASON suffices for us. Depart from us!"

How has God punished this execrable madness? He has punished it, as He created the light, by a single word. He spake, LET IT BE DONE!—and the political world has crumbled.

Europe is guilty, for having closed her eyes against these great truths; and it is because she is guilty, that she suffers. Yet she still repels the light, and acknowledges not the arm which gives the blow. Few men, indeed, among this material generation, are in a condition to know the *date, nature, and enormity,* of certain crimes, committed by individuals, by nations, and by sovereignties; still less to comprehend the kind of expiation which these crimes demand, and the adorable prodigy which compels EVIL to purify, with its own hands, the place which the eternal architect has already measured by the eye for His marvelous constructions.

A Harlot High and Low

Honore de Balzac

Honore de Balzac was one of the originators of the realistic novel that characterized nineteenth-century European literature. He entitled his enormous collective works The Human Comedy. *In this selection from* Harlot High and Low, *he mercilessly portrays the upwardly mobile bourgeoisie of the early-nineteenth century. His novels consistently provide a sense of enormous social change, as one world breaks down and another takes shape. Balzac concentrates on the consequences.*

Contenson

The famous banker was taking tea, nibbling slices of bread and butter like a man whose teeth had not been sharpened by appetite for a long time, when he heard a carriage stopping at the little door to his garden. Presently Nucingen's secretary brought in Contenson, whom he had eventually located in a café near Saint Pelagia's, where the agent was lunching on the tip given him by a debtor incarcerated with certain privileges which have to be paid for. Contenson, you must know, was a real poem, a Parisian poem. From his looks, you would have seen at first glance that the Figaro of Beaumarchais, the Mascarillo of Molière, Marivaux's Frontins and Dancourt's Lafleurs, those great exemplars of audacious knavery, of cunning brought to bay, of the setback turned to advantage, were mediocrities by contrast with this colossus of wretchedness and wit. When, in Paris, you meet a type, it is no mere man, it is a spectacle! it is no longer a moment in life, but a whole existence, several existences! Cook a plaster cast three times in a furnace, and you get a sort of bastard appearance of Florentine bronze; in the same way, the crackle of innumerable misfortunes, the grip of intolerable situations had bronzed Contenson's head as though the light of three furnaces had paled upon his visage. The tight lines could no longer be unwrinkled, they were eternal creases, white at the bottom. His yellow face was all lines. His skull, a bit like Voltaire's, was as unfeeling as a death's head, and, but for a little hair at the back, could hardly have been taken for that of a living man. Beneath a motionless brow, expressing nothing, moved the eyes of a Chinaman displayed under glass at the door of a tea-shop, artificial eyes pretending to be alive, their expression unchanging. The nose, flat like death's, defied Fate, and the mouth, tight-lipped as a miser's, was at once open and discreet like the rictus of a letter-box. Calm as a man of the wilderness, his hands deeply weathered, Contenson, a small, thin, dry man, had that attitude of Diogenic indifference which never bows to the forms of respect. And what commentary upon his life and customs was written into his dress, for those who know how to decipher a man's costume! . . . What breeches, particularly! . . . a bailiff's breeches, black and shiny like the stuff called *voile* of which barristers' gowns are made! . . . a waistcoat bought in the Temple, but embroidered and with lapels! . . . a coat of black turning red! . . . And all brushed, clean-looking, set off by a watch on a pinchbeck chain. On a pleated shirt-front of yellow cambric shone an artificial diamond pin! Upon the yoke of the velvet collar obtruded the raw folds of flesh like a Carib's. The silk hat shone like satin, but its lining would have yielded oil for two small lamps if some grocer had bought it and had it boiled. It serves little purpose to enumerate accessories, one should be able to

From: Honore de Balzac, *A Harlot High and Low* (New York: Penguin Books, 1970), pp. 111–116 paint the enormous pretentiousness imprinted on them by Contenson. There was something tremendously smart about the coat collar, about the newly polished boots with their gaping soles, which no expression in the language can render. In the end, trying to fit these various pieces together, an intelligent man, studying Contenson, would have seen that, if he had been a thief and not a police-spy, these rags, instead of bringing a smile to the lips, would have aroused horror. About his costume, an observer might have said to himself: 'There goes a squalid person, he drinks, he gambles, he has vices, but he doesn't get drunk, he doesn't cheat, he isn't a thief or a murderer.' And Contenson was indeed indefinable until the word 'spy' came into one's mind. The man had professed as many unknown trades as there are known ones. The faint smile on his pale lips, the blink of his greenish eyes, the twitching of his flat nose, showed that he did not lack intelligence. His tin-plate face must conceal a soul of identical substance. The movements of his physiognomy were grimaces drawn out of him by politeness, not the expression of emotions within. He would have aroused fear, if he had not been risible. Contenson, one of the most curious products of the scum which floats upon the waters of the Parisian sink, where everything is in ferment, prided himself above all on being a philosopher. He said without bitterness: 'I have great talents, but they go for nothing, as though I were an idiot!' And he condemned himself instead of accusing others. Find many spies with as little gall as Contenson. 'Circumstances are against us,' he repeatedly said to his superiors, 'we might be fine crystal, we are so many grains of sand, that is all.' His indifference in the matter of costume had a meaning, he cared as little about his everyday wear as actors do about theirs; he excelled in disguise, in make-up; he could have given lessons to Frederick Lemaître, for he could turn himself out stylishly when there was need. In his youth he had forcibly adopted the bohemianism of the back streets. He displayed a lordly contempt for the Judicial Police, for under the Empire he had worked for Fouché, whom he considered a great man. Since the suppression of the Ministry of Police, he had made the best of commercial investigations; but his known ability, his fine touch, made him a useful instrument, and the unknown heads of the Political Police kept his name on their books. Contenson, together with many of the same calibre, played only extras in the drama whose leading parts were allocated elsewhere, when political work was afoot.

The Goal of Passion

'Leaf us,' said Nucingen dismissing his secretary with a movement of the hand.

'Why does this man live in a mansion while I'm in a furnished room . . . ?' Contenson said to himself. 'He's ruined his creditors three times, he's stolen money, I've never taken a penny. . . I am more highly gifted than he is . . .'

'Gontenson, my luf,' said the baron, 'you tittled me a note off *tausend* francs . . .'

'My mistress was in debt up to the eyes . . .'

'You hef a mistress?' cried Nucingen eyeing Contenson with mingled admiration and envy.

'I'm only sixty-six,' replied Contenson, a man whom Vice had kept young, as a fatal example.

'End what does she?'

'Helps me,' said Contenson. 'If you're a thief and an honest woman loves you, either she becomes a thief, or you go straight. Me, I'm still an investigator, semi-private.'

'Hallways you hef need of money?' asked Nucingen.

'Always,' replied Contenson with a smile, 'it's my natural condition to want money, the way it's yours to make it; we ought to suit each other: you give me the stuff, I spend it. You're the well, me the bucket . . .'

'Do you wish earn note of fife *hundert* francs?'

'That's a fine question! but do I look stupid? . . . You're not offering it by way of repairing fortune's injustice in my favour.'

'Not at oll, I add it to *ze tausand* franc note you hef olready cheat me off; *also* fifteen *hundert* francs I gif you.'

'Good, you give me the thousand francs I took, and you add five hundred francs . . .'

'Yo, yo, is *gut*,' said Nucingen nodding his head.

'It's only five hundred francs,' said Contenson imperturbably.

'To gif? . . .' replied the baron.

'To take. Ah, well, what does Monsieur le Baron propose to buy with that?'

'I hef been dolt zet in Baris is a man gapable of discover ze woman I lof, end zet you know hiss eddress . . . Shortly, he iss master spy?'

'That's right . . .'

'Well, gif me z' eddress, end I gif you five *hundert* franc.'

'No kidding?' replied Contenson briskly.

'Here are,' the baron continued, taking a note from his pocket.

'Well, then, give,' said Contenson, holding out his hand.

'Gif I am, let us go see zis man, *und* you hef *ze* money, for you could sell me many eddress at zat price.'

Contenson began to laugh.

'As a matter of fact, you've got every right to think that of me,' said he with an air of greed. 'The more dastardly our condition, the more need we have of probity. But, look, Monsieur le Baron, make it six hundred francs, and I'll give you a piece of advice.'

'Gif it, end trust to my chenerosity . . .'

'I'll chance it,' said Contenson; 'but it's a big risk I'm taking. In police work, you know, you've got to keep your feet on the ground. You say: Come on, let's be off! . . . You're rich, you think everything gives way before money. Money counts, that's certain. But with money, in the opinion of one or two leading thinkers in our lot, you've only got men. There are things maybe you never think of, and they can't be bought! . . . You can't nobble good luck. So, in police work, you don't do things that way. Do you want to be seen with me in a carriage? we'd be met. Luck can be on your side, or it can be against you.'

'So?' said the baron.

'Lord! yes, sir. It was a horseshoe picked up in the street which led the Prefect of Police to the discovery of the infernal machine. Well! if we was to go at night in a four-wheeler to see M. de Saint-Germain, he'd no more care to see you walk in than you would to be seen going there.'

'Is true,' said the baron.

'Ah! he's the man all right, the famous Corentin's right hand, Fouché's strong arm, some say his natural son, he must have had one being a priest; but that's all rubbish: Fouché knew how to be a priest, same as he knew how to be Minister. Well, now, look, you won't get him on the job, see, for less than ten thousand franc notes . . . think about it . . . But the job will be done, and done well. And nobody the wiser, as they say. I shall have to warn Monsieur de Saint-Germain, and he'll arrange a meeting with you in some place where nobody'll either hear nor see, for it's risky for him to do police work for private individuals. But, there, what d'you expect? . . . he's a fine fellow, the king of men, and one who's had to put up with persecution on a big scale, all for being the saviour of France, what's more! . . . like me, like all the saviours of their country!'

'Well, *so*, you will write me when is ze ospicious hour,' said the baron smiling at his own witticism.

'Isn't Monsieur le Baron going to grease my palm? . . .' said Contenson with an air of threatening humility.

'Jean,' the baron called out to his gardener, 'go esk Georges twenty francs ent pring zem here . . .'

'If M. le Baron has no more information than what he has given me, I doubt all the same if the maestro will be able to help him.'

'I hef more!' replied the baron with a secretive air.

'I have the honour to salute Monsieur le Baron,' said Contenson taking the twenty-franc piece, 'I shall have the honour of coming and telling Georges where Monsieur should betake himself this evening, for on police work you should never put things in writing.'

'Is *komisch* how witty zese lads are,' said the baron to himself, 'in police is altogether much as in business.'

PART THREE

Eugene Delacroix, "Lady Liberty"

This famous painting of the July 1830 uprising in Paris is an eyewitness account and displays aspects both of liberalism and Romanticism. The young man in the opera hat holding a rifle to the left of Lady Liberty represents Delacroix himself, who took part in the events. The voluptuous figure of Liberty is meant as an abstract representation of what is highly desirable, in Delacroix's view, liberty itself. The violence of the painting suggests the cost of attaining freedom against the old regime.

Liberalism and Romanticism

The late eighteenth-century revolutions provided glimpses of a freer world. Tensions immediately arose between two competing world views—one aimed at retaining a hierarchical society dominated by hereditary elites and autocrats (see Part Two) and the other at creating a fluid society ruled by constitutions that favored those of recent prosperity and education. The latter view more closely fit the realities of post-1815 Europe: an energetic, often crude middle class, motivated by the attainment of wealth and prestige, refused to be bypassed politically. "Lady Liberty" (1830), the symbolic painting by Eugene Delacroix (1798–1863) of France's July 1830 uprising, suggests the middle class passion for greater freedom and a heftier role in politics. Middle-class politics found its expression in the writings of sophisticated political philosophers deeply grounded in Enlightenment writings. Simultaneously, in the cultural realm Romantic writers, composers, and painters also turned their backs on the old world in favor of new exploration. Liberalism, a political movement, and romanticism, a cultural one, shared many outlooks. Both welcomed change, focused on the individual and on individual nations, and rejected the old world.

The new century's foremost liberal philosopher, John Stuart Mill (1806–1873), welcomed freer society and politics in his *On Liberty* (1859). He emphasized the rights of the individual and, with other progressive thinkers, wished to enlist everyone's talents. In her novel *Middlemarch* (1871–1872), George Eliot (1819–1880) detailed the personal, working, and political lives of all classes in a small English town. In her view, empowering the people and bringing about reform caused raucous, but free, politics. The Sadler Commission (1832) members' questions and their working-class interviewees' answers testify to problems in a Europe undergoing rapid industrial growth and evolution toward parliamentary rule. The selection (which foreshadows issues raised in Part Four) suggests liberalism's inherent reformism which led it to question laissez faire, its own central tenet. In *The Sorrows of Young Werther* (1774), the German writer Johann von Goethe (1749–1832) helped create the Romantic era's new sensibility, which rejected the earlier reliance on Reason in favor of an emphasis on inner emotions and individual expression. Despairing of attaining his high personal goals, the romantic Werther commits suicide, an act that inspired many real life imitators among European youth still unused to individual freedom and unbridled sentiment. In *The Poor Fiddler* (1847), written at the other end of the Romantic era, Franz Grillparzer (1791–1872) raises different questions. His narrator, an educated person, displays a new sensitivity to the poor and suggests culture as a potentially equalizing element. By portraying a political event in the stormy style of the era's literature, music, and painting, Delacroix's "Lady Liberty" combined liberal and romantic outlooks. Romanticism's focus on national culture is the subject of later sections of this volume.

Study Questions

1. How does Mill's view of the individual differ from Metternich's?
2. What does Eliot's *Middlemarch* tell us about political campaigns?
3. What do the Sadler Commission's findings imply about liberalism's relationship to laissez faire?
4. Why is Young Werther representative of the era's Romantic Movement?
5. What do Goethe's and Grillparzer's novels suggest about literary fiction and reality?
6. Image: What does "Lady Liberty" reveal about the era's liberal and Romantic movements?

On Liberty

John Stuart Mill

In the early nineteenth century, the ideology of liberalism had many theorists, including John Stuart Mill. Mill was educated by his father according to stern principles. His intense education led to a nervous break-down at age 20, when he decided that there was more to life than devotion to the public good and a sharp intellect. Because of this, John Stuart Mill represents a merging of rationalist ideas with those of poets and other imaginative writers of the Romantic Era. His On Liberty *aroused a great deal of controversy, both in support and in opposition. Here Mill portrays his fears of middle-class conformism, which cared little for individual liberty.*

The object of this Essay is to assert one very simple principle, as entitled to govern absolutely the dealings of society with the individual in the way of compulsion and control, whether the means used be physical force in the form of legal penalties, or the moral coercion of public opinion. That principle is, that the sole end for which mankind are warranted, individually or collectively, in interfering with the liberty of action of any of their number, is self-protection. That the only purpose for which power can be rightfully exercised over any member of a civilised community, against his will, is to prevent harm to others. His own good, either physical or moral, is not a sufficient warrant. He cannot rightfully be compelled to do or forbear because it will be better for him to do so, because it will make him happier, because, in the opinions of others, to do so would be wise, or even right. These are good reasons for remonstrating with him, or reasoning with him, or persuading him, or entreating him, but not for compelling him, or visiting him with any evil in case he do otherwise. To justify that, the conduct from which it is desired to deter him must be calculated to produce evil to some one else. The only part of the conduct of any one, for which he is amenable to society, is that which concerns others. In the part which merely concerns himself, his independence is, of right, absolute. Over himself, over his own body and mind, the individual is sovereign.

It is, perhaps hardly necessary to say that this doctrine is meant to apply only to human beings in the maturity of their faculties. We are not speaking of children, or of young persons below the age which the law may fix as that of manhood or womanhood. Those who are still in a state to require being taken care of by others, must be protected against their own actions as well as against external injury. For the same reason, we may leave out of consideration those backward states of society in which the race itself may be considered as in its nonage. The early difficulties in the way of spontaneous progress are so great, that there is seldom any choice of means for overcoming them; and a ruler full of the spirit of improvement is warranted in the use of any expedients that will attain an end, perhaps otherwise unattainable. Despotism is a legitimate mode of government in dealing with barbarians, provided the end be their improvement, and the means justified by actually effecting that end. Liberty, as a principle, has no application to any state of things anterior to the time when mankind have become capable of being improved by free and equal discussion. Until then, there is nothing for them but implicit obedience to an

From: *Mill, Texts and Commentaries*, ed. Alan Ryan (New York, London: W.W. Norton & Company, 1997), pp. 48–59, 82–83.

Akbar or a Charlemagne, if they are so fortunate as to find one. But as soon as mankind have attained the capacity of being guided to their own improvement by conviction or persuasion (a period long since reached in all nations with whom we need here concern ourselves), compulsion, either in the direct form or in that of pains and penalties for non-compliance, is no longer admissible as a means to their own good, and justifiable only for the security of others.

It is proper to state that I forego any advantage which could be derived to my argument from the idea of abstract right, as a thing independent of utility. I regard utility as the ultimate appeal on all ethical questions; but it must be utility in the largest sense, grounded on the permanent interests of man as a progressive being. Those interests, I contend, authorise the subjection of individual spontaneity to external control, only in respect to those actions of each, which concern the interest of other people. If any one does an act hurtful to others, there is a *prima facie* case for punishing him, by law, or, where legal penalties are not safely applicable, by general disapprobation. There are also many positive acts for the benefit of others, which he may rightfully be compelled to perform; such as to give evidence in a court of justice: to bear his fair share in the common defence, or in any other joint work necessary to the interest of the society of which he enjoys the protection; and to perform certain acts of individual beneficence, such as saving a fellow-creature's life, or interposing to protect the defenceless against ill-usage, things which whenever it is obviously a man's duty to do, he may rightfully be made responsible to society for not doing. A person may cause evil to others not only by his actions but by his inaction, and in either case he is justly accountable to them for the injury. The latter case, it is true, requires a much more cautious exercise of compulsion than the former. To make any one answerable for doing evil to others is the rule: to make him answerable for not preventing evil is, comparatively speaking, the exception. Yet there are many cases clear enough and grave enough to justify that exception. In all things which regard the external relations of the individual, he is *de jure* amenable to those whose interests are concerned,

and, if need be, to society as their protector. There are often good reasons for not holding him to the responsibility; but these reasons must arise from the special expediencies of the case: either because it is a kind of case in which he is on the whole likely to act better, when left to his own discretion, than when controlled in any way in which society have it in their power to control him: or because the attempt to exercise control would produce other evils, greater than those which it would prevent. When such reasons as these preclude the enforcement of responsibility, the conscience of the agent himself should step into the vacant judgment seat, and protect those interests of others which have no external protection; judging himself all the more rigidly, because the case does not admit of his being made accountable to the judgment of his fellow-creatures.

But there is a sphere of action in which society, as distinguished from the individual, has, if any, only an indirect interest; comprehending all that portion of a person's life and conduct which affects only himself, or if it also affects others, only with their free, voluntary, and undeceived consent and participation. When I say only himself, I mean directly, and in the first instance; for whatever affects himself, may affect others *through* himself; and the objection which may be grounded on this contingency, will receive consideration in the sequel. This, then, is the appropriate region of human liberty. It comprises, first, the inward domain of consciousness: demanding liberty of conscience in the most comprehensive sense: liberty of thought and feeling; absolute freedom of opinion and sentiment on all subjects, practical or speculative, scientific, moral or theological. The liberty of expressing and publishing opinions may seem to fall under a different principle, since it belongs to that part of the conduct of an individual which concerns other people; but, being almost of as much importance as the liberty of thought itself, and resting in great part on the same reasons, is practically inseparable from it. Secondly, the principle requires liberty of tastes and pursuits: of framing the plan of our life to suit our own character; of doing as we like, subject to such consequences as may follow: without impediment from our fellow-creatures, so long as what we do does not harm them, even though they should think our conduct foolish, perverse, or wrong. Thirdly, from this liberty of each individual, follows the liberty, within the same limits, of combination among individuals; freedom to unite, for any purpose not involving harm to others: the persons combining being supposed to be of full age, and not forced or deceived.

No society in which these liberties are not, on the whole, respected, is free, whatever may be its form of government; and none is completely free in which they do not exist absolute and unqualified. The only freedom which deserves the name, is that of pursuing our own good in our own way, so long as we do not attempt to deprive others of theirs, or impede their efforts to obtain it. Each is the proper guardian of his own health, whether bodily, or mental and spiritual. Mankind are greater gainers by suffering each other to live as seems good to themselves, than by compelling each to live as seems good to the rest.

Though this doctrine is anything but new, and, to some persons, may have the air of a truism, there is no doctrine which stands more directly opposed to the general tendency of existing opinion and practice. Society has expended fully as much effort in the attempt (according to its lights) to compel people to conform to its notions of personal as of social excellence. The ancient commonwealths thought themselves entitled to practise, and the ancient philosophers countenanced, the regulation of every part of private conduct by public authority, on the ground that the State had a deep interest in the whole bodily and mental discipline of every one of its citizens: a mode of thinking which may have been admissible in small republics surrounded by powerful enemies, in constant peril of being subverted by foreign attack or internal commotion, and to which even a short interval of relaxed energy and self-command might so easily be fatal that they could not afford to wait for the salutary permanent effects of freedom. In the modern world, the greater size of political communities, and, above all, the separation between spiritual and temporal authority (which placed the direction of men's consciences in other hands than those which controlled their worldly affairs), prevented so great an interference by law in the details of private life; but the engines of moral repression have been wielded more strenuously against divergence from the reigning opinion

in self-regarding, than even in social matters; religion, the most powerful of the elements which have entered into the formation of moral feeling, having almost always been governed either by the ambition of a hierarchy, seeking control over every department of human conduct, or by the spirit of Puritanism. And some of those modern reformers who have placed themselves in strongest opposition to the religions of the past, have been noway behind either churches or sects in their assertion of the right of spiritual domination: M. Comte, in particular, whose social system, as unfolded in his *Système de Politique Positive*, aims at establishing (though by moral more than by legal appliances) a despotism of society over the individual, surpassing anything contemplated in the political ideal of the most rigid disciplinarian among the ancient philosophers.

Apart from the peculiar tenets of individual thinkers, there is also in the world at large an increasing inclination to stretch unduly the powers of society over the individual, both by the force of opinion and even by that of legislation; and as the tendency of all the changes taking place in the world is to strengthen society, and diminish the power of the individual, this encroachment is not one of the evils which tend spontaneously to disappear, but, on the contrary, to grow more and more formidable. The disposition of mankind, whether as rulers or as fellow-citizens, to impose their own opinions and inclinations as a rule of conduct on others, is so energetically supported by some of the best and by some of the worst feelings incident to human nature, that it is hardly ever kept under restraint by anything but want of power; and as the power is not declining, but growing, unless a strong barrier of moral conviction can be raised against the mischief, we must expect, in the present circumstances of the world, to see it increase.

It will be convenient for the argument, if, instead of at once entering upon the general thesis, we confine ourselves in the first instance to a single branch of it, on which the principle here stated is, if not fully, yet to a certain point, recognised by the current opinions. This one branch is the Liberty of Thought: from which it is impossible to separate the cognate liberty of speaking and of writing. Although these liberties, to some considerable amount, form part of the political morality of all countries which profess religious toleration and free institutions, the grounds, both philosophical and practical, on which they rest, are perhaps not so familiar to the general mind, nor so thoroughly appreciated by many even of the leaders of opinion, as might have been expected. Those grounds, when rightly understood, are of much wider application than to only one division of the subject, and a thorough consideration of this part of the question will be found the best introduction to the remainder. Those to whom nothing which I am about to say will be new, may therefore, I hope, excuse me, if on a subject which for now three centuries has been so often discussed, I venture on one discussion more.

Of the Liberty of Thought and Discussion

The time, it is to be hoped, is gone by, when any defence would be necessary of the "liberty of the press" as one of the securities against corrupt or tyrannical government. No argument, we may suppose, can now be needed, against permitting a legislature or an executive, not identified in interest with the people, to prescribe opinions to them, and determine what doctrines or what arguments they shall be allowed to hear. This aspect of the question, besides, has been so often and so triumphantly enforced by preceding writers, that it needs not be specially insisted on in this place. Though the law of England, on the subject of the press, is as servile to this day as it was in the time of the Tudors, there is little danger of its being actually put in force against political discussion, except during some temporary panic, when fear of insurrection drives ministers and judges from their propriety, and, speaking generally, it is not, in constitutional countries, to be apprehended, that the government, whether completely responsible to the people or not, will often attempt to control the expression of opinion, except when in doing so it makes itself the organ of the general intolerance of the public. Let us suppose, therefore, that the government is entirely at one with the people, and never thinks of exerting any power of coercion unless in agreement with what it conceives to be their voice. But I deny the right of the people to exercise such coercion, either by themselves or by their government. The power itself is

illegitimate. The best government has no more title to it than the worst. It is as noxious, or more noxious, when exerted in accordance with public opinion, than when in opposition to it. If all mankind minus one were of one opinion, and only one person were of the contrary opinion, mankind would be no more justified in silencing that one person, than he, if he had the power, would be justified in silencing mankind. Were an opinion a personal possession of no value except to the owner; if to be obstructed in the enjoyment of it were simply a private injury, it would make some difference whether the injury was inflicted only on a few persons or on many. But the peculiar evil of silencing the expression of an opinion is, that it is robbing the human race; posterity as well as the existing generation; those who dissent from the opinion, still more than those who hold it. If the opinion is right, they are deprived of the opportunity of exchanging error for truth: if wrong, they lose, what is almost as great a benefit, the clearer perception and livelier impression of truth, produced by its collision with error.

It is necessary to consider separately these two hypotheses each of which has a distinct branch of the argument corresponding to it. We can never be sure that the opinion we are endeavouring to stifle is a false opinion; and if we were sure, stifling it would be an evil still.

First: the opinion which it is attempted to suppress by authority may possibly be true. Those who desire to suppress it, of course deny its truth; but they are not infallible. They have no authority to decide the question for all mankind, and exclude every other person from the means of judging. To refuse a hearing to an opinion, because they are sure that it is false, is to assume that *their* certainty, is the same thing as *absolute* certainty. All silencing of discussion is an assumption of infallibility. Its condemnation may be allowed to rest on this common argument, not the worse for being common.

Unfortunately for the good sense of mankind, the fact of their fallibility is far from carrying the weight in their practical judgment which is always allowed to it in theory; for while every one well knows himself to be fallible, few think it necessary to take any precautions against their own fallibility, or admit the supposition that any opinion, of which they feel very certain, may be one of the examples of the error to which they acknowledge themselves to be liable. Absolute princes, or others who are accustomed to unlimited deference, usually feel this complete confidence in their own opinions on nearly all subjects. People more happily situated, who sometimes hear their opinions disputed, and are not wholly unused to be set right when they are wrong, place the same unbounded reliance only on such of their opinions as are shared by all who surround them, or to whom they habitually defer; for in proportion to a man's want of confidence in his own solitary judgment, does he usually repose, with implicit trust, on the infallibility of "the world" in general. And the world, to each individual, means the part of it with which he comes in contact; his party, his sect, his church, his class of society; the man may be called, by comparison, almost liberal and large-minded to whom it means anything so comprehensive as his own country or his own age. Nor is his faith, in this collective authority at all shaken by his being aware that other ages, countries, sects, churches, classes, and parties have thought, and even now think, the exact reverse. He devolves upon his own world the responsibility of being in the right against the dissentient worlds of other people; and it never troubles him that mere accident has decided which of these numerous worlds is the object of his reliance, and that the same causes which make him a Churchman in London, would have made him a Buddhist or a Confucian in Pekin. Yet it is as evident in itself, as any amount of argument can make it, that ages are no more infallible than individuals; every age having held many opinions which subsequent ages have deemed not only false but absurd; and it is as certain that many opinions now general will be rejected by future ages, as it is that many, once general, are rejected by the present.

The objection likely to be made to this argument would probably take some such form as the following. There is no greater assumption of infallibility in forbidding the propagation of error, than in any other thing which is done by public authority on its own judgment and responsibility. Judgment is given to men that they may use it. Because it may be used erroneously, are men to be told that they ought not to use it at all? To prohibit what they think pernicious, is not claiming exemption from error, but ful-

filling the duty incumbent on them, although fallible, of acting on their conscientious conviction. If we were never to act on our opinions, because those opinions may be wrong, we should leave all our interests uncared for, and all our duties unperformed. An objection which applies to all conduct can be no valid objection to any conduct in particular. It is the duty of governments, and of individuals, to form the truest opinions they can: to form carefully, and never impose them upon others unless they are quite sure of being right. But when they are sure (such reasoners may say), it is not conscientiousness but cowardice to shrink from acting on their opinions, and allow doctrines which they honestly think dangerous to the welfare of mankind, either in this life or in another, to be scattered abroad without restraint, because other people, in less enlightened times, have persecuted opinions now believed to be true. Let us take care, it may be said, not to make the same mistake: but governments and nations have made mistakes in other things, which are not denied to be fit subjects for the exercise of authority: they have laid on bad taxes, made unjust wars. Ought we therefore to lay on no taxes, and, under whatever provocation, make no wars? Men and governments must act to the best of their ability. There is no such thing as absolute certainty, but there is assurance sufficient for the purposes of human life. We may, and must, assume our opinion to be true for the guidance of our own conduct: and it is assuming no more when we forbid bad men to pervert society by the propagation of opinions which we regard as false and pernicious.

I answer, that it is assuming very much more. There is the greatest difference between presuming an opinion to be true, because, with every opportunity for contesting it, it has not been refuted, and assuming its truth for the purpose of not permitting its refutation. Complete liberty of contradicting and disproving our opinion is the very condition which justifies us in assuming its truth for purposes of action: and on no other terms can a being with human faculties have any rational assurance of being right.

When we consider either the history of opinion, or the ordinary conduct of human life, to what is it to be ascribed that the one and the other are no worse than they are? Not certainly to the inherent force of the human understanding: for, on any matter not self-evident, there are ninety-nine persons totally incapable of judging of it for one who is capable; and the capacity of the hundredth person is only comparative: for the majority of the eminent men of every past generation held many opinions now known to be erroneous, and did or approved numerous things which no one will now justify. Why is it, then, that there is on the whole a preponderance among mankind of rational opinions and rational conduct? If there really is this preponderance—which there must be unless human affairs are, and have always been, in an almost desperate state—it is owing to a quality of the human mind, the source of everything respectable in man either as an intellectual or as a moral being, namely, that his errors are corrigible. He is capable of rectifying his mistakes, by discussion and experience. Not by experience alone. There must be discussion, to show how experience is to be interpreted. Wrong opinions and practices gradually yield to fact and argument; but facts and arguments, to produce any effect on the mind, must be brought before it. Very few facts are able to tell their own story, without comments to bring out their meaning. The whole strength and value, then, of human judgment, depending on the one property, that it can be set right when it is wrong, reliance can be placed on it only when the means of setting it right are kept constantly at hand. In the case of any person whose judgment is really deserving of confidence, how has it become so? Because he has kept his mind open to criticism on his opinions and conduct. Because it has been his practice to listen to all that could be said against him; to profit by as much of it as was just, and expound to himself, and upon occasion to others, the fallacy of what was fallacious. Because he has felt, that the only way in which a human being can make some approach to knowing the whole of a subject, is by hearing what can be said about it by persons of every variety of opinion, and studying all modes in which it can be looked at by every character of mind. No wise man ever acquired his wisdom in any mode but this; nor is it in the nature of human intellect to become wise in any other manner. The steady habit of correcting and completing his own opinion by collating it with those of others, so far from causing doubt and hesitation in carrying it into practice, is the only stable foundation for a just reliance on it: for, being cognisant of all that can, at least obviously, be said against him, and having taken up his position against all gainsayers—knowing that he has sought for objections and difficulties, instead of avoiding them, and has shut out no light which can be thrown upon the subject from any quarter—he has a right to think his judgment better than that of any person, or any multitude, who have not gone through a similar process.

It is not too much to require that what the wisest of mankind, those who are best entitled to trust their own judgment, find necessary to warrant their relying on it, should be submitted to by that miscellaneous collection of a few wise and many foolish individuals, called the public. The most intolerant of churches, the Roman Catholic Church, even at the canonisation of a saint, admits, and listens patiently to, a "devil's advocate." The holiest of men, it appears, cannot be admitted to posthumous honours, until all that the devil could say against him is known and weighed. If even the Newtonian philosophy were not permitted to be questioned, mankind could not feel as complete assurance of its truth as they now do. The beliefs which we have most warrant for have no safeguard to rest on, but a standing invitation to the whole world to prove them unfounded. If the challenge is not accepted, or is accepted and the attempt fails, we are far enough from certainty still: but we have done the best that the existing state of human reason admits of: we have neglected nothing that could give the truth a chance of reaching us: if the lists are kept open, we may hope that if there be a better truth, it will be found when the human mind is capable of receiving it; and in the meantime we may rely on having attained such approach to truth as is possible in our own day. This is the amount of certainty attainable by a fallible being, and this the sole way of attaining it.

Strange it is, that men should admit the validity of the arguments for free discussion, but object to their being "pushed to an extreme": not seeing that unless the reasons are good for an extreme case, they are not good for any case. Strange that they should imagine that they are not assuming infallibility, when they acknowledge that there should be free discussion on all subjects which can possibly be *doubtful*, but think that some particular principle or doctrine should be forbidden to be questioned because it is so *certain,* that is, because *they are certain* that it is certain. To call any proposition certain, while there is any one who would deny its certainty if permitted, but who is not permitted, is to assume that we ourselves; and those who agree with us, are the judges of certainty, and judges without hearing the other side.

In the present age—which has been described as "destitute of faith, but terrified at scepticism"—in which people feel sure, not so much that their opinions are true, as that they should not know what to do without them—the claims of an opinion to be protected from public attack are rested not so much on its truth, as on its importance to society. There are, it is alleged, certain beliefs so useful, not to say indispensable, to well-being that it is as much the duty of governments to uphold those beliefs, as to protect any other of the interests of society. In a case of such necessity, and so directly in the line of their duty, something less than infallibility may, it is maintained, warrant, and even bind, governments to act on their own opinion, confirmed by the general opinion of mankind. It is also often argued, and still oftener thought that none but bad men would desire to weaken these salutary beliefs; and there can be nothing wrong, it is thought, in restraining bad men, and prohibiting what only such men would wish to practise. This mode of thinking makes the justification of restraints on discussion not a question of the truth of doctrines, but of their usefulness; and flatters itself by that means to escape the responsibility of claiming to be an infallible judge of opinions. But those who thus satisfy themselves, do not perceive that the assumption of infallibility is merely shifted from one point to another. The usefulness of an opinion is itself matter of opinion: as disputable, as open to discussion, and requiring discussion as much as the opinion itself. There is the same need of an infallible judge of opinions to decide an opinion to be noxious, as to decide it to be false, unless the opinion condemned has full opportunity of defending itself. And it will not do to say that the heretic may be allowed to maintain the utility or harmlessness of his opinion, though forbidden to maintain its truth. The truth of an opinion is part of its utility. If we would know whether or not it is desirable that a proposition should be believed, is it possible to exclude the consideration

of whether or not it is true? In the opinion, not of bad men, but of the best men, no belief which is contrary to truth can be really useful: and can you prevent such men from urging that plea, when they are charged with culpability for denying some doctrine which they are told is useful, but which they believe to be false? Those who are on the side of received opinions never fail to take all possible advantage of this plea: you do not find *them* handling the question of utility as if it could be completely abstracted from that of truth: on the contrary, it is, above all, because their doctrine is "the truth," that the knowledge or the belief of it is held to be so indispensable. There can be no fair discussion of the question of usefulness when an argument so vital may be employed on one side, but not on the other. And in point of fact, when law or public feeling do not permit the truth of an opinion to be disputed, they are just as little tolerant of a denial of its usefulness. The utmost they allow is an extenuation of its absolute necessity, or of the positive guilt of rejecting it.

In order more fully to illustrate the mischief of denying a hearing to opinions because we, in our own judgment, have condemned them, it will be desirable to fix down the discussion to a concrete case; and I choose, by preference, the cases which are least favourable to me—in which the argument against freedom of opinion, both on the score of truth and on that of utility, is considered the strongest. Let the opinions impugned be the belief in a God and in a future state, or any of the commonly received doctrines of morality. To fight the battle on such ground gives a great advantage to an unfair antagonist; since he will be sure to say (and many who have no desire to be unfair will say it internally). Are these the doctrines which you do not deem sufficiently certain to be taken under the protection of law? Is the belief in a God one of the opinions to feel sure of which you hold to be assuming infallibility? But I must be permitted to observe, that it is not the feeling sure of a doctrine (be it what it may) which I call an assumption of infallibility. It is the undertaking to decide that question *for others*, without allowing them to hear what can be said on the contrary side. And I denounce and reprobate this pretension not the less, if put forth on the side of my most solemn convictions. However positive any one's persuasion may be, not only of the falsity but of the pernicious consequences—not only of the pernicious consequences, but (to adopt expressions which I altogether condemn) the immorality and impiety of an opinion; yet if, in pursuance of that private judgment, though backed by the public judgment of his country or his contemporaries, he prevents the opinion from being heard in its defence, he assumes infallibility. And so far from the assumption being less objectionable or less dangerous because the opinion is called immoral or impious, this is the case of all others in which it is most fatal. These are exactly the occasions on which the men of one generation commit those dreadful mistakes which excite the astonishment and horror of posterity. It is among such that we find the instances memorable in history, when the arm of the law has been employed to root out the best men and the noblest doctrines; with deplorable success as to the men, though some of the doctrines have survived to be (as if in mockery) invoked in defence of similar conduct towards those who dissent from *them*, or from their received, interpretation.

*   *   *

We have now recognised the necessity to the mental well-being of mankind (on which all their other well-being depends) of freedom of opinion, and freedom of the expression of opinion, on four distinct grounds; which we will now briefly recapitulate.

First, if any opinion is compelled to silence, that opinion may, for aught we can certainly know, be true. To deny this is to assume our own infallibility.

Secondly, though the silenced opinion be an error, it may, and very commonly does, contain a portion of truth; and since the general or prevailing opinion on any subject is rarely or never the whole truth, it is only by the collision of adverse opinions that the remainder of the truth has any chance of being supplied.

Thirdly, even if the received opinion be not only true, but the whole truth: unless it is suffered to be, and actually is, vigorously and earnestly contested, it will, by most of those who receive it, be held in the manner of a prejudice, with little comprehension or feeling of its rational grounds. And not only this, but, fourthly, the meaning of the doctrine itself will

be in danger of being lost, or enfeebled, and deprived of its vital effect on the character and conduct; the dogma becoming a mere formal profession, inefficacious for good, but cumbering the ground, and preventing the growth of any real and heartfelt conviction, from reason or personal experience.

Before quitting the subject of freedom of opinion, it is fit to take some notice of those who say that the free expression of all opinions should be permitted, on condition that the manner be temperate, and do not pass the bounds of fair discussion. Much might be said on the impossibility of fixing where these supposed bounds are to be placed; for if the test be offence to those whose opinions are attacked, I think experience testifies that this offence is given whenever the attack is telling and powerful, and that every opponent who pushes them hard, and whom they find it difficult to answer, appears to them, if he shows any strong feeling on the subject, an intemperate opponent. But this, though an important consideration in a practical point of view, merges in a more fundamental objection. Undoubtedly the manner of asserting an opinion, even though it be a true one, may be very objectionable, and may justly incur severe censure. But the principal offences of the kind are such as it is mostly impossible, unless by accidental self-betrayal, to bring home to conviction. The gravest of them is, to argue sophistically, to suppress facts or arguments, to misstate the elements of the case, or misrepresent the opposite opinion. But all this, even to the most aggravated degree, is so continually done in perfect good faith, by persons who are not considered, and in many other respects may not deserve to be considered, ignorant or incompetent, that it is rarely possible, on adequate grounds, conscientiously to stamp the misrepresentation as morally culpable; and still less could law presume to interfere with this kind of controversial misconduct. With regard to what is commonly meant by intemperate discussion, namely invective, sarcasm, personality, and the like, the denunciation of these weapons would deserve more sympathy *if it were ever* proposed to interdict them equally to both sides; but it is only desired to restrain the employment of them against the prevailing opinion: against the unprevailing they may not only be used without general disapproval, but will be likely to obtain for him who uses them the praise of honest zeal and righteous indignation. Yet whatever mischief arises from their use is greatest when they are employed against the comparatively defenceless: and whatever unfair advantage can be derived by any opinion from this mode of asserting it, accrues almost exclusively to received opinions. The worst offence of this kind which can be committed by a polemic is to stigmatise those who hold the contrary opinion as bad and immoral men. To calumny of this sort, those who hold any unpopular opinion are peculiarly exposed, because they are in general few and uninfluential, and nobody but themselves feels much interested in seeing justice done them; but this weapon is, from the nature of the case, denied to those who attack a prevailing opinion: they can neither use it with safety to themselves, nor, if they could, would it do anything but recoil on their own cause. In general, opinions contrary to those commonly received can only obtain a hearing by studied moderation of language, and the most cautious avoidance of unnecessary offence, from which they hardly ever deviate even in a slight degree without losing ground: while unmeasured vituperation employed on the side of the prevailing opinion really does deter people from professing contrary opinions, and from listening to those who profess them. For the interest, therefore, of truth and justice, it is far more important to restrain this employment of vituperative language than the other; and, for example, if it were neccessary to choose, there would be much more need to discourage offensive attacks on infidelity than on religion. It is, however, obvious that law and authority have no business with restraining either, while opinion ought, in every instance, to determine its verdict by the circumstances of the individual case; condemning every one, on whichever side of the argument he places himself, in whose mode of advocacy either want of candour, or malignity, bigotry, or intolerance of feeling manifest themselves; but not inferring these vices from the side which a person takes, though it be the contrary side of the question to our own; and giving merited honour to every one, whatever opinion he may hold, who has calmness to see and honesty to state what his opponents and their opinions really are, exaggerating nothing to their discredit, keeping nothing back which tells, or can be supposed to tell, in their favour. This is the real morality of public discussion: and if often violated, I am happy to think that there are many controversialists who to a great extent observe it, and a still greater number who conscientiously strive towards it.

Middlemarch

George Eliot

George Eliot, born Mary Ann Evans, became one of the greatest novelists of the English language. Her novel Middlemarch *is set in England in the 1830s, a time of great conflict between the forces of change and those of the status quo. The influence of the industrial revolution makes itself felt throughout this work, as does the struggle for reform in England's political realm.*

Ladislaw, a talented and eligible but penniless young man of Polish-English descent, makes his career as a journalist and political advisor. A mutual attraction develops between himself and a young married woman of wealth and status. Later her husband, an older, unsympathetic character, dies, opening the way for future happiness. The personal stories of these and other characters work their way out against the backdrop of a local political campaign during the years prior to the 1832 reforms.

The Dead Hand

Party is Nature too, and you shall see
By force of Logic how they both agree:
The Many in the One, the One in Many;
All is not Some, nor Some the same as
 Any:
Genus holds species, both are great or
 small;
One genus highest, one not high at all;
Each species has its differentia too,
This is not That, and He was never You,
Though this and that are AYES, and
 you and he
Are like as one to one, or three to three.

No gossip about Mr Casaubon's will had yet reached Ladislaw: the air seemed to be filled with the dissolution of Parliament and the coming election, as the old wakes and fairs were filled with the rival clatter of itinerant shows; and more private noises were taken little notice of. The famous "dry election" was at hand, in which the depths of public feeling might be measured by the low flood-mark of drink. Will Ladislaw was one of the busiest at this time; and though Dorothea's widowhood was continually in his thought, he was so far from wishing to be spoken to on the subject, that when Lydgate sought him out to tell him what had passed about the Lowick living, he answered rather waspishly—

"Why should you bring me into the matter? I never see Mrs Casaubon, and am not likely to see her, since she is at Freshitt. I never go there. It is Tory ground, where I and the 'Pioneer' are no more welcome than a poacher and his gun."

The fact was that Will had been made the more susceptible by observing that Mr Brooke, instead of wishing him, as before, to come to the Grange oftener than was quite agreeable to himself, seemed now to contrive that he should go there as little as possible. This was a shuffling concession of Mr Brooke's to Sir James Chettam's indignant remonstrance; and Will, awake to the slightest hint in this direction, concluded that he was to be kept

From: George Eliot, *Middlemarch* (Oxford, England: Clarendon Press, 1986), pp. 487–499.

away from the Grange on Dorothea's account. Her friends, then, regarded him with some suspicion? Their fears were quite superfluous: they were very much mistaken if they imagined that he would put himself forward as a needy adventurer trying to win the favour of a rich woman.

Until now Will had never fully seen the chasm between himself and Dorothea—until now that he was come to the brink of it, and saw her on the other side. He began, not without some inward rage, to think of going away from the neighbourhood: it would be impossible for him to show any further interest in Dorothea without subjecting himself to disagreeable imputations—perhaps even in her mind, which others might try to poison.

"We are for ever divided," said Will. "I might as well be at Rome; she would be no farther from me." But what we call our despair is often only the painful eagerness of unfed hope. There were plenty of reasons why he should not go—public reasons why he should not quit his post at this crisis, leaving Mr Brooke in the lurch when he needed "coaching" for the election, and when there was so much canvassing, direct and indirect, to be carried on. Will could not like to leave his own chessmen in the heat of a game; and any candidate on the right side, even if his brain and marrow had been as soft as was consistent with a gentlemanly bearing, might help to turn a majority. To coach Mr Brooke and keep him steadily to the idea that he must pledge himself to vote for the actual Reform Bill, instead of insisting on his independence and power of pulling up in time, was not an easy task. Mr Farebrother's prophecy of a fourth candidate "in the bag" had not yet been fulfilled, neither the Parliamentary Candidate Society nor any other power on the watch to secure a reforming majority seeing a worthy nodus for interference while there was a second reforming candidate like Mr Brooke, who might be returned at his own expense; and the fight lay entirely between Pinkerton the old Tory member, Bagster the new Whig member returned at the last election, and Brooke the future independent member, who was to fetter himself for this occasion only. Mr Hawley and his party would bend all their forces to the return of Pinkerton, and Mr Brooke's success must depend either on plumpers which would leave Bagster in the rear, or on the new

minting of Tory votes into reforming votes. The latter means, of course, would be preferable.

This prospect of converting votes was a dangerous distraction to Mr Brooke: his impression that waverers were likely to be allured by wavering statements, and also the liability of his mind to stick afresh at opposing arguments as they turned up in his memory, gave Will Ladislaw much trouble.

"You know there are tactics in these things," said Mr Brooke; "meeting people half-way—tempering your ideas—saying, 'Well now, there's something in that,' and so on. I agree with you that this is a peculiar occasion—the country with a will of its own—political unions—that sort of thing—but we sometimes cut with rather too sharp a knife, Ladislaw. These ten-pound householders, now: why ten? Draw the line somewhere—yes: but why just at ten? That's a difficult question, now, if you go into it."

"Of course it is," said Will, impatiently. "But if you are to wait till we get a logical Bill, you must put yourself forward as a revolutionist, and then Middlemarch would not elect you, I fancy. As for trimming, this is not a time for trimming."

Mr Brooke always ended by agreeing with Ladislaw, who still appeared to him a sort of Burke with a leaven of Shelley; but after an interval the wisdom of his own methods reasserted itself, and he was again drawn into using them with much hopefulness. At this stage of affairs he was in excellent spirits, which even supported him under large advances of money; for his powers of convincing and persuading had not yet been tested by anything more difficult than a chairman's speech introducing other orators, or a dialogue with a Middlemarch voter, from which he came away with a sense that he was a tactician by nature, and that it was a pity he had not gone earlier into this kind of thing. He was a little conscious of defeat, however, with Mr Mawmsey, a chief representative in Middlemarch of that great social power, the retail trader, and naturally one of the most doubtful voters in the borough—willing for his own part to supply an equal quality of teas and sugars to reformer and anti-reformer, as well as to agree impartially with both, and feeling like the burgesses of old that this necessity of electing members was a great burthen to a town; for even if there were no danger in holding out hopes to all parties beforehand, there would be the painful necessity at last of disappointing respectable people whose names were on his books. He was accustomed to receive large orders from Mr Brooke of Tipton; but then, there were many of Pinkerton's committee whose opinions had a great weight of grocery on their side. Mr Mawmsey thinking that Mr Brooke, as not too "clever in his intellects," was the more likely to forgive a grocer who gave a hostile vote under pressure, had become confidential in his back parlour.

"As to Reform, sir, put it in a family light," he said, rattling the small silver in his pocket, and smiling affably. "Will it support Mrs Mawmsey, and enable her to bring up six children when I am no more? I put the question *fictiously,* knowing what must be the answer. Very well, sir. I ask you what, as a husband and a father, I am to do when gentlemen come to me and say, 'Do as you like, Mawmsey; but if you vote against us, I shall get my groceries elsewhere: when I sugar my liquor I like to feel that I am benefiting the country by maintaining tradesmen of the right colour.' Those very words have been spoken to me, sir, in the very chair where you are now sitting. I don't mean by your honourable self, Mr Brooke."

"No, no, no—that's narrow, you know. Until my butler complains to me of your goods, Mr Mawmsey," said Mr Brooke, soothingly, "until I hear that you send bad sugars, spices—that sort of thing—I shall never order him to go elsewhere."

"Sir, I am your humble servant, and greatly obliged," said Mr Mawmsey, feeling that politics were clearing up a little. "There would be some pleasure in voting for a gentleman who speaks in that honourable manner."

"Well, you know, Mr Mawmsey, you would find it the right thing to put yourself on our side. This Reform will touch everybody by-and-by—a thoroughly popular measure—a sort of A, B, C, you know, that must come first before the rest can follow. I quite agree with you that you've got to look at the thing in a family light: but public spirit, now. We're all one family, you know—it's all one cupboard. Such a thing as a vote, now: why, it may help to make men's fortunes at the Cape—there's no knowing what may be the effect of a vote," Mr Brooke ended, with a sense of being a little out at sea,

though finding it still enjoyable. But Mr Mawmsey answered in a tone of decisive check.

"I beg your pardon, sir, but I can't afford that. When I give a vote I must know what I'm doing; I must look to what will be the effects on my till and ledger, speaking respectfully. Prices, I'll admit, are what nobody can know the merits of—the sudden falls after you've bought in currants, which are a goods that will not keep—I've never myself seen into the ins and outs there; which is a rebuke to human pride. But as to one family, there's debtor and creditor, I hope; they're not going to reform that away; else I should vote for things staying as they are. Few men have less need to cry for change than I have, personally speaking—that is, for self and family. I am not one of those who have nothing to lose: I mean as to respectability both in parish and private business, and noways in respect of your honourable self and custom, which you was good enough to say you would not withdraw from me, vote or no vote, while the article sent in was satisfactory."

After this conversation Mr Mawmsey went up and boasted to his wife that he had been rather too many for Brooke of Tipton, and that he didn't mind so much now about going to the poll.

Mr Brooke on this occasion abstained from boasting of his tactics to Ladislaw, who for his part was glad enough to persuade himself that he had no concern with any canvassing except the purely argumentative sort, and that he worked no meaner engine than knowledge. Mr Brooke, necessarily, had his agents, who understood the nature of the Middlemarch voter and the means of enlisting his ignorance on the side of the Bill—which were remarkably similar to the means of enlisting it on the side against the Bill. Will stopped his ear occasionally; Parliament, like the rest of our lives, even to our eating and apparel, could hardly go on if our imaginations were too active about processes. There were plenty of dirty-handed men in the world to do dirty business; and Will protested to himself that his share in bringing Mr Brooke through would be quite innocent.

But whether he should succeed in that mode of contributing to the majority on the right side was very doubtful to him. He had written out various speeches and memoranda for speeches, but he had begun to perceive that Mr Brooke's mind, if it had the burthen of remembering any train of thought, would let it drop, run away in search of it, and not easily come back again. To collect documents is one mode of serving your country, and to remember the contents of a document is another. No! the only way in which Mr Brooke could be coerced into thinking of the right arguments at the right time was to be well plied with them till they took up all the room in his brain. But here there was the difficulty of finding room, so many things having been taken in beforehand. Mr Brooke himself observed that his ideas stood rather in his way when he was speaking.

However, Ladislaw's coaching was forthwith to be put to the test, for before the day of nomination Mr Brooke was to explain himself to the worthy electors at Middlemarch from the balcony of the White Hart, which looked out advantageously at an angle of the market-place, commanding a large area in front and two converging streets. It was a fine May morning, and everything seemed hopeful: there was some prospect of an understanding between Bagster's committee and Brooke's, to which Mr Bulstrode, Mr Standish as a Liberal lawyer, and such manufacturers as Mr Plymdale and Mr Vincy, gave a solidity which almost counterbalanced Mr Hawley and his associates who sat for Pinkerton at the Green Dragon. Mr Brooke, conscious of having weakened the blasts of the 'Trumpet' against him, by his reforms as a landlord in the last half-year, and hearing himself cheered a little as he drove into the town, felt his heart tolerably light under his buff-coloured waistcoat. But with regard to critical occasions, it often happens that all moments seem comfortably remote until the last.

"This looks well, eh?" said Mr Brooke as the crowd gathered. "I shall have a good audience, at any rate. I like this, now—this kind of public made up of one's own neighbours, you know."

The weavers and tanners of Middlemarch, unlike Mr Mawmsey, had never thought of Mr Brooke as a neighbour, and were not more attached to him than if he had been sent in a box from London. But they listened without much disturbance to the speakers who introduced the candidate, though one of them—a political personage from Brassing, who came to tell Middlemarch its duty—spoke so fully, that it was alarming to think what the candidate could find to say after him. Meanwhile the crowd

became denser, and as the political personage neared the end of his speech, Mr Brooke felt a remarkable change in his sensations while he still handled his eye-glass, trifled with documents before him, and exchanged remarks with his committee, as a man to whom the moment of summons was indifferent.

"I'll take another glass of sherry, Ladislaw." he said, with an easy air, to Will, who was close behind him, and presently handed him the supposed fortifier. It was ill-chosen; for Mr Brooke was an abstemious man, and to drink a second glass of sherry quickly at no great interval from the first was a surprise to his system which tended to scatter his energies instead of collecting them. Pray pity him: so many English gentlemen make themselves miserable by speechifying on entirely private grounds! whereas Mr Brooke wished to serve his country by standing for Parliament—which, indeed, may also be done on private grounds, but being once undertaken does absolutely demand some speechifying.

It was not about the beginning of his speech that Mr Brooke was at all anxious: this, he felt sure, would be all right; he should have it quite pat, cut out as nearly as a set of couplets from Pope. Embarking would be easy, but the vision of open sea that might come after was alarming. "And questions, now," hinted the demon just waking up in his stomach, "somebody may put questions about the schedules.—Ladislaw," he continued, aloud, "just hand me the memorandum of the schedules."

When Mr Brooke presented himself on the balcony, the cheers were quite loud enough to counterbalance the yells, groans, brayings, and other expressions of adverse theory, which were so moderate that Mr Standish (decidedly an old bird) observed in the ear next to him, "This looks dangerous, by God! Hawley has got some deeper plan than this." Still, the cheers were exhilarating, and no candidate could look more amiable than Mr Brooke, with the memorandum in his breast-pocket, his left hand on the rail of the balcony, and his right trifling with his eye-glass. The striking points in his appearance were his buff waistcoat, short-clipped blond hair, and neutral physiognomy. He began with some confidence.

"Gentlemen—Electors of Middlemarch!"

This was so much the right thing that a little pause after it seemed natural.

"I'm uncommonly glad to be here—I was never so proud and happy in my life—never so happy, you know."

This was a bold figure of speech, but not exactly the right thing; for, unhappily, the pat opening had slipped away—even couplets from Pope may be but "failings from us, vanishings," when fear clutches us, and a glass of sherry is hurrying like smoke among our ideas. Ladislaw, who stood at the window behind the speaker, thought, "It's all up now. The only chance is that, since the best thing won't always do, floundering may answer for once." Mr Brooke, meanwhile, having lost other clues, fell back on himself and his qualifications—always an appropriate graceful subject for a candidate.

"I am a close neighbour of yours, my good friends—you've known me on the bench a good while—I've always gone a good deal into public questions—machinery, now, and machine-breaking—you're many of you concerned with machinery, and I've been going into that lately. It won't do, you know, breaking machines: everything must go on—trade, manufactures, commerce, interchange of staples—that kind of thing—since Adam Smith, that must go on. We must look all over the globe:—'Observation with extensive view,' must look everywhere, 'from China to Peru,' as somebody says—Johnson, I think, 'The Rambler,' you know. That is what I have done up to a certain point—not as far as Peru; but I've not always stayed at home—I saw it wouldn't do. I've been in the Levant, where some of your Middlemarch goods go—and then, again, in the Baltic. The Baltic, now."

Plying among his recollections in this way, Mr Brooke might have got along easily to himself, and would have come back from the remotest seas without trouble; but a diabolical procedure had been set up by the enemy. At one and the same moment there had risen above the shoulders of the crowd, nearly opposite Mr Brooke, and within ten yards of him, the effigy of himself; buff-coloured waistcoat, eyeglass, and neutral physiognomy, painted on rag; and there had arisen, apparently in the air, like the note of the cuckoo, a parrot-like, Punch-voiced echo of his words. Everybody looked up at the open windows in the houses at the opposite angles of the converging streets; but they were either blank, or filled by laughing listeners. The most innocent echo has an impish mockery in it when it follows a gravely persistent speaker, and this echo was not at all innocent; if it did not follow with the precision of a natural echo, it had a wicked choice of the words it overtook. By the time it said, "The Baltic, now," the laugh which had been running through the audience became a general shout, and but for the sobering effects of party or that great public cause which the entanglement of things had identified with "Brooke of Tipton," the laugh might have caught his committee. Mr Bulstrode asked, reprehensively, what the new police was doing; but a voice could not well be collared, and an attack on the effigy of the candidate would have been too equivocal, since Hawley probably meant it to be pelted.

Mr Brooke himself was not in a position to be quickly conscious of anything except a general slipping away of ideas within himself: he had even a little singing in the ears, and he was the only person who had not yet taken distinct account of the echo or discerned the image of himself. Few things hold the perceptions more thoroughly captive than anxiety about what we have got to say. Mr Brooke heard the laughter; but he had expected some Tory efforts at disturbance, and he was at this moment additionally excited by the tickling, stinging sense that his lost exordium was coming back to fetch him from the Baltic.

"That reminds me," he went on, thrusting a hand into his side-pocket, with an easy air, "if I wanted a precedent, you know—but we never want a precedent for the right thing—but there is Chatham, now; I can't say I should have supported Chatham, or Pitt, the younger Pitt—he was not a man of ideas, and we want ideas, you know."

"Blast your ideas! we want the Bill," said a loud rough voice from the crowd below.

Immediately the invisible Punch, who had hitherto followed Mr Brooke, repeated, "Blast your ideas! we want the Bill." The laugh was louder than ever, and for the first time Mr Brooke being himself silent, heard distinctly the mocking echo. But it seemed to ridicule his interrupter, and in that light was encouraging; so he replied with amenity—

"There is something in what you say, my good friend, and what do we meet for but to speak our minds—freedom of opinion, freedom of the press, liberty—that kind of thing? The Bill, now—you shall have the Bill"—here Mr Brooke paused a moment to fix on his eye-glass and take the paper from his breast-pocket, with a sense of being practical and coming to particulars. The invisible Punch followed:—

"You shall have the Bill, Mr Brooke, per electioneering contest, and a seat outside Parliament as delivered, five thousand pounds, seven shillings, and fourpence."

Mr Brooke, amid the roars of laughter, turned red, let his eye-glass fall, and looking about him confusedly, saw the image of himself, which had come nearer. The next moment he saw it dolorously bespattered with eggs. His spirit rose a little, and his voice too.

"Buffoonery, tricks, ridicule the test of truth—all that is very well"—here an unpleasant egg broke on Mr Brooke's shoulder, as the echo said, "All that is very well;" then came a hail of eggs, chiefly aimed at the image, but occasionally hitting the original, as if by chance. There was a stream of new men pushing among the crowd; whistles, yells, bellowings, and fifes made all the greater hubbub because there was shouting and struggling to put them down. No voice would have had wing enough to rise above the uproar, and Mr Brooke, disagreeably anointed, stood his ground no longer. The frustration would have been less exasperating if it had been less gamesome and boyish: a serious assault of which the newspaper reporter "can aver that it endangered the learned gentleman's ribs," or can respectfully bear witness to "the soles of that gentleman's boots having been visible above the railing," has perhaps more consolations attached to it.

Mr Brooke re-entered the committee-room, saying, as carelessly as he could, "This is a little too bad, you know. I should have got the ear of the people by-and-by—but they didn't give me time. I should have gone into the Bill by-and-by, you know," he added, glancing at Ladislaw. "However, things will come all right at the nomination."

But it was not resolved unanimously that things would come right; on the contrary, the committee looked rather grim, and the political personage from Brassing was writing busily, as if he were brewing new devices.

"It was Bowyer who did it," said Mr Standish, evasively. "I know it as well as if he had been adver-tised. He's uncommonly good at ventriloquism, and he did it uncommonly well, by God! Hawley has been having him to dinner lately: there's a fund of talent in Bowyer."

"Well, you know, you never mentioned him to me, Standish, else I would have invited him to dine," said poor Mr Brooke, who had gone through a great deal of inviting for the good of his country.

"There's not a more paltry fellow in Middlemarch than Bowyer," said Ladislaw, indignantly, "but it seems as if the paltry fellows were always to turn the scale."

Will was thoroughly out of temper with himself as well as with his "principal," and he went to shut himself in his rooms with a half-formed resolve to throw up the 'Pioneer' and Mr Brooke together. Why should he stay? If the impassable gulf between himself and Dorothea were ever to be filled up, it must rather be by his going away and getting into a thoroughly different position than by his staying here and slipping into deserved contempt as an understrapper of Brooke's. Then came the young dream of wonders that he might do—in five years, for example: political writing, political speaking, would get a higher value now public life was going to be wider and more national, and they might give him such distinction that he would not seem to be asking Dorothea to step down to him. Five years:—if he could only be sure that she cared for him more than for others; if he could only make her aware that he stood aloof until he could tell his love without lowering himself—then he could go away easily, and begin a career which at five-and-twenty seemed probable enough in the inward order of things, where talent brings fame, and fame everything else which is delightful. He could speak and he could write; he could master any subject if he chose, and he meant always to take the side of reason and justice, on which he would carry all his ardour. Why should he not one day be lifted above the shoulders of the crowd, and feel that he had won that eminence well? Without doubt he would leave Middlemarch, go to town, and make himself fit for celebrity by "eating his dinners."

But not immediately: not until some kind of sign had passed between him and Dorothea. He could not be satisfied until she knew why, even if he were the man she would choose to marry, he would not marry her. Hence he must keep his post and bear with Mr Brooke a little longer.

But he soon had reason to suspect that Mr Brooke had anticipated him in the wish to break up their connexion. Deputations without and voices within had concurred in inducing that philanthropist to take a stronger measure than usual for the good of mankind; namely, to withdraw in favour of another candidate, to whom he left the advantages of his canvassing machinery. He himself called this a strong measure, but observed that his health was less capable of sustaining excitement than he had imagined.

"I have felt uneasy about the chest—it won't do to carry that too far," he said to Ladislaw in explaining the affair. "I must pull up. Poor Casaubon was a warning, you know. I've made some heavy advances, but I've dug a channel. It's rather coarse work—this electioneering, eh, Ladislaw? I dare say you are tired of it. However, we have dug a channel with the 'Pioneer'—put things in a track, and so on. A more ordinary man than you might carry it on now—more ordinary, you know."

"Do you wish me to give it up?" said Will, the quick colour coming in his face, as he rose from the writing-table, and took a turn of three steps with his hands in his pockets. "I am ready to do so whenever you wish it."

"As to wishing, my dear Ladislaw, I have the highest opinion of your powers, you know. But about the 'Pioneer,' I have been consulting a little with some of the men on our side, and they are inclined to take it into their hands—indemnify me to a certain extent—carry it on, in fact. And under the circumstances, you might like to give up—might find a better field. These people might not take that high view of you which I have always taken, as an *alter ego*, a right hand—though I always looked forward to your doing something else. I think of having a run into France. But I'll write you any letters, you know—to Althorpe and people of that kind. I've met Althorpe."

"I am exceedingly obliged to you," said Ladislaw, proudly. "Since you are going to part with the 'Pioneer,' I need not trouble you about the steps I shall take. I may choose to continue here for the present."

After Mr Brooke had left him Will said to himself, "The rest of the family have been urging him to get rid of me, and he doesn't care now about my going. I shall stay as long as I like. I shall go of my own movement, and not because they are afraid of me."

Evidence Given Before the Sadler Committee

In 1832 British member of Parliament Michael Sadler initiated a parliamentary investigation of conditions in British textile factories. The Sadler Commission's findings lay the basis for 1833 laws that limited women's and children's work hours in the textile industry and helped set in motion a gradual withdrawal from pure laissez-faire.

Joshua Drake, called in; and Examined.

You say you would prefer moderate labour and lower wages; are you pretty comfortable upon your present wages?—I have no wages, but two days a week at present; but when I am working at some jobs we can make a little, and at others we do very poorly.

When a child gets 3s. a week, does that go much towards its subsistence?—No, it will not keep it as it should do.

When they got 6s. or 7s. when they were pieceners, if they reduced the hours of labour, would they not get less?—They would get a half-penny a day less, but I would rather have less wages and less work.

Do you receive any parish assistance?—No.

Why do you allow your children to go to work at those places where they are ill-treated or over-worked?—Necessity compels a man that has children to let them work.

Then you would not allow your children to go to those factories under the present system, if it was not from necessity?—No.

Supposing there was a law passed to limit the hours of labour to eight hours a day, or something of that sort, of course you are aware that a manufacturer could not afford to pay them the same wages?—No, I do not suppose that they would, but at the same time I would rather have it, and I believe that it would bring me into employ: and if I lost 5d. a day from my children's work, and I got half-a-crown myself, it would be better.

From: Jonathan F. Scott and Alexander Baltzly, eds., *Readings in European History since 1814* (New York: F.S. Crofts & Co., 1930), pp. 78–83

How would it get you into employ?—By finding more employment at the machines, and work being more regularly spread abroad, and divided amongst the people at large. One man is now regularly turned off into the street, whilst another man is running day and night.

You mean to say, that if the manufacturers were to limit the hours of labour, they would employ more people?—Yes.

Mr. Matthew Crabtree, called in; and Examined.

What age are you?—Twenty-two.

What is your occupation?—A blanket manufacturer.

Have you ever been employed in a factory?—Yes.

At what age did you first go to work in one?—Eight.

How long did you continue in that occupation?—Four years.

Will you state the hours of labour at the period when you first went to the factory, in ordinary times?—From 6 in the morning to 8 at night.

Fourteen hours?—Yes.

With what intervals for refreshment and rest?—An hour at noon.

When trade was brisk what were your hours?—From 5 in the morning to 9 in the evening.

Sixteen hours?—Yes.

With what intervals at dinner?—An hour.

How far did you live from the mill?—About two miles.

Was there any time allowed for you to get your breakfast in the mill?—No.

Did you take it before you left your home?—Generally.

During those long hours of labour could you be punctual; how did you awake?—I seldom did awake spontaneously; I was most generally awoke or lifted out of bed, sometimes asleep, by my parents.

Were you always in time?—No.

What was the consequence if you had been too late?—I was most commonly beaten.

Severely?—Very severely, I thought.

In those mills is chastisement towards the latter part of the day going on perpetually?—Perpetually.

So that you can hardly be in a mill without hearing constant crying?—Never an hour, I believe.

Do you think that if the overlooker were naturally a humane person it would be still found necessary for him to beat the children, in order to keep up their attention and vigilance at the termination of those extraordinary days of labour?—Yes; the machine turns off a regular quantity of cardings, and of course they must keep as regularly to their work the whole of the day; they must keep with the machine, and therefore however humane the slubber may be, as he must keep up with the machine or be found fault with, he spurs the children to keep up also by various means but that which he commonly resorts to is to strap them when they become drowsy.

At the time when you were beaten for not keeping up with your work, were you anxious to have done it if you possibly could?—Yes; the dread of being beaten if we could not keep up with our work was a sufficient impulse to keep us to it if we could.

When you got home at night after this labour, did you feel much fatigued?—Very much so.

Had you any time to be with your parents, and to receive instruction from them?—No.

What did you do?—All that we did when we got home was to get the little bit of supper that was provided for us and go to bed immediately. If the supper had not been ready directly, we should have gone to sleep while it was preparing.

Did you not, as a child, feel it a very grievous hardship to be roused so soon in the morning?—I did.

Were the rest of the children similarly circumstanced?—Yes, all of them; but they were not all of them so far from their work as I was.

And if you had been too late you were under the apprehension of being cruelly beaten?—I generally was beaten when I happened to be too late; and when I got up in the morning the apprehension of

that was so great, that I used to run, and cry all the way as I went to the mill.

Mr. John Hall, called in; and Examined.

Will you describe to the Committee the position in which the children stand to piece in a worsted mill, as it may serve to explain the number and severity of those cases of distortion which occur?—At the top of the spindle there is a fly goes across, and the child takes hold of the fly by the ball of his left hand, and he throws the left shoulder up and the right knee inward; he has the thread to get with the right hand, and he has to stoop his head down to see what he is doing; they throw the right knee inward in that way, and all the children I have seen, that bend in the right knee. I knew a family, the whole of whom were bent outwards as a family complaint, and one of those boys was sent to a worsted-mill, and first he became straight in his right knee, and then he became crooked in it the other way.

Elizabeth Bentley, called in; and Examined.

What age are you?—Twenty-three.

Where do you live?—At Leeds.

What time did you begin to work at a factory?—When I was six years old.

At whose factory did you work?—Mr. Busk's.

What kind of mill is it?—Flax-mill.

What was your business in that mill?—I was a little doffer.

What were your hours of labour in that mill?—From 5 in the morning till 9 at night, when they were thronged.

For how long a time together have you worked that excessive length of time?—For about half a year.

What were your usual hours of labour when you were not so thronged?—From 6 in the morning till 7 at night.

What time was allowed for your meals?—Forty minutes at noon.

Had you any time to get your breakfast or drinking?—No, we got it as we could.

And when your work was bad, you had hardly any time to eat it at all?—No; we were obliged to leave it or take it home, and when we did not take it, the overlooker took it, and gave it to his pigs.

Do you consider doffing a laborious employment?—Yes.

Explain what it is you had to do?—When the frames are full, they have to stop the frames, and take the flyers off, and take the full bobbins off, and carry them to the roller; and then put empty ones on, and set the frame going again.

Does that keep you constantly on your feet?—Yes, there are so many frames, and they run so quick.

Your labour is very excessive?—Yes; you have not time for any thing.

Suppose you flagged a little, or were too late, what would they do?—Strap us.

Are they in the habit of strapping those who are last in doffing?—Yes.

Constantly?—Yes.

Girls as well as boys?—Yes.

Have you ever been strapped?—Yes.

Severely?—Yes.

Could you eat your food well in that factory?—No, indeed I had not much to eat, and the little I had I could not eat it, my appetite was so poor, and being covered with dust; and it was no use to take it home, I could not eat it, and the overlooker took it, and gave it to the pigs.

You are speaking of the breakfast?—Yes.

How far had you to go for dinner?—We could not go home to dinner.

Where did you dine?—In the mill.

Did you live far from the mill?—Yes, two miles.

Had you a clock?—No, we had not.

Supposing you had not been in time enough in the morning at these mills, what would have been the consequence?—We should have been quartered.

What do you mean by that?—If we were a quarter of an hour too late, they would take off half an hour; we only got a penny an hour, and they would take a halfpenny more.

The fine was much more considerable than the loss of time?—Yes.

Were you also beaten for being too late?—No, I was never beaten myself, I have seen the boys beaten for being too late.

Were you generally there in time?—Yes; my mother has been up at 4 o'clock in the morning, and at 2 o'clock in the morning; the colliers used to go to their work about 3 or 4 o'clock, and when she heard them stirring she has got up out of her warm bed, and gone out and asked them the time; and I have sometimes been at Hunslet Car at 2 o'clock in the morning, when it was streaming down with rain, and we have had to stay till the mill was opened.

Peter Smart, called in; and Examined.

You say you were locked up night and day?—Yes.

Do the children ever attempt to run away?—Very often.

Were they pursued and brought back again?—Yes, the overseer pursued them, and brought them back.

Did you ever attempt to run away?—Yes, I ran away twice.

And you were brought back?—Yes; and I was sent up to the master's loft, and thrashed with a whip for running away.

Were you bound to this man?—Yes, for six years.

By whom were you bound?—My mother got 15s. for the six years.

Do you know whether the children were, in point of fact, compelled to stop during the whole time for which they were engaged?—Yes, they were.

By law?—I cannot say by law; but they were compelled by the master; I never saw any law used there but the law of their own hands.

To what mill did you next go?—To Mr. Webster's, at Battus Den, within eleven miles of Dundee.

In what situation did you act there?—I acted as an overseer.

At 17 years of age?—Yes.

Did you inflict the same punishment that you yourself had experienced?—I went as an overseer; not as a slave, but as a slave-driver.

What were the hours of labour in that mill?—My master told me that I had to produce a certain quantity of yarn; the hours were at that time fourteen; I said that I was not able to produce the quantity of yarn that was required; I told him if he took the timepiece out of the mill I would produce that quantity, and after that time I found no difficulty in producing the quantity.

How long have you worked per day in order to produce the quantity your master required?—I have wrought nineteen hours.

Was this a water-mill?—Yes, water and steam both.

To what time have you worked?—I have seen the mill going till it was past 12 o'clock on the Saturday night.

So that the mill was still working on the Sabbath morning?—Yes.

Were the workmen paid by the piece, or by the day?—No, all had stated wages.

Did not that almost compel you to use great severity to the hands then under you?—Yes; I was compelled often to beat them, in order to get them to attend to their work, from their being over-wrought.

Were not the children exceedingly fatigued at that time?—Yes, exceedingly fatigued.

Were the children bound in the same way in that mill?—No; they were bound from one year's end to another, for twelve months.

Did you keep the hands locked up in the same way in that mill?—Yes, we locked up the mill; but we did not lock the bothy.

Did you find that the children were unable to pursue their labour properly to that extent?—Yes; they have been brought to that condition, that I have gone and fetched up the doctor to them, to see what was the matter with them, and to know whether they were able to rise or not able to rise; they were not at all able to rise; we have had great difficulty in getting them up.

When that was the case, how long have they been in bed, generally speaking?—Perhaps not above four or five hours in their beds.

The Sorrows of Young Werther
Johann Wolfgang von Goethe

Johann Wolfgang von Goethe was a famous German writer and also a politician, humanist, scientist, and philosopher. He was one of the main figures in German literature during the era of European Romanticism. The Sorrows of Young Werther is a loosely autobiographical novel, which turned Goethe into a celebrity almost overnight. The story consists of confidential diary entries and letters to a trusted friend, as Goethe touches on the Romantic subjects of love, religion, nature, and man's relationship with God and his fellow men. To Goethe's dismay, Werther's novelistic suicide led to a wave of imitative, or in today's terms "copycat," suicides.

Werther, a young man of the educated middle class, falls in love with Lotte, the wife of a friend. To escape the situation, he takes up employment at the court of a prince, where his brashness scandalizes the aristocrats, forcing him to resign. Failed in love and career and filled with high sentiment that merely hides his egoism, he commits suicide.

The way he describes nature makes me feel the love.

August 18

Must it so be that whatever makes man happy must later become the source of his misery?

That generous and warm feeling for living Nature which flooded my heart with such bliss, so that I saw the world around me as a Paradise, has now become an unbearable torment, a sort of demon that persecutes me wherever I go. When I formerly looked from the rock far across the river and the fertile valleys to the distant hills, and saw everything on all sides sprout and spring forth—the mountains covered with tall, thick trees from base to summit, the valleys winding between pleasant shading woods, the gently flowing river gliding among the whispering reeds and reflecting light clouds which sailed across the sky under the mild evening breeze; when I listened to the birds that bring the forest to life, while millions of midges danced in the red rays of a setting sun whose last flare roused the buzzing beetle from the grass; and all the whirring and weaving around me drew my attention to the ground underfoot where the moss, which wrests its nourishment from my hard rock, and the broom plant, which grows on the slope of the arid sand hill, revealed to me the inner, glowing, sacred life of Nature—how fervently did I take all this into my warm heart, feeling like a god in that overflowing abundance, while the beautiful forms of the infinite universe stirred and inspired my soul. Huge mountains surrounded me, precipices opened before me, and torrents gushed downward; the rivers streamed below, and wood and mountains sang; and I saw them at their mutual work of creation in the depths of the earth, all these unfathomable forces. And above the earth and below the sky swarms the variety of creatures, multifarious and multiform. Everything, everything populated with a thousand shapes; and mankind, huddled together in the security of its little houses, nesting throughout and dominating the wide world in its own way. Poor fool who belittles everything because

From: Johann Wolfgang von Goethe, *The Sorrows of Young Werther* (New York: Vintage Books, 1973), pp. 64–69, 88–94, 166–167.

Takes a turn towards more of a upsetting look to love.

you are yourself so small! From the inaccessible mountains, across the wasteland untrod by human foot, to the end of the unexplored seas breathes the spirit of the eternal Creator who rejoices in every atom of dust that divines Him and lives.—Oh, the times when I longed to fly on the crane's wings, as it passed overhead, to the shores of the illimitable ocean, in order to drink from the foaming cup of the Infinite an elating sensation of life, and to feel, if only for a moment, in the cramped forces of my being one drop of the bliss of that Being who creates everything in and through Himself.

My friend, only the memory of those hours eases my heart. Even the effort to recall and to express again in words those inexpressible sensations lifts my soul above itself, but also intensifies the anguish of my present state.

It is as if a curtain has been drawn away from my soul, and the scene of unending life is transformed before my eyes into the pit of the forever-open grave. Can you say: "This is!" when everything passes, everything rolls past with the speed of lightning and so rarely exhausts the whole power of its existence, alas, before it is swept away by the current, crowned and smashed on the rocks? There is not one moment which does not consume you and yours, and not one moment when you yourself are not inevitably destructive; the most harmless walk costs the lives of thousands of poor, minute worms; *one* step of your foot annihilates the painstaking constructions of ants, and stamps a small world into its ignominious grave. Ha! It is not the notable catastrophes of the world, the floods that wash away our villages, the earthquakes that swallow up our town which move me; my heart is instead worn out by the consuming power latent in the whole of Nature which has formed nothing that will not destroy its neighbor and itself. So I stagger with anxiety, Heaven and Earth and their weaving powers around me! I see nothing but an eternally devouring and ruminating monster.

August 21

In vain do I stretch my arms out for her in the morning, when I try to arouse myself from troubled dreams; in vain do I seek her at night in my bed, deluded by some happy and innocent dream in

Why did he not try to find someone else?

which I am sitting beside her in the meadow, holding her hand and covering it with a thousand kisses. And when, still heavy with sleep, I grope for her and suddenly find myself fully awake, a torrent of tears bursts from my oppressed heart, and I weep bitterly in view of a hopeless future.

August 22

It is disastrous, Wilhelm! All my energies are tuned to another pitch, have changed to a restless inactivity; I cannot be idle and yet the same time cannot set to work at anything. My power of imagination fails me; I am insensible to Nature, and I am sick of books. If we fail ourselves, everything fails us. I swear that I should sometimes like to be a workman so that I could see, when I wake up in the morning, some prospect for the coming day, some impetus, some hope. I often envy Albert, whom I see buried up to his ears in documents; and I imagine that I should be better off were I in his place. Already more than once the thought of writing to you and to the Minister flashed through my mind, in order to apply for the post at the Legation which, you have assured me, I would not be refused. So I myself believe. The Minister has liked me for a long time, and has frequently urged me to devote myself to some work; and sometimes, for an hour or so, it seems the thing to do. But when I come to consider it a little later, I remember the fable of the horse which, tired of freedom let itself be saddled and harnessed and was ridden to death. I don't *know what* to do. And, my dear fellow, isn't my longing for a change in my situation an innate, uneasy impatience that will pursue me wherever I go?

August 28

One thing is certain; if my disease could be cured, these people would cure it. Today is my birthday, and very early in the morning I received a little parcel from Albert. When I opened it I saw immediately one of the bows of pink ribbon Lotte had been wearing when I first met her and which I had often implored her to give me. The parcel also contained two books in duodecimo: the small Homer printed by Wetstein, which I had often wished to possess, so that I should not have to drag about with me on my walks the large volume edited by Ernesti. You see! that is how they anticipate my wishes, how well they select the small tokens of friendship which are a thousand times more precious than the dazzling presents which humiliate us, betraying the vanity of the giver. I kiss the ribbon over and over again and drink in with every breath the memory of the few blissful moments in those happy and irretrievable days. Wilhelm, so it is, and I do not complain—the blossoms of life are only phantoms. How many fade, leaving no trace behind; how few bear fruit, and how few of these fruits ripen! But still enough are left; but still—O my brother! should we neglect the ripe fruit, refuse to enjoy it, and let it rot?

Farewell! It is a glorious summer, and I often sit up in the trees of Lotte's orchard and take down with a long pole the pears from the highest branches. She stands below and catches them when I lower the pole.

*   *   *

March 15

Something has so humiliated me that I shall be forced to leave this place, and I gnash my teeth! The Devil! The harm is done, and it is *your* fault alone—*you* spurred me on, pushed and tormented me into accepting a position that was not congenial to me. Well, here I am! and you have had your way! And in order to prevent you from telling me that it was my eccentric ideas which ruined everything, I here recount, dear sir, the story, plain and clear, as a chronicler would put it down.

Count C. is very fond of me and singles me out, as is well known, and as I have written you many times. He had invited me for dinner at his house yesterday, on the very day when the whole aristocratic set, ladies and gentlemen, are accustomed to meet there late in the evening. I had completely forgotten this fact; and it also did not occur to me that subordinate officials like myself are not welcome on such occasions. Very well. I dined with the Count, and afterward we walked up and down the great hall in conversation and were joined later by Colonel B.; so the hour of the party drew near. God knows, I did not suspect anything. Then the more-than-gracious Lady S. entered with her spouse and

her nobly hatched little goose of a flat-bosomed and tight-laced daughter. *En passant*, they opened their eyes wide and turned up their noses in the traditional highly aristocratic manner. As that clique is entirely repulsive to me, I had decided to leave, only waiting until the Count could free himself from trivial chatter, when Fräulein von B. entered the room. Since I become always a little more cheerful when I see her, I stayed on, took my place behind her chair, and noticed only after some time had passed that she was not talking to me with her usual frankness but with some embarrassment. This took me by surprise. "Is she really like the rest of these people?" I asked myself and was piqued. I wanted to leave, but stayed on, because I should have liked to free her from a blame I did not believe, and still hoped for a kind word from her and—whatever you wish. Meanwhile, more and more people were filling the room. Baron F. all gotten up in a complete outfit dating back to the coronation of Francis I, Hofrat R. (but here in *qualitate* called Herr von N.) with his deaf wife, not to mention the badly-reduced-in-circumstances J., who had patched up the worn places in his old-fashioned clothes with brand-new material—all these people kept arriving in swarms; and I spoke to some of those I knew who were, however, very laconic, I thought—and paid attention only to my Fräulein von B. I did not notice that the dames at the far end of the room were whispering into each other's ears or that this whispering spread to the gentlemen; that Lady S. was talking to the Count (Fräulein von B. recounted all this to me afterward), until he finally came up to me and drew me into a window recess. "You know our strange social conventions," he said, "and I notice that the company is displeased to see you here, although I should not want you, for anything in the world—" —"Your Excellency!" I interrupted, "I apologize exceedingly; I should have thought of this before, and I know you will forgive me my inconsequence. I wanted to leave some time ago, but a malicious spirit held me back," I added, smiling and bowing to him. The Count pressed my hand with a warmth that expressed everything. I turned my back on the illustrious company, slipped away and took a cabriolet to M., to see the sunset from the hill, while reading in Homer the magnificent passage which describes how Odysseus is entertained by the faithful swineherd. All this was perfect.

In the evening I returned to the inn for supper. There were only a few people in the taproom, playing at dice at the corner of a table, having turned back the tablecloth. The honest Adelin then came in, put down his hat when he saw me, and, coming up closer, said to me in a low voice: "Did something annoy you?" "Annoy me?" I said.—"The Count asked you to leave his party."—"The Devil take it!" I said. "I was glad to get out into the fresh air."—"Good that you take it so lightly," he said. "The thing that worries me is that everyone is already talking." Now for the first time the whole thing began to irritate me. I imagined that everyone who came in for supper glanced at me and seemed to know about the incident. My blood was up.

And today when everyone pities me wherever I go and when I hear that my triumphant rivals are saying, "You see where arrogance leads, when proud people who boast of their little share of brains think they can ignore all conventions" (and whatever else these gossiping dogs may invent), one would like to take a knife and plunge it into one's heart; for, whatever one may say about independence, I should like to see the person who can allow rascals to slander him when they have the upper hand. When it is only empty talk, it is easy to ignore them.

March 16

Everything is against me. Today I met Fräulein von B in the avenue. I could not keep myself from speaking to her; to tell her, as soon as we were at some distance from her companions, how much she had hurt me the other day. "O Werther," she said with deep feeling, "how could you, knowing my heart, interpret my confusion in such a way? How I suffered for you from the moment I entered the room! I foresaw everything, and a warning word was on the tip of my tongue a dozen times. I knew that Lady S. and Lady T. would leave with their husbands rather than remain while you were there; and I knew that the Count cannot risk their displeasure—and now all this scandal!"—"What do you mean?" I asked, concealing my alarm, because everything that Adelin had told me the previous day made me suddenly feel very uneasy.—"How much it

has already cost me," said the sweet creature with tears in her eyes.—I was no longer master of myself, and was ready to throw myself at her feet. "Do tell me the truth," I cried. The tears ran down her cheeks, and I was almost out of my mind. She dried her tears without trying to conceal them. "You know my aunt," she began. "She was at the party and with her keen eyes kept a close watch on everything. Werther, I had to suffer for it last night, and this morning I was given a lecture on my friendship with you, and was forced to listen to the degrading, discrediting things she said about you, and could not—was not allowed to—defend you half as much as I wished."

Every word she spoke pierced my heart like a sword. She did not sense how charitable it would have been to keep all this from me; and she went on to say that more gossip would soon begin to run wild, and mentioned the sort of people who would gloat over it. How delighted they all would be about the punishment I had received for my arrogance and haughty contempt toward others, for which they had often blamed me. All this, Wilhelm, I had to hear from her, spoken in a tone of sincerest sympathy. I was completely crushed, and am still furious. I wish that someone would have the courage to blame me openly so that I could thrust my dagger through his body; if I saw blood, I should certainly feel better. Today I have taken up a knife a dozen times, intending to relieve with it my suffocating heart. I have been told that a noble breed of horses, when overheated and hunted almost to death, will by instinct bite open a vein and so recover their breath. I often feel the same. I should like to open one of my veins and gain eternal freedom for myself.

March 24

I have sent in my resignation to the Court, and I hope that it will be accepted. You will forgive me for not asking your permission first. It is absolutely necessary for me to leave; and everything you will say, to persuade me to stay, I myself know. And therefore—sugar the bitter pill for my mother. I cannot help myself, and she must put up with the fact that I cannot help her either. Of course, it is going to hurt her. To see the beginning brilliant career of her son, which might have mounted, perhaps, to the office of privy councilor and envoy, stop so suddenly, and the little horse brought back to its stable! Now think of the matter as you will and try to figure out, the possible conditions under which I might and should have stayed. Enough, I am going. But that you may know where I am going, let me tell you that Prince—, who likes my company extremely, when he heard of my intention, invited me to accompany him to his estates, and to spend the lovely springtime there. He has promised that I will be completely left alone, and as we understand one another very well, up to a certain point, I shall take my chance and go with him.

*   *   *

[handwritten: Decides to ~~reave~~ leave and "escape" the pain.]

December 20, after eleven

. . . a neighbor saw the flash of the powder and heard the shot; but, as everything remained quiet, he did not pay further attention to it.

Next morning, around six o'clock, the servant entered the room with a candle. He found his master lying on the floor, the pistol beside him, and blood everywhere. He called, he touched him; no answer came, only a rattling in the throat. He ran for a doctor and for Albert. Lotte heard the bell; a tremor seized all her limbs. She woke her husband; they got up, and the servant, sobbing and stammering, told the news. Lotte fainted and fell to the ground at Albert's feet.

When the doctor arrived, he found the unfortunate young man on the floor, past help; his pulse was still beating; all his limbs were paralyzed. He

[handwritten: A painful death. Surprised he didn't pass sooner than he did.]

had shot himself through the head above the right eye, and his brain was laid bare. They bled him needlessly; the blood flowed; he was still breathing.

From the blood on the back of the armchair they concluded that he had committed the act while sitting at his writing desk. He had then slid down and rolled around the chair in convulsions. He was lying on his back, facing the window, enfeebled, fully dressed, in his boots, his blue coat and yellow waistcoat.

The house, the neighborhood, the town, was in a tumult. Albert came in. They had laid Werther on his bed and bandaged his forehead; his face was already the face of a dead man; he did not move. His lungs still gave forth a dreadful rattling sound, now weak, now stronger; they expected the end.

He had drunk only one glass of the wine. Lessing's *Emilia Galotti* lay open on his desk.

I cannot describe Albert's consternation, Lotte's distress.

On hearing the news, the old bailiff rode up to the house at full speed; he kissed his dying friend and wept bitter tears. His older sons arrived soon afterward on foot; they knelt beside the bed with expressions of uncontrollable grief and kissed Werther's hands and mouth; the oldest, whom Werther had always loved most, clung to him to the bitter end, when they had to tear the boy away by force. Werther died at noon. The presence of the bailiff and the arrangements he made prevented a public disturbance. That night around eleven the bailiff had Werther buried at the place he himself had chosen. The old man and his sons followed the body to the grave; Albert was unable to. Lotte's life was in danger. Workmen carried the coffin. No clergyman attended.

[handwritten: How was Lotte's life ~~was~~ in danger when he killed himself because she didn't love him and his career?]

The Poor Fiddler

Franz Grillparzer

Franz Grillparzer represents the transition in literary writing during the first half of the nineteenth century, as writers struggled to define a new era that had not yet quite arrived. This transition in literature represents the changes in society underway during a period we call the Age of Metternich and the Age of Revolutions.

The violinist in *The Poor Fiddler* attempts, without much success, to satisfy his desire for perfection in his own compositions and to please the general public with his playing of popular songs.

In Vienna the Sunday after the July full moon is a genuine people's holiday, if ever there was one. Every year on that day and the day after, the people give themselves a party; they are at once hosts and guests, and any members of the upper classes who put in an appearance can do so only as part of the people. This is no occasion for being standoffish; at least it wasn't as recently as a few years ago.

On this day the people of Brigittenau celebrate the dedication of their own saint's church, and with them those of Augarten, Leopoldstadt and the Prater, all linked together in one unbroken chain of jollification. St. Bridget's fair marks happy days for the working folk and they look forward to it from one year to the next. Long awaited, this Saturnalian revel comes round at last. A great uproar then takes possession of the quiet, easygoing town. A swell of people fills the streets, with a clatter of footsteps and a rumble of talk pierced now and then by a cry or shout. Distinctions of calling vanish: citizen and soldier alike are borne on by the tide. At the city gates the push gathers force. The way out is captured, lost, then recaptured, and finally conquered. But next the Danube bridge presents a new obstacle. Another

victory, and at last two rivers flow on triumphantly over and under each other—the Danube Canal follows its old river bed, the more swollen stream of people bursts forth from the narrows of the bridge in an all-submerging flood, to form a wide, turbulent lake. A stranger might find the portents dangerous. But the uproar is one of joy, of pleasure unconfined.

Between the city and the bridge hackney-cabriolets are drawn up waiting for the real hierophants of these celebrations—the children of labor and service. Overloaded as they are, the cabs fly through the throng at a gallop, and the crowd divides just in time and closes up again at once, unafraid and unharmed. For in Vienna there is an unwritten pact between vehicle and man, an agreement not to run anyone over, however fast the pace, and not to be run over, however inattentive one may be.

Every second the interval between one cab and the next gets smaller. Smart, upper-class turnouts begin to join the procession, which comes to a halt again and again. The cabs don't fly any more. At last, five or six hours before nightfall, the individual molecules of horses and carriages are compressed into one solid row of traffic, which obstructs itself and is further obstructed by arrivals from all the side streets, and makes nonsense of the old proverb that it is better to be poorly driven than to walk.

From: Franz Grillparzer, *The Poor Fiddler* (New York: Frederick Ungar Publishing Co., 1967), pp. 29–43.

The ladies in their finery sit in the seemingly motionless vehicles, stared at, pitied, made fun of. Unused to the everlasting waiting, a Holstein black suddenly rears up, as though it wanted to make its way out over the top of the cab blocking its way in front—which is obviously what the screaming women and children populating the plebeian vehicle seem to fear. The darting *fiaker*, for once untrue to his nature, angrily tots up his loss in having to take three hours on a journey he normally whisks through in five minutes. The drivers quarrel, shout, exchange insults, with every now and then a lash of the whip.

At length, since it's in the nature of things for the most obstinate standstill to be an unperceived advance all the same, a ray of hope appears even in this *status quo*. The first trees of the Augarten and Brigittenau come into view. Land! Land in sight! Land ahoy! All troubles are forgotten. Those who have come by carriage get out and join the crowd on foot. Sounds of distant dance music float across and are greeted with cheers by the newcomers. And so on and onward until the wide harbor opens ahead, the harbor of pleasure where woods and meadows, music and dancing, wine and victuals, galanty shows and tightrope walkers, lights and fireworks all come together in one Land of Cockayne, an Eldorado, a Cloud-Cuckoo-Land, which regrettably or, if you will, fortunately, lasts only one day and the next and then vanishes like a midsummer night's dream, to survive only as a memory and maybe as a hope.

I don't lightly miss taking part in this holiday. I am a passionate lover of my fellow men, and especially of the common people—so much so that even as a dramatist I find the straightforward, if rowdy, response of the public in a packed theater ten times as interesting and indeed as instructive as the excogitated judgment of some literary matador, crippled in body and soul and bloated like a spider with the blood sucked from authors. As a lover of my fellow men, I say, especially when in a crowd they forget their private purposes for a while and feel themselves part of the whole wherein, ultimately, lies the divine, every popular celebration is to me a true spiritual celebration, a pilgrimage, an act of devotion. As though from some vast Plutarch which has escaped from the bounds of the book and lies in an open scroll before me, I read the collective biographies of men

unknown to fame. I read them in their faces, cheerful or worried by some secret, in their sprightly or dragging step, in the behavior of members of a family toward each other, in some unpremeditated remark. In truth, no one can understand the lives of the famous unless he has entered into the feelings of the humble. An invisible but continuous thread connects the brawling of drunken market porters with the strife of the sons of the gods, and Juliet, Dido or Medea exist in embryo within every young servant girl who, half against her will, follows her insistent lover out of the dancing crowd.

Two years ago I had, as usual, gone on foot to join the merrymakers at the fair. The main difficulties of the journey had been overcome and I was already at the end of the Augarten, with my longed for goal, Brigittenau, immediately ahead. At this point one more battle, the last, is still to be fought. A narrow causeway running between impassable enclosures forms the only connection between the two pleasure grounds, whose common boundary is marked midway by a wooden gate. On ordinary days there is more than enough room on this path for the ordinary walker. But during the fair, even were the path four times as wide, it would still be too narrow for the endless crowd which, pushed and pushing vigorously from behind and squeezed in front by those returning in the opposite direction, only manages to sort itself out at all thanks to the universal good humor.

I had abandoned myself to the drifting throng and was in the middle of the causeway, on classical ground already, but, alas, still having to stop again and again, to get out of the way and wait. Thus I had time and to spare to watch what was going on by the roadside.

So that the pleasure-hungry crowd should not lack a foretaste of the delights to come, a number of musicians had stationed themselves to the left, on the slope of the raised causeway; doubtless they were anxious to avoid serious competition and hoped that here, at the temple gates, they might gather the first fruits of the people's as yet unspent generosity. There was a woman harpist with repulsive, glassy eyes. There was an old cripple with a wooden leg, who labored away at a frightful, obviously homemade instrument, half zither and half barrel-organ, to bring home to the general sympathy by due means the aches and pains of his injury. There was a lame, misshapen boy, hunched inextricably over his fiddle, who played an unending stream of waltzes with all the feverish frenzy of his deformed breast. And finally—he captured my whole attention—there was an old man of at least seventy, in a threadbare but decent overcoat of Molton cloth and with a smiling, self-congratulating expression. He was bareheaded and bald, and, in the way of such people, he had placed his hat on the ground as a collecting box. He sawed away at an old, much cracked violin, and beat time not only by lifting and dropping his foot, but by a corresponding movement of his whole bowed body. Yet all his efforts to give some shape to his performance were fruitless, because what he played seemed nothing but a disjointed sequence of sounds, keeping to no time or tune. For all that, he was utterly absorbed in his task; his lips twitched, his eyes were rigidly fixed on the sheet of music before him—he really did have a piece of music! All the other musicians, whose playing was incomparably more pleasing, relied on their memory, but the old man, in the midst of the throng, had set up a small, easily portable music stand supporting grubby, tattered scores which doubtless contained in perfect order what he rendered in so disordered a fashion. It was precisely the unusual nature of his equipment which drew my attention, just as it aroused the mirth of the passing crowds who made fun of him and left empty his collecting hat, while the rest of the orchestra were bringing in loads of coppers. In order to observe this eccentric undisturbed I had walked a little way off along the slope of the causeway. He went on playing for a while. At last he stopped, and as though recovering his wits after a long trance, he glanced up at the sky which was beginning to show signs of approaching evening, then down at his hat, noticed that it was empty, and with undisturbed cheerfulness put it on and laid the bow between the strings. "*Sunt certi denique fines*," he said, grabbed his music stand and went off, working his way through the crowd coming to the fair, against the stream, like someone who is going home.

The old man and everything about him were just made to excite my anthropological avidity to the utmost: his needy, though distinguished appearance,

his unconquerable cheerfulness combined with so much zeal for his art and so much clumsiness, and the fact that he turned homeward at precisely the hour when others of his kind were just starting on their real harvest, and finally the few words of Latin, pronounced with exactly the right accentuation and complete fluency. So the man had enjoyed a fairly good education, had acquired some learning—and now was a begging, itinerant musician! I was eager for the explanation.

But already there was a dense pack of people between me and him. Small as he was, with his music stand getting in the way all over the place, he was pushed from one person to another, and the exit gate had swallowed him while I was still in the middle of the causeway, struggling against the opposing current of people. So he escaped me, and when I, too, at last got out into the open, there was nowhere any sign of the fiddler.

Cheated of my would-be adventure, I had lost all pleasure in the fair. I wandered about the Augarten in every direction, and finally decided to go home.

As I approached the little gate that leads from the Augarten to Taborstrasse, I suddenly heard once more the familiar sound of the old violin. I hastened my steps, and there before me was the object of my curiosity, playing for all he was worth amid a ring of boys who impatiently demanded a waltz.

"Play a waltz," they cried. "A waltz! Don't you hear?"

The old man fiddled away, apparently unheeding, until his little audience, shouting abuse and derision, left him and collected about an organ-grinder who had set up his barrel-organ nearby.

"They don't want to dance," said the old man, as though cast down, while he gathered up his things. I came up to him, and said: "It's just that the children don't know any dances except the waltz."

"I was playing a waltz," he answered, and pointed with his bow to the music of the piece he had just played. "One has to provide such things, to please the crowd. But the children have no ear," he said, sadly shaking his head.

"Won't you let me make up for their ingratitude," I said, taking a silver coin from my pocket and holding it out to him.

"Please, please!" said the old man, nervously fending it off with his hands. "In the hat, in the hat!"

I placed the coin in the hat that lay before him, from which the old man at once took it and pocketed it with obvious satisfaction. "For once I'll be going home with good takings," he said, chuckling.

"That reminds me," I said, "of something I was already curious about. Your takings today don't seem to have been of the best, and yet you go away just when the crop is ready to be picked. I suppose you know the fair goes on all night, and you could easily earn more then than during a whole week of ordinary days. What's the explanation?"

"What's the explanation?" the old man repeated. "Pardon me, I don't know who you are, though you must be a kind gentleman and a music lover." And he took the coin out of his pocket again and held it between his hands which he raised to his breast. "So I will tell you the reason, even though it often makes people laugh at me. In the first place, I was never given to reveling at night and don't think it right to incite others with music and song to such sinful doings. Secondly, one must maintain a certain order in all things, or else one slides into undisciplined ways, into sheer anarchy. And finally, in the third place—well, sir, all day long I play for the rowdy people and barely make a living out of it, but the evening belongs to me and my poor art. In the evening I stay at home and (he spoke more and more softly, and a blush spread over his face, while he looked at the ground) then I play from imagination, for myself, without a score. Improvising, I believe it's called in music books."

We both fell silent: he from shame at having given away his inmost secret, and I from astonishment at this reference to the highest level of art from a man who could not give a recognizable rendering of the simplest waltz. Meanwhile, he was getting ready to depart.

"Where do you live?" I said. "I should very much like to join you at your solitary exercises some time."

"Oh," he replied, almost imploringly, "prayer is private, you know."

"Let me call on you during the day, then," I said.

"All day I'm out getting my living," he answered.

"Early in the morning, perhaps?"

"It almost seems," said the old man with a smile, "as though you, my dear sir, were the one to receive a favor and I, if I may presume to say so, were the benefactor. You are so kind and I'm so disagreeable as to retreat into my shell. My abode will be honored to receive such a distinguished visitor at any time. I would only ask that you be so very obliging as to notify me in advance of the day of your advent, so that you will suffer no unseemly loss of time, nor I the inconvenience of having to interrupt whatever I may have begun to do. You see, my mornings are also apportioned. I always consider it my duty to offer my patrons and benefactors some not entirely unworthy return for their gifts. I don't want to be a beggar, my dear sir. Other street musicians, I know, are content to learn by heart a few popular hits, German waltzes, or indeed the tune of some lewd song, and to start over and over again at the same point and play through the whole lot, until people give them something just to get rid of them, or perhaps because the tunes revive the pleasant memory of a dance or some other disorderly diversion. That's why they play from memory, never mind if they get a note wrong every now and then, or indeed often. But so far as I am concerned, far be it from me to cheat. For that reason, I myself made these clean copies of music scores, partly because my memory is not exactly of the best, and partly because it must be difficult for anyone to keep in mind every note of intricate compositions by respected composers."

At that he pointed to his music book and turned over the pages. I was flabbergasted to see compositions by old and famous masters, fantastically difficult and thick with fast runs and double stoppings, all copied out meticulously in a hideous, stiff hand. And this was the sort of thing the old man played with his clumsy fingers!

"By playing these pieces," he went on, "I show my veneration for masters and composers long-since dead and rightly held in high regard. I also satisfy myself and live in the pleasant hope that the offerings most kindly made to me are not left unrequited, thanks to the refining of taste and feeling in a public which otherwise is confused and misled from so many quarters. But as that kind of thing, to come back to what I was saying"—and he smiled with self-satisfaction—"as that kind of thing requires practice, my morning hours are allotted exclusively to this *exercitium*. I think it is no unfair division of my time to give the first three hours of the day to practice, the middle to earning a living, and the evening to myself and God." As he spoke his eyes glistened as though they were moist; but he smiled.

"All right," I said, "I will call on you one of these mornings. Where do you live?"

In Gärtnergasse, he said.

"What number?"

"Number 34, first floor."

"Really," I exclaimed, "on the best floor?"

"As a matter of fact," he said, "it's a one-story house, but next to the loft there's a little room which I share with two journeymen."

"Three people in one room?"

PART FOUR

Claude Monet, "Gare Saint-Lazare"
This painting, one of several that Monet did of the St. Lazare Station during the 1870s, captures the power, energy, and beauty of steam power. This one invention transformed production, communications, transportation, and travel. Perhaps more than any of the other applications, the railroad engine symbolizes the Industrial Revolution. Little did Monet know that within a few decades internal combustion would supplant steam as a source of power.

Industrialization and Socialism

Beginning before 1800, technological innovations transformed European economies, as suggested by the 1870s image of a railroad station by Claude Monet (1840–1926). The Industrial Revolution enriched investors, owners, and managers but ruined artisanry and cottage industry, neither of which could compete with the new machines. Those who turned to industry for work faced the ruthless exploitation of an entrepreneurial middle-class with its noninterventionist (*laissez-faire*) mentality. The plight of the proletariat—men, women, and children workers—dismayed a conscience-stricken educated elite. Even before the full achievement of a liberal, representative government, some thinkers offered socialism as an allegedly more humane alternative to the bourgeoisie's unlimited sway. At first depending on moral persuasion, later on violent revolution, socialists sought to attain economic equality as a necessary corollary of political and legal equality.

In his famous 1798 essay on demographics, the British economist Thomas Malthus (1766–1834) defended *laissez-faire* while abandoning Adam Smith's prediction that its application would benefit the poor. Malthus blamed British workers' continued poverty on their ignorance, bad morals, and prolific childbearing, arguing that excess population depressed salaries. The French socialist Flora Tristan (1803–1844) visited England and witnessed the horrors of early industrialization there. As an antidote, she promoted workers' unions to enlist social support and worker self-help. Like other pre–1848 socialists, Tristan's voluntaristic ideas, outlined in her 1843 essays "Factory Workers" and "How to Constitute a Working Class," visualized that workers would eventually organize labor and production under communal arrangements. In his *Communist Manifesto,* Karl Marx (1796–1877) accused the earlier socialists of "utopianism," abandoned nonviolence, and predicted proletarian revolution as the carrier of a new just world. This definitive formulation of socialism uneasily balanced scientific analysis and moral cause. Elizabeth Gaskell (1810–1865), wife of a minister, based *Mary Barton* (1848) on observation of the early industrial metropolis, Manchester. The novel starkly contrasts middle-class prosperity with the daily horrors faced by laborers.

Study Questions

1. What does Malthus see as the solution to working-class poverty?
2. How do Tristan's views on relieving workers' poverty differ from those of Marx?
3. Was Marx a revolutionary activist or a theorist?
4. Where do these authors stand on Adam Smith's belief that laissez-faire would benefit everyone?
5. Does *Mary Barton* suggest that Gaskell was a follower of Karl Marx or Flora Tristan?
6. Image: How is Monet's powerful image of a railroad steam engine emblematic of nineteenth-century Europe?

An Essay on the Principle of Population

Thomas Malthus

In earlier decades, Adam Smith had confidently predicted that the introduction of full laissez-faire would lift up whole populations by providing jobs for everyone, after which all forms of welfare would be unnecessary. Already by the end of the eighteenth century, after years of industrial growth under free enterprise principles, Malthus admitted that Smith had been wrong. Poverty and unemployment had not ceased to exist despite strong economic growth. Malthus offered demographic explanations and blamed the poor morals and discipline of working class people for their continued hardship. If they would learn to limit the number of children they had, wages would rise as labor grew scarcer and ultimately poverty would end.

The professed object of Dr. Adam Smith's inquiry is the nature and causes of the wealth of nations. There is another inquiry, however, perhaps still more interesting, which he occasionally mixes with it, I mean an inquiry into the causes which affect the happiness of nations or the happiness and comfort of the lower orders of society, which is the most numerous class in every nation. I am sufficiently aware of the near connection of these two subjects, and that the causes which tend to increase the wealth of a State tend also, generally speaking, to increase the happiness of the lower classes of the people. But perhaps Dr. Adam Smith has considered these two inquiries as still more nearly connected than they really are; at least he has not stopped to take notice of those instances where the wealth of a society may increase (according to his definition of wealth) without having any tendency to increase the comforts of the labouring part of it. I do not mean to enter into a philosophical discussion of what constitutes the proper happiness of man, but shall merely consider two universally acknowledged ingredients, health, and the command of the necessaries and conveniences of life.

From: Thomas Robert Malthus, *An Essay on the Principle of Population,* ed. Philip Appleman (New York: W.W. Norton & Company, 1976), pp.103–105, 131–139.

Little or no doubt can exist that the comforts of the labouring poor depend upon the increase of the funds destined for the maintenance of labour, and will be very exactly in proportion to the rapidity of this increase. The demand for labour which such increase would occasion, by creating a competition in the market, must necessarily raise the value of labour, and, till the additional number of hands required were reared, the increased funds would be distributed to the same number of persons as before the increase, and therefore every labourer would live comparatively at his ease. But perhaps Dr. Adam Smith errs in representing every increase of the revenue or stock of a society as an increase of these funds. Such surplus stock or revenue will, indeed, always be considered by the individual possessing it as an additional fund from which he may maintain more labour; but it will not be a real and effectual fund for the maintenance of an additional number of labourers, unless the whole, or at least a great part of this increase of the stock or revenue of the society, be convertible into a proportional quantity of provisions; and it will not be so convertible where the increase has arisen merely from the produce of labour, and not from the produce of land. A distinction will in this case occur, between the number of hands which the stock of the society could employ, and the number which its territory can maintain.

To explain myself by an instance. Dr. Adam Smith defines the wealth of a nation to consist in the annual produce of its land and labour. This definition evidently includes manufactured produce, as well as the produce of the land. Now supposing a nation for a course of years was to add what it saved from its yearly revenue to its manufacturing capital solely, and not to its capital employed upon land, it is evident that it might grow richer according to the above definition, without a power of supporting a greater number of labourers, and therefore, without an increase in the real funds for the maintenance of labour. There would, notwithstanding, be a demand for labour from the power which each manufacturer would possess, or at least think he possessed, of extending his old stock in trade or of setting up fresh works. This demand would of course raise the price of labour, but if the yearly stock of provisions in the country was not increasing, this rise would soon turn out to be merely nominal, as the price of provisions must necessarily rise with it. The demand for manufacturing labourers might, indeed, entice many from agriculture and thus tend to diminish the annual produce of the land, but we will suppose any effect of this kind to be compensated by improvements in the instruments of agriculture, and the quantity of provisions therefore to remain the same. Improvements in manufacturing machinery would of course take place, and this circumstance, added to the greater number of hands employed in manufactures, would cause the annual produce of the labour of the country to be upon the whole greatly increased. The wealth therefore of the country would be increasing annually, according to the definition, and might not, perhaps, be increasing very slowly.

The question is whether wealth, increasing in this way, has any tendency to better the condition of the labouring poor. It is a self-evident proposition that any general rise in the price of labour, the stock of provisions remaining the same, can only be a nominal rise, as it must very shortly be followed by a proportional rise in provisions. The increase in the price of labour therefore, which we have supposed, would have little or no effect in giving the labouring poor a greater command over the necessaries and conveniences of life. In this respect they would be nearly in the same state as before. In one other respect they would be in a worse state. A greater

proportion of them would be employed in manufactures, and fewer, consequently, in agriculture. And this exchange of professions will be allowed, I think, by all, to be very unfavourable in respect of health, one essential ingredient of happiness, besides the greater uncertainty of manufacturing labour, arising from the capricious taste of man, the accidents of war, and other causes.

It may be said, perhaps, that such an instance as I have supposed could not occur, because the rise in the price of provisions would immediately turn some additional capital into the channel of agriculture. But this is an event which may take place very slowly, as it should be remarked that a rise in the price of labour had preceded the rise of provisions, and would therefore impede the good effects upon agriculture, which the increased value of the produce of the land might otherwise have occasioned.

It might also be said, that the additional capital of the nation would enable it to import provisions sufficient for the maintenance of those whom its stock could employ. A small country with a large navy, and great inland accommodations for carriage, such as Holland, may indeed import and distribute an effectual quantity of provisions; but the price of provisions must be very high to make such an importation and distribution answer in large countries less advantageously circumstanced in this respect.

An instance, accurately such as I have supposed, may not, perhaps, ever have occurred, but I have little doubt that instances nearly approximating to it may be found without any very laborious search. Indeed I am strongly inclined to think that England herself, since the revolution, affords a very striking elucidation of the argument in question.

The commerce of this country, internal as well as external, has certainly been rapidly advancing during the last century. The exchangeable value in the market of Europe of the annual produce of its land and labour has, without doubt, increased very considerably. But upon examination it will be found that the increase has been chiefly in the produce of labour and not in the produce of land, and therefore, though the wealth of the nation has been advancing with a quick pace, the effectual funds for the maintenance of labour have been increasing very slowly, and the result is such as might be expected. The increasing wealth of the nation has had little or no tendency to better the condition of the labouring poor.

*   *   *

Of Moral Restraint, and Our Obligation to Practise This Virtue

As it appears that, in the actual state of every society which has come within our review, the natural progress of population has been constantly and powerfully checked: and as it seems evident that no improved form of government, no plans of emigration, no benevolent institutions, and no degree or direction of national industry, can prevent the continued action of a great check to population in some form or other; it follows that we must submit to it as an inevitable law of nature; and the only inquiry that remains is, how it may take place with the least possible prejudice to the virtue and happiness of human society.

All the immediate checks to population, which have been observed to prevail in the same and different countries, seem to be resolvable into moral restraint, vice and misery; and if our choice be confined to these three, we cannot long hesitate in our decision respecting which it would be most eligible to encourage.

In the first edition of this essay I observed, that as from the laws of nature it appeared, that some check to population must exist, it was better that this check should arise from a foresight of the difficulties attending a family and the fear of dependent poverty, than from the actual presence of want and sickness. This idea will admit of being pursued farther; and I am inclined to think that, from the prevailing opinions respecting population, which undoubtedly originated in barbarous ages, and have been continued and circulated by that part of every community which may be supposed to be interested in their support, we have been prevented from attending to the clear dictates of reason and nature on this subject.

Natural and moral evil seem to be the instruments employed by the Deity in admonishing us to avoid any mode of conduct which is not suited to our being, and will consequently injure our happiness. If we are intemperate in eating and drinking, our health is disordered; if we indulge the transports of anger, we seldom fail to commit acts of which we afterwards repent; if we multiply too fast, we die miserably of poverty and contagious diseases. The laws of nature in all these cases are similar and uniform. They indicate to us that we have followed these impulses too far, so as to trench upon some other law, which equally demands attention. . . .

From the inattention of mankind hitherto to the consequences of increasing too fast, it must be presumed, that these consequences are not so immediately and powerfully connected with the conduct which leads to them, as in the other instances; but the delayed knowledge of particular effects does not alter their nature, or our obligation to regulate our conduct accordingly, as soon as we are satisfied of what this conduct ought to be. . . .

. . . It is of the very utmost importance to the happiness of mankind, that population should not increase too fast; but it does not appear, that the object to be accomplished would admit of any considerable diminution in the desire of marriage. It is clearly the duty of each individual not to marry till he has a prospect of supporting his children; but it is at the same time to be wished that he should retain undiminished his desire of marriage, in order that he may exert himself to realise this prospect, and be stimulated to make provision for the support of greater numbers.

It is evidently therefore regulation and direction which are required with regard to the principle of population, not diminution or alteration. And if moral restraint be the only virtuous mode of avoiding the incidental evils arising from this principle, our obligation to practise it will evidently rest exactly upon the same foundation as our obligation to practise any of the other virtues.

Whatever indulgence we may be disposed to allow to occasional failures in the discharge of a duty of acknowledged difficulty, yet of the strict line of duty we cannot doubt. Our obligation not to marry till we have a fair prospect of being able to support our children will appear to deserve the attention of the moralist, if it can be proved that an attention to this obligation is of most powerful effect in the prevention of misery; and that, if it were the general custom to follow the first impulse of nature, and marry at the age of puberty, the universal prevalence of every known virtue in the greatest conceivable degree, would fail of rescuing society from the most wretched and desperate state of want, and all the diseases and famines which usually accompany it.

*   *   *

Of the Only Effectual Mode of Improving the Condition of the Poor

. . . The object of those who really wish to better the condition of the lower classes of society must be to raise the relative proportion between the price of labour and the price of provisions, so as to enable the labourer to command a larger share of the necessaries and comforts of life. We have hitherto principally attempted to attain this end by encouraging the married poor and consequently increasing the number of labourers, and overstocking the market with a commodity which we still say that we wish to be dear. It would seem to have required no great spirit of divination to foretell the certain failure of such a plan of proceeding. There is nothing however like experience. It has been tried in many different countries, and for many hundred years, and the success has always been answerable to the nature of the scheme. It is really time now to try something else.

When it was found that oxygen, or pure vital air, would not cure consumptions as was expected, but rather aggravated their symptoms, trial was made of an air of the most opposite kind. I wish we had acted with the same philosophical spirit in our attempts to cure the disease of poverty: and having found that the pouring in of fresh supplies of labour only tended to aggravate the symptoms, had tried what would be the effect of withholding a little these supplies.

In all old and fully-peopled states it is from this method, and this alone, that we can rationally expect any essential and permanent melioration in the condition of the labouring classes of the people.

In an endeavour to raise the proportion of the quantity of provisions to the number of consumers in any country, out attention would naturally be first directed to the increasing of the absolute quantity of provisions; but finding that, as fast as we did this, the number of consumers more than kept pace with it, and that with all our exertions we were still

as far as ever behind, we should be convinced that our efforts directed only in this way would never succeed. It would appear to be setting the tortoise to catch the hare. Finding, therefore, that from the laws of nature we could not proportion the food to the population, our next attempt should naturally be to proportion the population to the food. If we can persuade the hare to go to sleep the tortoise may have some chance of overtaking her.

We are not, however, to relax our efforts in increasing the quantity of provisions, but to combine another effort with it: that of keeping the population, when once it has been overtaken, at such a distance behind as to effect the relative proportion which we desire: and thus unite the two grand *desiderata*, a great actual population and a state of society in which abject poverty and dependence are comparatively but little known: two objects which are far from being incompatible.

If we be really serious in what appears to be the object of such general research, the mode of essentially and permanently bettering the condition of the poor, we must explain to them the true nature of their situation, and show them that the withholding of the supplies of labour is the only possible way of really raising its price, and that they themselves, being the possessors of this commodity, have alone the power to do this.

*   *   *

Plan of the Gradual Abolition of the Poor Laws Proposed

If the principles in the preceding chapters should stand the test of examination, and we should ever feel the obligation of endeavouring to act upon them, the next inquiry would be in what way we ought practically to proceed. The first grand obstacle which presents itself in this country is the system of the poor-laws, which has been justly stated to be an evil in comparison of which the national debt, with all its magnitude of terror, is of little moment. The rapidity with which the poor's rates have increased of late years presents us indeed with the prospect of such an extraordinary proportion of paupers in the society as would seem to be incredible in a nation flourishing in arts, agriculture, and commerce, and with a government which has generally been allowed to be the best that has hitherto stood the test of experience.

*   *   *

I have reflected much on the subject of the poor-laws, and hope therefore that I shall be excused in venturing to suggest a mode of their gradual abolition to which I confess that at present I can see no material objection. Of this indeed I feel nearly convinced that, should we ever become so fully sensible of the widespreading tyranny, dependence, indolence, and unhappiness which they create as seriously to make an effort to abolish them, we shall be compelled by a sense of justice to adopt the principle, if not the plan, which I shall mention. It seems impossible to get rid of so extensive a system of support, consistently with humanity, without applying ourselves directly to its vital principle, and endeavouring to counteract that deeply-seated cause which occasions the rapid growth of all such establishments and invariably renders them inadequate to their object.

As a previous step even to any considerable alteration in the present system, which would contract or stop the increase of the relief to be given, it appears to me that we are bound in justice and honour formally to disclaim the *right* of the poor to support.

To this end, I should propose a regulation to be made, declaring that no child born from any marriage, taking place after the expiration of a year from the date of the law, and no illegitimate child born two years from the same date, should ever be entitled to parish assistance. And to give a more general knowledge of this law, and to enforce it more strongly on the minds of the lower classes of people, the clergyman of each parish should, after the publication of banns, read a short address stating the strong obligation on every man to support his own children; the impropriety, and even immorality, of marrying without a prospect of being able to do this; the evils which had resulted to the poor themselves from the attempt which had been made to assist by public institutions in a duty which ought to be exclusively appropriated to parents; and the absolute necessity which had at length appeared of abandoning all such institutions, on account of their producing effects totally opposite to those which were intended.

This would operate as a fair, distinct, and precise notice, which no man could well mistake; and, without pressing hard on any particular individuals, would at once throw off the rising generation from that miserable and helpless dependence upon the government and the rich, the moral as well as physical consequences of which are almost incalculable.

After the public notice which I have proposed had been given, and the system of poor-laws had ceased with regard to the rising generation, if any man chose to marry, without a prospect of being able to support a family, he should have the most perfect liberty so to do. Though to marry, in this case, is, in my opinion, clearly an immoral act, yet it is not one which society can justly take upon itself to prevent or punish; because the punishment provided for it by the laws of nature falls directly and most severely upon the individual who commits the act, and through him, only more remotely and feebly, on the society. When nature will govern and punish for us, it is a very miserable ambition to wish to snatch the rod from her hand and draw upon ourselves the odium of executioner. To the punishment therefore of nature he should be left, the punishment of want. He has erred in the face of a most clear and precise warning, and can have no just reason to complain of any person but himself when he feels the consequences of his error. All parish assistance should be denied him; and he should be left to the uncertain support of private charity. He should be taught to know that the laws of nature, which are the laws of God, had doomed him and his family to suffer for disobeying their repeated admonitions; that he had no claim of *right* on society for the smallest portion of food, beyond that which his labour would fairly purchase; and that if he and his family were saved from feeling the natural consequences of his imprudence he would owe it to the pity of some kind benefactor, to whom, therefore, he ought to be bound by the strongest ties of gratitude.

If this system were pursued, we need be under no apprehensions that the number of persons in extreme want would be beyond the power and the will of the benevolent to supply. The sphere for the exercise of private charity would, probably, not be greater than it is at present; and the principal difficulty would be to restrain the hand of benevolence from assisting those in distress in so indiscriminate a manner as to encourage indolence and want of foresight in others.

With regard to illegitimate children, after the proper notice had been given, they should not be allowed to have any claim to parish assistance, but be left entirely to the support of private charity. If the parents desert their child, they ought to be made answerable for the crime. The infant is, comparatively speaking, of little value to the society, as others will immediately supply its place. . . .

Of the Modes of Correcting the Prevailing Opinions on Population

It is not enough to abolish all the positive institutions which encourage population; but we must endeavour, at the same time, to correct the prevailing opinions which have the same, or perhaps even a more powerful effect. This must necessarily be a work of time; and can only be done by circulating juster notions on these subjects in writing and conversation; and by endeavouring to impress as strongly as possible on the public mind that it is not the duty of man simply to propagate his species, but to propagate virtue and happiness; and that, if he has not a tolerably fair prospect of doing this, he is by no means called upon to leave descendants.

. . . The fairest chance of accomplishing this end would probably be by the establishment of a system of parochial education upon a plan similar to that proposed by Adam Smith. In addition to the usual subjects of instruction, and those which he has mentioned, I should be disposed to lay considerable stress on the frequent explanation of the real state of the lower classes of society as affected by the principle of population, and their consequent dependence on themselves for the chief part of their happiness or misery. . . .

The principal argument which I have heard advanced against a system of national education in England is, that the common people would be put in a capacity to read such works as those of Paine, and that the consequences would probably be fatal to government. But on this subject I agree most cordially with Adam Smith in thinking that an instructed and well-informed people would be much less likely to be led away by inflammatory writings, and much better able to detect the false declamation of interested and ambitious demagogues, than an ignorant people. . . .

In most countries, among the lower classes of people, there appears to be something like a standard of wretchedness, a point below which they will not continue to marry and propagate their species. This standard is different in different countries, and is formed by various concurring circumstances of soil, climate, government, degree of knowledge, and civilisation, etc. The principal circumstances which contribute to raise it are liberty, security of property, the diffusion of knowledge, and a taste for the conveniences and the comforts of life. Those which contribute principally to lower it are despotism and ignorance.

In an attempt to better the condition of the labouring classes of society our object should be to raise this standard as high as possible, by cultivating a spirit of independence, a decent pride, and a taste for cleanliness and comfort. The effect of a good government in increasing the prudential habits and personal respectability of the lower classes of society has already been insisted on; but certainly this effect will always be incomplete without a good system of education; and, indeed, it may be said that no government can approach to perfection that does not provide for the instruction of the people. The benefits derived from education are among those which may be enjoyed without restriction of numbers; and, as it is in the power of governments to confer these benefits, it is undoubtedly their duty to do it.

Of Our Rational Expectations Respecting the Future Improvement of Society

*   *   *

It is less the object of the present work to propose new plans of improving society than to inculcate the necessity of resting contented with that mode of improvement which already has in part been acted upon as dictated by the course of nature, and of not obstructing the advances which would otherwise be made in this way.

It would be undoubtedly highly advantageous that all our positive institutions, and the whole tenour of our conduct to the poor, should be such as actively to cooperate with that lesson of prudence inculcated by the common course of human events; and if we take upon ourselves sometimes to mitigate the natural punishments of imprudence, that we could balance it by increasing the rewards of an opposite conduct. But much would be done if merely the institutions which directly tend to encourage marriage were gradually changed, and we ceased to circulate opinions and inculcate doctrines which positively counteract the lessons of nature.

The limited good which it is sometimes in our power to effect, is often lost by attempting too much, and by making the adoption of some particular plan essentially necessary even to a partial degree of success. In the practical application of the reasonings of this work, I hope that I have avoided this error. I wish to press on the recollection of the reader that, though I may have given some new views of old facts, and may have indulged in the contemplation of a considerable degree of *possible* improvement, that I might not shut out that prime cheerer hope; yet in my expectations of probable improvement and in suggesting the means of accomplishing it, I have been very cautious. . . .

From a review of the state of society in former periods compared with the present, I should certainly say that the evils resulting from the principle of population have rather diminished than increased, even under the disadvantage of an almost total ignorance of the real cause. And if we can indulge the hope that this ignorance will be gradually dissipated, it does not seem unreasonable to expect that they will be still further diminished. The increase of absolute population, which will of course take place, will evidently tend but little to weaken this expectation, as everything depends upon the relative proportion between population and food, and not on the absolute number of people. In the former part of this work it appeared that the countries which possessed the fewest people often suffered the most from the effects of the principle of population; and it can scarcely be doubled that, taking Europe throughout, fewer famines and fewer diseases arising from want have prevailed in the last century than in those which preceded it.

On the whole, therefore, though our future prospects respecting the mitigation of the evils arising from the principle of population may not be so bright as we could wish, yet they are far from being entirely disheartening, and by no means preclude that gradual and progressive improvement in human society which, before the late wild speculations on this subject, was the object of rational expectation. To the laws of property and marriage, and to the apparent narrow principle of self-interest which prompts each individual to exert himself in bettering his condition, we are indebted for all the noblest exertions of human genius, for everything that distinguishes the civilised from the savage state. A strict inquiry into the principle of population obliges us to conclude that we shall never be able to throw down the ladder by which we have risen to this eminence; but it by no means proves that we may not rise higher by the same means. The structure of society, in its great features, will probably always remain unchanged. We have every reason to believe that it will always consist of a class of proprietors and a class of labourers; but the condition of each, and the proportion which they bear to each other, may be so altered as greatly to improve the harmony and beauty of the whole. It would indeed be a melancholy reflection that, while the views of physical science are daily enlarging, so as scarcely to be bounded by the most distant horizon, the science of moral and political philosophy should be confined within such narrow limits, or at best be so feeble in its influence, as to be unable to counteract the obstacles to human happiness arising from a single cause. But however formidable these obstacles may have appeared in some parts of this work, it is hoped that the general result of the inquiry is such as not to make us give up the improvement of human society in despair. The partial good which seems to be attainable is worthy of all our exertions; is sufficient to direct our efforts, and animate our prospects. And although we cannot expect that the virtue and happiness of mankind will keep pace with the brilliant career of physical discovery; yet, if we are not wanting to ourselves, we may confidently indulge the hope that, to no unimportant extent, they will be influenced by its progress and will partake in its success.

Two Essays: Factory Workers and How to Constitute a Working Class

Flora Tristan

Of the educated middle class, Tristan lived in France of the early decades of the nineteenth century before industrialization had made its mark in France. After a trip to England, she began to address the workers' question, along with her concerns about the status of women. Tristan's radical solution to the workers' questions involved economic arrangements in which workers would join together in large productive unions that would compete with privately owned business. Although Tristan died before the 1848 Revolutions, many believe that her ideas helped inspire the uprising in France that overthrew King Louis Philippe.

Factory Workers

Slavery shows itself at the dawn of every society. The evils it produces make it essentially transitory, and its duration is inversely proportional to its severity. If our ancestors had had no more humanity for their serfs than the English manufacturers have for their workers, serfdom would not have lasted through the Middle Ages. The English proletariat, in whatever occupation, has such an atrocious existence that the negroes who have left the sugar plantations of Guadaloupe and Martinique in order to partake of English liberty on Dominique and Saint-Lucia return to their former masters whenever they can. Far be it from me to have the sacrilegious thought of defending any kind of slavery! I only want to prove by this example that English law is harder on the proletariat than the *arbitrary will* of the French master toward his negro. The English wage slave has an infinitely worse time earning his daily bread and paying the taxes that are imposed on him.

The negro is exposed only to the caprices of his master, while the existence of the English proletarian, his wife, and his children is at the mercy of the producer. Should calico or some such article be low-ered in price, those immediately affected by the drop, whether spinners, cutters, potters, etc., of one accord reduce wages, with no consideration at all for the subsistence of the workers; they also increase the number of work hours. Where pieceworkers are concerned, the producers demand more highly finished work while paying less, and when all the conditions are not exactly fulfilled the work is not paid for. Cruelly exploited by his employer, the worker is further pressured by the tax collector and starved by the landowners. He almost always dies at an early age. His life is shortened by the excess and nature of his work. His wife and children do not long survive him; tied to the factory, they succumb for the same reasons. If they have no work in the winter, they die of hunger in the street.

The division of labor pushed to its extreme limit, which has been the cause of such progress in manufacturing, has destroyed intelligence and reduced man to being only a gear of the machine. If the worker could still do different parts of one or several manufacturing processes, he would derive satisfaction from being more independent; the cupidity of the master would have fewer means of torturing him; his body would be able to resist the deleterious effects of an occupation that lasted only a few hours. Tool-grinders in English factories do not live past thirty-five years of age; the use of the grindstone does not harm our Châtellerault workers

From: Flora Tristan, *Utopian Feminist: Her Travel Diaries and Personal Crusade,* selected by Doris and Paul Beik (Bloomington: Indiana University Press, 1993), pp. 61–67, 107–111.

because the grinding is only a part of their work and of their time, whereas in the English workshops, the grinders do nothing else. If the worker could be employed in several parts of the manufacturing process instead of repeating the same thing all day long, he would not be overwhelmed by his own unimportance and by the perpetual inactivity of his mind. He would no longer need strong brandies to rouse him from the torpor into which the monotony of his work plunges him, and drunkenness would not be the last degree of his misfortune.

To get a good idea of the physical sufferings and moral debasement of this class of the population, one must visit the manufacturing cities and see the worker in Birmingham, Manchester, Glasgow, Sheffield, and in Staffordshire, etc. It is impossible to judge the lot of the English worker by that of the French worker. In England life is half again as expensive as in France, and since 1825 wages have gone down so much that most workers must ask for help from the parish to sustain their families, and since parishes are overburdened by the amount of aid they give, they ration it according to the workers' wages and the number of children he has; not in relation to the price of bread but to the price of potatoes, for to the proletarian bread is a luxury! More favored workers, excluded because of their wages from parish aid, are not much better off. The average pay they earn is, I am told, not more than three or four shillings (three francs, seventy-five centimes to five francs) a day, and the average family has four children. By comparing these two facts with the cost of food in England, one quickly gets an idea of their distress.

Most of the workers lack clothing, a bed, furniture, a fire, wholesome food, and often even potatoes! They are shut up twelve to fourteen hours a day in mean rooms where they breathe in, along with foul air, cotton, wool, and linen fibers, particles of copper, lead, iron, etc., and frequently go from insufficient nourishment to excessive drinking. These unfortunates are also pale, rickety, and sickly; they have thin, feeble bodies with weak arms, wan complexions, and dull eyes; one cannot help thinking that all of them must have lung disease. I do not know whether the painful expression that is so general among the workers should be attributed to permanent fatigue or to their utter despair. It is difficult

to meet their gaze; they all have their eyes continuously lowered and only look at you stealthily by throwing you a sideways glance in an underhand manner*—which gives a somewhat dazed, wild, and horribly evil look to these cold, impassive faces, enveloped in great sadness. In English factories there isn't any singing, chatting, or laughter, such as there is in ours. The master does not want his workers distracted for a minute by any reminders of life; he demands silence, and a deadly silence there is, so much does the hunger of the worker give weight to the word of the master! No friendly, polite relationship exists between the worker and the heads of the establishment, none of that interest that we have in our country, which softens the feelings of hate and envy that are borne in the hearts of the poor for the disdain, hardness, arbitrary demands, and luxury of the rich. In English workshops one never hears the master say to the worker, "Good-morning, Baptiste; how is your poor wife?—and the child? Good, so much the better! We will hope that the mother will recover quickly. Tell her to come and see me as soon as she can go out." A master would feel demeaned to speak thus to his workers. The worker sees in every factory boss a man who can have him put out of the workshop where he is employed, and so he greets the manufacturers with servility when he meets them; but the latter would feel their honor compromised if they returned the greeting.

Since I have known the English proletariat I no longer think that slavery is the greatest human misfortune: the slave is *sure of his bread all his life,* and of care when he is sick; whereas there exists no bond between the worker and the English master. If the latter has no work to give out, the worker dies of hunger; if he is sick, he succumbs on the straw of his pallet, unless, near death, he is received in a hospital; for it is a favor to be admitted there. If he grows old, or is crippled as the result of an accident, he is fired, and he turns to begging furtively for fear of being arrested. So horrible is this situation that

---

*This look, which I have also seen among the slaves in America, is not particular to factory workers in the British Isles. It is found wherever people are dependent and subordinate; it is one of the characteristic features of the twenty million proletarians. Nevertheless there are exceptions, nearly always encountered in *women.*

one has to believe that the worker has superhuman courage or complete apathy to bear it.

English manufacturing works are generally on small sites; the space in which the worker is to move is measured parsimoniously. The courtyards are small and the stairways narrow. The worker is obliged to pass *sideways* around machines and pieces of work. It is easy to see upon visiting a factory that the comfort and well-being, let alone the health of the men destined to be in a factory, have had no part in the builder's thought. Cleanliness, the best aid to health, is greatly neglected. The machines are just as carefully painted, varnished, cleaned, and polished as the courtyards are dirty and full of stagnant water, the floors dusty, and the windowpanes dirty. To tell the truth, if the buildings and the workshops were clean and neat and kept up like the factories of Alsace, the rags of the English worker would appear still more hideous. But it does not matter whether it is from negligence or from calculation; that dirt makes matters worse for the worker.

England's principal grandeur is its industry, but that is positively gigantic as one encounters it in the machines made possible by the mathematical spirit of modern times—magical instruments that dominate everything around them! The docks, the railroads, and the immensity of the factories announce the importance of British commerce and industry.

The power of the machines and their application to everything astonish and stupify the imagination! Human skill, incorporated in thousands of forms, replaces the functions of the intelligence. With machines and the division of labor, one only needs motors: reasoning and reflection are useless.

I have seen a steam engine with the power of 500 horses!* Nothing is more awe-inspiring than the sight of the motion imparted to these masses of iron whose colossal forms frighten the imagination and seem to go beyond the power of man! This motor of hyperbolical force is situated in a vast building where it drives a considerable number of machines for working iron and wood. These enormous bars of polished iron, which go up and down forty to fifty times a minute and activate a coming and going movement of the tongue of a monster that seems to want to engulf everything, the terrible groans it utters, the rapid revolutions of the immense wheel that leaves the abyss in order to reenter it immediately, never allowing more than half of its circumference to be seen, intimidate one's soul. In the presence of the monster one sees only it, hears only its breathing.

Upon recovering from your stupor and fright, you look for man. He can hardly be seen, reduced by the proportions of everything around him to the size of an ant. He is occupied in putting under the cutting edge of the two large curves in the form of a shark's jaw some enormous iron bars, which that machine cuts with the neatness of a Damascus blade slicing a turnip.

If at first I experienced humiliation at seeing man destroyed, no longer functioning other than as a machine, I soon appreciated the immense improvement that would one day come from these scientific discoveries: brute force eliminated, work with material things finished in less time, and more leisure for man to cultivate his mind; but for these great benefits to be realized there will have to be a social revolution. It will come! For God has not revealed these admirable inventions to men in order to make them slaves of a few manufacturers and landowners.

Beer and gas are two great divisions of consumption in London. I went to visit the superb Barclay-Perkins brewery, which is certainly worth seeing. This establishment is very extensive; nothing has been spared in its construction. I was unable to learn how many liters of beer it makes each year, but to judge by the size of the vats, it must be an extraordinary amount. It was in one of the largest of these vats that the Messrs. Barclay-Perkins gave a dinner for one of the English royal highnesses and invited more than fifty guests. That vat is thirty meters (ninety feet) high. Wherever steam operates, man's strength is excluded; what was most striking in this brewery was the small number of workers employed to do such prodigious work.

---

*I saw it in Birmingham. The owners of the factory assured me that the force of this steam engine could be raised to 500 horsepower. It turns more than 200 pulleys and operates powersaws for planks, shears for cutting iron, rollers of all sizes, an assortment of machines to make ladles for zinc, etc. A *sixpence* was put under a press to give me the idea of the force of the pressure; there came out forty-two yards of a small band of *silver paper* as thin as an onion skin.

One of the large gas plants is in Horse Ferry Road, Westminster (I have forgotten the name of the company). One visits this plant only with a ticket of admission.

In this manufacturing palace, there is a great profusion of machines and of iron. Everything is of iron: the walks, the corner posts, the stairways, certain floors, the roofs of the sheds, etc., and one realizes that everything has been done to make the buildings and equipment strong. I saw vats in cast iron and in zinc as high and wide as a four-storyed house. I would have liked very much to know how many thousands of tons they contain, but the foreman who accompanied me was as reserved about this as the one in the Barclay-Perkins had been about the number of liters of beer—absolute silence.

We entered the great heating room. The two rows of furnaces on each side were lighted. That fiery furnace calls to mind rather well the descriptions that the ancient poets have left us of Vulcan's forges, except that divine activity and intelligence animated the Cyclops, whereas the black servants of the English furnaces are morose, silent, and exhausted. There were about twenty men working there, accurately, but slowly. Those not occupied stood motionless, their eyes on the ground. They did not even have enough energy to dry the perspiration that poured off them. Three or four looked at me with eyes that immediately shifted from mine. The others did not turn their heads. The foreman told me that the stokers were chosen from the strongest men but that, even so, all became consumptive at the end of seven or eight years of the work and died of tuberculosis. That explained the sadness and apathy on the faces and in the movements of these unfortunates.

A kind of work is required of them that the human physique cannot bear. They are naked except for a small loincloth. When they leave, they throw a jacket over their shoulders.

Although the space between the two rows of furnaces seemed to me to be fifty or sixty feet, the floor was so hot that the heat immediately penetrated my shoes so much that I had to lift my feet as if I were stepping on burning coals. I had to step up onto a large stone and even though it was off the ground, it was *hot*. I could not stay in this hell; my lungs were full, the smell of gas went to my head, and the heat

suffocated me. The foreman took me to the back of the furnace room, to a balcony from which I could see everything without being so uncomfortable.

We made the tour of the establishment. I had great admiration for all these machines, this perfection and order with which the work is done. However, the precautions taken do not prevent all accidents, and frequently there are great disasters, injuring the men and sometimes killing them. My God! Progress, then, can only take place at the expense of the lives of a certain number of individuals!

The gas from this factory goes in pipes to light the district from Oxford Street to Regent Street.

The air that one breathes in this factory is really poisonous! Every minute noxious fumes assail you. I left the shed, hoping to breathe purer air in the courtyard; but everywhere I was pursued by the infectious exhalations of gas and the odors of oil, tar, etc.

I must say also that the site is very dirty. The courtyard full of stagnant water and pieces of garbage shows extreme negligence in everything concerning the property. In truth, the nature of the materials from which one obtains gas is such as to require a very active cleaning service but two men would be enough for the job, and with only a slight increase in expense the establishment would be made healthful.

I was asphyxiated and I was hurrying to get out of this stench when the foreman said to me: "Stay a minute more—you will see something interesting. The firemen are going to take the coke from the ovens."

I again perched on the balcony. From there I saw one of the most frightening sights I had ever witnessed.

The heating room is on the second floor; below is the chamber to receive the coke. The stokers, armed with long iron rakes, opened the ovens and drew out the coke, which, all fiery, fell in torrents into the chamber. Nothing could be more terrible or majestic than those mouths vomiting forth flames! Nothing could be more magical than the chamber suddenly illuminated by burning coals plunging like the waters of a cataract from a high rock and, like them, being swallowed in the abyss! Nothing could be more frightening than the sight of the stokers dripping as if they were emerging from water, lighted on all sides by those horrible coals whose fiery tongues seem to advance as if to devour them. No, one could not see anything more frightening!

When the furnaces were half empty, men on top of the vats at the four corners of the chamber threw down water to extinguish the fires; then the scene in the heating room changed: a whirlwind of black, thick, glowing smoke rose majestically from the hole and went out through the roof, which had been expressly opened for it. I could no longer see the mouths of the ovens except through this cloud that made the flames redder and the tongues of flame more frightening. The white bodies of the firemen became black and those unfortunates, whom one would have thought to be devils, became lost in this infernal chaos. Surprised by the smoke from the coke, I just had time to get down in a hurry.

I waited for the end of the operation, curious to know what was going to become of the poor stokers. I was amazed to see no woman arrive. My God, I thought, these workers, then, have no mothers, sisters, wives, or daughters waiting at the door when they leave this fiery furnace, to bathe them in warm water, wrap them in flannel shirts, make them drink a nourishing, strengthening beverage, and then give them such words of friendship and love as may console, encourage, and help man to bear the cruelest miseries. I was concerned; not a woman appeared. I asked the foreman if these men, drenched in sweat, were going to get some rest.

"They are going to throw themselves on a bed in this shed," he answered me coldly, "and at the end of a couple of hours they will fire up again."

This shed, open to every wind, only keeps out the rain; it was icy cold in there. A kind of mattress, hardly distinguishable from the coal around it, was in one of the corners. I saw the stokers stretch out on this hard-as-a-stone mattress. They were covered with very dirty overcoats, impregnated with so much sweat and coal dust that one couldn't even guess the color of them. "There," the foreman said to me, "that is how the men become consumptive—by going from hot to cold without precautions."

The foreman's last observation had such an effect on me that I left the factory in a complete state of exasperation.

That is how men's lives are bought for money; and when the exacted task causes deaths, the industrialist suffers no inconvenience except having to raise wages! Why, that is even worse than the negro *slave trade!* I see nothing surpassing this enormous monstrosity except cannibalism! The owners of factories and manufacturing plants can, with no legal impediment, have at their disposal the youth and the vigor of hundreds of men, purchase their lives and sacrifice them, in order to gain money! All at wages of seven to eight shillings a day, eight francs, seventy-five centimes to ten francs!

I do not know that any heads of factories such as those of whom I have just been speaking have had the humanity to make available a room moderately heated, with baths of warm water, mattresses, and wool covers, where the stokers could go, on leaving their furnaces, to wash and rest, well wrapped up, in an atmosphere not unlike the one they had left. It is really a shame and a national disgrace for such things as I have just described to occur.

In England when the horses arrive at the post stations, someone hurries to throw a blanket over them, dry their sweat and wash their feet; then they are put in a closed stable well lined with very dry straw.

A few years ago relay stations were placed closer together after it was realized that too great distances between them shortened the lives of the horses; yes, but a horse costs the industralist forty to fifty pounds sterling, whereas the country furnishes him men *for nothing!*

How to Constitute the Working Class

It is very important that the workers understand clearly the difference between the WORKERS' UNION as I have conceived of it and what exists today under various names such as *association, compagnonnage, union, mutual aid,* etc.

The common aim of all these distinct and differing associations is simply for *members of the same society* to provide each other with aid and assistance, mutually and individually. And so these societies were established in preparation for cases of *sickness, accidents,* and *long periods of unemployment.*

Given the present state of isolation, abandonment, and poverty characteristic of the working class, these societies are very useful, for their aim is to help, in small ways, the most needy, and thereby to lessen personal suffering that often exceeds the strength and courage of its victims. I therefore heartily approve of these societies, and I encourage workers to increase their number while at the same time purifying them of the abuses to which they can be subject. But to *relieve distress* is not to *destroy it;* to lessen an evil is not to *remove* it. If at last one decides to attack the evil at its root, clearly something more is needed than *private organizations* whose only purpose is to *minister to the sufferings of individuals.* . . .

Workers, you must therefore abandon as quickly as possible your habits of division and isolation and march courageously and fraternally in the only direction that is suitable for you—toward *unity.* The project of union as I have conceived of it rests on a broad base, and its spirit is capable of fully satisfying the moral and material requirements of a great people.

What is the objective and what will be the result of the *universal union of workingmen and workingwomen?*

It has as objectives: (1) To CONSTITUTE the compact, indissoluble UNITY of the WORKING CLASS; (2) to make the WORKERS' UNION the possessor of an enormous capital, by means of a voluntary contribution from each worker; (3) to acquire, by means of this capital, some real power, that of money; (4) by means of this power, to prevent poverty and to eradicate the evil at its root, in giving children of the working class a solid, rational education, capable of making them into trained, reasonable, intelligent men and women who art also skillful in their professions; (5) to compensate all sorts of labor amply and worthily.

This is too beautiful! someone will cry. It is too beautiful: *it is impossible.*

Readers, before paralyzing the impulses of your heart and imagination by this glacial phrase, *it is impossible,* always keep in mind that France contains seven to eight million workers; that at two francs apiece there will accumulate at the end of a year fourteen million; at four francs, twenty-eight million; at eight francs, fifty-six million. This result is in no way chimerical. Among the workers some

are well-to-do, and very many are generous; some will give two francs, others four, eight, ten, or twenty francs, and think of your number, seven million! . . . * I have said by means of this capital the WORKERS' UNION could gain real power, that which money gives. Let us see how.

For example, the Irish people by means of their union have been able to establish and maintain what is called THE ASSOCIATION . . . ; moreover, they have been able to set up, by voluntary contributions, . . . a colossal fortune, at the disposition of a man of heart and talent, O'Connell. . . .

What is the social position of the working class in France today, and what rights remain for it to claim?

In principle the organic law that has regulated French society since the Declaration of the Rights of Man of 1791 is the highest expression of justice and equity, for this law is the solemn recognition that legitimates the sanctity of the principle of absolute equality, and not only the equality before God demanded by Jesus but also that *living equality* practiced in the name of both the spirit and the flesh in the presence of humanity. . . .

. . . But let us hasten to say that to enjoy equality and liberty *in principle* is to live *in spirit,* and if he who brought to the world *the law of the spirit* spoke wisely in saying that "man does not live by bread alone," I believe that it is also wise to say that "man does not live by spirit alone."

In reading the Charter of 1830 one is struck by a serious omission. Our constitutional legislators forgot that prior to the rights of man and of the citizen there exists an imperious, imprescriptible right that precedes and governs all the others, the *right to live.* Now, for the poor worker who possesses neither land nor houses, nor capital, nor absolutely anything except *his arms,* the rights of man and citizen are of no value (and in this case they even become for him a bitter mockery), if first one does not recognize *his*

---

*The WORKERS' UNION, in my view, would have for its aim, at first, "to constitute the working class, properly speaking," and eventually to "*rally*" to the same cause the twenty-five million French working people of all kinds who are "not proprietors," in order that they might defend their interests and demand their rights. The working class is not the only one to suffer from the privileges of property. . . .

right to live, and, for the worker, the right to live is *the right to work, the only one* that can give him the possibility of *eating,* and consequently of living.

The first of the rights belonging to everyone from birth is precisely that which was *overlooked* in the writing of the charter. It is therefore *this first right* that is still to be proclaimed.*

Today the working class must concentrate on a single demand because this demand is based on the strictest equity and because this claim cannot be refused without violating the *right to life.* What, in fact, does the working class demand?

The Right to Work

Its own property, the only one that it can ever possess, is *its arms.* Yes, its arms! They are its patrimony, its unique wealth! Its arms are the *only instruments of labor* in its possession. They therefore constitute *its property,* and the *legitimacy,* and above all the *utility,* of this property cannot, I think, be contested, for if the earth produces, it is thanks to *the work people's arms.*

To deny that *arms are property* is to refuse to understand the *spirit* of article 8 of the charter. Nevertheless, arms as a form of property cannot be contested, and when the day comes that this matter can be discussed, there can be on this subject only one conclusion. But for the working class to be *secure* and *guaranteed* in the enjoyment of its property (as article 8 stipulates), the *free use* and guarantee of that property must be recognized in *principle* (and also in reality). Now the actual free use of this property would consist, for the working class, in being able to *make use of its arms,* whenever and however it wished, and to make this possible it must possess the *right to work.* And as for the guarantee of this property, it consists of a wise and equitable ORGANIZATION OF LABOR.

---

*The National Convention had "almost" recognized "the right to work" or at least "to public assistance." Art. XXI: "Public assistance is a sacred obligation. Society owes subsistence to unfortunate citizens, whether by finding work for them, or by guaranteeing the means of existence to those who are unable to work." *Declaration of the Rights of Man and of the Citizen,* June 27, 1793.

The working class has therefore two important claims to make: (1) THE RIGHT TO WORK; (2) THE ORGANIZATION OF LABOR.

But, someone is going to say again, what you demand for the working class is impossible. The right to work! They won't get it. This claim, however just and legal, will be considered an attack on property properly so called (land, houses, capital), and the organization of labor will be considered an attack on the rights of free competition. Now since those who manage the governmental machine are the owners of land and capital, it is evident that they will never consent to grant such rights to the working class.

Let us understand each other. If in their present condition of division and isolation the workers decide to demand the *right to work* and *the organization of labor,* the proprietors will not even do them the honor of considering their demand as an attack: they will simply not listen. A worker of merit (Adolphe Boyer) wrote a little book in which he made both demands: no one read his book. The unfortunate man, from chagrin and poverty, and possibly with the thought that his tragic end would move people to read his proposals, killed himself. Briefly the press took notice, for four days, perhaps eight; then the suicide and Adolphe Boyer's little book were completely forgotten. . . . Boyer was a poor worker who wrote all alone in his corner; he defended the cause of his unfortunate brothers, that is true, but he was not linked to them by shared thoughts or even by shared emotions or interests; and so he killed himself because he lacked 200 francs to pay the expenses of his small book. Can you believe that this would have happened if Boyer had been part of a vast union? Without doubt, no. . . .

Workers, you see the situation. If you want to save yourselves, you have only one means: you must UNITE.

If I preach UNION to you, it is because I understand the strength and capacity you will find in it. Open your eyes, look around you, and see the advantages enjoyed by all those who have formed a UNION in order to serve the same cause and the same interests.

Notice the procedure adopted by all men of intelligence, for example the founders of religions. Their first preoccupation was with the founding of a

UNION. Moses unites his people, and by attachments so strong that time itself cannot break them.... What does Jesus do before his death? He gathers his twelve apostles and UNITES them.... The master dies. No matter! THE UNION IS CONSTITUTED.... Jesus Christ *lives in his apostles* with an *eternal life,* for after John comes Peter, and after Peter comes Paul, and so on, to the end of time.

Twelve men UNITED established the *Catholic Church,* a vast union that became so powerful that for 2,000 years this union has governed most of the earth.

Examine on a smaller scale the same principle of strength in operation: Luther, Calvin, and all of the Catholic dissidents. From the moment of their joining together in a UNION they become powerful.

And now, another order of events: the revolution of '89 breaks out. Like a torrent that sweeps everything before it, it overthrows, it exiles, it kills. But the ROYALIST UNION is *constituted.* Although overwhelmingly outnumbered, it is so strong that it survives the destructions of '93, and twenty years later it returns to France, *its king as its head!* And in the face of such accomplishments you would persist in remaining in your isolation! No, no! Short of madness, you can persist no longer.

In '89 the bourgeois class won its independence. Its own charter dates from the taking of the Bastille. Workers, for 200 years and more the bourgeois fought with courage and persistence against the privileges of the nobility and for the triumph of their *rights.* But with victory achieved, although they recognized equality of rights for everyone, *in fact they seized for themselves alone* all the gains and advantages of this conquest.

Since '89 the bourgeois class HAS BEEN CONSTITUTED. Notice what force a body united by the same interests can have. Once this class IS CONSTITUTED it becomes so strong that it can appropriate every power in the land. Finally, in 1830, its strength reaches its peak, and without regard for consequences it pronounces the *dismissal the last king of France;* it chooses its *own* king, arranges for his selection without consulting the rest of the nation, and finally, being in fact *sovereign,* takes charge of affairs and governs the country according to its own tastes.

This bourgeois-proprietor class *represents itself* in the Chamber and before the nation, not in order to *defend its interests* there, for no one threatens them, but in order to *impose* its conditions on the twenty-five million proletarians, its subordinates. In a word, it makes itself *judge* and *party,* absolutely as the feudal lords behaved whom it has overthrown. As proprietor of the soil, it makes laws relating to the *products it markets,* and thus, regulates *as it pleases* the prices of the wine, the meat, and even the *bread* consumed by the people.

You see, the *noble class* has been succeeded by the *bourgeois class,* already much *more numerous* and *more useful;* it now remains to CONSTITUTE THE WORKING CLASS. It is necessary, therefore, for the workers, the enduring part of the nation, in their turn to form a vast UNION and CONSTITUTE THEMSELVES IN UNITY. Oh, then the working class will be strong, then it will be able to demand of messieurs the bourgeois both its RIGHT TO WORK and the ORGANIZATION OF LABOR; and insist on being heard.

The advantage enjoyed by all of the great *constituted* bodies is to be able to count for something in the state and thereby to *enjoy representation.* Today the ROYALIST UNION has its representative in the Chamber, its delegate before the nation to defend its interests; and that defender is the most eloquent man in France, M. Berryer. THE COLONIAL UNION has its representatives in the Chamber, its delegates before the mother country to defend its interests. Well, why then should not the working class, once it is CONSTITUTED AS A BODY, the class that by its number, and especially its importance, is certainly the equal of the royalists and the colonial proprietors, have, too, its representative in the Chamber and its delegate before the nation *to defend its interests there?*

Workers, consider this well: the first thing you must do is to have yourselves *represented before the nation.*

I said above that the WORKERS' UNION would enjoy real power, that of money. It will in fact be easy for it, out of twenty to thirty million francs, to devote 500,000 a year to the ample rapport of a defender worthy of serving its cause!

We need not doubt that there will easily be found in our beautiful France, so generous, so chivalrous, men with the devotion and talents of an O'Connel.

If, then, the WORKERS' UNION really understands its position and its true interests, its first act must be a solemn APPEAL to those men possessed of sufficient love, strength, courage, and talent to dare assume the defense of the holiest of causes, that of the workers.

Oh, who knows what France still possesses in the way of generous hearts and capable men! Who could foresee the effect of an appeal in the name of seven million workers demanding the RIGHT TO WORK?

Poor workers! Isolated, you count for nothing in the nation; but once the WORKERS' UNION IS CONSTITUTED the working class will become a powerful and respectable body; and men of the highest merit will solicit the honor of being chosen as defenders of the WORKERS' UNION. . . .

The Communist Manifesto
Karl Marx

By 1848, when the famous Manifesto was written and published, Marx had rejected the ideas of earlier reformist socialists that change could come about voluntarily. He criticized nonviolent socialists as "utopians," a characterization that remains in force today. Change, he insisted, would have to come by revolution, the engine for which was class conflict. When impoverished workers overthrew the owning class, the bourgeoisie, they would establish a democracy of equal wealth. Marx's ideas became the bible of socialism for the following century or more.

 Benefit.

A spectre is haunting Europe—the spectre of Communism. All the powers of old Europe have entered into a holy alliance to exorcise this spectre: Pope and Tsar, Metternich and Guizot, French Radicals and German police-spies. → *Only wanted power over all people*

Where is the party in opposition that has not been decried as communistic by its opponents in power? Where is the Opposition that has not hurled back the branding reproach of Communism, against the more advanced opposition parties, as well as against its reactionary adversaries?

Two things result from this fact:

1. Communism is already acknowledged by all European powers to be itself a power.

2. It is high time that Communists should openly, in the face of the whole world, publish their views, their aims, their tendencies, and meet this nursery tale of the spectre of Communism with a manifesto of the party itself.

To this end, Communists of various nationalities have assembled in London, and sketched the following manifesto, to be published in the English, French, German, Italian, Flemish and Danish languages:

(left margin handwritten note: was acknowledged but rulers wanted power.)

From: Karl Marx, *The Communist Manifesto*, commentary and notes by Emile Burns (New York: Avenel Books, 1982), pp.22–59. NOTE: The footnotes were written by Engels for the English edition of 1888.

I: Bourgeois and Proletarians*

The history of all hitherto existing society[†] is the history of class struggles.

Freeman and slave, patrician and plebeian, lord and serf, guild-master[‡] and journeyman, in a word, oppressor and oppressed, stood in constant opposition to one another, carried on an uninterrupted,

---

*By bourgeoisie is meant the class of modern capitalists, owners of the means of social production and employers of wage-labour. By proletariat, the class of modern wage-labourers who, having no means of production of their own, are reduced to selling their labour power in order to live.

†That is, all *written* history. In 1847, the pre-history of society, the social organisation existing previous to recorded history, was all but unknown. Since then Haxthausen [August von, 1792–1866] discovered common ownership of land in Russia, Maurer [Georg Ludwig von] proved it to be the social foundation from which all Teutonic races started in history, and, by and by, village communities were found to be, or to have been, the primitive form of society everywhere from India to Ireland. The inner organization of this primitive communistic society was laid bare, in its typical form, by Morgan's [Henry, 1818–1881] crowning discovery of the true nature of the *gens* and its relation to the *tribe*. With the dissolution of these primæval communities, society begins to be differentiated into separate and finally antagonistic classes. I have attempted to retrace this process of dissolution in *Der Ursprung der Familie, des Privaleigenthums und des Staats*, 2nd edition, Stuttgart, 1886. (*The Origin of the Family, Private Property and the State.*)

‡Guild-master, that is a full member of a guild, a master within, not a head of a guild.

now hidden, now open fight, a fight that each time ended, either in a revolutionary reconstitution of society at large, or in the common ruin of the contending classes.

In the earlier epochs of history, we find almost everywhere a complicated arrangement of society into various orders, a manifold gradation of social rank. In ancient Rome we have patricians, knights, plebeians, slaves; in the Middle Ages, feudal lords, vassals, guild-masters, journeymen, apprentices, serfs; in almost all of these classes, again, subordinate gradations.

The modern bourgeois society that has sprouted from the ruins of feudal society has not done away with class antagonisms. It has but established new classes, new conditions of oppression, new forms of struggle in place of the old ones.

Our epoch, the epoch of the bourgeoisie, possesses, however, this distinctive feature: it has simplified the class antagonisms. Society as a whole is more and more splitting up into two great hostile camps, into two great classes directly facing each other—bourgeoisie and proletariat.

From the serfs of the Middle Ages sprang the chartered burghers of the earliest towns. From these burgesses the first elements of the bourgeoisie were developed.

The discovery of America, the rounding of the Cape, opened up fresh ground for the rising bourgeoisie. The East-Indian and Chinese markets, the colonisation of America, trade with the colonies, the increase in the means of exchange and in commodities generally, gave to commerce, to navigation, to industry, an impulse never before known, and thereby, to the revolutionary element in the tottering feudal society, a rapid development.

The feudal system of industry, in which industrial production was monopolised by closed guilds, now no longer sufficed for the growing wants of the new markets. The manufacturing system took its place. The guild-masters were pushed aside by the manufacturing middle class; division of labour between the different corporate guilds vanished in the face of division of labour in each single workshop.

Meantime the markets kept ever growing, the demand ever rising. Even manufacture no longer sufficed. Thereupon, steam and machinery revolutionised industrial production. The place of manufacture was taken by the giant, modern industry, the place of the industrial middle class, by industrial millionaires, the leaders of whole industrial armies, the modern bourgeois.

Modern industry has established the world market, for which the discovery of America paved the way. This market has given an immense development to commerce, to navigation, to communication by land. This development has, in its turn, reacted on the extension of industry; and in proportion as industry, commerce, navigation, railways extended, in the same proportion the bourgeoisie developed, increased its capital, and pushed into the background every class handed down from the Middle Ages.

We see, therefore, how the modern bourgeoisie is itself the product of a long course of development, of a series of revolutions in the modes of production and of exchange.

Each step in the development of the bourgeoisie was accompanied by a corresponding political advance of that class. An oppressed class under the sway of the feudal nobility, an armed and self-governing association in the mediæval commune;* here independent urban republic (as in Italy and Germany), there taxable "third estate" of the monarchy (as in France); afterwards, in the period of manufacture proper, serving either the semi-feudal or the absolute monarchy as a counterpoise against the nobility, and, in fact, corner-stone of the great monarchies in general, the bourgeoisie has at last, since the establishment of Modern Industry and of the world market, conquered for itself, in the modern representative State, exclusive political sway. The executive of the modern State is but a committee for managing the common affairs of the whole bourgeoisie.

The bourgeoisie, historically, has played a most revolutionary part.

The bourgeoisie, wherever it has got the upper hand, has put an end to all feudal, patriarchal, idyllic

---

*"Commune" was the name taken, in France, by the nascent town even before they had conquered from their feudal lords and masters, local self-government and political rights as "the Third Estate." Generally speaking, for the economical development of the bourgeoisie, England is here taken as the typical country, for its political development France.

relations. It has pitilessly torn asunder the motley feudal ties that bound man to his "natural superiors," and has left no other nexus between man and man than naked self-interest, than callous "cash payment." It has drowned the most heavenly ecstasies of religious fervour, of chivalrous enthusiasm, of philistine sentimentalism, in the icy water of egotistical calculation. It has resolved personal worth into exchange value, and in place of the numberless indefeasible chartered freedoms, has set up that single, unconscionable freedom—Free Trade. In one word, for exploitation, veiled by religious and political illusions, it has substituted naked, shameless, direct, brutal exploitation.

The bourgeoisie has stripped of its halo every occupation hitherto honoured and looked up to with reverent awe. It has converted the physician, the lawyer, the priest, the poet, the man of science, into its paid wage-labourers.

The bourgeoisie has torn away from the family its sentimental veil, and has reduced the family relation to a mere money relation.

The bourgeoisie has disclosed how it came to pass that the brutal display of vigour in the Middle Ages, which reactionaries so much admire, found its fitting complement in the most slothful indolence. It has been the first to show what man's activity can bring about. It has accomplished wonders far surpassing Egyptian pyramids, Roman aqueducts, and Gothic cathedrals; it has conducted expeditions that put in the shade all former Exoduses of nations and crusades.

The bourgeoisie cannot exist without constantly revolutionising the instruments of production, and thereby the relations of production, and with them the whole relations of society. Conservation of the old modes of production in unaltered form, was, on the contrary, the first condition of existence for all earlier industrial classes. Constant revolutionising of production, uninterrupted disturbance of all social conditions, everlasting uncertainty and agitation distinguish the bourgeois epoch from all earlier ones. All fixed, fast-frozen relations, with their train of ancient and venerable prejudices and opinions, are swept away, all new-formed ones become antiquated before they can ossify. All that is solid melts into air, all that is holy is profaned, and man is at last compelled to face with sober senses his real conditions of life and his relations with his kind.

The need of a constantly expanding market for its products chases the bourgeoisie over the whole surface of the globe. It must nestle everywhere, settle everywhere, establish connections everywhere.

The bourgeoisie has through its exploitation of the world market given a cosmopolitan character to production and consumption in every country. To the great chagrin of reactionaries, it has drawn from under the feet of industry the national ground on which it stood. All old-established national industries have been destroyed or are daily being destroyed. They are dislodged by new industries, whose introduction becomes a life and death question for all civilised nations, by industries that no longer work up indigenous raw material, but raw material drawn from the remotest zones; industries whose products are consumed, not only at home, but in every quarter of the globe. In place of the old wants, satisfied by the production of the country, we find new wants, requiring for their satisfaction the products of distant lands and climes. In place of the old local and national seclusion and self-sufficiency, we have intercourse in every direction, universal interdependence of nations. And as in material, so also in intellectual production. The intellectual creations of individual nations become common property. National one-sidedness and narrow-mindedness become more and more impossible, and from the numerous national and local literatures there arises a world literature.

The bourgeois, by the rapid improvement of all instruments of production, by the immensely facilitated means of communication, draws all, even the most barbarian, nations into civilisation. The cheap prices of its commodities are the heavy artillery with which it batters down all Chinese walls, with which it forces the barbarians' intensely obstinate hatred of foreigners to capitulate. It compels all nations, on pain of extinction, to adopt the bourgeois mode of production; it compels them to introduce what it calls civilisation into their midst, i.e., to become bourgeois themselves. In one word, it creates a world after its own image.

The bourgeoisie has subjected the country to the rule of the towns. It has created enormous cities, has greatly increased the urban population as compared with the rural, and has thus rescued a considerable part of the population from the idiocy of

Everyone begins to rely on each other.

people had gained more freedom

rural life. Just as it has made the country dependent on the towns, so it has made barbarian and semi-barbarian countries dependent on the civilised ones, nations of peasants on nations of bourgeois, the East on the West.

The bourgeoisie keeps more and more doing away with the scattered state of the population, of the means of production, and of property. It has agglomerated population, centralised means of production, and has concentrated property in a few hands. The necessary consequence of this was political centralisation. Independent, or but loosely connected provinces, with separate interests, laws, governments and systems of taxation, became lumped together into one nation, with one government, one code of laws, one national class interest, one frontier and one customs tariff.

The bourgeoisie, during its rule of scarce one hundred years, has created more massive and more colossal productive forces than have all preceding generations together. Subjection of nature's forces to man, machinery, application of chemistry to industry and agriculture, steam-navigation, railways, electric telegraphs, clearing of whole continents for cultivation, canalisation of rivers, whole populations conjured out of the ground—what earlier century had even a presentiment that such productive forces slumbered in the lap of social labour?

We see then; the means of production and of exchange, on whose foundation the bourgeoisie built itself up, were generated in feudal society. At a certain stage in the development of these means of production and of exchange, the conditions under which feudal society produced and exchanged, the feudal organisation of agriculture and manufacturing industry, in one word, the feudal relations of property became no longer compatible with the already developed productive forces; they became so many fetters. They had to be burst asunder; they were burst asunder.

Into their place stepped free competition, accompanied by a social and political constitution adapted to it, and by the economical and political sway of the bourgeois class.

A similar movement is going on before our own eyes. Modern bourgeois society with its relations of production, of exchange and of property, a society that has conjured up such gigantic means of production and of exchange, is like the sorcerer who is no longer able to control the powers of the nether world whom he has called up by his spells. For many a decade past the history of industry and commerce is but the history of the revolt of modern productive forces against modern conditions of production, against the property relations that are the conditions for the existence of the bourgeoisie and of its rule. It is enough to mention the commercial crises that by their periodical return put the existence of the entire bourgeois society on its trial, each time more threateningly. In these crises a great part not only of the existing products, but also of the previously created productive forces, are periodically destroyed. In these crises there breaks out an epidemic that, in all earlier epochs, would have seemed an absurdity—the epidemic of over-production. Society suddenly finds itself put back into a state of momentary barbarism; it appears as if a famine, a universal war of devastation had cut off the supply of every means of subsistence; industry and commerce seem to be destroyed. And why? Because there is too much civilisation, too much means of subsistence, too much industry, too much commerce. The productive forces at the disposal of society no longer tend to further the development of the conditions of bourgeois property; on the contrary, they have become too powerful for these conditions, by which they are fettered, and so soon as they overcome these fetters, they bring disorder into the whole of bourgeois society, endanger the existence of bourgeois property. The conditions of bourgeois society are too narrow to comprise the wealth created by them. And how does the bourgeoisie get over these crises? On the one hand by enforced destruction of a mass of productive forces; on the other, by the conquest of new markets, and by the more thorough exploitation of the old ones. That is to say, by paving the way for more extensive and more destructive crises, and by diminishing the means whereby crises are prevented.

The weapons with which the bourgeoisie felled feudalism to the ground are now turned against the bourgeoisie itself.

But not only has the bourgeoisie forged the weapons that bring death to itself; it has also called into existence the men who are to wield those weapons—the modern working class—the proletarians.

In proportion as the bourgeoisie, i.e., capital, is developed, in the same proportion is the proletariat, the modern working class, developed—a class of labourers, who live only so long as they find work, and who find work only so long as their labour increases capital. These labourers, who must sell themselves piecemeal, are a commodity, like every other article of commerce, and are consequently exposed to all the vicissitudes of competition, to all the fluctuations of the market.

Owing to the extensive use of machinery and to division of labour, the work of the proletarians has lost all individual character, and, consequently, all charm for the workman. He becomes an appendage of the machine, and it is only the most simple, most monotonous, and most easily acquired knack, that is required of him. Hence, the cost of production of a workman is restricted, almost entirely, to the means of subsistence that he requires for his maintenance, and for the propagation of his race. But the price of a commodity, and therefore, also of labour, is equal to its cost of production. In proportion, therefore, as the repulsiveness of the work increases, the wage decreases. Nay, more, in proportion as the use of machinery and division of labour increases, in the same proportion the burden of toil also increases, whether by prolongation of the working hours, by increase of the work exacted in a given time, or by increased speed of the machinery, etc.

Modern industry has converted the little workshop of the patriarchal master into the great factory of the industrial capitalist. Masses of labourers, crowded into the factory are organised like soldiers. As privates of the industrial army they are placed under the command of a perfect hierarchy of officers and sergeants. Not only are they slaves of the bourgeois class, and of the bourgeois state; they are daily and hourly enslaved by the machine, by the over looker, and, above all, by the individual bourgeois manufacturer himself. The more openly this despotism proclaims gain to be its end and aim, the more petty, the more hateful and the more embittering it is.

The less the skill and exertion of strength implied in manual labour, in other words, the more modern industry becomes developed, the more is the labour of men superseded by that of women. Differences of age and sex have no longer any distinctive social validity for the working class. All are instruments of labour, more or less expensive to use, according to their age and sex.

No sooner is the exploitation of the labourer by the manufacturer so far at an end that he receives his wages in cash than he is set upon by the other portions of the bourgeoisie, the landlord, the shopkeeper, the pawnbroker, etc.

The lower strata of the middle class—the small tradespeople, shopkeepers, and retired tradesmen generally, the handicraftsmen and peasants—all these sink gradually into the proletariat, partly because their diminutive capital does not suffice for the scale on which modern industry is carried on, and is swamped in the competition with the large capitalists, partly because their specialised skill is rendered worthless by new methods of production. Thus the proletariat is recruited from all classes of the population.

The proletariat goes through various stages of development. With its birth begins its struggle with the bourgeoisie. At first the contest is carried on by individual labourers, then by the work people of a factory, then by the operatives of one trade, in one locality, against the individual bourgeois who directly exploits them. They direct their attacks not against the bourgeois conditions of production, but against the instruments of production themselves; they destroy imported wares that compete with their labour, they smash to pieces machinery, they set factories ablaze, they seek to restore by force the vanished status of the workman of the Middle Ages.

At this stage the labourers still form an incoherent mass scattered over the whole country, and broken up by their mutual competition. If anywhere they unite to form more compact bodies, this is not yet the consequence of their own active union, but of the union of the bourgeoisie, which class, in order to attain its own political ends, is compelled to set the whole proletariat in motion, and is moreover yet, for a time, able to do so. At this stage, therefore, the proletarians do not fight their enemies, but the enemies of their enemies, the remnants of absolute monarchy, the landowners, the non-industrial bourgeois, the petty bourgeoisie. Thus the whole historical movement is concentrated in the hands of the bourgeoisie; every victory so obtained is a victory for the bourgeoisie.

But with the development of industry the proletariat not only increases in number; it becomes concentrated in greater masses, its strength grows, and it feels that strength more. The various interests and conditions of life within the ranks of the proletariat are more and more equalised, in proportion as machinery obliterates all distinctions of labour, and nearly everywhere reduces wages to the same low level. The growing competition among the bourgeois, and the resulting commercial crises, make the wages of the workers ever more fluctuating. The unceasing improvement of machinery, ever more rapidly developing, makes their livelihood more and more precarious; the collisions between individual workmen and individual bourgeois take more and more the character of collisions between two classes. Thereupon the workers begin to form combinations (trades' unions) against the bourgeois; they club together in order to keep up the rate of wages; they found permanent associations in order to make provision beforehand for these occasional revolts. Here and there the contest breaks out into riots.

Now and then the workers are victorious, but only for a time. The real fruit of their battles lies, not in the immediate result, but in the ever expanding union of the workers. This union is helped on by the improved means of communication that are created by modern industry, and that place the workers of different localities in contact with one another. It was just this contact that was needed to centralise the numerous local struggles, all of the same character, into one national struggle between classes. But every class struggle is a political struggle. And that union, to attain which the burghers of the Middle Ages, with their miserable highways, required centuries, the modern proletarians, thanks to railways, achieve in a few years.

This organisation of the proletarians into a class, and consequently into a political party, is continually being upset again by the competition between the workers themselves. But it ever rises up again, stronger, firmer, mightier. It compels legislative recognition of particular interests of the workers, by taking advantage of the divisions among the bourgeoisie itself. Thus the ten-hours' bill in England was carried.

Altogether, collisions between the classes of the old society further in many ways the course of development of the proletariat. The bourgeoisie finds itself involved in a constant battle. At first with the aristocracy; later on, with those portions of the bourgeoisie itself, whose interests have become antagonistic to the progress of industry; at all times with the bourgeoisie of foreign countries. In all these battles it sees itself compelled to appeal to the proletariat, to ask for its help, and thus to drag it into the political arena. The bourgeoisie itself, therefore, supplies the proletariat with its own elements of political and general education, in other words, it furnishes the proletariat with weapons for fighting the bourgeoisie.

Further, as we have already seen, entire sections of the ruling classes are, by the advance of industry, precipitated into the proletariat, or are at least threatened in their conditions of existence. These also supply the proletariat with fresh elements of enlightenment and progress.

Finally, in times when the class struggle nears the decisive hour, the process of dissolution going on within the ruling class, in fact within the whole range of old society, assumes such a violent, glaring character that a small section of the ruling class cuts itself adrift and joins the revolutionary class, the class that holds the future in its hands. Just as, therefore, at an earlier period, a section of the nobility went over to the bourgeoisie, so now a portion of the bourgeoisie goes over to the proletariat, and, in particular, a portion of the bourgeois ideologists, who have raised themselves to the level of comprehending theoretically the historical movement as a whole.

Of all the classes that stand face to face with the bourgeoisie to-day, the proletariat alone is a really revolutionary class. The other classes decay and finally disappear in the face of modern industry; the proletariat is its special and essential product.

The lower middle class, the small manufacturer, the shopkeeper, the artisan, the peasant, all these fight against the bourgeoisie, to save from extinction their existence as fractions of the middle class. They are therefore not revolutionary, but conservative.

Nay, more, they are reactionary, for they try to roll back the wheel of history. If by chance they are revolutionary, they are so only in view of their impending transfer into the proletariat; they thus defend not their present, but their future interests; they desert their own standpoint to place themselves at that of the proletariat.

The "dangerous class," the social scum, that passively rotting mass thrown off by the lowest layers of old society, may, here and there, be swept into the movement by a proletarian revolution; its conditions of life, however, prepare it far more for the part of a bribed tool of reactionary intrigue.

In the conditions of the proletariat, those of old society at large are already virtually swamped. The proletarian is without property; his relation to his wife and children has no longer anything in common with the bourgeois family relations; modern industrial labour, modern subjection to capital, the same in England as in France, in America as in Germany, has stripped him of every trace of national character. Law, morality, religion, are to him so many bourgeois prejudices, behind which lurk in ambush just as many bourgeois interests.

All the preceding classes that got the upper hand, sought to fortify their already acquired status by subjecting society at large to their conditions of appropriation. The proletarians cannot become masters of the productive forces of society, except by abolishing their own previous mode of appropriation, and thereby also every other previous mode of appropriation. They have nothing of their own to secure and to fortify; their mission is to destroy all previous securities for, and insurances of, individual property.

All previous historical movements were movements of minorities, or in the interest of minorities. The proletarian movement is the self-conscious, independent movement of the immense majority, in the interest of the immense majority. The proletariat, the lowest stratum of our present society, cannot stir, cannot raise itself up, without the whole superincumbent strata of official society being sprung into the air.

Though not in substance, yet in form, the struggle of the proletariat with the bourgeoisie is at first a national struggle. The proletariat of each country must, of course, first of all settle matters with its own bourgeoisie.

In depicting the most general phases of the development of the proletariat, we traced the more or less veiled civil war, raging within existing society, up to the point where that war breaks out into open revolution, and where the violent overthrow of the bourgeoisie lays the foundation for the sway of the proletariat.

Hitherto, every form of society has been based, as we have already seen, on the antagonism of oppressing and oppressed classes. But in order to oppress a class, certain conditions must be assured to it under which it can, at least, continue its slavish existence. The serf, in the period of serfdom, raised himself to membership in the commune, just as the petty bourgeois, under the yoke of feudal absolutism, managed to develop into a bourgeois. The modern labourer, on the contrary, instead of rising with the progress of industry, sinks deeper and deeper below the conditions of existence of his own class. He becomes a pauper, and pauperism develops more rapidly than population and wealth. And here it becomes evident that the bourgeoisie is unfit any longer to be the ruling class in society and to impose its conditions of existence upon society as an over-riding law. It is unfit to rule because it is incompetent to assure an existence to its slave within his slavery, because it cannot help letting him sink into such a state, that it has to feed him, instead of being fed by him. Society can no longer live under this bourgeoisie; in other words, its existence is no longer compatible with society.

The essential condition for the existence and for the sway of the bourgeois class is the formation and augmentation of capital; the condition for capital is wage-labour. Wage-labour rests exclusively on competition between the labourers. The advance of industry, whose involuntary promoter is the bourgeoisie, replaces the isolation of the labourers, due to competition, by their revolutionary combination, due to association. The development of modern industry, therefore, cuts from under its feet the very foundation on which the bourgeoisie produces and appropriates products. What the bourgeoisie therefore produces, above all, are its own grave-diggers. Its fall and the victory of the proletariat are equally inevitable.

II: Proletarians and Communists

In what relation do the Communists stand to the proletarians as a whole?

The Communists do not form a separate party opposed to other working class parties.

They have no interests separate and apart from those of the proletariat as a whole.

They do not set up any sectarian principles of their own, by which to shape and mould the proletarian movement.

The Communists are distinguished from the other working class parties by this only: 1. In the national struggles of the proletarians of the different countries, they point out and bring to the front the common interests of the entire proletariat, independently of all nationality. 2. In the various stages of development which the struggle of the working class against the bourgeoisie has to pass through, they always and everywhere represent the interests of the movement as a whole.

The Communists, therefore, are on the one hand, practically, the most advanced and resolute section of the working class parties of every country, that section which pushes forward all others; on the other hand, theoretically, they have over the great mass of the proletariat the advantage of clearly understanding the line of march, the conditions, and the ultimate general results of the proletarian movement.

The immediate aim of the Communists is the same as that of all the other proletarian parties: formation of the proletariat into a class, overthrow of the bourgeois supremacy, conquest of political power by the proletariat.

The theoretical conclusions of the Communists are in no way based on ideas or principles that have been invented, or discovered, by this or that would-be universal reformer.

They merely express, in general terms, actual relations springing from an existing class struggle, from a historical movement going on under our very eyes. The abolition of existing property relations is not at all a distinctive feature of Communism.

All property relations in the past have continually been subject to historical change consequent upon the change in historical conditions.

The French revolution, for example, abolished feudal property in favour of bourgeois property.

The distinguishing feature of Communism is not the abolition of property generally but the abolition of bourgeois property. But modern bourgeois private property is the final and most complete expression of the system of producing and appropriating products that is based on class antagonisms, on the exploitation of the many by the few.

In this sense, the theory of the Communists may be summed up in the single sentence: Abolition of private property.

We Communists have been reproached with the desire of abolishing the right of personally acquiring property as the fruit of a man's own labour, which property is alleged to be the groundwork of all personal freedom, activity and independence.

Hard-won, self-acquired, self-earned property! Do you mean the property of the petty artisan and of the small peasant, a form of property that preceded the bourgeois form? There is no need to abolish that; the development of industry has to a great extent already destroyed it, and is still destroying it daily.

Or do you mean modern bourgeois private property?

But does wage-labour create any property for the labourer? Not a bit. It creates capital, i.e., that kind of property which exploits wage-labour and which cannot increase except upon condition of begetting a new supply of wage-labour for fresh exploitation. Property, in its present form, is based on the antagonism of capital and wage-labour. Let us examine both sides of this antagonism.

To be a capitalist is to have not only a purely personal, but a social, *status* in production. Capital is a collective product, and only by the united action of many members, nay, in the last resort, only by the united action of all members of society, can it be set in motion.

Capital is therefore not a personal, it is a social power.

When, therefore, capital is converted into common property, into the property of all members of society, personal property is not thereby transformed into social property. It is only the social character of the property that is changed. It loses its class character.

Let us now take wage-labour.

The average price of wage-labour is the minimum wage, i.e., that quantum of the means of subsistence which is absolutely requisite to keep the labourer in bare existence as a labourer. What, therefore, the wage-labourer appropriates by means of his labour merely suffices to prolong and reproduce a bare existence. We by no means intend to abolish this personal appropriation of the products of labour, an appropriation that is made for the maintenance and reproduction of human life, and that leaves no surplus wherewith to command the labour of others. All that we want to do away with is the miserable character of this appropriation, under which the labourer lives merely to increase capital, and is allowed to live only in so far as the interest of the ruling class requires it.

In bourgeois society, living labour is but a means to increase accumulated labour. In Communist society, accumulated labour is but a means to widen, to enrich, to promote the existence of the labourer.

In bourgeois society, therefore, the past dominates the present; in Communist society, the present dominates the past. In bourgeois society capital is independent and has individuality, while the living person is dependent and has no individuality.

And the abolition of this state of things is called by the bourgeois abolition of individuality and freedom! And rightly so. The abolition of bourgeois individuality, bourgeois independence, and bourgeois freedom is undoubtedly aimed at.

By freedom is meant, under the present bourgeois conditions of production, free trade, free selling and buying.

But if selling and buying disappears, free selling and buying disappears also. This talk about free selling and buying, and all the other "brave words" of our bourgeoisie about freedom in general, have a meaning, if any, only in contrast with restricted selling and buying, with the fettered traders of the Middle Ages, but have no meaning when opposed to the Communist abolition of buying and selling, of the bourgeois conditions of production, and of the bourgeoisie itself.

You are horrified at our intending to do away with private property. But in your existing society, private property is already done away with for nine-tenths of the population; its existence for the few is solely due to its non-existence in the hands of those nine-tenths. You reproach us, therefore, with intending to do away with a form of property, the necessary condition for whose existence is the non-existence of any property for the immense majority of society.

In one word, you reproach us with intending to do away with your property. Precisely so; that is just what we intend.

From the moment when labour can no longer be converted into capital, money, or rent, into a social power capable of being monopolised, i.e., from the moment when individual property can no longer be transformed into bourgeois property, into capital, from that moment, you say, individuality vanishes.

You must, therefore, confess that by "individual" you mean no other person than the bourgeois, than the middle class owner of property. This person must, indeed, be swept out of the way, and made impossible.

Communism deprives no man of the power to appropriate the products of society; all that it does is to deprive him of the power to subjugate the labour of others by means of such appropriation.

It has been objected that upon the abolition of private property all work will cease, and universal laziness will overtake us.

According to this, bourgeois society ought long ago to have gone to the dogs through sheer idleness; for those of its members who work acquire nothing, and those who acquire anything do not work. The whole of this objection is but another expression of the tautology: There can no longer be any wage-labour when there is no longer any capital.

All objections urged against the Communistic mode of producing and appropriating material products have, in the same way, been urged against the Communistic modes of producing and appropriating intellectual products. Just as to the bourgeois the disappearance of class property is the disappearance of production itself so the disappearance of class culture is to him identical with the disappearance of all culture.

That culture, the loss of which he laments, is, for the enormous majority, a mere training to act as a machine.

But don't wrangle with us so long as you apply, to our intended abolition of bourgeois property, the standard of your bourgeois notions of freedom, culture, law, etc. Your very ideas are but the outgrowth of the conditions of your bourgeois production and bourgeois property, just as your jurisprudence is but the will of your class made into a law for all, a will whose essential character and direction are determined by the economical conditions of existence of your class.

The selfish misconception that induces you to transform into eternal laws of nature and of reason, the social forms springing from your present mode of production and form of property—historical relations that rise and disappear in the progress of production—this misconception you share with every ruling class that has preceded you. What you see clearly in the case of ancient property, what you admit in the case of feudal property, you are of course forbidden to admit in the case of your own bourgeois form of property.

Abolition of the family! Even the most radical flare up at this infamous proposal of the Communists.

On what foundation is the present family, the bourgeois family, based? On capital, on private gain. In its completely developed form this family exists only among the bourgeoisie. But this state of things finds its complement in the practical absence of the family among the proletarians, and in public prostitution.

The bourgeois family will vanish as a matter of course when its complement vanishes, and both will vanish with the vanishing of capital.

Do you charge us with wanting to stop the exploitation of children by their parents? To this crime we plead guilty.

But, you will say, we destroy the most hallowed of relations, when we replace home education by social.

And your education! Is not that also social, and determined by the social conditions under which you educate, by the intervention, direct or indirect, of society, by means of schools, etc.? The Communists have not invented the intervention of society in education; they do but seek to alter the character of that intervention, and to rescue education from the influence of the ruling class.

The bourgeois claptrap about the family and education, about the hallowed correlation of parent and child, becomes all the more disgusting the more, by the action of modern industry, all family ties among the proletarians are torn asunder, and their children transformed into simple articles of commerce and instruments of labour.

But you Communists would introduce community of women, screams the whole bourgeoisie in chorus.

The bourgeois sees in his wife a mere instrument of production. He hears that the instruments of production are to be exploited in common, and, naturally, can come to no other conclusion than that the lot of being common to all will likewise fall to the women.

He has not even a suspicion that the real point aimed at is to do away with the status of women as mere instruments of production.

For the rest, nothing is more ridiculous than the virtuous indignation of our bourgeois at the community of women which, they pretend, is to be openly and officially established by the Communists. The Communists have no need to introduce community of women; it has existed almost from time immemorial.

Our bourgeois, not content with having the wives and daughters of their proletarians at their disposal, not to speak of common prostitutes, take the greatest pleasure in seducing each other's wives.

Bourgeois marriage is in reality a system of wives in common and thus, at the most, what the Communists might possibly be reproached with is that they desire to introduce, in substitution for a hypocritically concealed, an openly legalised community of women. For the rest, it is self-evident that the abolition of the present system of production must bring with it the abolition of the community of women springing from that system, i.e., of prostitution both public and private.

The Communists are further reproached with desiring to abolish countries and nationality.

The working men have no country. We cannot take from them what they have not got. Since the proletariat must first of all acquire political supremacy, must rise to be the leading class of the nation, must constitute itself *the* nation, it is, so far, itself national, though not in the bourgeois sense of the word.

National differences and antagonisms between peoples are daily more and more vanishing, owing to the development of the bourgeoisie, to freedom of commerce, to the world market, to uniformity in mode of production and in the conditions of life corresponding thereto.

The supremacy of the proletariat will cause them to vanish still faster. United action of the leading civilised countries at least is one of the first conditions for the emancipation of the proletariat.

In proportion as the exploitation of one individual by another is put an end to, the exploitation of one nation by another will also be put an end to. In proportion as the antagonism between classes within the nation vanishes, the hostility of one nation to another will come to an end.

The charges against Communism made from a religious, a philosophical and, generally, from an ideological standpoint are not deserving of serious examination.

Does it require deep intuition to comprehend that man's ideas, views, and conceptions, in one word, man's consciousness, changes with every change in the conditions of his material existence, in his social relations and in his social life?

What else does the history of ideas prove than that intellectual production changes its character in proportion as material production is changed? The ruling ideas of each age have ever been the ideas of its ruling class.

When people speak of ideas that revolutionise society, they do but express the fact that within the old society the elements of a new one have been created, and that the dissolution of the old ideas keeps even pace with the dissolution of the old conditions of existence.

When the ancient world was in its last throes, the ancient religions were overcome by Christianity. When Christian ideas succumbed in the eighteenth century to rationalist ideas, feudal society fought its death-battle with the then revolutionary bourgeoisie. The ideas of religious liberty and freedom of conscience merely gave expression to the sway of free competition within the domain of knowledge.

"Undoubtedly," it will be said, "religious, moral, philosophical and juridical ideas have been modified in the course of historical development. But religion, morality, philosophy, political science, and law constantly survived this change."

"There are, besides, eternal truths, such as Freedom, Justice, etc., that are common to all states of society. But Communism abolishes eternal truths, it abolishes all religion, and all morality, instead of constituting them on a new basis; it therefore acts in contradiction to all past historical experience."

What does this accusation reduce itself to? The history of all past society has consisted in the development of class antagonisms, antagonisms that assumed different forms at different epochs.

But whatever form they may have taken, one fact is common to all past ages, viz., the exploitation of one part of society by the other. No wonder, then, that the social consciousness of past ages, despite all the multiplicity and variety it displays, moves within certain common forms, or general ideas, which cannot completely vanish except with the total disappearance of class antagonisms.

The Communist revolution is the most radical rupture with traditional property relations; no wonder that its development involves the most radical rupture with traditional ideas.

But let us have done with the bourgeois objections to Communism.

We have seen above that the first step in the revolution by the working class is to raise the proletariat to the position of ruling class, to win the battle of democracy.

The proletariat will use its political supremacy to wrest, by degrees, all capital from the bourgeoisie, to centralise all instruments of production in the hands of the State, i.e., of the proletariat organised as the ruling class; and to increase the total of productive forces as rapidly as possible.

Of course, in the beginning, this cannot be effected except by means of despotic inroads on the rights of property, and on the conditions of bourgeois production; by means of measures, therefore, which appear economically insufficient and untenable, but which, in the course of the movement, outstrip themselves, necessitate further inroads upon the old social order, and are unavoidable as a means of entirely revolutionising the mode of production.

These measures will, of course, be different in different countries.

MARX   The Communist Manifesto   111

Nevertheless in the most advanced countries, the following will be pretty generally applicable:

1. Abolition of property in land and application of all rents of land to public purposes.
2. A heavy progressive or graduated income tax.
3. Abolition of all right of inheritance.
4. Confiscation of the property of all emigrants and rebels.
5. Centralisation of credit in the hands of the State, by means of a national bank with State capital and an exclusive monopoly.
6. Centralisation of the means of communication and transport in the hands of the State.
7. Extension of factories and instruments of production owned by the State; the bringing into cultivation of waste lands, and the improvement of the soil generally in accordance with a common plan.
8. Equal obligation of all to work. Establishment of industrial armies, especially for agriculture.
9. Combination of agriculture with manufacturing industries; gradual abolition of the distinction between town and country, by a more equable distribution of the population over the country.
10. Free education for all children in public schools. Abolition of children's factory labour in its present form. Combination of education with industrial production, etc.

When, in the course of development, class distinctions have disappeared, and all production has been concentrated in the hands of a vast association of the whole nation, the public power will lose its political character. Political power, properly so called, is merely the organised power of one class for oppressing another. If the proletariat during its contest with the bourgeoisie is compelled, by the force of circumstances, to organise itself as a class; if, by means of a revolution, it makes itself the ruling class, and, as such, sweeps away by force the old conditions of production, then it will, along with these conditions, have swept away the conditions for the existence of class antagonisms and or classes generally, and will thereby have abolished its own supremacy as a class.

In place of the old bourgeois society, with its classes and class antagonisms, we shall have an association in which the free development of each is the condition for the free development of all.

III: Socialist and Communist Literature

1. Reactionary Socialism

a. Feudal Socialism

Owing to their historical position, it became the vocation of the aristocracies of France and England to write pamphlets against modern bourgeois society. In the French revolution of July 1830, and in the English reform agitation, these aristocracies again succumbed to the hateful upstart. Thenceforth, a serious political struggle was altogether out of the question. A literary battle alone remained possible. But even in the domain of literature the old cries of the restoration period* had become impossible.

In order to arouse sympathy, the aristocracy was obliged to lose sight, apparently, of its own interests, and to formulate its indictment against the bourgeoisie in the interest of the exploited working class alone. Thus the aristocracy took their revenge by singing lampoons on their new master, and whispering in his ears sinister prophecies of coming catastrophe.

In this way arose feudal socialism: half lamentation, half lampoon; half echo of the past, half menace of the future; at times, by its bitter, witty and incisive criticism, striking the bourgeoisie to the very heart's core, but always ludicrous in its effect, through total incapacity to comprehend the march of modern history.

The aristocracy, in order to rally the people to them, waved the proletarian alms-bag in front for a banner. But the people so often as it joined them saw on their hindquarters the old feudal coats of arms, and deserted with loud and irreverent laughter.

One section of the French Legitimists and "Young England," exhibited this spectacle.

In pointing out that their mode of exploitation was different to that of the bourgeoisie, the feudalists forget that they exploited under circumstances and conditions that were quite different, and that are now antiquated. In showing that, under their rule, the modern proletariat never existed, they forget that the modern bourgeoisie is the necessary offspring of their own form of society.

---

*Not the English Restoration, 1660 to 1689, but the French Restoration, 1814 to 1830.

For the rest, so little do they conceal the reactionary character of their criticism that their chief accusation against the bourgeoisie amounts to this, that under the bourgeois regime a class is being developed which is destined to cut up root and branch the old order of society.

What they upbraid the bourgeoisie with is not so much that it creates a proletariat as that it creates a *revolutionary* proletariat.

In political practice, therefore, they join in all coercive measures against the working class; and in ordinary life, despite their high-faluting phrases, they stoop to pick up the golden apples dropped from the tree of industry, and to barter truth, love, and honour for traffic in wool, beetroot-sugar, and potato spirits.*

As the parson has ever gone hand in hand with the land lord, so has Clerical Socialism with Feudal Socialism.

Nothing is easier than to give Christian asceticism a Socialist tinge. Has not Christianity declaimed against private property, against marriage, against the State? Has it not preached in the place of these, charity and poverty, celibacy and mortification of the flesh, monastic life and Mother Church? Christian Socialism is but the holy water with which the priest consecrates the heart-burnings of the aristocrat.

b. Petty Bourgeois Socialism

The feudal aristocracy was not the only class that was ruined by the bourgeoisie, not the only class whose conditions of existence pined and perished in the atmosphere of modern bourgeois society. The mediæval burgesses and the small peasant proprietors were the precursors of the modern bourgeoisie. In those countries which are but little developed, industrially and commercially, these two classes still vegetate side by side with the rising bourgeoisie.

In countries where modern civilisation has become fully developed, a new class of petty bourgeois has been formed fluctuating between proletariat and bourgeoisie, and ever renewing itself as a supplementary part of bourgeois society. The individual members of this class, however, are being constantly hurled down into the proletariat by the action of competition, and, as modern industry develops, they even see the moment approaching when they will completely disappear as an independent section of modern society, to be replaced, in manufactures, agriculture and commerce, by overlookers, bailiffs and shopmen.

In countries like France, where the peasants constitute far more than half of the population, it was natural that writers who sided with the proletariat against the bourgeoisie should use, in their criticism of the bourgeois régime the standard of the peasant and petty bourgeois, and from the standpoint of these intermediate classes should take up the cudgels for the working class. Thus arose petty bourgeois Socialism. Sismondi was the head of this school, not only in France but also in England.

This school of Socialism dissected with great acuteness the contradictions in the conditions of modern production. It laid bare the hypocritical apologies of economists. It proved, incontrovertibly, the disastrous effects of machinery and division of labour; the concentration of capital and land in a few hands; overproduction and crises; it pointed out the inevitable ruin of the petty bourgeois and peasant, the misery of the proletariat, the anarchy in production, the crying inequalities in the distribution of wealth, the industrial war of extermination between nations, the dissolution of old moral bonds, of the old family relations, of the old nationalities.

In its positive aims, however, this form of Socialism aspires either to restoring the old means of production and of exchange, and with them the old property relations, and the old society, or to cramping the modern means of production and of exchange within the framework of the old property relations that have been, and were bound to be exploded by those means. In either case, it is both reactionary and Utopian.

Its last words are: Corporate guilds for manufacture; patriarchal relations in agriculture.

---

*This applies chiefly to Germany where the landed aristocracy and squirearchy have large portions of their estates cultivated for their own account by stewards, and are, moreover, extensive beetroot-sugar manufacturers and distillers of potato spirits. The wealthier British aristocracy are, as yet, rather above that; but they, too, know how to make up for declining rents by lending their names to floaters of more or less shady joint-stock companies.

Ultimately, when stubborn historical facts had dispersed all intoxicating effects of self-deception, this form of Socialism ended in a miserable fit of the blues.

c. German or "True" Socialism

The Socialist and Communist literature of France, a literature that originated under the pressure of a bourgeoisie in power, and that was the expression of the struggle against this power, was introduced into Germany at a time when the bourgeoisie in that country had just begun its contest with feudal absolutism.

German philosophers, would-be philosophers, and men of letters eagerly seized on this literature, only forgetting that when these writings immigrated from France into Germany, French social conditions had not immigrated along with them. In contact with German social conditions, this French literature lost all its immediate practical significance, and assumed a purely literary aspect. Thus, to the German philosophers of the eighteenth century, the demands of the "Practical Reason" in general—and the utterance of the will of the first French Revolution were nothing more than the demands of revolutionary French bourgeoisie—signified in their eyes the laws of pure will, of will as it was bound to be, of true human will generally.

The work of the German *literati* consisted solely in bringing the new French ideas into harmony with their ancient philosophical conscience, or, rather, in annexing the French ideas without deserting their own philosophic point of view.

This annexation took place in the same way in which a foreign language is appropriated, namely, by translation.

It is well known how the monks wrote silly lives of Catholic saints *over* the manuscripts on which the classical works of ancient heathendom had been written. The German *literati* reversed this process with the profane French literature. They wrote their philosophical nonsense beneath the French original. For instance, beneath the French criticism of the economic functions of money, they wrote "alienation of humanity," and beneath the French criticism of the bourgeois State they wrote, "dethronement of the category of the general," and so forth.

The introduction of these philosophical phrases at the back of the French historical criticisms they

dubbed "Philosophy of Action," "True Socialism," "German Science of Socialism," "Philosophical Foundation of Socialism," and so on.

The French Socialist and Communist literature was thus completely emasculated. And, since it ceased in the hands of the German to express the struggle of one class with the other, he felt conscious of having overcome "French onesidedness" and of representing, not true requirements, but the requirements of truth; not the interests of the proletariat, but the interests of human nature, of man in general, who belongs to no class, has no reality, who exists only in the misty realm of philosophical phantasy.

This German Socialism, which took its schoolboy task so seriously and solemnly, and extolled its poor stock-in-trade in such mountebank fashion, meanwhile gradually lost its pedantic innocence.

The fight of the German and especially of the Prussian bourgeoisie against feudal aristocracy and absolute monarchy, in other words, the liberal movement, became more earnest.

By this, the long-wished-for opportunity was offered to "True" Socialism of confronting the political movement with the Socialist demands, of hurling the traditional anathemas against liberalism, against representative government, against bourgeois competition, bourgeois freedom of the press, bourgeois legislation, bourgeois liberty and equality, and of preaching to the masses that they had nothing to gain, and everything to lose, by this bourgeois movement. German Socialism forgot, in the nick of time, that the French criticism, whose silly echo it was, presupposed the existence of modern bourgeois society, with its corresponding economic conditions of existence, and the political constitution adapted thereto, the very things whose attainment was the object of the pending struggle in Germany.

To the absolute governments, with their following of parsons, professors, country squires and officials, it served as a welcome scarecrow against the threatening bourgeoisie.

It was a sweet finish after the bitter pills of floggings and bullets with which these same governments, just at that time, dosed the German working class risings.

While this "True" Socialism thus served the governments as a weapon for fighting the German bourgeoisie, it, at the same time, directly represented a reactionary interest, the interest of the German Philistines. In Germany the petty bourgeois class, a relic of the sixteenth century, and since then constantly cropping up again under various forms, is the real social basis of the existing state of things.

To preserve this class is to preserve the existing state of things in Germany. The industrial and political supremacy of the bourgeoisie threatens it with certain destruction—on the one hand, from the concentration of capital; on the other, from the rise of a revolutionary proletariat. "True" Socialism appeared to kill these two birds with one stone. It spread like an epidemic.

The robe of speculative cobwebs, embroidered with flowers of rhetoric, steeped in the dew of sickly sentiment, this transcendental robe in which the German Socialists wrapped their sorry "eternal truths," all skin and bone, served to wonderfully increase the sale of their goods amongst such a public.

And on its part, German Socialism recognised, more and more, its own calling as the bombastic representative of the petty bourgeois Philistine.

It proclaimed the German nation to be the model nation, and the German petty Philistine to be the typical man. To every villainous meanness of this model man it gave a hidden, higher, socialistic interpretation, the exact contrary of its real character. It went to the extreme length of directly opposing the "brutally destructive" tendency of Communism, and of proclaiming its supreme and impartial contempt of all class struggles. With very few exceptions, all the so-called Socialist and Communist publications that now (1847) circulate in Germany belong to the domain of this foul and enervating literature.

2. Conservative or Bourgeois Socialism

A part of the bourgeoisie is desirous of redressing social grievances, in order to secure the continued existence of bourgeois society.

To this section belong economists, philanthropists, humanitarians, improvers of the condition of the working class, organisers of charity, members of societies for the prevention of cruelty to animals, temperance fanatics, hole-and-corner reformers of every imaginable kind. This form of Socialism has, moreover, been worked out into complete systems.

We may cite Proudhon's *Philosophie de la Misère* (Philosophy of Poverty) as an example of this form.

The socialistic bourgeois want all the advantages of modern social conditions without the struggles and dangers necessarily resulting therefrom. They desire the existing state of society minus its revolutionary and disintegrating elements. They wish for a bourgeoisie without a proletariat. The bourgeoisie naturally conceives the world in which it is supreme to be the best; and bourgeois Socialism develops this comfortable conception into various more or less complete systems. In requiring the proletariat to carry out such a system, and thereby to march straightway into the social New Jerusalem, it but requires in reality that the proletariat should remain within the bounds of existing society, but should cast away all its hateful ideas concerning the bourgeoisie.

A second and more practical, but less systematic, form of this Socialism sought to depreciate every revolutionary movement in the eyes of the working class, by showing that no mere political reform, but only a change in the material conditions of existence, in economical relations, could be of any advantage to them. By changes in the material conditions of existence, this form of Socialism, however, by no means understands abolition of the bourgeois relations of production, an abolition that can be effected only by a revolution, but administrative reforms, based on the continued existence of these relations; reforms, therefore, that in no respect affect the relations between capital and labour, but, at the best, lessen the cost, and simplify the administrative work of bourgeois government.

Bourgeois Socialism attains adequate expression, when, and only when, it becomes a mere figure of speech.

Free trade: for the benefit of the working class. Protective duties: for the benefit of the working class. Prison reform: for the benefit of the working class. This is the last word and the only seriously meant word of bourgeois Socialism.

It is summed up in the phrase: the bourgeois is a bourgeois—for the benefit of the working class.

3. Critical-Utopian Socialism and Communism

We do not here refer to that literature which, in every great modern revolution, has always given voice to the demands of the proletariat, such as the writings of Babeuf and others.

The first direct attempts of the proletariat to attain its own ends, made in times of universal excitement, when feudal society was being overthrown—these attempts necessarily failed, owing to the then undeveloped state of the proletariat, as well as to the absence of the economic conditions for its emancipation, conditions that had yet to be produced, and could be produced by the impending bourgeois epoch alone. The revolutionary literature that accompanied these first movements of the proletariat had necessarily a reactionary character. It inculcated universal asceticism and social levelling in its crudest form.

The Socialist and Communist systems properly so called, those of St. Simon, Fourier, Owen and others, spring into existence in the early undeveloped period, described above, of the struggle between proletariat and bourgeoisie (see Section I. Bourgeois and Proletarians).

The founders of these systems see, indeed, the class antagonisms, as well as the action of the decomposing elements in the prevailing form of society. But the proletariat, as yet in its infancy, offers to them the spectacle of a class without any historical initiative or any independent political movement.

Since the development of class antagonism keeps even pace with the development of industry, the economic situation, as they find it, does not as yet offer to them the material conditions for the emancipation of the proletariat. They therefore search after a new social science, after new social laws, that are to create these conditions.

Historical action is to yield to their personal inventive action; historically created conditions of emancipation to phantastic ones; and the gradual, spontaneous class organisation of the proletariat to an organisation of society specially contrived by these inventors. Future history resolves itself, in their eyes, into the propaganda and the practical carrying out of their social plans.

In the formation of their plans they are conscious of caring chiefly for the interests of the working class, as being the most suffering class. Only from the point of view of being the most suffering class does the proletariat exist for them.

The undeveloped state of the class struggle, as well as their own surroundings, causes Socialists of this kind to consider themselves far superior to all class antagonisms. They want to improve the condition of every member of society, even that of the most favoured. Hence, they habitually appeal to society at large, without distinction of class; nay, by preference, to the ruling class. For how can people, when once they understand their system, fail to see in it the best possible plan of the best possible state of society?

Hence, they reject all political, and especially all revolutionary action; they wish to attain their ends by peaceful means, and endeavour, by small experiments, necessarily doomed to failure, and by the force of example, to pave the way for the new social gospel.

Such phantastic pictures of future society, painted at a time when the proletariat is still in a very undeveloped state and has but a phantastic conception of its own position, correspond with the first instinctive yearnings of that class for a general reconstruction of society.

But these Socialist and Communist publications contain also a critical element. They attack every principle of existing society. Hence they are full of the most valuable materials for the enlightenment of the working class. The practical measures proposed in them—such as the abolition of the distinction between town and country, of the family, of the carrying on of industries for the account of private individuals, and of the wage-system, the proclamation of social harmony, the conversion of the functions of the State into a mere superintendence of production—all these proposals point solely to the disappearance of class antagonisms which were, at that time, only just cropping up, and which, in these publications, are recognised in their earliest, indistinct and undefined forms only. These proposals, therefore, are of a purely Utopian character.

The significance of Critical-Utopian Socialism and Communism bears an inverse relation to historical development. In proportion as the modern class struggle develops and takes definite shape, this phantastic standing apart from the contest, these phantastic attacks on it, lose all practical value and all theoretical justification. Therefore, although the originators of these systems were, in many respects, revolutionary, their disciples have, in every case, formed mere reactionary sects. They hold fast by the original views of their masters, in opposition to the progressive historical development of the proletariat. They, therefore, endeavour, and that consistently, to deaden the class struggle and to reconcile the class antagonisms. They still dream of experimental realization of their social Utopias, of founding isolated *phalansteres,* of establishing "Home Colonies," or setting up a "Little Icaria"*—pocket editions of the New Jerusalem—and to realise all these castles in the air, they are compelled to appeal to the feelings and purses of the bourgeois. By degrees they sink into the category of the reactionary conservative Socialists depicted above, differing from these only by more systematic pedantry, and by their fanatical and superstitious belief in the miraculous effects of their social science.

They, therefore, violently oppose all political action on the part of the working class; such action, according to them, can only result from blind unbelief in the new gospel.

The Owenites in England, and the Fourierists in France, respectively, oppose the Chartists and the *Reformistes.*

IV: Position of the Communists in Relation to the Various Existing Opposition Parties

Section II has made clear the relations of the Communists to the existing working class parties, such as the Chartists in England and the Agrarian Reformers in America.

The Communists fight for the attainment of the immediate aims, for the enforcement of the momentary interests of the working class; but in the movement of the present, they also represent and take care of the future of that movement. In France the Communists ally themselves with the Social-Democrats,† against the conservative and radical bourgeoisie, reserving, however, the right to take up a critical position in regard to phrases and illu-

sions traditionally handed down from the great Revolution.

In Switzerland they support the Radicals, without losing sight of the fact that this party consists of antagonistic elements, partly of Democratic Socialists, in the French sense, partly of radical bourgeois.

In Poland they support the party that insists on an agrarian revolution as the prime condition for national emancipation, that party which fomented the insurrection of Cracow in 1846.

In Germany they fight with the bourgeoisie whenever it acts in a revolutionary way, against the absolute monarchy, the feudal squirearchy, and the petty bourgeoisie.

But they never cease, for a single instant, to instil into the working class the clearest possible recognition of the hostile antagonism between bourgeoisie and proletariat, in order that the German workers may straightway use, as so many weapons against the bourgeoisie, the social and political conditions that the bourgeoisie must necessarily introduce along with its supremacy, and in order that, after the fall of the reactionary classes in Germany, the fight against the bourgeoisie itself may immediately begin.

The Communists turn their attention chiefly to Germany, because that country is on the eve of a bourgeois revolution that is bound to be carried out under more advanced conditions of European civilisation and with a much more developed proletariat than that of England was in the seventeenth, and of France in the eighteenth century, and because the bourgeois revolution in Germany will be but the prelude to an immediately following proletarian revolution.

In short, the Communists everywhere support every revolutionary movement against the existing social and political order of things.

In all these movements they bring to the front, as the leading question in each, the property question, no matter what its degree of development at the time.

Finally, they labour everywhere for the union and agreement of the democratic parties of all countries.

The Communists disdain to conceal their views and aims. They openly declare that their ends can be attained only by the forcible overthrow of all existing social conditions. Let the ruling classes tremble at a Communist revolution. The proletarians have nothing to lose but their chains. They have a world to win.

Working men of all countries, unite!

Phalansteres were socialist colonies on the plan of Charles Fourier; Icaria was the name given by Cabet to his Utopia and, later on, to his American Communist colony.

†The party then represented in Parliament by Ledru-Rollin, in literature by Louis Blanc [1811–1882], in the daily press by the *Reform.* The name of Social-Democracy signifies, with these its inventors, a section of the Democratic or Republican Party more or less tinged with Socialism.

Mary Barton: A Tale of Manchester Life
Elizabeth Gaskell

The wife of a minister, the middle-class Elizabeth Gaskell dedicated herself to making people aware of the terrible suffering of working-class people in industrial Manchester, where she lived. Gaskell offers no easy solutions to the problem, although she would probably have preferred the ideas of the so-called utopian socialists to those of Marx. Regardless, her insights into the stark contrast between the lives of the working poor and the owning class served to strengthen the idea of class conflict.

The Barton family are textile workers in Manchester mills. Tom Barton, whose wife has died, is determined that their daughter Mary will never toil in the mills. Meanwhile, the mill owner's son plots to seduce the innocent Mary. These characters' interactions disclose the startling differences in their lives.

'How little can the rich man know
Of what the poor man feels,
When Want, like some dark demon foe,
    Nearer and nearer steals!
He never tramp'd the weary round,
A stroke of work to gain,
And sicken'd at the dreaded sound
Telling him 'twas in vain.
Foot-sore, heart-sore, he never came
Back through the winter's wind,
To a dark cellar, there no flame,
No light, no food, to find.
He never saw his darlings lie
Shivering, the grass their bed;
He never heard that maddening cry,
"Daddy, a bid of bread!"'

MANCHESTER SONG

John Barton was not far wrong in his idea that the Messrs Carson would not be over much grieved for the consequences of the fire in their mill. They were well insured; the machinery lacked the improvements of late years, and worked but poorly in comparison with that which might now be procured. Above all, trade was very slack; cottons could find no market, and goods lay packed and piled in many a warehouse. The mills were merely worked to keep the machinery, human and metal, in some kind of order and readiness for better times. So this was an excellent time, Messrs Carson thought, for refitting their factory with first-rate improvements, for which the insurance money would amply pay. They were in no hurry about the business, however. The weekly drain of wages given for labour, useless in the present state of the market, was stopped. The partners had more leisure than they had known for years; and promised wives and daughters all manner of pleasant excursions, as soon as the weather should become more genial. It was a pleasant thing to be able to lounge over breakfast with a review or newspaper in hand; to have time for becoming acquainted with agreeable and accomplished daughters, on whose education no money had been spared, but whose fathers, shut up during a long day with calicoes and accounts, had so seldom had leisure to enjoy their daughters' talents. There were happy

From: Elizabeth Gaskell, *Mary Barton: A Tale of Manchester Life* (London: Penguin, 1970), pp.95–113.

family evenings, now that the men of business had time for domestic enjoyments. There is another side to the picture. There were homes over which Carsons' fire threw a deep, terrible gloom; the homes of those who would fain work, and no man gave unto them—the homes of those to whom leisure was a curse. There, the family music was hungry wails, when week after week passed by, and there was no work to be had, and consequently no wages to pay for the bread the children cried aloud for in their young impatience of suffering. There was no breakfast to lounge over; their lounge was taken in bed, to try and keep warmth in them that bitter March weather, and, by being quiet, to deaden the gnawing wolf within. Many a penny that would have gone little way enough in oatmeal or potatoes, bought opium to still the hungry little ones, and make them forget their uneasiness in heavy troubled sleep. It was mothers mercy. The evil and the good of our nature came out strongly then. There were desperate fathers; there were bitter-tongued mothers (O God! what wonder!); there were reckless children; the very closest bonds of nature were snapt in that time of trial and distress. There was Faith such as the rich can never imagine on earth; there was 'Love strong as death'; and self-denial, among rude, coarse men, akin to that of Sir Philip Sidney's most glorious deed. The vices of the poor sometimes astound us *here;* but when the secrets of all hearts shall be made known, their virtues will astound us in far greater degree. Of this I am certain.

As the cold bleak spring came on (spring, in name alone), and consequently as trade continued dead, other mills shortened hours, turned off hands, and finally stopped work altogether.

Barton worked short hours; Wilson, of course, being a hand in Carsons' factory, had no work at all. But his son, working at an engineer's, and a steady man, obtained wages enough to maintain all the family in a careful way. Still it preyed on Wilson's mind to be so long indebted to his son. He was out of spirits and depressed. Barton was morose, and soured towards mankind as a body, and the rich in particular. One evening, when the clear light at six o'clock contrasted strangely with the Christmas cold, and when the bitter wind piped down every entry, and through every cranny, Barton sat brooding over his stinted fire, and listening for Mary's step, in unac-

knowledged trust that her presence would cheer him. The door was opened, and Wilson came breathless in.

'You've not got a bit o' money by you, Barton?' asked he.

'Not I; who has now, I'd like to know. Whatten you want it for?'

'I donnot want it for mysel, tho' we've none to spare. But don ye know Ben Davenport as worked at Carsons'? He's down wi' the fever, and ne'er a stick o' fire, nor a cowd potato in the house.'

'I han got no money, I tell ye,' said Barton. Wilson looked disappointed. Barton tried not to be interested, but he could not help it in spite of his gruffness. He rose, and went to the cupboard (his wife's pride long ago). There lay the remains of his dinner, hastily put there ready for supper. Bread, and a slice of cold fat boiled bacon. He wrapped them in his handkerchief, put them in the crown of his hat, and said—'Come, let's be going.'

'Going—art thou going to work this time o' day?'

'No, stupid, to be sure not. Going to see the fellow thou spoke on.' So they put on their hats and set out. On the way Wilson said Davenport was a good fellow, though too much of the Methodee; that his children were too young to work, but not too young to be cold and hungry; that they had sunk lower and lower, and pawned thing after thing, and that now they lived in a cellar in Berry Street, off Store Street. Barton growled inarticulate words of no benevolent import to a large class of mankind, and so they went along till they arrived in Berry Street. It was unpaved; and down the middle a gutter forced its way, every now and then forming pools in the holes with which the street abounded. Never was the Old Edinburgh cry of 'Gardez l'eau,' more necessary than in this street. As they passed, women from their doors tossed household slops of *every* description into the gutter; they ran into the next pool, which overflowed and stagnated. Heaps of ashes were the stepping-stones, on which the passer-by, who cared in the least for cleanliness, took care not to put his foot. Our friends were not dainty, but even they picked their way till they got to some steps leading down into a small area, where a person standing would have his head about one foot below the level of the street, and might at the same time, without the least motion of his body, touch the window of the cellar and the damp

muddy wall right opposite. You went down one step
even from the foul area into the cellar in which a
family of human beings lived. It was very dark
inside. The window-panes were many of them broken and stuffed with rags, which was reason enough
for the dusky light that pervaded the place even at
mid-day. After the account I have given of the state
of the street, no one can be surprised that on going
into the cellar inhabited by Davenport, the smell
was so foetid as almost to knock the two men
down Quickly recovering themselves, as those
inured to such things do, they began to penetrate
the thick darkness of the place, and to see three or
four little children rolling on the damp, nay wet,
brick floor, through which the stagnant, filthy moisture of the street oozed up; the fire-place was empty
and black; the wife sat on her husband's chair, and
cried in the dank loneliness.

'See, missis, I'm back again.—Hold your noise,
children, and don't mither your mammy for bread,
here's a chap as has got some for you.'

In that dim light, which was darkness to strangers,
they clustered round Barton, and tore from him the
food he had brought with him. It was a large hunch
of bread, but it had vanished in an instant.

'We mun do summut for 'em,' said he to Wilson.
'Yo stop here, and I'll be back in half-an-hour.'

So he strode, and ran, and hurried home. He
emptied into the ever-useful pocket-handkerchief
the little meal remaining in the mug. Mary would
have her tea at Miss Simmonds'; her food for the
day was safe. Then he went up-stairs for his better
coat, and his one, gay, red-and-yellow silk pocket-
handkerchief—his jewels, his plate, his valuables,
these were. He went to the pawn-shop; he pawned
them for five shillings; he stopped not, nor stayed, till
he was once more in London Road, within five minutes' walk of Berry Street—then he loitered in his
gait, in order to discover the shops he wanted. He
bought meat, and a loaf of bread, candles, chips, and
from a little retail yard he purchased a couple of hun-
dredweights of coals. Some money, yet remained—
all destined for them, but he did not yet know how
best to spend it. Food, light, and warmth, he had
instantly seen were necessary; for luxuries he would
wait. Wilson's eyes filled with tears when he saw Barton enter with his purchases. He understood it all,
and longed to be once more in work, that he might

help in some of these material ways, without feeling
that he was using his son's money. But though 'silver
and gold he had none,' he gave heart-service, and
love-works of far more value. Nor was John Barton
behind in these. 'The fever' was (as it usually is in
Manchester), of a low, putrid, typhoid kind; brought
on by miserable living, filthy neighbourhood, and
great depression of mind and body. It is virulent,
malignant, and highly infectious. But the poor are
fatalists with regard to infection; and well for them it
is so, for in their crowded dwellings no invalid can be
isolated. Wilson asked Barton if he thought he
should catch it, and was laughed at for his idea.

The two men, rough, tender nurses as they were,
lighted the fire, which smoked and puffed into the
room as if it did not know the way up the damp,
unused chimney. The very smoke seemed purifying
and healthy in the thick clammy air. The children
clamoured again for bread; but this time Barton
took a piece first to the poor, helpless, hopeless
woman, who still sat by the side of her husband, listening to his anxious miserable mutterings. She took
the bread, when it was put into her hand, and broke
a bit, but could not eat. She was past hunger. She fell
down on the floor with a heavy unresisting bang.
The men looked puzzled. 'She's well-nigh clemmed,'
said Barton. 'Folk do say one mustn't give clemmed
people much to eat; but, bless us, she'll eat naught.'

'I'll tell you what I'll do,' said Wilson. 'I'll take
these two big lads, as does nought but fight, home
to my missis's for to-night, and I will get a jug o' tea.
Them women always does best with tea and such
like slop.'

So Barton was now left alone with a little child,
crying (when it had done eating) for mammy; with a
fainting, dead-like woman; and with the sick man,
whose mutterings were rising up to screams and
shrieks of agonized anxiety. He carried the woman
to the fire, and chafed her hands. He looked around
for something to raise her head. There was literally
nothing but some loose bricks. However, those he
got; and taking off his coat he covered them with it
as well as he could. He pulled her feet to the fire,
which now began to emit some faint heat. He
looked round for water, but the poor woman had
been too weak to drag herself out to the distant
pump, and water there was none. He snatched the
child, and ran up the area-steps to the room above,

and borrowed their only saucepan with some water in it. Then he began, with the useful skill of a working-man, to make some gruel; and when it was hastily made he seized a battered iron table-spoon (kept when many other little things had been sold in a lot), in order to feed baby, and with it he forced one or two drops between her clenched teeth. The mouth opened mechanically to receive more, and gradually she revived. She sat up and looked round; and recollecting all, fell down again in weak and passive despair. Her little child crawled to her, and wiped with its fingers the thick-coming tears which she now had strength to weep. It was now high time to attend to the man. He lay on straw, so damp and mouldy no dog would have chosen it in preference to flags; over it was a piece of sacking, coming next to his worn skeleton of a body; above him was mustered every article of clothing that could be spared by mother or children this bitter weather; and in addition to his own, these might have given as much warmth as one blanket, could they have been kept on him; but as he restlessly tossed to and fro, they fell off and left him shivering in spite of the burning heat of his skin. Every now and then he started up in his naked madness, looking like the prophet of woe in the fearful plague-picture; But he soon fell again in exhaustion, and Barton found he must be closely watched, lest in these falls he should injure himself against the hard brick floor. He was thankful when Wilson reappeared, carrying in both hands a jug of steaming tea, intended for the poor wife; but when the delirious husband saw drink, he snatched at it with animal instinct, with a selfishness he had never shown in health.

Then the two men consulted together. It seemed decided without a word being spoken on the subject, that both should spend the night with the forlorn couple; that was settled. But could no doctor be had? In all probability no; the next day an infirmary order might be begged, but meanwhile the only medical advice they could have must be from a druggist's. So Barton (being the moneyed man) set out to find a shop in London Road.

It is a pretty sight to walk through a street with lighted shops; the gas is so brilliant, the display of goods so much more vividly shown than by day, and of all shops a druggist's looks the most like the tales of our childhood, from Aladdin's garden of enchanted fruits to the charming Rosamond with her purple jar. No such associations had Barton; yet he felt the contrast between the well-filled, well-lighted shops and the dim gloomy cellar, and it made him moody that such contrasts should exist. They are the mysterious problem of life to more than him. He wondered if any in all the hurrying crowd, had come from such a house of mourning. He thought they all looked joyous, and he was angry with them. But he could not, you cannot, read the lot of those who daily pass you by in the street. How do you know the wild romances of their lives; the trials, the temptations they are even now enduring, resisting, sinking under? You may be elbowed one instant by the girl desperate in her abandonment, laughing in mad merriment with her outward gesture, while her soul is longing for the rest of the dead, and bringing itself to think of the cold-flowing river as the only mercy of God remaining to her here. You may pass the criminal, meditating crimes at which you will to-morrow shudder with horror as you read them. You may push against one, humble and unnoticed, the last upon earth, who in Heaven will for ever be in the immediate light of God's countenance. Errands of mercy—errands of sin— did you ever think where all the thousands of people you daily meet are bound? Barton's was an errand of mercy; but the thoughts of his heart were touched by sin, by bitter hatred of the happy, whom he, for the time, confounded with the selfish.

He reached a druggist's shop, and entered. The druggist (whose smooth manners seemed to have been salved over with his own spermaceti) listened attentively to Barton's description of Davenport's illness; concluded it was typhus fever, very prevalent in that neighbourhood; and proceeded to make up a bottle of medicine, sweet spirits of nitre, or some such innocent potion, very good for slight colds, but utterly powerless to stop, for an instant, the raging fever of the poor man it was intended to relieve. He recommended the same course they had previously determined to adopt, applying the next morning for an infirmary order; and Barton left the shop with comfortable faith in the physic given him; for men of his class, if they believe in physic at all, believe that every description is equally efficacious.

Meanwhile, Wilson had done what he could at Davenport's home. He had soothed, and covered

the man many a time; he had fed and hushed the little child, and spoken tenderly to the woman, who
lay still in her weakness and her weariness. He had
opened a door but only for an instant; it led into a
back cellar, with a grating instead of a window,
down which dropped the moisture from pigstyes,
and worse abominations. It was not paved; the floor
was one mass of bad smelling mud. It had never
been used, for there was not an article of furniture
in it; nor could a human being, much less a pig,
have lived there many days. Yet the 'back apartment' made a difference in the rent. The Davenports
paid threepence more for having two rooms. When
he turned round again, he saw the woman suckling
the child from her dry, withered breast.

'Surely the lad is weaned!' exclaimed he, in surprise. 'Why, how old is he?'

'Going on two year,' she faintly answered. 'But,
Oh! it keeps him quiet when I've nought else to gi'
him, and he'll get a bit of sleep lying there, if he's
getten nought beside. We han done our best to gi'
the childer food, howe'er we pinched ourselves.'

'Han ye had no money fra th' town?'

'No, my master is Buckinghamshire born; and
he's feared the town would send him back to his
parish, if he went to th' board; so we've just borne
on in hope o' better times. But I think they'll never
come in my day'; and the poor woman began her
weak high-pitched cry again.

'Here, sup this drop o' gruel, and then try and
get a bit o' sleep. John and I'll watch by your master
to-night.'

'God's blessing be on you.'

She finished the gruel, and fell into a dead sleep.
Wilson covered her with his coat as well as he
could, and tried to move lightly for fear of disturbing her; but there need have been no such dread, for
her sleep was profound and heavy with exhaustion.
Once only she roused to pull the coat round her little child.

And now all Wilson's care, and Barton's to boot,
was wanted to restrain the wild mad agony of the
fevered man. He started up, he yelled, he seemed
infuriated by overwhelming anxiety. He cursed and
swore, which surprised Wilson, who knew his piety
in health, and who did not know the unbridled
tongue of delirium. At length he seemed exhausted,
and fell asleep; and Barton and Wilson drew near

the fire, and talked together in whispers. They sat on
the floor, for chairs there were none; the sole table
was an old tub turned upside-down. They put out
the candle and conversed by the flickering fire-light.

'Han yo known this chap long?' asked Barton.

'Better nor three year. He's worked wi' Carsons
that long, and were alway a steady, civil-spoken fellow, though, as I said afore, somewhat of a Methodee. I wish I'd gotten a letter he sent his missis, a
week or two agone, when he were on tramp for
work. It did my heart good to read it; for, yo see, I
were a bit grumbling mysel; it seemed hard to be
spunging on Jem, and taking a' his flesh-meat
money to buy bread for me and them as I ought to
be keeping. But, yo know, though I can earn
nought, I mun eat summut. Well, as I told ye, I
were grumbling, when she (indicating the sleeping
woman by a nod) brought me Ben's letter, for she
could na read hersel. It were as good as Bible-
words; ne'er a word o' repining; a' about God being
our father, and that we mun bear patiently whate'er
he sends.'

'Don ye think he's th' masters' father, too? I'd be
loath to have 'em for brothers.'

'Eh, John I donna talk so; sure there's many and
many a master as good or better nor us.'

'If you think so, tell me this. How comes it
they're rich, and we're poor? I'd like to know that.
Han they done as they'd be done by for us?'

But Wilson was no arguer. No speechifier as he
would have called it. So Barton, seeing he was likely
to have it his own way, went on.

'You'll say (at least many a one does), they'n getten capital an' we'n getten none. I say, our labour's
our capital and we ought to draw interest on that.
They get interest on their capital somehow a' this
time, while ourn is lying idle, else how could they all
live as they do? Besides, there's many on 'em as had
nought to begin wi'; there's Carsons, and Dun-
combes, and Mengles, and many another, as comed
into Manchester with clothes to their back, and that
were all, and now they're worth their tens of thousands, a' getten out of our labour; why the very land
as fetched but sixty pound twenty year agone is now
worth six hundred, and that, too, is owing to our
labour: but look at yo, and see me, and poor Davenport yonder; whatten better are we? They'n screwed
us down to th' lowest peg, in order to make their

great big fortunes, and build their great big houses, and we, why we're just clemming, many and many of us. Can you say there's nought wrong in this?'

'Well, Barton, I'll not gainsay ye. But Mr Carson spoke to me after th' fire, and says he, "I shall ha' to retrench, and be very careful in my expenditure during these bad times, I assure ye"; so yo see th' masters suffer too.'

'Han they ever seen a child o' their'n die for want o' food?' asked Barton, in a low, deep voice.

'I donnot mean,' continued he, 'to say as I'm so badly off. I'd scorn to speak for mysel; but when I see such men as Davenport there dying away, for very clemming, I cannot stand it. I've but gotten Mary, and she keeps hersel pretty much. I think we'll ha' to give up house-keeping; but that I donnot mind.'

And in this kind of talk the night, the long heavy night of watching, wore away. As far as they could judge, Davenport continued in the same state, although the symptoms varied occasionally. The wife slept on, only roused by a cry of her child now and then, which seemed to have power over her, when far louder noises failed to disturb her. The watchers agreed, that as soon as it was likely Mr Carson would be up and visible, Wilson should go to his house, and beg for an Infirmary order. At length the grey dawn penetrated even into the dark cellar; Davenport slept, and Barton was to remain there until Wilson's return; so stepping out into the fresh air, brisk and reviving, even in that street of abominations, Wilson took his way to Mr Carson's.

Wilson had about two miles to walk before he reached Mr Carson's house, which was almost in the country. The streets were not yet bustling and busy. The shop-men were lazily taking down the shutters, although it was near eight o'clock; for the day was long enough for the purchases people made in that quarter of the town, while trade was so flat. One or two miserable-looking women were setting off on their day's begging expedition. But there were few people abroad. Mr Carson's was a good house, and furnished with disregard to expense. But in addition to lavish expenditure, there was much taste shown, and many articles chosen for their beauty and elegance adorned his rooms. As Wilson passed a window which a housemaid had thrown open, he saw pictures and gilding, at which he was tempted to stop

and look; but then he thought it would not be respectful. So he hastened on to the kitchen door. The servants seemed very busy with preparations for breakfast; but good-naturedly, though hastily, told him to step in, and they could soon let Mr Carson know he was there. So he was ushered into a kitchen hung round with glittering tins, where a roaring fire burnt merrily, and where numbers of utensils hung round, at whose nature and use Wilson amused himself by guessing. Meanwhile, the servants bustled to and fro; an out-door man-servant came in for orders, and sat down near Wilson; the cook broiled steaks, and the kitchen-maid toasted bread, and boiled eggs.

The coffee steamed upon the fire, and altogether the odours were so mixed and appetizing, that Wilson began to yearn for food to break his fast, which had lasted since dinner the day before. If the servants had known this, they would have willingly given him meat and bread in abundance; but they were like the rest of us, and not feeling hunger themselves, forgot it was possible another might. So Wilson's craving turned to sickness, while they chattered on, making the kitchen's free and keen remarks upon the parlour.

'How late you were last night, Thomas!'

'Yes, I was right weary of waiting; they told me to be at the rooms by twelve; and there I was. But it was two o'clock before they called me.'

'And did you wait all that time in the street?' asked the housemaid who had done her work for the present, and come into the kitchen for a bit of gossip.

'My eye as like! you don't think I'm such a fool as to catch my' death of cold, and let the horses catch their death too, as we should ha' done if we'd stopped there. No! I put th' horses up in th' stables at th' Spread Eagle, and went mysel', and got a glass or two by th' fire. They're driving a good custom, them, wi' coachmen. There were five on us, and we'd many a quart o' ale, and gin wi' it, to keep out cold.'

'Mercy on us, Thomas; you'll get a drunkard at last!'

'If I do, I know whose blame it will be. It will be missis's, and not mine. Flesh and blood can't sit to be starved to death on a coach-box, waiting for folks as don't know their own mind.'

A servant, semi-upper-housemaid, semi-lady's-maid, now came down with orders from her mistress.

'Thomas, you must ride to the fishmonger's, and say missis can't give above half-a-crown a pound for salmon for Tuesday; she's grumbling because trade's so bad. And she'll want the carriage at three to go to the lecture, Thomas; at the Royal Execution, you know.'

'Ay, ay, I know.'

'And you'd better all of you mind your P's and Q's, for she's very black this morning. She's got a bad headache.'

'It's a pity Miss Jenkins is not here to match her. Lord! how she and missis did quarrel which had got the worst headaches, it was that Miss Jenkins left for; she would not give up having bad headaches, and missis could not abide any one to have 'em but herself.'

'Missis will have her breakfast up-stairs, cook, and the cold partridge as was left yesterday, and put plenty of cream in her coffee, and she thinks there's a roll left, and she would like it well buttered.'

So saying, the maid left the kitchen to be ready to attend to the young ladies' bell when they chose to ring, after their late assembly the night before.

In the luxurious library, at the well-spread breakfast-table, sat the two Mr Carsons, father and son. Both were reading; the father a newspaper, the son a review, while they lazily enjoyed their nicely prepared food. The father was a prepossessing-looking old man; perhaps self-indulgent you might guess. The son was strikingly handsome, and knew it. His dress was neat and well appointed, and his manners far more gentlemanly than his father's. He was the only son, and his sisters were proud of him; his father and mother were proud of him: he could not set up his judgement against theirs; he was proud of himself.

The door opened and in bounded Amy, the sweet youngest daughter of the house, a lovely girl of sixteen, fresh and glowing, and bright as a rosebud. She was too young to go to assemblies, at which her father rejoiced, for he had little Amy with her pretty jokes, and her bird-like songs, and her playful caresses all the evening to amuse him in his loneliness; and she was not too much tired, like Sophy and Helen, to give him her sweet company at breakfast the next morning.

He submitted willingly while she blinded him with her hands, and kissed his rough red face all over. She took his newspaper away after a little pre-

tended resistance and would not allow her brother Harry to go on with his review.

'I'm the only lady this morning, papa, so you know you must make a great deal of me.'

'My darling, I think you have your own way always, whether you're the only lady or not.'

'Yes, papa, you're pretty good and obedient, I must say that; but I'm sorry to say Harry is very naughty, and does not do what I tell him; do you, Harry?'

'I'm sure I don't know what you mean to accuse me of, Amy; I expected praise and not blame; for did not I get you that eau de Portugal from town, that you could not meet with at Hughes', you little ungrateful puss?'

'Did you! Oh sweet Harry; you're as sweet as eau de Portugal yourself; you're almost as good as papa; but still you know you did go and forget to ask Bigland for that rose, that new rose they say he has got.'

'No, Amy, I did not forget. I asked him, and he has got the Rose, *sans reproche;* but do you know, little Miss Extravagance, a very small one is half a guinea?'

'Oh, I don't mind. Papa will give it me, won't you, dear father? He knows his little daughter can't live without flowers and scents?'

Mr Carson tried to refuse his darling, but she coaxed him into acquiescence, saying she must have it, it was one of her necessaries. Life was not worth having without flowers.

'Then, Amy,' said her brother, 'try and be content with peonies and dandelions.'

'Oh you wretch! I don't call them flowers. Besides, you're every bit as extravagant. Who gave half-a-crown for a bunch of lilies of the valley at Yates', a month ago, and then would not let his poor little sister have them, though she went on her knees to beg them? Answer me that, Master Hal.'

'Not on compulsion,' replied her brother, smiling with his mouth, while his eyes had an irritated expression, and he went first red, then pale, with vexed embarrassment.

'If you please, sir,' said a servant, entering the room, 'here's one of the mill people wanting to see you; his name is Wilson, he says.'

'I'll come to him directly; stay, tell him to come in here.'

Amy danced off into the conservatory which opened out of the room, before the gaunt, pale, unwashed, unshaven weaver was ushered in. There he stood at the door, sleeking his hair with old country habit, and every now and then stealing a glance round at the splendour of the apartment.

'Well, Wilson, and what do you want today, man?'

'Please, sir, Davenport's ill of the fever, and I'm come to know if you've got an Infirmary order for him?'

'Davenport—Davenport; who is the fellow? I don't know the name.'

'He's worked in your factory better nor three year, sir.'

'Very likely, I don't pretend to know the names of the men I employ; that I leave to the overlooker. So he's ill, eh?'

'Ay, sir, he's very bad; we want to get him in at the fever wards.'

'I doubt if I have an in-patients order to spare; they're always wanted for accidents, you know. But I'll give you an out-patient's, and welcome.'

So saying, he rose up, unlocked a drawer, pondered a minute, and then gave Wilson an out-patient's order to be presented the following Monday. Monday! How many days there were before Monday!

Meanwhile, the younger Mr Carson had ended his review, and began to listen to what was going on. He finished his breakfast, got up, and pulled five shillings out of his pocket, which he gave to Wilson as he passed him, for the 'poor fellow'. He went past quickly, and calling for his horse, mounted gaily, and rode away. He was anxious to be in time to have a look and a smile from lovely Mary Barton, as she went to Miss Simmonds'. But today he was to be disappointed. Wilson left the house, not knowing whether to be pleased or grieved. It was long to Monday, but they had all spoken kindly to him, and who could tell if they might not remember this, and do something before Monday. Besides, the cook, who, when she had had time to think, after breakfast was sent in, had noticed his paleness, had had meat and bread ready to put in his hand when he came out of the parlour; and a full stomach makes every one of us more hopeful.

When he reached Berry Street, he had persuaded himself he bore good news, and felt almost elated in his heart. But it fell when he opened the cellar-door, and saw Barton and the wife both bending over the sick man's couch with awe-struck, saddened look.

'Come here,' said Barton. 'There's a change comed over him sin' yo left, is there not?'

Wilson looked. The flesh was sunk, the features prominent, bony, and rigid. The fearful clay-colour of death was over all. But the eyes were open and sensible, though the films of the grave were settling upon them.

'He wakened fra his sleep, as yo left him in, and began to mutter and moan; but he soon went off again, and we never knew he were awake till he called his wife, but now she's here he's gotten nought to say to her.'

Most probably, as they all felt, he could not speak, for his strength was fast ebbing. They stood round him still and silent; even the wife checked her sobs, though her heart was like to break. She held her child to her breast, to try and keep him quiet. Their eyes were all fixed on the yet living one, whose moments of life were passing so rapidly away. At length he brought, (with jerking, convulsive effort) his two hands into the attitude of prayer. They saw his lips move, and bent to catch the words, which came in gasps, and not in tones.

'Oh Lord God! I thank thee, that the hard struggle of living is over.'

'Oh, Ben! Ben!' wailed forth his wife, 'have you no thought for me? Oh, Ben! Ben! do say one word to help me through life.'

He could not speak again. The trump of the archangel would set his tongue free; but not a word more would it utter till then. Yet he heard, he understood, and though sight failed, he moved his hand gropingly over the covering. They knew what he meant, and guided it to her head, bowed and hidden in her hands, when she had sunk in her woe. It rested there, with a feeble pressure of endearment. The face grew beautiful, as the soul neared God. A peace beyond understanding came over it. The hand was a heavy, stiff weight on the wife's head. No more grief or sorrow for him. They reverently laid out the corpse—Wilson fetching his only spare shirt to array it in. The wife still lay hidden in the clothes, in a stupor of agony.

There was a knock at the door, and Barton went to open it. It was Mary, who had received a message from her father, through a neighbour, telling her where he was; and she had set out early to come and have a word with him before her day's work; but some errands she had to do for Miss Simmonds had detained her until now.

'Come in, wench!' said her father. 'Try if thou canst comfort yon poor, poor woman, kneeling down there. God help her.' Mary did not know what to say, or how to comfort; but she knelt down by her, and put her arm round her neck, and in a little while fell to crying herself so bitterly, that the source of tears was opened by sympathy in the widow, and her full heart was, for a time, relieved.

And Mary forgot all purposed meeting with her gay lover, Harry Carson; forgot Miss Simmonds' errands, and her anger, in the anxious desire to comfort the poor lone woman. Never had her sweet face looked more angelic, never had her gentle voice seemed so musical as when she murmured her broken sentences of comfort.

'Oh, don't cry so, dear Mrs Davenport, pray don't take on so. Sure he's gone where he'll never know care again. Yes, I know how lonesome you must feel; but think of your children. Oh! we'll all help to earn food for 'em. Think how sorry *he'd* be, if he sees you fretting so. Don't cry so, please don't.'

And she ended by crying herself, as passionately as the poor widow.

It was agreed that the town must bury him; he had paid to a burial club as long as he could; but by a few weeks' omission, he had forfeited his claim to a sum of money now. Would Mrs Davenport and the little child go home with Mary? The latter brightened up as she urged this plan; but no! where the poor, fondly loved remains were, there would the mourner be; and all that they could do was to make her as comfortable as their funds would allow, and to beg a neighbour to look in and say a word at times. So she was left alone with her dead, and they went to work that had work, and he who had none, took upon him the arrangements for the funeral.

Mary had many a scolding from Miss Simmonds that day for her absence of mind. To be sure Miss Simmonds was much put out by Mary's non-appearance in the morning with certain bits of muslin, and shades of silk which were wanted to complete a dress to be worn that night; but it was true enough that Mary did not mind what she was about; she was too busy planning how her old black gown (her best when her mother died) might be spunged, and turned, and lengthened into something like decent mourning for the widow. And when she went home at night (though it was very late, as a sort of retribution for her morning's negligence), she set to work at once, and was so busy, and so glad over her task, that she had, every now and then, to check herself in singing merry ditties, that she felt little accorded with the sewing on which she was engaged.

So when the funeral day came, Mrs Davenport was neatly arrayed in black, a satisfaction to her poor heart in the midst of her sorrow. Barton and Wilson both accompanied her, as she led her two elder boys, and followed the coffin. It was a simple walking funeral, with nothing to grate on the feelings of any; far more in accordance with its purpose, to my mind, than the gorgeous hearses, and nodding plumes, which form the grotesque funeral pomp of respectable people. There was no 'rattling the bones over the stones', of the pauper's funeral. Decently and patiently was he followed to the grave by one determined to endure her woe meekly for his sake. The only mark of pauperism attendant on the burial concerned the living and joyous, far more than the dead, or the sorrowful. When they arrived in the churchyard, they halted before a raised and handsome tombstone; in reality a wooden mockery of stone respectabilities which adorned the burial-ground. It was easily raised in a very few minutes, and below was the grave in which pauper bodies were piled until within a foot or two of the surface; when the soil was shovelled over, and stamped down, and the wooden cover went to do temporary duty over another hole.* But little they recked of this who now gave up their dead.

---

*The case, to my certain knowledge, in one churchyard in Manchester. There may be more.

PART FIVE

Print of the 1848 Uprising in Frankfurt
Participants in this violent uprising hoped for unification of Germany and some form of representative government. Later in the year, the famous Frankfurt Parliament met to try to write a constitution for a German constitutional monarchy. In the end, all of this came to nothing. The print reminds us of the stark divisions about politics that still separated segments of European populations and the willingness of both sides to use force to attain their goals. The cost of progress was heavy.

1848 and Nationalism

The year 1848 abruptly closed the curtain on the era of Metternich and revolutions. From the English Channel to the Russian frontier, uprisings swept away monarchies in favor of liberal political goals and national self-determination. Angry middle classes found allies among workers with socialist slogans and, sometimes, peasants attacking serfdom's last vestiges. Frightened by the anarchy, millions soon welcomed back the recently overturned old regimes. One commentator described 1848 as the "turning point in history when history failed to turn." Even so, the 1848 tumult forewarned elites about widespread, irresistible popular aspirations. Of special note was the sharp rise of nationalism in association with the Romantic Movement, with its focus on the history, language, and culture of individual peoples and on the idea that people sharing a language and culture should constitute a nation-state. Beginning in 1820 and accelerating after 1848, national aspirations in many parts of Europe achieved recognition.

Now a commonplace, the idea of national self-rule played little role in pre-1800 thinking about states and peoples. Earlier writers focused on all Europe as "Christendom" and the Enlightenment stressed common rational capacities. Monarchies ruled over whatever territories and peoples they inherited or obtained. Inspired by German romantic writers, Madame (Anne-Louise-Germaine) de Staël (1766–1817), daughter of a famous prerevolutionary statesman, first popularized the idea of national character. Published between 1810 and 1818, her evenhanded descriptions of the German, English, and Russian peoples highlighted individual national histories and cultures and forecast subsequent concerns about national identity. In 1834, the poet Adam Mickiewicz (1798–1855) published what came to be known as the Polish national epic, *Pan Tadeuzs*. Two years later in a speech to the British Parliament, Daniel O'Connell (1775–1847) appealed for justice for his native Ireland. By the middle of the century, Giuseppe Mazzini (1805–1872) preached the full-fledged nationalist cause. His writings, such as *The Duties of Man* (1844), spurred the 1848 Italian uprisings and inspired Italian national unification a few years later. These and other writers about nations and nationalism created the intellectual and psychological basis for the nation-state. A first-hand observer from England, Percy B. St. John (1821–1889), described the 1848 revolt in Paris and its brutal repression, a turn of events that symbolizes the failure of most 1848 uprisings, whether national or liberal. The print of the 1848 Uprising in Frankfurt reminds us of how liberal and nationalist ideas came together in 1848 to bring about the wave of unrest.

Study Questions

1. In her analyses of nations, what attracts de Staël's attention?
2. What do Mickiewicz and O'Connell tell us about pre-1848 nationalism?
3. Why does Mazzini believe that duties come before rights?
4. How do these authors define "the nation"?
5. What do these documents suggest as the underlying causes of the 1848 revolutions?
6. Image: What does this image of the Frankfurt uprising reveal about German nationalist goals?

Three Essays: Germany, England, and Russia
Madame de Staël

The idea of the nation-state became a dominant theme during the nineteenth century, as nations began to define themselves as single ethnic groups with the right to self-rule. Early in the century, Madame de Staël had participated in the transition in peoples' expectations from multiethnic monarchies toward clearly defined separate nations. Her descriptions of Germany, England, and Russia may have been her personal opinion, but the fact that she identified these "nations" with certain characteristics helped stimulate a growing interest in nationhood.

Germany

The Customs and the Character of the Germans

Only a few basic characteristics are held in common by the entire German nation, for the diversities of this country are such that one is at a loss to combine from one viewpoint religions, governments, climates, and even peoples so different. The Germany of the South is, in many respects, entirely distinct from the North; the commercial cities are unlike the cities famous for their universities; the small states differ considerably from the two great monarchies of Prussia and Austria. Germany was an aristocratic federation. This domain had no common center of enlightenment and public spirit; it was not a solid nation, for the separate elements were not tied together. This division of Germany, fatal to her political influence, was nevertheless very favorable to all efforts of talent and the imagination. In respect to literary and metaphysical ideas, there was a sort of mild and peaceful anarchy that permitted each person to develop fully his own way of looking at things.

Since there is no capital where the elite of Germany gathers, the spirit of society exercises little power there: the sway of taste and the weapon of

From: Madame de Staël-Holstein, *On Politics, Literature, and National Character*, ed. Monroe Berger (Garden City, NJ: Doubleday, 1964), pp. 277–285, 342–348, 362–369.

ridicule have no influence. Most writers and thinkers work in solitude or surrounded only by a little circle that they dominate.

In literature, as in politics, the Germans have too much consideration for foreigners and not enough national predilections. This self-abnegation and esteem of others is a virtue in individuals, but the patriotism of nations ought to be self-centered.

I shall examine separately the Germany of the South and of the North but I shall confine myself now to some reflections applicable to the whole nation. The Germans are in general sincere and faithful; they rarely break their word, and deceit is foreign to them.

The power of work and reflection is another distinctive trait of the German nation. They are naturally literary and philosophical; but the separation of the classes, which is more pronounced in Germany than anywhere else because society does not subdue its distinctions, is in some respects harmful to the understanding properly so called. The nobility have too few ideas and the men of letters too little practical experience. It is imagination, rather than understanding, that characterizes the Germans.

In leaving France, it is very difficult to get used to the slowness and dullness of the German people. They never hurry, and they find obstacles to everything. You hear "it is impossible" a hundred times in Germany for one time in France. When it comes to action, the Germans do not know how to wrestle with difficulties. Their respect for power arises more from its resemblance to destiny than from self-interest. The lower classes have rather coarse manners, especially when they are rubbed the wrong way. They naturally feel, more than the nobility, that holy antipathy for foreign manners, customs, and languages that strengthens the national bond in every country. The offer of money does not disturb their usual ways, nor does fear; in short, they are very capable of that steadiness in all things that is an excellent basis for morality; for the man who is always moved by fear, and even more by hope, passes easily from one opinion to another whenever his interest requires it.

Once we rise a little above the lowest class of people in Germany, we can easily observe the inner life, the poetry of the soul, that characterizes the Germans. Almost all the inhabitants of town and country, the soldiers and the peasants, know music. I had the experience of entering poor homes blackened by tobacco-smoke and of suddenly hearing not only the mistress but also the master of the house improvising on the harpsichord, as the Italians improvise in verse.

We must also be grateful to the Germans for the good will they display in the respectful bows and in politeness filled with formalities that foreigners have so often held up to ridicule. They might easily have substituted cold and indifferent manners for the grace and elegance they are accused of being unable to reach. Indifference always silences mockery, for mockery applies itself especially to useless efforts. But benevolent people would rather expose themselves to mockery than preserve themselves from it by the haughty and reserved air so easy for anyone to assume.

One is constantly struck, in Germany, by the contrast between sentiments and habits, between talents and tastes: civilization and nature do not yet seem to be well blended. Sometimes the most truthful men are affected in their expressions and appearance, as if they had something to hide. Sometimes, on the other hand, gentleness of soul does not prevent rudeness in manners: often this contradiction goes still further, and weakness of character reveals itself through the rough language and conduct. Enthusiasm for the arts and poetry is joined to rather common behavior in social life. There is no country where the men of letters or the young people studying in the universities are better acquainted with ancient languages and antiquity, but also there is none where superannuated practices more generally still persist. The memories of Greece and the taste for the fine arts seem to have reached them indirectly, but feudal institutions and the old customs of the Germans are still held in honor there, although, unhappily for the military power of the country, they no longer have the same strength.

There is no more bizarre combination than the military appearance of all Germany—the soldiers one meets at every step, and the kind of domesticated life people lead there. They are afraid of hardship and bad weather, as though the nation were entirely made up of merchants and men of letters; yet all their institutions tend—and necessarily so—to give the nation military habits.

Stoves, beer, and tobacco-smoke surround the lower classes of Germany with a heavy and hot atmosphere from which they do not like to emerge. This atmosphere is harmful to alertness, which is no less important than courage in war. Determination is sluggish and discouragement is easy because such a generally melancholy life does not afford much confidence in fortune.

The demarcation of classes, much more positive in Germany than it was in France, necessarily destroyed the military spirit in the middle class. This demarcation is not offensive, for, I repeat, amiability suffuses everything in Germany, even aristocratic pride. Differences in rank are reduced to a few court privileges, to a few gatherings that do not afford enough pleasure to warrant much regret. Nothing is bitter, no matter how regarded, when society—and through it, ridicule—has little influence. Men can wound their own souls only by duplicity or mockery; in a serious and truthful country there is always justice and happiness. But the barrier in Germany that separated the nobles from the citizens necessarily made the entire nation less warlike.

Imagination, which is the dominant feature of artistic and literary Germany, inspires the fear of danger if this natural emotion is not combated by the influence of judgment and the exaltation of honor. It is important to know whether domestic affections, the habit of reflection, and the very gentleness of soul do not lead to the fear of death; and if all the power of a state consists in its military spirit, it is essential to examine the causes that have weakened this spirit in the German nation.

Three chief motives usually lead men to battle: love of country and of freedom, love of glory, and religious fanaticism.

There cannot be much love of country in a realm divided for several centuries, where Germans fought Germans almost always through foreign instigation. Love of glory has little vitality where there is no center, no capital, no society. The type of impartiality, a luxury of justice, that characterizes the Germans makes them susceptible to being more inflamed by abstract ideas than by the concerns of life. The general who loses a battle is more certain of indulgence than the general who wins one is of applause. In such a nation there is not enough difference between success and failure to excite much ambition.

Religion in Germany is deep-seated, but it has a character of meditation and self-containment that does not inspire the vigor necessary to exclusive feelings. That same separateness in opinion, individuals, and states, so harmful to the power of the German Empire, is found in religion too: a large number of different sects divide Germany. Even Catholicism, which by its nature exerts a uniform and strict discipline, is interpreted by each one in his own way. A political and social bond among peoples, one government, one religion, one law, common interests, a classical literature, a prevailing point of view—none of these things is found among the Germans.

The love of liberty is not developed among the Germans; they have not learned its value through possession or deprivation of it. There are several examples of federated governments that lend as much vigor to public spirit as does unity in government, but they are associations of equal states and of free citizens. The German federation was composed of strong and weak states, citizens and serfs, rivals and even enemies—these were old elements joined by circumstances and respected by men.

The very independence enjoyed in Germany, in almost all respects, made the Germans indifferent to liberty. Independence is a possession, and liberty is a right. And precisely because no one in Germany was injured in respect to his rights or possessions, no need was felt for any means to preserve this happy condition.

The Germans, with a few exceptions, are hardly able to succeed in anything that calls for tact and facility. Everything makes them anxious, everything hinders them, and they feel the need of a method in doing things just as much as they feel the need of independence in ideas. The French, on the contrary, approach action with the freedom of art, and ideas with the bondage of custom. The Germans, who cannot endure the yoke of rules in literature, prefer everything to be laid out for them in advance when it comes to behavior. They do not know how to deal with people; and the less occasion they have in this respect to decide for themselves, the more satisfied they are.

Only political institutions can shape the character of a nation. The nature of the government of Germany was antithetical to the philosophical enlightenment of the Germans. That is why they combine boldness of thought with the most obedient character. The pre-eminence of the military regime and the distinctions of rank have accustomed them to the strictest submission in the relations of social life. Among them obedience is a matter of regularity, not servility; they are scrupulous in the execution of the orders they receive, as though every order were a duty.

The enlightened men of Germany heatedly argue among themselves in the domain of theory, where they will brook no interference. But they rather willingly abandon to the powerful of this earth all the realities of life. These realities, which they so despise, nonetheless find purchasers, who then disturb and repress the realm of the imagination. The mind and character of the Germans appear not to be in touch with each other: the one cannot bear any restriction, the other submits to every yoke. The one is very venturesome, the other very timid. In short, the enlightenment of the one rarely lends strength to the other, and that is easily explained. The spread of knowledge in modern times only weakens character when the latter is not fortified by the practice of business and the exercise of the will. To see and understand everything is a great cause of uncertainty; and vigor of action develops only in those free and powerful countries where patriotic sentiments are to the soul like blood to the veins and grow cold only as life ends.

The Women

Nature and society have given women a great capacity for endurance, and it seems to me that it cannot be denied that in our day they are in general more meritorious than men.

German women have a charm all their own—a touching voice, fair hair, a dazzling complexion. They are modest, but less timid than English women; it seems that they less often meet men who are superior to them and that, moreover, they have less to fear from harsh judgments of the public. They seek to please by their sensibility and to interest by their imagination. They are familiar with the language of poetry and the fine arts. They flirt wholeheartedly, whereas French women do so wittily and jokingly. The perfect loyalty that is peculiar to the character of the Germans makes love less dangerous for the happiness of women, and they possibly approach this sentiment with more confidence because it is clothed in more romantic colors, and disdain and infidelity are less to be feared there than elsewhere.

Love is a religion in Germany, but a poetic religion that too readily tolerates whatever sensibility excuses. It cannot be denied that the ease of divorce in Protestant areas strikes at the sacredness of marriage. Husbands and wives are changed there as calmly as if it were a matter of arranging the incidents of a play. Owing to the good nature of men and women, no bitterness enters into these easy separations; and since the Germans have more imagination than genuine passion, the most bizarre events occur with extraordinary tranquillity. But it is in this way that manners and character lose all solidity. The spirit of paradox shakes the most sacred institutions, and there are no fixed rules on any subject.

One may justifiably laugh at the absurdities of some German women who become enthusiastic to the point of affectation, and whose saccharine expressions obliterate everything pointed and striking in mind and character. They are not frank, yet neither are they false. It is merely that they see and judge nothing accurately, and real events pass before their eyes like a phantasmagoria. Even when it occurs to them to be gay, they still maintain a tinge of that sentimentality that is so honored in their country.

Despite these absurdities, there are many German women with genuine feelings and simple manners. Their careful upbringing and natural purity of soul make them a gentle and steady influence. But we seldom find among them the quick wit that animates conversation and stimulates ideas; this kind of delight is hardly to be found except in the smartest and wittiest Paris society.

*   *   *

England

The Prosperity of England and the Causes That Have Hitherto Increased It

Reaching England, I was thinking of no particular person: I knew hardly anyone there, but I went with confidence. I was persecuted by an enemy of liberty, so I believed myself certain of honorable sympathy in a country whose every institution was in harmony with my political sentiments. I counted much, also, on the memory of my father to protect me, and I was not deceived. The waves of the North Sea, which I crossed in coming from Sweden, still filled me with terror as I made out from afar the green island that alone had resisted the enslavement of Europe. Those who will not acknowledge the influence of liberty in the power of England constantly repeat that the English would have been conquered by Bonaparte, like all the Continental nations, had they not been protected by the sea. This opinion cannot be refuted by experience. I have no doubt that if, by a stroke of Leviathan, Great Britain had been joined to the European continent, it would certainly have suffered more and its wealth would have diminished. But the public spirit of a free nation is such that it would never have yielded to the yoke of foreigners.

From Harwich to London one travels a highway about seventy miles long bordered almost entirely by country houses to the right and left: a succession of dwellings with gardens, interrupted by towns. Almost everyone is well-clothed, hardly a cottage is in decay; even the animals seem peaceful and thriving, as if there were rights for them, too, in this great structure of social order. The price of everything is necessarily very high, but most of these prices are fixed; there is in this country such an aversion for anything arbitrary that, besides the law itself, a rule and then a custom are established to ensure, as far as possible, in the smallest details, some degree of exactness and stability. The high cost of living resulting from extremely high taxes is of course a disadvantage. But assuming the war was absolutely necessary, what other nation—that is, what other form of government—could be equal to it?

The amount accomplished in England through private contributions is enormous: hospitals, educational establishments, missions, Christian societies were not only maintained but increased during the war; and foreigners who underwent disasters from it—the Swiss, Germans, Dutch—constantly received private aid from England, the result of voluntary gifts.

But to what are these miracles of liberal prosperity to be attributed? To liberty—that is, to the nation's trust in a government that makes publicity the first principle of finances, in a government enlightened by discussion and by freedom of the press. The nation, which cannot be deceived under such an arrangement, knows the use of the taxes it pays, and public credit supports the unbelievable weight of the English debt. If something proportionately similar were tried in any non-representative state on the European continent, it would not be able to go far in such an undertaking. Five hundred thousand owners of government bonds constitute a strong guarantee of payment of the debt in a country where each man's opinion and interest is influential.

The government never meddles in anything that private individuals can do just as well. Respect for individual freedom extends to the exercise of everyone's abilities, and the people are so anxious to manage their own affairs, when it is possible, that in many respects London lacks the police necessary for the convenience of the city because the ministers may not encroach upon the local authorities.

Political security, without which there can be neither credit nor capital accumulation, is still not enough to develop all the resources of a nation: emulation must stimulate men to labor, while the law assures them of its fruit. Commerce and industry must be honored, not by rewards to this or that individual—this presupposes two classes in a country, one of which thinks it has the right to reward the other—but by an order of things that allows each man to rise to the highest level if he deserves it. In fact, the absurd prejudice that forbade the nobility of France to go into business did more harm to the growth of French fortunes than any other abuse of the Old Regime. In England peerages have been recently granted to leading businessmen. Once peers, they do not remain in commerce, because they are expected to serve the country in another way; but it is their function as government officials, and not the prejudices of caste, that divorces them from business, into which the younger sons of the highest nobility enter without hesitation when circumstances call them to it. The same family often has peers on one side and on the other the most ordinary merchants of some provincial town. This political order enhances all the faculties of every individual, because there are no limits to the advantages that wealth and talent can bring, and because the lowest English citizen, if he is worthy of being the highest, is barred from no marriage, employment, society, or title.

All classes of well-bred men in England meet often in various committees engaged in some venture or charity supported by private contributions. Publicity in all matters is a principle so widely accepted that, though the English are by nature the most reserved of men and the most reluctant to speak before others, there are almost always, in the rooms where the committees meet, seats for spectators and a platform from which the speakers address the assembly.

I attended one of these discussions, in which the reasons calculated to stimulate the listeners' generosity were forcefully presented. It concerned the sending of help to the people of Leipzig after the battle fought beneath its walls. The first speaker was the Duke of York, second son of the king. After the Duke of York, the Duke of Sussex, the fifth son of the king, who expresses himself with much elegance and ease, also spoke in his turn; and the most beloved and respected man in all of England, Mr. Wilberforce, could hardly make himself heard above the applause. Humble men, and with no other status in society than their wealth or devotion to humanity, followed these illustrious names. The listeners contributed as they left, and considerable sums were the result of this meeting. Thus are formed the ties that strengthen the unity of the nation and thus the social order bases itself upon reason and humanity.

The object of these worthy assemblies is not merely to encourage works of charity; some of them serve especially to strengthen the union of the nobility and the businessmen, the nation and the government.

Liberty and Public Spirit among the English

The greatest support of liberty is individual security, and nothing is finer than English legislation in this respect. A criminal trial is a horrible spectacle anywhere. In England the excellence of the procedure, the humanity of the judges, the precautions of every kind taken to protect the lives of the innocent, and the means of defense of the guilty inject a feeling of admiration into the anguish of such a trial. The admirable institution of the jury, which goes back in England to remote antiquity, introduces equity into justice.

English civil law is much less worthy of praise; the trials are too costly and too long. It will certainly be improved with time, as it already has been in several respects, for what distinguishes English government above all is the possibility of orderly improvement.

"Very well," exclaim the enemies of all public virtue, "even if praise of England were fully warranted, it would only mean that it is a skillfully and wisely governed country, just as any other country might be. But it is not free in the way that the *philosophes* understand freedom, for the ministers are the masters of everything, there as elsewhere. They buy the votes of Parliament in such a way as always to assure themselves a majority, and the whole English constitution of which people speak with admiration is nothing but the art of putting political venality to work."

Can anyone honestly convince himself that the English ministers give money to the members of the House of Commons or of the higher chamber to vote with the government? How could the English ministers, who account for public funds so exactly, find sums large enough to corrupt men of such great wealth, to say nothing of their character?

Fidelity to party is one of the virtues based upon public spirit, from which comes the greatest advantage for English liberty. If tomorrow the ministers with whom one voted go out of office, those to whom they have given posts leave with them. A man would be disgraced in England if he parted from his political allies for his private interest. One never hears the same mouth uttering two opposite opinions; but in the present state of things in England differences are a matter of shades rather than colors. The Tories, it has been said, approve liberty and love the monarchy, while the Whigs approve the monarchy and love liberty. But between these two parties there is no question as to a republic or a monarchy, the old or the new dynasty, liberty or servitude.

For nearly fifty years the members of the Opposition have held ministerial office only three or four years, yet their fidelity to party has not been shaken.

The existence of a Government party and an Opposition party, though it cannot be prescribed by law, is an essential support of liberty based on the nature of things. In every country where you see an assembly of men always in agreement, be certain that there is a despotism, or that despotism will be the result of unanimity if it is not the cause of it. Now, since power and the favors it disposes have attraction for men, liberty could exist only with this fidelity to party which imposes, so to speak, a discipline of honor in the ranks of the deputies enrolled under various banners.

But if opinions are settled in advance, how can truth and eloquence influence the assembly? How can the majority change when circumstances require it to do so, and of what use is debate if no one can vote according to his conviction? That is not the situation. What is called fidelity to party means that one must not separate one's personal interests from the interests of one's political allies, nor deal separately with the men in power. But it often happens that circumstances or arguments influence the bulk of the assembly and that the considerable number of neutrals, that is, those who do not play an active role in politics, are able to change the majority. It is in the nature of English government that the ministers cannot stay in office without this majority in their favor. Yet Mr. Pitt, though he temporarily lost it at the time of the King's first illness, could remain in office because public opinion, which was favorable to him, enabled him to dissolve Parliament and to resort to a new election. In short, opinion rules in England; it is this that establishes the liberty of a state.

Enlightenment and the strength of public spirit are a more than adequate answer to the arguments of those who maintain that, if England were a Continental power, the army would encroach upon its liberty. It is undoubtedly an advantage to the English that their strength lies in the navy rather than in ground forces. It requires greater knowledge to be a captain of a ship than a colonel, and the habits acquired at sea do not lead to the desire to interfere in the internal affairs of one's country. But if nature, turned lavish, created ten Lord Wellingtons and if the world saw ten more Battles of Waterloo, it would not occur to those who so readily give their lives for their country to turn their power against it; if they did, they would face an insuperable obstacle in men just as brave as themselves and more enlightened, who detest the military spirit though they admire and practice warlike qualities.

The kind of prejudice that convinced the French nobility that they could serve their country only in a military career does not exist at all in England. A great many sons of peers are lawyers; the bar shares the respect felt for the law, and in all walks of life civil occupations are respected. In such a country people need not yet fear the inroads of military power; only unenlightened nations have a blind admiration for the sword.

*   *   *

Russia

The Road from Kiev to Moscow

I have seen nothing barbaric in these people. On the contrary, their manners have something elegant and gentle that is not found elsewhere. I am quite aware that one may reasonably raise, in objection to my view, the great atrocities found in Russian history. But, first, I should place the blame for them upon the Boyars, depraved by the despotism they practiced or suffered, rather than upon the nation itself. Moreover, political dissension, in all places and times, perverts the national character. Nothing in history is more deplorable than a succession of masters elevated and overturned by crime. But such is the inevitable condition of absolute power upon this earth.

If tyranny had on its side only its fully convinced advocates, it could never maintain itself. The astonishing thing, which more than anything else reveals human wretchedness, is that most ordinary men are at the service of success. They do not have the power to think beyond a bare fact, and when an oppressor has triumphed and a victim is destroyed, they hasten to justify not the tyrant, precisely, but the fate of which he is the instrument. Weakness of mind and character is no doubt the cause of this servility, but there is also in man a certain need to justify fate, whatever it may be, as if that were a way to live in peace with it.

Everywhere in Europe one sees the contrast between wealth and poverty, but in Russia neither the one nor the other, so to speak, is conspicuous. The populace are not poor; the upper class can, when necessary, lead the same life as the populace. What characterizes this country is the mixture of the severest hardships and the most exquisite pleasures. Those very noblemen whose houses combine the most striking luxuries from various parts of the world live, while traveling, on much worse food than do our French peasants and can endure a very disagreeable physical existence not only in war but in many circumstances of life. The severity of the climate, the marshlands, forests, and deserts, which make up a large part of the country, put man in a struggle against nature. What the English call *comfort*, and what we call *l'aisance*, is hardly to be found in Russia. You will find nothing of any kind perfect enough to satisfy the fancy of the Russian nobles. But when this poetry of abundance falls short, they drink hydromel, sleep on a plank, and travel day and night in an open carriage without missing the luxury to which one would think them accustomed. They love wealth for its magnificence rather than for the pleasures it affords; in this too they are like Orientals, who practice hospitality toward strangers, overwhelm them with presents, and often neglect their own ordinary comfort. This is one of the reasons that explain the great courage with which they have borne the ruin inflicted upon them by the burning of Moscow. More accustomed to external pomp than to solicitude for themselves, they are not debilitated by luxury; to give away money satisfies their pride as much as or more than lavish spending. A gigantic quality in all things characterizes this nation; ordinary dimensions do not at all apply to it. I do not mean by this that neither true greatness nor stability are to be found in it. But the boldness, the imagination, of the Russians knows no bounds. Among them everything is colossal rather than proportional, audacious rather than thoughtful, and if the target is not hit it is because it is overshot.

Appearance of the Country.
Character of the Russian People

On the eve of my arrival in Moscow, I stopped, the night of a very warm day, in a pleasant enough meadow. Some peasant women, dressed picturesquely in accordance with the habit of the locality, were returning from their labors singing Ukrainian tunes whose words praise love and liberty with a kind of melancholy akin to regret. I asked them to dance and they consented to do so. I was struck by the gentle gaiety of these peasant women, as I had been by that of most of the common people I met in Russia. I can well believe that they are terrible when their passions are aroused; and as they have no education, they do not know how to curb their violence. As a result of this ignorance, they have few moral principles, and theft is very frequent in Russia, but so is hospitality. They give to you as they take from you, according to whether trickery or generosity strikes their fancy; both arouse the admiration of this nation. There is a little resemblance to uncivilized people in this way of living, but it seems to me that at present the only vigorous European nations are those that are called either barbarous—that is to say, unenlightened—or free.

One thing worth noting is the degree to which public spirit is marked in Russia. The reputation for invincibility which a great many successes have given this nation, the pride natural to the nobility, the self-sacrifice ingrained in the character of the nation, the profound influence of religion, the hatred of foreigners which Peter I tried to destroy in order to enlighten and civilize his country but which remains nonetheless in the blood of the Russians and is occasionally aroused—all these causes combine to make this nation a very energetic one. Some wretched anecdotes about earlier reigns, some Russians who ran up debts in Paris, and some *bon mots* of Diderot put it into the heads of Frenchmen that Russia consisted only of a corrupt Court, officers and chamberlains, and a population of slaves. This is a great error.

The welcome the Russians extend is so kind that from the first day one thinks he is intimate with them, but very likely one would not really know them even after ten years. Russian silence is absolutely extraordinary; it is induced only by what arouses their deep interest. Of everything else, they talk as much as one would like, but their conversation reveals only their politeness: it betrays neither their feelings nor their opinions. Moreover, as they are in general not highly educated, they find little pleasure in serious conversation and do not take pride in scintillating by the wit that may be displayed in it. Poetry, eloquence, and literature are not found in Russia. Luxury, power, and courage are the main goals of pride and ambition; all other ways of distinguishing oneself still seem effeminate and hollow to this nation.

But, it will be said, the people are slaves. What kind of character can they be credited with? I certainly do not have to point out that all enlightened people hope that the Russian nation will emerge from this condition, and the one who probably desires it most is Emperor Alexander. But this Russian slavery does not resemble the kind we are familiar with in the West. It is not, as under the feudal *régime*, a matter of conquerors who imposed their harsh laws upon the conquered. The relationship between the nobles and the populace is more like what was called the family of slaves among the ancients than the status of serfs among the moderns. There is no third estate in Russia. This is a great hindrance to the progress of literature and the fine arts, for it is usually in this middle class that learning is developed. But the result of this absence of an intermediary between the nobility and the populace is that they have greater affection for each other.

The distance between the two classes seems the greater because there is nothing between these two extremes, but in actual fact they are the closer to one another for not being separated by a middle class. This is a social organization entirely unfavorable to the enlightenment of the upper classes but not to the happiness of the lower. Moreover, where there is no representative government, that is, in countries where the monarch still decrees the laws he is to execute, men are often more degraded by the loss of their reason and their character than in this vast domain where a few simple religious and patriotic ideas govern a large mass guided by a few leaders. The immense extent of the Russian realm also prevents the despotism of the nobles from bearing heavily upon the people in everyday affairs. Finally, above all, the religious and military spirit is so predominant in the nation that many faults may be forgiven in consideration of these two great sources of noble deeds.

Moscow

Gilded cupolas announced Moscow from afar; yet, as the surrounding country is only a plain like all of Russia, one can reach that large city without being impressed by its extent. Someone has said with reason that Moscow is rather a province than a city. Indeed, one sees there huts, houses, palaces, a bazaar as in the Orient, churches, public buildings, bodies of water, woods, and parks. The diversity of manners and of nations that make up Russia is revealed in this vast region. I was asked: Would you like to buy some Kashmir shawls in the Tartar district? Have you seen Chinatown? Asia and Europe are combined in this immense city. People in it enjoy more liberty than in Petersburg, where the Court necessarily exercises great influence. The nobles settled in Moscow do not strive for high places; but they show their patriotism by large gifts to the state, whether for public purposes in time of peace or for relief in time of war. The colossal fortunes of the Russian nobles are used for building up collections of all kinds, for commercial enterprises, and for entertainments modeled after the *Thousand and One Nights,* and these fortunes are also very often lost through the unrestrained passions of their owners.

When I arrived in Moscow, there was talk of nothing but the sacrifices made for the war.

No sooner does a Russian become a soldier than his beard is cut, and from this moment he is free. People wished that everyone who served in the militia would also be regarded as free, but then the whole nation would have been free, for it rose up almost in its entirety. Let us hope that this liberation, so much desired, will be brought about peacefully. But, in the meantime, one wishes the beards would be preserved, so much strength and dignity do they lend the face.

The Kremlin, that citadel where the emperors of Russia defended themselves against the Tartars, is surrounded by a high wall crenelated and flanked with turrets whose unusual shapes recall a Turkish minaret rather than a fortress like most of those in the West. But though the external character of the city's buildings is Oriental, the imprint of Christianity is found in the multitude of churches, so revered, which attract one's notice at every step.

The Russians played no role in the Age of Chivalry; they were not involved in the Crusades. Constantly at war with the Tartars, Poles, and Turks, the military spirit took shape among them in the midst of atrocities of all kinds brought about by the barbarity of the Asian nations and of the tyrants who governed Russia. In social relations, which are so new to them, the Russians do not distinguish themselves by the spirit of chivalry as the peoples of the West conceive it; rather, they have always shown themselves to be unmerciful toward their enemies. So many massacres took place in the interior of Russia down to and after the reign of Peter the Great that the morality of the nation, and especially that of the nobility, necessarily suffered much from them. These despotic governments, whose only limit is the assassination of the despot, overthrow the principles of honor and duty in the minds of men. But patriotism and attachment to religious beliefs have maintained themselves in all their strength through the wreckage of this bloody history, and the nation that preserves such virtues may yet astonish the world.

In Moscow I saw the most enlightened men in the field of the sciences and literature. But there, as at Petersburg, almost all the professorial posts are filled by Germans. There is a great scarcity of educated men in every field in Russia. The young people, for the most part, do not go to the university except to enter the military profession sooner. Civil offices in Russia confer a rank corresponding to a grade in the army; the spirit of the nation is entirely directed toward the war. In everything else, in administration, political economy, public education, etc., the other nations have until now surpassed the Russians. They are, however, making attempts in literature. The softness and vividness of the sounds of their language are obvious even to those who do not understand it; it should be well suited to music and poetry. But the Russians, like so many other nations on the Continent, make the mistake of imitating French literature which, by its very beauty, is appropriate only to the French. It seems to me that the Russians should find their literary heritage in the Greeks rather than in the Latins. The letters of Russian script, which are so much like those of the Greeks, the former connections between the Russians and the Byzantine empire, their future destinies, which may lead them toward the illustrious monuments of Athens and Sparta—all this should induce the Russians to study Greek. But above all their writers must draw their poetry from the deepest source in their own souls. Their works, until now, have been composed, so to speak, only from their lips, but so vigorous a nation can never be stirred by such weak notes.

The Duties of Man

Giuseppe Mazzini

Giuseppe Mazzini is considered the intellectual father of Italian nationalism. He founded the movement Young Italy and led the Italian Risorgimento—resurgence—that aimed at establishing an Italian nation-state out of the many Italian states of the early nineteenth century. His writings led Italians to begin to think of themselves as a nation. In this book, Mazzini addressed the workingmen of Italy and explained that the solution to their problems lay in Italian nationhood.

To the Italian Working-Men

I want to speak to you of your duties. I want to speak to you, as my heart dictates to me, of the most sacred things which we know—of God, of Humanity, of the Fatherland, of the Family. Listen to me with love, even as I shall speak to you with love. My words are words of conviction matured by long years of sorrow and of observation and of study. The duties which I am going to point out to you I strive and shall strive as long as I live to fulfil, to the utmost of my power. I may make mistakes, but my heart is true. I may deceive myself, but I will not deceive you. Hear me therefore as a brother; judge freely among yourselves, whether it seems to you that I speak the truth; abandon me if you think that I preach what is false; but follow me and do according to my teaching if you find me an apostle of truth. To be mistaken is a misfortune to be pitied; but to know the truth and not to conform one's actions to it is a crime which Heaven and Earth condemn.

Why do I speak to you of your *duties* before speaking to you of your *rights*? Why in a society in which all, voluntarily or involuntarily, oppress you, in which the exercise of all the rights which belong to man is constantly denied you, in which misery is your lot, and what is called happiness is for other classes of men, why do I speak to you of self-sacrifice and not of conquest; of virtue, moral improvement,

From: Joseph Mazzini, *The Duties of Man and Other Essays* (New York: Dutton, 1966), pp. 7–20, 51–59.

education, and not of material *well-being?* This is a question which I must answer before going further, because here precisely lies the difference between our school and many others which are being preached to-day in Europe; because, moreover, it is a question which rises readily in the indignant mind of the suffering working-man.

We are poor, enslaved, unhappy; speak to us of better material conditions, of liberty, of happiness. Tell us if we are doomed to suffer for ever, or if we too may enjoy in our turn. Preach Duty to our masters, to the classes above us which treat us like machines, and monopolise the blessings which belong to all. To us speak of rights; speak of the means of vindicating them; speak of our strength. Wait till we have a recognized existence; then you shall speak to us of duties and of sacrifice. This is what many of our working-men say, and follow teachers and associations which respond to their desires. They forget one thing only, and that is, that the doctrine which they invoke has been preached for the last fifty years without producing the slightest material improvement in the condition of the working-people.

For the last fifty years whatever has been done for the cause of progress and of good against absolute governments and hereditary aristocracies has been done in the name of the Rights of Man; in the name of liberty as the means, and of *well-being* as the object of existence. All the acts of the French Revolution and of the revolutions which followed and imitated it were consequences of a Declaration of the

Rights of Man. All the works of the philosophers who prepared it were based upon a theory of liberty, and upon the need of making known to every individual his own rights. All the revolutionary schools preached that man is born for happiness, that he has the right to seek it by all the means in his power, that no one has the right to impede him in this search, and that he has the right of overthrowing all the obstacles which he may encounter on his path. And the obstacles were overthrown; liberty was conquered. It endured for years in many countries; in some it still endures. Has the condition of the people improved? Have the millions who live by the daily labour of their hands gained the least fraction of the well-being hoped for and promised to them?

No; the condition of the people has not improved; rather it has grown and grows worse in nearly every country, and especially here where I write the price of the necessaries of life has gone on continually rising, the wages of the working-man in many branches of industry falling, and the population multiplying. In nearly every country the lot of workers has become more uncertain, more precarious, and the labour crises which condemn thousands of working-men to idleness for a time have become more frequent. The yearly increase of emigration from one country to another, and from Europe to other parts of the world, and the ever-growing number of beneficent institutions, the increase of poor rates and provisions for the destitute, are enough to prove this. The latter prove also that public attention is waking more and more to the ills of the people; but their inability to lessen those ills to any visible extent points to a no less continual increase of poverty among the classes which they endeavour to help.

And nevertheless, in these last fifty years, the sources of social wealth and the sum of material blessings have steadily increased. Production has doubled. Commerce, amid continual crises, inevitable in the utter absence of organisation, has acquired a greater force of activity and a wider sphere for its operations. Communication has almost everywhere been made secure and rapid, and the price of commodities has fallen in consequence of the diminished cost of transport. And, on the other hand, the idea of rights inherent in human nature is to-day generally accepted; accepted in word and, hypocritically, even by those who seek to evade it in deed. Why, then, has the condition of the people not improved? Why is the consumption of products, instead of being divided equally among all the members of the social body in Europe, concentrated in the hands of a small number of men forming a new aristocracy? Why has the new impulse given to industry and commerce produced, not the well-being of the many, but the luxury of the few?

The answer is clear to those who will look a little closely into things. Men are creatures of education, and act only according to the principle of education given to them. The men who have promoted revolutions hitherto have based them upon the idea of the rights belonging to the individual; the revolutions conquered liberty—individual liberty, liberty of teaching, liberty of belief, liberty of trade, liberty in everything and for everybody. But of what use was the recognition of their rights to those who had no means of exercising them? What did liberty of teaching mean to those who had neither time nor means to profit by it, or liberty of trade to those who had nothing to trade with, neither capital nor credit? In all the countries where these principles were proclaimed society was composed of a small number of individuals who possessed the land, the credit, the capital, and of vast multitudes of men who had nothing but their own hands and were forced to give the labour of them to the former class, on any terms, in order to live, and forced to spend the whole day in material and monotonous toil. For these, constrained to battle with hunger, what was liberty but an illusion and a bitter irony? To make it anything else it would have been necessary for the men of the well-to-do classes to consent to reduce the hours of labour, to increase the remuneration, to institute free and uniform education for the masses, to make the instruments of labour accessible to all, and to provide a bonus fund for the working-man endowed with capacity and good intentions. But why should they do it? Was not *well-being* the supreme object in life? Were not material blessings desirable before all other things? Why should they lessen their own enjoyment for the advantage of others? Let those who could, help themselves. When society has secured to everybody who can use them the free exercise of the rights belonging to human nature, it does all that is required of it. If there be any one who is unable from the fatality of his own circumstances to exercise any of these rights, he must resign himself and not blame others.

It was natural that they should say thus, and thus, in fact, they did say. And this attitude of mind towards the poor in the classes privileged by fortune soon became the attitude of every individual towards every other. Each man looked after his own rights and the improvement of his own condition without seeking to provide for others; and when his rights clashed with those of others, there was war; not a war of blood, but of gold and of cunning; a war less manly than the other, but equally destructive; cruel war, in which those who had the means and were strong relentlessly crushed the weak or the unskilled. In this continual warfare, men were educated in egoism and in greed for material welfare exclusively. Liberty of belief destroyed all community of faith. Liberty of education produced moral anarchy. Men without a common tie, without unity of religious belief and of aim, and whose sole vocation was enjoyment, sought every one his own road, not heeding if in pursuing it they were trampling upon the heads of their brothers—brothers in name and enemies in fact. To this we are come to-day, thanks to the theory of *rights*.

Certainly rights exist; but where the rights of an individual come into conflict with those of another, how can we hope to reconcile and harmonise them, without appealing to something superior to all rights? And where the rights of an individual, or of many individuals, clash with the rights of the Country, to what tribunal are we to appeal? If the right to *well-being*, to the greatest possible well-being, belongs to every living person, who will solve the difficulty between the workingman and the manufacturer? If the right to existence is the first and inviolable right of every man, who shall demand the sacrifice of that existence for the benefit of other men? Will you demand it in the name of Country, of Society, of the multitude of your brothers? What is Country, in the opinion of those of whom I speak, but the place in which our individual rights are most secure? What is Society but a collection of men who have agreed to bring the strength of the many in support of the rights of each? And after having taught the individual for fifty years that Society is

established for the purpose of *assuring to him the exercise of his rights,* would you ask him to sacrifice them all to Society, to submit himself, if need be, to continuous toil, to prison, to exile, for the sake of improving it? After having preached to him everywhere that the object of life is *well-being,* would you all at once bid him give up well-being and life itself to free his country from the foreigner, or to procure better conditions for a class which is not his own? After having talked to him for years of *material* interests, how can you maintain that, finding wealth and power in his reach, he ought not to stretch out his hand to grasp them, even to the injury of his brothers?

Italian Working-men, this is not a chance thought of my mind, without a foundation in fact. It is history, the history of our own times, a history the pages of which drip with blood, the blood of the people. Ask all the men who transformed the revolution of 1830 into a mere substitution of one set of persons for another, and, for example, made the bodies of your French comrades, who were killed fighting in the Three Days, into stepping-stones to raise themselves to power; all their doctrines, before 1830, were founded on the old theory of the *rights* of man, not upon a belief in his *duties.* You call them to-day traitors and apostates, and yet they were only consistent with their own doctrine. They fought with sincerity against the Government of Charles X, because that Government was directly hostile to the classes from which they sprang, and violated and endeavoured to suppress their rights. They fought in the name of the well-being which they did not possess as much of as they thought they ought to have. Some were persecuted for freedom of thought; others, men of powerful mind, saw themselves neglected, shut out from offices occupied by men of capacity inferior to their own. Then the wrongs of the people angered them also. Then they wrote boldly and in good faith about the rights which belong to every man. Afterwards, when their own political and intellectual rights had been secured, when the path to office was opened to them, when they had conquered the *well-being* which they sought, they forgot the people, forgot that the millions, inferior to them in education and in aspirations, were seeking the exercise of other rights and the achievement of *well-being* of another sort, and they set their minds at rest and troubled no longer about anybody but themselves. Why call them traitors? Why not rather call their doctrine treacherous?

There lived and wrote at that time in France a man whom you ought never to forget, more powerful in mind than all of them put together. He was our opponent then; but he believed in Duty; in the duty of sacrificing the whole existence to the common good, to the pursuit and triumph of Truth. He studied the men and the circumstances of the time deeply, and did not allow himself to be led astray by applause, or to be discouraged by disappointment. When he had tried one way and failed, he tried yet another for the amelioration of the masses. And when the course of events had shown him that there was one power alone capable of achieving it, when the people had proved themselves in the field of action more virtuous and more believing than all those who had pretended to deal with their cause, he, Lamennais, author of the *Words of a Believer,* which you have all read, became the best apostle of the cause in which we are brothers. There you see in him, and in the men of whom I have been speaking, the difference between the men of *rights* and those of *duty.* To the first the acquisition of their individual rights, by withdrawing stimulus, proves a sufficient check to further effort; the work of the second only ceases here on earth with life.

And among the peoples who are completely enslaved, where the conflict has very different dangers, where every step made towards a better state of things is signed with the blood of a martyr, where the operations against injustice in high places are necessarily secret and lack the consolation of publicity and of praise, what obligation, what stimulus to constancy can maintain upon the path of progress men who degrade the holy social war which we carry on to a mere battle for their *rights?* I speak, be it understood, of the generality and not of the exceptions to be met with in all schools of thought. When the hot blood and the impulse of reaction against tyranny which naturally draw youth into the conflict have calmed down, what can prevent these men, after a few years of effort, after the disappointments inevitable in any such enterprise, from grow-

ing weary? Why should they not prefer any sort of repose to an unquiet existence, agitated by continual struggles and danger, and liable to end any day in imprisonment, or the scaffold, or exile? It is the too common story of most of the Italians of to-day, imbued as they are with the old French ideas; a very sad story, but how can it be altered except by changing the principle with which they start as their guide? How and in whose name are they to be convinced that danger and disappointment ought to make them stronger, that they have got to fight not for a few years, but for their whole lives? Who shall say to a man, *Go on struggling for your rights,* when to struggle for them costs him dearer than to abandon them?

And even in a society constituted on a juster basis than our own, who shall convince a believer in the theory of *rights* solely that he has to work for the common purpose and devote himself to the development of the social *idea?* Suppose he should rebel; suppose he should feel himself strong and should say to you: *I break the social compact; my inclinations, my faculties, call me elsewhere; I have a sacred and inviolable right to develop them, and I choose to be at war with everybody:* what answer can you give him while he keeps to his theory of rights? What right have you, because you are a majority, to compel his obedience to laws which do not accord with his desires and with his individual aspirations? What right have you to punish him if he violates them? Rights belong equally to every individual; the fact of living together in a community does not create a single one. Society has greater strength, not more rights, than the individual. How, then, are you going to prove to the individual that he must merge his will in the will of those who are his brothers, whether in the Country or in the wider fellowship of Humanity? By means of the executioner, of the prison? Societies existing up till now have used such means. But that is war, and we want peace; that is tyrannical repression, and we want education.

Education, we have said; and this is the great word which sums up our whole doctrine. The vital question agitating our century is a question of education. What we have to do is not to establish a new order of things by violence. An order of things so established is always tyrannical even when it is better than the old. *We have to overthrow by force the brute force which opposes itself to-day to every attempt at improvement,* and then propose for the approval of the nation, free to express its will, what we believe to be the best order of things and by every possible means educate men to develop it and act in conformity with it. The theory of *rights* enables us to rise and overthrow obstacles, but not to found a strong and lasting accord between all the elements which compose the nation. With the theory of happiness, of *well-being,* as the primary aim of existence we shall only form egoistic men, worshippers of the material, who will carry the old passions into the new order of things and corrupt it in a few months. We have therefore to find a principle of education superior to any such theory, which shall guide men to better things, teach them constancy in self-sacrifice and link them with their fellow men without making them dependent on the ideas of a single man or on the strength of all. And this principle is Duty. We must convince men that they, sons of one only God, must obey one only law, here on earth; that each one of them must live, not for himself, but for others; that the object of their life is not to be more or less happy, but to make themselves and others better; that to fight against injustice and error for the benefit of their brothers is not only a *right,* but a *duty;* a duty not to be neglected without sin,—the duty of their whole life.

Italian Working-men, my Brothers! understand me fully. When I say that the knowledge of their *rights* is not enough to enable men to effect any appreciable or lasting improvement, I do not ask you to renounce these rights; I only say that they cannot exist except as a consequence of duties fulfilled, and that one must begin with the latter in order to arrive at the former. And when I say that by proposing *happiness, well-being,* or *material* interest as the aim of existence, we run the risk of producing egoists, I do not mean that you should never strive after these things. I say that material interests pursued alone, and not as a means, but as an end, lead always to this most disastrous result. When under the Emperors, the old Romans asked for nothing but *bread* and *amusements,* they became the most abject race conceivable, and after submitting to the stupid and ferocious tyranny of the Emperors they basely fell into slavery to the invading Barbarians. In France and elsewhere the enemies of all social progress have sown corruption and tried to divert men's minds from ideas of change by furthering the development of *material* activity. And shall we help the enemy with our own hands? Material improvement is essential, and we shall strive to win it for ourselves; but not because the one thing necessary for man is to be well fed and housed, but rather because you cannot have a sense of your own dignity or any moral development while you are engaged, as at the present day, in a continual duel with want. You work ten or twelve hours a day: how can you find *time* to educate yourselves? Most of you earn hardly enough to keep yourselves and your families: how can you then find *means* to educate yourselves? The uncertainty of your employment and the frequent interruptions in it cause you to alternate between too much work and periods of idleness: how are you to acquire habits of order, regularity, and assiduity? The scantiness of your earnings does away with any hope of saving enough to be useful some day to your children, or to your own old age: how are you to educate yourselves into habits of economy? Many of you are compelled by poverty to separate your children, we will not say from the careful bringing-up—what sort of bringing-up can the poor wives of working-men give their children?—but from the love and the watchful eye of their mothers, and to send them out, for the sake of a few halfpence, to unwholesome labour in factories: how, in such conditions, can family affection unfold itself and be ennobled? You have not the rights of citizens, nor any participation, by election or by vote, in the laws which regulate your actions and your life: how should you feel the pride of citizenship or have any zeal for the State, or sincere affection for the laws? Justice is not dealt out to you with the same equal hand as to the other classes: whence, then, are you to learn respect and love for justice? Society treats you without a shadow of sympathy: whence are you to learn sympathy with society? You need, then, a change in your material conditions to enable you to develop morally; you need to work less so as to have some hours of your day to devote to the improvement of your minds;

you need a sufficient remuneration of your labour to put you in a position to accumulate savings, and so set your minds at rest about the future, and to purify yourselves above all of every sentiment of *retaliation,* every impulse of revenge, every thought of injustice towards those who have been unjust to you. You must strive, then, for this change, and you will obtain it, but you must strive for it as a *means,* not as an *end;* strive for it from a sense of *duty,* not only as a *right;* strive for it in order to make yourselves better, not only to make yourselves *materially* happy. If not, what difference would there be between you and your tyrants? They are tyrants precisely because they do not think of anything but *well-being,* pleasure and power.

To make yourselves better; this must be the aim of your life. You cannot make yourselves permanently less unhappy except by improving yourselves. Tyrants will arise by the thousand among you, if you fight only in the name of material interests, or of a particular organisation. A change of social organisation makes little difference if you and the other classes keep the passions and the egoism of to-day; organisations are like certain plants which yield poison or remedies according to the way in which they are administered. Good men make bad organisations good, and bad men make good organisations bad. You have got to improve the classes which, voluntarily or involuntarily, oppress you to-day, and convince them of their duties; but you will never succeed in this unless you begin by making yourselves better as far as possible.

When therefore you hear men who preach the necessity of a social transformation telling you that they can accomplish it by invoking your *rights* only, be grateful to them for their good intentions, but distrustful of the outcome. The ills of the poor man are known, in part at least, to the well-to-do classes; *known* but not *felt.* In the general indifference born of the absence of a common faith; in the egoism, inevitably resulting from the continual preaching through so many years of the doctrine of material *well-being,* those who do not suffer have grown accustomed little by little to consider these ills as a sad necessity of the social order and to leave the trouble of remedying them to the generations to come. The difficulty is not to convince them, but to shake them out of inertia and to induce them, when they are convinced, to *act,* to associate themselves, to unite with you in brotherly fellowship for the purpose of creating such a social organisation as shall put an end, as far as the conditions of humanity allow, to your ills and to their own fears. Now, this is a work of faith, of faith in the mission which God has given to the human creature here upon earth; of faith in the responsibility weighing upon all those who do not fulfil that mission, and in the duty which bids every one work continually, and with self-sacrifice, for the cause of Truth. All possible theories of rights and of material *well-being* can only lead you to attempts which, so long as they remain isolated and dependent on your strength only, will not succeed, but can only bring about the worst of social crimes, a civil war between class and class.

Italian Working-men, my Brothers! When Christ came and changed the face of the world, He did not speak of rights to the rich, who had no need to conquer them; nor to the poor, who would perhaps have abused them, in imitation of the rich. He did not speak of utility or of self-interest to a people whom utility and self-interest had corrupted. He spoke of Duty, He spoke of Love, of Sacrifice, of Faith: He said that *they only should be first among all who had done good to all by their work.* And these thoughts, breathed into the ear of a society which had no longer any spark of life, reanimated it, conquered the millions, conquered the world, and caused the education of the human race to progress a degree. Italian Working-men! we live in an epoch like Christ's. We live in the midst of a society rotten as that of the Roman Empire, and feel in our souls the need of reviving and transforming it, of associating all its members and its workers in one single faith, under one single law, and for one purpose; the free and progressive development of all the faculties which God has planted in His creatures. We seek the reign of God upon earth as in heaven, or better, that the earth shall be a preparation for heaven, and society an endeavour towards a progressive approach to the Divine Idea.

But every act of Christ's represented the faith which He preached, and round Him there were apostles who embodied in their acts the faith which they had accepted. Be such as they, and you will conquer. Preach Duty to the men of the classes above you, and fulfil, as far as possible, your own duties; preach virtue, sacrifice, love; and be yourselves virtuous and prompt to self-sacrifice and love. Declare with courage your needs and your ideas; but without wrath, without vindictiveness, without threats. The most powerful threat, if there are any who need threats, is firm, not angry, speech. While you propagate among your companions the conception of their future destinies, the conception of a nation which will give them a name, education, work, and fair wages, together with the self-respect and vocation of men, while you kindle their spirit for the inevitable struggle for which they must prepare themselves, so that they may conquer all this in spite of all the forces of our evil government and of the foreigner, strive to instruct yourselves, to grow better, and to educate yourselves to the full knowledge and to the practice of your duties. This is an impossible task for the masses in a great part of Italy; no plan of popular education could be realised among us without a change in the material condition of the people, and without a political revolution; they who deceive themselves into hoping for it, and preach it as an indispensable preparation for any attempt at emancipation, preach a gospel of inertia, nothing else. But the few among you whose circumstances are somewhat better, and to whom a sojourn in foreign lands has afforded more liberal means of education, can do it, and therefore ought to do it. And these few, once imbued with the true principles upon which the education of a people depends, will be enough to spread them among the thousands as a guide for their path and a protection from the fallacies and the false doctrines which will come to waylay them.

*   *   *

Duties to Country

Your first Duties—first, at least, in importance—are, as I have told you, to Humanity. You are *men* before you are *citizens* or *fathers*. If you do not embrace the whole human family in your love, if you do not confess your faith in its unity—consequent on the unity of God—and in the brotherhood of the Peoples who are appointed to reduce that unity to fact—if wherever one of your fellowmen groans, wherever the dignity of human nature is violated by falsehood or tyranny, you are not prompt, being able, to succour that wretched one, or do not feel yourself called, being able, to fight for the purpose of relieving the deceived or oppressed—you disobey your law of life, or do not comprehend the religion which will bless the future.

But what can *each* of you, with his isolated powers, *do* for the moral improvement, for the progress of Humanity? You can, from time to time, give sterile expression to your belief; you may, on some rare occasion, perform an act of *charity* to a brother not belonging to your own land, no more. Now, *charity* is not the watchword of the future faith. The watchword of the future faith is *association*, fraternal cooperation towards a common aim, and this is as much superior to *charity* as the work of many uniting to raise with one accord a building for the habitation of all together would be superior to that which you would accomplish by raising a separate hut each for himself, and only helping one another by exchanging stones and bricks and mortar. But divided as you are in language tendencies, habits, and capacities, you cannot attempt this common work. The *individual* is too weak, and Humanity too vast. *My God,* prays the Breton mariner as he puts out to sea, *protect me, my ship is so little, and Thy ocean so great!* And this prayer sums up the condition of each of you, if no means is found of multiplying your forces and your powers of action indefinitely. But God gave you this means when he gave you a Country, when, like a wise overseer of labour, who distributes the different parts of the work according to the capacity of the workmen, he divided Humanity into distinct groups upon the face of our globe, and thus planted the seeds of nations. Bad governments have disfigured the design of God, which you may see clearly marked out, as far, at least, as regards Europe, by the courses of the great rivers, by the lines of the lofty mountains, and by other geographical conditions; they have disfigured it by conquest, by greed, by jealousy of the just sovereignty of others; disfigured it so much that to-day there is perhaps no nation except England and France whose confines correspond to this design.

They did not, and they do not, recognise any country except their own families and dynasties, the egoism of caste. But the divine design will infallibly be fulfilled. Natural divisions, the innate spontaneous tendencies of the peoples will replace the arbitrary divisions sanctioned by bad governments. The map of Europe will be remade. The Countries of the People will rise, defined by the voice of the free, upon the ruins of the Countries of Kings and privileged castes. Between these Countries there will be harmony and brotherhood. And then the work of Humanity for the general amelioration, for the discovery and application of the real law of life, carried on in association and distributed according to local capacities, will be accomplished by peaceful and progressive development; then each of you, strong in the affections and in the aid of many millions of men speaking the same language, endowed with the same tendencies, and educated by the same historic tradition, may hope by your personal effort to benefit the whole of Humanity.

To you, who have been born in Italy, God has allotted, as if favouring you specially, the best-defined country in Europe. In other lands, marked by more uncertain or more interrupted limits, questions may arise which the pacific vote of all will one day solve, but which have cost, and will yet perhaps cost, tears and blood; in yours, no. God has stretched round you sublime and indisputable boundaries; on one side the highest mountains of Europe, the Alps; on the other the sea, the immeasurable sea. Take a map of Europe and place one point of a pair of compasses in the north of Italy on Parma; point the other to the mouth of the Var, and describe a semicircle with it in the direction of the Alps; this point, which will fall, when the semicircle is completed, upon the mouth of the Isonzo, will have marked the frontier which God has given you. As far as this frontier your language is spoken and understood; beyond this you have no rights. Sicily, Sardinia, Corsica, and the smaller islands between them and the mainland of Italy belong undeniably to you. Brute force may for a little while contest these frontiers with you, but they have been recognised from of old by the tacit general consent of the peoples; and the day when, rising with one accord for the final trial, you plant your tricoloured flag

upon that frontier, the whole of Europe will acclaim re-risen Italy, and receive her into the community of the nations. To this final trial all your efforts must be directed.

Without Country you have neither name, token, voice, nor rights, no admission as brothers into the fellowship of the Peoples. You are the bastards of Humanity. Soldiers without a banner, Israelites among the nations, you will find neither faith nor protection; none will be sureties for you. Do not beguile yourselves with the hope of emancipation from unjust social conditions if you do not first conquer a Country for yourselves; where there is no Country there is no common agreement to which you can appeal; the egoism of self-interest rules alone, and he who has the upper hand keeps it, since there is no common safeguard for the interests of all. Do not be led away by the idea of improving your material conditions without first solving the national question. You cannot do it. Your industrial associations and mutual help societies are useful as a means of educating and disciplining yourselves; as an economic fact they will remain barren until you have an Italy. The economic problem demands, first and foremost, an increase of capital and production; and while your Country is dismembered into separate fragments—while shut off by the barrier of customs and artificial difficulties of every sort, you have only restricted markets open to you—you cannot hope for this increase. To-day—do not delude yourselves—you are not the working-class of Italy; you are only fractions of that class; powerless, unequal to the great task which you propose to yourselves. Your emancipation can have no practical beginning until a National Government, understanding the signs of the times, shall, seated in Rome, formulate a Declaration of Principles to be the guide for Italian progress, and shall insert into it these words, *Labour is sacred, and is the source of the wealth of Italy.*

Do not be led astray, then, by hopes of material progress which in your present conditions can only be illusions. Your Country alone, the vast and rich Italian Country, which stretches from the Alps to the farthest limit of Sicily, can fulfil these hopes. You cannot obtain your *rights* except by obeying the commands of *Duty*. Be worthy of them, and you will have them. O my Brothers! love your Country.

Our Country is our home, the home which God has given us, placing therein a numerous family which we love and are loved by, and with which we have a more intimate and quicker communion of feeling and thought than with others; a family which by its concentration upon a given spot, and by the homogeneous nature of its elements, is destined for a special kind of activity. Our Country is our field of labour; the products of our activity must go forth from it for the benefit of the whole earth; but the instruments of labour which we can use best and most effectively exist in it, and we may not reject them without being unfaithful to God's purpose and diminishing our own strength. In labouring according to true principles for our Country we are labouring for Humanity; our Country is the fulcrum of the lever which we have to wield for the common good. If we give up this fulcrum we run the risk of becoming useless to our Country and to Humanity. Before *associating* ourselves with the Nations which compose Humanity we must exist as a Nation. There can be no association except among equals; and you have no recognised collective existence.

Humanity is a great army moving to the conquest of unknown lands, against powerful and wary enemies. The Peoples are the different corps and divisions of that army. Each has a post entrusted to it; each a special operation to perform; and the common victory depends on the exactness with which the different operations are carried out. Do not disturb the order of the battle. Do not abandon the banner which God has given you. Wherever you may be, into the midst of whatever people circumstances may have driven you, fight for the liberty of that people if the moment calls for it; but fight as Italians, so that the blood which you shed may win honour and love, not for you only, but for your Country. And may the constant thought of your soul be for Italy, may all the acts of your life be worthy of her, and may the standard beneath which you range yourselves to work for Humanity be Italy's. Do not say *I;* say *we.* Be every one of you an incarnation of your Country, and feel himself and make himself responsible for his fellow-countrymen; let each one of you learn to act in such a way that in him men shall respect and love his Country.

Your Country is one and indivisible. As the members of a family cannot rejoice at the common table if one of their number is far away, snatched from the affection of his brothers, so you should have no joy or repose as long as a portion of the territory upon which your language is spoken is separated from the Nation.

Your Country is the token of the mission which God has given you to fulfil in Humanity. The faculties, the strength of *all* its sons should be united for the accomplishment of this mission. A certain number of common duties and rights belong to every man who answers to the *Who are you?* of the other peoples, *I am an Italian.* Those duties and those rights cannot be represented except by one *single* authority resulting from your votes. A Country must have, then, a single government. The politicians who call themselves federalists, and who would make Italy into a brotherhood of different states, would dismember the Country, not understanding the idea of Unity. The States into which Italy is divided to-day are not the creation of our own people; they are the result of the ambitions and calculations of princes or of foreign conquerors, and serve no purpose but to flatter the vanity of local aristocracies for which a narrower sphere than a great Country is necessary. What you, the people, have created, beautified, and consecrated with your affections, with your joys, with your sorrows, and with your blood, is the City and the Commune, not the Province or the State. In the City, in the Commune, where your fathers sleep and where your children will live, where you exercise your faculties and your personal rights, you live out your lives as *individuals.* It is of your City that each of you can say what the Venetians say of theirs: *Venezia la xe nostra : l'avemo fatta nu.* In your City you have need of *liberty* as in your Country you have need of *association.* The Liberty of the Commune and the Unity of the Country—let that, then, be your faith. Do not say Rome and Tuscany, Rome and Lombardy, Rome and Sicily; say Rome and Florence, Rome and Siena, Rome and Leghorn, and so through all the Communes of Italy. Rome for all that represents Italian life; your Commune for whatever represents the *individual* life. All the other divisions are artificial, and are not confirmed by your national tradition.

A Country is a fellowship of free and equal men bound together in a brotherly concord of labour towards a single end. You must make it and maintain it such. A Country is not an aggregation, it is an *association.* There is no true Country without a uniform right. There is no true Country where the uniformity of that right is violated by the existence of caste, privilege, and inequality—where the powers and faculties of a large number of individuals are suppressed or dormant—where there is no common principle accepted, recognised, and developed by all. In such a state of things there can be no Nation, no People, but only a multitude, a fortuitous agglomeration of men whom circumstances have brought together and different circumstances will separate. In the name of your love for your Country you must combat without truce the existence of every privilege, every inequality, upon the soil which has given you birth. One privilege only is lawful—the privilege of Genius when Genius reveals itself in brotherhood with Virtue; but it is a privilege conceded by God and not by men, and when you acknowledge it and follow its inspirations, you acknowledge it freely by the exercise of your own reason and your own choice. Whatever privilege claims your submission in virtue of force or heredity, or any right which is not a common right, is a usurpation and a tyranny, and you ought to combat it and annihilate it. Your Country should be your Temple. God at the summit, a People of equals at the base. Do not accept any other formula, any other moral law, if you do not want to dishonour your Country and yourselves. Let the secondary laws for the gradual regulation of your existence be the progressive application of this supreme law.

And in order that they should be so, it is necessary that *all* should contribute to the making of them. The laws made by one fraction of the citizens only can never by the nature of things and men do otherwise than reflect the thoughts and aspirations and desires of that fraction; they represent, not the whole country, but a third, a fourth part, a class, a zone of the country. The law must express the general aspiration, promote the good of all, respond to a beat of the nation's heart. The whole nation therefore should be, directly or indirectly, the legislator. By yielding this mission to a few men, you put the egoism of one class in the place of the Country, which is the union of *all* the classes.

A Country is not a mere territory; the particular territory is only its foundation. The Country is the idea which rises upon that foundation; it is the sentiment of love, the sense of fellowship which binds together all the sons of that territory. So long as a single one of your brothers is not represented by his own vote in the development of the national life—so long as a single one vegetates uneducated among the educated—so long as a single one able and willing to work languishes in poverty for want of work—you have not got a Country such as it ought to be, the Country of all and for all. *Votes, education, work* are the three main pillars of the nation; do not rest until your hands have solidly erected them.

And when they have been erected—when you have secured for every one of you food for both body and soul—when freely united, entwining your right hands like brothers round a beloved mother, you advance in beautiful and holy concord towards the development of your faculties and the fulfilment of the Italian mission—remember that that mission is the moral unity of Europe; remember the immense duties which it imposes upon you. Italy is the only land that has twice uttered the great word of unification to the disjoined nations. Twice Rome has been the metropolis, the temple, of the European world; the first time when our conquering eagles traversed the known world from end to end and prepared it for union by introducing civilised institutions; the second time when, after the Northern conquerors had themselves been subdued by the potency of Nature, of great memories and of religious inspiration, the genius of Italy incarnated itself in the Papacy and undertook the solemn mission—abandoned four centuries ago—of preaching the union of souls to the peoples of the Christian world. To-day a third mission is dawning for our Italy; as much vaster than those of old as the Italian People, the free and united Country which you are going to found, will be greater and more powerful than Caesars or Popes. The presentiment of this mission agitates Europe and keeps the eye and the thought of the nations chained to Italy.

Your duties to your Country are proportioned to the loftiness of this mission. You have to keep it pure from egoism, uncontaminated by falsehood and by the arts of that political Jesuitism which they call diplomacy.

The government of the country will be based through your labours upon the worship of principles, not upon the idolatrous worship of interests and of opportunity. There are countries in Europe where Liberty is sacred within, but is systematically violated without; peoples who say, *Truth is one thing, utility another: theory is one thing, practice another.* Those countries will have inevitably to expiate their guilt in long isolation, oppression, and anarchy. But you know the mission of our Country, and will pursue another path. Through you Italy will have, with one only God in the heavens, one only truth, one only faith, one only rule of political life upon earth. Upon the edifice, sublimer than Capitol or Vatican, which the people of Italy will raise, you will plant the banner of Liberty and of Association, so that it shines in the sight of all the nations, nor will you lower it ever for terror of despots or lust for the gains of a day. You will have boldness as you have faith. You will speak out aloud to the world, and to those who call themselves the lords of the world, the thought which thrills in the heart of Italy. You will never deny the sister nations. The life of the Country shall grow through you in beauty and in strength, free from servile fears and the hesitations of doubt, keeping as its *foundation* the people, as its *rule* the consequences of its principles logically deduced and energetically applied, as its *strength* the strength of all, as its *outcome* the amelioration of all, as its *end* the fulfilment of the mission which God has given it. And because you will be ready to die for Humanity, the life of your Country will be immortal.

Pan Tadeusz

Adam Mickiewicz

Some consider Adam Mickiewicz's Polish national epic, Pan Tadeusz, *to be Europe's last great epic poem (the selection presented here is in prose). The story is set in 1811, when Poland was partitioned between Russia, Prussia, and Austria. Most of the action takes place in a Lithuanian village, previously part of Poland and at that time subject to Russian rule. This highlights the degree to which nationality had not determined state boundaries in the past, a circumstance that caused enormous problems as the new nationalism took hold of people's imaginations. Mickiewicz was an active participant in the cause of Polish liberation.*

The master kept quickening the time and playing with greater power, but suddenly he struck a false chord like the hiss of a snake, like the grating of iron on glass—it sent a shudder through every one, and mingled with the general gaiety an ill-omened foreboding. Disturbed and alarmed, the hearers wondered whether the instrument might not be out of tune, or the musician be making a blunder. Such a master had not blundered! He purposely kept touching that traitorous string and breaking up the melody, striking louder and louder that angry chord, confederated against the harmony of the tones; at last the Warden understood the master, covered his face in his hands, and cried, "I know, I know those notes; that is *Targowica*!" And suddenly the ill-omened string broke with a hiss; the musician rushed to the treble notes, broke up and confused the measure, abandoned the treble notes, and hurried his hammers to the bass strings.

One could hear louder and louder a thousand noises, measured marching, war, an attack, a storm; one could hear the reports of guns, the groans of children, the weeping of mothers. So finely did the wonderful master render the horrors of a storm that

the village girls trembled, calling to mind with tears of grief the Massacre of Praga, which they knew from song and story; they were glad when finally the master thundered with all the strings at once, and choked the outcries as though he had crushed them into the earth.

Hardly did the hearers have time to recover from their amazement, when once more the music changed: at first there were once more light and gentle hummings; a few thin strings complained together, like flies striving to free themselves from the spider's web. But more and more strings joined them; now the scattered tones were blended and legions of chords were united; now they advanced measuredly with harmonious notes, forming the mournful melody of that famous song of the wandering soldier who travels through woods and through forests, ofttimes fainting with woe and with hunger: at last he falls at the feet of his faithful steed, and the steed with his foot digs a grave for him. A poor old song, yet very dear to the Polish troops! The soldiers recognized it, and the privates crowded about the master; they hearkened, and they remembered that dreadful season when over the grave of their country they had sung this song and departed for the ends of the earth; they called to mind their long years of wandering, over lands and seas, over frosts and burning sands, amid foreign peoples, where often in camp they had been cheered

From: Adam Mickiewicz, *Pan Tadeusz* (London and Toronto: J.M. Dent & Sons Ltd., 1917), pp. 325–328.

and heartened by this folk song. So thinking, they sadly bowed their heads!

But they raised them straightway, for the master was playing stronger and higher notes; he changed his measure, and proclaimed something quite different from what had preceded. Once more he looked down and measured the strings with his eye; he joined his hands and smote with the two hammers in unison: the blow was so artistic, so powerful, that the strings rang like brazen trumpets, and from the trumpets a well-known song floated to the heavens, a triumphal march, "Poland has not yet perished; march, Dombrowski, to Poland!"—And all clapped their hands, and all shouted in chorus, "March, Dombrowski!"

The musician seemed amazed at his own song; he dropped the hammers from his hands and raised his arms aloft; his fox-skin cap dropped from his head to his shoulders; his uplifted beard waved majestically; his cheeks glowed with a strange flush; in his glance, full of spirit, shone the fire of youth. At last, when the old man turned his eyes on Dombrowski, he covered them with his hands, and from under his hands gushed a stream of tears.

"General," said he, "long has our Lithuania awaited thee—long, even as we Jews have awaited the Messiah; of thee in olden times minstrels prophesied among the folk; thy coming was heralded by a marvel in the sky. Live and wage war, O thou our—"

As he spoke, he sobbed; the honest Jew loved his country like a Pole! Dombrowski extended his hand to him and thanked him; Jankiel, doffing his cap, kissed the leader's hand.

It was time to begin the polonaise.—The Chamberlain stepped forward, and, lightly throwing back the flowing sleeves of his kontusz and twirling his mustache, he offered his arm to Zosia; with a polite bow he invited her to lead off in the first couple. Behind the Chamberlain a long line of couples formed; the signal was given and the dance began— he was its leader.

Over the greensward glittered his crimson boots, the light gleamed from his sabre and his rich girdle shone; he advanced slowly, with seeming carelessness—yet in every step and every motion one could read the feelings and the thoughts of the dancer. He stopped, as if he wished to question his lady; he bent his head down towards her as if wishing to whisper in her ear; the lady averted her head, was bashful, would not listen; he doffed his white cap and bowed humbly; the lady deigned to gaze upon him, but still kept a stubborn silence; he slackened his pace, followed her glances with his eyes, and at last he laughed.— Happy in her reply, he advanced more quickly, gazing down at his rivals; now he hung his white cap with its heron's plumes over his brow, now he shook it above his brow; at last he cocked it over his ear and twirled his mustache. He strode on; all felt envious of him and pressed upon him in pursuit; he would have been glad to steal away from the throng with his lady; at times he stood still, courteously raised his hand, and humbly begged them to pass by; sometimes he meditated withdrawing adroitly to one side; he often changed his course, and would have been glad to elude his comrades, but they importunately followed him with swift steps, and encircled him from all sides in the evolutions of the dance: so he grew angry, and laid his right hand on his sword hilt, as if to say: "I care not for you; woe to those who are jealous of me!" He turned about with a haughty brow and with a challenge in his eye, and made straight for the throng; the throng of dancers did not dare withstand him, but retired from his path—and, changing their formation, they started again in pursuit of him.—

Cries rang out on all sides: "Ah, perhaps he is the last—watch, watch, you young men—perhaps he is the last who can lead the polonaise in such fashion!" And the couples followed one another merrily and uproariously; the circle would disperse and then contract once more! As when an immense serpent twines into a thousand folds, so there was seen a perpetual change amid the gay, parti-coloured garments of the ladies, the gentlemen, and the soldiers, like glittering scales gilded by the beams of the western sun and relieved against the dark pillows of turf. Brisk was the dance and loud the music, the applause, and the drinking of healths.

Justice for the Irish

Daniel O'Connell

In 1836 Daniel O'Connell, sometimes called the liberator of Ireland, gave the following speech in support of a status for Ireland similar to that already enjoyed by Scotland and England. O'Connell had also struggled for Catholic emancipation in a country in which before 1829 Roman Catholics could not be members of the British House of Commons. After the Catholic Emancipation Act of 1829 and his election to Parliament, O'Connell devoted himself to the Irish cause.

On February 4, 1836, O'Connell gave this speech in the House of Commons calling for equal justice.

━━━━━━━━━━━━━━━━━━━━━━━━━━━━━━━━━━━

It appears to me impossible to suppose that the House will consider me presumptuous in wishing to be heard for a short time on this question, especially after the distinct manner in which I have been alluded to in the course of the debate. If I had no other excuse, that would be sufficient; but I do not want it; I have another and a better—the question is one in the highest degree interesting to the people of Ireland. It is, whether we mean to do justice to that country—whether we mean to continue the injustice which has been already done to it, or to hold out the hope that it will be treated in the same manner as England and Scotland. That is the question. We know what "lip service" is; we do not want that. There are some men who will even declare that they are willing to refuse justice to Ireland; while there are others who, though they are ashamed to say so, are ready to consummate the iniquity, and they do so.

England never did do justice to Ireland—she never did. What we have got of it we have extorted from men opposed to us on principle—against which principle they have made us such concessions as we have obtained from them. The right honorable baronet opposite [Sir Robert Peel] says he does not distinctly understand what is meant by a principle. I believe him. He advocated religious exclusion on religious motives; he yielded that point at length, when we were strong enough to make it prudent for him to do so.

Here am I calling for justice to Ireland; but there is a coalition tonight—not a base unprincipled one—God forbid!—it is an extremely natural one; I mean that between the right honorable baronet and the noble lord the member for North Lancashire [Lord Stanley]. It is a natural coalition, and it is impromptu; for the noble lord informs us he had not even a notion of taking the part he has until the moment at which he seated himself where he now is. I know his candor; he told us it was a sudden inspiration which induced him to take part against Ireland. I believe it with the most potent faith, because I know that he requires no preparation for voting against the interests of the Irish people. [Groans.] I thank you for that groan—it is just of a piece with the rest. I regret much that I have been thrown upon arguing this particular question, because I should have liked to have dwelt upon the speech which has been so graciously delivered from the throne today—to have gone into its details, and to have pointed out the many great

From: *Modern History Sourcebook:* O'Connell: Justice for Ireland, 1836. http://www.fordham.edu/halsall/mod/1836oconnell.html

and beneficial alterations and amendments in our existing institutions which it hints at and recommends to the House. The speech of last year was full of reforms in words, and in words only; but this speech contains the great leading features of all the salutary reforms the country wants; and if they are worked out fairly and honestly in detail, I am convinced the country will require no further amelioration of its institutions, and that it will become the envy and admiration of the world. I, therefore, hail the speech with great satisfaction.

It has been observed that the object of a king's speech is to say as little in as many words as possible; but this speech contains more things than words—it contains those great principles which, adopted in practice, will be most salutary not only to the British Empire, but to the world. When speaking of our foreign policy, it rejoices in the cooperation between France and this country; but it abstains from conveying any ministerial approbation of alterations in the domestic laws of that country which aim at the suppression of public liberty, and the checking of public discussion, such as call for individual reprobation, and which I reprobate as much as any one. I should like to know whether there is a statesman in the country who will get up in this House and avow his approval of such proceedings on the part of the French government. I know it may be done out of the House amid the cheers of an assembly of friends; but the government have, in my opinion, wisely abstained from reprobating such measures in the speech, while they have properly exulted in such a union of the two countries as will contribute to the national independence and the public liberty of Europe.

Years are coming over me, but my heart is as young and as ready as ever in the service of my country, of which I glory in being the pensionary and the hired advocate. I stand in a situation in which no man ever stood yet—the faithful friend of my country—its servant—its stave, if you will—I speak its sentiments by turns to you and to itself. I require no L20,000,000 on behalf of Ireland—I ask you only for justice: will you—can you—I will not say dare you refuse, because that would make you turn the other way. I implore you, as English gentlemen, to take this matter into consideration now, because you never had such an opportunity of conciliating. Experience makes fools wise; you are not fools, but you have yet to be convinced. I cannot forget the year 1825. We begged then as we would for a beggar's boon; we asked for emancipation by all that is sacred amongst us, and I remember how my speech and person were treated on the Treasury Bench, when I had no opportunity of reply. The other place turned us out and sent us back again, but we showed that justice was with us. The noble lord says the other place has declared the same sentiments with himself; but he could not use a worse argument. It is the very reason why we should acquiesce in the measure of reform, for we have no hope from that House—all our hopes are centered in this; and I am the living representative of those hopes. I have no other reason for adhering to the ministry than because they, the chosen representatives of the people of England, are anxiously determined to give the same measure of reform to Ireland as that which England has received. I have not fatigued myself, but the House, in coming forward upon this occasion. I may be laughed and sneered at by those who talk of my power; but what has created it but the injustice that has been done in Ireland? That is the end and the means of the magic, if you please—the groundwork of my influence in Ireland. If you refuse justice to that country, it is a melancholy consideration to me to think that you are adding substantially to that power and influence, while you are wounding my country to its very heart's core; weakening that throne, the monarch who sits upon which, you say you respect; severing that union which, you say, is bound together by the lightest links, and withholding that justice from Ireland which she will not cease to seek till it is obtained; every man must admit that the course I am taking is the legitimate and proper course—I defy any man to say it is not. Condemn me elsewhere as much as you please, but this you must admit. You may taunt the ministry with having coalesced me, you may raise the vulgar cry of "Irishman and Papist" against me, you may send out men called ministers of God to slander and calumniate me; they may assume whatever garb they please, but the question comes into this narrow compass. I demand, I respectfully insist: on equal justice for Ireland, on the same principle by which it has been administered to Scotland and England. I will not take less. Refuse me that if you can.

The French Revolution in 1848
Percy St. John

An Englishman, Percy B. St. John witnessed the 1848 revolution in France. As elsewhere in 1848, the revolutionaries wanted more liberty, a more clearly defined nation, or some combination of the two. The revolutions seemed to be a final break with the ancien regime, *but, as St. John reported, the French revolution and many others across Europe would be countered and defeated by conservative forces.*

Percy B. St. John was an eyewitness to the events herein described, and the following were taken from his notes compiled at the time.

Tuesday, February 22. The journals of the opposition appeared with the notice, in large letters, at the head of their papers, that the banquet was given up, and an appeal to the population of Paris to keep order, formed a very prominent part of the announcement. The Left were evidently alarmed, while ministers were confident and their journals sang a triumphant song of victory. From an early hour detachments of municipal guard, troops of the line and cavalry, were seen moving toward the boulevards and the Chamber of Deputies; it became known that heavy squadrons of cavalry had entered Paris during the night, while others were concealed within the Hippodrome, or were bivouacked round the fortifications. The spies of the government reported during the night that there was a total absence of conspiracy....

The weather was disagreeable, even wet. A somber and threatening sky hung over the town, but from six in the morning the boulevards presented an animated appearance. Crowds of workingmen, of shopkeepers, began to move toward the

Church of the Madeleine, in front of which the procession was to have met and formed. Many were not aware that the banquet was given up, and went to witness the departure of the cortege, while those who knew that the opposition had abandoned their intention of holding the meeting, went with a vague desire to see what would happen. Hundreds went with a settled determination to bring things to an issue; for early on Tuesday morning I saw swords, and daggers, and pistols concealed under the blouses of the workingmen....

Between nine and ten I walked to the Place de la Madeleine. It was covered with knots of men and women of all classes, talking, whispering, looking about with a vague air of uncertainty and alarm....

The neighborhood of the Chamber of Deputies were then occupied militarily. A strong force was placed upon the Pont de la Concorde, and on attempting to pass, I and others were driven back by the military. No one was allowed to cross save deputies, who carried their medals, or persons bearing tickets. The other approaches to the legislature were equally well guarded. Between the Quai d'Orsay and the Invalides, two regiments of the line and six pieces of artillery were stationed.

Meanwhile, everywhere the crowd increased; all Paris seemed moving to the boulevards, to the

From: *Modern History Sourcebook:* Percy B. St. John: The French Revolution in 1848. http://www.fordham.edu/halsall/mod/1848johnson.html

Madeleine, to the Champs Elysees, and to the Place de la Concorde. As yet there was no menacing aspect in the masses, many artisans, with their wives on their arms, hung about looking on and listening. Not a policeman in uniform was seen, but many a *mouchard* face could be distinguished in the crowd.

About ten o'clock, a considerable body of workmen, and young men belonging to the different schools of Paris collected on the Place du Pantheon, and set out for the Madeleine by the Rues St. Jacques, des Gres, the Pont Neuf, the Rue St. Honore, etc., crying as they went, Vive la Reforme, and singing the Marseillaise and the chant of the Girondins. . . .

This procession, which had gradually swelled as it went, came out upon the boulevards by the Rue Duphot, and as they passed, it was impossible not to admire the courage of this body of young men, who, wholly unarmed, thus braved the strict orders of a government, backed by an immense army and whole parks of artillery. They were liable at every moment to be charged or fired on. . . .

Having reached the Madeleine, the procession halted before the house in which the central committee of the electors of the opposition were in the habit of assembling, and asked for Barrot, who, however, was not there. The Ministry of Foreign Affairs, up to the time this procession passed before its door, had the gate open, with soldiers standing before utterly unarmed. . . .

An officer of dragoons advanced alone to a large group of spectators, who were collected in the basin of one of the fountains, and begged them to retire, which many of them at once did. A few persisted; but suddenly the water beginning to play, they jumped out amid loud laughter. In fact, with few exceptions, the crowd, amidst whom were many well-dressed ladies and gentlemen, were excessively good humored. The majority seemed persuaded that the vast display of unarmed Parisians who had turned out would induce the ministry to give way. The municipal guard, however, like the gendarmes and Swiss of the July Revolution, seemed doomed to mar all. This body, detested by the Parisians as police, kept up continued charges upon the crowd as it gradually dispersed.

About twelve, passing by the Ministry of Foreign Affairs, I noticed, in the back court, a heavy detachment of dragoons, in addition to which, soon after, the front door was closed and guarded by numerous sentries. A powerful mob, with sticks and iron bars, strove to burst open the gate and inflict summary vengeance on Guizot. The windows were broken with stones. Loud cries of *Vive la Reforme!* were followed by *a bas Guizot!* A single municipal guard strove to get out at the front gate, as if to go for a reinforcement. He was pelted with stones and driven back within shelter of the hotel [i.e., the Ministry].

About this time a most imposing military force marched down upon the hotel, which assumed the air of a fortress. A line of soldiers, with their arms loaded and bayonets fixed, occupied the pavement. The long garden wall was guarded by a cordon of troops, and municipal guards on horseback stood before the door. These latter took up their position with so much carelessness, as to knock down and severely wound one of the crowd. Shortly after, one of these police having rushed out to seize a rioter, was unhorsed and severely handled, after which he was taken to the same doctor's shop where was the wounded man of the people. From that moment all disturbance finished on this point for the day, and Guizot was able to go to the Chamber of Deputies. The passengers were in this neighborhood compelled to turn out on to the carriage way, the whole pavement being occupied by soldiers. . . .

At this very time [about three], having returned to my residence to write a letter, I was witness to a scene, which described minutely, may give an idea of many similar events. My residence is situated in the Rue St. Honore. . . . Called to my window by a noise, I saw several persons standing at the horses' heads of an omnibus. The driver whipped, and tried to drive on. The people insisted. At length, several policemen in plain clothes interfered, and as the party of the people was small, disengaged the omnibus, ordered the passengers to get out, and sent the vehicle home amid the hootings of the mob. A few minutes later, a cart full of stones and gravel came up. A number of boys seized it, undid the harness, and it was placed instantly in the middle of the street, amid loud cheering. A brewer's dray and hackney cab were in brief space of time added, and the barricade was made. The passers-by continued to move along with the most perfect indifference. . . .

Next door to me is an armorer's. Suddenly the people perceived the words *Prelat, armourier*, over the door. A rush is made at his shutters, stones are raised at his windows, and those of the house he occupied, many of which smash the panes in neighboring houses. Every window is, however, filled by anxious spectators. Suddenly the shutters of the shop give way, they are torn down and borne to the barricade, while the windows being smashed, the people rush into the warehouse. There are no arms! The night before they have been removed or concealed. Still, a few horns of gunpowder, and some swords and pistols are taken. Though the mob was through the whole of the vast hotel, a portion of which was occupied by the armorer, nothing but arms were taken away. . . .

On Wednesday, however, it was impossible to conceal from the Iiing that the movement was general, that the people were flying to arms, that barricades were rising in every quarter, and worse than all, the colonels of the national guard reported, one after another, that their men demanded, nay, insisted on the dismissal of Guizot. The generals of the line were interrogated. Not one would answer for the troops if the national guard sided with the people. The saying of an artillery officer near the Hotel de Ville was reported "Fire on the people? No! Fire on the people who pay us? We shall do nothing of the kind. If we have to choose between massacring our brothers and abandoning the monarchy, there can be no hesitation." Louis Philippe saw the critical nature of the position, and hesitated no longer. Guizot and his colleagues were dismissed. . . .

Toward seven o'clock, the general aspect of Paris was peaceable. On the Petit Bourse, near the Opera, the funds had risen forty centimes on the arrival of the news that the ministry had been dismissed. Aides-de-camp and general officers galloped here and there, proclaiming the intelligence. Everywhere the people delivered the prisoners made during the day, and then they went away rejoicing.

Nevertheless, the barricades were not abandoned. The strongest and most artistically made were guarded by some hundreds of young men, between the Rue du Temple and the Rue St. Martin, and about the Rue Transnonain. Though repeatedly told of the dismissal of Guizot, they replied that they must have guarantees, and with this they posted sentries at every issue, and prepared to bivouac for the night, many without food, many without fire. Among these were numbers of the better classes, who had placed blouses over their clothes and joined the people, to encourage and direct them.

Between eight and nine o'dock, darkness having completely set in, the streets began to present an unusual aspect—that of an illumination. With rare exceptions, at every window of the lofty houses on the quarter of the Tuileries, candles or lamps were placed, and by their light could be seen ladies and gentlemen looking down upon the dense and happy crowd who filled the streets to overflowing. Loud cheers greeted the presence of the spectators, while groans and threats of demolishing their windows were the punishment of the sulky few who refused to join in the general manifestation. They gained nothing by it but to let their ill will be seen, for the populace compelled them to follow the general example. All, however, was gayety and good humor.

After witnessing the fine *coup-d'oeil* presented by the Rue St. Honore, the longest street in the world, I believe, I attempted to gain the boulevards by the Place Vendome. I found it, however, occupied by a dense mass of some ten thousand men, who were striving to force the denizens of the Hotel de Justice to light up. As no attention was paid to their demand, and Hebert [minister of Justice] was peculiarly hated, they began to break his windows, and even set fire to the planks which shelved off from the door, as well as to the sentry box. A heavy body of cuirassiers however, and several detachments of national guards came down, and using vigorous, but gentle measures, re-established order. To lessen the crowd, they drew a line across the Rue Castiglione, and allowed no one to pass. Standing in the crowd, I heard many republicans conversing. Their tone was that of bitter disappointment. They said that the people were deceived, that a Molé ministry was a farce, and that if the populace laid down their arms, it would be but to take them up again. Still, the majority rejoiced. To have carried this point was a great thing, and no greater proof of the patriotism of the workingmen can be given. They gained nothing by the change but mental satisfaction, with which a vast majority seemed amply satisfied.

But a terrible and bloody tragedy was about to change the aspect of the whole scene. . . .

Wednesday, February 23d. About a quarter past ten, while on my way, by another route, to the boulevards, I suddenly, with others, was startled by the aspect of a gentleman who, without his hat, ran madly into the middle of the street, and began to harangue the passersby. "To arms!" he cried, "we are betrayed. The soldiers have slaughtered a hundred unarmed citizens by the Hôtel des Capucines. Vengeance!" and having given the details of the affair, he hurried to carry the intelligence to other quarters. The effect was electric; each man shook his neighbor by the hand, and far and wide the word was given that the whole system must fall.

As this tragic event sealed the fate of the Orleans dynasty, I have been at some pains to collect a correct version of it, and I have every reason to believe those who were eyewitnesses will bear me out in my description. I went immediately as near to the spot as possible, I conversed to numerous parties who saw it, and myself saw many of the immediate consequences.

The boulevards were, like all the other streets, brilliantly illuminated, and everywhere immense numbers of promenaders walked up and down, men, women, and children, enjoying the scene, and rejoicing that the terrific struggle of the day had ceased. The footpaths were quite covered, while the carriage way, in part occupied by cavalry, was continually filled by processions of students, working men, and others, who sang songs of triumph at their victory. Round the Hôtel des Capucines, where Guizot resided, there was a heavy force of military, of troops of the line, dragoons, and municipal guard, who occupied the pavement and forced everyone on to the carriage way. A vast crowd, principally of accidental spectators, ladies, gentlemen, English, etc., in fact curious people in general, were stationed watching a few men and boys who tried to force the inmates to light up.

For some time all was tranquil, but presently a column of students and artisans, unarmed, but singing *"Mourir pour la patrie,"* came down the boulevards; at the same instant a gun was heard, and the 14th Regiment of Line leveled their muskets and fired. The scene which followed was awful. Thousands of men, women, children, shrieking, bawling, raving, were seen flying in all directions, while sixty-two men, women, and lads, belonging to every class of society, lay weltering in their blood upon the pavement. Next minute an awful roar, the first breath of popular indignation was heard, and then flew the students, artisans, the shopkeepers, all, to carry the news to the most distant parts of the city, and to rouse the population to arms against a government whose satellites murdered the people in this atrocious manner.

A squadron of cuirassiers now charged, sword in hand, over dead and wounded, amid useless cries of "Mind the fallen," and drove the people before them. The sight was awful. Husbands were seen dragging their fainting wives from the scene of massacre; fathers snatching up their children, with pale faces and clenched teeth, hurried away to put their young ones in safety, and then to come out in arms against the monarchy. Women clung to railings, trees, or to the wall, or fell fainting on the stones. More than a hundred persons who saw the soldiers level, fell in time to save their lives, and then rose and hastened to quit the spot. Utter strangers shook hands and congratulated one another on their escape.

In a few minutes, a deputy of the opposition, Courtais, now commanding the national guard, was on the spot and making inquiries into the cause of this fearful affair. "Sir," said he, warmly addressing the colonel in command, "you have committed an action, unworthy of a French soldier." The Colonel, overwhelmed with sorrow and shame, replied, that the order to fire was a mistake. It appeared that a ball, from a gun which went off accidentally, had struck his horse's leg, and that thinking he was attacked, he had ordered a discharge. "Monsieur le Colonel," added the honorable deputy, "you are a soldier, I believe in your good faith; but remember that an awful responsibility rests on your head." Tremendous indeed, for he had sealed the fate of the tottering monarchy!

A word before we proceed. When the proclamation was made that the Guizot ministry had been dismissed, the military were gradually withdrawn, and wherever this occurred, tranquility followed. No serious attacks were made upon any public building; in fact, the people contented themselves with breaking a few windows; everywhere the cry "Light the lamps," was not obeyed. Guizot, however, conscious of the intense hatred which was felt toward him, kept his house guarded like a fortress. The display of military force was tremendously imposing, both within and without the hotel. Had none been stationed outside, whatever he had in, the causes which kept crowds standing round, would have been removed, and the people would not have been irritated. It was the overcare of his own person shown by Guizot, which caused this frightful catastrophe. Like every other event of this great week, with all its momentous conse-quences, this is to be traced to the utter incapacity of Guizot, in politics. . . .

Meanwhile, Courtais had hurried to the *National* office, while a body of men, now no longer hindered by the soldiers, proceeded to remove the heaps of dead and dying, whose groans must have been plainly heard by the ex-minister in his hotel. The wounded, and those bodies which were claimed, were borne to houses in the neighborhood, while some of the national guards in uniform were carried to their respective town halls, everywhere as the bloody banner of insurrections. Seventeen corpses, however, were retained and placed upon a cart. Ghastly was the spectacle of torch and gaslight, of that heap of dead, a few minutes before alive, merry, anxious, full of hopes, and perhaps, lofty aspirations for their country. Round about were men, no less pale and ghastly, bearing pikes and torches, while others drew the awful cartload along.

PART SIX

Photograph of the Arrest of Emmeline Pankhurst

Once again a picture captures a reality better than words. Victorian England had an almost courtly attitude toward the interrelationships between men and women. It was unthinkable that in public a woman, indeed a woman of a privileged class, could be arrested and literally picked up bodily and hauled away by men. That this occured suggests the extent to which women such as the Pankhursts challenged male-dominated society.

Gender: Women's Spheres and the Male Role

A few exceptional women made their mark in nineteenth-century Europe. As always, poor rural and urban women toiled arduously. Millions entered the industrial workforce, only to face a new stark exploitation. Middle- and upper-class women contended with male control. Society fully accepted women's endeavors only on the domestic scene (household tasks, raising children, and pleasing husbands), charitable work being a single exception. Regardless, European liberation movements eventually addressed the plight of women, especially of the laboring classes. Later in the century, with the advent of universal male suffrage, a powerful movement arose for female voting rights. After World War I, this movement finally attained its goal, although full equal rights for women came neither easily, quickly, nor fully. European women's problems played out against the backdrop of society's attitudes about male roles: men firmly occupied a predominant position in the public and private spheres.

Before mid-century, social commentator Flora Tristan (1803–1844) portrayed the plight of laboring women, as did Gaskell's *Mary Barton* (see earlier section). In her 1840 essay "Why I Mention Women," Tristan noted the historically debased status of women, often viewed as bestial in mental and spiritual capacities. Only equal rights and education, claimed Tristan, would eliminate poor women's frequent resort to prostitution and criminality. In her *The Book of Household Management* (1861), Isabella Beeton (1836–1865) meticulously detailed Victorian conceptions of middle class women's roles. During later decades, women of an educated English family, Emmeline, Sylvia, and Christabel Pankhurst, fashioned a critical analysis to include questions of suffrage for all women, an example of which is "Why We Are Militant" (1913) by Emmeline Pankhurst (1858–1928). The Pankhursts also resorted to militant activism. Society's response is illustrated by the image of the police unceremoniously carrying the arrested Emmeline from the site of one of her demonstrations. In *Anna Karenina* (1878), Leo Tolstoy (1828–1910) meticulously sketches the problems confronting upper-class women despite their privilege. In almost contemporary terms, Henrik Ibsen (1828–1906) presents an unflattering picture of middle-class married life in *A Doll's House* (1879). Although not impoverished, the women in this play face toil, sacrifice, and risk. Ibsen's portrayal of a woman abandoning her husband, children, and home for the purpose of self-fulfillment shocked contemporary Europe. Throughout the century, novelists such as Balzac, Hardy, Eliot, and many others portrayed women's experiences. The short story "Carsten Curator" (1877) by Theodor Storm (1817–1888) elucidates expectations about males as honorable men of affairs and managers of women's financial lives: responsibilities were great and the cost of failure high.

Study Questions

1. What issues faced all nineteenth-century women?
2. What problems separated Tristan's women from those portrayed by Mrs. Beeton and Tolstoy?
3. Why did Pankhurst insist on violence in support of women's voting rights?
4. How would Ibsen's heroine be viewed in today's society?
5. What stands out in Storm's portrayal of a middle-class man?
6. Image: What does the image of Pankhurst's arrest suggest about social attitudes towards women?

Why I Mention Women

Flora Tristan

Tristan coupled her concern for the plight of workers with her feminism. In writings such as this selection, Tristan revealed the horrendous oppression visited upon women, who were considered to be morally incompetent and virtual beasts of burden. In this case, she specifically addressed working men, who had good reason to know the hardships of women in their own families. Full equality and education were the solutions.

Workers, you my brothers, for whom I work with love, because you represent the most vital, numerous, and useful part of humanity, and because from that point of view I find my own satisfaction in serving your cause, I beg you earnestly to read this with the greatest attention. For, you must be persuaded, it concerns your material interests to understand why when I mention women I always designate them as *female workers* or *all the women*.

The intelligent person enlightened by rays of divine love and love for humanity, can easily grasp the logical chain of relationships that exist between causes and effects. For him, all of philosophy and religion can be summed up by two questions: First, how can and must one love God and serve Him for the universal well-being of all men and women? Second, how can and must one love and treat woman, for the sake of all men and women? Asked in this manner, these two questions, with respect to natural order, underlie everything produced in the moral and physical worlds (one results or flows from the other).

I don't believe this is the place to answer these two questions. Later, if the workers wish it, I shall gladly treat metaphysically and philosophically questions of the highest order. But, for the time being, one need only pose the questions, as the formal declaration of an absolute principle. Without going directly back to causes, let us limit our analysis to the effects.

From: Flora Tristan, *The Workers' Union*, translated by Beverly Livingston (Urbana: University of Illinois Press, 1983), pp. 75–88.

Up to now, woman has counted for nothing in human society. What has been the result of this? That the priest, the lawmaker, and the philosopher have treated her as a true *pariah*. Woman (one half of humanity) has been cast out of the Church, out of the law, out of society. For her, there are no functions in the Church, no representation before the law, no functions in the State. The priest told her, "Woman, you are temptation, sin, and evil; you represent flesh, that is, corruption and rottenness. Weep for your condition, throw ashes on your head, seek refuge in a cloister, and mortify your heart, which is made for love, and your female organs, which are made for motherhood. And when thus you have mutilated your heart and body, offer them all bloody and dried up to your God for remission from the original sin committed by your mother Eve." Then the lawmaker tells her, "Woman, by yourself you are nothing; you have no active role in human affairs; you cannot expect to find a seat at the social banquet. If you want to live, you must serve as an appendage to your lord and master, man. So, young girl, you will obey your father; when married you shall obey your husband; widowed and old, you will be left alone." Then, the learned philosopher tells her, "Woman, it has been scientifically observed that, according to your constitution, you are inferior to man. Now, you have no intelligence, no comprehension for lofty questions, no logic in ideas, no ability for the so-called exact sciences, no aptitude for serious endeavors. Finally, you are a feeble-minded and weak-bodied being, cowardly, superstitious; in a word, you are nothing but a capricious child, spontaneous, frivolous, for ten or fifteen years of your life you are a nice little doll, but full of faults and vices. That is why, woman, man must be your master and have complete authority over you."

So that is how for the six thousand years the world has existed, the wisest among the wise have judged the female race.

Such a terrible condemnation, repeated for six thousand years, is likely to impress the masses, for the sanction of time has great authority over them. However, what must make us hope that this sentence can be repealed is that the wisest of the wise have also for six thousand years pronounced a no less horrible verdict upon another race of humanity—the proletariat. Before 1789, what was the proletarian in French society? A serf, a peasant, who was made into a taxable, drudging beast of burden. Then came the Revolution of 1789, and all of a sudden the wisest of the wise proclaimed that the lower orders are to be called the *people,* that the serfs and peasants are to be called *citizens.* Finally, they proclaimed the *rights of man* in full national assembly.

The proletarian, considered until then a brute, was quite surprised to learn that it had been the neglect and scorn for his rights that had caused all the world's misfortunes. He was quite surprised to learn that he would enjoy civil, political, and social rights, and finally would become the *equal* of his former lord and master. His surprise grew when he was told that he possessed a brain of the same quality as the royal prince's. What a change! However, it did not take long to realize that this second judgment on the proletariat was truer than the first. Hardly had they proclaimed that proletarians were capable of all kinds of civil, military, and social functions, than out of their ranks came generals the likes of which Charlemagne, Henri IV, and Louis XIV could not recruit from the ranks of their proud and brilliant nobility. Then, as if by magic, from the ranks of the proletariat surged learned men, artists, poets, writers, statesmen, and financiers who gave France a luster she had never had. Then military glory came upon her like a halo; scientific discoveries enriched her; the arts embellished her; her commerce made immense strides, and in less than thirty years the wealth of the country trebled. These facts cannot be disputed: everyone agrees today that men are born indistinct, with essentially equal faculties, and that the sole thing we should be concerned about is how to develop an individual's total faculties for the sake of the general well-being.

What happened to the proletariat, it must be agreed, is a good omen for women when their "1789" rings out. According to a very simple calculation, it is obvious that wealth will increase immeasurably on the day women are called upon to participate with their intelligence, strength, and ability in the social process. This is as easy to understand as two is the double of one. But, alas! We are not yet there. Meanwhile, let us take a look at what is happening in 1843.

The Church having said that woman was sin; the lawmaker that by herself she was nothing, that she was to enjoy no rights; the learned philosopher that by her constitution she had no intellect, it was concluded that she is a poor being disinherited by God; so men and society treated her as such.

Once woman's inferiority was proclaimed and postulated, notice what disastrous consequences resulted for the universal well-being of all men and women.

Those who believed that woman by nature lacked the strength, intelligence, and capacity to do serious and useful work, very logically deduced that it would be a waste of time to give her a rational, solid, and strict education, the kind that would make her a useful member of society. So she has been raised to be a nice doll and a slave destined for amusing and serving her master. In truth, from time to time some intelligent, sensitive men, showing empathy with their mothers, wives, and daughters, have cried out against the barbarity and absurdity of such an order of things, energetically protesting against such an iniquitous condemnation. On several occasions, society has been moved for a moment; but when pushed by logic, has replied, "Well then! Let us suppose that women are not what the wise men have believed, that they have great moral strength and intelligence. Well, in that case, what good would it be to develop their faculties, since they would not be able to employ them usefully in this society which rejects them? What an awful torture, to feel one has force and power to act, and to see oneself condemned to inaction!"

This reasoning was irrefutably true. So everyone repeated, "It's true, women would suffer too much if their God-given talents were developed, if from childhood on they were raised to understand their dignity and to be conscious of their value as members of society. Then never would they be able to bear the degradation imposed upon them by the Church, the law, and prejudice. It is better to treat them like children and leave them in the dark about themselves: they will suffer less."

Follow closely, and you will see what horrible consequences result from accepting a false premise.

In order not to stray too far from my subject, even though it is a good opportunity to speak from a general standpoint, I am returning to the question of the working class.

In the life of the workers, woman is everything. She is their sole providence. If she is gone, they lack everything. So they say, "It is woman who makes or unmakes the home," and this is the clear truth: that is why it has become a proverb. However, what education, instruction, direction, moral or physical development does the working-class woman receive? None. As a child, she is left to the mercy of a mother and grandmother who also have received no education. One of them might have a brutal and wicked disposition and beat and mistreat her for no reason; the other might be weak and uncaring, and let her do anything. (As with everything I am suggesting, I am speaking in general terms; of course, there are numerous exceptions.) The poor child will be raised among the most shocking contradictions—hurt by unfair blows and treatment one day, then pampered and spoiled no less perniciously the next.

Instead of being sent to school, she is kept at home in deference to her brothers and so that she can share in the housework, rock the baby, run errands, or watch the soup, etc. At the age of twelve she is made an apprentice. There she continues to be exploited by her mistress and often continues to be as mistreated as she was at home.

Nothing embitters the character, hardens the heart, or makes the spirit so mean as the continuous suffering a child endures from unfair and brutal treatment. First, the injustice hurts, afflicts, and causes despair; then when it persists, it irritates and exasperates us and finally, dreaming only of revenge, we end up by becoming hardened, unjust, and wicked. Such will be the normal condition for a poor girl of twenty. Then she will marry, without

love, simply because one must marry in order to get out from under parental tyranny. What will happen? I suppose she will have children, and she, in turn, will be unable to raise them suitably. She will be just as brutal to them as her mother and grandmother were to her.

Working class women, take note, I beg you, that by mentioning your ignorance and incapacity to raise your children, I have no intention in the least of accusing *you* or *your nature*. No, I am accusing society for leaving you uneducated—you, women and mothers, who actually need so much to be instructed and formed in order to be able to instruct and develop the men and children entrusted to your care.

Generally women of the masses are brutal, mean, and sometimes hard. This being true, where does this situation come from, so different from the sweet, good, sensitive, and generous nature of woman?

Poor working women! They have so many reasons to be irritated! First, their husbands. (It must be agreed that there are few working-class couples who are happily married.) Having received more instruction, being the head by law and also by the money he brings home, the husband thinks he is (and he is, in fact) very superior to his wife, who only brings home her small daily wage and is merely a very humble servant in her home.

Consequently, the husband treats his wife with nothing less than great disdain. Humiliated by his every word or glance, the poor woman either openly or silently revolts, depending upon her personality. This creates violent, painful scenes that end up producing an atmosphere of constant irritation between the master and the slave (one can indeed say *slave,* because the woman is, so to speak, her husband's property). This state becomes so painful that, instead of staying home to talk with his wife, the husband hurries out; and as if he had no other place to go, he goes to the tavern to drink blue wine in the hope of getting drunk, with the other husbands who are just as unhappy as he.

This type of distraction makes things worse. The wife, waiting for payday (Sunday) to buy weekly provisions for the family, is in despair seeing her husband spend most of the money at the tavern. Then she reaches a peak of irritation, and her brutality and wickedness redouble. You have to have personally seen these working-class households (especially the bad ones) to have an idea of the husband's misfortune and the wife's suffering. It passes from reproaches and insults to blows, then tears; from discouragement to despair.

And following the acute chagrins caused by the husband come the pregnancies, illnesses, unemployment, and poverty, planted by the door like Medusa's head. Add to all that the endless tension provoked by four or five loud, turbulent, and bothersome children clamoring about their mother, in a small worker's room too small to turn around in. My! One would have to be an angel from heaven not to be irritated, not to become brutal and mean in such a situation. However, in this domestic setting, what becomes of the children? They see their father only in the evening or on Sunday. Always either upset or drunk, their father speaks to them only angrily and gives them only insults and blows. Hearing their mother continuously complain, they begin to feel hatred and scorn for her. They fear and obey her, but they do not love her, for a person is made that way—he cannot love someone who mistreats him. And isn't it a great misfortune for a child not to be able to love his mother! If he is unhappy, to whose breast will he go to cry? If he thoughtlessly makes a bad mistake or is led astray, in whom can he confide? Having no desire to stay close to his mother, the child will seek any pretext to leave the parental home. Bad associations are easy to make, for girls as for boys. Strolling becomes vagrancy, and vagrancy often becomes thievery.

Among the poor girls in houses of prostitution and the poor men moaning in jails, how many can say, "If we had had a *mother able to raise us*, then we would not be here."

I repeat, woman is everything in the life of a worker. As mother, she can influence him during his childhood. She and only she is the one from whom he gets his first notions of that science which is so important to acquire—the science of life, which teaches us how to live well for ourselves and for others, according to the milieu in which fate has placed us. As lover, she can influence him during his youth, and what a powerful influence could be exerted by a young, beautiful, and beloved girl! As wife, she can have an effect on him for three-quarters of his life. Finally, as daughter, she can act upon him in his old age. Note that the worker's

position is very different from an idle person's. If the rich child has a mother unable to raise him, he is placed in a boarding school or given a governess. If the young rich fellow has no mistress, he can busy his heart and imagination with studying the arts and sciences. If the rich man has no spouse, he does not fail to find distractions in society. If the old rich man has no daughter, he finds some old friends or young nephews who willingly come and play cards with him; whereas the worker, for whom all these pleasures are denied, has only the company of the women in his family, his companions in misfortune, for all his joy and solace. The result of this situation is that it would be most important, from the point of view of intellectually, morally, and materially improving the working class, that the women receive from childhood a rational and solid education, apt to develop all their potential so that they can become skilled in their trades, good mothers capable of raising and guiding their children and to be for them, as *La Presse* says, free and natural schoolteachers, and also so that they can serve as moralizing agents for the men whom they influence from birth to death.

Are you beginning to understand, you men, who cry scandal before being willing to examine the issue, why I demand rights for women? Why I would like women placed in society on a footing of *absolute equality* with men to enjoy the legal birthright all beings have? I call for woman's rights because I am convinced that *all* the misfortunes in the world come from this neglect and scorn shown until now for the natural and inalienable rights of woman. I call for woman's rights because it is the only way to have her educated, and woman's education depends upon man's in general, and particularly the working-class man's. I call for woman's rights because it is the only way to obtain her rehabilitation before the church, the law, and society, and this rehabilitation is necessary before working men themselves can be rehabilitated. All working-class ills can be summed up in two words: poverty and ignorance. Now in order to get out of this maze, I see only one way: begin by educating women, because the women are in charge of instructing boys and girls.

Workers, in the current state of things, you know what goes on in your households. You, the master with rights over your wife, do you live with her with a contented heart? Say, are you happy? No, it is easy to see, in spite of your rights, you are neither contented nor happy. Between master and slave there can only be the weariness of the chain's weight tying them together. Where the lack of freedom is felt, happiness cannot exist.

Men always complain about the bad moods and the devious and silently wicked characters women show in all their relationships. Oh, would I have a very bad opinion of women, if in the state of abjection where the law and customs place them, they were to submit without a murmur to the yoke weighing on them! Thanks be to God, that it is not so! Their protest, since the beginning of time, has always been relentless. But since the declaration of the rights of man, a solemn act proclaiming the neglect and scorn the new men gave to women, their protest has taken on new energy and violence which proves that the slave's exasperation has peaked.

Workers, you who have good sense and with whom one can reason, because, as Fourier says, you do not have minds stuffed with systems, suppose for a moment that by right woman is the equal of man? What would come of that? (1) That as soon as one would no longer have to fear the dangerous consequences necessarily caused by the moral and physical development of woman's faculties because of her current enslavement, she would be carefully educated so as to bring out the best possible in her intelligence and work; (2) that you, men of the people, you would have clever workers for mothers, earning a good wage, instructed, well-raised and very able to teach and raise you, workers, as it is appropriate for free men; (3) that your sisters, lovers, wives, and friends would be educated, well-raised women whose daily companionship would be most pleasant for you, for nothing is sweeter or gentler to a man's heart than a woman's conversation when she is well educated, good, and speaks with logic and benevolence.

We have quickly glanced over what is currently going on in the workers' households. Let us now examine what would occur in these same households if woman were man's equal.

Knowing that his wife has rights equal to his, the husband would not treat her anymore with the disdain and scorn shown to inferiors. On the contrary, he would treat her with the respect and deference one grants to equals. Then the woman will no longer have cause for irritation; and once that is destroyed, she will no longer appear brutal, devious, grouchy, angry, exasperated, or mean. No longer considered the husband's servant at home, but his associate, friend, and companion, she will naturally take an interest in the association and do all she can to make the little household flourish. With theoretical and practical knowledge, she will employ all her intelligence to keep her house neat, economical, and pleasant. Educated and aware of the utility of an education, she will put all her ambition into raising her children well. She will lovingly teach them herself, watch over their schoolwork, and place them in good apprenticeships; and finally, she will always guide them with care, tenderness, and discernment. Then what a contented heart, peace of mind, and happy soul the man, the husband, the worker will have who possesses such a woman! Finding his wife has intelligence, common sense and educated opinions, he will be able to talk with her about serious subjects, tell her about his plans, and work with her to further improve their position. Flattered by his confidence in her, she will help him with good advice or collaboration in his endeavors and business. The worker, also educated and well brought up, will find it delightful to teach and develop his young children. Workers in general are kindhearted and love children very much. How diligently a man will work all week knowing that he is to spend Sunday in his wife's company, that he will enjoy his two little mischievous, affectionate girls and his two already educated boys who are able to talk with their father about serious things! How hard this father will work to earn a few extra cents to buy pretty bonnets for his little girls, a book for his sons, an engraving or something else which he knows will please them? With what joyful ecstasy these little gifts will be received, and what happiness for the mother to see the reciprocal love between father and children! It is clear that this, hypothetically, would be the most desirable domestic life for the worker. Comfortable at home, happy and satisfied in the company of his kind, old mother and young wife and children, it would never occur to him to leave the house to seek a good time at the tavern, that place of perdition which wastes the worker's time, money and health, and dulls his intellect. With half of what a drunkard spends in the tavern, a worker's whole family living together could go for meals in the country in summer. So little is necessary for people who know how to live soberly. Out in the open air, the children would all be happy to run with their father and mother, who would be like children to amuse them; and in the evening, with contented hearts and limbs slightly weary from the week's work, the family would return home very satisfied with their day. In winter, the family would go to a show. These amusements offer a dual advantage: they instruct children while entertaining them. How many objects of study an intelligent mother can find to teach her children in a day spent in the country or an evening at the theater!

Under the circumstances I have just outlined, the home would create well-being rather than ruin for the worker. Who doesn't know how love and contentment of the heart treble or quadruple a man's strength? We have seen it in a few rare cases. It has happened that a worker, adoring his family and getting the idea of teaching his children, did the work that three unmarried men would not have been able to do in order to attain this noble goal. Then there is the question of deprivations. Single men spend generously; they don't deny themselves anything. What does it matter, they say, after all, we can gaily live and drink since we have no one to feed. But the married man who loves his family finds satisfaction in depriving himself and lives with exemplary frugality.

Workers, this vaguely sketched picture of the situation the proletariat would enjoy if woman were recognized as man's equal must lead to thought about the evil existing and the goodness which might exist. That ought to make you become very determined.

Workers, you probably have no power to abrogate the old laws or to make new ones. But you have the power to protest against the inequity and absurdity of laws that impede humanity's progress and make you in particular suffer. You can and must then energetically use thought, speaking, and writing to protest the laws oppressing you for it is your sacred duty. So now, try to understand: the law which enslaves woman and deprives her of education oppresses you, proletarian men.

To be raised, educated, and taught the science of the world, the son of the wealthy has governesses and knowledgeable teachers, able advisers and finally, beautiful *marquises,* elegant, witty women whose functions in high society consist in taking over the son's education after he leaves school. It's a very useful role for the well-being of those gentlemen of high nobility. These ladies teach them to have proper manners, tact, finesse, wit; in a word, they make them into men who *know how to live,* the right kind of men. No matter how capable a young man is, if he is fortunate enough to be the protégé of one of these amiable ladies, his fortune is made. At thirty-five he is certain of becoming an ambassador or a minister. While you, poor workers, to rear and teach you, you have only your mother; to make you into civilized men, you only have women of your class, your companions in ignorance and misery.

Thus it is not in the name of woman's superiority (as I will unfailingly be accused) that I tell you to demand rights for women; not really. First of all, before discussing her superiority, one must recognize her social individuality. My support has a more solid basis. In the name of your own interest and improvement, men; and finally in the name of the universal well-being of all men and women, I invite you to appeal for women's rights, and meanwhile at least to recognize them in principle.

Thus, workers, it is up to you, who are the victims of real inequality and injustice, to establish the rule of justice and absolute equality between man and woman on this earth. Give a great example to the world, an example that will prove to your oppressors that you want to triumph through your right and not by brute force. You seven, ten, fifteen million proletarians, could avail yourselves of that brute force! In calling for justice, prove that you are just and equitable. You, the strong men, the men with bare arms, proclaim your recognition that woman is your equal, and as such, you recognize her equal right to the benefits of the *universal union of working men and women.*

Workers, perhaps in three or four years you will have your first palace, ready to admit six hundred old persons and six hundred children. Well! Proclaim through your statutes, which will become your charter, the rights of women for equality. Let it be written in your charter that an equal number of girls and boys will be admitted to the Workers' Union palace to receive intellectual and vocational training.

Workers, in 1791, your fathers proclaimed the immortal declaration of the *rights of man,* and it is to that solemn declaration that today you owe your being free and equal men before the law. May your fathers be honored for this great work! But, proletarians, there remains for you men of 1843 a no less great work to finish. In your turn, emancipate the last slaves still remaining in French society; proclaim the *rights of woman,* in the same terms your fathers proclaimed yours:

"We, French proletarians, after fifty-three years of experience, recognize that we are duly enlightened and convinced that the neglect and scorn perpetrated upon the natural rights of woman are the only cause of unhappiness in the world, and we have resolved to expose her sacred and inalienable rights in a solemn declaration inscribed in our charter. We wish women to be informed of our declaration, so that they will not let themselves be oppressed and degraded any more by man's injustice and tyranny, and so that men will respect the freedom and equality they enjoy in their wives and mothers.

1. The goal of society necessarily being the common happiness of men and women, the Workers' Union guarantees them the enjoyment of their rights as working men and women.

2. Their rights include equal admission to the Workers' Union palaces, whether they be children, or disabled or elderly.

3. Woman being man's equal, we understand that girls will receive as rational, solid, and extensive (though different) an education in moral and professional matters as the boys.

4. As for the disabled and the elderly, in every way, the treatment will be the same for women as for men.

Workers, rest assured, if you have enough equity and justice to inscribe in your Charter the few lines I have just traced, this declaration of the rights of woman will soon become custom, then law, and within twenty-five years you will see absolute equality of man and woman inscribed at the head of the book of law.

Then, my brothers, and only then, will human unity be established.

Sons of '89, that is the work your fathers bequeathed to you!

Book of Household Management
Isabella Beeton

Mrs. Beeton's advice on running a middle-class household achieved instant fame. The tasks she ascribes to women are daunting and in certain respects match male roles telescoped down to the level of household. "As with the commander of an army, or the leader of any enterprise," states Beeton, "so is it with the mistress of a house." What had started out as a cookbook became a virtual manual for middle-class home life in all its aspects.

Chapter I

The Mistress

"Strength, and honour are her clothing; and she shall rejoice in time to come. She openeth her mouth with wisdom; and in her tongue is the law of kindness. She looketh well to the ways of her household; and eateth not the bread of idleness. Her children arise up, and call her blessed; her husband also, and he praiseth her."—Proverbs, xxxi. 25–28.

1. AS WITH THE COMMANDER OF AN ARMY, or the leader of any enterprise, so is it with the mistress of a house. Her spirit will be seen through the whole establishment; and just in proportion as she performs her duties intelligently and thoroughly, so will her domestics follow in her path. Of all those acquirements, which more particularly belong to the feminine character, there are none which take a higher rank, in our estimation, than such as enter into a knowledge of household duties; for on these are perpetually dependent the happiness, comfort, and well-being of a family. In this opinion we are borne out by the author of "The Vicar of Wakefield," who says: "The modest virgin, the prudent wife, and the careful matron, are much more serviceable in life than petticoated philosophers, blustering heroines, or virago queens. She

who makes her husband and her children happy, who reclaims the one from vice and trains up the other to virtue, is a much greater character than ladies described in romances, whose whole occupation is to murder mankind with shafts from their quiver, or their eyes."

2. PURSUING THIS PICTURE, we may add, that to be a good housewife does not necessarily imply an abandonment of proper pleasures or amusing recreation; and we think it the more necessary to express this, as the performance of the duties of a mistress may, to some minds, perhaps seem to be incompatible with the enjoyment of life. Let us, however, now proceed to describe some of those home qualities and virtues which are necessary to the proper management of a Household, and then point out the plan which may be the most profitably pursued for the daily regulation of its affairs.

3. EARLY RISING IS ONE OF THE MOST ESSENTIAL QUALITIES which enter into good Household Management, as it is not only the parent of health, but of innumerable other advantages. Indeed, when a mistress is an early riser, it is almost certain that her house will be orderly and well-managed. On the contrary, if she remain in bed till a late hour, then the domestics, who, as we have before observed, invariably partake somewhat of their mistress's character, will surely become sluggards. To self-indulgence all are more or less disposed, and it is not to be expected that servants are freer from this fault than the heads of houses. The great Lord Chatham thus gave his advice in

From: Isabella Beeton, *Book of Household Management,* http://www.gutenberg.org/dirs/1/0/1/3/10136/10136-8.txt

reference to this subject:—"I would have inscribed on the curtains of your bed, and the walls of your chamber, 'If you do not rise early, you can make progress in nothing.'"

4. CLEANLINESS IS ALSO INDISPENSABLE TO HEALTH, and must be studied both in regard to the person and the house, and all that it contains. Cold or tepid baths should be employed every morning, unless, on account of illness or other circumstances, they should be deemed objectionable. The bathing of children will be treated of under the head of "MANAGEMENT OF CHILDREN."

5. FRUGALITY AND ECONOMY ARE HOME VIRTUES, without which no household can prosper. Dr. Johnson says: "Frugality may be termed the daughter of Prudence, the sister of Temperance, and the parent of Liberty. He that is extravagant will quickly become poor, and poverty will enforce dependence and invite corruption." The necessity of practicing economy should be evident to every one, whether in the possession of an income no more than sufficient for a family's requirements, or of a large fortune, which puts financial adversity out of the question. We must always remember that it is a great merit in housekeeping to manage a little well. "He is a good waggoner," says Bishop Hall, "that can turn in a little room. To live well in abundance is the praise of the estate, not of the person. I will study more how to give a good account of my little, than how to make it more." In this there is true wisdom, and it may be added, that those who can manage a little well, are most likely to succeed in their management of larger matters. Economy and frugality must never, however, be allowed to degenerate into parsimony and meanness.

6. THE CHOICE OF ACQUAINTANCES is very important to the happiness of a mistress and her family. A gossiping acquaintance, who indulges in the scandal and ridicule of her neighbours, should be avoided as a pestilence. It is likewise all-necessary to beware, as Thomson sings,

"The whisper'd tale,
That, like the fabling Nile, no fountain knows;—
Fair-laced Deceit, whose wily, conscious aye
Ne'er looks direct; the tongue that licks the dust
But, when it safely dares, as prompt to sting."

If the duties of a family do not sufficiently occupy the time of a mistress, society should be formed of such a kind as will tend to the mutual interchange of general and interesting information.

7. FRIENDSHIPS SHOULD NOT BE HASTILY FORMED, nor the heart given, at once, to every new-comer. There are ladies who uniformly smile at, and approve everything and everybody, and who possess neither the courage to reprehend vice, nor the generous warmth to defend virtue. The friendship of such persons is without attachment, and their love without affection or even preference. They imagine that every one who has any penetration is ill-natured, and look coldly on a discriminating judgment. It should be remembered, however, that this discernment does not always proceed from an uncharitable temper, but that those who possess a long experience and thorough knowledge of the world, scrutinize the conduct and dispositions of people before they trust themselves to the first fair appearances. Addison, who was not deficient in a knowledge of mankind, observes that "a friendship, which makes the least noise, is very often the most useful; for which reason, I should prefer a prudent friend to a zealous one." And Joanna Baillie tells us that

"Friendship is no plant of hasty growth,
Though planted in esteem's deep-fixed soil,
The gradual culture of kind intercourse
Must bring it to perfection."

8. HOSPITALITY IS A MOST EXCELLENT VIRTUE; but care must be taken that the love of company, for its own sake, does not become a prevailing passion; for then the habit is no longer hospitality, but dissipation. Reality and truthfulness in this, as in all other duties of life, are the points to be studied; for, as Washington Irving well says, "There is an emanation from the heart in genuine hospitality, which cannot be described, but is immediately felt, and puts the stranger at once at his ease." With respect to the continuance of friendships, however, it may be found necessary, in some cases, for a mistress to relinquish, on assuming the responsibility of a household, many of those commenced in the earlier part of her life. This will be the more requisite, if the number still retained be quite equal to her means and opportunities.

— READING 28 —
Why We Are Militant
Emmeline Pankhurst

The Pankhurst family was of the educated British upper-middle class, a group whose women suffered far less than others from discrimination. Even so, women of this class had no right to political participation, control their own property or children in marriage, or play more than a restricted role in the civil and economic life of the nation. By the late nineteenth and early twentieth century, the Pankhursts settled on very militant and even violent means to make their cause heard. The goal was the vote, without which other oppressions would never be addressed. Eventually, the publicity spurred by the Pankhursts' tactics played a role in women's emancipation.

A Speech Delivered in New York October 21st, 1913

I know that in your minds there are questions like these: you are saying, 'Woman Suffrage is sure to come; the emancipation of humanity is an evolutionary process, and how is it that some women, instead of trusting to that evolution, instead of educating the masses of people of their country, instead of educating their own sex to prepare them for citizenship, how is it that these militant women are using violence and upsetting the business arrangements of the country in their undue impatience to attain their end?'

Let me try to explain to you the situation.

Although we have a so-called democracy, and so-called representative government there, England is the most conservative country on earth. Why, your forefathers found that out a great many years ago! If you had passed your life in England as I have, you would know that there are certain words which certainly, during the last two generations, certainly till about ten years ago, aroused a feeling of horror and fear in the minds of the mass of the people. The word revolution, for instance, was identified in Eng-

land with all kind of horrible ideas. The idea of change, the idea of unsettling the established order of things was repugnant.

Now, in America it is the proud boast of some of the most conservative men and women that I have met, that they are descended from the heroes of the Revolution. You have an organisation, I believe, called the Daughters of the Revolution, whose members put an interpretation upon the word revolution which is quite different from the interpretation given to it in Great Britain. Perhaps that will help you to realise how extremely difficult it is in Great Britain to get anything done. All my life I have heard people talking in advocacy of reforms which it was self-evident would be for the good of the people, and yet it has all ended in talk; they are still talking about these reforms, and unless something happens of a volcanic nature they will go on talking about them until the end of time. Nothing ever has been got out of the British Parliament without something very nearly approaching a revolution. You need something dynamic in order to force legislation through the House of Commons; in fact, the whole machinery of government in England may almost be said to be an elaborate arrangement for not doing anything.

From: *Suffrage and the Pankhursts*, ed. Jane Marcus (London: Routledge & Kegan Paul, 1984), pp. 153–162.

The extensions of the franchise to the men of my country have been preceded by very great violence, by something like a revolution, by something like civil war. In 1832, you know we were on the edge of a civil war and on the edge of revolution, and it was at the point of the sword—no, not at the point of the sword—it was after the practice of arson on so large a scale that half the city of Bristol was burned down in a single night, it was because more and greater violence and arson were feared that the Reform Bill of 1832 was allowed to pass into law. In 1867, John Bright urged the people of London to crowd the approaches to the Houses of Parliament in order to show their determination, and he said that if they did that no Parliament, however obdurate, could resist their just demands. Rioting went on all over the country, and as the result of that rioting, as the result of that unrest, which resulted in the pulling down of the Hyde Park railings, as a result of the fear of more rioting and violence the Reform Act of 1867 was put upon the statute books.

In 1884 came the turn of the agricultural labourer. Joseph Chamberlain, who afterwards became a very conservative person, threatened that, unless the vote was given to the agricultural labourer, he would march 100,000 men from Birmingham to know the reason why. Rioting was threatened and feared, and so the agricultural labourers got the vote.

Meanwhile, during the '80's, women, like men, were asking for the franchise. Appeals, larger and more numerous than for any other reform, were presented in support of Woman's Suffrage. Meetings of the great corporations, great town councils, and city councils, passed resolutions asking that women should have the vote. More meetings were held, and larger, for Woman Suffrage than were held for votes for men, and yet the women did not get it. Men got the vote because they were and would be violent. The women did not get it because they were constitutional and law-abiding. Why, is it not evident to everyone that people who are patient where mis-government is concerned may go on being patient! Why should anyone trouble to help them? I take to myself some shame that through all those years, at any rate from the early '80's, when I first came into the Suffrage movement, I did not learn my political lessons.

I believed, as many women still in England believe, that women could get their way in some mysterious manner, by purely peaceful methods. We have been so accustomed, we women, to accept one standard for men and another standard for women, that we have even applied that variation of standard to the injury of our political welfare.

Having had better opportunities of education, and having had some training in politics, having in political life come so near to the 'superior' being as to see that he was not altogether such a fount of wisdom as they had supposed, that he had his human weaknesses as we had, the twentieth century women began to say to themselves, 'Is it not time, since our methods have failed and the men's have succeeded, that we should take a leaf out of their political book?'

We were led to that conclusion, we older women, by the advice of the young—you know there is a French proverb which says, 'If youth knew; if age could,' but I think that when you can bring together youth and age, as we have done, and get them to adopt the same methods and take the same point of view, then you are on the high road to success.

Well, we in Great Britain, on the eve of the General Election of 1905, a mere handful of us—why, you could almost count us on the fingers of both hands—set out on the wonderful adventure of forcing the strongest Government of modern times to give the women the vote. Only a few in number; we were not strong in influence, and we had hardly any money, and yet we quite gaily made our little banners with the words 'Votes for Women' upon them, and we set out to win the enfranchisement of the women of our country.

The Suffrage movement was almost dead. The women had lost heart. You could not get a Suffrage meeting that was attended by members of the general public. We used to have about 24 adherents in the front row. We carried our resolutions and heard no more about them.

Two women changed that in a twinkling of an eye at a great Liberal demonstration in Manchester, where a Liberal leader, Sir Edward Grey, was explaining the programme to be carried out during the Liberals' next turn of office. The two women put the fateful question, 'When are you going to give votes to women?' and refused to sit down until they had been answered. These two women were sent to gaol, and from that day to this the women's movement, both militant and constitutional, has never looked back. We had little more than one moribund society for Woman Suffrage in those days. Now we have nearly 50 societies for Woman Suffrage, and they are large in membership, they are rich in money, and their ranks are swelling every day that passes. That is how militancy has put back the clock of Woman Suffrage in Great Britain.

Now, some of you have said how wicked it is (the immigration commissioners told me that on Saturday afternoon), how wicked it is to attack the property of private individuals who have done us no harm. Well, you know there is a proverb which says that you cannot make omelettes without breaking eggs. I wish we could.

I want to say here and now that the only justification for violence, the only justification for damage to property, the only justification for risk to the comfort of other human beings is the fact that you have tried all other available means and have failed to secure justice, and as a law-abiding person—and I am by nature a law-abiding person, as one hating violence, hating disorder—I want to say that from the moment we began our militant agitation to this day I have felt absolutely guiltless in this matter.

I tell you that in Great Britain there is no other way. We can show intolerable grievances. The Chancellor of the Exchequer, Mr Lloyd George, who is no friend of the woman's movement, although a professed one, said a very true thing when speaking of the grievances of his own country, of Wales. He said that there comes a time in the life of human beings suffering from intolerable grievances when the only way to maintain their self respect is to revolt against that injustice.

Well, I say the time is long past when it became necessary for women to revolt in order to maintain their self respect in Great Britain. The women who are waging this war are women who would fight, if it were only for the idea of liberty—if it were only that they might be free citizens of a free country—I myself would fight for that idea alone. But we have, in addition to this love of freedom, intolerable grievances to redress.

We do not feel the weight of those grievances in our own persons. I think it is very true that people who are crushed by personal wrongs are not the right people to fight for reform. The people who can fight best are the people who have happy lives themselves, the fortunate ones. At any rate, in our revolution it is the happy women, the fortunate women, the women who have drawn prizes in the lucky bag of life, in the shape of good fathers, good husbands and good brothers, they are the women who are fighting this battle. They are fighting it for the sake of others more helpless than themselves, and it is of the grievances of those helpless ones that I want to say a few words to-night to make you understand the meaning of our militant campaign.

Those grievances are so pressing that, so far from it being a duty to be patient and to wait for evolution, in thinking of those grievances the idea of patience is intolerable. We feel that patience is something akin to crime when our patience involves continued suffering on the part of the oppressed.

We are fighting to get the power to alter bad laws; but some people say to us, 'Go to the representatives in the House of Commons, point out to them that these laws are bad, and you will find them quite ready to alter them.'

Ladies and gentlemen, there are women in my country who have spent long and useful lives trying to get reforms, and because of their voteless condition, they are unable even to get the ear of Members of Parliament, much less are they able to secure those reforms.

Our marriage and divorce laws are a disgrace to civilisation. I sometimes wonder, looking back from the serenity of past middle age, at the courage of women. I wonder that women have the courage to take upon themselves the responsibilities of marriage and motherhood when I see how little protection the law of my country affords them. I wonder that a woman will face the ordeal of childbirth with the knowledge that after she has risked her life to bring a child into the world she has absolutely no parental rights over the future of that child. Think what trust women have in men when a woman will marry a man, knowing, if she has knowledge of the law, that if that man is not all she in her love for him thinks him, he may even bring a strange woman into the house, bring his mistress into the house to live with her, and she cannot get legal relief from such a marriage as that.

How often is women's trust misplaced, and yet how whole-hearted and how touching that trust must be when a woman, in order to get love and companionship, will run such terrible risks in entering into marriage! Yet women have done it, and as we get to know more of life we militant Suffragists have nerved ourselves and forced ourselves to learn something of how other people live. As we get that knowledge we realise how political power, how political influence, which would enable us to get better laws, would make it possible for thousands upon thousands of unhappy women to live happier lives.

Well, you may say, the laws may be inadequate, the laws may be bad, but human nature, after all, is not much influenced by laws, and upon the whole, people are fairly happy. Now, for those who are fortunate it is very comfortable to have that idea, but if you will really look at life as we see it in our centralised civilisation in Europe, you will find that after all the law is a great educator, and if men are brought up to think the law allows them to behave badly to those who should be nearest and dearest to them, the worst kind of man is very apt to take full advantage of all the laxity of the law.

What have we been hearing of so much during the last few years! It is a very remarkable thing, ladies, and gentlemen, that along with this woman's movement, along with this woman's revolt, you are having a great uncovering of social sores. We are having light let into dark places, whether it is in the United States or whether it is in the old countries of Europe, you find the social ills from which humanity suffers, are very much the same. Every civilised country has been discussing how to deal with that most awful slavery, the white slave traffic.

When I was a very tiny child the great American people were divided into hostile sections on the question of whether it was right that one set of human beings of one colour should buy and sell human beings of another colour, and you had a bloody war to settle that question. I tell you that throughout the civilised world to-day there is a slavery more awful than negro slavery in its worst form ever was. It is called prostitution, but in that awful slavery there are slaves of every shade and colour, and they are all of one sex.

Well, in my country we have been having legislation to deal with it. We have now a White Slave Act, and in that Act of Parliament they have put a flogging clause. Certain men are to be flogged if they are convicted and found guilty under that Act of Parliament, and the British House of Commons, composed of men of varying moral standard, waxed highly eloquent on the need of flogging these tigers of the human race, men engaged in the white slave traffic.

Well, we women looked on and we read their speeches, but in our hearts we said, 'Why don't they decide to go to the people for whom the white slave traffic exists? What is the use of dealing with the emissaries, with the slave hunters, with the purveyors? Why don't they go to the very foundation of the evil; why don't they attack the customers? If there was no demand there would be no traffic, because business does not exist if there is no demand for it?' And so we women said, 'It's no use, gentlemen, trying to put us off with sentimental legislation on the white slave traffic. We don't trust you to settle it; we want to have a hand in settling it ourselves, because we think we know how.' And we have a right to distrust that legislation. They passed the Act very, very quickly; they put it on the Statute Book, and we have seen it in operation, and we know that the time of Parliament and the time of the nation was wasted on a piece of legislation which I fear was never intended to be taken very seriously; something to keep the women quiet, something to lull us into a sense of security, something to make us believe that now, at least, the Government were really grappling with the situation.

And so we attacked this great evil. We said, 'How can we expect real legislation to deal with the white slave traffic on a small scale when the Government of the country is the biggest white slave trading firm that we have got?'

And it is true; because you know, although we have suppressed such regulation of vice in England, we have got it in full swing in the great dependencies that we own all over the world, and we have only to turn to India and look to other places where our Army is stationed to find the Government, which is in no way responsible to women, actually taking part in that awful trade, in absolute cold bloodedness where native women are concerned, all, forsooth, in the name of the health of the men of our forces.

Well, we have been speaking out, ladies and gentlemen; we have been saying to our nation and the rulers of our nation, 'We will not have the health of one-half of the community, their pretended health, maintained at the expense of the degradation and sorrow and misery of the other half.'

I want to ask you whether, in all the revolutions of the past, in your own revolt against British rule, you had deeper or greater reasons for revolt than women have to-day?

Take the industrial side of the question: have men's wages for a hard day's work ever been so low and inadequate as are women's wages to-day? Have men ever had to suffer from the laws, more injustice than women suffer? Is there a single reason which men have had for demanding liberty that does not also apply to women?

Why, if you were talking to the *men* of any other nation you would not hesitate to reply in the affirmative. There is not a man in this meeting who has not felt sympathy with the uprising of the men of other lands when suffering from intolerable tyranny, when deprived of all representative rights. You are full of sympathy with men in Russia. You are full of sympathy with nations that rise against the domination of the Turk. You are full of sympathy with all struggling people striving for independence. How is it, then, that some of you have nothing but ridicule and contempt and reprobation for women who are fighting for exactly the same thing?

All my life I have tried to understand why it is that men who value their citizenship as their dearest possession seem to think citizenship ridiculous when it is to be applied to the women of their race. And I find an explanation, and it is the only one I can think of. It came to me when I was in a prison cell, remembering how I had seen men laugh at the idea of women going to prison. Why they would confess they could not bear a cell door to be shut upon themselves for a single hour without asking to be let out. A thought came to me in my prison cell, and it was this: that to men women are not human beings like themselves. Some men think we are superhuman; they put us on pedestals; they revere us; they think we are too fine and too delicate to come down into the hurly-burly of life. Other men think us sub-human; they think we are a strange species unfortunately having to exist for the perpetuation of the race. They think that we are fit for drudgery, but that in some strange way our minds are not like

theirs, our love for great things is not like theirs, and so we are a sort of sub-human species.

We are neither superhuman nor are we sub-human. We are just human beings like yourselves.

Our hearts burn within us when we read the great mottoes which celebrate the liberty of your country; when we go to France and we read the words, liberty, fraternity and equality, don't you think that we appreciate the meaning of those words? And then when we wake to the knowledge that these things are not for us, they are only for our brothers, then there comes a sense of bitterness into the hearts of some women, and they say to themselves, 'Will men never understand?' But so far as we in England are concerned, we have come to the conclusion that we are not going to leave men any illusions upon the question.

When we were patient, when we believed in argument and persuasion, they said, 'You don't really want it because, if you did, you would do something unmistakable to show you were determined to have it.' And then when we did something unmistakable they said, 'You are behaving so badly that you show you are not fit for it.'

Now, gentlemen, in your heart of hearts you do not believe that. You know perfectly well that there never was a thing worth having that was not worth fighting for. You know perfectly well that if the situation were reversed, if you had no constitutional rights and we had all of them, if you had the duty of paying and obeying and trying to look as pleasant, and we were the proud citizens who could decide our fate and yours, because we knew what was good for you better than you knew yourselves, you know perfectly well that you wouldn't stand it for a single day, and you would be perfectly justified in rebelling against such intolerable conditions.

Well, in Great Britain, we have tried persuasion, we have tried the plan of showing (by going upon public bodies, where they allowed us to do work they hadn't much time to do themselves) that we are capable people. We did it in the hope that we should convince them and persuade them to do the right and proper thing. But we had all our labour for our pains, and now we are fighting for our rights, and we are growing stronger and better women in the process. We are getting more fit to use our rights because we have such difficulty in getting them.

And now may I say a word about the reason for my coming to America.

Always when human beings have been struggling for freedom they have looked to happier parts of the world for support and sympathy. In your hour of trouble you went to other peoples and asked them for help. It seems to me, looking into the past, into my recollections of history, that a great man named Benjamin Franklin went to France to ask the French people to help in the struggle for American independence. You didn't apologise for sending him, and I am sure he didn't apologise for going. There may have been people in France who said, 'Why does this pestilent, rebellious fellow come over trying to stir up people here in our peaceful country?' But, in the main, the people of France welcomed him. Their hearts thrilled at the idea of a brave and courageous struggle, and they sent money and they sent men to help to fight and win the independence of the American people.

Those who have been struggling for freedom in other lands have come to you, and I can't help remembering that right through the struggle of the Irish people they sent law-breakers to plead with you for help for law-breakers in Ireland.

Yes, and like all political law breaking done by men, the form their violence has taken has not been merely to break some shop windows or to set on fire the house of some rich plutocrat, but it has found its expression in the taking of human life, in the injury even of poor, dumb animals who could have no part in the matter. And yet you looked at that agitation in a large way. You said, 'In times of revolution and revolt you cannot curb the human spirit, you cannot bind men and women down to narrow rules of conduct which are proper and right in times of peace,' and you sent help and cheer to the Irish people in their struggle for greater freedom.

Why, then, should not I come to ask for help for British women? Whatever helps them is going to help women all over the world. It will be the hastening of your victory. It has not as yet been necessary in the United States for women to be militant in the sense that we are, and perhaps one of the reasons why it is not necessary and why it may never be necessary is that we are doing the militant work for you. And we are glad to do that work. We are proud to do that work. If there are any men who are fighters in this hall, any men who have taken part in warfare, I tell you, gentlemen, that amongst the other good things that you, consciously or unconsciously, have kept from women, you have kept the joy of battle.

We know the joy of battle. When we have come out of the gates of Holloway at the point of death, battered, starved, forcibly fed as some of our women have been—their mouths forced open by iron gags—their bodies bruised, they have felt when the prison bars were broken and the doors have opened, even at the point of death, they have felt the joy of battle and the exultation of victory.

People have said that women could never vote, never share in the government, because government rests upon force. We have proved that is not true. Government rests not upon force; government rests upon the consent of the governed; and the weakest woman, the very poorest woman, if she withholds her consent cannot be governed.

They sent me to prison, to penal servitude for three years. I came out of prison at the end of nine days. I broke my prison bars. Four times they took me back again; four times I burst the prison door open again. And I left England openly to come and visit America, with only three or four weeks of the three years' sentence of penal servitude served. Have we not proved, then, that they cannot govern human beings who withhold their consent?

And so we are glad we have had the fighting experience, and we are glad to do all the fighting for all the women all over the world. All that we ask of you is to back us up. We ask you to show that although, perhaps, you may not mean to fight as we do, yet you understand the meaning of our fight; that you realise we are women fighting for a great idea; that we wish the betterment of the human race, and that we believe this betterment is coming through the emancipation and uplifting of women.

Anna Karenina
Leo Tolstoy

In the seemingly idyllic world of upper-class women in Tolstoy's novel, women's concerns have to do with husband, family, children, and social reputation. These women's status does not ultimately conceal their helplessness in the face of legal, political, and customary factors they cannot control. If a woman struggled against society's mores, she faced utter disaster.

Kitty Shcherbatsky, youngest daughter of a highly placed Petersburg family, confronts possible serious illness and the troubled family life of her sister, Dolly.

Chapter Two

Soon after the doctor left, Dolly arrived. She knew that there was to be a consultation that day, and though she was just up after her confinement (she had another baby, a little girl, born at the end of the winter), though she had trouble and anxiety enough of her own, she had left her tiny baby and a sick child to come and hear Kitty's fate, which was to be decided that day.

"Well, well?" she said, coming into the drawing room without taking off her hat. "You're all in good spirits. Good news, then?"

They tried to tell her what the doctor had said, but it appeared that though the doctor had talked distinctly enough and at great length, it was utterly impossible to report what he had said. The only point of interest was that it was settled that they should go abroad.

Dolly could not help sighing. Her dearest friend, her sister, was going away. And her life was not a cheerful one. Her relations with Stepan Arkadyevich after their reconciliation had become humiliating. The union Anna had cemented turned out to be less than solid, and family harmony was breaking down

again at the same point. There had been nothing definite, but Stepan Arkadyevich was hardly ever at home; money, too, was hardly ever forthcoming, and Dolly was continually tortured by suspicions of infidelity, which she tried to dismiss, dreading the agonies of jealousy she had already been through. The first onslaught of jealousy, once lived through, could never come back again, and even the discovery of infidelities could never now affect her as it had the first time. Such a discovery now would only mean breaking up family habits, and she let herself be deceived, despising him and still more herself for the weakness. Besides this, the care of her large family was a constant worry to her: first, the nursing of her young baby did not go well, then the nurse had gone away, now one of the children had fallen ill.

"Well, how are all of you?" asked her mother.

"Ah, Mama, we have plenty of troubles of our own. Lily is ill, and I'm afraid it's scarlet fever. I have come here now to hear about Kitty, and then I shall shut myself up entirely, if—God forbid—it should be scarlet fever."

The old prince too had come in from his study after the doctor's departure, and after presenting his cheek to Dolly and saying a few words to her, he turned to his wife:

"How have you settled it? You're going? Well, and what do you mean to do with me?"

From: Leo Tolstoy, *Anna Karenina* (New York: Random House, Inc., 1965), pp. 128–134.

"I suppose you had better stay here, Aleksander," said his wife.

"Just as you like."

"Mama, why shouldn't Father come with us?" said Kitty. "It'll be nicer for him and for us too."

The old prince got up and stroked Kitty's hair. She lifted her head and looked at him with a forced smile. It always seemed to her that he understood her better than anyone in the family, though he did not say much about her. Being the youngest, she was her father's favorite, and she imagined that his love gave him insight. When now her glance met his blue kindly eyes looking intently at her, it seemed to her that he saw right through her, and understood all that was not good that was going on within her. Reddening, she stretched out toward him, expecting a kiss, but he only patted her hair and said:

"These stupid chignons! There's no getting at the real daughter, one simply strokes the bristles of dead women. Well, Dolinka," he said, turning to his elder daughter, "what's your young buck doing, hey?"

"Nothing, Father," answered Dolly, understanding that he meant her husband. "He's always out; I scarcely ever see him," she could not resist adding with a sarcastic smile.

"Why, hasn't he gone into the country yet—to see about selling that forest?"

"No, he's still getting ready for the journey."

"Oh, that's it!" said the prince. "And so am I to be getting ready for a journey too? At your service," he said to his wife, sitting down. "And I tell you what, Katya," he went on to his younger daughter, "you must wake up one fine day and say to yourself: 'Why, I'm very well, and happy, and going out again with Father for an early morning walk in the frost.' Hey?"

What her father said seemed simple enough, yet at these words Kitty became confused and overcome like a detected criminal. "Yes, he sees it all, he understands it all, and in these words he's telling me that though I'm ashamed, I must get over my shame." She could not pluck up spirit to make any answer. She tried to begin, and all at once burst into tears, and rushed out of the room.

"See what comes of your jokes!" the princess pounced down on her husband. "You're always . . ." she began a string of reproaches.

The prince listened to the princess's scolding rather a long while without speaking, but he frowned more and more.

"She's so much to be pitied, poor child, so much to be pitied, and you don't feel how it hurts her to hear the slightest reference to the cause of it. Ah! To be so mistaken in people!" said the princess, and by the change in her tone both Dolly and the prince knew she was speaking of Vronsky. "I don't know why there aren't laws against such base, dishonorable people."

"Ah, I can't bear to hear you!" said the prince gloomily, getting up from his low chair, and seeming anxious to get away, yet stopping in the doorway. "There are laws, madam, and since you've challenged me to it, I'll tell you who's to blame for it all: you, you, you and nobody else. Laws against such young gallants there have always been, and there still are! Yes, if there has been nothing that ought not to have been, old as I am, I'd have challenged him, the young fop. Yes, and now you dose her and call in these quacks."

The prince apparently had plenty more to say, but as soon as the princess heard his tone she subsided at once, and became penitent, as she always did on serious occasions.

"Aleksandr, Aleksandr," she whispered, moving toward him and beginning to weep.

As soon as she began to cry the prince too calmed down. He went up to her.

"There, that's enough, that's enough! You're wretched too, I know. It can't be helped. There's no great harm done. God is merciful . . . thanks . . ." he said, not knowing what he was saying, as he responded to the tearful kiss of the princess that he felt on his hand. And the prince went out of the room.

Before this, as soon as Kitty went out of the room in tears, Dolly, with her motherly, family instincts, had promptly perceived that here a woman's work lay before her, and she prepared to do it. She took off her hat, and, mentally, rolled up her sleeves and prepared for action. While her mother was attacking her father, she tried to restrain her mother, so far as filial reverence would allow. During the prince's outburst she was silent; she felt ashamed for her mother, and tender toward her father for so quickly being kind again. But when her father left them she prepared for what was most needed—to go to Kitty and console her.

"I'd been meaning to tell you something for a long while, Mama: did you know that Levin meant to propose to Kitty when he was here the last time? He told Stiva so."

"Well, so what? I don't understand . . ."

"So did Kitty perhaps refuse him? . . . She didn't tell you?"

"No, she has said nothing to me either of one or the other; she's too proud. But I know it's all on account of the other."

"Yes, but suppose she has refused Levin, and she wouldn't have refused him if it hadn't been for the other, I know. And then, he has deceived her so horribly."

It was too terrible for the princess to think of how she had sinned against her daughter, and she broke out angrily:

"Oh, I really don't understand! Nowadays they all go their own way, and mothers haven't a word to say in anything, and then—"

"Mama, I'll go to her."

"Well, do. Did I tell you not to?" said her mother.

Chapter Three

When she went into Kitty's room, a pretty, pink little room, full of knickknacks made of *vieux saxe,** as fresh and pink and white and gay as Kitty herself had been two months ago, Dolly remembered how they had decorated the room the year before together, with what love and gaiety. Her heart turned cold when she saw Kitty sitting on a low chair near the door, her eyes fixed immovably on a corner of the rug. Kitty glanced at her sister, and the cold, rather severe expression of her face did not change.

"I'm going now, and I shall have to stay in and you won't be able to come to see me," said Dolly, sitting down beside her. "I want to talk to you."

"What about?" Kitty asked swiftly, lifting her head in dismay.

"What should it be but your trouble?"

"I have no trouble."

"Nonsense, Kitty. Do you suppose I could help knowing? I know all about it. And believe me, it's of so little consequence . . . We've all been through it."

Kitty did not speak, and her face had a stern expression.

"He's not worth your grieving over him," pursued Darya Aleksandrovna, coming straight to the point.

"No, because he has treated me with contempt," said Kitty, in a breaking voice. "Don't talk of it! Please, don't talk of it!"

"But who can have told you so? No one has said that. I'm certain he was in love with you, and would still be in love with you, if it hadn't—"

"Oh, the most awful thing of all for me is this sympathizing!" shrieked Kitty, suddenly flying into a passion. She turned around on her chair, flushed crimson, and, rapidly moving her fingers, pinched the buckle of her belt first with one hand and then with the other. Dolly knew this habit her sister had of clenching her hands when she was very excited; she knew, too, that in moments of excitement Kitty was capable of forgetting herself and saying a great deal too much, and Dolly would have soothed her, but it was too late.

"What, what is it you want to make me feel, eh?" said Kitty quickly. "That I've been in love with a man who didn't care a straw for me, and that I'm dying of love for him? And this is said to me by my own sister, who imagines that . . . that . . . that she's sympathizing with me! . . . I don't want this commiseration and this hypocrisy!"

"Kitty, you're unfair."

"Why are you tormenting me?"

"But I . . . quite the contrary . . . I see you're unhappy . . ."

But Kitty in her fury did not hear her.

"I've nothing to grieve over and be comforted about. I am too proud ever to allow myself to care for a man who does not love me."

"Yes, I don't say so, either . . . Only one thing. Tell me the truth," said Darya Aleksandrovna, taking her by the hand: "tell me, did Levin speak to you? . . ."

The mention of Levin's name seemed to deprive Kitty of the last vestige of self-control. She leaped up from her chair, and flinging her buckle on the ground, she gesticulated rapidly with her hands and said:

"Why bring Levin in too? I can't understand why you want to torment me. I've told you, and I say it again, that I have some pride, and never, *never*

*"Old Saxony," i.e., porcelain.

would I do as you're doing—go back to a man who's deceived you, who has cared for another woman. I can't understand it. You may, but I can't!"

And saying these words, she glanced at her sister, and seeing that Dolly sat silent, her head mournfully bowed, Kitty, instead of running out of the room, as she had meant to do, sat down near the door and hid her face in her handkerchief.

The silence lasted for a minute or two. Dolly was thinking of herself. That humiliation of which she was always conscious came back to her with a peculiar bitterness when her sister reminded her of it. She had not expected such cruelty from her sister, and she was angry with her. But suddenly she heard the rustle of a skirt, and with it the sound of heart-rending, smothered sobbing, and felt arms about her neck. Kitty was on her knees before her.

"Dolinka, I am so, so wretched!" she whispered penitently. And the sweet face covered with tears hid itself in Darya Aleksandrovna's skirt.

As though tears were the indispensable oil without which the machinery of mutual confidence could not run smoothly between the two sisters, the sisters after their tears talked, not of what was uppermost in their minds, but, though they talked of outside matters, they understood each other. Kitty knew that the word she had uttered in anger about her husband's infidelity and her humiliating position had cut her poor sister to the heart, but that she had forgiven her. Dolly for her part knew all she had wanted to find out. She felt certain that her surmises were correct; that Kitty's misery, her inconsolable misery, was due precisely to the fact that Levin had made her a proposal and she had refused him, and Vronsky had deceived her, and that she was fully prepared to love Levin and to detest Vronsky. Kitty said not a word of that; she talked of nothing but her state of mind.

"I have nothing to make me miserable," she said, getting calmer; "but can you understand that everything has become hateful, loathsome, coarse to me, and I myself most of all? You can't imagine what loathsome thoughts I have about everything."

"Why, whatever loathsome thoughts can you have?" asked Dolly, smiling.

"The most utterly loathsome and coarse: I can't tell you. It's not unhappiness, or low spirits, but much worse. As though everything that was good in me was all hidden away, and nothing was left but the most loathsome. Come, how am I to tell you?" she went on, seeing the puzzled look in her sister's eyes. "Father began saying something to me just now . . . It seems to me he thinks all I want is to be married. Mother takes me to a ball: it seems to me she only takes me to get me married off as soon as possible, and be rid of me. I know it's not the truth, but I can't drive away such thoughts. Eligible suitors, as they call them—I can't bear to see them. It seems to me they're taking stock of me and summing me up. In old days to go anywhere in a ball dress was a simple joy to me, I admired myself; now I feel ashamed and awkward. And then! The doctor . . . Then . . ." Kitty hesitated; she wanted to say further that ever since this change had taken place in her, Stepan Arkadyevich had become insufferably repulsive to her, and that she could not see him without the grossest and most hideous conceptions rising before her imagination.

"Oh, well, everything presents itself to me in the coarsest, most loathsome light," she went on. "That's my illness. Perhaps it will pass."

"But you mustn't think about it."

"I can't help it. I'm never happy except with the children at your house."

"What a pity you can't be with me!"

"Oh, yes, I'm coming. I've had scarlet fever, and I'll persuade Mama to let me."

Kitty insisted on having her way, and went to stay at her sister's and nursed the children all through the scarlet fever, for that is what it turned out to be. The two sisters brought all six children successfully through it, but Kitty was no better in health, and in Lent the Shcherbatskys went abroad.

A Doll's House

Henrik Ibsen

Written just a year later than Tolstoy's novel, Ibsen's play recreates roughly the same situation for his female characters as Tolstoy did but with a very different outcome. In this case, the heroine decides to escape the trap, the doll's house, of husband, children, and security. This rejection in the play shocked contemporary audiences and yet as time went by more and more women chose independence over dependence. If Tolstoy's novel summarized the past as it culminates in the (then) present, Ibsen's play predicted the future.

Nora Helmer, wife of Torvald Helmer, a loving but uncomprehending husband, informs him that she is leaving him and the children to create a life of her own.

You mustn't worry about anything. Nora—only be absolutely frank with me, and I'll be both your will and your conscience. . . . Why, what's this? Not in bed? You've changed your clothes!

NORA [*in her everyday things*]: Yes, Torvald, I've changed my clothes.

HELMER: But why? At *this* hour!

NORA: I shan't sleep tonight.

HELMER: But, my dear Nora—

NORA: [*looking at her watch*]: It's not so very late. Sit down here, Torvald—you and I have a lot to talk over. [*She sits down at one side of the table.*]

HELMER: Nora—what is all this? Why do you look so stern?

NORA: Sit down—this'll take some time. I have a lot to talk to you about.

HELMER: [*sitting across the table from her*]: Nora, you frighten me—I don't understand you.

NORA: No, that's just it—you don't understand me. And I've never understood you—until tonight. No, you mustn't interrupt—just listen to what I have to say. Torvald, this is a reckoning.

HELMER: What do you mean by that?

NORA: [*after a short pause*]: Doesn't it strike you that there's something strange about the way we're sitting here?

HELMER: No . . . what?

NORA: We've been married for eight years now. Don't you realize that this is the first time that we two—you and I, man and wife—have had a serious talk together?

HELMER: Serious? What do you mean by that?

NORA: For eight whole years—no, longer than that—ever since we first met, we've never exchanged a serious word on any serious subject.

HELMER: Was I to keep forever involving you in worries that you couldn't possibly help me with?

NORA: I'm not talking about worries; what I'm saying is that we've never sat down in earnest together to get to the bottom of a single thing.

HELMER: But, Nora dearest, what good would that have been to you?

NORA: That's just the point—you've never understood me. I've been dreadfully wronged, Torvald—first by Papa, and then by you.

HELMER: What? By your father and me? The two people who loved you more than anyone else in the world.

From: Henrik Ibsen, *The League of Youth. A Doll's House. The Lady from the Sea* (New York: Penguin Books, 1965), pp. 224-232.

NORA: [*shaking her head*]: You've never loved me, you've only found it pleasant to be in love with me.

HELMER: Nora—what are you saying?

NORA: It's true, Torvald. When I lived at home with Papa, he used to tell me his opinion about everything, and so I had the same opinion. If I thought differently, I had to hide it from him, or he wouldn't have liked it. He called me his little doll, and he used to play with me just as I played with my dolls. Then I came to live in your house—

HELMER: That's no way to talk about our marriage!

NORA: [*undisturbed*]: I mean when I passed out of Papa's hands into yours. You arranged everything to suit your own tastes, and so I came to have the same tastes as yours . . . or I pretended to. I'm not quite sure which . . . perhaps it was a bit of both—sometimes one and sometimes the other. Now that I come to look at it, I've lived here like a pauper—simply from hand to mouth. I've lived by performing tricks for you, Torvald. That was how you wanted it. You and Papa have committed a grievous sin against me: it's your fault that I've made nothing of my life.

HELMER: That's unreasonable, Nora—and ungrateful. Haven't you been happy here?

NORA: No, that's something I've never been. I thought I had, but really I've never been happy.

HELMER: Never . . . happy?

NORA: No, only gay. And you've always been so kind to me. But our home has been nothing but a play-room. I've been your doll-wife here, just as at home I was Papa's doll-child. And the children have been my dolls in their turn. I liked it when you came and played with me, just as they liked it when I came and played with them. That's what our marriage has been, Torvald.

HELMER: There is some truth in what you say, though you've exaggerated and overstated it. But from now on, things will be different. Playtime's over, now comes lesson-time.

NORA: Whose lessons? Mine or the children's?

HELMER: Both yours and the children's, Nora darling.

NORA: Ah, Torvald, you're not the man to teach me to be a real wife to you—

HELMER: How can you say that?

NORA: —and how am I fitted to bring up the children?

HELMER: Nora!

NORA: Didn't you say yourself, a little while ago, that you daren't trust them to me?

HELMER: That was in a moment of anger—you mustn't pay any attention to that.

NORA: But you were perfectly right—I'm not fit for it. There's another task that I must finish first—I must try to educate myself. And you're not the man to help me with that; I must do it alone. That's why I'm leaving you.

HELMER: [*leaping to his feet*]: What's that you say?

NORA: I must stand on my own feet if I'm to get to know myself and the world outside. That's why I can't stay here with you any longer.

HELMER: Nora—Nora . . . !

NORA: I want to go at once. I'm sure Kristina will take me in for the night.

HELMER: You're out of your mind. I won't let you—I forbid it.

NORA: It's no good your forbidding me anything any longer. I shall take the things that belong to me, but I'll take nothing from you—now or later.

HELMER: But this is madness . . .

NORA: Tomorrow I shall go home—to my old home, I mean—it'll be easier for me to find something to do there.

HELMER: Oh, you blind, inexperienced creature . . . !

NORA: I must try to *get* some experience, Torvald.

HELMER: But to leave your home—your husband and your children. . . . You haven't thought of what people will say.

NORA: I can't consider that. All I know is that this is necessary for me.

HELMER: But this is disgraceful. Is this the way you neglect your most sacred duties?

NORA: What do you consider is my most sacred duty?

HELMER: Do I have to tell you that? Isn't it your duty to your husband and children?

NORA: I have another duty, just as sacred.

HELMER: You can't have. What duty do you mean?

NORA: My duty to myself.

HELMER: Before everything else, you're a wife and a mother.

NORA: I don't believe that any longer. I believe that before everything else I'm a human being—just as much as you are . . . or at any rate I shall try to become one. I know quite well that most people would agree with you, Torvald, and that you have warrant for it in books; but I can't be satisfied any longer with what most people say, and with what's in books. I must think things out for myself and try to understand them.

HELMER: Shouldn't you first understand your place in your own home? Haven't you an infallible guide in such matters—your religion?

NORA: Ah, Torvald, I don't really know what religion is.

HELMER: What's that you say?

NORA: I only know what Pastor Hansen taught me when I was confirmed. He told me that religion was this, that, and the other. When I get away from all this, and am on my own, I want to look into that too. I want to see if what Pastor Hansen told me was right—or at least, if it is right for me.

HELMER: This is unheard-of from a young girl like you. But if religion can't guide you, then let me rouse your conscience. You must have *some* moral sense. Or am I wrong? Perhaps you haven't.

NORA: Well, Torvald, it's hard to say; I don't really know—I'm so bewildered about it all. All I know is that I think quite differently from you about things; and now I find that the law is quite different from what I thought, and I simply can't convince myself that the law is right. That a woman shouldn't have the right to spare her old father on his deathbed, or to save her husband's life! I can't believe things like that.

HELMER: You're talking like a child; you don't understand the world you live in.

NORA: No, I don't. But now I mean to go into that, too. I must find out which is right—the world or I.

HELMER: You're ill, Nora—you're feverish. I almost believe you're out of your senses.

NORA: I've never seen things so clearly and certainly as I do tonight.

HELMER: Clearly and certainly enough to forsake your husband and your children?

NORA: Yes.

HELMER: Then there's only one possible explanation . . .

NORA: What?

HELMER: You don't love me any more.

NORA: No, that's just it.

HELMER: Nora! How can you say that?

NORA: I can hardly bear to, Torvald, because you've always been so kind to me—but I can't help it. I don't love you any more.

HELMER: [*with forced self-control*]: And are you clear and certain about that, too?

NORA: Yes, absolutely clear and certain. That's why I won't stay here any longer.

HELMER: And will you also be able to explain how I've forfeited your love?

NORA: Yes, I can indeed. It was this evening, when the miracle didn't happen—because then I saw that you weren't the man I'd always thought you.

HELMER: I don't understand that. Explain it.

NORA: For eight years I'd waited so patiently—for, goodness knows, I realized that miracles don't happen every day. Then this disaster overtook me, and I was completely certain that now the miracle would happen. When Krogstad's letter was lying out there, I never imagined for a moment that you would submit to his conditions. I was completely certain that you would say to him 'Go and publish it to the whole world!' And when that was done . . .

HELMER: Well, what then? When I'd exposed my own wife to shame and disgrace?

NORA: When that was done, I thought—I was completely certain—that you would come forward and take all the blame—that you'd say 'I'm the guilty one.'

HELMER: Nora!

NORA: You think that I should never have accepted a sacrifice like that from you? No, of course I shouldn't. But who would have taken my word against yours? That was the miracle I hoped for . . . and dreaded. It was to prevent *that* that I was ready to kill myself.

HELMER: Nora, I'd gladly work night and day for you, and endure poverty and sorrow for your sake. But no man would sacrifice his *honour* for the one he loves.

NORA: Thousands of women have.

HELMER: Oh, you're talking and thinking like a stupid child.

NORA: Perhaps . . . But you don't talk or think like the man I could bind myself to. When your first panic was over—not about what threatened me, but about what might happen to *you*—and when there was no more danger, then, as far as you were concerned, it was just as if nothing had happened at all. I was simply your little songbird, your doll, and from now on you would handle it more gently than ever because it was so delicate and fragile. [*Rising*] At that moment, Torvald, I realized that for eight years I'd been living here with a strange man, and that I'd borne him three children. Oh, I can't bear to think of it—I could tear myself to little pieces!

HELMER: [*sadly*]: Yes. I see—I see. There truly is a gulf between us. . . . Oh, but Nora, couldn't we somehow bridge it?

NORA: As I am now, I'm not the wife for you.

HELMER: I could change . . .

NORA: Perhaps—if your doll is taken away from you.

HELMER: But to lose you—to lose you, Nora! No, no, I can't even imagine it . . .

NORA: [*going out to the right*]: That's just why it *must* happen. [*She returns with her outdoor clothes, and a little bag which she puts on a chair by the table.*]

HELMER: Nora! Not now, Nora—wait till morning.

NORA: [*putting on her coat*]: I couldn't spend the night in a strange man's house.

HELMER: But couldn't we live here as brother and sister?

NORA: [*putting her hat on*]: You know quite well that that wouldn't last. [*She pulls her shawl round her.*] Good-bye, Torvald. I won't see my children—I'm sure they're in better hands than mine. As I am now, I'm no good to them.

HELMER: But some day, Nora—some day . . . ?

NORA: How can I say? I've no idea what will become of me.

HELMER: But you're my wife—now, and whatever becomes of you.

NORA: Listen, Torvald: I've heard that when a wife leaves her husband's house as I'm doing now, he's legally freed from all his obligations to her. Anyhow, *I* set you free from them. You're not to feel yourself bound in any way, and nor shall I. We must both be perfectly free. Look, here's your ring back—give me mine.

HELMER: Even that?

NORA: Even that.

HELMER: Here it is.

NORA: There. Now it's all over. Here are your keys. The servants know all about running the house—better than I did. Tomorrow, when I've gone, Kristina will come and pack my things that I brought from home; I'll have them sent after me.

HELMER: Over! All over! Nora, won't you ever think of me again?

NORA: I know I shall often think of you—and the children, and this house.

HELMER: May I write to you, Nora?

NORA: No . . . you must never do that.

HELMER: But surely I can send you—

NORA: Nothing—nothing.

HELMER: —or help you, if ever you need it?

NORA: No, I tell you, I couldn't take anything from a stranger.

HELMER: Nora—can't I ever be anything more than a stranger to you?

NORA: [*picking up her bag*]: Oh, Torvald—there would have to be the greatest miracle of all . . .

HELMER: What would that be—the greatest miracle of all?

NORA: Both of us would have to be so changed that—Oh, Torvald, I don't believe in miracles any longer.

HELMER: But I'll believe. Tell me: 'so changed that . . .'?

NORA: That our life together could be a real marriage. Good-bye. [*She goes out through the hall.*]

HELMER: [*sinking down on a chair by the door and burying his face in his hands*]: Nora! Nora! [*He rises and looks round.*] Empty! She's not here any more! [*With a glimmer of hope*] 'The greatest miracle of all . . .'?

[*From below comes the noise of a door slamming.*]

Carsten Curator

Theodor Storm

Storm's short story about an ordinary middle-class man in an early-nineteenth-century German city serves to delineate expectations about manhood and society then and, in contrast, now. In his business capacity, Carsten advises women about their financial status and looks after their business affairs.

Carsten faces complications in his life when he falls in love with a young woman, his client, whose father has died.

His name was really Carsten Carstens and he was the son of a small merchant, from whom he had inherited a house that his grandfather had built and which stood on the .side street by the harbor, and a business in knitted woolens and such clothing as the boatmen from the nearby islands needed for their sea voyages. But as he was of a rather brooding nature and, like many a North Frisian, born with a liking for neutral work, he had busied himself from his youth with all sorts of books and writings and had gradually gained the reputation among his fellows of being a man from whom you could get sound advice in doubtful situations. If, as it might happen, his reading led his thoughts along paths on which those about him could not follow him, he invited no one to do so; consequently he incurred nobody's distrust. And so he had become the curator to a host of widows and unmarried ladies who, according to the laws of the time, had need of such aid in their legal affairs.

Since his principal concern in the administration of other people's affairs was not his own gain but his interest in the job itself, he differed essentially from the men who usually performed such services; and soon those who approached death knew of no

better man whom they could appoint as guardian of their children, and the courts could find no better administrator of bankrupt or hereditary estates than Carsten Carstens from the alley, who was now generally known by the name of "Carsten Curator," as a man of impeccable honor.

With so many offices of trust claiming his time, his little business naturally declined into a subsidiary affair and was run almost single-handed by an unmarried sister, who had remained with him in their parents' home.

For the rest, Carstens was a man of few words and quick decisions, and, when he felt he was in the presence of base intentions, he was inexorable, even to his own cost. One day a so-called ox-grazer, who for years had rented a field of his at a price that was in those times considered to be low, solemnly declared that he would not be able to exist next year if he had to pay the same rent. When he got no reply, he agreed to pay the former price; when this offer was now declined, he agreed to pay an even higher rent. But Carstens explained to him that he had no desire to make anyone suffer a loss because of a thoughtless act involving a field that belonged to him; then he offered the land at the old price to a man who had approached him about it earlier.

And yet there had been a period in his life when people had shaken their heads over him. Not

From: *Ten German Novellas,* translated and edited by Harry Steiner Garden City, NY: Doubleday & Co., Inc., 1969), pp. 189-193.

because he in any way neglected the affairs entrusted to him, but because he seemed to become uncertain in the conduct of his own. But after a few years, Death, exploiting one of his fairly common experiences, brought things back to an even keel. It was during the continental blockade, in the so-called Blockade Era, when the little harbor town was filled with Danish officers and French seafolk and with many foreign speculators. One of the latter had been found hanged in the attic of his warehouse. That this was the work of his own hand was beyond any doubt; for the deceased man's affairs had ended in ruin after a series of losses that he had incurred in rapid succession. The only asset from his estate, it was said, was his daughter, the attractive Juliane; so far, many viewers had turned up, but no buyers.

On the very next morning this daughter sent Carstens a message inviting him to undertake the regulation of her affairs; but he curtly declined: "I want to have nothing to do with these people." But when the old longshoreman who had transmitted the request returned in the afternoon and said, "Don't be so hard, Carstens; there's no one left but the girl. She cries she'll have to do herself an injury," he got up quickly, took his cane and followed the messenger to the dead man's house.

In the middle of the room into which he was led stood the open coffin with the corpse; beside it on a low stool sat a beautiful girl, half dressed, her knees drawn up under her. She had a tortoise-shell comb in her hand and was drawing it through her heavy golden hair, which hung down loose over her back; her eyes were red and her lips trembled from vehement weeping, whether from helplessness or from grief over her father it was difficult to decide.

When Carstens went up to her, she stood up and received him with reproaches: "You won't help me?" she cried. "And I understand nothing about all these things. What am I to do? My father had a lot of money but I don't suppose there's any left. There he lies now. Do you want me to lie like that too?" She sat down on her stool again, and Carstens looked at her almost in astonishment. "But you see, miss," he then said, "I'm here to help you. Will you entrust your father's books to me?"

"Books? I know nothing about that, but I'll look." She went into an adjoining room and soon returned with a key ring. "There," she said, laying it on the table before Carstens. "They say you're a good man. Do what you wish. From now on I care about nothing."

Carstens saw in astonishment how charming she looked as she spoke these flippant words; for a sigh of relief went through her whole body and a smile like sudden sunshine passed over her pretty face.

And it turned out as she had said: Carstens worked and she cared about nothing; he could never find out how she spent her time. But the fresh red lips laughed once more, and her black mourning dress became a seductive piece of finery on her. Once when he heard her sigh, he said that if she had worries, she could tell him about them. She looked at him half smiling. "Oh, Herr Carstens," she said, sighing again, "it's so boring when you mustn't dance in these black clothes." Then, like a child wanting to have its fun, she asked him if he thought she might change them some time soon, at least for one evening; her father had always permitted her to dance, and now he was buried long ago.

When Carstens said no, she went away pouting. She had noticed long before that she could best punish him in this way for his strict morals. For under his hand the deceased man's financial confusion had at least straightened out to the extent that debit and credit seemed to balance each other; but he himself had fallen into another sort of confusion— the laughing eyes of the beautiful Juliane had befuddled the man of forty. What would normally have made him hesitate, seemed to him at this time, when the even course of his life was completely upset, far less dubious; and since the girl was unaccustomed to work and preferred a safe refuge to the troubles she would otherwise encounter, a swift marriage bond was tied between these two unequally matched people, in spite of sister Brigitte's headshaking. To be sure, the sister, who was now all the more indispensable in the household, gained nothing from the arrangement but a double burden of work. But the sudden possession of so much youth and beauty, to which in his own opinion he was entitled neither by his own person nor by his years, filled the brother with an overflowing sense of gratitude, which made him only too indulgent toward the wishes of his young wife. So it happened that the usually quiet man was soon to be found at every party arranged by the officers who were foreign to the city and the country to make their idle hours pass. Not only was this social activity above his position and means, but having been drawn into it solely because of his wife, he played an insignificant and awkward role in it.

However, Juliane died giving birth to her first child. "If only I could dance again!" she had said several times during her pregnancy. But she was never to dance again, and in this way the danger that threatened Carstens was removed. His happiness too, of course; for no matter how much she had to be scolded, and though she had scarcely belonged to him, as she perhaps belonged to no one, she had been the one who had shone the light of her beauty into his everyday world; a strange butterfly that flew over his garden and which his eyes continued to follow long after it disappeared from view. For the rest, Carstens again became, even more than before, a sensible, calm and judicious man. The boy the dead woman left behind, who soon revealed himself as the physical and also the mental heir of his beautiful mother, was raised by Carstens with a strictness which cost him some effort. The good-natured but easily seduced darling was spared none of the punishment he earned; but when the boy's beautiful eyes looked up at him with a kind of helpless terror, as always happened in such instances, the father had to restrain himself from locking the child at once in his arms with passionate tenderness.

PART SEVEN

Print of A Schematic History of Evolution

The evolution of humans from lesser animal forms was implied by Darwin's theories. The images in A Schematic History of Evolution portray primitive life forms changing into lesser animals, apes, and then a black African or perhaps Australian Aboriginal person, a posing of the matter that suggests white sensitivities. Whatever one makes of Darwinian evolution, in recent decades genetic science has done much to establish relationships between species living and extinct only hinted at in this drawing.

Science and Technology

By the mid-nineteenth century, obvious technological transformations of everyday life had won enormous prestige for science. Even political philosophers such as Marx now wished to be understood as scientific. The restless twin spirits of scientific quest and technological innovation had another aspect. During the decades before and after 1800, scientific speculation and genuine findings gradually brought into question religiously inspired ideas about the recent origins of the earth and life. Some found this deeply disturbing and others found it liberating.

One of the founders of modern geology, Charles Lyell (1797–1875), wrote his *The Principles of Geology* (1830) in order to inform the public of the scientifically demonstrable ancient origins of the planet. In 1859 Charles Darwin (1809–1882) published *The Origin of Species,* which offered a scientific account for the rise and differentiation of species. Minute differences adapted individuals within existing species to specific environments and, claimed Darwin, promoted survival. Widespread varied cumulative adaptations eventually resulted in species proliferation. Although Darwin made no direct connections between his theory of evolution and human societies, the mechanisms of change in the natural world described by him reflected a sort of competition, which fit industrial Europe's capitalist, laissez-faire economics.

The writings of Florence Nightingale (1820–1910) provide another example of the application of science to human technologies, in this case in the realm of hygiene. Her insistence upon basic sanitary measures in military environments during the Crimean War saved untold lives and utterly transformed the practice of medicine. In her *Rural Hygiene* (1859), Nightingale extended these insights into everyday life, with equally profound effect. In his *The Life of a German Inventor: The Discovery of the Automobile* (1925), Karl Benz (1844–1929) recalled his contemporaries' indifference to the idea of the self-moving carriage. The first halting trips of the new automobile with its noisy internal-combustion engine and less than reliable equipment inspired superstitious fear rather than admiration.

Study Questions

1. What links the ideas of Lyell and Darwin?
2. What religious views did Darwin challenge?
3. What were Nightingale's objectives in improving hygiene?
4. How has the public perception of technological change altered since the time of Benz?
5. What goals did Lyell, Darwin, Nightingale, and Benz have in common?
6. Image: What information, accurate or misleading, does A Schematic History of Evolution bring to viewers?

The Principles of Geology

Charles Lyell

The subtitle of Lyell's The Principles of Geology, *"An Attempt to Explain the Former Changes of the Earth's Surface by Reference to Causes now in Operation," explains his main subject matter. Lyell believed that at that time theories of geology relied too much on interpretations of the book of Genesis. He hoped to prove that, with the use of scientific methods that he helped develop, the study of geology would allow us to extend geological history back millions of years.*

Uniformity in the Series of Past Changes in the Animate and Inanimate World*

Origin of the doctrine of alternate periods of repose and disorder.—It has been truly observed that when we arrange the fossiliferous formations in chronological order, they constitute a broken and defective series of monuments; we pass without any intermediate gradations from systems of strata which are horizontal, to other systems which are highly inclined—from rocks of peculiar mineral composition to others which have a character wholly distinct—from one assemblage of organic remains to another, in which frequently nearly all the species, and a large part of the genera, are different. These violations of continuity are so common as to constitute in most regions the rule rather than the exception, and they have been considered by many geologists as conclusive in favour of sudden revolutions in the inanimate and animate world. We have already seen that according to the speculations of some writers, there have been in the past history of the planet alternate periods of tranquility and convulsion, the former enduring for ages, and resembling the state of things now experienced by man; the other brief, transient, and paroxysmal, giving rise to new mountains, seas, and valleys, annihilating one set of organic beings and ushering in the creation of another.

It will be the object of the present chapter to demonstrate that these theoretical views are not borne out by a fair interpretation of geological monuments. It is true that in the solid framework of the globe we have a chronological chain of natural records, many links of which are wanting: but a careful consideration of all the phenomena leads to the opinion that the series was originally defective— that it has been rendered still more so by time—that a great part of what remains is inaccessible to man, and even of that fraction which is accessible ninetenths or more are to this day unexplored.

The readiest way, perhaps, of persuading the reader that we may dispense with great and sudden revolutions in the geological order of events is by showing him how a regular and uninterrupted series of changes in the animate and inanimate world must give rise to such breaks in the sequence, and such unconformability of stratified rocks, as are usually thought to imply convulsions and catastrophes. It is scarcely necessary to state that the order of events thus assumed to occur, for the sake of illustration, should be in harmony with all the conclusions legitimately drawn by geologists from the structure of the earth, and must be equally in accordance with the changes observed by man to be now going on in the living as well as in the inorganic creation. It may be necessary in the present state of science to

From: *Classics of Modern Science (from Copernicus to Pasteur),* ed. By William S. Knickerbocker (New York: F.S. Crofts & Co., 1936), pp. 206–225.
*From the *Principles of Geology*, Bk. I, Ch. XIII.

supply some part of the assumed course of nature hypothetically; but if so, this must be done without any violation of probability, and always consistently with the analogy of what is known both of the past and present economy of our system. Although the discussion of so comprehensive a subject must carry the beginner far beyond his depth, it will also, it is hoped, stimulate his curiosity, and prepare him to read some elementary treatises on geology with advantage, and teach him the bearing on that science of the changes now in progress on the earth. At the same time it may enable him the better to understand the intimate connection between the Second and Third Books of this work, one of which is occupied with the changes of the inorganic, the latter with those of the organic creation.

In pursuance, then, of the plan above proposed, I will consider in this chapter, first, the laws which regulate the denudation of strata and the deposition of sediment; secondly, those which govern the fluctuation in the animate world; and thirdly, the mode in which subterranean movements affect the earth's crust.

Uniformity of change considered, first, in reference to denudation and sedimentary deposition.— First, in regard to the laws governing the deposition of new strata. If we survey the surface of the globe, we immediately perceive that it is divisible into areas of deposition and non-deposition; or, in other words, at any given time there are spaces which are the recipients, others which are not the recipients, of sedimentary matter. No new strata, for example, are thrown down on dry land, which remains the same from year to year; whereas, in many parts of the bottom of seas and lakes, mud, sand, and pebbles are annually spread out by rivers and currents. There are also great masses of limestone growing in some seas, chiefly composed of corals and shells, or, as in the depths of the Atlantic, of chalky mud made up of foraminifera and diatomaceæ.

As to the dry land, so far from being the receptacle of fresh accessions of matter, it is exposed almost everywhere to waste away. Forests may be as dense and lofty as those of Brazil, and may swarm with quadrupeds, birds, and insects, yet at the end of thousands of years one layer of black mould a few inches thick may be the sole representative of those myriads of trees, leaves, flowers, and fruits, those innumerable bones and skeletons of birds, quadrupeds, and reptiles, which tenanted the fertile region. Should this land be at length submerged, the waves of the sea may wash away in a few hours the scanty covering of mould, and it may merely import a darker shade of colour to the next stratum of marl, sand, or other matter newly thrown down. So also at the bottom of the ocean where no sediment is accumulating, seaweed, zoophytes, fish, and even shells, may multiply for ages and decompose, leaving no vestige of their form or substance behind. Their decay, in water, although more slow, is as certain and eventually as complete as in the open air. Nor can they be perpetuated for indefinite periods in a fossil state, unless imbedded in some matrix which is impervious to water, or which at least does not allow a free percolation of that fluid, impregnated as it usually is, with a slight quantity of carbonic or other acid. Such a free percolation may be prevented either by the mineral nature of the matrix itself, or by the superposition of an impermeable stratum; but if unimpeded, the fossil shell or bone will be dissolved and removed, particle after particle, and thus entirely effaced, unless petrification or the substitution of some mineral for the organic matter happen to take place.

That there has been land as well as sea at all former geological periods, we know from the fact that fossil trees and terrestrial plants are imbedded in rocks of every age, except those which are so ancient as to be very imperfectly known to us. Occasionally lacrustine and fluviatile shells, or the bones of amphibious or land reptiles, point to the same conclusion. The existence of dry land at all periods of the past implies, as before mentioned, the partial deposition of sediment, or its limitation to certain areas; and the next point to which I shall call the reader's attention is the shifting of these areas from one region to another.

First, then, variations in the site of sedimentary deposition are brought about independently of subterranean movements. There is always a slight change from year to year, or from century to century. The sediment of the Rhone, for example, thrown in the Lake of Geneva, is now conveyed to a spot a mile and a half distant from that where it accumulated in the tenth century, and six miles from the point where the delta began originally to form. We may look forward to the period when this lake will be filled up, and then the distribution of the transported matter will be suddenly altered, for the mud and sand brought down from the Alps will thenceforth, instead of being deposited near Geneva, be carried nearly 200 miles southwards, where the Rhone enters the Mediterranean.

In the deltas of large rivers, such as those of the Ganges and Indus, the mud is first carried down for many centuries through one arm, and on this being stopped up it is discharged by another, and may then enter the sea at a point 50 or 100 miles distant from its first receptacle. The direction of marine currents is also liable to be changed by various accidents, as by the heaping up of new sandbanks, or the wearing away of cliffs and promontories.

But, secondly, all these causes of fluctuation in the sedimentary areas are entirely subordinate to those great upward or downward movements of lands, which will be presently spoken of, as prevailing over large tracts of the globe. By such elevation or subsidence certain spaces are gradually submerged, or made gradually to emerge: in the one case sedimentary deposition may be suddenly renewed after having been suspended for one or more geological periods, in the other as suddenly made to cease after having continued for ages.

If deposition be renewed after a long interval, the new strata will usually differ greatly from the sedimentary rocks previously formed in the same place, and especially if the older rocks have suffered derangement, which implies a change in the physical geography of the district since the previous conveyance of sediment to the same spot. It may happen, however, that, even where the two groups, the superior and the inferior, are horizontal and conformable to each other, they may still differ entirely in mineral character, because, since the origin of the older formation, the geography of some distant country has been altered. In that country rocks before concealed may have become exposed by denudation; volcanoes may have burst out and covered the surface with scoriæ and lava; or new lakes, intercepting the sediment previously conveyed from the upper country, may have been formed by subsidence; and other fluctuations may have occurred, by which the materials brought down from thence by rivers to the sea have acquired a distinct mineral character.

It is well known that the stream of the Mississippi is charged with sediment of a different colour from that of the Arkansas and Red Rivers, which are tinged with red mud, derived from rocks of porphyry and red gypseous clays in "the far west." The waters of the Uruguay, says Darwin, draining a granitic country, are clear and black, those of the Parana, red. The mud with which the Indus is loaded, says Burnes, is of a clayey hue, that of the Chenab, on the other hand, is reddish, that of the Sutlej is more pale. The same causes which make these several rivers, sometimes situated at no great distance the one from the other, to differ greatly in the character of their sediment, will make the waters draining the same country at different epochs, especially before and after great revolutions in physical geography, to be entirely dissimilar. It is scarcely necessary to add that marine currents will be affected in an analogous manner in consequence of the formation of new shoals, the emergence of new islands, the subsidence of others, the gradual waste of neighbouring coasts, the growth of new deltas, the increase of coral reefs, volcanic eruptions, and other changes.

Uniformity of change considered, secondly, in reference to the living creation.—Secondly, in regard to the vicissitudes of the living creation, all are agreed that the successive groups of sedimentary strata found in the earth's new crust are not only dissimilar in mineral composition for reasons above alluded to, but are likewise distinguishable from each other by their organic remains. The general inference drawn from the study and comparison of the various groups, arranged in chronological order, is this: that at successive periods distinct tribes of animals and plants have inhabited the land and waters, and that the organic types of the newer formations are more analogous to species now existing than those of more ancient rocks. If we then turn to the present state of the animate creation, and inquire whether it has now become fixed and stationary, we discover that, on the contrary, it is in a state of continual flux—that there are many causes in action which tend to the extinction of species, and which are conclusive against the doctrine of their unlimited durability.

There are also causes which give rise to new varieties and races in plants and animals, and new forms are continually supplanting others which had endured for ages. But natural history has been successfully cultivated for so short a period, that a few examples only of local, and perhaps but one or two of absolute, extirpation of species can as yet be proved, and these only where the interference of man has been conspicuous. It will nevertheless appear evident, from the facts and arguments detailed in the chapters which treat of the geographical distribution of species in the next volume, that man is not the only exterminating agent; and that, independently of his intervention, the annihilation of species is promoted by the multiplication and gradual diffusion of every animal or plant. It will also appear that every alteration in the physical geography and climate of the globe cannot fail to have the same tendency. If we proceed still farther, and inquire whether new species are substituted from time to time for those which die out, we find that the successive introduction of new forms appears to have been a constant part of the economy of the terrestrial system, and if we have no direct proof of the fact it is because the changes take place so slowly as not to come within the period of exact scientific observation. To enable the reader to appreciate the gradual manner in which a passage may have taken place from an extinct fauna to that now living, I shall say a few words on the fossils of successive Tertiary periods. When we trace the series of formations from the more ancient to the more modern, it is in these Tertiary deposits that we first meet with assemblages of organic remains having a near analogy to the fauna of certain parts of the globe in our own time. In the Eocene, or oldest subdivisions, some few of the testacea belong to existing species, although almost all of them, and apparently all the associated vertebrata, are now extinct. These Eocene strata are succeeded by a great number of more modern deposits, which depart gradually in the character of their fossils from the Eocene type, and approach more and more to that of the living creation. In the present state of science, it is chiefly by the aid of shells, that we are enabled to arrive at these results, for of all classes the testacea are the most generally diffused in a fossil state, and may be called the medals principally employed by nature in recording the chronology of past events. In the Upper Miocene rocks we begin to find a considerable number, although still a minority, of recent species, intermixed with some fossils common to the preceding, or Eocene, epoch. We then arrive at the Pliocene strata, in which species now contemporary with man begin to preponderate, and in the newest of which nine-tenths of the fossils agree with species still inhabiting the neighbouring sea. It is in the Post-Tertiary strata, where all the shells agree with species now living, that we have discovered the first or earliest known remains of man associated with the bones of quadrupeds, some of which are of extinct species.

In thus passing from the older to the newer members of the Tertiary system, we meet with many chasms, but none which separate entirely, by a broad line of demarcation, one state of the organic world from another. There are no signs of an abrupt termination of one fauna and flora, and the starting into life of new and wholly distinct forms. Although we are far from being able to demonstrate geologically an insensible transition from the Eocene to the Miocene, or even from the latter to the recent fauna, yet the more we enlarge and perfect our general survey, the more nearly do we approximate to such a continuous series, and the more gradually are we conducted from times when many of the genera and nearly all the species were extinct, to those in which scarcely a single species flourished, which we do not know to exist at present. Dr. A. Philippi, indeed, after an elaborate comparison of the fossil tertiary shells of Sicily with those now living in the Mediterranean, announced, as the result of his examination, that there are strata in that island which attest a very gradual passage from a period when only thirteen in a hundred of the shells were like the species now living in the sea, to an era when the recent species had attained a proportion of ninety-five in a hundred. There is, therefore, evidence, he says, in Sicily of this revolution in the animate world having been effected "without the intervention of any convulsion or abrupt changes, certain species having from time died out, and others having been introduced, until at length the existing fauna was elaborated."

In no part of Europe is the absence of all signs of man or his works, in strata of comparatively modern date, more striking than in Sicily. In the central parts of that island we observe a lofty table-land and hills, sometimes rising to the height of 3,000 feet, capped with a limestone, in which from 70 to 85 per cent of the fossil testacea are specifically identical with those now inhabiting the Mediterranean. These calcareous and other argillaceous strata of the same age are intersected by deep valleys which appear to have been gradually formed by denudation, but have not varied materially in width or depth since Sicily was first colonized by the Greeks. The limestone, moreover, which is of so late a date in geological chronology, was quarried for building those ancient temples of Girgenti and Syracuse, of which the ruins carry us back to a remote era in human history. If we are lost in conjectures when speculating on the ages required to lift up these formations to the height of several thousand feet above the sea, and to excavate the valleys, how much more remote must be the era when the same rocks were gradually formed beneath the waters!

The intense cold of the Glacial period was spoken of in the tenth chapter. Although we have not yet succeeded in detecting proofs of the origin of man antecedently to that epoch, we have yet found evidence that most of the testacea, and not a few of the quadrupeds, which preceded, were of the same species as those which followed the extreme cold. To whatever local disturbances this cold may have given rise in the distribution of species, it seems to have done little in effecting their annihilation. We may conclude, therefore, from a survey of the tertiary and modern strata, which constitute a more complete and unbroken series than rocks of older date, that the extinction and creation of species have been, and are, the result of a slow and gradual change in the organic world.

Uniformity of change considered, thirdly, in reference to subterranean movements.—Thirdly, to pass on to the last of the three topics before proposed for discussion, the reader will find, in the account given in the Second Book, Vol. II., of the earthquakes recorded in history, that certain countries have, from time immemorial, been rudely shaken again and again; while others, comprising by far the largest part of the globe, have remained to all appearance motionless. In the regions of convulsion rocks have been rent asunder, the surface has been forced up into ridges, chasms have opened, or the ground throughout large spaces has been permanently lifted up above or let down below its former level. In the regions of tranquillity some areas have remained at rest, but others have been ascertained, by a comparison of measurements made at different periods, to have arisen by an insensible motion, as in Sweden, or to have subsided very slowly, as in Greenland. That these same movements, whether ascending or descending, have continued for ages in the same direction has been established by historical or geological evidence. Thus we find on the opposite coasts of Sweden that brackish water deposits, like those now forming in the Baltic, occur on the eastern side, and upraised strata filled with purely marine shells, now proper to the ocean, on the western coast. Both of these have been lifted up to an elevation of several hundred feet above high-water mark. The rise within the historical period has not amounted to many yards, but the greater extent of antecedent upheaval is proved by the occurrence in inland spots, several hundred feet high, of deposits filled with fossil shells of species now living either in the ocean or the Baltic.

It must in general be more difficult to detect proofs of slow and gradual subsidence than of elevation, but the theory which accounts for the form of circular coral reefs and lagoon islands, and which will be explained in the concluding chapter of this work, will satisfy the reader that there are spaces on the globe, several thousand miles in circumference, throughout which the downward movement has predominated for ages, and yet the land has never, in a single instance, gone down suddenly for several hundred feet at once. Yet geology demonstrates that the persistency of subterranean movements in one direction has not been perpetual throughout all past time. There have been great oscillations of level, by which a surface of dry land has been submerged to a depth of several thousand feet, and then at a period long subsequent raised again and made to emerge. Nor have the regions now motionless been always at rest; and some of those which are at present the theatres of reiterated earthquakes have formerly enjoyed a long continuance of tranquillity. But, although disturbances have ceased after having long prevailed, or have recommenced after a suspension of ages, there has been no universal disruption of the earth's crust or desolation of the surface since times the most remote. The non-occurrence of such a general convulsion is proved by the perfect horizontality now retained by some of the most ancient fossiliferous strata throughout wide areas.

That the subterranean forces have visited different parts of the globe at successive periods is inferred chiefly from the unconformability of strata belonging to groups of different ages. Thus, for example, on the borders of Wales and Shropshire, we find the slaty beds of the ancient Silurian system inclined and vertical, while the beds of the overlying carboniferous shale and sandstone are horizontal. All are agreed that in such a case the older set of strata had suffered great disturbance before the deposition of the newer or carboniferous beds, and that these last have never since been violently fractured, nor have ever been bent into folds, whether by sudden or continuous lateral pressure. On the other hand, the more ancient or Silurian group suffered only a local derangement, and neither in Wales nor elsewhere are all the rocks of that age found to be curved or vertical.

In various parts of Europe, for example, and particularly near Lake Wener in the south of Sweden, and in many parts of Russia, the Silurian strata maintain the most perfect horizontality; and a similar observation may be made respecting limestones and shales of like antiquity in the great lake district of Canada and the United States. These older rocks are still as flat and horizontal as when first formed; yet, since their origin, not only have most of the actual mountain-chains been uplifted, but some of the very rocks of which those mountains are composed have been formed, some of them by igneous and others by aqueous action.

It would be easy to multiply instances of similar unconformability in formations of other ages; but a few more will suffice. The carboniferous rocks before alluded to as horizontal on the borders of Wales are vertical in the Mendip hills in Somersetshire, where the overlying beds of the New Red Sandstone are horizontal. Again, in the Wolds of Yorkshire the last-mentioned sandstone supports on its curved and inclined beds the horizontal Chalk.

The Chalk again is vertical on the flanks of the Pyrenees, and the tertiary strata repose unconformably upon it.

As almost every country supplies illustrations of the same phenomena, they who advocate the doctrine of alternate periods of disorder and repose may appeal to the facts above described, as proving that every district has been by turns convulsed by earthquakes and then respited for ages from convulsions. But so it might with equal truth be affirmed that every part of Europe has been visited alternately by winter and summer, although it has always been winter and always summer in some part of the planet, and neither of these seasons has ever reigned simultaneously over the entire globe. They have been always shifting from place to place; but the vicissitudes which recur thus annually in a single spot are never allowed to interfere with the invariable uniformity of seasons throughout the whole planet.

So, in regard to subterranean movements, the theory of the perpetual uniformity of the force which they exert on the earth's crust is quite consistent with the admission of their alternate development and suspension for long and indefinite periods within limited geographical areas.

If, for reasons before stated, we assume a continual extinction of species and appearance of others on the globe, it will then follow that the fossils of strata formed at two distant periods on the same spot will differ even more certainly than the mineral composition of those strata. For rocks of the same kind have sometimes been reproduced in the same district after a long interval of time; whereas all the evidence derived from fossil remains is in favour of the opinion that species which have once died out have never been reproduced. The submergence, then, of land must be often attended by the commencement of a new class of sedimentary deposits, characterized by a new set of fossil animals and plants, while the reconversion of the bed of the sea into land may arrest at once and for an indefinite time the formation of geological monuments. Should the land again sink, strata will again be formed; but one or many entire revolutions in animal or vegetable life may have been completed in the interval.

As to the want of completeness in the fossiliferous series, which may be said to be almost universal, we have only to reflect on what has been already said of the laws governing sedimentary deposition, and those which give rise to fluctuations in the animate world, to be convinced that a very rare combination of circumstances can alone give rise to such a superposition and preservation of strata as will bear testimony to the gradual passage from one state of organic life to another. To produce such strata nothing less will be requisite than the fortunate coincidence of the following conditions: first, a never-failing supply of sediment in the same region throughout a period of vast duration; secondly, the fitness of the deposit in every part for the permanent preservation of imbedded fossils; and, thirdly, a gradual subsidence to prevent the sea or lake from being filled up and converted into land.

It will appear in the chapter on coral reefs, that, in certain parts of the Pacific and Indian Oceans, most of these conditions, if not all, are complied with, and the constant growth of coral, keeping pace with the sinking of the bottom of the sea, seems to have gone on so slowly, for such indefinite periods, that the signs of a gradual change in organic life might probably be detected in that quarter of the globe if we could explore its submarine geology. Instead of the growth of coralline limestone, let us suppose, in some other place, the continuous deposition of fluviatile mud and sand, such as the Ganges and Brahmapootra have poured for thousands of years into the Bay of Bengal. Part of this bay, although of considerable depth, might at length be filled up before an appreciable amount of change was effected in the fish, mollusca, and other inhabitants of the sea and neighbouring land. But if the bottom be lowered by sinking at the same rate that it is raised by fluviatile mud, the bay can never be turned into dry land. In that case one new layer of matter may be superimposed upon another for a thickness of many thousand feet, and the fossils of the inferior beds may differ greatly from those entombed in the uppermost, yet every intermediate gradation may be indicated in the passage from an older to a newer assemblage of species. Granting, however, that such an unbroken sequence of monuments may thus be elaborated in certain parts of the sea, and that the strata happen to be all of them well

adapted to preserve the included fossils from decomposition, how many accidents must still concur before these submarine formations will be laid open to our investigation! The whole deposit must first be raised several thousand feet, in order to bring into view the very foundation; and during the process of exposure the superior beds must not be entirely swept away by denudation.

In the first place, the chances are nearly as three to one against the mere emergence of the mass above the waters, because nearly three-fourths of the globe are covered by the ocean. But if it be upheaved and made to constitute part of the dry land, it must also, before it can be available for our instruction, become part of that area already surveyed by geologists. In this small fraction of land already explored, and still very imperfectly known, we are required to find a set of strata deposited under peculiar conditions, and which, having been originally of limited extent, would have been probably much lessened by subsequent denudation.

Yet it is precisely because we do not encounter at every step the evidence of such gradations from one state of the organic world to another, that so many geologists have embraced the doctrine of great and sudden revolutions in the history of the animate world. Not content with simply availing themselves, for the convenience of classification, of those gaps and chasms which here and there interrupt the continuity of the chronological series, as at present known, they deduce, from the frequency of these breaks in the chain of records, an irregular mode of succession in the events themselves, both in the organic and inorganic world. But, besides that some links of the chain which once existed are now entirely lost and others concealed from view, we have good reason to suspect that it was never complete originally. It may undoubtedly be said that strata have been always forming somewhere, and therefore at every moment of past time Nature has added a page to her archives; but, in reference to this subject, it should be remembered that we can never hope to compile a consecutive history by gathering together monuments which were originally detached and scattered over the globe. For, as the species of organic beings contemporaneously inhabiting remote regions are distinct, the fossils of the first of several periods which may be preserved in any one country, as in America for example, will have no connection with those of a second period found in India, and will therefore no more enable us to trace the signs of a gradual change in the living creation, than a fragment of Chinese history will fill up a blank in the political annals of Europe.

The absence of any deposits of importance containing recent shells in Chili, or anywhere on the western shore of South America, naturally led Mr. Darwin to the conclusion that "where the bed of the sea is either stationary or rising, circumstances are far less favourable than where the level is sinking to the accumulation of conchiferous strata of sufficient thickness and extension to resist the average vast amount of denudation." In like manner the beds of superficial sand, clay, and gravel, with recent shells, on the coasts of Norway and Sweden, where the land has risen in Post-tertiary times, are so thin and scanty as to incline us to admit a similar proposition. We may in fact assume that in all cases where the bottom of the sea has been undergoing continuous elevation, the total thickness of sedimentary matter accumulating at depths suited to the habitation of most of the species of shells can never be great, nor can the deposits be thickly covered with superincumbent matter, so as to be consolidated by pressure. When they are upheaved, therefore, the waves on the beach will bear down and disperse the loose materials; whereas, if the bed of the sea subsides slowly, a mass of strata containing abundance of such species as live at moderate depths, may be formed and may increase in thickness to any amount. It may also extend horizontally over a broad area, as the water gradually encroaches on the subsiding land.

Hence it will follow that great violations of continuity in the chronological series of fossiliferous rocks will always exist, and the imperfection of the record, though lessened, will never be removed by future discoveries. For not only will no deposits originate on the dry land, but those formed in the sea near land, which is undergoing constant upheaval, will usually be too slight in thickness to endure for ages.

In proportion as we become acquainted with larger geographical areas, many of the gaps, by which a chronological table is rendered defective, will be removed. We were enabled by aid of the labours of Prof. Sedgwick and Sir Roderick Murchison, to intercalate, in 1838, the marine strata of the Devonian period, with their fossil shells, corals, and fish, between the Silurian and Carboniferous rocks. Previously the marine fauna of these last-mentioned formations wanted the connecting links which now render the passage from the one to the other much less abrupt. In like manner the Upper Miocene has no representative in England, but in France, Germany, and Switzerland it constitutes a most instructive link between the living creation and the middle of the great Tertiary period. Still we must expect, for reasons before stated, that chasms will forever continue to occur, in some parts of our sedimentary series.

Concluding remarks on the consistency of the theory of gradual change with the existence of great breaks in the series.—To return to the general argument pursued in this chapter, it is assumed, for reasons above explained, that a slow change of species is in simultaneous operation everywhere throughout the habitable surface of sea and land; whereas the fossilization of plants and animals is confined to those areas where new strata are produced. These areas, as we have seen, are always shifting their position, so that the fossilizing process, by means of which the commemoration of the particular state of the organic world, at any given time, is effected, may be said to move about, visiting and revisiting different tracts in succession.

To make still more clear the supposed working of this machinery, I shall compare it to a somewhat analogous case that might be imagined to occur in the history of human affairs. Let the mortality of the population of a large country represent the successive extinction of species, and the births of new individuals the introduction of new species. While these fluctuations are gradually taking place everywhere, suppose commissioners to be appointed to visit each province of the country in succession, taking an exact account of the number, names and individual peculiarities of all the inhabitants, and leaving in each district a register containing a record of this information. If, after the completion of one census, another is immediately made on the same plan, and then another, there will at last be a series of statistical documents in each province. When those belonging to any one province are arranged in chronological order, the contents of such as stand next to each other will differ according to the length of the intervals of time between the taking of each census. If, for example, there are sixty provinces, and all the registers are made in a single year and renewed annually, the number of births and deaths will be so small, in proportion to the whole of the inhabitants, during the interval between the compiling of two consecutive documents, that the individuals described in such documents will be nearly identical; whereas, if the survey of each of the sixty provinces occupies all the commissioners for a whole year, so that they are unable to revisit the same place until the expiration of sixty years, there will then be an almost entire discordance between the persons enumerated in two consecutive registers in the same province. There are, undoubtedly, other causes, besides the mere quantity of time, which may augment or diminish the amount of discrepancy. Thus, at some periods, a pestilential disease may have lessened the average duration of human life; or a variety of circumstances may have caused the births to be unusually numerous, and the population to multiply; or a province may be suddenly colonized by persons migrating from surrounding districts.

These exceptions may be compared to the accelerated rate of fluctuations in the fauna and flora of a particular region, in which the climate and physical geography may be undergoing an extraordinary degree of alteration.

But I must remind the reader that the case above proposed has no pretensions to be regarded as an exact parallel to the geological phenomena which I desire to illustrate; for the commissioners are supposed to visit the different provinces in rotation; whereas the commemorating processes by which organic remains become fossilized, although they are always shifting from one area to the other, are yet very irregular in their movements. They may abandon and revisit many spaces again and again, before they once approach another district; and, besides this source of irregularity, it may often happen that, while the depositing process is suspended, denudation may take place, which may be compared to the occasional destruction by fire or other causes of some of the statistical documents before mentioned. It is evident that where such accidents occur the want of continuity in the series may

become indefinitely great, and that the monuments which follow next in succession will by no means be equidistant from each other in point of time.

If this train of reasoning be admitted, the occasional distinctness of the fossil remains, in formations immediately in contact, would be a necessary consequence of the existing laws of sedimentary deposition and subterranean movement, accompanied by a constant dying-out and renovation of species.

As all the conclusions above insisted on are directly opposed to opinions still popular, I shall add another comparison, in the hope of preventing any possible misapprehension of the argument. Suppose we had discovered two buried cities at the foot of Vesuvius, immediately superimposed upon each other, with a great mass of tuff and lava intervening, just as Portici and Resina, if now covered with ashes, would overlie Herculaneum. An antiquary might possibly be entitled to infer, from the inscriptions on public edifices, that the inhabitants of the inferior and older city were Greeks, and those of the modern town Italians. But he would reason very hastily if he also concluded from these data, that there had been a sudden change from the Greek to the Italian language in Campania. But if he afterwards found three buried cities, one above the other, the intermediate one being Roman, while, as in the former example, the lowest was Greek and the uppermost Italian, he would then perceive the fallacy of his former opinion and would begin to suspect that the catastrophes, by which the cities were inhumed, might have no relation whatever to the fluctuations in the language of the inhabitants; and that, as the Roman tongue had evidently intervened between the Greek and Italian, so many other dialects may have been spoken in succession, and the passage from the Greek to the Italian may have been very gradual, some terms growing obsolete, while others were introduced from time to time.

If this antiquary could have shown that the volcanic paroxysms of Vesuvius were so governed as that cities should be buried one above the other, just as often as any variation occurred in the language of the inhabitants, then, indeed, the abrupt passage from a Greek to a Roman, and from a Roman to an Italian city, would afford proof of fluctuations no less sudden in the language of the people.

So, in Geology, if we could assume that it is part of the plan of Nature to preserve, in every region of the globe, an unbroken series of monuments to commemorate the vicissitudes of the organic creation, we might infer the sudden extirpation of species, and the simultaneous introduction of others, as often as two formations in contact are found to include dissimilar organic fossils. But we must shut our eyes to the whole economy of the existing causes, aqueous, igneous, and organic, if we fail to perceive that such is not the plan of Nature.

I shall now conclude the discussion of a question with which we have been occupied since the beginning of the fifth chapter—namely, whether there has been any interruption, from the remotest periods, of one uniform and continuous system of change in the animate and inanimate world. We were induced to enter into that inquiry by reflecting how much the progress of opinion in Geology had been influenced by the assumption that the analogy was slight in kind, and still more slight in degree, between the causes which produced the former revolutions of the globe, and those now in every-day operation. It appeared clear that the earlier geologists had not only a scanty acquaintance with existing changes, but were singularly unconscious of the amount of their ignorance. With the presumption naturally inspired by this unconsciousness, they had no hesitation in deciding at once that time could never enable the existing powers of nature to work out changes of great magnitude, still less such important revolutions as those which are brought to light by Geology. They therefore felt themselves at liberty to indulge their imaginations in guessing at what might be, rather than inquiring what is; in other words, they employed themselves in conjecturing what might have been the course of Nature at a remote period, rather than in the investigation of what was the course of Nature in their own times.

It appeared to them far more philosophical to speculate on the possibilities of the past, than patiently to explore the realities of the present; and having invented theories under the influences of such maxims, they were consistently unwilling to test their validity by the criterion of their accordance with the ordinary operations of Nature. On the contrary, the claims of each new hypothesis to credibility appeared enhanced by the great contrast, in kind or intensity, of the causes referred to and those now in operation.

Never was there a dogma more calculated to foster indolence, and to blunt the keen edge of curiosity, than this assumption of the discordance between the ancient and existing causes of change. It produced a state of mind unfavourable in the highest degree to the candid reception of the evidence of those minute but incessant alterations which every part of the earth's surface is undergoing, and by which the condition of its living inhabitants is continually made to vary. The student, instead of being encouraged with the hope of interpreting the enigmas presented to him in the earth's structure—instead of being prompted to undertake laborious inquiries into the natural history of the organic world, and the complicated effects of the igneous and aqueous causes now in operation—was taught to despond from the first. Geology, it was affirmed, could never rise to the rank of an exact science; the greater number of phenomena must forever remain inexplicable, or only be partially elucidated by ingenious conjectures. Even the mystery which invested the subject was said to constitute one of its principal charms, affording, as it did, full scope to the fancy to indulge in a boundless field of speculation.

The course directly opposed to this method of philosophizing consists in an earnest and patient inquiry, how far geological appearances are reconcilable with the effect of changes now in progress, or which may be in progress in regions inaccessible to us, but of which the reality is attested by volcanoes and subterranean movements. It also endeavours to estimate the aggregate result of ordinary operations multiplied by time, and cherishes a sanguine hope that the resources to be derived from observation and experiment, or from the study of Nature such as she now is, are very far from being exhausted. For this reason all theories are rejected which involve the assumption of sudden and violent catastrophes and revolutions of the whole earth, and its inhabitants—theories which are restrained by no reference to existing analogies, and in which a desire is manifested to cut, rather than patiently to untie, the Gordian knot.

We have now, at least, the advantage of knowing, from experience, that an opposite method has always put geologists on the road that leads to truth—suggesting views which, although imperfect at first, have been found capable of improvement, until at last adopted by universal consent; while the method of speculating on a former distinct state of things and causes has led invariably to a multitude of contradictory systems, which have been overthrown one after the other—have been found incapable of modification—and which have often required to be precisely reversed.

The remainder of this work will be devoted to an investigation of the changes now going on in the crust of the earth and its inhabitants. The importance which the student will attach to such researches will mainly depend on the degree of confidence which he feels in the principles above expounded. If he firmly believes in the resemblance or identity of the ancient and present system of terrestrial changes, he will regard every fact collected respecting the causes in diurnal action as affording him a key to the interpretation of some mystery in the past. Events which have occurred at the most distant periods in the animate and inanimate world will be acknowledged to throw light on each other, and the deficiency of our information respecting some of the most obscure parts of the present creation will be removed. For as, by studying the external configuration of the existing land and its inhabitants, we may restore in imagination the appearance of the ancient continents which have passed away, so may we obtain from the deposits of ancient seas and lakes an insight into the nature of the subaqueous processes now in operation, and of many forms of organic life which, though now existing, are veiled from sight. Rocks, also, produced by subterranean fire in former ages, at great depths in the bowels of the earth, present us, when upraised by gradual movements, and exposed to the light of heaven, with an image of those changes which the deep-seated volcano may now occasion in the nether regions. Thus, although we are mere sojourners on the surface of the planet, chained to a mere point in space, enduring but for a moment of time, the human mind is not only enabled to number worlds beyond the unassisted ken of mortal eye, but to trace the events of indefinite ages before the creation of our race, and is not even withheld from penetrating into the dark secrets of the ocean, or the interior of the solid globe; free, like the spirit which the poet described as animating the universe,

—*ire per omnes*
Terrasque, tractusque maris, coelumque profundum.

The Origin of Species

Charles Darwin

The Origin of Species is one of the most famous and controversial books of the last two centuries. In it Darwin describes scientifically the rise and differentiation of species—his understanding of natural selection. Today Darwin's explanation of evolutionary theory is often portrayed in stark contrast to a religious understanding of creation. Darwin himself was sharply aware of potential religious controversy and attempted to reconcile his views on the origins of species with religious views of the divine origins of the universe.

Recapitulation and Conclusion

As this whole volume is one long argument, it may be convenient to the reader to have the leading facts and inferences briefly recapitulated.

That many and serious objections may be advanced against the theory of descent with modification through variation and natural selection, I do not deny. I have endeavoured to give to them their full force. Nothing at first can appear more difficult to believe than that the more complex organs and instincts have been perfected, not by means superior to, though analogous with, human reason, but by the accumulation of innumerable slight variations, each good for the individual possessor. Nevertheless, this difficulty, though appearing to our imagination insuperably great, cannot be considered real if we admit the following propositions, namely, that all parts of the organisation and instincts offer, at least, individual differences—that there is a struggle for existence leading to the preservation of profitable deviations of structure or instinct—and, lastly, that gradations in the state of perfection of each organ may have existed, each good of its kind. The truth of these propositions cannot, I think, be disputed.

It is, no doubt, extremely difficult even to conjecture by what gradations many structures have been perfected, more especially amongst broken and failing groups of organic beings, which have suffered much extinction, but we see so many strange gradations in nature, that we ought to be extremely cautious in saying that any organ or instinct, or any whole structure, could not have arrived at its present state by many graduated steps. There are, it must be admitted, cases of special difficulty opposed to the theory of natural selection; and one of the most curious of these is the existence in the same community of two or three defined castes of workers or sterile female ants; but I have attempted to show how these difficulties can be mastered.

* * *

Turning to geographical distribution, the difficulties encountered on the theory of descent with modification are serious enough. All the individuals of the same species, and all the species of the same genus, or even higher group, are descended from common parents; and therefore, in however distant and isolated parts of the world they may now be found, they must in the course of successive generations have travelled from some one point to all the others. We are often wholly unable even to conjecture how this could have been effected. Yet, as we have reason to believe that some species have retained the same specific form for very long periods of time, immensely long as measured by years, too much stress ought

From: Charles Darwin, *The Origin of Species by Means of Natural Selection; or, The Preservation of Favored Races in the Struggle for Life* (New York: The Modern Library, 1936), p. 353, pp. 355–374.

not to be laid on the occasional wide diffusion of the same species; for during very long periods there will always have been a good chance for wide migration by many means. A broken or interrupted range may often be accounted for by the extinction of the species in the intermediate regions. It cannot be denied that we are as yet very ignorant as to the full extent of the various climatal and geographical changes which have affected the earth during modern periods; and such changes will often have facilitated migration. As an example, I have attempted to show how potent has been the influence of the Glacial period on the distribution of the same and of allied species throughout the world. We are as yet profoundly ignorant of the many occasional means of transport. With respect to distinct species of the same genus inhabiting distant and isolated regions, as the process of modification has necessarily been slow, all the means of migration will have been possible during a very long period; and consequently the difficulty of the wide diffusion of the species of the same genus is in some degree lessened.

As according to the theory of natural selection an interminable number of intermediate forms must have existed, linking together all the species in each group by gradations as fine as are our existing varieties, it may be asked: Why do we not see these linking forms all around us? Why are not all organic beings blended together in an inextricable chaos? With respect to existing forms, we should remember that we have no right to expect (excepting in rare cases) to discover *directly* connecting links between them, but only between each and some extinct and supplanted form. Even on a wide area, which has during a long period remained continuous, and of which the climatic and other conditions of life change insensibly in proceeding from a district occupied by one species into another district occupied by a closely allied species, we have no just right to expect often to find intermediate varieties in the intermediate zones. For we have reason to believe that only a few species of a genus ever undergo change; the other species becoming utterly extinct and leaving no modified progeny. Of the species which do change, only a few within the same country change at the same time; and all modifications are slowly effected. I have also shown that the intermediate varieties which probably at first

existed in the intermediate zones, would be liable to be supplanted by the allied forms on either hand; for the latter, from existing in greater numbers, would generally be modified and improved at a quicker rate than the intermediate varieties, which existed in lesser numbers; so that the intermediate varieties would, in the long run, be supplanted and exterminated.

On this doctrine of the extermination of an infinitude of connecting links, between the living and extinct inhabitants of the world, and at each successive period between the extinct and still older species, why is not every geological formation charged with such links? Why does not every collection of fossil remains afford plain evidence of the gradation and mutation of the forms of life? Although geological research has undoubtedly revealed the former existence of many links, bringing numerous forms of life much closer together, it does not yield the infinitely many fine gradations between past and present species required on the theory; and this is the most obvious of the many objections which may be urged against it. Why, again, do whole groups of allied species appear, though this appearance is often false, to have come in suddenly on the successive geological stages? Although we now know that organic beings appeared on this globe, at a period incalculably remote, long before the lowest bed of the Cambrian system was deposited, why do we not find beneath this system great piles of strata stored with the remains of the progenitors of the Cambrian fossils? For on the theory, such strata must somewhere have been deposited at these ancient and utterly unknown epochs of the world's history.

I can answer these questions and objections only on the supposition that the geological record is far more imperfect than most geologists believe. The number of specimens in all our museums is absolutely as nothing compared with the countless generations of countless species which have certainly existed. The parent-form of any two or more species would not be in all its characters directly intermediate between its modified offspring, any more than the rock-pigeon is directly intermediate in crop and tail between its descendants, the pouter and fantail pigeons. We should not be able to recognise a species as the parent of another and modified species, if we were to examine the two ever so closely, unless we possessed most of the intermediate links; and owing to the imperfection of the geological record, we have no just right to expect to find so many links. If two or three, or even more linking forms were discovered, they would simply be ranked by many naturalists as so many new species, more especially if found in different geological substages, let their differences be ever so slight. Numerous existing doubtful forms could be named which are probably varieties; but who will pretend that in future ages so many fossil links will be discovered, that naturalists will be able to decide whether or not these doubtful forms ought to be called varieties? Only a small portion of the world has been geologically explored. Only organic beings of certain classes can be preserved in a fossil condition, at least in any great number. Many species when once formed never undergo any further change but become extinct without leaving modified descendants; and the periods, during which species have undergone modification, though long as measured by years, have probably been short in comparison with the periods during which they retain the same form. It is the dominant and widely ranging species which vary most frequently and vary most, and varieties are often at first local—both causes rendering the discovery of intermediate links in any one formation less likely. Local varieties will not spread into other and distant regions until they are considerably modified and improved; and when they have spread and are discovered in a geological formation, they appear as if suddenly created there, and will be simply classed as new species. Most formations have been intermittent in their accumulation; and their duration has probably been shorter than the average duration of specific forms. Successive formations are in most cases separated from each other by blank intervals of time of great length; for fossiliferous formations thick enough to resist future degradations can as a general rule be accumulated only where much sediment is deposited on the subsiding bed of the sea. During the alternate periods of elevation and of stationary level the record will generally be blank. During these latter periods there will probably be more variability in the forms of life; during periods of subsidence, more extinction.

With respect to the absence of strata rich in fossils beneath the Cambrian formation, I can recur only to the hypothesis given in the tenth chapter; namely, that though our continents and oceans have endured for an enormous period in nearly their present relative positions, we have no reason to assume that this has always been the case; consequently formations much older than any now known may lie buried beneath the great oceans. With respect to the lapse of time not having been sufficient since our planet was consolidated for the assumed amount of organic change, and this objection, as urged by Sir William Thompson, is probably one of the gravest as yet advanced, I can only say, firstly, that we do not know at what rate species change as measured by years, and secondly, that many philosophers are not as yet willing to admit that we know enough of the constitution of the universe and of the interior of our globe to speculate with safety on its past duration.

That the geological record is imperfect all will admit; but that it is imperfect to the degree required by our theory, few will be inclined to admit. If we look to long enough intervals of time, geology plainly declares that species have all changed; and they have changed in the manner required by the theory, for they have changed slowly and in a graduated manner. We clearly see this in the fossil remains from consecutive formations invariably being much more closely related to each other, than are the fossils from widely separated formations.

Such is the sum of the several chief objections and difficulties which may be justly urged against the theory; and I have now briefly recapitulated the answers and explanations which, as far as I can see, may be given. I have felt these difficulties far too heavily during many years to doubt their weight. But it deserves especial notice that the more important objections relate to questions on which we are confessedly ignorant; nor do we know how ignorant we are. We do not know all the possible transitional gradations between the simplest and the most perfect organs; It cannot be pretended that we know all the varied means of Distribution during the long lapse of years, or that we know how imperfect is the Geological Record. Serious as these several objections are, in my judgment they are by no means sufficient to overthrow the theory of descent with subsequent modification.

Now let us turn to the other side of the argument. Under domestication we see much variability, caused, or at least excited, by changed conditions of life; but often in so obscure a manner, that we are tempted to consider the variations as spontaneous. Variability is governed by many complex laws,—by correlated growth, compensation, the increased use and disuse of parts, and the definite action of the surrounding conditions. There is much difficulty in ascertaining how largely our domestic productions have been modified; but we may safely infer that the amount has been large, and that modifications can be inherited for long periods. As long as the conditions of life remain the same, we have reason to believe that a modification, which has already been inherited for many generations, may continue to be inherited for an almost infinite number of generations. On the other hand, we have evidence that variability when it has once come into play, does not cease under domestication for a very long period; nor do we know that it ever ceases, for new varieties are still occasionally produced by our oldest domesticated productions.

Variability is not actually caused by man; he only unintentionally exposes organic beings to new conditions of life, and then nature acts on the organisation and causes it to vary. But man can and does select the variations given to him by nature, and thus accumulates them in any desired manner. He thus adapts animals and plants for his own benefit or pleasure. He may do this methodically, or he may do it unconsciously by preserving the individuals most useful or pleasing to him without any intention of altering the breed. It is certain that he can largely influence the character of a breed by selecting, in each successive generation, individual differences so slight as to be inappreciable except by an educated eye. This unconscious process of selection has been the great agency in the formation of the most distinct and useful domestic breeds. That many breeds produced by man have to a large extent the character of natural species, is shown by the inextricable doubts whether many of them are varieties or aboriginally distinct species.

There is no reason why the principles which have acted so efficiently under domestication should not have acted under nature. In the survival of favoured individuals and races, during the constantly-recurrent Struggle for Existence, we see a powerful and ever-acting form of Selection. The struggle for existence inevitably follows from the high geometrical ratio of increase which is common to all organic beings. This high rate of increase is proved by calculation,—by the rapid increase of many animals and plants during a succession of peculiar seasons, and when naturalised in new countries. More individuals are born than can possibly survive. A grain in the balance may determine which individuals shall live and which shall die,—which variety or species shall increase in number, and which shall decrease, or finally become extinct. As the individuals of the same species come in all respects into the closest competition with each other, the struggle will generally be most severe between them; it will be almost equally severe between the varieties of the same species, and next in severity between the species of the same genus. On the other hand the struggle will often be severe between beings remote in the scale of nature. The slightest advantage in certain individuals, at any age or during any season, over those with which they come into competition, or better adaptation in however slight a degree to the surrounding physical conditions, will, in the long run, turn the balance.

With animals having separated sexes, there will be in most cases a struggle between the males for the possession of the females. The most vigorous males, or those which have most successfully struggled with their conditions of life, will generally leave most progeny. But success will often depend on the males having special weapons, or means of defence, or charms; and a slight advantage will lead to victory.

As geology plainly proclaims that each land has undergone great physical changes, we might have expected to find that organic beings have varied under nature, in the same way as they have varied under domestication. And if there has been any variability under nature, it would be an unaccountable fact if natural selection had not come into play. It has often been asserted, but the assertion is incapable of proof, that the amount of variation under nature is a strictly limited quantity. Man, though acting on external characters alone and often capriciously, can produce within a short period a great result by adding up mere individual differences in his domestic productions; and every one admits that species present individual differences. But, besides such differences, all naturalists admit that natural varieties exist, which are considered sufficiently distinct to be worthy of record in systematic works. No one has drawn any clear distinction between individual differences and slight varieties; or between more plainly marked varieties and sub-species, and species. On separate continents, and on different parts of the same continent when divided by barriers of any kind, and on outlying islands, what a multitude of forms exist, which some experienced naturalists rank as varieties, others as geographical races or sub-species, and others as distinct, though closely allied species!

If then, animals and plants do vary, let it be ever so slightly or slowly, why should not variations or individual differences, which are in any way beneficial, be preserved and accumulated through natural selection, or the survival of the fittest? If man can by patience select variations useful to him, why, under changing and complex conditions of life, should not variations useful to nature's living products often arise, and be preserved or selected? What limit can be put to this power, acting during long ages and rigidly scrutinising the whole constitution, structure, and habits of each creature,—favouring the good and rejecting the bad? I can see no limit to this power, in slowly and beautifully adapting each form to the most complex relations of life. The theory of natural selection, even if we look no farther than this, seems to be in the highest degree probable. I have already recapitulated, as fairly as I could, the opposed difficulties and objections: now let us turn to the special facts and arguments in favour of the theory.

On the view that species are only strongly marked and permanent varieties, and that each species first existed as a variety, we can see why it is that no line of demarcation can be drawn between species, commonly supposed to have been produced by special acts of creation, and varieties which are acknowledged to have been produced by secondary laws. On this same view we can understand how it is that in a region where many species of a genus have been produced, and where they now flourish, these same species should present many varieties; for where the manufactory of species has been active, we might expect, as a general rule, to find it still in action; and this is the case if varieties be incipient species. Moreover, the species of the larger genera, which afford the greater number of varieties or incipient species, retain to a certain degree the character of varieties; for they differ from each other by a less amount of difference than do the species of smaller genera. The closely allied species also of the larger genera apparently have restricted ranges, and in their affinities they are clustered in little groups round other species—in both respects resembling varieties. These are strange relations on the view that each species was independently created, but are intelligible if each existed first as a variety.

As each species tends by its geometrical rate of reproduction to increase inordinately in number; and as the modified descendants of each species will be enabled to increase by as much as they become more diversified in habits and structure, so as to be able to seize on many and widely different places in the economy of nature, there will be a constant tendency in natural selection to preserve the most divergent offspring of any one species. Hence, during a long-continued course of modification, the slight differences characteristic of varieties of the same species, tend to be augmented into the greater differences characteristic of the species of the same genus. New and improved varieties will inevitably supplant and exterminate the older, less improved, and intermediate varieties; and thus species are rendered to a large extent defined and distinct objects. Dominant species belonging to the larger groups within each class tend to give birth to new and dominant forms; so that each large group tends to become still larger, and at the same time more divergent in character. But as all groups cannot thus go on increasing in size, for the world would not hold them, the more dominant groups beat the less dominant. This tendency in the large groups to go on increasing in size and diverging in character, together with the inevitable contingency of much extinction, explains the arrangement of all the forms of life in groups subordinate to groups, all within a few great classes, which has prevailed throughout all time. This grand fact of the grouping of all organic beings under what is called the Natural System, is utterly inexplicable on the theory of creation.

As natural selection acts solely by accumulating slight, successive, favourable variations, it can produce no great or sudden modifications; it can act only by short and slow steps. Hence, the canon of "Natura non facit saltum," which every fresh addition to our knowledge tends to confirm, is on this theory intelligible. We can see why throughout nature the same general end is gained by an almost infinite diversity of means, for every peculiarity when once acquired is long inherited, and structures already modified in many different ways have to be adapted for the same general purpose. We can, in short, see why nature is prodigal in variety, though niggard in innovation. But why this should be a law of nature if each species has been independently created no man can explain.

Many other facts are, as it seems to me, explicable on this theory. How strange it is that a bird, under the form of a woodpecker, should prey on insects on the ground; that upland geese which rarely or never swim should possess webbed feet; that a thrush-like bird should dive and feed on sub-aquatic insects; and that a petrel should have the habits and structure fitting it for the life of an awk! and so in endless other cases. But on the view of each species constantly trying to increase in number, with natural selection always ready to adapt the slowly varying descendants of each to any unoccupied or ill-occupied place in nature, these facts cease to be strange, or might even have been anticipated.

We can to a certain extent understand how it is that there is so much beauty throughout nature; for this may be largely attributed to the agency of selection. That beauty, according to our sense of it, is not universal, must be admitted by every one who will look at some venomous snakes, at some fishes, and at certain hideous bats with a distorted resemblance to the human face. Sexual selection has given the most brilliant colours, elegant patterns, and other ornaments to the males, and sometimes to both sexes of many birds, butterflies, and other animals. With birds it has often rendered the voice of the male musical to the female, as well as to our ears. Flowers and fruit have been rendered conspicuous by brilliant colours in contrast with the green foliage, in order that the flowers may be readily seen, visited and fertilised by insects, and the seeds disseminated by birds. How it comes that certain colours, sounds, and forms should give pleasure to man and the lower animals,—that is, how the sense of beauty in its simplest form was first acquired,—

we do not know any more than how certain odours and flavours were first rendered agreeable.

As natural selection acts by competition, it adapts and improves the inhabitants of each country only in relation to their co-inhabitants; so that we need feel no surprise at the species of any one country, although on the ordinary view supposed to have been created and specially adapted for that country, being beaten and supplanted by the naturalised productions from another land. Nor ought we to marvel if all the contrivances in nature be not, as far as we can judge, absolutely perfect, as in the case even of the human eye; or if some of them be abhorrent to our ideas of fitness. We need not marvel at the sting of the bee, when used against an enemy, causing the bee's own death; at drones being produced in such great numbers for one single act, and being then slaughtered by their sterile sisters; at the astonishing waste of pollen by our fir-trees; at the instinctive hatred of the queen-bee for her own fertile daughters; at the ichneumonidæ feeding within the living bodies of caterpillars; or at other such cases. The wonder indeed is, on the theory of natural selection, that more cases of the want of absolute perfection have not been detected.

The complex and little known laws governing the production of varieties are the same, as far as we can judge, with the laws which have governed the production of distinct species. In both cases physical conditions seem to have produced some direct and definite effect, but how much we cannot say. Thus, when varieties enter any new station, they occasionally assume some of the characters proper to the species of that station. With both varieties and species, use and disuse seem to have produced a considerable effect; for it is impossible to resist this conclusion when we look, for instance, at the logger-headed duck, which has wings incapable of flight, in nearly the same condition as in the domestic duck; or when we look at the burrowing tucu-tucu, which is occasionally blind, and then at certain moles, which are habitually blind and have their eyes covered with skin; or when we look at the blind animals inhabiting the dark caves of America and Europe. With varieties and species, correlated variation seems to have played an important part, so that when one part has been modified other parts have been necessarily modified. With both varieties and species, reversions to long-lost characters occasionally occur. How inexplicable on the theory of creation is the occasional appearance of stripes on the shoulders and legs of the several species of the horse-genus and of their hybrids! How simply is this fact explained if we believe that these species are all descended from a striped progenitor, in the same manner as the several domestic breeds of the pigeon are descended from the blue and barred rock-pigeon!

On the ordinary view of each species having been independently created, why should specific characters, or those by which the species of the same genus differ from each other, be more variable than generic characters in which they all agree? Why, for instance, should the colour of a flower be more likely to vary in any one species of a genus, if the other species possess differently coloured flowers, than if all possessed the same coloured flowers? If species are only well-marked varieties, of which the characters have become in a high degree permanent, we can understand this fact; for they have already varied since they branched off from a common progenitor in certain characters, by which they have come to be specifically distinct from each other; therefore these same characters would be more likely again to vary than the generic characters which have been inherited without change for an immense period. It is inexplicable on the theory of creation why a part developed in a very unusual manner in one species alone of a genus, and therefore, as we may naturally infer, of great importance to that species, should be eminently liable to variation; but, on our view, this part has undergone, since the several species branched off from a common progenitor, an unusual amount of variability and modification, and therefore we might expect the part generally to be still variable. But a part may be developed in the most unusual manner, like the wing of a bat, and yet not be more variable than any other structure, if the part be common to many subordinate forms, that is, if it has been inherited for a very long period; for in this case, it will have been rendered constant by long-continued natural selection.

Glancing at instincts, marvellous as some are, they offer no greater difficulty than do corporeal structures on the theory of the natural selection of successive slight, but profitable modifications. We can thus understand why nature moves by graduated steps in endowing different animals of the same class with their several instincts. I have attempted to show how much light the principle of gradation throws on the admirable architectural powers of the hive-bee. Habit no doubt often comes into play in modifying instincts; but it certainly is not indispensable, as we see in the case of neuter insects, which leave no progeny to inherit the effects of long-continued habit. On the view of all the species of the same genus having descended from a common parent, and having inherited much in common, we can understand how it is that allied species, when placed under widely different conditions of life, yet follow nearly the same instincts; why the thrushes of tropical and temperate South America, for instance, line their nests with mud like our British species. On the view of instincts having been slowly acquired through natural selection, we need not marvel at some instincts being not perfect and liable to mistakes, and at many instincts causing other animals to suffer.

If species be only well-marked and permanent varieties, we can at once see why their crossed offspring should follow the same complex laws in their degrees and kinds of resemblance to their parents,—in being absorbed into each other by successive crosses, and in other such points,—as do the crossed offspring of acknowledged varieties. This similarity would be a strange fact, if species had been independently created and varieties had been produced through secondary laws.

If we admit that the geological record is imperfect to an extreme degree, then the facts, which the record does give, strongly support the theory of descent with modification. New species have come on the stage slowly and at successive intervals; and the amount of change, after equal intervals of time, is widely different in different groups. The extinction of species and of whole groups of species which has played so conspicuous a part in the history of the organic world, almost inevitably follows from the principle of natural selection; for old forms are supplanted by new and improved forms. Neither single species nor groups of species reappear when the chain of ordinary generation is once broken. The gradual diffusion of dominant forms, with the slow modification of their descendants, causes the forms of life, after long intervals of time, to appear as if they had changed simultaneously throughout the world. The fact of the fossil remains of each formation being in some degree intermediate in character between the fossils in the formations above and below, is simply explained by their intermediate position in the chain of descent. The grand fact that all extinct beings can be classed with all recent beings, naturally follows from the living and the extinct being the offspring of common parents. As species have generally diverged in character during their long course of descent and modification, we can understand why it is that the more ancient forms, or early progenitors of each group, so often occupy a position in some degree intermediate between existing groups. Recent forms are generally looked upon as being, on the whole, higher in the scale of organisation than ancient forms; and they must be higher, in so far as the later and more improved forms have conquered the older and less improved forms in the struggle for life; they have also generally had their organs more specialised for different functions. This fact is perfectly compatible with numerous beings still retaining simple and but little improved structures, fitted for simple conditions of life; it is likewise compatible with some forms having retrograded in organisation, by having become at each stage of descent better fitted for new and degraded habits of life. Lastly, the wonderful law of the long endurance of allied forms on the same continent,—of marsupials in Australia, of edentata in America, and other such cases,—is intelligible, for within the same country the existing and the extinct will be closely allied by descent.

Looking to geographical distribution, if we admit that there has been during the long course of ages much migration from one part of the world to another, owing to former climatal and geographical changes and to the many occasional and unknown means of dispersal, then we can understand, on the theory of descent with modification, most of the great leading facts in Distribution. We can see why there should be so striking a parallelism in the distribution of organic beings throughout space, and in their geological succession throughout time; for in both cases the beings have been connected by the bond of ordinary generation, and the means of modification have been the same. We see the full meaning of the wonderful fact, which has struck every traveller, namely, that on the same continent, under the most diverse conditions, under heat and cold, on mountain and lowland, on deserts and marshes, most of the inhabitants within each great class are plainly related; for they are the descendants of the same progenitors and early colonists. On this same principle of former migration, combined in most cases with modification, we can understand, by the aid of the Glacial period, the identity of some few plants, and the close alliance of many others, on the most distant mountains, and in the northern and southern temperate zones; and likewise the close alliance of some of the inhabitants of the sea in the northern and southern temperate latitudes, though separated by the whole intertropical ocean. Although two countries may present physical conditions as closely similar as the same species ever require, we need feel no surprise at their inhabitants being widely different, if they have been for a long period completely sundered from each other; for as the relation of organism to organism is the most important of all relations, and as the two countries will have received colonists at various periods and in different proportions, from some other country or from each other, the course of modification in the two areas will inevitably have been different.

On this view of migration, with subsequent modification, we see why oceanic islands are inhabited by only few species, but of these, why many are peculiar or endemic forms. We clearly see why species belonging to those groups of animals which cannot cross wide spaces of the ocean, as frogs and terrestrial mammals, do not inhabit oceanic islands; and why, on the other hand, new and peculiar species of bats, animals which can traverse the ocean, are found on islands far distant from any continent. Such cases as the presence of peculiar species of bats on oceanic islands and the absence of all other terrestrial mammals, are facts utterly inexplicable on the theory of independent acts of creation.

The existence of closely allied or representative species in any two areas, implies, on the theory of descent with modification, that the same parent-forms formerly inhabited both areas; and we almost invariably find that wherever many closely allied species inhabit two areas, some identical species are still common to both. Wherever many closely allied yet distinct species occur, doubtful forms and varieties belonging to the same groups likewise occur. It is a rule of high generality that the inhabitants of each area are related to the inhabitants of the nearest source whence immigrants might have been derived. We see this in the striking relation of nearly all plants and animals of the Galapagos archipelago, of Juan Fernandez, and of the other American islands, to the plants and animals of the neighbouring American mainland; and of those of the Cape de Verde archipelago, and of the other African islands to the African mainland. It must be admitted that these facts receive no explanation on the theory of creation.

The fact, as we have seen, that all past and present organic beings can be arranged within a few great classes, in groups subordinate to groups, and with the extinct groups often falling in between the recent groups, is intelligible on the theory of natural selection with its contingencies of extinction and divergence of character. On these same principles we see how it is, that the mutual affinities of the forms within each class are so complex and circuitous. We see why certain characters are far more serviceable than others for classification;—why adaptive characters, though of paramount importance to the beings, are of hardly any importance in classification; why characters derived from rudimentary parts, though of no service to the beings, are often of high classificatory value; and why embryological characters are often the most valuable of all. The real affinities of all organic beings, in contradistinction to their adaptive resemblances, are due to inheritance or community of descent. The Natural System is a genealogical arrangement, with the acquired grades of difference, marked by the terms, varieties, species, genera, families, &c.; and we have to discover the lines of descent by the most permanent characters whatever they may be and of however slight vital importance.

The similar framework of bones in the hand of a man, wing of a bat, fin of the porpoise, and leg of the horse,—the same number of vertebræ forming the neck of the giraffe and of the elephant,—and innumerable other such facts, at once explain themselves on the theory of descent with slow and slight successive modifications. The similarity of pattern in the wing and in the leg of a bat, though used for such different purpose,—in the jaws and legs of a crab,—in the petals, stamens, and pistils of a flower, is likewise, to a large extent, intelligible on the view of the gradual modification of parts or organs, which were aboriginally alike in an early progenitor in each of these classes. On the principle of successive variations not always supervening at an early age, and being inherited at a corresponding not early period of life, we clearly see why the embryos of mammals, birds, reptiles, and fishes should be so closely similar, and so unlike the adult forms. We may cease marvelling at the embryo of an air-breathing mammal or bird having branchial slits and arteries running in loops, like those of a fish which has to breathe the air dissolved in water by the aid of well-developed branchiæ.

Disuse, aided sometimes by natural selection, will often have reduced organs when rendered useless under changed habits or conditions of life; and we can understand on this view the meaning of rudimentary organs. But disuse and selection will generally act on each creature, when it has come to maturity and has to play its full part in the struggle for existence, and will thus have little power on an organ during early life; hence the organ will not be reduced or rendered rudimentary at this early age. The calf, for instance, has inherited teeth, which never cut through the gums of the upper jaw, from an early progenitor having well-developed teeth; and we may believe, that the teeth in the mature animal were formerly reduced by disuse, owing to the tongue and palate, or lips having become excellently fitted through natural selection to browse without their aid; whereas in the calf, the teeth have been left unaffected, and on the principle of inheritance at corresponding ages have been inherited from a remote period to the present day. On the view of each organism with all its separate parts having been specially created, how utterly inexplicable is it that organs bearing the plain stamp of inutility, such as the teeth in the embryonic calf or the shrivelled wings under the soldered wing-covers of many beetles, should so frequently occur. Nature may be said to have taken pains to reveal her scheme of modification, by means of rudimentary organs, of embryological and homologous structures, but we are too blind to understand her meaning.

I have now recapitulated the facts and considerations which have thoroughly convinced me that species have been modified, during a long course of descent. This has been effected chiefly through the natural selection of numerous successive, slight, favourable variations; aided in an important manner by the inherited effects of the use and disuse of parts; and in an unimportant manner, that is in relation to adaptive structures, whether past or present, by the direct action of external conditions, and by variations which seem to us in our ignorance to arise spontaneously. It appears that I formerly underrated the frequency and value of these latter forms of variation, as leading to permanent modifications of structure independently of natural selection. But as my conclusions have lately been much misrepresented, and it has been stated that I attribute the modification of species exclusively to natural selection, I may be permitted to remark that in the first edition of this work, and subsequently, I placed in a most conspicuous position—namely, at the close of the Introduction—the following words: "I am convinced that natural selection has been the main but not the exclusive means of modification." This has been of no avail. Great is the power of steady misrepresentation; but the history of science shows that fortunately this power does not long endure.

It can hardly be supposed that a false theory would explain, in so satisfactory a manner as does the theory of natural selection, the several large classes of facts above specified. It has recently been objected that this is an unsafe method of arguing; but it is a method used in judging of the common events of life, and has often been used by the greatest natural philosophers. The undulatory theory of light has thus been arrived at; and the belief in the revolution of the earth on its own axis was until lately supported by hardly any direct evidence. It is no valid objection that science as yet throws no light on the far higher problem of the essence or origin of life. Who can explain what is the essence of the attraction of gravity? No one now objects to following out the results consequent on this unknown element of attraction; notwithstanding that Leibnitz formerly accused Newton of introducing "occult qualities and miracles into philosophy."

I see no good reason why the views given in this volume should shock the religious feelings of any one. It is satisfactory, as showing how transient such impressions are, to remember that the greatest discovery ever made by man, namely, the law of the attraction of gravity, was also attacked by Leibnitz, "as subversive of natural, and inferentially of revealed, religion." A celebrated author and divine has written to me that "he has gradually learnt to see that it is just as noble a conception of the Deity to believe that He created a few original forms capable of self-development into other and needful forms, as to believe that He required a fresh act of creation to supply the voids caused by the action of His laws."

Why, it may be asked, until recently did nearly all the most eminent living naturalists and geologists disbelieve in the mutability of species? It cannot be asserted that organic beings in a state of nature are subject to no variation; it cannot be proved that the amount of variation in the course of long ages is a limited quality; no clear distinction has been, or can be, drawn between species and well-marked varieties. It cannot be maintained that species when intercrossed are invariably sterile, and varieties invariably fertile; or that sterility is a special endowment and sign of creation. The belief that species were immutable productions was almost unavoidable as long as the history of the world was thought to be of short duration; and now that we have acquired some idea of the lapse of time, we are too apt to assume, without proof, that the geological record is so perfect that it would have afforded us plain evidence of the mutation of species, if they had undergone mutation.

But the chief cause of our natural unwillingness to admit that one species has given birth to clear and distinct species, is that we are always slow in admitting great changes of which we do not see the steps. The difficulty is the same as that felt by so many geologists, when Lyell first insisted that long lines of inland cliffs had been formed, and great valleys excavated, by the agencies which we see still at work. The mind cannot possibly grasp the full meaning of the term of even a million years; it cannot add up and perceive the full effects of many slight variations, accumulated during an almost infinite number of generations.

Although I am fully convinced of the truth of the views given in this volume under the form of an abstract, I by no means expect to convince experienced naturalists whose minds are stocked with a multitude of facts all viewed, during a long course of years, from a point of view directly opposite to mine. It is so easy to hide our ignorance under such expressions as the "plan of creation," "unity of design," &c., and to think that we give an explanation when we only re-state a fact. Any one whose disposition leads him to attach more weight to unexplained difficulties than to the explanation of a certain number of facts will certainly reject the theory. A few naturalists, endowed with much flexibility of mind, and who have already begun to doubt the immutability of species, may be influenced by this volume; but I look with confidence to the future,—to young and rising naturalists, who will be able to view both sides of the question with impartiality. Whoever is led to believe that species are mutable will do good service by conscientiously expressing his conviction; for thus only can the load of prejudice by which this subject is overwhelmed be removed.

Several eminent naturalists have of late published their belief that a multitude of reputed species in each genus are not real species; but that other species are real, that is, have been independently created. This seems to me a strange conclusion to arrive at. They admit that a multitude of forms, which till lately they themselves thought were special creations, and which are still thus looked at by the majority of naturalists, and which consequently have all the external characteristic features of true species,—they admit that these have been produced by variation, but they refuse to extend the same view to other and slightly different forms. Nevertheless they do not pretend that they can define, or even conjecture, which are the created forms of life, and which are those produced by secondary laws. They admit variation as a *vera causa* in one case, they arbitrarily reject it in another, without assigning any distinction in the two cases. The day will come when this will be given as a curious illustration of the blindness of preconceived opinion. These authors seem no more startled at a miraculous act of creation than at an ordinary birth. But do they really believe that at innumerable periods in the earth's history certain elemental atoms have been commanded suddenly to flash into living tissues? Do they believe that at each supposed act of creation one individual or many were produced? Were all the infinitely numerous kinds of animals and plants cre-

ated as eggs or seed, or as full grown? and in the case of mammals, were they created bearing the false marks of nourishment from the mother's womb? Undoubtedly some of these same questions cannot be answered by those who believe in the appearance or creation of only a few forms of life, or of some one form alone. It has been maintained by several authors that it is as easy to believe in the creation of a million beings as of one; but Maupertuis' philosophical axiom "of least action" leads the mind more willingly to admit the smaller number; and certainly we ought not to believe that innumerable beings within each great class have been created with plain, but deceptive, marks of descent from a single parent.

As a record of a former state of things, I have retained in the foregoing paragraphs, and elsewhere, several sentences which imply that naturalists believe in the separate creation of each species; and I have been much censured for having thus expressed myself. But undoubtedly this was the general belief when the first edition of the present work appeared. I formerly spoke to very many naturalists on the subject of evolution, and never once met with any sympathetic agreement. It is probable that some did then believe in evolution, but they were either silent, or expressed themselves so ambiguously that it was not easy to understand their meaning. Now things are wholly changed, and almost every naturalist admits the great principle of evolution. There are, however, some who still think that species have suddenly given birth, through quite unexplained means, to new and totally different forms: but, as I have attempted to show, weighty evidence can be opposed to the admission of great and abrupt modifications. Under a scientific point of view, and as leading to further investigation, but little advantage is gained by believing that new forms are suddenly developed in an inexplicable manner from old and widely different forms, over the old belief in the creation of species from the dust of the earth.

It may be asked how far I extend the doctrine of the modification of species. The question is difficult to answer, because the more distinct the forms are which we consider, by so much the arguments in favour of community of descent become fewer in number and less in force. But some arguments of the greatest weight extend very far. All the members of whole classes are connected together by a chain of affinities, and all can be classed on the same principle, in groups subordinate to groups. Fossil remains sometimes tend to fill up very wide intervals between existing orders.

Organs in a rudimentary condition plainly show that an early progenitor had the organ in a fully developed condition; and this in some cases implies an enormous amount of modification in the descendants. Throughout whole classes various structures are formed on the same pattern, and at a very early age the embryos closely resemble each other. Therefore I cannot doubt that the theory of descent with modification embraces all the members of the same great class or kingdom. I believe that animals are descended from at most only four or five progenitors, and plants from an equal or lesser number.

Analogy would lead me one step farther, namely, to the belief that all animals and plants are descended from some one prototype. But analogy may be a deceitful guide. Nevertheless all living things have much in common, in their chemical composition, their cellular structure, their laws of growth, and their liability to injurious influences. We see this even in so trifling a fact as that the same poison often similarly affects plants and animals; or that the poison secreted by the gall-fly produces monstrous growths on the wild rose or oak-tree. With all organic beings excepting perhaps some of the very lowest, sexual production seems to be essentially similar. With all, as far as is at present known the germinal vesicle is the same; so that all organisms start from a common origin. If we look even to the two main divisions—namely, to the animal and vegetable kingdoms—certain low forms are so far intermediate in character that naturalists have disputed to which kingdom they should be referred. As Professor Asa Gray has remarked, "the spores and other reproductive bodies of many of the lower algæ may claim to have first a characteristically animal, and then an unequivocally vegetable existence." Therefore, on the principle of natural selection with divergence of character, it does not seem incredible that, from such low and intermediate form, both animals and plants may have been developed; and, if we admit this, we must likewise admit that all the organic beings which have ever

lived on this earth may be descended from some one primordial form. But this inference is chiefly grounded on analogy and it is immaterial whether or not it be accepted. No doubt it is possible, as Mr. G. H. Lewes has urged, that at the first commencement of life many different forms were evolved; but if so we may conclude that only a very few have left modified descendants. For, as I have recently remarked in regard to the members of each great kingdom, such as the Vertebrata Articulata &c., we have distinct evidence in their embryological homologous and rudimentary structures that within each kingdom all the members are descended from a single progenitor.

When the views advanced by me in this volume, and by Mr. Wallace, or when analogous views on the origin of species are generally admitted, we can dimly foresee that there will be a considerable revolution in natural history. Systematists will be able to pursue their labours as at present; but they will not be incessantly haunted by the shadowy doubt whether this or that form be a true species. This, I feel sure and I speak after experience, will be no slight relief. The endless disputes whether or not some fifty species of British brambles are good species will cease. Systematists will have only to decide (not that this will be easy) whether any form be sufficiently constant and distinct from other forms, to be capable of definition; and if definable, whether the differences be sufficiently important to deserve a specific name. This latter point will become a far more essential consideration than it is at present; for differences, however slight, between any two forms if not blended by intermediate gradations, are looked at by most naturalists as sufficient to raise both forms to the rank of species.

Hereafter we shall be compelled to acknowledge that the only distinction between species and well-marked varieties is, that the latter are known, or believed, to be connected at the present day by intermediate gradations, whereas species were formerly thus connected. Hence, without rejecting the consideration of the present existence of intermediate gradations between any two forms we shall be led to weigh more carefully and to value higher the actual amount of difference between them. It is quite possible that forms now generally acknowledged to be merely varieties may hereafter be thought worthy of specific names; and in this case scientific and common language will come into accordance. In short, we shall have to treat species in the same manner as those naturalists treat genera, who admit that genera are merely artificial combinations made for convenience. This may not be a cheering prospect; but we shall at least be free from the vain search for the undiscovered and undiscoverable essence of the term species.

The other and more general departments of natural history will rise greatly in interest. The terms used by naturalists, of affinity, relationship, community of type, paternity, morphology, adaptive characters, rudimentary and aborted organs, &c., will cease to be metaphorical, and will have a plain signification. When we no longer look at an organic being as a savage looks at a ship, as something wholly beyond his comprehension; when we regard every production of nature as one which has had a long history; when we contemplate every complex structure and instinct as the summing up of many contrivances, each useful to the possessor, in the same way as any great mechanical invention is the summing up of the labour, the experience, the reason, and even the blunders of numerous workmen; when we thus view each organic being, how far more interesting—I speak from experience—does the study of natural history become!

A grand and almost untrodden field of inquiry will be opened, on the causes and laws of variation, on correlation, on the effects of use and disuse, on the direct action of external conditions, and so forth. The study of domestic productions will rise immensely in value. A new variety raised by man will be a more important and interesting subject for study than one more species added to the infinitude of already recorded species. Our classifications will come to be, as far as they can be so made, genealogies; and will then truly give what may be called the plan of creation. The rules for classifying will no doubt become simpler when we have a definite object in view. We possess no pedigrees or armorial bearings; and we have to discover and trace the many diverging lines of descent in our natural genealogies, by characters of any kind which have long been inherited. Rudimentary organs will speak

infallibly with respect to the nature of long-lost structures. Species and groups of species which are called aberrant, and which may fancifully be called living fossils, will aid us in forming a picture of the ancient forms of life. Embryology will often reveal to us the structure, in some degree obscured, of the prototype of each great class.

When we feel assured that all the individuals of the same species, and all the closely allied species of most genera, have within a not very remote period descended from one parent, and have migrated from some one birth-place; and when we better know the many means of migration, then, by the light which geology now throws, and will continue to throw, on former changes of climate and of the level of the land, we shall surely be enabled to trace in an admirable manner the former migrations of the inhabitants of the whole world. Even at present, by comparing the differences between the inhabitants of the sea on the opposite sides of a continent, and the nature of the various inhabitants on that continent, in relation to their apparent means of immigration, some light can be thrown on ancient geography.

The noble science of Geology loses glory from the extreme imperfection of the record. The crust of the earth with its imbedded remains must not be looked at as a well-filled museum, but as a poor collection made at hazard and at rare intervals. The accumulation of each great fossiliferous formation will be recognised as having depended on an unusual concurrence of favourable circumstances, and the blank intervals between the successive stages as having been of vast duration. But we shall be able to gauge with some security the duration of these intervals by a comparison of the preceding and succeeding organic forms. We must be cautious in attempting to correlate as strictly contemporaneous two formations, which do not include many identical species, by the general succession of the forms of life. As species are produced and exterminated by slowly acting and still existing causes, and not by miraculous acts of creation; and as the most important of all causes of organic change is one which is almost independent of altered and perhaps suddenly altered physical conditions, namely, the mutual relation of organism to organism,—the improvement of one organism entailing the improvement or the extermination of others; it follows, that the amount of organic change in the fossils of consecutive formations probably serves as a fair measure of the relative though not actual lapse of time. A number of species, however, keeping in a body might remain for a long period unchanged, whilst within the same period several of these species by migrating into new countries and coming into competition with foreign associates, might become modified; so that we must not overrate the accuracy of organic change as a measure of time.

In the future I see open fields for far more important researches. Psychology will be securely based on the foundation already well laid by Mr. Herbert Spencer, that of the necessary acquirement of each mental power and capacity by gradation. Much light will be thrown on the origin of man and his history.

Authors of the highest eminence seem to be fully satisfied with the view that each species has been independently created. To my mind it accords better with what we know of the laws impressed on matter by the Creator, that the production and extinction of the past and present inhabitants of the world should have been due to secondary causes, like those determining the birth and death of the individual. When I view all beings not as special creations, but as the lineal descendants of some few beings which lived long before the first bed of the Cambrian system was deposited, they seem to me to become ennobled. Judging from the past, we may safely infer that not one living species will transmit its unaltered likeness to a distant futurity. And of the species now living very few will transmit progeny of any kind to a far distant futurity; for the manner in which all organic beings are grouped, shows that the greater number of species in each genus, and all the species in many genera, have left no descendants, but have become utterly extinct. We can so far take a prophetic glance into futurity as to foretell that it will be the common and widely-spread species, belonging to the larger and dominant groups within each class, which will ultimately prevail and procreate new and dominant species. As all the living forms of life are the lineal descendants of those which lived long before the Cambrian epoch, we may feel certain that the ordinary succession by generation has never once been broken, and that no cataclysm has desolated the whole world. Hence we may look with some confidence to a secure future of great length. And as natural selection works solely by and for the good of each being, all corporeal and mental endowments will tend to progress towards perfection.

It is interesting to contemplate a tangled bank, clothed with many plants of many kinds, with birds singing on the bushes, with various insects flitting about, and with worms crawling through the damp earth, and to reflect that these elaborately constructed forms, so different from each other, and dependent upon each other in so complex a manner, have all been produced by laws acting around us. These laws, taken in the largest sense, being Growth with Reproduction; Inheritance which is almost implied by reproduction; Variability from the indirect and direct action of the conditions of life, and from use and disuse: a Ratio of Increase so high as to lead to a Struggle for Life, and as a consequence to Natural Selection, entailing Divergence of Character and the Extinction of less-improved forms. Thus, from the war of nature, from famine and death, the most exalted object which we are capable of conceiving, namely, the production of the higher animals, directly follows. There is grandeur in this view of life, with its several powers, having been originally breathed by the Creator into a few forms or into one; and that, whilst this planet has gone cycling on according to the fixed law of gravity, from so simple a beginning endless forms most beautiful and most wonderful have been, and are being evolved.

Rural Hygiene

Florence Nightingale

Florence Nightingale was one of the most influential women of the nineteenth century. Her work as a nurse during the Crimean War (1851–1854) is perhaps the best-known aspect of her life, but it was only the beginning of a long career. In 1859, from her experience in the Crimean War, she wrote Rural Hygiene *and argued in support of sanitary reform and public health.*

We will now deal with the PRESENT STATE OF RURAL HYGIENE, which is indeed a pitiful and disgusting story, dreadful to tell.

For the sake of giving actual facts—it is no use lecturing upon drainage, watersupply, wells, pigsties, storage of excrement, storage of refuse, etc., etc., *in general;* they are dreadfully concrete,—I take leave to give the facts of one rural district, consisting of villages and one small market town, as described by a Local Government Board official this year; and I will ask the ladies here present whether they could not match these facts in every county in the kingdom. Perhaps, too, the lady lecturers on Rural Hygiene will favour us with some of their experiences.

A large number of the poorcottages have been recently condemned as "unfit for human habitation," but though "unfit" many are still "inhabited," from lack of other accommodation.

Provision for conveying away surface and slopwater is conspicuous either by its absence or defect. The slopwater stagnates and sinks into the soil all round the dwellings, aided by the droppings from the thatch. (It has been known that the bedroom slops are sometimes emptied out of window.) There *are* inside sinks, but the wastepipe is often either untrapped or not disconnected.

It is a Government Official who says all this.

Watersupply almost entirely from shallow wells, often uncovered, mostly in the cottagegarden, not far from a pervious privy pit, a pigsty, or a huge collection of house refuse, polluted by the foulness soaking into it. The liquid manure from the pigsty trickles through the ground into the well. Often after heavy rain the cottagers complain that their wellwater becomes thick.

The water in many shallow wells has been analysed. And some have been closed; others *cleaned out.* But when no particular impurity is detected, no care has been taken to stop the too threatening pollution, or to prohibit the supply. In one village which *had* a pump, it was so far from one end that a pond in an adjoining field was used for their supply.

It may be said that, up to the present time, *practically* nothing has been done by the Sanitary Authorities to effect the removal of house refuse, etc.

In these days of investigation and statistics, where results are described with microscopic exactness and tabulated with mathematical accuracy, we seem to think figures will do instead of facts, and calculation instead of action. We remember the policeman who watched his burglar enter the house, and waited to make quite sure whether he was going to commit robbery with violence or without, before interfering with his operations. So as we read such an account as this we seem to be watching, not robbery, but murder going on, and to be waiting for the rates of mortality to go up before we interfere; we wait to see how many of

From: *Selected Writings of Florence Nightingale*, ed. by Lucy Ridgely Seymer (New York: The Macmillan Co., 1954), pp. 382–387.

the children playing round the houses shall be stricken down. We wait to see whether the filth will really trickle into the well, and whether the foul water really will poison the family, and how many will die of it. And then, when enough have died, we think it time to spend some money and some trouble to stop the murders going further, and we enter the results of our "masterly inactivity" neatly in tables; but we do not analyse and tabulate the saddened lives of those who remain, and the desolate homes in our "*sanitary*" "districts."

Storage of Excrement in These Villages. This comes next. And it is so disgustingly inefficient that I write it on a separate sheet, to be omitted if desired. But we must remember that if we cannot bear with it, the national health has to bear with it, and especially the children's health. And I add, as a fact in another Rural District to the one quoted above, that, in rainy weather, the little children may play in the privy or in the socalled "bam" or small outhouse, where may be several privies, several pigs, and untold heaps of filth. And as the little faces are very near the ground, children's diarrhœa and diseases have been traced to this miasma.

Cesspit Privies. The *cesspits are excavations* in the ground; often left unlined. Sometimes the privy is a wooden sentrybox, placed so that the fœcal matter falls directly into a ditch. Cesspits often very imperfectly or not at all covered. Some privies with a cubic capacity of 18 or 20 feet are emptied from once to thrice yearly. But we are often told that all the contents "ran away," and that therefore emptying was not required!

These privies are often close to the well—one within a yard of the cottagers' pump.

Earth closets are the exception, cesspit privies the rule. (In another place 109 cesspit privies were counted to 120 cottages. And, as might be expected, there was hardly a pure well in the place.)

In one, a market town, there *are* waterclosets, so called from being without water.

Storage of Refuse and Ashes. Ashpits are conspicuous by their absence. Huge heaps of accumulated refuse are found piled up near the house, sometimes under the windows, or near the well, into which these refuse heaps soak. Where there *are* ashpits, they are piled up and overflowing. Privy contents are often mixed up with the refuse or buried in a hole in the refuseheap.

As to the final disposal, in most cases the cottagers have allotments, but differing in distance from but a few yards to as much as two miles from their homes. Their privy contents and ash refuse are therefore valuable as manure, and they would "strongly resent" any appropriation of it by the Sanitary Authority.

And we might take this into account by passing a byelaw to the effect that house refuse must be removed at least once a quarter, and that if the occupier neglected to do this, the Sanitary Authority would do it, *and would appropriate* it. This amount of pressure is thoroughly legitimate to protect the lives of the children.

Health Missioners might teach the value of cooperation in sanitary matters. For instance, suppose the hire of a sewagecart is 1s. the first day, and sixpence every other day. If six houses, adjacent to each other, subscribed for the use of the sewagecart, they would each get it far cheaper than by single orders.

The usual practice is to wait until there is a sufficient accumulation to make worth while the hiring of a cart. The ashes, and often the privy contents too, are then taken away to the allotments. A statement that removal takes place as much as two or three times a year is often too obviously untrue.

But, as a rule, the occupiers have sufficient garden space, i.e., curtilage, for the proper utilisation of their privy contents. (I would urge the reading of Dr. Poore's "Rural Hygiene" on this particular point.)

Often the garden is large enough for the utilisation of ashes and house refuse too. But occupiers almost always take both privy and ashpit contents to their allotments. Thus hoardingup of refuse matters occurs. In some cases the cost of hiring horse and cart—the amount depending on the distance of the allotment from the dwelling—is so serious a consideration that if byelaws compelled the occupiers to remove their refuse to their allotments, say every month, either the value of the manure would be nothing, or the scavenging must be done at the expense of the Sanitary Authority. From the public health point of view, the Sanitary Authority should of course do the scavenging in all the villages.

The health Economy of the Community demands the most profitable use of manure for the land. Now the most profitable use is that which permits of least waste, and if we could only regard economy in this matter in its true and broad sense, we should acknowledge that the Community is advantaged by the frequent removal of sewage refuse from the houses, where it is dangerous, to the land, where it is an essential. And if the Community is advantaged, the Community should pay for that advantage. The gain is a double one—safety in the matter of health—increase in the matter of food, besides the untold gain, moral as well as material, which results from the successful cultivation of land.

There are some villages without any gardens— barely room for a privy and ashpit. But even in these cases the occupiers generally have allotments.

Plenty of byelaws may be imposed, but byelaws are not in themselves active agents. And in many, perhaps in most, cases they are impossible of execution, and remain a dead letter.

Now let us come to WHAT THE WOMEN HAVE TO DO WITH IT—*i.e.*, how much the cottage mothers, if instructed by instructed women, can remedy or prevent these and other frightful evils.

And first

(I) OUR HOMES—The Cottage Homes of England being, after all, the most important of the homes of any class, should be pure in every sense.

Boys and girls must grow up healthy, with clean minds, and clean bodies, and clean skins. And the first teachings and impressions they have at home must all be pure, and gentle, and firm.

It is *home* that teaches the child after all, more than any other schooling. A child learns before it is three whether it shall obey its mother or not. And before it is seven its character is a good way to being formed.

When a child has lost its health, how often the mother says: "O, if I had only known, but there was no one to tell me!" God did not intend all mothers to be accompanied by doctors, but He meant all children to be cared for by mothers.

(a) Back Yard and Garden. Where and how are slops emptied? The following are some of the essential requisites: slops to be poured slowly down a drain, not hastily thrown down to make a pool round the drain; gratings of drain to be kept clean and passage free; soil round the house kept pure, that pure air may come in at the window; bedroom slops not to be thrown out of window; no puddles to be allowed to stand round walls; privy contents to be got into the soil as soon as possible—most valuable for your garden; cesspools not to be allowed to filter into your shallow wells; pumpwater wells must be taken care of, they are upright drains, so soil round them should be pure. Bad smells are danger signals. Pigsties—Moss litter to absorb liquid manure, cheap and profitable; danger from pools of liquid manure making the whole soil foul.

The Life of a German Inventor:
The Invention of the Automobile
Karl Benz

The German mechanical engineer Karl Benz built the first practical automobile powered by an internal-combustion engine. Unlike other automobile inventors, such as his fellow countryman Gottlieb Daimler (1834-1900), Benz designed not only the engine but the whole vehicle. In 1888 he produced the first automobile designed for public sale. In the following selection, published in 1925, Benz describes the reaction to a self-moving carriage.

Resistance

Always when something great was to be achieved in the area of technology, major blows were necessary. Resistance needed to be overcome, public opinions needed to be confronted, in order that the creative power of the new idea could come into being, even in defiance of financial inhibitions and the resistance of business.

This was also my experience.

The world still had no idea at this time about the great future of the internal combustion engine. Exactly the opposite! The more knowledgeable and smarter the people, the more enthused they were about the steam engine and the more disparagingly they looked down upon the gasoline engine. Even in my circle of acquaintances in Mannheim I did not find anyone who wanted to prove his trust in motors by "the investing of a certain amount of money."

The two-stroke engine was surely a good business-like springboard. Yet my heart did not lie with the two-stroke engine, but rather with the self-moving vehicle. But exactly against this dream the resistance was intense.

From: Karl Benz, *Lebesfahrt eines deutschen Erfinders. Die Erfindung des Automobils. Erinnerungen eines Achtigjaerigen* (Leipzig: Roehler & Smeling, 1925), transl. by John C. Swanson, pp. 43–44, 74–75, 104–105.

My business partners were great Realpolitiker and had no understanding for my favorite idea—the motorized carriage. Benz-Motors: yes, that was okay. That produced money. But Benz-Carriages: no, that would be a great loss of every Pfennig invested.

The First Journeys

In the Factory Courtyard

The year 1884/1885 became the birth-year of the motorized carriage. Already in the spring of 1885, my life-long dream, as part of the grace of a great moment, took on a concrete form and a viable shape. Out of the world of ideas and into the world of reality, the youngest product of technology stood one beautiful day in the factory courtyard.

On the Street

Beep, beep, beep! A new greeting of a new era. A first sound of an epoch, in which the motor [engine] became the master, first on land, then on water, and finally in the air. The world takes notice! People remain standing on the street, they stare and watch. How can this happen? A carriage without horses, running, and rolling? Miraculously puffs the carriage down the street. The driver is as proud as a king. And with the pride of a king he sends down from his elevated seat his greetings to the starring public below.

All of a sudden came the disaster—in the form of the first "flat tire." The carriage moved more slowly, and then? Yes, the carriage stood motionless. The driver dismounted, kneeled down, tinkered around, and fixed the flat. The public gathered around, smiled, and laughed. . . .

How at the Beginning it Haunted the Country Roads

"When one takes a trip, then one can have stories to tell." This saying was especially meaningful for the first automobile [motorized carriage] trips. From my vast memory I want to provide only a few of my experiences. One has to imagine, how strange this new unusual carriage must have appeared to animals and people during the early period of the automobile. Horses, which showed little love and understanding for their new competition, shied away and wanted nothing of it. When the carriage passed different villages, the children screamed: "Witch cart, Witch cart!" and darted into the houses. They slammed the doors behind them, as fast as they could, and bolted them out of fear of bad spirits. A woman in the Black forest always repeatedly made the sign of the cross when I approached, as if I were the personification of "the Evil One." . . .

PART EIGHT

Print of Early Cinematography

New technologies for transmitting information and images became and remain today a central part of civilization in Europe and elsewhere. Just as machinery to some degree freed humans from the natural world in the realm of production, photography and cinematography (moving pictures) freed them from the natural world in culture. By a kind of machine, human beings and their lives could be captured and reproduced in endless situations on film. Film could manipulate the human situations portrayed and, for better or worse, manipulate the audience. This early print of people in the dress of a past century watching with fascination and responding to moving images on a screen marks the beginning of a cultural transformation that we have still neither controlled nor measured.

European Civilization, 1850-1914

European civilization changed dramatically in the decades before World War I. Feverish industrial development and the rise of mass politics profoundly transformed economic, social, and political life. Despite severe economic fluctuations, by century's end the introduction of the internal combustion engine, the telephone, and the gramophone constituted a virtual second industrial revolution. Europe's population increased and more people moved to cities. The late nineteenth-century also witnessed the growing influence of political parties. European lives and views altered irrevocably. After World War I, some reminisced about the good old days, "la belle époque," while others recalled, more darkly, the "fin de siècle," an end of the century cultural crisis.

Darwin did not apply his theories to human society but, as noted, others did. Herbert Spencer (1820–1903), later known as a Social Darwinist, shared Darwin's interest in evolutionary theory, except that he applied the concept of evolutionary competition to human society. His *Social Growth* (1897) argues that states, like animal species, struggle to survive and only the most highly developed prevail. Spencer emphasized the phrase "survival of the fittest" as equivalent to Darwin's "natural selection." By the late nineteenth century, evolutionary theory heavily influenced people's social views. This and the demise of other traditional values led to a European-wide cultural crisis, accompanied by an increase in nervous disorders, alcoholism, and drug use. Sigmund Freud (1856-1939), a Viennese doctor, used his *Introductory Lectures on Psychoanalysis* (1915–1917) to seek explanations for society's problems in the human unconscious, a strategy that implied the inadequacy of the Enlightenment's rationalism. Friedrich Nietzsche (1844–1900) went even further by arguing in *Beyond Good and Evil* (1886) that humankind progressed only under the often brutal leadership of outstanding individuals. He denounced concepts of "equal and inalienable rights to life, liberty, and the pursuit of happiness" and urged instead an aristocracy of supermen willing to act decisively and mercilessly for mankind's betterment. The image of viewers fascinated by an early film suggests the deeply unsettling cultural, as well as material, transformations people experienced. When the ideas of Darwin, Freud, and Nietzsche, high-powered intellectuals, intersected with cinematography for the masses, for better or worse a new civilization was in the making.

Study Questions

1. How did Spencer distort Darwin's central idea?
2. What role does rationalism play in the works of Freud and Nietzsche?
3. Does Nietzsche's evident denial of morality exclude all possibility of moral behavior?
4. What do these selections tell us about late nineteenth-century civilization?
5. How do the ideas of Spencer, Freud, and Nietzsche relate to science and technology?
6. Image: What does the print, The Invention of Cinematography, suggest about late nineteenth-century European society and culture?

Social Growth

Herbert Spencer

Today Herbert Spencer is probably best remembered for his political thought, such as his defense of natural rights. He was also a staunch supporter of evolutionary theory. Whereas Darwin emphasized "natural selection" in the natural world, Spencer applied evolutionary theory to the study of societies. This argument provided support for later proponents, including politicians, of the idea of the "survival of the fittest" and the "laws of nature," which were used to support wars of conquest and imperialism.

Societies, like living bodies, begin as germs—originate from masses which are extremely minute in comparison with the masses some of them eventually reach. That out of small wandering hordes have arisen the largest societies, is a conclusion not to be contested. The implements of prehistoric peoples, ruder even than existing savages use, imply absence of those arts by which alone great aggregations of men are made possible. Religious ceremonies that survived among ancient historic races pointed back to a time when the progenitors of those races had flint knives, and got fire by rubbing together pieces of wood, and must have lived in such small clusters as are alone possible before the rise of agriculture.

The implication is that by integrations, direct and indirect, there have in course of time been produced social aggregates a million times in size the aggregates which alone existed in the remote past. Here, then, is a growth reminding us, by its degree, of growth in living bodies.

Between this trait of organic evolution and the answering trait of super-organic evolution, there is a further parallelism: the growths in aggregates of different classes are extremely various in their amounts.

Glancing over the entire assemblage of animal types, we see that the members of one large class, the *Protozoa*, rarely increase beyond the microscopic

From: *The Evolution of Society: Selections from Herbert Spencer's Principles of Sociology*, ed. Robert L. Carneiro (Chicago: The University of Chicago Press, 1967), pp. 9–13, 214–217.

size with which every higher animal begins. Among the multitudinous kinds of *Coelenterata*, the masses range from that of the small hydra to that of the large medusa. The annulose and molluscous types respectively show us immense contrasts between their superior and inferior members. And the vertebrate animals, much larger on the average than the rest, display among themselves enormous differences.

Kindred unlikenesses of size strike us where we contemplate the entire assemblage of human societies. Scattered over many regions there are minute hordes—still extant samples of the primordial type of society. We have Wood Veddas living sometimes in pairs, and only now and then assembling; we have Bushmen wandering about in families, and forming larger groups but occasionally; we have Fuegians clustered by the dozen or the score. Tribes of Australians, of Tasmanians, of Andamanese, are variable within the limits of perhaps twenty to fifty. And similarly, if the region is inhospitable, as with the Eskimos, or if the arts of life are undeveloped, as with the Digger Indians, or if adjacent higher races are obstacles to growth, as with Indian Hill tribes like the Juangs, this limitation to primitive size continues. Where a fruitful soil affords much food, and where a more settled life, leading to agriculture, again increases the supply of food, we meet with larger social aggregates: instance those in the Polynesian Islands and in many parts of Africa. Here a hundred or two, here several thousands, here many thousands, are held together more or less completely as one mass. And then in the highest societies, instead of partially aggregated thousands, we have completely aggregated millions.

The growths of individual and social organisms are allied in another respect. In each case size augments by two processes which go on sometimes separately, sometimes together. There is increase by simple multiplication of units, causing enlargement of the group; there is increase by union of groups, and again by union of groups of groups. The first parallelism is too simple to need illustration but the facts which show us the second must be set forth.

Organic integration . . . must be here summarized to make the comparison intelligible. . . . The smallest animal, like the smallest plant, is essentially a minute group of living molecules. There are many forms and stages showing us the clustering of such smallest animals. Sometimes, as in the compound *Vorticellae* and in the sponges, their individualities are scarcely at all masked; but as evolution of the composite aggregate advances, the individualities of the component aggregates become less distinct. In some *Coelenterata*, though they retain considerable independence, which they show by moving about like amoebae when separated, they have their individualities mainly merged in that of the aggregate formed of them: for instance the common hydra. Tertiary aggregates similarly result from the massing of secondary ones. . . .

Social growth proceeds by an analogous compounding and recompounding. The primitive social group, like the primitive group of living molecules with which organic evolution begins, never attains any considerable size by simple increase. Where, as among Fuegians, the supplies of wild food yielded by an inclement habitat will not enable more than a score or so to live in the same place—where, as among Andamanese, limited to a strip of shore backed by impenetrable bush, forty is about the number of individuals who can find prey without going too far from their temporary abode . . . — where, as among Bushmen, wandering over barren tracts, small hordes are alone possible and even families "are sometimes obliged to separate, since the same spot will not afford sufficient sustenance for all". . . we have extreme instances of the limitation of simple groups, and the formation of migrating groups when the limit is passed.

Even in tolerably productive habitats, fission of the groups is eventually necessitated in a kindred manner. Spreading as its number increases, a primitive tribe presently reaches a diffusion at which its parts become incoherent, and it then gradually separates into tribes that become distinct as fast as their continually diverging dialects pass into different languages. Often nothing further happens than repetition of this. Conflicts of tribes, dwindlings or extinctions of some, growths and spontaneous divisions of others, continue.

The formation of a larger society results only by the joining of such smaller societies, which occurs without obliterating the divisions previously caused by separations. This process may be seen now going on among uncivilized races, as it once went on among the ancestors of the civilized races. Instead of absolute independence of small hordes, such as the lowest savages show us, more advanced savages show us slight cohesions among larger hordes. In North America each of the three great tribes of Comanches consists of various bands having such feeble combination only as results from the personal character of the great chief. . . . So of the Dakotas there are, according to Burton . . . , seven principal bands, each including minor bands, numbering altogether, according to Catlin, forty-two. . . . And in like manner the five Iroquois nations had severally eight tribes.

Closer unions of these slightly coherent original groups arise under favorable conditions, but they only now and then become permanent. A common form of the process is that described by Mason as occurring among the Karens. . . . "Each village, with its scant domain, is an independent state, and every chief a prince; but now and then a little Napoleon arises, who subdues a kingdom to himself, and builds up an empire. The dynasties, however, last only with the controlling mind." The like happens in Africa. Livingstone says, "Formerly all the Maganja were united under the government of their great Chief, Undi; . . . but after Undi's death it fell to pieces. . . . This has been the inevitable fate of every African Empire from time immemorial.". . .

Only occasionally does there result a compound social aggregate that endures for a considerable period, as Dahomey or as Ashanti, which is "an assemblage of states owing a kind of feudal obedience to the sovereign".... The histories of Madagascar and of sundry Polynesian islands also display these transitory compound groups, out of which at length come in some cases permanent ones. During the earliest times of the extinct civilized races, like stages were passed through. In the words of Maspero, Egypt was "divided at first into a great number of tribes, which at several points simultaneously began to establish small independent states, every one of which had its laws and its worship".... The compound groups of Greeks first formed were those minor ones resulting from the subjugation of weaker towns by stronger neighboring towns. And in northern Europe during pagan days the numerous German tribes, each with its cantonal divisions, illustrated this second stage of aggregation.

After such compound societies are consolidated, repetition of the process on a larger scale produces doubly compound societies which, usually cohering but feebly, become in some cases quite coherent. Maspero infers that the Egyptian nomes described above as resulting from integrations of tribes, coalesced into the two great principalities, Upper Egypt and Lower Egypt, which were eventually united, the small states becoming provinces. The boasting records of Mesopotamian kings similarly show us this union of unions going on. So, too, in Greece the integration at first occurring locally, began afterwards to combine the minor societies into two confederacies. During Roman days there arose for defensive purposes federations of tribes which eventually consolidated, and subsequently these were compounded into still larger aggregates. Before and after the Christian era, the like happened throughout Northern Europe. Then after a period of vague and varying combinations, there came, in later times, as is well illustrated by French history, a massing of small feudal territories into provinces, and a subsequent massing of these into kingdoms.

So that in both organic and superorganic growths we see a process of compounding and recompounding carried to various stages. In both cases, after some consolidation of the smallest aggregates there comes the process of forming larger aggregates by union of them; in both cases repetition of this process makes secondary aggregates into tertiary ones.

Organic growth and superorganic growth have yet another analogy. As above said, increase by multiplication of individuals in a group and increase by union of groups may go on simultaneously, and it does this in both cases.

The original clusters, animal and social, are not only small, but they lack density. Creatures of low types occupy large spaces considering the small quantities of animal substance they contain, and low-type societies spread over areas that are wide relatively to the numbers of their component individuals. But as integration in animals is shown by concentration as well as by increase of bulk, so that social integration which results from the clustering of clusters is joined with augmentation of the number contained by each cluster. If we contrast the sprinklings in regions inhabited by wild tribes with the crowds filling equal regions in Europe or if we contrast the density of population in England under the Heptarchy with its present density, we see that besides the growth produced by union of groups there has gone on interstitial growth. Just as the higher animal has become not only larger than the lower but more solid, so, too, has the higher society.

Social growth, then, equally with the growth of a living body, shows us the fundamental trait of evolution under a twofold aspect. Integration is displayed both in the formation of a larger mass and in the progress of such mass towards that coherence due to closeness of parts.

It is proper to add, however, that there is a model of social growth to which organic growth affords no parallel—that caused by the migration of units from one society to another. Among many primitive groups and a few developed ones this is a considerable factor but, generally, its effect bears so small a ratio to the effects of growth by increase of population and coalescence of groups that it does not much qualify the analogy.

*   *   *

Summary

... We [have seen] ... that societies are aggregates which grow; that in the various types of them there are great varieties in the growths reached; that types of successively larger sizes result from the aggregation and reaggregation of those of smaller sizes; and that this increase by coalescence, joined with interstitial increase, is the process through which have been formed the vast civilized nations.

Along with increase of size in societies goes increase of structure. Primitive hordes are without established distinctions of parts. With growth of them into tribes habitually come some unlikenesses, both in the powers and occupations of their members. Unions of tribes are followed by more unlikenesses, governmental and industrial—social grades running through the whole mass, and contrasts between the differently occupied parts in different localities. Such differentiations multiply as the compounding progresses. They proceed from the general to the special. First the broad division between ruling and ruled; then within the ruling part divisions into political, religious, military, and within the ruled part divisions into food-producing classes and handicraftsmen; then within each of these divisions minor ones, and so on.

Passing from the structural aspect to the functional aspect, we note that so long as all parts of a society have like natures and activities, there is hardly any mutual dependence, and the aggregate scarcely forms a vital whole. As its parts assume different functions they become dependent on one another, so that injury to one hurts others, until, in highly evolved societies, general perturbation is caused by derangement of any portion. This contrast between undeveloped and developed societies arises from the fact that with increasing specialization of functions comes increasing inability in each part to perform the functions of other parts.

The organization of every society begins with a contrast between the division which carries on relations habitually hostile with environing societies and the division which is devoted to procuring necessaries of life, and during the earlier stages of development these two divisions constitute the whole. Eventually there arises an intermediate division serving to transfer products and influences from part to part. And in all subsequent stages, evolution of the two earlier systems of structures depends on evolution of this additional system.

While the society as a whole has the character of its sustaining system determined by the character of its environment, inorganic and organic, the respective parts of this system differentiate in adaptation to local circumstances, and, after primary industries have been thus localized and specialized, secondary industries dependent on them arise in conformity with the same principle. Further, as fast as societies become compounded and recompounded and the distributing system develops, the parts devoted to each kind of industry, originally scattered, aggregate in the most favorable localities, and the localized industrial structures, unlike the governmental structures, grow regardless of the original lines of division.

Increase of size, resulting from the massing of groups, necessitates means of communication, both for achieving combined offensive and defensive actions, and for exchange of products. Faint tracks, then paths, rude roads, finished roads, successively arise, and as fast as intercourse is thus facilitated, there is a transition from direct barter to trading carried on by a separate class, out of which evolves a complex mercantile agency of wholesale and retail distributors. The movement of commodities effected by this agency, beginning as a slow flux to and reflux from certain places at long intervals, passes into rhythmical, regular, rapid currents, and materials for sustentation distributed hither and thither, from being few and crude become numerous and elaborated. Growing efficiency of transfer with greater variety of transferred products, increases the mutual dependence of parts at the same time that it enables each part to fulfil its function better.

Unlike the sustaining system, evolved by converse with the organic and inorganic environments, the regulating system is evolved by converse, offensive and defensive, with environing societies. In primitive headless groups temporary chieftainship results from temporary war; chronic hostilities generate permanent chieftainship; and gradually from the military control results the civil control. Habitual war, requiring prompt combination in the actions of parts, necessitates subordination. Societies in which there is little subordination disappear, and leave outstanding those in which subordination is great, and so there are produced societies in which the habit fostered by war and surviving in peace brings about permanent submission to a government. The centralized regulating system thus evolved, is in early stages the sole regulating system. But in large societies which have become predominantly industrial there is added a decentralized regulating system for the industrial structures, and this, at first subject in every way to the original system, acquires at length substantial independence. Finally there arises for the distributing structures also an independent controlling agency.

Societies fall firstly into the classes of simple, compound, doubly compound, trebly compound, and from the lowest the transition to the highest is through these stages. Otherwise, though less definitely, societies may be grouped as militant and industrial, of which the one type in its developed form is organized on the principle of compulsory cooperation, while the other in its developed form is organized on the principle of voluntary cooperation. The one is characterized not only by a despotic central power, but also by unlimited political control of personal conduct, while the other is characterized not only by a democratic or representative central power, but also by limitation of political control over personal conduct.

Lastly we noted the corollary that change in the predominant social activities brings metamorphosis. If, where the militant type has not elaborated into so rigid a form as to prevent change, a considerable industrial system arises, there come mitigations of the coercive restraints characterizing the militant type, and weakening of its structure. Conversely, where an industrial system largely developed has established freer social forms, resumption of offensive and defensive activities causes reversion towards the militant type. . . .

The many facts contemplated unite in proving that social evolution forms a part of evolution at large. Like evolving aggregates in general, societies show *integration*, both by simple increase of mass and by coalescence and recoalescence of masses. The change from *homogeneity* to *heterogeneity* is multitudinously exemplified, up from the simple tribe, alike in all its parts, to the civilized nation, full of structural and functional unlikenesses. With progressing integration and heterogeneity goes increasing *coherence*. We see the wandering group dispersing, dividing, held together by no bonds; the tribe with parts made more coherent by subordination to a dominant man; the cluster of tribes united into a political plexus under a chief with subchiefs; and so on up to the civilized nation, consolidated enough to hold together for a thousand years or more. Simultaneously comes increasing *definiteness*. Social organization is at first vague; advance brings settled arrangements which grow slowly more precise; customs pass into laws which, while gaining fixity, also become more specific in their applications to varieties of actions; and all institutions, at first confusedly intermingled, slowly separate, at the same time that each within itself marks off more distinctly its component structures. Thus in all respects is fulfilled the formula of evolution. There is progress towards greater size, coherence, multiformity, and definiteness.

Besides these general truths, a number of special truths have been disclosed by our survey. Comparisons of societies in their ascending grades have made manifest certain cardinal facts respecting their growths, structures, and functions—facts respecting the systems of structures, sustaining, distributing, regulating, of which they are composed; respecting the relations of these structures to the surrounding conditions and the dominant forms of social activities entailed; and respecting the metamorphoses of types caused by changes in activities. The inductions arrived at, thus constituting in rude outline an empirical sociology, show that in social phenomena there is a general order of co-existence and sequence, and that therefore social phenomena form the subject matter of a science. . . .

A General Introduction to Psychoanalysis

Sigmund Freud

At the end of the nineteenth century, various philosophers as well as medical doctors were attempting to explain the problems of European society. Sigmund Freud, a Viennese doctor, searched for answers in the human unconscious, as described in this selection from lectures delivered at the University of Vienna. Freud explains how the solutions to society's problems can be discovered, scientifically, by studying the unconscious, which, of course, operates unscientifically or irrationally. Freud's work continues the earlier emphasis on scientific certainty, with a new focus on uncertainty.

First Lecture

Introduction

I do not know what knowledge any of you may already have of psycho-analysis, either from reading or from hearsay. But having regard to the title of my lectures—Introductory Lectures on Psycho-Analysis—I am bound to proceed as though you knew nothing of the subject and needed instruction, even in its first elements.

One thing, at least, I may pre-suppose that you know—namely, that psycho-analysis is a method of medical treatment for those suffering from nervous disorders; and I can give you at once an illustration of the way in which psycho-analytic procedure differs from, and often even reverses, what is customary in other branches of medicine. Usually, when we introduce a patient to a new form of treatment we minimize its difficulties and give him confident assurances of its success. This is, in my opinion, perfectly justifiable, for we thereby increase the probability of success. But when we undertake to treat a neurotic psycho-analytically we proceed otherwise. We explain to him the difficulties of the method, its long duration, the trials and sacrifices which will be required of him; and, as to the result, we tell him

that we can make no definite promises, that success depends upon his endeavours, upon his understanding, his adaptability and his perseverance. We have, of course, good reasons, into which you will perhaps gain some insight later on, for adopting this apparently perverse attitude.

Now forgive me if I begin by treating you in the same way as I do my neurotic patients, for I shall positively advise you against coming to hear me a second time. And with this intention I shall explain to you how of necessity you can obtain from me only an incomplete knowledge of psycho-analysis and also what difficulties stand in the way of your forming an independent judgment on the subject. For I shall show you how the whole trend of your training and your accustomed modes of thought must inevitably have made you hostile to psycho-analysis, and also how much you would have to overcome in your own minds in order to master this instinctive opposition. I naturally cannot foretell what degree of understanding of psycho-analysis you may gain from my lectures, but I can at least assure you that by attending them you will not have learnt how to conduct a psycho-analytic investigation, nor how to carry out a psycho-analytic treatment. And further, if any one of you should feel dissatisfied with a merely cursory acquaintance with psycho-analysis and should wish to form a permanent connection with it, I shall not merely discourage him, but I shall actually warn him against it. For as things are at the present time, not only would the

From: Sigmund Freud, *A General Introduction to Psychoanalysis: A Course of Twenty-Eight Lectures Delivered at the University of Vienna*, trans. Joan Riviere (New York: Liveright Publishing Corporation, 1920), pp.17–24, 75–89.

choice of such a career put an end to all chances of academic success, but, upon taking up work as a practitioner, such a man would find himself in a community which misunderstood his aims and intentions, regarded him with suspicion and hostility, and let loose upon him all the latent evil impulses harboured within it. Perhaps you can infer from the accompaniments of the war now raging in Europe what a countless host that is to reckon with.

However, there are always some people to whom the possibility of a new addition to knowledge will prove an attraction strong enough to survive all such inconveniences. If there are any such among you who will appear at my second lecture in spite of my words of warning they will be welcome. But all of you have a right to know what these inherent difficulties of psycho-analysis are to which I have alluded.

First of all, there is the problem of the teaching and exposition of the subject. In your medical studies you have been accustomed to use your eyes. You see the anatomical specimen, the precipitate of the chemical reaction, the contraction of the muscle as the result of the stimulation of its nerves. Later you come into contact with the patients; you learn the symptoms of disease by the evidence of your senses; the results of pathological processes can be demonstrated to you, and in many cases even the exciting cause of them in an isolated form. On the surgical side you are witnesses of the measures by which the patient is helped, and are permitted to attempt them yourselves. Even in psychiatry, demonstration of patients, of their altered expression, speech and behaviour, yields a series of observations which leave a deep impression on your minds. Thus a teacher of medicine acts for the most part as an exponent and guide, leading you as it were through a museum, while you gain in this way a direct relationship to what is displayed to you and believe yourselves to have been convinced by your own experience of the existence of the new facts.

But in psycho-analysis, unfortunately, all this is different. In psycho-analytic treatment nothing happens but an exchange of words between the patient and the physician. The patient talks, tells of his past experiences and present impressions, complains, and expresses his wishes and his emotions. The physician listens, attempts to direct the patient's thought-processes, reminds him, forces his attention in certain directions, gives him explanations and observes the reactions of understanding or denial thus evoked. The patient's unenlightened relatives—people of a kind to be impressed only by something visible and tangible, preferably by the sort of 'action' that may be seen at a cinema—never omit to express their doubts of how "mere talk can possibly cure anybody." Their reasoning is of course as illogical as it is inconsistent. For they are the same people who are always convinced that the sufferings of neurotics are purely "in their own imagination." Words and magic were in the beginning one and the same thing, and even to-day words retain much of their magical power. By words one of us can give to another the greatest happiness or bring about utter despair; by words the teacher imparts his knowledge to the student; by words the orator sweeps his audience with him and determines its judgements and decisions. Words call forth emotions and are universally the means by which we influence our fellow-creatures. Therefore let us not despise the use of words in psycho-therapy and let us be content if we may overhear the words which pass between the analyst and the patient.

But even that is impossible. The dialogue which constitutes the analysis will admit of no audience; the process cannot be demonstrated. One could, of course, exhibit a neurasthenic or hysterical patient to students at a psychiatric lecture. He would relate his case and his symptoms, but nothing more. He will make the communications necessary to the analysis only under the conditions of a special affective relationship to the physician; in the presence of a single person to whom he was indifferent he would become mute. For these communications relate to all his most private thoughts and feelings, all that which as a socially independent person he must hide from others, all that which, being foreign to his own conception of himself, he tries to conceal even from himself.

It is impossible, therefore, for you to be actually present during a psycho-analytic treatment; you can only be told about it, and can learn psycho-analysis, in the strictest sense of the word, only by hearsay. This tuition at second hand, so to say, puts you in a very unusual and difficult position as regards forming your own judgement on the subject, which will therefore largely depend on the reliance you can place on your informant.

Now imagine for a moment that you were present at a lecture in history instead of in psychiatry, and that the lecturer was dealing with the life and conquests of Alexander the Great. What reason would you have to believe what he told you? The situation would appear at first sight even more unsatisfactory than in the case of psycho-analysis, for the professor of history had no more part in Alexander's campaigns than you yourselves; the psycho-analyst at least informs you of matters in which he himself has played a part. But then we come to the question of what evidence there is to support the historian. He can refer you to the accounts of early writers who were either contemporaries or who lived not long after the events in question, such as Diodorus, Plutarch, Arrian, and others; he can lay before you reproductions of the preserved coins and statues of the king, and pass round a photograph of the mosaic at Pompeii representing the battle at Issus. Yet, strictly speaking, all these documents only prove that the existence of Alexander and the reality of his deeds were already believed in by former generations of men, and your criticism might begin anew at this point. And then you would find that not everything reported of Alexander is worthy of belief or sufficiently authenticated in detail, but I can hardly suppose that you would leave the lecture-room in doubt altogether as to the reality of Alexander the Great. Your conclusions would be principally determined by two considerations: first, that the lecturer could have no conceivable motive for attempting to persuade you of something which he did not himself believe to be true, and secondly, that all the available authorities agree more or less in their accounts of the facts. In questioning the accuracy of the early writers you would apply these tests again, the possible motives of the authors and the agreement to be found between them. The result of such tests would certainly be convincing in the case of Alexander, probably less so in regard to figures like Moses and Nimrod. Later on you will perceive clearly enough what doubts can be raised against the credibility of an exponent of psycho-analysis.

Now you will have a right to ask the question: If no objective evidence for psycho-analysis exists and no possibility of demonstrating the process, how is it possible to study it at all or to convince oneself of its truth? The study of it is indeed not an easy matter, nor are there many people who have thoroughly learned it; still, there is, of course, some way of learning it. Psycho-analysis is learnt first of all on oneself, through the study of one's own personality. This is not exactly what is meant by introspection, but it may be so described for want of a better word. There is a whole series of very common and well-known mental phenomena which can be taken as material for self-analysis when one has acquired some knowledge of the method. In this way one may obtain the required conviction of the reality of the processes which psycho-analysis describes, and of the truth of its conceptions, although progress on these lines is not without its limitations. One gets much further by submitting oneself to analysis by a skilled analyst, undergoing the working of the analysis in one's own person and using the opportunity to observe the finer details of the technique which the analyst employs. This, eminently the best way, is of course only practicable for individuals and cannot be used in a class of students.

The second difficulty you will find in connection with psycho-analysis is not, on the other hand, inherent in it, but is one for which I must hold you yourselves responsible, at least in so far as your medical studies have influenced you. Your training will have induced in you an attitude of mind very far removed from the psycho-analytical one. You have been trained to establish the functions and disturbances of the organism on an anatomical basis, to explain them in terms of chemistry and physics, and to regard them from a biological point of view; but no part of your interest has ever been directed to the mental aspects of life, in which, after all, the development of the marvellously complicated organism culminates. For this reason a psychological attitude of mind is still foreign to you, and you are accustomed to regard it with suspicion, to deny it a scientific status, and to leave it to the general public, poets, mystics, and philosophers. Now this limitation in you is undoubtedly detrimental to your medical efficiency; for on meeting a patient it is the mental aspects with which one first comes into contact, as in most human relationships, and I am afraid you will pay the penalty of having to yield a part of the curative influence at which you aim to the quacks, mystics, and faith-healers whom you despise.

I quite acknowledge that there is an excuse for this defect in your previous training. There is no auxiliary philosophical science that might be of service to you in your profession. Neither speculative philosophy nor descriptive psychology, nor even the so-called experimental psychology which is studied in connection with the physiology of the sense-organs, as they are taught in the schools, can tell you anything useful of the relations existing between mind and body, or can give you a key to comprehension of a possible disorder of the mental functions. It is true that the psychiatric branch of medicine occupies itself with describing the different forms of recognizable mental disturbances and grouping them in clinical pictures, but in their best moments psychiatrists themselves are doubtful whether their purely descriptive formulations deserve to be called science. The origin, mechanism, and interrelation of the symptoms which make up these clinical pictures are undiscovered: either they cannot be correlated with any demonstrable changes in the brain, or only with such changes as in no way explain them. These mental disturbances are open to therapeutic influence only when they can be identified as secondary effects of some organic disease.

This is the lacuna which psycho-analysis is striving to fill. It hopes to provide psychiatry with the missing psychological foundation, to discover the common ground on which a correlation of bodily and mental disorder becomes comprehensible. To this end it must dissociate itself from every foreign preconception, whether anatomical, chemical, or physiological, and must work throughout with conceptions of a purely psychological order, and for this very reason I fear that it will appear strange to you at first.

For the next difficulty I shall not hold you, your training or your mental attitude, responsible. There are two tenets of psycho-analysis which offend the whole world and excite its resentment; the one conflicts with intellectual, the other with moral and æsthetic prejudices. Let us not underestimate these prejudices; they are powerful things, residues of valuable, even necessary, stages in human evolution. They are maintained by emotional forces, and the fight against them is a hard one.

The first of these displeasing propositions of psycho-analysis is this: that mental processes are essentially unconscious, and that those which are conscious are merely isolated acts and parts of the whole psychic entity. Now I must ask you to remember that, on the contrary, we are accustomed to identify the mental with the conscious. Consciousness appears to us as positively the characteristic that defines mental life, and we regard psychology as the study of the content of consciousness. This even appears so evident that any contradiction of it seems obvious nonsense to us, and yet it is impossible for psycho-analysis to avoid this contradiction, or to accept the identity between the conscious and the psychic. The psycho-analytical definition of the mind is that it comprises processes of the nature of feeling, thinking, and wishing, and it maintains that there are such things as unconscious thinking and unconscious wishing. But in doing so psycho-analysis has forfeited at the outset the sympathy of the sober and scientifically minded, and incurred the suspicion of being a fantastic cult occupied with dark and unfathomable mysteries. You yourselves must find it difficult to understand why I should stigmatize an abstract proposition, such as "The psychic is the conscious," as a prejudice; nor can you guess yet what evolutionary process could have led to the denial of the unconscious, if it does indeed exist, nor what advantage could have been achieved by this denial. It seems like an empty wrangle over words to argue whether mental life is to be regarded as co-extensive with consciousness or whether it may be said to stretch beyond this limit, and yet I can assure you that the acceptance of unconscious mental processes represents a decisive step towards a new orientation in the world and in science.

As little can you suspect how close is the connection between this first bold step on the part of psycho-analysis and the second to which I am now coming. For this next proposition, which we put forward as one of the discoveries of psycho-analysis, consists in the assertion that impulses, which can only be described as sexual in both the narrower and the wider sense, play a peculiarly large part, never before sufficiently appreciated, in the causation of nervous and mental disorders. Nay, more, that these sexual impulses have contributed invaluably to the highest cultural, artistic, and social achievements of the human mind.

In my opinion, it is the aversion from this conclusion of psycho-analytic investigation that is the most significant source of the opposition it has encountered. Are you curious to know how we ourselves account for this? We believe that civilization has been built up, under the pressure at the struggle for existence, by sacrifices in gratification of the primitive impulses, and that it is to a great extent for ever being re-created, as each individual, successively joining the community, repeats the sacrifice of his instinctive pleasures for the common good. The sexual are amongst the most important of the instinctive forces thus utilized: they are in this way sublimated, that is to say, their energy is turned aside from its sexual goal and diverted towards other ends, no longer sexual and socially more valuable. But the structure thus built up is insecure, for the sexual impulses are with difficulty controlled; in each individual who takes up his part in the work of civilization there is a danger that a rebellion of the sexual impulses may occur, against this diversion of their energy. Society can conceive of no more powerful menace to its culture than would arise from the liberation of the sexual impulses and a return of them to their original goal. Therefore society dislikes this sensitive place in its development being touched upon; that the power of the sexual instinct should be recognized, and the significance of the individual's sexual life revealed, is very far from its interests; with a view to discipline it has rather taken the course of diverting attention away from this whole field. For this reason, the revelations of psycho-analysis are not tolerated by it, and it would greatly prefer to brand them as æsthetically offensive, morally reprehensible, or dangerous. But since such objections are not valid arguments against conclusions which claim to represent the objective results of scientific investigation, the opposition must be translated into intellectual terms before it can be expressed. It is a characteristic of human nature to be inclined to regard anything which is disagreeable as untrue, and then without much difficulty to find arguments against it. So society pronounces the unacceptable to be untrue, disputes the results of psycho-analysis with logical and concrete arguments, arising, however, in affective sources, and clings to them with all the strength of prejudice against every attempt at refutation.

But we, on the other hand, claim to have yielded to no tendency in propounding this objectionable theory. Our intention has been solely to give recognition to the facts as we found them in the course of painstaking researches. And we now claim the right to reject unconditionally any such introduction of practical considerations into the field of scientific investigation, even before we have determined whether the apprehension which attempts to force these considerations upon us is justified or not.

These, now, are some of the difficulties which confront you at the outset when you begin to take an interest in psycho-analysis. It is probably more than enough for a beginning. If you can overcome their discouraging effect, we will proceed further.

*   *   *

Fifth Lecture

Difficulties and Preliminary Approach to the Subject

One day the discovery was made that the symptoms of disease in certain nervous patients have meaning. It was upon this discovery that the psycho-analytic method of treatment was based. In this treatment it happened that patients in speaking of their symptoms also mentioned their dreams, whereupon the suspicion arose that these dreams too had meaning.

However, we will not pursue this historical path, but will strike off in the opposite direction. Our aim is to demonstrate the meaning of dreams, in preparation for the study of the neuroses. There are good grounds for this reversal of procedure, since the study of dreams is not merely the best preparation for that of the neuroses, but a dream is itself a neurotic symptom and, moreover, one which possesses for us the incalculable advantage of occurring in all healthy people. Indeed, if all human beings were healthy and would only dream, we could gather almost all the knowledge from their dreams which we have gained from studying the neuroses.

So dreams become the object of psycho-analytic research—another of these ordinary, under-rated occurrences, apparently of no practical value, like "errors," and sharing with them the characteristic of occurring in healthy persons. But in other respects the conditions of work are rather less favourable. Errors had only been neglected by science, people had not troubled their heads much about them, but at least it was no disgrace to occupy oneself with them. True, people said, there are things more important but still something may possibly come of it. To occupy oneself with dreams, however, is not merely unpractical and superfluous, but positively scandalous: it carries with it the taint of the unscientific and arouses the suspicion of personal leanings towards mysticism. The idea of a medical student troubling himself about dreams when there is so much in neuropathology and psychiatry itself that is more serious—tumours as large as apples compressing the organ of the mind, hæmorrhages, chronic inflammatory conditions in which the alterations in the tissues can be demonstrated under the microscope! No, dreams are far too unworthy and trivial to be objects of scientific research.

There is yet another factor involved which, in itself, sets at defiance all the requirements of exact investigation. In investigating dreams even the object of research, the dream itself, is indefinite. A delusion, for example, presents clear and definite outlines. "I am the Emperor of China," says your patient plainly. But a dream? For the most part it cannot be related at all. When a man tells a dream, has he any guarantee that he has told it correctly, and not perhaps altered it in the telling or been forced to invent part of it on account of the vagueness of his recollection? Most dreams cannot be remembered at all and are forgotten except for some tiny fragments. And is a scientific psychology or a method of treatment for the sick to be founded upon material such as this?

A certain element of exaggeration in a criticism may arouse our suspicions. The arguments brought against the dream as an object of scientific research are clearly extreme. We have met with the objection

of triviality already in "errors," and have told ourselves that great things may be revealed even by small indications. As to the indistinctness of dreams, that is a characteristic like any other—we cannot dictate to things their characteristics; besides, there are also dreams which are clear and well-defined. Further, there are other objects of psychiatric investigation which suffer in the same way from the quality of indefiniteness, e.g. the obsessive ideas of many cases, with which nevertheless many psychiatrists of repute and standing have occupied themselves. I will recall the last case of the kind which came before me in medical practice. The patient, a woman, presented her case in these words: "I have a certain feeling, as if I had injured, or had meant to injure, some living creature—perhaps a child—no, no, a dog rather, as if perhaps I had pushed it off a bridge—or done something else." Any disadvantage resulting from the uncertain recollection of dreams may be remedied by deciding that exactly what the dreamer tells is to count as the dream, and by ignoring all that he may have forgotten or altered in the process of recollection. Finally, one cannot maintain in so sweeping a fashion that dreams are unimportant things. We know from our own experience that the mood in which we awake from a dream may last throughout the day, and cases have been observed by medical men in which mental disorder began with a dream, the delusion which had its source in this dream persisting; further, it is told of historical persons that impulses to momentous deeds sprang from their dreams. We may therefore ask: what is the real cause of the disdain in which dreams are held in scientific circles? In my opinion it is the reaction from the over-estimation of them in earlier times. It is well known that it is no easy matter to reconstruct the past, but we may assume with certainty (you will forgive my jest) that as early as three thousand years ago and more our ancestors dreamt in the same way as we do. So far as we know, all ancient peoples attached great significance to dreams and regarded them as of practical value; they obtained from them auguries of the future and looked for portents in them. For the Greeks and other Orientals, it was at times as unthinkable to undertake a campaign without a dream-interpreter as it would be to-day without air-scouts for intelligence. When Alexander the Great set out on his campaign of conquest the most famous interpreters of dreams were in his following. The city of Tyre, still at that time on an island, offered so stout a resistance to the king that he entertained the idea of abandoning the siege; then one night he dreamed of a satyr dancing in triumph, and when he related this dream to his interpreters they informed him that it foretold his victory over the city; he gave the order to attack and took Tyre by storm. Among the Etruscans and Romans other methods of foretelling the future were employed, but during the whole of the Græco-Roman period the interpretation of dreams was practised and held in high esteem. Of the literature on this subject the principal work at any rate has come down to us, namely, the book of Artemidorus of Daldis, who is said to have lived at the time of the Emperor Hadrian. How it happened that the art of dream-interpretation declined later and dreams fell into disrepute, I cannot tell you. The progress of learning cannot have had very much to do with it, for in the darkness of the middle ages things far more absurd than the ancient practice of the interpretation of dreams were faithfully retained. The fact remains that the interest in dreams gradually sank to the level of superstition and could hold its own only amongst the uneducated. In our day, there survive, as a final degradation of the art of dream-interpretation, the attempts to find out from dreams numbers destined to draw prizes in games of chance. On the other hand, exact science of the present day has repeatedly concerned itself with the dream, but always with the sole object of illustrating *physiological* theories. By medical men, naturally, a dream was never regarded as a mental process but as the mental expression of physical stimuli. Binz in 1876 pronounced the dream to be "a physical process, always useless and in many cases actually morbid, a process above which the conception of the world-soul and of immortality stands as high as does the blue sky above the most low-lying, weed-grown stretch of sand." Maury compares dreams with the spasmodic jerkings of St. Vitus' dance, contrasted with the co-ordinated movements of the normal human being; in an old comparison a parallel is drawn between the content of a dream and the sounds which would be produced if "someone ignorant of music let his ten fingers wander over the keys of an instrument."

"Interpretation" means discovering a hidden meaning, but there can be no question of attempting this while such an attitude is maintained towards the dream-performance. Look up the description of dreams given in the writings of Wundt, Jodl and other recent philosophers: they are content with the bare enumeration of the divergences of the dream-life from waking thought with a view to depreciating the dreams: they emphasize the lack of connection in the associations, the suspended exercise of the critical faculty, the elimination of all knowledge, and other indications of diminished functioning. The single valuable contribution to our knowledge about dreams for which we are indebted to exact science relates to the influence upon the dream-content of physical stimuli operating during sleep. We have the work of a Norwegian author who died recently—J. Mourly Vold—two large volumes on experimental investigation of dreams (translated into German in 1910 and 1912), which are concerned almost entirely with the results obtained by change in the position of the limbs. These investigations have been held up to us as models of exact research in the subject of dreams. Now can you imagine what would be the comment of exact science on learning that we intend to try to find out the *meaning* of dreams? The comment that has perhaps been made already! However, we will not allow ourselves to be appalled at the thought. If it was possible for errors to have an underlying meaning, it is possible that dreams have one too; and errors have, in very many cases, a meaning which has eluded the researches of exact science. Let us adopt the assumption of the ancients and of simple folk, and follow in the footsteps of the dream-interpreters of old.

First of all, we must take our bearings in this enterprise, and make a survey of the field of dreams. What exactly is a dream? It is difficult to define it in a single phrase. Yet we need not seek after a definition, when all we need is to refer to something familiar to everyone. Still we ought to pick out the essential features in dreams. How are we to discover these features? The boundaries of the region we are entering comprise such vast differences, differences whichever way we turn. That which we can show to be common to all dreams is probably what is essential.

Well then—the first common characteristic of all dreams would be that we are asleep at the time. Obviously, the dream is the life of the mind during sleep, a life bearing certain resemblances to our waking life and, at the same time, differing from it widely. That, indeed, was Aristotle's definition. Perhaps dream and sleep stand in yet closer relationship to each other. We can be waked by a dream; we often have a dream when we wake spontaneously or when we are forcibly roused from sleep. Dreams seem thus to be an intermediate condition between sleeping and waking. Hence, our attention is directed to sleep itself: what then is sleep?

That is a physiological or biological problem concerning which much is still in dispute. We can come to no decisive answer, but I think we may attempt to define one psychological characteristic of sleep. Sleep is a condition in which I refuse to have anything to do with the outer world and have withdrawn my interest from it. I go to sleep by retreating from the outside world and warding off the stimuli proceeding from it. Again, when I am tired by that world I go to sleep. I say to it as I fall asleep: "Leave me in peace, for I want to sleep." The child says just the opposite: "I won't go to sleep yet; I'm not tired, I want more things to happen to me!" Thus the biological object of sleep seems to be recuperation, its psychological characteristic the suspension of interest in the outer world. Our relationship with the world which we entered so unwillingly seems to be endurable only with intermission; hence we withdraw again periodically into the condition prior to our entrance into the world: that is to say, into intra-uterine existence. At any rate, we try to bring about quite similar conditions—warmth, darkness and absence of stimulus—characteristic of that state. Some of us still roll ourselves tightly up into a ball resembling the intra-uterine position. It looks as if we grown-ups do not belong wholly to the world, but only by two-thirds; one-third of us has never yet been born at all. Every time we wake in the morning it is as if we were newly born. We do, in fact, speak of the condition of waking from sleep in these very words: we feel "as if we were newly born,"—and in this we are probably quite mistaken in our idea of the general sensations of the new-born infant; it may be assumed on the contrary that it feels

extremely uncomfortable. Again, in speaking of birth we speak of "seeing the light of day."

If this is the nature of sleep, then dreams do not come into its scheme at all, but seem rather to be an unwelcome supplement to it; and we do indeed believe that dreamless sleep is the best, the only proper sleep. There should be no mental activity during sleep; if any such activity bestirs itself, then in so far have we failed to reach the true prenatal condition of peace; we have not been able to avoid altogether some remnants of mental activity, and the act of dreaming would represent these remnants. In that event it really does seem that dreams do not need to have meaning. With errors it was different, for they were at least activities manifested in waking life; but if I sleep and have altogether suspended mental activity, with the exception of certain remnants which I have not been able to suppress, there is no necessity whatever that they should have any meaning. In fact, I cannot even make use of any such meaning, seeing that the rest of my mind is asleep. It can really then be a matter of spasmodic reactions only, of such mental phenomena only as have their origin in physical stimulation. Hence, dreams must be remnants of the mental activity of waking life disturbing sleep, and we might as well make up our minds forthwith to abandon a theme so unsuited to the purposes of psycho-analysis.

Superfluous as dreams may be, however, they do exist nevertheless, and we can try to account for their existence to ourselves. Why does not mental life go off to sleep? Probably because there is something that will not leave the mind in peace; stimuli are acting upon it and to these it is bound to react. Dreams therefore are the mode of reaction of the mind to stimuli acting upon it during sleep. We note here a possibility of access to comprehension of dreams. We can now endeavour to find out, in various dreams, what are the stimuli seeking to disturb sleep, the reaction to which takes the form of dreams. By doing this we should have worked out the first characteristic common to all dreams.

Is there any other common characteristic? Yes, there is another, unmistakable, and yet much harder to lay hold of and describe. The character of mental processes during sleep is quite different from that of waking processes. In dreams we go through many experiences, which we fully believe in, whereas in reality we are perhaps only experiencing the single disturbing stimulus. For the most part our experiences take the form of visual images; there may be feeling as well, thoughts, too, mixed up with them, and the other senses may be drawn in; but for the most part dreams consist of visual images. Part of the difficulty of reciting a dream comes from the fact that we have to translate these images into words. "I could draw it," the dreamer often says to us, "but I do not know how to put it into words." Now this is not exactly a diminution in the mental capacity, as seen in a contrast between a feeble-minded person and a man of genius. The difference is rather a qualitative one, but it is difficult to say precisely wherein it lies. G. T. Fechner once suggested that the stage whereon the drama of the dream (within the mind) is played out is other than that of the life of waking ideas. That is a saying which we really do not understand, nor do we know what it is meant to convey to us, but it does actually reproduce the impression of strangeness which most dreams make upon us. Again, the comparison of the act of dreaming with the performances of an unskilled hand in music breaks down here, for the piano will certainly respond with the same notes, though not with melodies, to a chance touch on its keys. We will keep this second common characteristic of dreams carefully in view, even though we may not understand it.

Are there any other qualities common to all dreams? I can think of none, but can see differences only, whichever way I look, differences too in every respect—in apparent duration, definiteness, the part played by affects, persistence in the mind, and so forth. This is really not what we should naturally expect in the case of a compulsive attempt, at once meagre and spasmodic, to ward off a stimulus. As regards the length of dreams, some are very short, containing only one image, or very few, or a single thought, possibly even a single word; others are peculiarly rich in content, enact entire romances and seem to last a very long time. There are dreams as distinct as actual experiences, so distinct that for some time after waking we do not realize that they were dreams at all; others, which are ineffably faint, shadowy and blurred; in one and the same dream, even, there may be some parts of extraordinary vividness alternating with others so indistinct as to be almost wholly elusive. Again, dreams may be quite consistent or at any rate coherent, or even witty or fantastically beautiful; others again are confused, apparently imbecile, absurd or often absolutely mad. There are dreams which leave us quite cold, others in which every affect makes itself felt—pain to the point of tears, terror so intense as to wake us, amazement, delight, and so on. Most dreams are forgotten soon after waking; or they persist throughout the day, the recollection becoming fainter and more imperfect as the day goes on; others remain so vivid (as, for example, the dreams of childhood) that thirty years later we remember them as clearly as though they were part of a recent experience. Dreams, like people, may make their appearance once and never come back; or the same person may dream the same thing repeatedly, either in the same form or with slight alterations. In short, these scraps of mental activity at night-time have at command an immense repertory, can in fact create everything that by day the mind is capable of—only, it is never the same.

One might attempt to account for these diversities in dream by assuming that they correspond to different intermediate states between sleeping and waking, different levels of imperfect sleep. Very well; but then in proportion as the mind approached the waking state there should be not merely an increase in the value, content, and distinctness of the dream-performance, but also a growing perception that it *is* a dream; and it ought not to happen that side by side with a clear and sensible element in the dream there is one which is nonsensical or indistinct, followed again by a good piece of work. It is certain that the mind could not vary its depth of sleep so rapidly as that. This explanation therefore does not help; there is in fact no short cut to an answer.

For the present we will leave the "meaning" of the dream out of question, and try instead, by starting from the common element in dreams, to clear a path to a better understanding of their nature. From the relationship of dreams to sleep we have drawn the conclusion that dreams are the reaction to a stimulus disturbing sleep. As we have heard, this is also the single point at which exact experimental psychology can come to our aid; it affords proof of the fact that stimuli brought to bear during sleep make their appearance in dreams. Many investigations have been made on these lines, culminating in those of Mourly Vold whom I mentioned earlier; we have all, too, been in a position to confirm their results by occasional observations of our own. I will choose some of the earlier experiments to tell you. Maury had tests of this kind carried out upon himself. Whilst dreaming, he was made to smell some eau de Cologne, whereupon he dreamt he was in Cairo, in the shop of Johann Maria Farina, and this was followed by some crazy adventures. Again, someone gave his neck a gentle pinch, and he dreamt of the application of a blister and of a doctor who had treated him when he was a child. Again, they let a drop of water fall on his forehead and he was immediately in Italy, perspiring freely and drinking the white wine of Orvieto.

The striking feature about these dreams produced under experimental conditions will perhaps become still clearer to us in another series of "stimulus"-dreams. These are three dreams of which we have an account by a clever observer, Hildebrandt, and all three are reactions to the sound of an alarum-clock:

"I am going for a walk on a spring morning, and I saunter through fields just beginning to grow green, till I come to a neighbouring village, where I see the inhabitants in holiday attire making their way in large numbers to the church, their hymnbooks in their hands. Of course! it is Sunday and the morning service is just about to begin. I decide to take part in it, but first as I am rather overheated I think I will cool down in the churchyard which surrounds the church. Whilst reading some of the epitaphs there I hear the bell-ringer go up into the tower, where I now notice, high up, the little village bell which will give the signal for the beginning of the service. For some time yet it remains motionless, then it begins to swing, and suddenly the strokes ring out, clear and piercing—so clear and piercing that they put an end to my sleep. But the sound of the bell comes from the alarum-clock."

Here is another combination of images. "It is a bright winter day, and the roads are deep in snow. I

have promised to take part in a sleighing expedition, but I have to wait a long time before I am told that the sleigh is at the door. Now follow the preparations for getting in, the fur rug is spread out and the foot-muff fetched and finally I am in my place. But there is still a delay while the horses wait for the signal to start. Then the reins are jerked and the little bells, shaken violently, begin their familiar janizary music, so loudly that in a moment the web of the dream is rent. Again it is nothing but the shrill sound of the alarum-clock."

Now for the third example! "I see a kitchen-maid with dozens of piled-up plates going along the passage to the dining-room. It seems to me that the pyramid of china in her arms is in danger of over-balancing. I call out a warning: 'Take care, your whole load will fall to the ground.' Of course I receive the usual answer: that they are accustomed to carrying china in that way, and so on; meanwhile I follow her as she goes with anxious looks. I thought so—the next thing is a stumble on the threshold, the crockery falls, crashing and clattering in a hundred pieces on the ground. But—I soon become aware that that interminably prolonged sound is no real crash, but a regular ringing—and this ringing is due merely to the alarum-clock, as I realize at last on awakening."

These dreams are very pretty, perfectly sensible, and by no means so incoherent as dreams usually are. We have no quarrel with them on those grounds. The thing common to them all is that in each case the situation arises from a noise, which the dreamer on waking recognizes as that of the alarum-clock. Hence we see here how a dream is produced, but we find out something more. In the dream there is no recognition of the clock, which does not even appear in it, but for the noise of the clock another noise is substituted; the stimulus which disturbs sleep is interpreted, but interpreted differently in each instance. Now why is this? There is no answer; it appears to be mere caprice. But to understand the dream we should be able to account for its choice of just this noise and no other to interpret the stimulus given by the alarum-clock. In analogous fashion we must object to Maury's experiments that, although it is clear that the stimulus brought to bear on the sleeper does appear in the dream, yet his experiments don't explain why it appears exactly in that form, which is one that does not seem explicable by the nature of the stimulus disturbing sleep. And further, in Maury's experiments there was mostly a mass of other dream-material attached to the direct result of the stimulus, for example, the crazy adventures in the eau de Cologne dream, for which we are at a loss to account.

Now will you reflect that the class of dreams which wake one up affords the best opportunity for establishing the influence of external disturbing stimuli. In most other cases it will be more difficult. We do not wake up out of all dreams, and if in the morning we remember a dream of the night before, how are we to assign it to a disturbing stimulus operating perhaps during the night? I once succeeded in subsequently establishing the occurrence of a sound-stimulus of this sort, but only, of course, because of peculiar circumstances. I woke up one morning at a place in the Tyrolese mountains knowing that I had dreamt that the Pope was dead. I could not explain the dream to myself, but later my wife asked me: "Did you hear quite early this morning the dreadful noise of bells breaking out in all the churches and chapels?" No, I had heard nothing, my sleep is too sound, but thanks to her telling me this I understood my dream. How often may such causes of stimulus as this induce dreams in the sleeper without his ever hearing of them afterwards? Possibly very often: and possibly not. If we can get no information of any stimulus we cannot be convinced on the point. And apart from this we have given up trying to arrive at an estimation of the sleep-disturbing external stimuli, since we know that they only explain a fragment of the dream and not the whole dream-reaction.

We need not on that account give up this theory altogether; there is still another possible way of following it out. Obviously it is a matter of indifference what disturbs sleep and causes the mind to dream. If it cannot always be something external acting as a stimulus to one of the senses, it is possible that, instead, a stimulus operates from the internal organs—a so-called somatic stimulus. This supposition lies very close, and moreover it corresponds to the view popularly held with regard to the origin of dreams, for it is a common saying that

they come from the stomach. Unfortunately, here again we must suppose that in very many cases information respecting a somatic stimulus operating during the night would no longer be forthcoming after waking, so that it would be incapable of proof. But we will not overlook the fact that many trustworthy experiences support the idea that dreams may be derived from somatic stimuli; on the whole it is indubitable that the condition of the internal organs can influence dreams. The relation of the content of many dreams to distention of the bladder or to a condition of excitation of the sex-organs is so plain that it cannot be mistaken. From these obvious cases we pass to others, in which, to judge by the content of the dream, we are at least justified in suspecting that some such somatic stimuli have been at work, since there is something in this content which can be regarded as elaboration, representation, or interpretation of these stimuli. Scherner, the investigator of dreams (1861), emphatically supported the view which traces the origin of dreams to organic stimuli, and contributed some excellent examples towards it. For instance, he sees in a dream "two rows of beautiful boys, with fair hair and delicate complexions, confronting each other pugnaciously, joining in combat, seizing hold of one another, and again letting go their hold, only to take up the former position and go through the whole process again"; his interpretation of the two rows of boys as the teeth is in itself plausible and seems to receive full confirmation when after this scene the dreamer "pulls a long tooth from his jaw." Again, the interpretation of "long, narrow, winding passages" as being suggested by a stimulus originating in the intestine seems sound and corroborates Scherner's assertion that dreams primarily endeavour to represent, by like objects, the organ from which the stimulus proceeds.

We must therefore be prepared to admit that internal stimuli can play the same rôle in dreams as external ones. Unfortunately, evaluation of this factor is open to the same objections. In a great number of instances the attribution of dreams to somatic stimuli must remain uncertain or incapable of proof; not all dreams, but only a certain number of them, rouse the suspicion that stimuli from internal organs have something to do with their origin;

and lastly, the internal somatic stimulus will suffice no more than the external sensory stimulus to explain any other part of the dream than the direct reaction to it. The origin of all the rest of the dream remains obscure.

Now, however, let us direct our attention to a certain peculiarity of the dream-life which appears when we study the operation of these stimuli. The dream does not merely reproduce the stimulus, but elaborates it, plays upon it, fits it into a context, or replaces it by something else. This is a side of the dream-work which is bound to be of interest to us because possibly it may lead us nearer to the true nature of dreams. The scope of a man's production is not necessarily limited to the circumstance which immediately gives rise to it. For instance, Shakespeare's *Macbeth* was written as an occasional drama on the accession of the king who first united in his person the crowns of the three kingdoms. But does this historical occasion cover the whole content of the drama, or explain its grandeur and its mystery? Perhaps in the same way the external and internal stimuli operating upon the sleeper are merely the occasion of the dream and afford us no insight into its true nature.

The other element common to all dreams, their peculiarity in mental life, is on the one hand very difficult to grasp and on the other seems to afford no clue for further inquiry. Our experiences in dreams for the most part take the form of visual images. Can these be explained by the stimuli? Is it really the stimulus that we experience? If so, why is the experience visual, when it can only be in the very rarest instance that any stimulus has operated upon our eyesight? Or, can it be shown that when we dream of speech any conversation or sounds resembling conversation reached our ears during sleep? I venture to discard such a possibility without any hesitation whatever.

If we cannot get any further with the common characteristics of dreams as a starting-point, let us try beginning with their differences. Dreams are often meaningless, confused, and absurd, yet there are some which are sensible, sober, and reasonable. Let us see whether these latter sensible dreams can help to elucidate those which are meaningless. I will tell you the latest reasonable dream which was told

to me, the dream of a young man: "I went for a walk in the Kärntnerstrasse and there I met Mr. X.; after accompanying him for a short time I went into a restaurant. Two ladies and a gentleman came and sat down at my table. At first I was annoyed and refused to look at them, but presently I glanced across at them and found that they were quite nice." The dreamer's comment on this was that the evening before he had actually been walking in the Kärntnerstrasse, which is the way he usually goes, and that he had met Mr. X. there. The other part of the dream was not a direct reminiscence, but only bore a certain resemblance to an occurrence of some time previously. Or here we have another prosaic dream, that of a lady. Her husband says to her: "Don't you think we ought to have the piano tuned?" and she replies: "It is not worth it, for the hammers need fresh leather anyhow." This dream repeats a conversation which took place in almost the same words between herself and her husband the day before the dream. What then do we learn from these two prosaic dreams? Merely that there occur in them recollections of daily life or of matters connected with it. Even that would be something if it could be asserted of all dreams without exception. But that is out of the question; this characteristic too belongs only to a minority of dreams. In most dreams we find no connection with the day before, and no light is thrown from this quarter upon meaningless and absurd dreams. All we know is that we have met with a new problem. Not only do we want to know what a dream is saying, but if as in our examples that is quite plain, we want to know further from what cause and to what end we repeat in dreams this which is known to us and has recently happened to us.

I think you would be as tired as I of continuing the kind of attempts we have made up to this point. It only shows that all the interest in the world will not help us with a problem unless we have also an idea of some path to adopt in order to arrive at a solution. Till now we have not found this path. Experimental psychology has contributed nothing but some (certainly very valuable) information about the significance of stimuli in the production of dreams. Of philosophy we have nothing to expect, unless it be a lofty repetition of the reproach that our object is intellectually contemptible; while from the occult sciences we surely do not choose to borrow. History and the verdict of the people tell us that dreams are full of meaning and importance, and of prophetic significance; but that is hard to accept and certainly does not lend itself to proof. So then our first endeavours are completely baffled.

But unexpectedly there comes a hint from a direction in which we have not hitherto looked. Colloquial speech, which is certainly no matter of chance but the deposit as it were, of ancient knowledge— a thing which must not indeed be made too much of—our speech, I say, recognizes the existence of something to which, strangely enough, it gives the name of "day-dreams." Day-dreams are phantasies (products of phantasy); they are very common phenomena, are observable in healthy as well as in sick persons, and they also can easily be studied by the subject himself. The most striking thing about these 'phantastic' creations is that they have received the name of "day-dreams," for they have nothing in common with the two universal characteristics of dreams. Their name contradicts any relationship to the condition of sleep and, as regards the second universal characteristic, no experience or hallucination takes place in them, we simply imagine something; we recognize that they are the work of phantasy, that we are not seeing but thinking. These day-dreams appear before puberty, often indeed in late childhood, and persist until maturity is reached when they are either given up or retained as long as life lasts. The content of these phantasies is dictated by a very transparent motivation. They are scenes and events which gratify either the egoistic cravings of ambition or thirst for power, or the erotic desires of the subject. In young men, ambitious phantasies predominate; in women, whose ambition centres on success in love, erotic phantasies; but the erotic requirement can often enough in men too be detected in the background, all their heroic deeds and successes are really only intended to win the admiration and favour of women. In other respects these day-dreams show great diversity and their fate varies. All of them are either given up after a short time and replaced by a new one, or retained, spun out into long stories, and adapted to changing circumstances in life. They march with the times; and they receive as it were "date-stamps" upon them which show the influence of new situations. They form the raw material of poetic production; for the writer by transforming, disguising, or curtailing them creates out of his day-dreams the situations which he embodies in his stories, novels, and dramas. The hero of a day-dream is, however, always the subject himself, either directly imagined in the part or transparently identified with someone else.

Perhaps day-dreams are so called on account of their similar relation to reality, as an indication that their content is no more to be accepted as real than is that of dreams. But it is possible that they share the name of dreams because of some mental characteristic of the dream which we do not yet know but after which we are seeking. On the other hand, it is possible that we are altogether wrong in regarding this similarity of name as significant. That is a question which can only be answered later.

Beyond Good and Evil
Friedrich Nietzsche

Friedrich Nietzsche's Beyond Good and Evil *was a devastating critique of contemporary philosophy, religion, science, politics, and ethics. Nietzsche is probably best known for the phrase "God is dead!" and such concepts as the* Übermensch *(superman) and the* Will to Power. *In this selection, he discusses the will to power as an expression of creative energy, which he believed was the driving force of nature. Even the philosopher's drive for objective truth was, in his view, a manifestation of the will to power. Nietzsche's insanity late in life has caused some to say that his ideas drove him insane and others to suggest that his insanity gave birth to his ideas. Regardless, some of his insights are still striking.*

Prejudices of Philosophers

1.

The Will to Truth, which is to tempt us to many a hazardous enterprise, the famous Truthfulness of which all philosophers have hitherto spoken with respect, what questions has this Will to Truth not laid before us! What strange, perplexing, questionable questions! It is already a long story; yet it seems as if it were hardly commenced. Is it any wonder if we at last grow distrustful, lose patience, and turn impatiently away? That this Sphinx teaches us at last to ask questions ourselves? *Who* is it really that puts questions to us here? *What* really is this "Will to Truth" in us? In fact we made a long halt at the question as to the origin of this Will—until at last we came to an absolute standstill before a yet more fundamental question. We inquired about the *value* of this Will. Granted that we want the truth: *why not rather* untruth? And uncertainty? Even ignorance? The problem of the value of truth presented itself before us—or was it we who presented ourselves before the problem? Which of us is the Œdipus here? Which the Sphinx? It would seem to be a rendezvous of questions and notes of interrogation. And could it be believed that it at last seems to us as if the problem had never been propounded before, as if we were the first to discern it, get a sight of it, and *risk raising* it. For there is risk in raising it, perhaps there is no greater risk.

2.

"*How could* anything originate out of its opposite? For example, truth out of error? or the Will to Truth out of the will to deception? or the generous deed out of selfishness? or the pure sun-bright vision of the wise man out of covetousness? Such genesis is impossible; whoever dreams of it is a fool, nay, worse than a fool; things of the highest value must have a different origin, an origin of *their own*—in this transitory, seductive, illusory, paltry world, in this turmoil of delusion and cupidity, they cannot have their source. But rather in the lap of Being, in the intransitory, in the concealed God, in the 'Thing-in-itself'—*there* must be their source, and nowhere else!"—This mode of reasoning discloses the typical prejudice by which metaphysicians of all times can be recognised, this mode of valuation is at the back of all their logical procedure; through this "belief" of theirs, they exert themselves for their "knowledge," for something that is in the end solemnly christened "the Truth." The fundamental belief of metaphysicians is *the belief in antitheses of*

From: Friedrich Nietzsche, *Beyond Good and Evil: Prelude to a Philosophy of the Future*, trans. Helen Zimmern (New York: Russell & Russell, Inc., 1964), pp.5–8, 20–22, 33–34, 223–232, 234–237, 255–256.

values. It never occurred even to the wariest of them to doubt here on the very threshold (where doubt, however, was most necessary); though they had made a solemn vow, "*de omnibus dubitandum.*" For it may be doubted, firstly, whether antitheses exist at all; and secondly, whether the popular valuations and antitheses of value upon which metaphysicians have set their seal, are not perhaps merely superficial estimates, merely provisional perspectives, besides being probably made from some corner, perhaps from below—"frog perspectives," as it were, to borrow an expression current among painters. In spite of all the value which may belong to the true, the positive, and the unselfish, it might be possible that a higher and more fundamental value for life generally should be assigned to pretence, to the will to delusion, to selfishness, and cupidity. It might even be possible that *what* constitutes the value of those good and respected things, consists precisely in their being insidiously related, knotted, and crocheted to these evil and apparently opposed things—perhaps even in being essentially identical with them. Perhaps! But who wishes to concern himself with such dangerous "Perhapses"! For that investigation one must await the advent of a new order of philosophers, such as will have other tastes and inclinations, the reverse of those hitherto prevalent—philosophers of the dangerous "Perhaps" in every sense of the term. And to speak in all seriousness, I see such new philosophers beginning to appear.

3.

Having kept a sharp eye on philosophers, and having read between their lines long enough, I now say to myself that the greater part of conscious thinking must be counted amongst the instinctive functions, and it is so even in the case of philosophical thinking; one has here to learn anew, as one learned anew about heredity and "innateness." As little as the act of birth comes into consideration in the whole process and procedure of heredity, just as little is "being-conscious" *opposed* to the instinctive in any decisive sense; the greater part of the conscious thinking of a philosopher is secretly influenced by his instincts, and forced into definite channels. And behind all logic and its seeming sovereignty of

movement, there are valuations, or to speak more plainly, physiological demands, for the maintenance of a definite mode of life. For example, that the certain is worth more than the uncertain, that illusion is less valuable than "truth": such valuations, in spite of their regulative importance for *us*, might notwithstanding be only superficial valuations, special kinds of *niaiserie*, such as may be necessary for the maintenance of beings such as ourselves. Supposing, in effect, that man is not just the "measure of things."

niaiserie : Silliness

*   *   *

13.

think → reflect

Psychologists should bethink themselves before putting down the instinct of self-preservation as the cardinal instinct of an organic being. A living thing seeks above all to *discharge* its strength—life itself is *Will to Power*; self-preservation is only one of the indirect and most frequent *results* thereof. In short, here, as everywhere else, let us beware of *superfluous* teleological principles!—one of which is the instinct of self-preservation (we owe it to Spinoza's inconsistency). It is thus, in effect, that method ordains, which must be essentially economy of principles.

14.

It is perhaps just dawning on five or six minds that natural philosophy is only a world-exposition and world-arrangement (according to us, if I may say so!) and *not* a world-explanation; but in so far as it is based on belief in the senses, it is regarded as more, and for a long time to come must be regarded as more—namely, as an explanation. It has eyes and fingers of its own, it has ocular evidence and palpableness of its own: this operates fascinatingly, persuasively, and *convincingly* upon an age with fundamentally plebeian tastes—in fact, it follows instinctively the canon of truth of eternal popular sensualism. What is clear, what is "explained"? Only that which can be seen and felt—one must pursue every problem thus far. Obversely, however, the charm of the Platonic mode of thought, which was an *aristocratic* mode, consisted precisely in *resistance to* obvious sense-evidence—perhaps among men who enjoyed even stronger and more fastidious senses than our contemporaries, but who knew how to find a higher triumph in remaining musters of them: and this by means of pale, cold, grey conceptional networks which they threw over the motley whirl of the senses—the mob of the senses, as Plato said. In this overcoming of the world, and interpreting of the world in the manner of Plato, there was an *enjoyment* different from that which the physicists of to-day offer us—and likewise the Darwinists and antiteleologists among the physiological workers, with their principle of the "smallest possible effort," and the greatest possible blunder. "Where there is nothing more to see or to grasp, there is also nothing more for men to do"—that is certainly an imperative different from the Platonic one, but it may notwithstanding be the right imperative for a hardy, laborious race of machinists and bridge-builders of the future, who have nothing but *rough* work to perform.

*   *   *

23.

All psychology hitherto has run aground on moral prejudices and timidities, it has not dared to launch out into the depths. In so far as it is allowable to recognise in that which has hitherto been written, evidence of that which has hitherto been kept silent, it seems as if nobody had yet harboured the notion of psychology as the Morphology and *Development-doctrine of the Will to Power,* as I conceive of it. The power of moral prejudices has penetrated deeply into the most intellectual world, the world apparently most indifferent and unprejudiced, and has obviously operated in an injurious, obstructive, blinding, and distorting manner. A proper physio-psychology has to contend with unconscious antagonism in the heart of the investigator, it has "the heart" against it: even a doctrine of the reciprocal conditionalness of the "good" and the "bad" impulses, causes (as refined immorality) distress and aversion in a still strong and manly conscience—still more so, a doctrine of the derivation of all good impulses from bad ones. If, however, a person should regard even the emotions of hatred, envy, covetousness, and imperiousness as life-conditioning emotions, as factors

which must be present, fundamentally and essentially, in the general economy of life (which must, therefore, be further developed if life is to be further developed), he will suffer from such a view of things as from sea-sickness. And yet this hypothesis is far from being the strangest and most painful in this immense and almost new domain of dangerous knowledge; and there are in fact a hundred good reasons why every one should keep away from it who *can* do so! On the other hand, if one has once drifted hither with one's bark, well! very good! now let us set our teeth firmly! let us open our eyes and keep our hand fast on the helm! We sail away right *over* morality, we crush out, we destroy perhaps the remains of our own morality by daring to make our voyage thither—but what do *we* matter! Never yet did a *profounder* world of insight reveal itself to daring travellers and adventurers, and the psychologist who thus "makes a sacrifice"—it is *not* the *sacrifizio dell' intelletto,* on the contrary!—will at least be entitled to demand in return that psychology shall once more be recognised as the queen of the sciences, for whose service and equipment the other sciences exist. For psychology is once more the path to the fundamental problems.

*   *   *

What is Noble?

257.

Every elevation of the type "man," has hitherto been the work of an aristocratic society—and so will it always be—a society believing in a long scale of gradations of rank and differences of worth among human beings, and requiring slavery in some form or other. Without the *pathos of distance,* such as grows out of the incarnated difference of classes, out of the constant outlooking and downlooking of the ruling caste on subordinates and instruments, and out of their equally constant practice of obeying and commanding, of keeping down and keeping at a distance—that other more mysterious pathos could never have arisen, the longing for an ever new widening of distance within the soul itself, the formation of ever higher, rarer, further, more extended, more comprehensive states, in short, just the elevation of the type "man," the continued "self-surmounting of man," to use a moral formula in a supermoral sense. To be sure, one must not resign oneself to any humanitarian illusions about the history of the origin of an aristocratic society (that is to say, of the preliminary condition for the elevation of the type "man"): the truth is hard. Let us acknowledge unprejudicedly how every higher civilisation hitherto has *originated!* Men with a still natural nature, barbarians in every terrible sense of the word, men of prey, still in possession of unbroken strength of will and desire for power, threw themselves upon weaker, more moral, more peaceful races (perhaps trading or cattle-rearing communities), or upon old mellow civilisations in which the final vital force was flickering out in brilliant fireworks of wit and depravity. At the commencement, the noble caste was always the barbarian caste: their superiority did not consist first of all in their physical, but in their psychical power—they were more *complete* men (which at every point also implies the same as "more complete beasts").

258.

Corruption—as the indication that anarchy threatens to break out among the instincts, and that the foundation of the emotions, called "life," is convulsed—is something radically different according to the organisation in which it manifests itself. When, for instance, an aristocracy like that of France at the beginning of the Revolution, flung away its privileges with sublime disgust and sacrificed itself to an excess of its moral sentiments, it was corruption:—it was really only the closing act of the corruption which had existed for centuries, by virtue of which that aristocracy had abdicated step by step its lordly prerogatives and lowered itself to a *function* of royalty (in the end even to its decoration and parade-dress). The essential thing, however, in a good and healthy aristocracy is that it should *not* regard itself as a function either of the kingship or the commonwealth, but as the *significance* and highest justification thereof—that it should therefore accept with a good conscience the sacrifice of a legion of individuals, who, *for its sake,* must be suppressed and reduced to imperfect men, to slaves and instruments. Its fundamental belief must be precisely that society is *not* allowed to exist

for its own sake, but only as a foundation and scaffolding, by means of which a select class of beings may be able to elevate themselves to their higher duties, and in general to a higher *existence:* like those sun-seeking climbing plants in Java—they are called *Sipo Matador,*—which encircle an oak so long and so often with their arms, until at last, high above it, but supported by it, they can unfold their tops in the open light, and exhibit their happiness.

259.

To refrain mutually from injury, from violence, from exploitation, and put one's will on a par with that of others: this may result in a certain rough sense in good conduct among individuals when the necessary conditions are given (namely, the actual similarity of the individuals in amount of force and degree of worth, and their co-relation within one organisation). As soon, however, as one wished to take this principle more generally, and if possible even as *the fundamental principle of society,* it would immediately disclose what it really is—namely, a Will to the *denial* of life, a principle of dissolution and decay. Here one must think profoundly to the very basis and resist all sentimental weakness: life itself is *essentially* appropriation, injury, conquest of the strange and weak, suppression, severity, obtrusion of peculiar forms, incorporation, and at the least, putting it mildest, exploitation;—but why should one for ever use precisely these words on which for ages a disparaging purpose has been stamped? Even the organisation within which, as was previously supposed, the individuals treat each other as equal—it takes place in every healthy aristocracy—must itself, if it be a living and not a dying organisation, do all that towards other bodies, which the individuals within it refrain from doing to each other: it will have to be the incarnated Will to Power, it will endeavour to grow, to gain ground, attract to itself and acquire ascendency—not owing to any morality or immorality, but because it *lives,* and because life *is* precisely Will to Power. On no point, however, is the ordinary consciousness of Europeans more unwilling to be corrected than on this matter; people now rave everywhere, even under the guise of science, about coming conditions of society in which "the exploiting character" is to be absent:—that sounds to my ears as if they promised to invent a mode of life which should refrain from all organic functions. "Exploitation" does not belong to a depraved, or imperfect and primitive society: it belongs to the *nature* of the living being as a primary organic function; it is a consequence of the intrinsic Will to Power, which is precisely the Will to Life.—Granting that as a theory this is a novelty—as a reality it is the *fundamental fact* of all history: let us be so far honest towards ourselves!

260.

In a tour through the many finer and coarser moralities which have hitherto prevailed or still prevail on the earth, I found certain traits recurring regularly together and connected with one another, until finally two primary types revealed themselves to me, and a radical distinction was brought to light. There is *master-morality* and *slave-morality;*—I would at once add, however, that in all higher and mixed civilisations, there are also attempts at the reconciliation of the two moralities; but one finds still oftener the confusion and mutual misunderstanding of them, indeed, sometimes their close juxtaposition—even in the same man, within one soul. The distinctions of moral values have either originated in a ruling caste, pleasantly conscious of being different from the ruled—or among the ruled class, the slaves and dependents of all sorts. In the first case, when it is the rulers who determine the conception "good," it is the exalted, proud disposition which is regarded as the distinguishing feature, and that which determines the order of rank. The noble type of man separates from himself the beings in whom the opposite of this exalted, proud disposition displays itself: he despises them. Let it at once be noted that in this first kind of morality the antithesis "good" and "bad" means practically the same as "noble" and "despicable";—the antithesis "good" and "*evil*" is of a different origin. The cowardly, the timid, the insignificant, and those thinking merely of narrow utility are despised; moreover, also, the distrustful, with their constrained glances, the self-abasing, the dog-like kind of men who let themselves be abused, the mendicant flatterers, and above all the liars:—it is a fundamental belief of all aristocrats that the common people are untruthful. "We truthful ones"—the

nobility in ancient Greece called themselves. It is obvious that everywhere the designations of moral value were at first applied to *men,* and were only derivatively and at a later period applied to *actions;* it is a gross mistake, therefore, when historians of morals start with questions like, "Why have sympathetic actions been praised?" The noble type of man regards *himself* as a determiner of values; he does not require to be approved of; he passes the judgment: "What is injurious to me is injurious in itself"; he knows that it is he himself only who confers honour on things; he is a *creator of values.* He honours whatever he recognises in himself: such morality is self-glorification. In the foreground there is the feeling of plenitude, of power, which seeks to overflow, the happiness of high tension, the consciousness of a wealth which would fain give and bestow:—the noble man also helps the unfortunate, but not—or scarcely—out of pity, but rather from an impulse generated by the superabundance of power. The noble man honours in himself the powerful one, him also who has power over himself, who knows how to speak and how to keep silence, who takes pleasure in subjecting himself to severity and hardness, and has reverence for all that is severe and hard. "Wotan placed a hard heart in my breast," says an old Scandinavian Saga: it is thus rightly expressed from the soul of a proud Viking. Such a type of man is even proud of *not* being made for sympathy; the hero of the Saga therefore adds warningly: "He who has not a hard heart when young, will never have one." The noble and brave who think thus are the furthest removed from the morality which sees precisely in sympathy, or in acting for the good of others, or in *désintéressement,* the characteristic of the moral; faith in oneself, pride in oneself, a radical enmity and irony towards "selflessness," belong as definitely to noble morality, as do a careless scorn and precaution in presence of sympathy and the "warm heart."—It is the powerful who *know* how to honour, it is their art, their domain for invention. The profound reverence for age and for tradition—all law rests on this double reverence,—the belief and prejudice in favour of ancestors and unfavourable to newcomers, is typical in the morality of the powerful; and if, reversely, men of "modern ideas" believe almost instinctively in "progress" and the "future," and are more and more lacking in respect for old age, the ignoble origin of these "ideas" has complacently betrayed itself thereby. A morality of the ruling class, however, is more especially foreign and irritating to present-day taste in the sternness of its principle that one has duties only to one's equals; that one may act towards beings of a lower rank, towards all that is foreign, just as seems good to one, or "as the heart desires," and in any case "beyond good and evil": it is here that sympathy and similar sentiments can have a place. The ability and obligation to exercise prolonged gratitude and prolonged revenge—both only within the circle of equals,—artfulness in retaliation, *raffinement* of the idea in friendship, a certain necessity to have enemies (as outlets for the emotions of envy, quarrelsomeness, arrogance—in fact, in order to be a good *friend*): all these are typical characteristics of the noble morality, which, as has been pointed out, is not the morality of "modern ideas," and is therefore at present difficult to realise, and also to unearth and disclose.—It is otherwise with the second type of morality, *slave-morality*. Supposing that the abused, the oppressed, the suffering, the unemancipated, the weary, and those uncertain of themselves, should moralise, what will be the common element in their moral estimates? Probably a pessimistic suspicion with regard to the entire situation of man will find expression, perhaps a condemnation of man, together with his situation. The slave has an unfavourable eye for the virtues of the powerful; he has a scepticism and distrust, a *refinement* of distrust of everything "good" that is there honoured—he would fain persuade himself that the very happiness there is not genuine. On the other hand, *those* qualities which serve to alleviate the existence of sufferers are brought into prominence and flooded with light; it is here that sympathy, the kind, helping hand, the warm heart, patience, diligence, humility, and friendliness attain to honour; for here these are the most useful qualities, and almost the only means of supporting the burden of existence. Slave-morality is essentially the morality of utility. Here is the seat of the origin of the famous antithesis "good" and "*evil*":—power and dangerousness are assumed to reside in the evil, a certain dreadfulness, subtlety, and strength, which do not admit of being despised. According to slave-morality, therefore, the "evil" man arouses fear; according to master-morality, it is precisely the "good" man who arouses fear and seeks to arouse it, while the bad man is regarded as the despicable being. The contrast attains its maximum when, in accordance with the logical consequences of slave-morality, a shade of depreciation—it may be slight and well-intentioned—at last attaches itself even to the "good" man of this morality; because, according to the servile mode of thought, the good man must in any case be the *safe* man: he is good-natured, easily deceived, perhaps a little stupid, *un bonhomme*. Everywhere that slave-morality gains the ascendency, language shows a tendency to approximate the significations of the words "good" and "stupid."—A last fundamental difference: the desire for *freedom*, the instinct for happiness and the refinements of the feeling of liberty belong as necessarily to slave-morals and morality, as artifice and enthusiasm in reverence and devotion are the regular symptoms of an aristocratic mode of thinking and estimating.—Hence we can understand without further detail why love *as a passion*—it is our European speciality—must absolutely be of noble origin; as is well known, its invention is due to the Provençal poet-cavaliers, those brilliant ingenious men of the "*gai saber*," to whom Europe owes so much, and almost owes itself.

*   *   *

262.

A *species* originates, and a type becomes established and strong in the long struggle with essentially constant *unfavourable* conditions. On the other hand, it is known by the experience of breeders that species which receive superabundant nourishment, and in general a surplus of protection and care, immediately tend in the most marked way to develop variations, and are fertile in prodigies and monstrosities (also in monstrous vices). Now look at an aristocratic commonwealth, say an ancient Greek *polis*, or Venice, as a voluntary or involuntary contrivance for the purpose of *rearing* human beings; there are there men beside one another, thrown upon their

own resources, who want to make their species prevail, chiefly because they *must* prevail, or else run
the terrible danger of being exterminated. The
favour, the superabundance, the protection are there
lacking under which variations are fostered; the
species needs itself as species, as something which,
precisely by virtue of its hardness, its uniformity,
and simplicity of structure, can in general prevail
and make itself permanent in constant struggle with
its neighbours, or with rebellious or rebellion-
threatening vassals. The most varied experience
teaches it what are the qualities to which it principally owes the fact that it still exists, in spite of all
Gods and men, and has hitherto been victorious:
these qualities it calls virtues, and these virtues
alone it develops to maturity. It does so with severity, indeed it desires severity; every aristocratic
morality is intolerant in the education of youth, in
the control of women, in the marriage customs, in
the relations of old and young, in the penal laws
(which have an eye only for the degenerating): it
counts intolerance itself among the virtues, under
the name of "justice." A type with few, but very
marked features, a species of severe, warlike, wisely
silent, reserved and reticent men (and as such, with
the most delicate sensibility for the charm and
nuances of society) is thus established, unaffected by
the vicissitudes of generations; the constant struggle
with uniform *unfavourable* conditions is, as already
remarked, the cause of a type becoming stable and
hard. Finally, however, a happy state of things
results, the enormous tension is relaxed; there are
perhaps no more enemies among the neighbouring
peoples, and the means of life, even of the enjoyment of life, are present in superabundance. With
one stroke the bond and constraint of the old discipline severs: it is no longer regarded as necessary, as
a condition of existence—if it would continue, it
can only do so as a form of *luxury,* as an archaïsing
taste. Variations, whether they be deviations (into
the higher, finer, and rarer), or deteriorations and
monstrosities, appear suddenly on the scene in the
greatest exuberance and splendour; the individual
dares to be individual and detach himself. At this
turning-point of history there manifest themselves,
side by side, and often mixed and entangled
together, a magnificent, manifold, virgin-forest-like
up-growth and up-striving, a kind of *tropical tempo*
in the rivalry of growth, and an extraordinary decay
and self-destruction, owing to the savagely opposing and seemingly exploding egoisms, which strive
with one another "for sun and light," and can no
longer assign any limit, restraint, or forbearance for
themselves by means of the hitherto existing morality. It was this morality itself which piled up the
strength so enormously, which bent the bow in so
threatening a manner:—it is now "out of date," it
is getting "out of date." The dangerous and disqui-
eting point has been reached when the greater, more
manifold, more comprehensive life *is lived beyond*
the old morality; the "individual" stands out, and
is obliged to have recourse to his own law-giving,
his own arts and artifices for self-preservation, self-
elevation, and self-deliverance. Nothing but new
"Whys," nothing but new "Hows," no common
formulas any longer, misunderstanding and disregard in league with each other, decay, deterioration,
and the loftiest desires frightfully entangled, the
genius of the race overflowing from all the cornu-
copias of good and bad, a portentous simultaneous-
ness of Spring and Autumn, full of new charms and
mysteries peculiar to the fresh, still inexhausted, still
unwearied corruption. Danger is again present, the
mother of morality, great danger; this time shifted
into the individual, into the neighbour and friend,
into the street, into their own child, into their own
heart, into all the most personal and secret recesses
of their desires and volitions. What will the moral
philosophers who appear at this time have to
preach? They discover, these sharp onlookers and
loafers, that the end is quickly approaching, that
everything around them decays and produces decay,
that nothing will endure until the day after tomorrow, except one species of man, the incurably
mediocre. The mediocre alone have a prospect of
continuing and propagating themselves—they will
be the men of the future, the sole survivors; "be like
them! become mediocre!" is now the only morality
which has still a significance, which still obtains a
hearing.—But it is difficult to preach this morality
of mediocrity! it can never avow what it is and what
it desires! it has to talk of moderation and dignity
and duty and brotherly love—it will have difficulty
in concealing its irony!

*　*　*

287.

—What is noble? What does the word "noble" still mean for us nowadays? How does the noble man betray himself, how is he recognised under this heavy overcast sky of the commencing plebeianism, by which everything is rendered opaque and leaden?—It is not his actions which establish his claim—actions are always ambiguous, always inscrutable; neither is it his "works." One finds nowadays among artists and scholars plenty of those who betray by their works that a profound longing for nobleness impels them; but this very *need of* nobleness is radically different from the needs of the noble soul itself, and is in fact the eloquent and dangerous sign of the lack thereof. It is not the works, but the *belief* which is here decisive and determines the order of rank—to employ once more an old religious formula with a new and deeper meaning,—it is some fundamental certainty which a noble soul has about itself, something which is not to be sought, is not to be found, and perhaps, also, is not to be lost.—*The noble soul has reverence for itself.*—

Good point

PART NINE

PUCK.

"THE REAL TROUBLE WILL COME WITH THE "WAKE""

Cartoon of Western Designs on China
This satirical cartoon with its symbolic representations of various industrialized nations competing to feed on the corpse of China seems to provide support for Lenin's cynical vision of capitalism and imperialism. Before turning to China, these same nations had divided up much of the rest of the world.

European Imperialism

In the 1880s, the centuries-old colonial question took on a new meaning. Europe (joined by Japan and the United States) entered a period of renewed imperialism, during which European and other powers carved up Africa, much of Asia, and the Pacific islands. In the decades before World War I, Europeans alone seized ten million square miles and subjugated half a billion people. Unlike the earlier forms of colonialism, the new imperialism had behind it popular support—the power of nationalism. The scramble for Africa turned into an inter-European competition that almost led to war. In 1885 the Berlin Conference established rules for the continued dismemberment of Africa, although tensions about global empires persisted.

To justify building new empires, most European states drew on the newly influential Social-Darwinist mentality developed by Herbert Spencer, which assumed the "superiority" of technologically advanced nations. The French talked about their "civilizing" mission, the Germans of spreading "culture," and the British of "the white man's burden." It was, however, King Leopold of the Belgians (1832–1905) who set off the new round of empire building when he seized the Congo in the early 1880s. Leopold masked purely commercial interests by proclaiming his intention to bring the benefits of modern European civilization to the so-called "Congo Free State." The stark reality of Leopold's rule in the Congo, characterized by historians as a virtual holocaust, raised a huge scandal. One informed observer with anti-imperialist views, Edmund Morel (1873–1924), wrote a book, *King Leopold's Rule in Africa* (1904), about the depopulation, slaughter, and disease that had accompanied the Congo's occupation, already confirmed by Leopold's own 1903 Investigative Commission. Unfortunately, scandals did nothing to end colonialism in the Congo or elsewhere. The poem "The White Man's Burden," written by Rudyard Kipling (1865–1936) in 1899, suggests the views of many Europeans about their empires. The new imperialism persisted for more than half the following century, deeply marking the post–1900 history of Europe and the rest of the globe. The story "Shooting an Elephant" (1936) by George Orwell (1903–1950) depicts the relationship between imperialists and a subject community, in this case Burma between 1922 and 1927. In his *Imperialism: the Highest Stage of World Capitalism* (1916), Vladimir Lenin (1870–1924) portrayed the phenomenon as the last desperate attempt of over-industrialized capitalist nations to avoid collapse.

Study Questions

1. What distinguishes the new imperialism after 1880 from past colonialism?
2. How did stated intentions of the new imperialists differ from reality?
3. Why didn't the findings of the 1903 Investigative Commission bring about serious reform?
4. How do Kipling's and Orwell's views about the imperial experience differ?
5. According to Lenin, how does imperialism extend the life of capitalism?
6. Image: What does this satirical cartoon about Western intentions toward China, a place that never fully succumbed to colonialism, tell us about the era's imperialism?

King Leopold's Rule in Africa
Edmund Morel

A British journalist in the Congo, Morel detailed the shocking abuses of Africans in his 1904 book, which continued the exposé he had begun in 1903 in The Black Man's Burden. *The horrendous facts, based upon his own observations and interviews with officials of the Belgian imperial bureaucracy and companies, caused a wave of horror throughout the world. Already in 1897, when Morel had seen ships from the Congo unloading ivory and other valuable products in the Port of Antwerp, he realized that slave labor was involved, since the only goods being loaded back on to the ships were guns and bullets.*

[E]verywhere [in the Congo] we see the same policy [of forced labor] at work, with the same results. What are the chief symptoms of the effects of that policy upon native life?

Outwardly the most striking effect is depopulation: slaughter, mutilation; emigration; sickness, largely aggravated by cruel and systematic oppression; poverty, and even positive starvation, induced by unlimited taxation in food-stuffs and live stock; a hopeless despair, and mental depression engendered by years of grinding tyranny; neglect of children by the general maltreatment of women, one of the most odious and disgraceful features of the system—these are some of the many recorded causes of depopulation which, in certain districts, has assumed gigantic proportions. . . .

What a sum total of human wretchedness does not lie behind that bald word "depopulation"! To my mind, the horror of this curse which has come upon the Congo peoples reaches its maximum of intensity when we force ourselves to consider its everyday concomitants; the crushing weight of perpetual, remorseless oppression; the gradual elimination of everything in the daily life of the natives which makes that life worth living. Under the prevailing system, every village is a penal settlement.

Armed soldiers are quartered in every hamlet; the men pass nearly the whole of their lives in satisfying the ceaseless demands of the "Administration," or its affiliates the Trusts. . . .

The cumulative effects of depopulation and infantile mortality by dragging women away from their homes for forced labour requisitions—seizing them as "hostages," and "tying them up," whether virgins, wives, mothers, or those about to become mothers, in order to bring pressure to bear upon brothers, husbands, and fathers for the adequate supply of rubber or food taxes; flinging them into "prison," together with their children, often to die of starvation and neglect; flogging them, sometimes even unto death; leaving them at the mercy of the soldiers; distributing them after punitive raids among hangers-on—must be enormous. There we have depopulation through the infamous torture of women—often enough shot outright or mutilated—and the neglect and the mutilation of young children and boys; most of whom, it may be presumed, when so mutilated do not survive the operation, in order to have "the bad taste to show their stumps to the missionaries,"* as one of the Belgian deputies said in the course of the Congo debate in the Belgian House last year.

What has come over the civilised people of the globe that they can allow their Governments to

From: Edmund Morel, *King Leopold's Rule in Africa* (1904)(reprinted Westport, Conn.: Negro University Press, 1970), pp. 236, 242, 247–249, 255–256.

*Amputation of a hand was a common form of punishment in the Belgian Congo.

remain inactive and apathetic in the face of incidents which recall in aggravated form the worst horrors of the over-sea slave trade, which surpass the exploits of Arab slave catchers? What could be worse than scenes such as these, which can be culled by the dozen. . . .

The Congo Government boasts that, in stopping intertribal warfare, it has stopped the selling of tribal prisoners of war into domestic slavery. The condition of the domestic slave under the African system is blissful beyond words, if you compare his lot with that of the degraded serf under the Leopoldian system. . . .

Enough has been said to show that under this system of "moral and material regeneration," constituting a monstrous invasion of primitive rights which has no parallel in the whole world, the family life and social ties of the people are utterly destroyed. . . .

If Gladstone* had been alive he would perhaps have found a phrase adequate to describe the revival of the slave trade under the aegis of a European Sovereign in Equatorial Africa, and the forms which that revival takes. But I doubt if even he could have found one more fittingly characterising it than that he so truly applied to other quarters. The "Negation of God" erected with a system—yes, indeed!

Why are these people allowed to suffer thus cruelly? What crime have they collectively committed in past ages that they should undergo to-day so terrible an expiation? Are they "groaning and dying" under this murderous system as a great object-lesson to Europe? What price, then, will

*William Gladstone (1809–1898), four-time British prime minister, who spoke eloquently against Turkish atrocities in the Balkans in the 1870s and in Armenia in the 1890s.

Europe later on have to pay for the teaching? Inscrutable are the decrees of Providence. One wonders whether the deepening horror of this colossal crime will end by a reaction so violent that an era of justice will, for the first time in the history of Caucasian relationship with the Dark Continent, arise, never to be eradicated, for the peoples of Africa. Or that some day tropical Africa may breed brains as she breeds muscles, and then . . . ? But it bodes little to dwell among the mists of conjecture. The future is closed to us. We grope in the dark, puzzled, incensed, impatient. The future is with God. To the past man may look and gather consolation in the knowledge that evils such as these bring their own Nemesis upon the nation whose moral guilt is primarily involved. Belgium, technically unconcerned, is morally responsible, and Belgium will suffer. . . .

If the policy of the Congo State were a rational policy, if the Congo tribes were being systematically bled to death either through distorted zeal . . . or through lust of conquest; if the Congo Basin were capable of being colonised by the Caucasian race, the policy we condemn and reprobate would still be a crime against humanity, an outrage upon civilisation. But the Congo territories can never be a white man's country; the "Congo State" is naught but a collection of individuals—with one supreme above them all—working for their own selfish ends, caring nothing for posterity, callous of the present, indifferent of the future, as of the past, animated by no fanaticism other than the fanaticism of dividends—and so upon the wickedness of this thing is grafted the fatuous stupidity and inhumanity of the Powers in allowing the extermination of the Congo races to go on unchecked, barely, if at all, reproved.

— READING 40 —
King Leopold's Investigative Commission

The Belgian Investigative Commission, which issued its report in 1903 after rumors began to spread about what the Belgians were inflicting on the inhabitants of the Congo, fully supported the picture given by Edmund Morel in his 1903 and 1904 studies. Among the results of the Belgian occupation of what was mis-named the Congo Free State was a drastic collapse in population.

"The State has absolute and exclusive ownership of the whole territory. . . . The economic condition of the natives is stagnant. . . . Often the natives are for-bidden to change their place of residence, or are merely granted permission to visit a neighbouring locality for a short time; a breach of these regula-tions exposes them to arrest or punishment; the demands of the agents are often excessive, for they have a personal interest in the yield of rubber. . . . In the majority of cases a native must march one or two days before he can reach the part of the forest where a fair number of rubber vines can be tapped; there he spends a few extremely disagreeable days, without food, without his wife, exposed to the severities of the weather and to the attacks of wild beasts. . . . He can hardly stay in his own village for as long as two or three days, . . . a monstrous

From: Ludwig Bauer, *Leopold the Unloved. King of the Belgians and of Money* (London: Cassell & Co., 1934), p. 292.

infringement of the regulation of forty hours' work per month. . . . The taking of hostages, imprison-ment of the chiefs, billeting of soldiers, punish-ments, military expeditions. It can hardly be denied that in all the settlements of the Abir the imprison-ment of women as hostages, the forcing of the chiefs to do degrading work, the flogging of the rubber collectors, brutality on the part of the black offi-cials, have been the general rule. . . . The complaints of murders by the black soldiers have been justified by various evidence and by official reports. . . . Impossible to say in how many instances. . . . Sinister character of the system. . . . 142 black sol-diers killed, desire for revenge. . . . The agents have never attempted to deny the charges made against their black soldiers. . . . In official reports concern-ing punitive expeditions we find the following expressions: 'Energetic measures. Numerous killed and wounded enemies. . . . Loot. . . . Villages taken by surprise. . . . Great abuses. . . . Men, women, and children shot while trying to escape.'"

The White Man's Burden (1899)

Rudyard Kipling

Although Kipling's famous poem reads like a satire today, Kipling seems to have been quite serious. He understood, of course, the hardship imposed on the inhabitants of the new colonies but also felt that Western nations had the responsibility to bring allegedly uncivilized peoples into the modern world. This poem was written in 1899 to urge the United States to go into the Philippines, which had revolted against Spanish rule.

[handwritten: somewhat understand but why?]

(THE UNITED STATES AND THE PHILIPPINE ISLANDS)

[handwritten margin note: out of control]

Take up the White Man's burden—
  Send forth the best ye breed—
Go bind your sons to exile
  To serve your captives' need;
To wait in heavy harness
  On fluttered folk and wild—
Your new-caught, sullen peoples, [handwritten: down in the dumps]
  Half devil and half child.

Take up the White Man's burden—
  In patience to abide, [handwritten: stamp fear but not too]
To veil the threat of terror [handwritten: proudly]
[handwritten: Love] And check the show of pride;
By open speech and simple,
  An hundred times made plain,
To seek another's profit,
  And work another's gain.

Take up the White Man's burden—
  The savage wars of peace—
Fill full the mouth of Famine
  And bid the sickness cease;

And when your goal is nearest
  The end for others sought,
Watch Sloth and heathen Folly
  Bring all your hope to nought.

Take up the White Man's burden—
  No tawdry rule of kings,
But toil of serf and sweeper—
  The tale of common things.
The ports ye shall not enter,
  The roads ye shall not tread,
Go make them with your living,
  And mark them with your dead!

Take up the White Man's burden—
  And reap his old reward:
The blame of those ye better,
  The hate of those ye guard—
The cry of hosts ye humour
  (Ah, slowly!) toward the light:—
'Why brought ye us from bondage,
  'Our loved Egyptian night?'

From: T. S. Eliot, *A Choice of Kipling's Verse* (New York: Charles Scribner's Sons, 1943), pp. 136–137.

Take up the White Man's burden—
  Ye dare not stoop to less—
Nor call too loud on Freedom
  To cloak your weariness;
By all ye cry or whisper,
  By all ye leave or do,
The silent, sullen peoples
  Shall weigh your Gods and you.

Take up the White Man's burden—
  Have done with childish days—
The lightly proffered laurel,
  The easy, ungrudged praise.
Comes now, to search your manhood
  Through all the thankless years,
Cold-edged with dear-bought wisdom,
  The judgment of your peers!

Imperialism: The Highest Stage of World Capitalism

V. I. Lenin

With his usual radicalism, Lenin brushed aside all the reasons imperial powers had given for empire-building. Instead, he suggested that the capitalist nations had developed their economies as far as they could go on their own. Competition among the industrialized nations threatened to unleash warfare and economic collapse, as predicted by Karl Marx. The great powers, suggested Lenin, had attempted to ward off the inevitable by seizing resources in Africa, Asia, and the Pacific. The world war reflected this last struggle of capitalist states to survive by dominating the world's resources.

Preface to the Russian Edition

The pamphlet here presented to the reader was written in Zürich in the spring of 1916. In the conditions in which I was obliged to work there I naturally suffered somewhat from a shortage of French and English literature and from a serious dearth of Russian literature. However, I made use of the principal English work, *Imperialism*, J. A. Hobson's book, with all the care that, in my opinion, that work deserves.

This pamphlet was written with an eye to the tsarist censorship. Hence, I was not only forced to confine myself strictly to an exclusively theoretical, mainly economic analysis of facts, but to formulate the few necessary observations on politics with extreme caution, by hints, in that Æsopian language—in that cursed Æsopian language—to which tsarism compelled all revolutionaries to have recourse whenever they took up their pens to write a "legal" work.

It is very painful, in these days of liberty, to read these cramped passages of the pamphlet, crushed, as they seem, in an iron vise, distorted on account of the censor. Of how imperialism is the eve of the socialist revolution; of how social-chauvinism (socialism in words, chauvinism in deeds) is the

From: V. I. Lenin, *Imperialism: The Highest Stage of World Capitalism* (New York: International Publishers, 1939), pp. 7–8, 15, 123–128.

utter betrayal of socialism, complete desertion to the side of the bourgeoisie; of how the split in the labour movement is bound up with the objective conditions of imperialism, etc., I had to speak in a "slavish" tongue. . . . In order to show, in a guise acceptable to the censors, how shamefully the capitalists and the social-chauvinist deserters (whom Kautsky opposes with so much inconsistency) lie on the question of annexations; in order to show with what cynicism they *screen* the annexations of *their* capitalists, I was forced to quote as an example—Japan! The careful reader will easily substitute Russia for Japan, and Finland, Poland, Courland, the Ukraine, Khiva, Bokhara, Estonia or other regions peopled by non-Great Russians, for Korea.

I trust that this pamphlet will help the reader to understand the fundamental economic question, *viz.*, the question of the economic essence of imperialism, for unless this is studied, it will be impossible to understand and appraise modern war and modern politics.

*　　*　　*

Imperialism, the Highest Stage of Capitalism

During the last fifteen or twenty years, especially since the Spanish-American War (1898), and the Anglo-Boer War (1899–1902), the economic and also the political literature of the two hemispheres has more and more often adopted the term "imperialism" in order to define the present era. In 1902, a book by the English economist, J. A. Hobson, *Imperialism,* was published in London and New York. This author, who adopts the point of view of bourgeois social reformism and pacifism which, in essence, is identical with the present point of view of the ex-Marxist, K. Kautsky, gives an excellent and comprehensive description of the principal economic and political characteristics of imperialism. In 1910, there appeared in Vienna the work of the Austrian Marxist, Rudolf Hilferding, *Finance Capital.* In spite of the mistake the author commits on the theory of money, and in spite of a certain inclination on his part to reconcile Marxism with opportunism, this work gives a very valuable theoretical analysis, as its sub-title tells us, of "the latest phase of capitalist development." Indeed, what has been said of imperialism during the last few years, especially in a great many magazine and newspaper articles, and also in the resolutions, for example, of the Chemnitz and Basle Congresses which took place in the autumn of 1912, has scarcely gone beyond the ideas put forward, or, more exactly, summed up by the two writers mentioned above.

Later on we shall try to show briefly, and as simply as possible, the connection and relationships between the *principal* economic features of imperialism. We shall not be able to deal with non-economic aspects of the question, however much they deserve to be dealt with. . . .

*   *   *

The Place of Imperialism in History

We have seen that the economic quintessence of imperialism is monopoly capitalism. This very fact determines its place in history, for monopoly that grew up on the basis of free competition, and precisely out of free competition, is the transition from the capitalist system to a higher social-economic order. We must take special note of the four principal forms of monopoly, or the four principal manifestations of monopoly capitalism, which are characteristic of the epoch under review.

Firstly, monopoly arose out of the concentration of production at a very advanced stage of development. This refers to the monopolist capitalist combines, cartels, syndicates and trusts. We have seen the important part that these play in modern economic life. At the beginning of the twentieth century, monopolies acquired complete supremacy in the advanced countries. And although the first steps towards the formation of the cartels were first taken by countries enjoying the protection of high tariffs (Germany, America), Great Britain, with her system of free trade, was not far behind in revealing the same basic phenomenon, namely, the birth of monopoly out of the concentration of production.

Secondly, monopolies have accelerated the capture of the most important sources of raw materials, especially for the coal and iron industries, which are the basic and most highly cartelised industries in capitalist society. The monopoly of the most important sources of raw materials has enormously increased the power of big capital, and has sharpened the antagonism between cartelised and noncartelised industry.

Thirdly, monopoly has sprung from the banks. The banks have developed from modest intermediary enterprises into the monopolists of finance capital. Some three or five of the biggest banks in each of the foremost capitalist countries have achieved the "personal union" of industrial and bank capital, and have concentrated in their hands the disposal of thousands upon thousands of millions which form the greater part of the capital and income of entire countries. A financial oligarchy, which throws a close net of relations of dependence over all the economic and political institutions of contemporary bourgeois society without exception—such is the most striking manifestation of this monopoly.

Fourthly, monopoly has grown out of colonial policy. To the numerous "old" motives of colonial policy, finance capital has added the struggle for the sources of raw materials, for the export of capital, for "spheres of influence," *i.e.,* for spheres for profitable deals, concessions, monopolist profits and so on; in fine, for economic territory in general. When the colonies of the European powers in Africa, for instance, comprised only one-tenth of that territory (as was the case in 1876), colonial policy was able to develop by methods other than those of monopoly—by the "free grabbing" of territories, so to speak. But when nine-tenths of Africa had been seized (approximately by 1900), when the whole world had been divided up, there was inevitably ushered in a period of colonial monopoly and, consequently, a period of particularly intense struggle for the division and the redivision of the world.

The extent to which monopolist capital has intensified all the contradictions of capitalism is generally known. It is sufficient to mention the high cost of living and the oppression of the cartels. This intensification of contradictions constitutes the most powerful driving force of the transitional period of history, which began from the time of the definite victory of world finance capital.

Monopolies, oligarchy, the striving for domination instead of the striving for liberty, the exploitation of an increasing number of small or weak nations by an extremely small group of the richest or most powerful nations—all these have given birth to those distinctive characteristics of imperialism which compel us to define it as parasitic or decaying capitalism. More and more prominently there emerges, as one of the tendencies of imperialism, the creation of the "bondholding" (rentier) state, the usurer state, in which the bourgeoisie lives on the proceeds of capital exports and by "clipping coupons." It would be a mistake to believe that this tendency to decay precludes the possibility of the rapid growth of capitalism. It does not. In the epoch of imperialism, certain branches of industry, certain strata of the bourgeoisie and certain countries betray, to a more or less degree, one or other of these tendencies. On the whole, capitalism is growing far more rapidly than before. But this growth is not only becoming more and more uneven in general; its unevenness also manifests itself, in particular, in the decay of the countries which are richest in capital (such as England).

In regard to the rapidity of Germany's economic development, Riesser, the author of the book on the big German banks, states.

"The progress of the preceding period (1848–70), which had not been exactly slow, stood in about the same ratio to the rapidity with which the whole of Germany's national economy, and with it German banking, progressed during this period (1870–1905) as the mail coach of the Holy Roman Empire of the German nation stood to the speed of the present-day automobile ... which in whizzing past, it must be said, often endangers not only innocent pedestrians in its path, but also the occupants of the car."

In its turn, this finance capital which has grown so rapidly is not unwilling (precisely because it has grown so quickly) to pass on to a more "tranquil" possession of colonies which have to be seized—and not only by peaceful methods—from richer nations. In the United States, economic development in the last decades has been even more rapid than in Germany, and *for this very reason* the parasitic character of modern American capitalism has stood out with particular prominence. On the other hand, a comparison of, say, the republican American bourgeoisie with the monarchist Japanese or German bourgeoisie shows that the most pronounced political distinctions diminish to an extreme degree in the epoch of imperialism—not because they are unimportant in general, but because in all these cases we are discussing a bourgeoisie which has definite features of parasitism.

The receipt of high monopoly profits by the capitalists in one of the numerous branches of industry, in one of numerous countries, etc., makes it economically possible for them to corrupt certain sections of the working class, and for a time a fairly considerable minority, and win them to the side of the bourgeoisie of a given industry or nation against all the others. The intensification of antagonisms between imperialist nations for the division of the world increases this striving. And so there is created that bond between imperialism and opportunism, which revealed itself first and most clearly in England, owing to the fact that certain features of imperialist development were observable there much earlier than in other countries.

Some writers, L. Martov, for example, try to evade the fact that there is a connection between imperialism and opportunism in the labour movement—which is particularly striking at the present time—by resorting to "official optimistic" arguments (*à la* Kautsky and Huysmans) like the following: the cause of the opponents of capitalism would be hopeless if it were precisely progressive capitalism that led to the increase of opportunism, or, if it were precisely the best paid workers who were inclined towards opportunism, etc. We must have no illusion regarding "optimism" of this kind. It is optimism in regard to opportunism; it is optimism which serves to conceal opportunism. As a matter of fact the extraordinary rapidity and the particularly revolting character of the development of opportunism is by no means a guarantee that its victory will be durable: the rapid growth of a malignant abscess on a healthy body only causes it to burst more quickly and thus to relieve the body of it. The most dangerous people of all in this respect are those who do not wish to understand that the fight against imperialism is a sham and humbug unless it is inseparably bound up with the fight against opportunism.

From all that has been said in this book on the economic nature of imperialism, it follows that we must define it as capitalism in transition, or, more precisely, as moribund capitalism. It is very instructive in this respect to note that the bourgeois economists, in describing modern capitalism, frequently employ terms like "interlocking," "absence of isolation," etc.; "in conformity with their functions and course of development," banks are "not purely private business enterprises; they are more and more outgrowing the sphere of purely private business regulation." And this very Riesser, who uttered the words just quoted, declares with all seriousness that the "prophecy" of the Marxists concerning "socialisation" has "not come true"!

What then does this word "interlocking" express? It merely expresses the most striking feature of the process going on before our eyes. It shows that the observer counts the separate trees, but cannot see the wood. It slavishly copies the superficial, the fortuitous, the chaotic. It reveals the observer as one who is overwhelmed by the mass of raw material and is utterly incapable of appreciating its meaning and importance. Ownership of shares and relations between owners of private property "interlock in a haphazard way." But the underlying factor of this interlocking, its very base, is the changing social relations of production. When a big enterprise assumes gigantic proportions, and, on the basis of exact computation of mass data, organises according to plan the supply of primary raw materials to the extent of two-thirds, or three-fourths of all that is necessary for tens of millions of people; when the raw materials are transported to the most suitable place of production, sometimes hundreds or thousands of miles away, in a systematic and organised manner; when a single centre directs all the successive stages of work right up to the manufacture of numerous varieties of finished articles; when these products are distributed according to a single plan among tens and hundreds of millions of consumers (as in the case of the distribution of oil in America and Germany by the American "oil trust")—then it becomes evident that we have socialisation of production, and not mere "interlocking"; that private economic relations and private property relations constitute a shell which is no longer suitable for its contents, a shell which must inevitably begin to decay if its destruction be delayed by artificial means; a shell which may continue in a state of decay for a fairly long period (particularly if the cure of the opportunist abscess is protracted), but which will inevitably be removed.

The enthusiastic admirer of German imperialism, Schulze-Gaevernitz, exclaims:

"Once the supreme management of the German banks has been entrusted to the hands of a dozen persons, their activity is even today more significant for the public good than that of the majority of the Ministers of State." (The "interlocking" of bankers, ministers, magnates of industry and rentiers is here conveniently forgotten.) . . . "If we conceive of the tendencies of development which we have noted as realised to the utmost: the money capital of the nation united in the banks; the banks themselves combined into cartels; the investment capital of the nation cast in the shape of securities, then the brilliant forecast of Saint-Simon will be fulfilled: 'The present anarchy of production caused by the fact that economic relations are developing without uniform regulation must make way for organisation in production. Production will no longer be shaped by isolated manufacturers, independent of each other and ignorant of man's economic needs, but by a social institution. A central body of management, being able to survey the large fields of social economy from a more elevated point of view, will regu-

late it for the benefit of the whole of society, will be able to put the means of production into suitable hands, and above all will take care that there be constant harmony between production and consumption. Institutions already exist which have assumed as part of their task a certain organisation of economic labour: the banks.' The fulfilment of the forecasts of Saint-Simon still lies in the future, *but we are on the way to its fulfilment—Marxism, different from what Marx imagined, but different only in form."*

A crushing "refutation" of Marx, indeed! It is a retreat from Marx's precise, scientific analysis to Saint-Simon's guesswork, the guesswork of a genius, but guesswork all the same.

Shooting an Elephant

George Orwell

Orwell's famous short story chronicles the awkward position young colonial administrators, such as himself in Burma, found themselves in as regards the native peoples. He did not know the customs but had to assert himself as part of the foreign ruling elite. This accounted for his decision to shoot the rampant elephant. Some among the European occupiers felt that an elephant was worth more than the Burmese villagers it might kill.

In Moulmein, in Lower Burma, I was hated by large numbers of people—the only time in my life that I have been important enough for this to happen to me. I was sub-divisional police officer of the town, and in an aimless, petty kind of way anti-European feeling was very bitter. No one had the guts to raise a riot, but if a European woman went through the bazaars alone somebody would probably spit betel juice over her dress. As a police officer I was an obvious target and was baited whenever it seemed safe to do so. When a nimble Burman tripped me up on the football field and the referee (another Burman) looked the other way, the crowd yelled with hideous laughter. This happened more than once. In the end the sneering yellow faces of young men that met me everywhere, the insults hooted after me when I was at a safe distance, got badly on my nerves. The young Buddhist priests were the worst of all. There were several thousands of them in the town and none of them seemed to have anything to do except stand on street corners and jeer at Europeans.

All this was perplexing and upsetting. For at that time I had already made up my mind that imperialism was an evil thing and the sooner I chucked up my job and got out of it the better. Theoretically—and secretly, of course—I was all for the Burmese

and all against their oppressors, the British. As for the job I was doing, I hated it more bitterly than I can perhaps make clear. In a job like that you see the dirty work of Empire at close quarters. The wretched prisoners huddling in the stinking cages of the lock-ups, the grey, cowed faces of the long-term convicts, the scarred buttocks of the men who had been flogged with bamboos—all these oppressed me with an intolerable sense of guilt. But I could get nothing into perspective. I was young and ill-educated and I had had to think out my problems in the utter silence that is imposed on every English-man in the East. I did not even know that the British Empire is dying, still less did I know that it is a great deal better than the younger empires that are going to supplant it. All I knew was that I was stuck between my hatred of the empire I served and my rage against the evil-spirited little beasts who tried to make my job impossible. With one part of my mind I thought of the British Raj as an unbreakable tyranny, as something clamped down, in *saecula saeculorum*, upon the will of prostrate peoples; with another part I thought that the greatest joy in the world would be to drive a bayonet into a Buddhist priest's guts. Feelings like these are the normal by-products of imperialism; ask any Anglo-Indian official, if you can catch him off duty.

One day something happened which in a round-about way was enlightening. It was a tiny incident in itself, but it gave me a better glimpse than I had had before of the real nature of imperialism—the

From: George Orwell, *A Collection of Essays* (New York: Doubleday Anchor Books, 1954), pp. 154–162.

real motives for which despotic governments act. Early one morning the sub-inspector at a police station the other end of the town rang me up on the 'phone and said that an elephant was ravaging the bazaar. Would I please come and do something about it? I did not know what I could do, but I wanted to see what was happening and I got on to a pony and started out. I took my rifle, an old .44 Winchester and much too small to kill an elephant, but I thought the noise might be useful *in terrorem*. Various Burmans stopped me on the way and told me about the elephant's doings. It was not, of course, a wild elephant, but a tame one which had gone "must." It had been chained up, as tame elephants always are when their attack of "must" is due, but on the previous night it had broken its chain and escaped. Its mahout, the only person who could manage it when it was in that state, had set out in pursuit, but had taken the wrong direction and was now twelve hours' journey away, and in the morning the elephant had suddenly reappeared in the town. The Burmese population had no weapons and were quite helpless against it. It had already destroyed somebody's bamboo hut, killed a cow and raided some fruit-stalls and devoured the stock; also it had met the municipal rubbish van and, when the driver jumped out and took to his heels, had turned the van over and inflicted violences upon it.

The Burmese sub-inspector and some Indian constables were waiting for me in the quarter where the elephant had been seen. It was a very poor quarter, a labyrinth of squalid bamboo huts, thatched with palm-leaf, winding all over a steep hillside. I remember that it was a cloudy, stuffy morning at the beginning of the rains. We began questioning the people as to where the elephant had gone and, as usual, failed to get any definite information. That is invariably the case in the East; a story always sounds clear enough at a distance, but the nearer you get to the scene of events the vaguer it becomes. Some of the people said that the elephant had gone in one direction, some said that he had gone in another, some professed not even to have heard of any elephant. I had almost made up my mind that the whole story was a pack of lies, when we heard yells a little distance away. There was a loud, scandalized cry of

"Go away, child! Go away this instant!" and an old woman with a switch in her hand came round the corner of a hut, violently shooing away a crowd of naked children. Some more women followed, clicking their tongues and exclaiming; evidently there was something that the children ought not to have seen. I rounded the hut and saw a man's dead body sprawling in the mud. He was an Indian, a black Dravidian coolie, almost naked, and he could not have been dead many minutes. The people said that the elephant had come suddenly upon him round the corner of the hut, caught him with its trunk, put its foot on his back and ground him into the earth. This was the rainy season and the ground was soft, and his face had scored a trench a foot deep and a couple of yards long. He was lying on his belly with arms crucified and head sharply twisted to one side. His face was coated with mud, the eyes wide open, the teeth bared and grinning with an expression of unendurable agony. (Never tell me, by the way, that the dead look peaceful. Most of the corpses I have seen looked devilish.) The friction of the great beast's foot had stripped the skin from his back as neatly as one skins a rabbit. As soon as I saw the dead man I sent an orderly to a friend's house nearby to borrow an elephant rifle. I had already sent back the pony, not wanting it to go mad with fright and throw me if it smelt the elephant.

The orderly came back in a few minutes with a rifle and five cartridges, and meanwhile some Burmans had arrived and told us that the elephant was in the paddy fields below, only a few hundred yards away. As I started forward practically the whole population of the quarter flocked out of the houses and followed me. They had seen the rifle and were all shouting excitedly that I was going to shoot the elephant. They had not shown much interest in the elephant when he was merely ravaging their homes, but it was different now that he was going to be shot. It was a bit of fun to them, as it would be to an English crowd; besides they wanted the meat. It made me vaguely uneasy. I had no intention of shooting the elephant—I had merely sent for the rifle to defend myself if necessary—and it is always unnerving to have a crowd following you. I marched down the hill, looking and feeling a fool, with the rifle over my shoulder and an ever-growing army of people jostling at my heels. At the bottom, when you got away from the huts, there was a metalled road and beyond that a miry waste of paddy fields a thousand yards across, not yet ploughed but soggy from the first rains and dotted with coarse grass. The elephant was standing eight yards from the road, his left side towards us. He took not the slightest notice of the crowd's approach. He was tearing up bunches of grass, beating them against his knees to clean them and stuffing them into his mouth.

I had halted on the road. As soon as I saw the elephant I knew with perfect certainty that I ought not to shoot him. It is a serious matter to shoot a working elephant—it is comparable to destroying a huge and costly piece of machinery—and obviously one ought not to do it if it can possibly be avoided. And at that distance, peacefully eating, the elephant looked no more dangerous than a cow. I thought then and I think now that his attack of "must" was already passing off; in which case he would merely wander harmlessly about until the mahout came back and caught him. Moreover, I did not in the least want to shoot him. I decided that I would watch him for a little while to make sure that he did not turn savage again, and then go home.

But at that moment I glanced round at the crowd that had followed me. It was an immense crowd, two thousand at the least and growing every minute. It blocked the road for a long distance on either side. I looked at the sea of yellow faces above the garish clothes—faces all happy and excited over this bit of fun, all certain that the elephant was going to be shot. They were watching me as they would watch a conjurer about to perform a trick. They did not like me, but with the magical rifle in my hands I was momentarily worth watching. And suddenly I realized that I should have to shoot the elephant after all. The people expected it of me and I had got to do it; I could feel their two thousand wills pressing me forward, irresistibly. And it was at this moment, as I stood there with the rifle in my hands, that I first grasped the hollowness, the futility of the white man's dominion in the East. Here was I, the white man with his gun, standing in front of the unarmed native crowd—seemingly the leading actor of the piece; but in reality I was only an absurd puppet pushed to and fro by the will of those yellow faces behind. I perceived in this moment that

when the white man turns tyrant it is his own freedom that he destroys. He becomes a sort of hollow, posing dummy, the conventionalized figure of a sahib. For it is the condition of his rule that he shall spend his life in trying to impress the "natives," and so in every crisis he has got to do what the "natives" expect of him. He wears a mask, and his face grows to fit it. I had got to shoot the elephant. I had committed myself to doing it when I sent for the rifle. A sahib has got to act like a sahib; he has got to appear resolute, to know his own mind and do definite things. To come all that way, rifle in hand, with two thousand people marching at my heels, and then to trail feebly away, having done nothing—no, that was impossible. The crowd would laugh at me. And my whole life, every white man's life in the East, was one long struggle not to be laughed at.

But I did not want to shoot the elephant. I watched him beating his bunch of grass against his knees, with that preoccupied grandmotherly air that elephants have. It seemed to me that it would be murder to shoot him. At that age I was not squeamish about killing animals, but I had never shot an elephant and never wanted to. (Somehow it always seems worse to kill a *large* animal.) Besides, there was the beast's owner to be considered. Alive, the elephant was worth at least a hundred pounds; dead, he would only be worth the value of his tusks, five pounds, possibly. But I had got to act quickly. I turned to some experienced-looking Burmans who had been there when we arrived, and asked them how the elephant had been behaving. They all said the same thing: he took no notice of you if you left him alone, but he might charge if you went too close to him.

It was perfectly clear to me what I ought to do. I ought to walk up to within, say, twenty-five yards of the elephant and test his behavior. If he charged, I could shoot; if he took no notice of me, it would be safe to leave him until the mahout came back. But also I knew that I was going to do no such thing. I was a poor shot with a rifle and the ground was soft mud into which one would sink at every step. If the elephant charged and I missed him, I should have about as much chance as a toad under a steamroller. But even then I was not thinking particularly of my own skin, only of the watchful yellow faces behind. For at that moment, with the crowd watching me, I was not afraid in the ordinary sense, as I would have been if I had been alone. A white man mustn't be frightened in front of "natives"; and so, in general, he isn't frightened. The sole thought in my mind was that if anything went wrong those two thousand Burmans would see me pursued, caught, trampled on and reduced to a grinning corpse like that Indian up the hill. And if that happened it was quite probable that some of them would laugh. That would never do. There was only one alternative. I shoved the cartridges into the magazine and lay down on the road to get a better aim.

The crowd grew very still, and a deep, low, happy sigh, as of people who see the theatre curtain go up at last, breathed from innumerable throats. They were going to have their bit of fun after all. The rifle was a beautiful German thing with cross-hair sights. I did not then know that in shooting an elephant one would shoot to cut an imaginary bar running from ear-hole to ear-hole. I ought, therefore, as the elephant was sideways on, to have aimed straight at his ear-hole; actually I aimed several inches in front of this, thinking the brain would be further forward.

When I pulled the trigger I did not hear the bang or feel the kick—one never does when a shot goes home—but I heard the devilish roar of glee that went up from the crowd. In that instant, in too short a time, one would have thought, even for the bullet to get there, a mysterious, terrible change had come over the elephant. He neither stirred nor fell, but every line of his body had altered. He looked suddenly stricken, shrunken, immensely old, as though the frightful impact of the bullet had paralysed him without knocking him down. At last, after what seemed a long time—it might have been five seconds, I dare say—he sagged flabbily to his knees. His mouth slobbered. An enormous senility seemed to have settled upon him. One could have imagined him thousands of years old. I fired again into the same spot. At the second shot he did not collapse but climbed with desperate slowness to his feet and stood weakly upright, with legs sagging and head drooping. I fired a third time. That was the shot that did for him. You could see the agony of it jolt his whole body and knock the last remnant of strength from his legs. But in falling he seemed for a moment to rise, for as his hind legs collapsed beneath him he seemed to tower upward like a huge rock toppling, his trunk reaching skywards like a tree. He trumpeted, for the first and only time. And then down he came, his belly towards me, with a crash that seemed to shake the ground even where I lay.

I got up. The Burmans were already racing past me across the mud. It was obvious that the elephant would never rise again, but he was not dead. He was breathing very rhythmically with long rattling gasps, his great mound of a side painfully rising and falling. His mouth was wide open—I could see far down into caverns of pale pink throat. I waited a long time for him to die, but his breathing did not weaken. Finally I fired my two remaining shots into the spot where I thought his heart must be. The thick blood welled out of him like red velvet, but still he did not die. His body did not even jerk when the shots hit him, the tortured breathing continued without a pause. He was dying, very slowly and in great agony, but in some world remote from me where not even a bullet could damage him further. I felt that I had got to put an end to that dreadful noise. It seemed dreadful to see the great beast lying there, powerless to move and yet powerless to die, and not even to be able to finish him. I sent back for my small rifle and poured shot after shot into his heart and down his throat. They seemed to make no impression. The tortured gasps continued as steadily as the ticking of a clock.

In the end I could not stand it any longer and went away. I heard later that it took him half an hour to die. Burmans were bringing dahs and baskets even before I left, and I was told they had stripped his body almost to the bones by the afternoon.

Afterwards, of course, there were endless discussions about the shooting of the elephant. The owner was furious, but he was only an Indian and could do nothing. Besides, legally I had done the right thing, for a mad elephant has to be killed, like a mad dog, if its owner fails to control it. Among the Europeans opinion was divided. The older men said I was right, the younger men said it was a damn shame to shoot an elephant for killing a coolie, because an elephant was worth more than any damn Coringhee coolie. And afterwards I was very glad that the coolie had been killed; it put me legally in the right and it gave me a sufficient pretext for shooting the elephant. I often wondered whether any of the others grasped that I had done it solely to avoid looking a fool.

—PART TEN—

Print of Bismarck Declaring the Second German Empire
Perhaps the most striking thing about the print of Bismarck standing in front of the new Hohenzollern emperor was that the event was taking place in the hall of mirrors at Versailles, symbol of the French monarchy. Germany had just defeated France in the Franco-Prussian War. The humiliation of using Versailles to proclaim the new German Empire added insult to the injury of military defeat and helped set the stage for World War I. Whereas in the past rulers had pitted themselves against other rulers, now nations vied with other nations.

Problems of National Identity

Questions of national identity and national self-determination, which arose sharply on the European scene after the Napoleanic era and reached a culmination in the 1848 revolutions, continued to characterize European life and politics thereafter. Following Italy's example, in 1870 Germany too achieved national unification on the basis of a combination of warfare, political maneuvering, and popular support at home as suggested by the image of Otto von Bismarck (1815–1898) declaring the new German Empire. The original idea that all nations contributed to the sum of human achievement and that all nations had the right to self-government gradually transformed into assertions of national superiority or chauvinism. Dynasties that ruled multiethnic states came to be perceived as associated with one predominant nationality. Poles, Jews, Hungarians, the Irish and many other subject national groups dreamed of escaping oppression. Ernest Renan (1823–1892) captured the era's sweeping claims about national identity and rights in the essay, What is a nation? (1882). The nation, he answered, is a "soul, decided by a daily plebiscite."

No sooner had the 1848 tumult begun to die out throughout much of Europe than the Hungarians rose up in an unsuccessful attempt to achieve independence from the Habsburg Empire. The Hungarian Declaration of Independence (April 1849) based its claim to statehood on alleged Habsburg oppression of Hungary's national rights. Continued pressures for Hungarian independence led to the Compromise (*Ausgleich*) of 1867 which established the dual monarchy of Austria-Hungary, with ruling centers in Vienna and Budapest. During this same time period, Leon Gambetta, future president of the 3rd French Republic, espoused a program of increased voting suffrage and free education for all French children as part of a national project to unify all segments of society in support of the state (see Part Thirteen). Toward the last decades of the century, Jewish populations of central and eastern European nations experienced a wave of anti-Semitism, itself a reflection of the era's chauvinism. In *The Jews' State* (1896), Theodore Herzl (1860–1904), founder of the Zionist movement, suggested that his people seek a home outside Europe, freed from the burdens of oppression and threatened persecution. Joseph Roth (1894–1939) describes remote late-nineteenth-century Austro-Hungarian towns, garrisons, and landscapes in his novel *The Radetzky March* (1932). The multiethnic reality of the dying monarchy, against the backdrop of a turn of the century world denuded of certainties, is one of the novel's principal themes.

Study Questions

1. Can late nineteenth-century nationalism still be tied to liberalism?
2. What role does national identity play in peoples' lives?
3. How do the problems that Herzl faced differ from those of other nationalists?
4. What does Roth tell us about national sensitivities by the end of the nineteenth century?
5. Is the nation a product of the modern world or has it always been present in history?
6. Image: What does this image of the declaration of the Second German Empire suggest about the relative roles of Bismarck and the emperor?

What is a Nation?

Ernest Renan

"What is a Nation?" was delivered in the form of a lecture in 1882 at the Sorbonne and is still considered a classic statement about the meaning of the concept of a nation. Renan rejects the common understanding of a nation as a state. Instead he describes the nation as a kind of spiritual entity, a soul. As he put it, the nation is a daily plebiscite, by which members affirm their connection to the whole.

A nation is a soul, a spiritual principle. Only two things, actually, constitute this soul, this spiritual principle. One is in the past, the other is in the present. One is the possession in common of a rich legacy of remembrances; the other is the actual consent, the desire to live together, the will to continue to value the heritage which all hold in common. Man, sirs, does not improvise. The nation, even as the individual, is the end product of a long period of work, sacrifice and devotion. The worship of ancestors is understandably justifiable, since our ancestors have made us what we are. A heroic past, of great men, of glory (I mean the genuine kind), that is the social principle on which the national idea rests. To have common glories in the past, a common will in the present; to have accomplished great things together, to wish to do so again, that is the essential condition for being a nation. One loves in proportion to the sacrifices which one has approved and for which one has suffered. One loves the house which he has built and which he has made over. The Spartan chant: 'We are what you make us; we are what you are' is simply the abbreviated hymn of the Fatherland.

In the past, a heritage of glory and a reluctance to break apart, to realize the same program in the future; to have suffered, worked, hoped together; that is worth more than common taxes and frontiers conforming to ideas of strategy; that is what one really understands despite differences of race and language. I have said 'having suffered together'; indeed, common suffering is greater than happiness. In fact, national sorrows are more significant than triumphs because they impose obligations and demand a common effort.

A nation is a grand solidarity constituted by the sentiment of sacrifices which one has made and those that one is disposed to make again. It supposes a past, it renews itself especially in the present by a tangible deed: the approval, the desire, clearly expressed, to continue the communal life. The existence of a nation (pardon this metaphor!) is an everyday plebiscite; it is, like the very existence of the individual, a perpetual affirmation of life. Oh! I know it, this is less metaphysical than the concept of divine right, less brutal than the so-called historic right. In the order of ideas that I submit to you, a nation has no more right than a king of a province to say: 'You appear to me, I take you.' A province for us is its inhabitants; if anyone in this matter has a right to be considered, it is the inhabitant. A nation never has a real interest in being annexed or holding on to a country despite itself. The desire of nations to be together is the only real criterion that must always be taken into account.

We have traced the politics of metaphysical and theological abstractions. What remains after that? Man remains, his desires, his needs.... Human desires change; but what does not change on this earth? Nations are not something eternal. They have begun, they will end. They will be replaced, in

From: Ernest Renan, *Qu'est-ce qu'une nation*, trans. by Ida Mae Snyder (Paris: Calmann-Levy, 1882), pp. 26–29.

all probability, by a European confederation. But such is not the law of the century in which we live. At the present time the existence of nations happens to be good, even necessary. Their existence is a guarantee of liberty, which would be lost if the world had only one law and only one master.

Through their varied, frequently opposing, abilities, nations serve the common cause of civilization; each holds one note in the concert of humanity, which, in the long run, is the highest ideal to which we can aspire. Isolated, they have their weaknesses. I often say to myself that a person who has these defects in quality that nations have, who nourishes himself on vainglory, who is jealous, egotistic and quarrelsome, who could support nothing without fighting; he would be the most intolerable of men.

But all these unharmonious details disappear when we are united. Poor humanity! How you have suffered! What ordeals await you yet! Can the spirit of wisdom guide you to prevent the many dangers that line your path?

I continue, sirs. Man is not enslaved, nor is his race nor his language, nor his religion, nor the course of the rivers, nor the direction of the mountain ranges. A great aggregation of men, with a healthy spirit and warmth of heart, creates a moral conscience which is called a nation. When this moral conscience proves its strength by sacrifices that demand abdication of the individual for the benefit of the community, it is legitimate, and it has a right to exist.

Hungarian Declaration of Independence

The revolutions of 1848 tried to further the cause of nationalism throughout much of Europe. National independence, constitutions, and an end of serfdom were common goals during the 1848 revolutions. The Hungarians, ruled by the German-speaking Habsburg Monarchy centered in Vienna, rebelled in 1848 and by 1849 had declared their independence. As with all 1848 revolutions, this revolt ended tragically. The Habsburgs, with the assistance of the Russians, put down the Hungarian uprising.

We, the legally constituted representatives of the Hungarian nation, assembled in Diet, do by these presents solemnly proclaim, in maintenance of the inalienable natural rights of Hungary, with all its dependencies, to occupy the position of an independent European State—that the House of Habsburg-Lorraine, as perjured in the sight of God and man, has forfeited its right to the Hungarian throne. At the same time we feel ourselves bound in duty to make known the motives and reasons which have impelled us to this decision, that the civilized world may learn we have taken this step not out of overweening confidence in our own wisdom, or out of revolutionary excitement, but that it is an act of the last necessity, adopted to preserve from utter destruction a nation persecuted to the limit of the most enduring patience.

Three hundred years have passed since the Hungarian nation, by free election, placed the house of Austria upon its throne, in accordance with stipulations made on both sides, and ratified by treaty. These three hundred years have been, for the country, a period of uninterrupted suffering.

The Creator has blessed this country with all the elements of wealth and happiness. Its area of 100,000 square miles presents in varied profusion innumerable sources of prosperity. Its population, numbering nearly fifteen millions, feels the glow of youthful strength within its veins, and has shown

temper and docility which warrant its proving at once the main organ of civilization in eastern Europe, and the guardian of that civilization when attacked. Never was a more grateful task appointed to a reigning dynasty by the dispensation of Providence, than that which devolved upon the House of Habsburg-Lorraine. It would have sufficed to do nothing that could impede the development of the country. Had this been the rule observed Hungary would now rank among the most prosperous nations. It was only necessary that it should not envy the Hungarians the moderate share of constitution liberty which they timidly maintained during the difficulties of a thousand years with rare fidelity to their sovereigns, and the House of Habsburg might long have counted this nation among the most faithful adherents of the throne.

This dynasty, however, which can at no epoch point to a ruler who based his power on the freedom of the people, adopted a course toward this nation from father to son, which deserves the appellation of perjury.

The house of Austria has publicly used every effort to deprive the country of its legitimate independence and constitution, designing to reduce it to a level with the other provinces long since deprived of all freedom, and to unite all in a common link of slavery. Foiled in this effort by the untiring vigilance of the people, it directed its endeavor to tame the power, to check the progress of Hungary, causing it to minister to the gain of the provinces of Austria, but only to the extent which enabled those provinces to bear the load of taxation with which the prodigal-

From: Henry M. De Puy, *Kossuth and His Generals* (Buffalo: Phinney & Co., 1852), pp. 202–209, 222–225.

ity of the imperial house weighed them down; having first deprived those provinces of all constitutional means of remonstrating against a policy which was not based upon the welfare of the subject, but solely intended to maintain despotism and crush liberty in every country of Europe.

It has frequently happened that the Hungarian nation, in spite of this systemized [sic] tyranny, has been obliged to take up arms in self-defense. Although constantly victorious in these constitutional struggles, yet so moderate has the nation ever been in its use of the victory, so strongly has it confided in the plighted word of the king, that it has ever laid down arms as soon as the king by new compact and fresh oaths has guaranteed the duration of its rights and liberty. But every new compact was as futile as those which preceded. Each oath which fell from the royal lips was but a renewal of previous perjuries. The policy of the house of Austria, which aimed at destroying the independence of Hungary as a state, has been pursued without alteration for three hundred years.

It was in vain that the Hungarian nation shed its blood for the deliverance of Austria whenever it was in danger; in vain were all the sacrifices which it made to serve the interests of the reigning house; in vain did it, on the renewal of the royal promises, forget the wounds which the past had inflicted; vain was the fidelity cherished by the Hungarians for their king, and which, in moments of danger, assumed a character of devotion;—they were in vain, because the history of the government of that dynasty in Hungary presents but an unbroken series of perjured acts from generation to generation.

In spite of such treatment, the Hungarian nation has all along respected the tie by which it was united to this dynasty; and in now decreeing its expulsion from the throne, it acts under the natural law of self-preservation, being driven to pronounce this sentence by the full conviction that the House of Habsburg-Lorraine is compassing the destruction of Hungary as an independent state; so that this dynasty has been the first to tear the bands by which it was united to the Hungarian nation, and to confess that it had torn them in the face of Europe. For many causes a nation is justified, before God and man, in expelling a reigning dynasty. Among such are the following:

When it forms alliances with the enemies of the country, with robbers, or partisan chieftains, to oppress the nation; when it attempts to annihilate the independence of the country and its constitution, solemnly sanctioned by oaths, attacking with an armed force the people who have committed no act of revolt; when the integrity of a country, which the sovereign has sworn to maintain, is violated, and its power diminished; when foreign armies are employed to murder the people, and to oppress their liberties.

Each of the grounds here enumerated would justify the exclusion of a dynasty from the throne. But the House of Habsburg-Lorraine is unexampled in the compass of its perjuries, and has committed every one of these crimes against the nation; and its determination to extinguish the independence of Hungary has been accompanied with a succession of criminal acts, comprising robbery, destruction of property by fire, murder, maiming, and personal ill-treatment of all kinds, besides setting the laws of the country at defiance, so that humanity will shudder when reading this disgraceful page of history.

The main impulse to this recent unjustifiable course was the passing of the laws adopted in the spring of 1848, for the better protection of the constitution of the country. These laws provided reforms in the internal government of the country, by which the commutation of servile services and of the tithe were decreed; a fair representation guaranteed to the people in the Diet, the constitution of which was, before that, exclusively aristocratical; equality before the law proclaimed; the privilege of exemption from taxation abolished; freedom of the press pronounced; and, to stem the torrent of abuses, trial by jury established, with other improvements. Notwithstanding that troubles broke out in every province of the Austrian empire, as a consequence of the French February Revolution, and the reigning dynasty was left without support, the Hungarian nation was too generous at such a moment to demand more privileges, and contented itself with enforcing the administration of its old rights upon a system of ministerial responsibility, and with maintaining them and the independence of the country against the often renewed and perjured attempts of the crown. These rights, and the independence sought to be maintained, were, however, no new acquisition, but were what the king, by his oath, and according to law, was bound to keep up, and which had not in the slightest degree been affected by the relation in which Hungary stood to the provinces of the empire.

In point of fact, Hungary and Transylvania, with all their possessions and dependencies, never were incorporated into the Austrian empire, but formed a separate, independent kingdom, even after the adoption of the pragmatic sanction by which the same law of succession was adopted for Hungary which obtained in the other countries and provinces.

The clearest proof of this legal fact is furnished by the law incorporated into the act of the pragmatic sanction, and which stipulates that the territory of Hungary and its dependencies, as well as its independence, self-government, constitution, and privileges, shall remain inviolate and specially guaranteed.

Another proof is contained in the stipulation of the pragmatic sanction, according to which the heir of the crown only becomes legally king of Hungary upon the conclusion of a coronation treaty with the nation, and upon his swearing to maintain the constitution and the laws of the country, whereupon he is to be crowned with the crown of St. Stephen. The act signed at the coronation contains the stipulation that all laws, privileges, and the entire constitution, shall be observed, together with the order of succession. Only one sovereign since the adoption of the pragmatic sanction refused to enter into the coronation compact, and swear to the constitution. This was Joseph II, who died without being crowned, but for that reason his name is not recorded among the kings of Hungary, and all his acts are considered illegal, null and void. His successor, Leopold II, was obliged, before ascending the Hungarian throne, to enter into the coronation compact, to take the oath, and to let himself be crowned. On this occasion it was distinctly declared in Art. IC, 1790, sanctioned upon oath by the king, that Hungary was a free and independent country with regard to its government, and not subordinate to any other state or people whatever, consequently that it was to be governed by its own customs and laws.

The same oath was taken by Francis I, who came to the throne in the year 1792. On the extinction of the imperial dignity in Germany, and the foundation of the Austrian empire, this emperor, who allowed himself to violate the law in innumerable instances,

had still sufficient respect for his oath, publicly to avow that Hungary formed no portion of the Austrian empire. For this reason Hungary was separated from the rest of the Austrian states by a chain of custom guards along the whole frontier, which still continues.

The same oath was taken on his accession to the throne by Ferdinand V, who, at the Diet held at Pressburg last year, of his own free-will, sanctioned the laws that were passed, but who, soon after, breaking that oath, entered into a conspiracy with the other members of his family with the intent of erasing Hungary from the list of independent nations.

Still the Hungarian nation preserved with useless piety its loyalty to its perjured sovereign, and during March last year, while the empire was on the brink of destruction, while its armies in Italy suffered one defeat after another, and he in his imperial palace had to fear at any moment that he, might be driven from it; Hungary did not take advantage of so favorable a moment to make increased demands; it only asked that its constitution might be guaranteed, and abuses rectified—a constitution, to maintain which fourteen kings of the Austrian dynasty had sworn a solemn oath, which every one of them had broken.

When the king undertook to guarantee those ancient rights, and gave his sanction to the establishment of a responsible ministry, the Hungarian nation flew enthusiastically to his support, and rallied its might around his tottering throne. At that eventful crisis, as at so many others, the house of Austria was saved by the fidelity of the Hungarians.

Scarcely, however, had this oath fallen from his lips when he conspired anew with his family, the accomplices of his crime, to compass the destruction of the Hungarian nation. This conspiracy did not take place on the ground that any new privileges were conceded by the recent laws which diminished the royal authority. From what has been said, it is clear that no such demands were made. The conspiracy was founded to get rid of the responsible ministry, which made it impossible for the Vienna cabinet to treat the Hungarian constitution any longer as a nullity.

*   *   *

. . . . Confiding in the justice of Eternal God, we, before the world, and relying on the natural rights of the Hungarian the power it has developed to maintain them, further impelled by that sense of duty which urges every nation to defend its existence, do hereby declare and proclaim in the name of the nation legally represented by us, the following:

1st. Hungary, with Transylvania, as legally united with it, and its dependencies, are hereby declared to constitute a free, independent, sovereign state. The territorial unity of this state is declared to be inviolable, and its territory to be indivisible.

2d. The House of Habsburg-Lorraine—having, by treachery, perjury, and levying of war against the Hungarian nation, as well as by its outrageous violation of all compacts, in breaking up the integral territory of the kingdom, in the separation of Transylvania, Croatia, Sclavonia, Fiume, and its districts from Hungary—further, by compassing the destruction of the independence of the country by arms, and by calling in the disciplined army of a foreign power, for the purpose of annihilating its nationality, by violation both of the Pragmatic Sanction and of treaties concluded between Austria and Hungary, on which the alliance between the two countries depended—is, as treacherous and perjured, forever excluded from the throne of the united states of Hungary and Transylvania, and, all their possessions and dependencies, and is hereby deprived of the style and title, as well as of the armorial bearings belonging to the crown of Hungary, and declared to be banished forever from the united countries and their dependencies and possessions. They are therefore declared to be deposed, degraded, and banished from the Hungarian territory.

3d. The Hungarian nation, in the exercise of its rights and sovereign will, being determined to assume the position of a free and independent state among the nations of Europe, declares it to be its intention to establish and maintain friendly and neighborly relations with those states with which it was formerly united under the same sovereign, as well as to contract alliances with all other nations.

4th. The form of government to be adopted for the future will be fixed by the Diet of the nation.

But until this shall be decided, on the basis of the ancient and received principles which have been recognized for ages, the government of the united countries, their possessions and dependencies, shall be conducted on personal responsibility, and under the obligation to render an account of all acts, by Louis Kossuth, who has by acclamation, and with the unanimous approbation of the Diet of the nation, been named Governing President, (Gubernator,) and the ministers whom he shall appoint.

And this resolution of ours we shall proclaim and make known to all the nations of the civilized world, with the conviction that the Hungarian nation will be received by them among the free and independent nations of the world, with the same friendship and free acknowledgment of its rights which the Hungarians proffer to other countries.

We also hereby proclaim and make known to all the inhabitants of the united states of Hungary and Transylvania, and their dependencies, that all authorities, communes, towns, and the civil officers both in the counties and cities, are completely set free and released from all the obligations under which they stood, by oath or otherwise, to the said House of Habsburg-Lorraine, and that any individual daring to contravene this decree, and by word or deed in any way to aid or abet any one violating it, shall be treated and punished as guilty of high treason. And by the publication of this decree, we hereby bind and oblige all the inhabitants of these countries to obedience to the government now instituted formally, and endowed with all necessary legal powers.

Debreczin, April 14, 1849.

The Jews' State

Theodore Herzl

Anti-Semitism was a growing problem in many parts of Europe by the late nineteenth century. Theodore Herzl witnessed some of its worst manifestations during the Dreyfus affair in France. From this experience and armed with the new ideas of nations and nationalism, Herzl founded the Zionist movement and worked towards establishing a Jewish homeland outside Europe. He had concluded that assimilation did not solve anti-Semitism.

Preamble

The concept with which I am dealing in this paper is very old. It is the establishment of the Jews' State.

The world resounds with clamor against Jews, and that arouses this concept out of its sleep.

At every stage of my argument, it should be kept clearly in mind that I am not making anything up. I am making up neither the situation of the Jews, which has developed historically, nor the means of overcoming it. The material components of the building, which I am designing, are available in real life; they can be seized with both hands; everyone can convince himself of this. If this attempt to solve the issue of the Jews is to be characterized in one word, then it should not be called a "fantasy," at most it may be called a "project."

First of all, I must defend my plan against the charge of being utopian. Strictly speaking, in doing so I am merely protecting superficial critics from committing an absurdity. For it would hardly be a shame to write a humane utopia. I could also give myself an easier literary success if to the reader, keen to be entertained, I brought this plan couched in the irresponsible form of a novel. But this is no charming utopian scheme, such as has been produced so often before and after Thomas More. I believe the situation of Jews in various countries is so bad as to render introductory trifles superfluous.

From: Theodor Herzl, *The Jews' State*, transl. by Henk Overberg (Northvale, N.J.: Jason Aronson Inc., 1997), pp. 123–138.

To throw some light on the difference between my construct and a utopian scheme, I choose an interesting book, recently published, *Freeland* by Dr. Theodor Hertzka. Conceived by a thoroughly modern scholar, trained in the area of national economics, this is a talented piece of fantasy, as far from real life as the Equator-Mountain, where this dreamland is situated. *Freeland* is a complicated machine with many cogs and wheels which even slot into each other, but nothing convinces me that it can be made to work. Even if I were to see the establishment of "Freeland-Societies," I would still regard them as a joke.

By contrast, the present plan is concerned with the application of a driving force which is present in real life. In all modesty, and being well aware of my inadequacy, I content myself with merely pointing out the cogs and wheels of the machine, trusting that there will be better practical mechanics than I am, who can build it.

The important point is the driving force. And what is this force? The plight of the Jews.

Who dares deny that this force exists? We will deal with it in the chapter about the basis of antisemitism.

We know the power of steam, developing in the teapot as the water heats, and lifting the lid. The Zionist experiments and the many other forms of associations "to ward off antisemitism": they are this phenomenon of the teapot.

Now I say that this force, properly applied, is powerful enough to drive a large machine, to profit people and things. It will not matter what this machine will look like.

I am convinced to the very depths of my being that I am right; I do not know whether I shall be proved correct during my lifetime. The first men who will start this movement will probably not see its glorious culmination. But even just by starting it, a great pride, an inner freedom, and joy will enter their lives.

I shall also be sparing in filling in the picture with picturesque details, so as to guard my plan against the suspicion of being utopian. In any case, I suspect that some will thoughtlessly try to mock and caricature what I have designed so as to rob everything of its power. An otherwise quite intelligent Jew, with whom I discussed the issue, thought that "potential detail portrayed as real is a characteristic of utopian" description. That is wrong. Every finance minister prepares his budget with future estimates—not merely with figures calculated from the averages of past years or derived from documents from other countries, but also with projected data that have no precedent, for example, when introducing a new tax. If you do not know that, you can never have studied a budget. Would you consider a financial bill utopian, even if you knew that the projections could never be precisely achieved?

But I put even more difficult challenges to my readers. From the educated persons whom I address, I demand that they rethink and relearn many old notions. I specifically challenge the best Jews who are involved in a practical way with solving the issue of the Jews to regard their attempts so far as failed and impractical.

In presenting the idea I have to be careful of a danger. If I practice discretion when I say all these things which lie in the future, then it could seem as if I do not believe they are possible. If, on the contrary, I announce their realization without reserve, then everything could look far-fetched.

So I say clearly and firmly: I believe it is possible to bring the idea to reality, even though I do not pretend to have found it in its final form. The world needs the Jews' State; consequently it will come about.

If pursued by a single individual, this idea would be insane, but if many Jews get involved at the same time, it is completely rational, and bringing it to fruition poses no difficulties to speak of. The idea merely depends on how many people support it. Perhaps our ambitious young people, to whom all avenues have been blocked and to whom the Jews' State offers the prospect of honor, freedom and happiness, perhaps they will take on the task of spreading the idea about.

Personally, I think that my task is completed with the publication of this paper. I will only speak to it if attacked by opponents of note, or if needed to counter unforeseen objections or to put aside errors.

Is what I say not yet appropriate for the present time? Am I ahead of my time? Are the sufferings of the Jews not yet great enough? We shall see.

At any rate, it depends on the Jews themselves whether for the time being this paper represents political fact or political fiction. If the present generation is still too apathetic, then another, higher, better one will come. Those Jews who want it will have their state, and they will deserve it.

Introduction

What practical men, standing in the midst of life, understand of economics is often startlingly little. This explains why even Jews faithfully repeat the slogan of the antisemites that we live off "host" populations, and that we would starve to death if we did not have a "host" population around us. Here is an instance that shows how unjust accusations can lower our self-esteem. So what is the real truth about the concept of "host" populations? Assuming the concept does not rest on old physiocratic limitations, it is based on the naïve misconception that economic life rests on the constant recirculation of the same wealth. Now unlike Rip van Winkle, we do not need to wake up out of a long sleep to realize that it is the constant production of new wealth which changes the world. In our wonderful times replete with technical progress even the most benighted person with his eyes shut can see the emerging new wealth. It has been created by the spirit of enterprise.

Labor without enterprise is old and stationary; the typical example is agriculture, which is standing still at the point reached by its precursors a thousand years ago. All material progress has come through entrepreneurs. You almost feel ashamed to write down such an obvious triviality. Even if we were all entrepreneurs, which is a foolish exaggeration, we would still not need a "host" population.

We do not depend on the constant recirculation of the same wealth, because we create new wealth.

In machines we possess slaves of enormous power, which have made their entry into the civilized world as deadly competitors for manual workers. Admittedly, you also need workers to operate the machines, but for this purpose we have more than enough people. Only those who are not familiar with the situation of Jews in the various regions of Eastern Europe would be so bold as to maintain that Jews are not suited to manual labor or are unwilling to perform it.

However, I really do not want to use this paper to defend the Jews. That would be useless. All that is reasonable and charitable has already been said about this subject. It is not enough to find the appropriate arguments to change intellect and attitudes; if your audience does not have the capacity to understand, you are a voice crying in the wilderness. If, however, your audience has a capacity for understanding, then the whole sermon is superfluous. I believe that humanity progresses to ever higher levels of morality, even though I consider this progress to be desperately slow. If we had to wait until the man in the street learns the tolerance shown by Lessing when he wrote *Nathan the Wise,* then we would be waiting a long time, as would our children, grandchildren and great-grandchildren. The spirit of the times assists us from another angle.

By virtue of its technical achievements, the present century has offered us a precious renaissance. Unfortunately, this fabulous progress has not yet affected our humanity. The earth has been conquered in all its vastness, yet we still suffer the pains of our own narrowness. We now speed in enormous steamships over formerly unknown seas without danger. Trains now lead us safely into the mountains, which we used to fear on foot. What happens in countries which were not even thought of when Europe already confined Jews to ghettos is now known within the hour. That is why the plight of the Jews is an anachronism—not because we had the Enlightenment a century ago, which in fact merely affected the greatest scholars.

In my opinion electricity was not discovered so that a few snobs could light up their ostentatious rooms, but rather so that we could solve the great questions of humanity by its light. The issue of the Jews is one of these, and not even the most insignificant one. In devising a solution, we do not only act for ourselves, but also for many others who are burdened and bothered.

The issue of the Jews does exist. It would be foolish to deny it. It is a worn-out relic from the Middle Ages, which the community of civilized nations still cannot leave behind with the best will in the world. They did show their generous disposition when they emancipated us. The issue of the Jews exists in all those places where Jews live in appreciable numbers. Where it does not exist, it is brought in by Jews that go to live there. Obviously, we go where they do not persecute us; but as soon as we appear, persecution sets in. That is true and will always be true, as long as the issue of the Jews is not solved on a political level. Even in highly developed countries: France provides the evidence. At this very moment the poor Jews carry antisemitism into England, they have already introduced it into America.

I believe I understand antisemitism, which is a highly complicated movement. I view this movement from the standpoint of a Jew, but without hatred or fear. I believe I can recognize those aspects of antisemitism which are a coarse joke, common jealousy, inherited prejudice, religious intolerance; but also those aspects born out of alleged self-defense. I consider the issue of the Jews neither in social nor religious terms, even though these things do come into it. It is a national issue, and if we are to find a solution, we must make it into a political question for the whole world, to be tackled in counsel with all civilized peoples.

We are a people, *one* people.

We have tried everywhere in all honesty to assimilate into the communities around us, while preserving the faith of our fathers. We are not allowed to. We are faithful and often even over-enthusiastic patriots—in vain. We make the same sacrifices in life and limb as our countrymen—in vain. We do our utmost to further the reputation of our home countries in the fields of arts and science—in vain. We toil to increase the wealth of our lands with our commerce and trade—in vain. In our home countries, where we have been living for centuries, we are decried as foreign, often by those whose forebears were not even living there when our forebears were already being persecuted. It is the majority which decides who is an alien in the land; it is a question of power, like all relations between peoples. By saying this as a single individual without a mandate I do not put any of our acquired rights on the line. Given the present state of the world, might will have precedence over right in the foreseeable future. Therefore we are good patriots everywhere in vain, just like the Huguenots, who were forced to go elsewhere. If they only left us in peace . . .

But I believe they will not leave us in peace.

Pressure and persecution will not eradicate us. No people in history has coped with such struggles and suffering as we have. Jew baiting has only ever persuaded our weak members to fall away. Strong Jews return defiantly back to their tribe once persecution breaks out. That became clear during the period immediately after the emancipation of the Jews. The more highly educated and wealthier Jews completely lost their feeling of solidarity. Given some lasting political well-being we assimilate everywhere; I do not believe that to be dishonorable. The statesman keen to have a touch of the Jewish race in his nation would have to look after our political well-being in the long run. And even a Bismarck could not manage that.

For deep down within the feelings of peoples there are old prejudices anchored against us. If you want evidence, you only need to listen where the people express themselves simply and truthfully: folktales and proverbs are antisemitic. Everywhere the common people is like a big child to be educated, but at best this education would take so much time that we can solve our problems far more quickly in other ways, as I have already said.

Assimilation—which I take to be not just external assimilation in dress, ways of living, customs and language, but rather becoming equal in mind and kind—such assimilation of Jews could only be achieved through mixed marriage. This, however, should be experienced by the majority as a need; it is not enough to simply permit mixed marriage in terms of the law. The liberals in Hungary, who have recently done this, are curiously mistaken. They illustrated this officially sanctioned mixed marriage by an early example of a baptized Jew marrying a Jewish woman. The difficulties with the present law

on marriage in Hungary have widened in many cases the divisions between Christians and Jews and harmed rather than promoted the mixing of the races. There is only one way if you want to see the decline of Jews through mixed marriage. Jews would first have to attain such a degree of economic power that the old social prejudice against them is conquered. The classic example is the aristocracy, in which most mixed marriages take place. The old aristocracy guilds itself with the money of Jews, and Jewish families are absorbed into it. But how would this phenomenon work with the middle-classes, where the issue of the Jews is most pertinent, in view of the fact that Jews are a middle-class people? In this context the prior need for Jews to attain status would be synonymous with Jews attaining a monopoly of economic power, which some think they have already, albeit wrongly. If the power the Jews hold at present already gives rise to the angry and distressed bleatings of the antisemites, how much worse would such outbreaks be if this Jewish power grew even bigger? Such a first stage of absorption is unattainable, for it would imply the subjugation of the majority by a minority, disdained until recently and not in possession of the instruments of war and administration. That is why I believe the absorption of Jews on the basis of their prosperity to be improbable. Jewish residents of present antisemitic countries would agree with me. My compatriots in those other countries, where Jews are doing well at present, will probably disagree violently with my opinion. They will only believe me when next confronted with Jew baiting. The longer antisemitism is kept at bay, the more furious it will be when it does break out. The infiltration of emigrating Jews, attracted by the seemingly secure conditions, coupled with the rising class movement of the local Jews, will then form a mighty movement and force a revolution. Nothing is more simple than this conclusion.

Because I fearlessly draw conclusions which are founded in truth, I anticipate in advance that there will be objections and hostility from those Jews living in better conditions. Insofar as these represent private interests of people who feel threatened by their own stupidity and cowardice, they can be brushed aside with a disdainful smile. For the cause of the poor and oppressed is more important. Even so, I would not want to give the wrong impression that well-off Jews would lose their property if this plan were ever realized. That is why I will provide detailed explanations of what will legally happen to property. If the whole concept remains on paper, then nothing will ever change.

A more serious objection would be that by calling Jews a people, or rather one people, I am giving a boost to the antisemites; that I am hindering the assimilation of Jews where it is about to occur, or that I am endangering in retrospect the position of those Jews already assimilated—as if one solitary writer is in a position to seriously hinder or endanger anything at all.

This objection is likely to come in the first instance from France. I also expect it from other places, but I will answer the French Jews in anticipation, because they provide the most striking example.

However much I venerate the individual, be it the unique, strong individual personality of the statesman, the discoverer, the artist, the philosopher or the general, or the collective personality of a historical group of human beings which we call *Volk,* I still do not mourn his destruction. Whoever can, wants to, must perish—should perish. The collective personality of the Jews as a people, however, cannot, will not, and must not perish. It cannot perish, because external enemies hold it together. It will not perish; it has demonstrated that during two millennia under enormous suffering. It must not perish; that is what I seek to demonstrate in this publication after many other Jews who never gave up hope. Whole branches of Jewry may well die away and fall off; the tree lives.

My answer to all or some of the French Jews who may object to my plan because they are already "assimilated" is simple: the entire issue is of no concern to them. They are Israelite Frenchmen, excellent! This, however, is an internal concern of Jews.

Of course, the movement toward statehood which I am proposing would harm neither Israelite Frenchmen nor "assimilated" Jews of other countries. On the contrary, it would be of great benefit to them. For, to use Darwin's expression, they would no longer be disturbed in their "chromatic function." They could go on assimilating in peace, for the antisemitism of today would stop for ever. Indeed, as persons assimilated to the innermost depths of

their soul, their credibility would be enhanced if they stay where they now live after the new state for Jews, with its better institutions, has become a fact of life.

Getting rid of the Jews who remain true to their group would be even more advantageous to assimilated Jews than to Christian citizens, for assimilated Jews would no longer have to cope with the worrisome, inevitable, incalculable competition of the Jewish proletariat, thrown about from place to place and country to country by political pressure and economic distress. This floating proletariat would become tied to one place. At present, many Christian citizens—commonly known as antisemites—are in a position to protest against the immigration of foreign Jews. The Israelite citizens cannot do so, even though they are the more heavily affected, because they are in competition with their own economic kind, who, apart from everything else, are responsible for importing antisemitism from abroad or even for increasing local antisemitism. This is the lament of assimilated Jews, to which they then give expression in "philanthropic" projects. They establish emigration societies for immigrating Jews. This phenomenon is a paradox, which might even be funny, were it not that suffering human beings are involved. In offering assistance, some of these societies do not work for but rather against persecuted Jews. The poorest among these must be taken away, very quickly and very far. Indeed when you go into it carefully you realize that many a would-be friend of the Jews is no more than an antisemite of Jewish background in disguise.

Yet even the colonizing efforts of really well-meaning individuals have thus far not taken root, even though they have been interesting as experiments. I do not really believe that they regarded these experiments of uprooting poor Jews as a sport in much the same way as horse racing. The issue is simply too serious and sad. These experiments were interesting insofar as they represent in a limited sense precursors of the idea of the Jews' State. And even the mistakes that were made have their use, for we now know what to avoid when the real thing takes place. Unfortunately, these experiments have also done some harm. That as the inevitable consequence of such artificial infiltration, antisemitism has been transplanted to new regions, I would regard as the least of the disadvantages. It is more serious that the unsatisfactory experiences have led the Jews themselves to cast doubt on the quality of Jewish human resources. Intelligent persons having this doubt may be answered quite simply as follows: what is impracticable or appropriate at a micro level, need not be so at a macro level. A small business may well experience losses under the same conditions that a large business makes a profit. You might not be able to float a rowing boat on a brook, yet the river into which it flows can carry stately iron ships.

No one person has sufficient strength or wealth to transplant a whole people from one domicile to another. Only an idea is powerful enough to do that. The idea of the state has such power. For the whole night of their history Jews have not stopped dreaming the royal dream. "Next year in Jerusalem" is our ancient watchword. The question now is to demonstrate that the dream can be turned into an idea as bright as day.

To achieve this, we must wipe our souls clean of all the old, superseded, confused, narrow-minded ideas. Some dull spirits may at first feel that wandering away from civilization must necessarily lead into the desert. Not true! Our emigration will take place in the midst of civilization. You do not go back to a lower stage, but advance to a higher stage of civilization. You do not occupy clay huts, but you build yourselves beautiful modern houses where you can live without fear. You do not lose your hard-earned wealth, but put it to good use. You only exchange your present rights for better rights. You do not give up the ways which have become dear to you, but you find them again. You do not leave the old house before the new one is ready. The only ones among us to leave are those who are certain to improve their situation by doing so. First the desperate among us, then the poor, then the well-off, then the wealthy. Those who leave first will be raised to the next social level as the inevitable consequence of such artificial infiltration, until people at this new level start sending their representatives. Apart from anything else, this emigration is an ascending class movement.

The emigration of the Jews will not lead to any economic disturbances, crises or persecutions, but will introduce a period of prosperity in the countries Jews leave behind. There will be a movement internally by Christian citizens into the positions the Jews leave vacant. The transformation will be gradual, free from trauma, and its intinial stages will mark the end of antisemitism. The Jews will be leaving as valued friends, and should some isolated individuals subsequently return, they will be received back in the civilized countries with kindness and treated like other foreign nationals. This emigration is not a flight, but an orderly transfer supported by public opinion. The movement must be based solely within a framework of law; indeed it can only be accomplished with the friendly cooperation of the participating governments, which themselves stand to gain substantially from it.

To guarantee the integrity of the idea and the power of putting it into practice, guarantees will be necessary which can only be found in so-called "moral" and "juridical" entities. I would like to keep these two categories, which in legal language are often bundled together, quite separate. As moral entity, which incorporates legal status outside the sphere of private property, I establish the Society of Jews. Beside it stands the juridical entity of the Jewish Company, whose purpose is to handle resources.

Any individual who thinks he could undertake this gigantic task on his own could only be a crook or a madman. The integrity of the moral entity is guaranteed by the good character of all its members. Whether the juridical entity has sufficient power is measured by the resources at its disposal.

With the above introductory remarks I have aimed to deflect the swarm of objections which the very term "Jews' State" is likely to evoke. We will now go on in a somewhat more leisurely fashion to explain things; we will tackle other objections and we will develop more fully many of the things which we have only hinted at so far. In the interest of this publication, which should take flight, we will try to stay clear of complicated matter and language as far as we possibly can. Short pithy chapters will be most suited to this objective.

If I want to build a new building on the site of an old one, I must first demolish before constructing. So I will stick to this sensible sequence. Initially, in the general part I will define ideas, clear away old concepts that have become meaningless, indicate the political and economic conditions, and develop the concept.

In the particular part, which is divided into three chapters, the practical issues will be presented. These three chapters are: Jewish Company, Local Groups and Society of Jews. The Society will be established first, the Company last of all; but they are best discussed the other way round, because the financial feasibility presents the most difficulties, which therefore have to be addressed first.

In the conclusion I will introduce those possible objections which we have not hitherto met. I hope my Jewish readers will follow me patiently to the end. Many readers will think of objections in a different order than I tackle them. If, however, your reservations have been intelligently dealt with, then you should commit yourself to the cause.

Though I try to be purely rational, I know very well that reason alone is not enough. Old prisoners find it difficult to leave the dungeon. We shall see whether our young people, whom we need, have the capacity to follow our lead—our youth, who will sweep the old along with them, carry them in their powerful arms, and who will transform our intellectual reasons into enthusiasm.

The Radetzky March

Joseph Roth

Despite the success of the idea of the nation-state, many multinational states still functioned by the early twentieth century. One such was the Habsburg Monarchy. In the Habsburg realm, individuals struggled with various identities. Along with their continued understanding of themselves as subjects of the Emperor, people had loyalties to their local towns or villages, to a sense of nation based on ethnicity, and to their religion. Roth's novel The Radetzky March *suggests the trials and tribulations of the monarchy during its last days.*

When Lieutenant-Baron von Trotta's only friend, the regimental doctor Demant, is killed in a senseless duel, he seeks reassignment to an area near the home village of his Slovene peasant grandfather, who was awarded a title for saving the emperor's life at the Battle of Solferino. Instead he is sent to the far eastern frontiers of the empire.

In those days before the Great War when the events narrated in this book took place, it had not yet become a matter of indifference whether a man lived or died. When one of the living had been extinguished another did not at once take his place in order to obliterate him: there was a gap where he had been, and both close and distant witnesses of his demise fell silent whenever they became aware of this gap. When fire had eaten away a house from the row of others in a street, the burnt-out space remained long empty. Masons worked slowly and cautiously. Close neighbors and casual passers-by alike, when they saw the empty space, remembered the aspect and walls of the vanished house. That was how things were then. Everything that grew took its time in growing and everything that was destroyed took a long time to be forgotten. And everything that had once existed left its traces so that in those days people lived on memories, just as now they live by the capacity to forget quickly and completely. . . .

From: Joseph Roth, *The Radetzky March* (Woodstock, NY: The Overlook Press, 1983), pp. 107–130.

*   *   *

Eastward to the frontiers of the Tsar, the Habsburg sun shot forth its rays. It was the same sun which had fostered the growth of the Trottas to nobility and esteem. Francis Joseph had a long memory for gratitude and his favor had a wide reach. If one of his favorite children was about to commit some folly, the servants and ministers of the Emperor intervened in good time to force the erring child into prudence and reason. It would scarcely have been fitting to permit the sole heir of this recently created baronetcy of Trotta von Sipolje to serve in the native province of the hero of Solferino, the grandson of illiterate Slovenian peasants, the son of a gendarmery sergeant-major. This young nobleman might, of course, if he chose, exchange his service in the Uhlans for a modest commission in an infantry regiment; it merely proved him faithful to the memory of his grandfather, who had saved his Emperor's life as a plain lieutenant in the line. But the prudence of the Imperial and Royal Ministry of War avoided sending the bearer of such a title, a title identical with the actual Slovenian village in which the first baron had been born, to serve in the neighborhood of the village. The District Commissioner, son of the hero of Solferino, agreed with the authorities. Though with a heavy heart he allowed his son to transfer to the infantry, he was not at all pleased with Carl Joseph's request to serve in the Slovenian province. He himself, the District Commissioner, had never felt any desire to see the home of his fathers. He was an Austrian, civil servant of the Habsburgs, his home the Imperial Hofburg in Vienna. Had he entertained political notions of any useful reshaping of the great and multifarious monarchy it would have seemed fitting to him that all the crownlands should simply form large and colorful outer courts of the Imperial Hofburg; and to see in all the nations of the monarchy subjects of the Habsburgs. He was a District Commissioner; within his district he represented the Apostolic Majesty. He wore the gold collar, cocked hat, and sword. He had no wish at all to drive a furrow into the blessed Slovenian earth. His final decisive letter to his son contained the following sentence: "Fate has raised our stock from peasant frontiersmen to Austrians. Let us remain such."

So it came about that Carl Joseph, Baron Trotta von Sipolje, found the southern frontiers inaccessible. He had only the choice between serving in the interior of Austria or on its eastern border. He chose a battalion of Jaeger stationed not more than two miles from the Russian frontier. Near it was the village of Burdlaki, Onufrij's home. This district was akin to the home of Ukrainian peasants, their melancholy concertinas and their unforgettable songs; it was the northern sister of Slovenia.

For seventeen hours Carl Joseph sat in the train. In the eighteenth there came into sight the last eastern railway station of the monarchy. Here he got out. His batman came with him. The Jaeger barracks stood at the center of the small town. Onufrij crossed himself three times before they entered the barrack square. It was morning. Spring, which had long since reached the inner provinces of the Empire, had only recently arrived here. The laburnum glowed on the arches of the railway viaduct. Violets flowered in the moist woods. Frogs croaked in the endless marshes. Storks circled above the low-thatched roofs of the village huts in search of old wheels to use as foundations for their summer nests.

At that time the borderland between Austria and Russia in the north-eastern corner was one of the most remarkable areas of the monarchy. Carl Joseph's Jaeger battalion garrisoned a town of ten thousand inhabitants. It lay around a wide circular market-place at whose center two main roads intersected, east to west, north to south. One led from the cemetery to the railway station, the other from the castle ruins to the steam mill. About a third of the town's ten thousand inhabitants were craftsmen of various kinds; another third lived in poverty off meager small holdings. The rest engaged in trade of a sort.

We call it "trade of a sort" since neither the goods nor the business methods corresponded in any way to the notions which the so-called civilized world has formed of trade. In these parts the tradesmen made their living far more by hazard than by design, more by the unpredictable grace of God than by any commercial reckonings in advance. Every trader was ready at any moment to seize on whatever floating merchandise heaven might throw in his way, or even to invent his goods if God had provided him with none. The livelihood of these traders was indeed a mystery. They displayed no shopfronts, they had no names. They had no credit. But they possessed a keen, miraculous sharp instinct for any remote and hidden sources of profit. Though they lived on other people's work, they created work for strangers. They were frugal. They lived as meanly as if they survived by the toil of their hands. And yet the toil was never theirs. Forever shifting, ever on the road, with glib tongues and clear, quick brains, they might have had possession of half the world if they had had any notion of the world. But they had none. They lived remote from it, wedged between East and West, cramped between day and night, themselves a species of living ghosts spawned by the night and haunting the day.

Cramped? The character of their native soil left them unconscious of it. Nature had forged endless horizons for these dwellers on the frontier, drawing around them a mighty circle of green forests and blue hills. When they walked in the twilight of pinewoods, they might even have felt themselves privileged by God, had their daily cares for the sustenance of wives and children left them time to perceive His goodness. But they entered their forests only to gather wood to trade with native shopkeepers as soon as winter drew near. For they also dealt in wood. They dealt in coral for the peasant girls of nearby villages and for those other peasants over the border, on Russian soil. They dealt in feathers for featherbeds, in tobacco, in horsehair, in bar silver, in jewelry, in Chinese tea, in fruit from the south, in cattle and horses, poultry and eggs, fish and vegetables, jute and wool, butter and cheese, woodlands and fields, Italian marble, human hair from China for making wigs, raw-silk and finished-silk merchandise, Manchester cotton and Brussels lace, galoshes from Moscow, Viennese linen, lead from Bohemia. No cheap bit of goods or splendid merchandise thrown up by the earth in profusion was unknown to the tradesmen of this district. What the law forbade them to come by and to sell, they would get one way or another in defiance of it—slick and secretive, adroitly prudent and bold. Some traded in live human flesh. They shipped off deserters from the Russian army to America and peasant girls to Brazil and Argentina. They had shipping agents and business connections with foreign brothels. Yet, with it all, their gains were meager, and they had no inkling of the vast superfluity in which a man may live. Their senses, so acutely edged for the sniffing out of petty gain, their hands which could strike gold from gravel like sparks from a flint, were not capable of bringing pleasure to their hearts or health to their bodies. The people in this district were swamp-begotten. For evil swamps lay far and wide to either side of the high-road and over the whole face of the land. Swamps that spawned frogs and fever, deceptive grass, dreadful enticements to a dreadful death for the unsuspecting stranger. Many had perished in the swamps with no one hearing their cries for help. But all who had been born here were familiar with the malignity of the marshland, and they themselves were tinged with this same malignity. In spring and summer, the air was thick with the deep and endless croaking of the frogs. Under the sky, equally jubilant larks rejoiced. It was an untiring dialogue between sky and marshland.

Many of these traders were Jews. A *lusus naturae*, perhaps a mysterious law obeyed by some secret branch of the legendary tribe of Khazars, determined that many among these frontier Jews were red-headed. The hair flamed from their heads.

Their beards were like torches. On the backs of their nimble hands wiry hairs bristled like minute spears. And delicate reddish wool burgeoned out of their ears, like fumes of the red fires which might be glowing in their heads.

A stranger who settled here was bound to degenerate in time. No one was as strong as the swamp. No one could hold out against the borderland. At this time gentlemen in high places in Vienna and St Petersburg were already beginning preparations for the Great War. The people at the frontier were conscious of its approach sooner than others, not only because they sensed the future out of habit, but because from day to day they observed omens of disaster. They turned these preparations to profit. Many lived by espionage and counterespionage, drew Austrian gulden from the Austrian police and Russian rubles from the Russian. The isolation and swampy boredom of the garrison sometimes drove an officer to despair, to gambling, to debt, and into the company of sinister men. The cemeteries of the frontier garrisons concealed many young corpses of weak men.

But here, as in every garrison in the monarchy, privates drilled. Every day the Jaeger battalion, bespattered with shiny mud, their boots gray with slime, turned back to barracks. Major Zoglauer rode at their head. Lieutenant Trotta was in charge of the first platoon of the second company. A long sober blast from the bugler set the pace for the marching Jaeger—not the proud fanfare which had pierced the clattering hoofs of the Uhlan horses, and had checked and surrounded them. Carl Joseph tramped along, persuading himself that he preferred it. Around him crunched the hobnail boots of the Jaeger, over sharp-edged gravel freshly strewn week after week in spring, by request of the military authorities, only to be sucked down by the swampy highroad. All the stones, millions of them, disappeared into the insatiable ground. And everywhere triumphant silver-gray shiny mud oozed up out of the depths, devouring mortar and gravel, slapping up around the stamping boots of the men.

The barracks stood behind the municipal park. Next to it on the left was the District Court, and facing it the official enclosure of the District Commissioner's office buildings. Behind those ornate but crumbling walls stood two churches, one Roman

Catholic, the other Greek Orthodox. To the right of the barracks stood the grammar school. The town was so small you could cross it in twenty minutes. The major buildings clustered together in irksome proximity. Like convicts in their prison yard, the townspeople exercised every evening round and round the unbroken ring of their park. It was a good half hour's walk to the station. The mess of the Jaeger officers was situated in two small rooms of a private house. Most preferred to eat in the station restaurant, including Carl Joseph. He was glad to tramp through the oozing slime if only to see a station. This was the last of all stations in the monarchy, but even so, it displayed two pairs of glittering lines stretching away without break into the heart of the monarchy. Like all the others, this station had shining signals of brightly colored glass, ringing with gentle messages from home; and there was a Morse keyboard ticking away incessantly on which the confused, delightful voices of a lost and distant world were hammered out, stitched as on some busy sewing machine.

This station, like all others, had its porter and this porter swung a clanging bell and the bell signified "All aboard, all aboard!" Once a day, at lunchtime, he went swinging his bell alongside a train on its way to Cracow, Oderberg, Vienna. A cozy, nice train. It stood there, almost the whole of lunch-time, just in front of the first-class refreshment-room windows, behind which the officers sat. Not until the coffee arrived did the engine whistle. Gray steam rolled against the windows. By the time it had begun to collect in drops and run down in streaks, the train had departed. They finished their coffee and went back in a slow, disconsolate group, through the silver slime. Even generals on tours of inspection took care not to come here. They did not come, nobody came. Only twice a year the one hotel in the town where most of the Jaeger officers were billeted was visited by rich hop merchants from Nuremberg and Prague and Saaz. When they had completed their incomprehensible deals, they hired a band and played cards in the only café, which belonged to the hotel.

Carl Joseph could see the whole town from his room on the second floor of the Hotel Brodnitzer. He could see the gable roofs of the District Court,

the little white tower of the District Commissioner's offices, the black-and-yellow flag over the barracks, the double cross of the Greek church, the weather-cock on the municipal building and all the slate-gray shingled roofs of the little, one-storied houses. The Hotel Brodnitzer was the tallest building in the area. It was as much a landmark as the church or the municipal and government buildings. The streets had no names and the little houses no numbers, so that anyone in search of a specific place had to find his way by vague description. So-and-so lived behind the church, so-and-so just opposite the jail. So-and-so somewhere to the right of the District Court. They lived like villagers. The secrets of the people in these low houses leaked out through chinks and rafters into the slimy streets and even into the ever-inaccessible barrack yard. So-and-so's wife had betrayed him, so-and-so had sold his daughter to a Russian cavalry captain; in this house they dealt in rotten eggs, the whole family over the way lived by contraband; so-and-so had been in jail, but the other had got off scot free. So-and-so lent officers money, and his neighbor collected a third of the pay. The officers, mainly middle class, of German parentage, had been stationed in this garrison for years. They were used to it and accepted the inevitable. Cut off from their homes and the German language, which here became merely an official language, exposed to the endless desolation of the swamps, they took up gambling and drank the fiery local brandy manufactured locally and sold under the label NINETY PERCENT. From the harmless mediocrity to which cadet schools and drill had educated them, they sank into the corruption of the area—already overcast by the vast breath of the hostile empire of the Tsars. They were scarcely fourteen kilometers out of Russia. Not infrequently Russian officers from the frontier garrison came across in their long pale-lemon and dove-gray army coats, with heavy gold and silver epaulettes on their broad shoulders, and shiny galoshes drawn over their shimmering top-boots in all weathers. Indeed, there was a certain amount of friendly exchange between the garrisons. Sometimes they would go in little canvas-roofed baggage carts across the frontier to watch the Cossacks display their horsemanship and drink the Russian brandy. Over there, in the Russian garrison, spirit casks stood on the edge of the wooden pavements, guarded by Russian privates with grounded rifles and long, triple-edged fixed bayonets. At dusk, these little casks rolled and bumped along uneven streets, kicked by Cossack boots to the Russian club, a soft slap and gurgle from inside betraying their contents to the townspeople. The officers of the Tsar showed the officers of His Apostolic Majesty what Russian hospitality really meant. And none of the Tsar's officers and none of His Apostolic Majesty's officers knew at that time how, above the goblets from which they drank, death was already crossing his haggard invisible hands.

In the open space between the two frontier woods, the sotnias of Cossacks galloped and wheeled like winds in military formation, uniformed winds on the swift little ponies of their native steppes, flourishing their lances above their tall fur caps like streaks of lightning on long wooden stems, coquettish blades with graceful pennons. On the soft swampy ground the clatter of hoofs was almost inaudible. The wet earth gave no more than a low sigh under the flying thud of their hoofs. The dark-green meadow grass scarcely bent beneath them. It was as though these Cossacks hovered above the plain. And when they crossed the dusty, coppery highway, there rose up a tall, bright-yellow, fine-grained sandstorm, glittering with sunlight, drifting wide, sinking to earth in myriad tiny clouds. The guests sat watching them from rough wooden stands. These riders' movements were almost quicker than the eyes of the watchers. The Cossacks ducked from their saddles to snatch blue and scarlet handkerchiefs off the ground in their strong tawny horse teeth, suddenly falling right under the bellies of their mounts in full gallop, their legs still pressing the flanks in glistening riding boots. Others flung their lances high in the air, and, far beyond them, the shafts glittered and twirled, to fall obediently back in the riders' hands, returning, as falcons might, to their masters. Others again, crouching down flat across their horses' backs, their mouths pressing the beasts' soft muzzles fraternally, jumped through iron hoops, astonishingly narrow, each just wide enough to girt a small beer keg. The horses stretched all four feet out from their bodies,

their manes soared like wings, their tails acting as rudders, their narrow heads like the slim bows of canoes skidding along. Another could jump his beast over twenty beer barrels set edge to edge. The horse whinnied before taking them. The rider came galloping from a distance; a gray speck, he grew in scorching speed to a streak. The body, the rider, became a huge, legendary bird, half-horse, half-man, a winged centaur, until at last, after the jump, he stood stock-still a hundred paces beyond the casks: a monument, a lifeless image. Others again fired at flying targets as they sped like arrows, themselves looking like arrows, targets which were held up to them on big white rounds by riders galloping away. The marksmen galloped, fired, and hit. Many tumbled to the earth. The men, coming from behind, sped gently across their bodies, no hoof touched them. There were riders with horses galloping beside them who could leap in full gallop from saddle to saddle, return to the first, suddenly tumble back into the second, until at last, with one band set on each horse, their legs dangling down between the galloping bodies, they pulled both up with a jerk at the given stopping place, reining them in to stand there motionless, like steeds in bronze.

Such displays of horsemanship were not the sole diversion provided by the outpost between the monarchy and Russia. A regiment of Dragoons was also stationed in the garrison. Between Jaeger officers, Dragoons and the gentlemen of the Russian regiment, Count Chojnicki established intimate relations. He was one of the wealthiest Polish landowners in the district.

Count Wojciech Chojnicki, a connection of the Ledochowskis and Potockis, a cousin of the Sternbergs, a friend of the Thuns, was a man of the world. Forty years old (though he might have been any age), a cavalry captain in the Reserve, a bachelor, he was frivolous and at the same time melancholy, a lover of horses, alcohol, society, both flippant and serious. He spent his winters in cities and in the gambling casinos of the Riviera. But he returned like a migrating bird to the home of his ancestors when the laburnum began to bloom on the railway bridges. He brought with him a faintly scented whiff of society and tales of gallantry and adventure. He was the kind of man who can have no enemies but no friends either; he had only associates, boon companions, or casual acquaintances. Chojnicki, with his pale, intelligent, rather prominent eyes, his shining baldness smooth as a pebble, his wisp of a yellow mustache, and his narrow shoulders, his thin, disproportionately long legs, could attract whomever he chose or whomever chance had set in his way.

He lived alternately in two houses, known to the townspeople and respected by them, as the old and the new Schloss. The so-called old Schloss was a huge dilapidated hunting lodge which, for mysterious reasons, the Count refused to put into repair. The new Schloss was a spacious, two-storey country house, the upper storey often filled with strange and sometimes rather shady-looking visitors. These were the Count's poor relations. The closest possible study of family history would never have enabled Count Chojnicki to trace the exact degrees of kinship of his guests. Gradually they had made it a habit to arrive and stay the summer at the new Schloss, as family pensioners and connections. Having rested and fed, sometimes clothed in new suits provided by the Count's local tailor, these guests departed when starlings twittered in the night and the time of cuckoo weed was approaching—back into the unknown regions from which they had come. The master of the house noticed neither their arrival, nor their presence, nor their departure. His Jewish steward had standing orders to examine their family credentials, regulate their habits, and get rid of them at the approach of winter. The house had two entrances. While the Count and any guest who was not a kinsman used the front door, the relations had to go the long way around, across the fruit garden and in by the little side door in its wall. Apart from this, these uninvited guests were free to do anything they pleased.

Twice a week, on Mondays and Thursdays, Count Chojnicki held his little evenings, and once a month he gave a party. On little evenings only six rooms were lit up, for the parties twelve. On little evenings the footmen wore drab yellow livery and no gloves. Parties meant white-gloved footmen in dark-brown coats with silver buttons and velvet facings. All occasions began with vermouth and dry Spanish wines from which the guests passed on to Burgundy and Bordeaux. Then it was time for the champagne, which was followed by cognac. An evening ended with a fitting tribute to local patriotism—namely the local product, Ninety Percent.

The officers of the ultrafeudal Dragoons and the chiefly middle-class Jaeger swore lifelong friendship with great emotion at Count Chojnicki's parties. Through the wide curved windows of the Schloss, summer dawns would witness a colorful confusion of infantry and cavalry uniforms. Toward five a.m. a swarm of despairing batmen came running to the Schloss to wake their masters; for regimental parades began at six. The host, in whom alcohol engendered no fatigue, had long since gone to his little hunting lodge. There he would fiddle about with weird test tubes, chemical apparatus, and minute flames. Local gossip had it that Chojnicki was trying to make gold. Indeed, it certainly looked as though he were occupied with some foolish experiment in alchemy. However, even if he failed to produce gold, he was certainly making money at roulette. Sometimes he would drop hints about infallible systems passed on to him by a deceased gambler.

For years he had been a deputy to the Reichsrat, always re-elected by his district, quelling any local opposition by money, influence, or sudden attack. He was the spoilt darling of every government and despised the parliament he served in. He had never made a speech nor asked a question. Unbelieving and contemptuous, fearless and without scruple, Chojnicki was in the habit of saying that the Emperor was a thoughtless old man, the government officials a set of fools, the Reichsrat a well-meaning assemblage of pathetic idiots, the Civil Service venal, cowardly, and indolent. German-Austrians were waltzing apes, Hungarians stank, Czechs were born lick-spittles, Ruthenians treacherous Russians in disguise, Croats and Slovenes, whom he always called Crovots and Schlaviners, were tinkers, peddlars, and sots. His own nation, the Poles, were snobs, hairdressers, and fashion-plate photographers.

After every return from Vienna, or any other part of that society in which he kicked his heels up so familiarly, the Count would give an ominous lecture, somewhat as follows:

"The monarchy is bound to end. The minute the Emperor is dead, we shall splinter into a hundred fragments. The Balkans will be more powerful than we are. Each nation will set up its own dirty little government, even the Jews will proclaim a king in Palestine. Vienna's begun to stink of the sweat of democrats—I can't stand the Ringstrasse any more. The workers all wave red flags and don't want to work any more. The mayor of Vienna is a pious shopkeeper. Even the parsons are going red, they've started preaching in Czech in the churches. At the Burgtheater all the performances are filthy Jewish plays. And every week another Hungarian water-closet manufacturer is made a baron. I tell you, gentlemen, if we don't start shooting pretty soon, it'll be the end. You just wait and see what's coming to us."

His listeners laughed and had another drink. They couldn't see what the fuss was all about. Now and again, of course, you did some shooting, at election times, for instance, to secure the safe return of Count Chojnicki, which proved that things were not being allowed to go to the dogs just like that. The Emperor was still alive. He would be followed by his successor. The army continued to drill, resplendent in every regulation hue. The people loved their dynasty and acclaimed it, in many different kinds of peasant costume. Chojnicki was a joker.

But Trotta was more sensitive than his comrades, sadder than they, his mind forever full of echoes, darkness, and the rustling wings of death he had already twice encountered. Lieutenant Trotta could sometimes feel the dismal force of these prophecies.

PART ELEVEN

John Constable, "The Cornfields"
This beautiful painting captures as a visual image what the written selections portray in words. Questions inevitably arise: is this picture accurate? Is it too idyllic? Should we yearn for the calm beauty of the past? Or does this image conceal the poverty, inequality, and ignorance of the past?

Europe's Landscapes: Rural, Town, and City

Throughout the nineteenth century, millions of rural dwellers moved to cities and adopted new ways. The rhythms and traditions of village life, as portrayed in "The Cornfields" (1826) by John Constable (1776–1837), faded among city people and seemed poised to pass away. In *Years of Childhood* (1856), Sergei Aksakov (1791–1859) recalled life on his Russian noble family's serf estates. His memoir evoked a way of life that endured in parts of Europe into the twentieth century. Settled life had only just conquered nature in Europe's uttermost eastern peripheries, to which Aksakov's grandfather had escaped the pettiness of social life. The memoirs of Savva Purlevskii (1800–1868) provide a rare picture of the experiences of an escaped serf who became a prosperous businessman. Here he describes the serf village of his youth. The novels of Thomas Hardy (1840–1928), such as *The Mayor of Casterbridge* (1886), trace their characters' life trajectories from agriculture through artisanry and petty commerce toward prosperity. A fall from grace into tragedy always threatens. In *Reeds in the Wind* (1913), Nobel prize-winning author, Grazia Deledda (1871–1936), depicts the timeless mores of Italian Sardinia. Both religious and superstitious in outlook, the peasants confront incomprehensible social and economic change. The Report on Sanitary Conditions (1842) sheds a stark light on how people lived when they moved to industrial areas. The selection from the novel *Effi Briest* (1895) by Theodor Fontane (1819–1898) suggests the advantages of city life, in this case modernizing Berlin, for those not in poverty. The novel also shows the continued plight of middle-class and elite women, a topic of concern in a later section. Kaleidoscopic rural, town, and urban scenes form the backdrop for the lives portrayed in these sources, as for those of Eliot's *Middlemarch*, Roth's *Radetzky March* (in an earlier section), and others of this text's sources.

Europe's landscapes were filled with such scenes, as the changes in people's lives paralleled transfigurations of the physical world—from golden fields, wooded expanses, and picturesque dwellings to drab crowded cities whose "satanic" mills poisoned air and water. Europe's cities had prosperous and elegant sections, always adjacent, however, to working class quarters. Chadwick's Report on Sanitary Conditions (1842) reminds us of modern European cities' shortcomings. Only toward century's end did public services begin to overcome the problems of inadequate water supplies, sewerage systems, waste collection, and lighting. Regardless, villagers entered the cities in droves and led lives their grandparents might have envied. In the end, not much remained of pristine early nineteenth-century Europe.

Study Questions

1. What awareness of the industrial revolution do these readings reveal?
2. In light of these readings, how would one compare or contrast the lives of the rural and urban poor?
3. What does Hardy's novel tell us about women's status in mid-nineteenth Europe?
4. How do Deledda's peasants suggest a premodern world?
5. Why do Chadwick's Report and *Effi Briest* provide such contrasting views of town and city life?
6. Is Constable's painting of country life idealistic or realistic?

Years of Childhood

Sergei Aksakov

The noble Aksakov family became prominent in nineteenth-century Russia as writers and as participants in the movement known as Slavophilism that emphasized Russia's past and culture. In this selection, Sergei Aksakov recalls life on his family's Urals estates early in the nineteenth century. Among his recollections are his grandfather's surprisingly positive outlooks on the peasant serfs on his estates.

Parashino

From level upper country the road suddenly ran downhill, and at last there before us, lying in a hollow, lay revealed the prosperous village of Parashino, with its stone church and a small mere where the spring waters had cut their channel. The manor farmyard with its rows of stacks of corn was just like a little town, and there were quite a number of stacks of last year's corn to be seen even in the peasants' own yards.

My father was delighted to see such quantities of corn. "There's peasants indeed!" he cried. "Those are the peasants for you! A delight to the heart!" I shared his pleasure, though it again struck me that my mother was quite indifferent to what he had just said.

At last we entered the village. At that very moment the priest was just setting out from the church to bless the waters of Jordan. He was in full canonicals, bearing the cross on his head, while in front of him processed the deacon with his censer and the icons and banners. A huge crowd of people followed. We at once reined in our carriage and got out to join the congregation. Mother held my hand, and Nurse carried my little sister, who stared at this sight, something she had never seen before, with unusual interest, and although I for my part had had the opportunity of seeing the like in Ufa, I nonetheless also watched most excitedly.

When the blessing of the waters was over, we all in turn kissed the cross and were aspersed with holy water; the priest then congratulated us on our safe arrival at journey's end, and we at last entered Parashino manor courtyard, which was only just across the road from the church. The folk crowded close around us, all of them as happy and pleased to see us as the peasants in the harvest fields had been. A group of senior men pressed their way forward, bowing and greeting us most cordially. The leader among them was a short-statured, broad-shouldered, elderly peasant with grizzled hair and eyes so unusual that I felt quite frightened when he looked hard at me. The concourse of peasants now conducted us to the porch of the manor guest house, when they dispersed, while this peasant with the unusual eyes ran up the steps, unlocked the door, and invited us to step inside, constantly assuring my parents how cordially welcome they were and addressing them as "little Father" and "little Mother" Alexey Stepanych and Sofia Nikolavna.

We stepped indoors. Everything seemed to have been got ready specially for our coming. But later I learned that my great-aunt's principal steward and manager regularly put up there whenever he happened to come to Parashino. My parents spoke rather familiarly of him as "Mikhailushka," but everybody else always referred to him with great respect as "Mikhail Maksimych"—anyway, he proved to be the real reason why the guest apartments at Parashino were always ready.

From something my father said I now guessed that the short-statured peasant with the terrible eyes

From: Sergei Aksakov, *Years of Childhood* (New York: Vintage Books, 1960), pp. 39–52.

was none other than the man they called Mironych
about whom I had made inquiries while we were still
in our carriage. Father was now inquiring of him
about all aspects of the farm management. At last,
dismissing him, Father said he would send for him
when he needed him, and told Mironych to send to
him a number of the older men, whom he indicated
by name. Small though I was, it struck me then that
Father's instructions were not much to Mironych's
liking. He said "Very well, sir" in such a way that I
can hear him to this very moment, and the words
really meant: "That's not at all the thing to do."

When Mironych had gone, I heard a conversation between my parents which absolutely flabbergasted me. Mother said that this man Mironych
must be a rogue, and Father just grinned and said it
did look rather like it: he had heard a lot of bad
things about the man previously, but Mironych was
a kinsman and pet of Mikhailushka's, and Aunt
Praskovia trusted Mikhailushka implicitly. Father
explained that he had given orders for elder men of
the Bagrovo peasants to be sent to him—men who
would tell him the full truth, knowing that he would
not betray their trust—and that this had not suited
Mironych's book at all. Father added that after dinner he thought he would drive around and have a
look at all the field work. He asked Mother if she
would go with him, but she said flatly she would
not, she could not bear the sight of it all, but if he
liked, he could take the boy. I was overjoyed, and
asked if I might go, and my Father readily consented. "Yes," he said, "and what's more, when
we've had a cup of tea, Sergey and I'll walk around
and have a look at the stables. From there we can go
round by the springs and the mill."

I need not say how welcome this additional sugges-
tion was to me, and what was still better was that my
mother agreed. We drank our tea; then we set out for
the stable yard, which was at the far end of the grass-
grown Parashino courtyard. At the stable doors we
were met by the chief horseman, Grigori Kovliaga,
waiting for us, together with the other stable men. At
first glance I liked Kovliaga very much; he was very
nice to me, too. But before we had had time even to go
inside the stables, there was that loathsome Mironych,
and from then on he did not leave my father all day.

Through the big doorway we entered a funny,
long building. There were passages down each side

of it, and off these, to left and right, between partitions, were huge, grown-up, fat horses. And in some
of these partitions there were also young horses, still
nice and slender. At this point I learned that the par-
titioned-off spaces were called "boxes." On the wall,
facing the entrance, there was an icon, and Kovliaga
told me this was "Nicholas the Miracle-performer."

When he had inspected both sides of the stables
and praised their cleanliness, my father went out into
the yard again and had some of the horses led out. It
was Kovliaga who did this, with the help of another
stable man. Well foddered and well rested, the proud
creatures reared on their hind legs and whinnied, lifting the two stable men up into the air, so they just
hung from their necks, their right hands holding fast
to the bridle. I was scared and pressed close to my
father, but when they made some of those glorious
horses run and jump at the end of a long rope that,
digging their heels into the ground and scarcely able to
manage, the stable man held, I loved watching them.

Mironych put his spoke in everywhere, and I was
very annoyed when familiarly and without any
respect instead of "Grigori Kovliaga" he called him
"Grishka Kovlazhenok," whereas Father called him
quite properly: Grigori. "And where do you turn
the horses out to pasture?" Father asked Grigori,
but it was Mironych who answered and said one
herd went out to "Koshelga" [the "Punnet"] and
the other to "Kamenni Vrag" ["Stony Hollow"],
and added: "But, perhaps, Batiushka Alexey Stepanych, you would like me to send 'em out to the fallow land—we mean to have the dedication service
tomorrow and start sowing—that won't be so far,
then we can have a look at the manor rye and
spring-wheat crops." Father said: "Very well."

From the stable yard we went to the springs. My
father was very fond of any sort of waters, but especially natural spring waters, while I could not even
see water running in the gutters in the street without
excitement, so the magnificent Parashino springs, of
which there were more than twenty, enraptured me.
Some of the springs were very powerful indeed,
breaking out of the hillside halfway up, others came
bubbling out at the foot of the hill, and those which
were up the slope were fenced in with piles and
roofed over, with troughs of limewood set in these
huts, and the troughs were full of water so clear that
they looked quite empty, the troughs were brimful,

with the water streaming over and down the sides like glass curtains.

I saw the peasant women bringing their buckets, saw how they tapped out the wooden plug at the end of the trough and put their buckets under the stream of water, which shot out in a big curve, because the end of the trough was high above the ground, as it stood on big stone blocks (the sides of the ravine consisted of nothing but natural blocks of stone). A bucket was full in a minute; then the other was filled. The water from all the springs flowed down into the mill pool. There were a lot of springs which were not built over, but they too all flowed to the mere in little brooks, over a shingly bed, and in these, Father and I found ever so many lovely stones, just as if polished. They were quite round and rather long, so they were like sugar leaves. They were called "devil's fingers." This was the first time I had ever seen any. I found them wonderful things and stuffed my pockets full, only Father could not give me any explanation of the name, and I plagued him with questions for a long time as to what sort of an animal a devil was to have such strong fingers.

Still full of new and pleasant impressions, now I suddenly passed on to new ones that, though not quite so pleasing, were nonetheless very interesting ones; my father took me to the mill, a thing about which I had no notion whatsoever. A mill pond was fed by the springs, and it was rather deep. The perpendicular-walled channel that the waters had cut was fenced across by a broad wall, which could be moved, and dammed it. In the center of it was a little wooden house, and in this mill there was the milling machinery, which only ground well at high water, though this, as my father explained to me, was not because there was not much water in the mere, but because the dam was all leaks.

This wretched little mill seemed to me to be a miracle of human artifice. The first thing I looked at was the stream of water which poured out of the sluice funnel on to the water wheel, which had become quite green from wetness and turned rather slowly with a lot of splashing and foaming, while with the noise of the water mingled some other humming and hissing. Then my father pointed out the wooden hopper, which was the box, broad at the top and narrower at the bottom (as I saw later), into which the wheat was poured. Then we went

downstairs, and I could see the mill stone turning and above it the hopper shaking away, out of which the grains of wheat poured under the stone. This had a wooden rim all around it, and it kept on turning and grinding the grains and turning them into flour, which poured out underneath onto a sort of wooden shovel. When I peeped in sideways, I could see another wheel, which was called the "dry wheel." This turned a lot faster than the bobbin wheel and kept catching at the trundle head with a sort of hands, so that it turned the stone that was fastened to it.

The mill house was full of flour dust and all a-quiver and sometimes it simply hopped up into the air. For a long time I was absolutely astounded, gazing at these wonderful things and remembering having seen something like it in children's toys. We spent a very long time in the mill, where there was an old man who was very feeble and bent, whom they called the "tipper-in"; he was all gray and tottering, and he was milling all the tailings for feeding the master's horses, he said. He was absolutely white from flour dust. I would have asked him all sorts of questions, but when I saw how often he coughed till he could not get his breath back, I felt very sorry for him, and I put all the rest of my questions to my father, but here, too, the loathsome Mironych would keep putting his word in, although I would rather not have heard a thing he said.

When we came out of the mill, I saw that we, too, were white with flour dust, though not as white as the tipper-in. I at once turned to ask my father to have the old man put to bed and given hot tea to drink. My father smiled, then, turning to Mironych, said: "Old Vassily Terentiev, the tipper-in, is frightfully old and ailing, isn't he? That cough has quite got him down, and the tail-wheat dust is no good for him. He ought to be retired from old man's work and not made to keep on being tipper-in." "It shall be as you wish, sir," was Mironych's response. "Only won't other old men be envious? If we retire him, then we ought to retire the others, too. There are a lot of men who don't earn their keep and idlers, you know. Who'll take on the old-man jobs?" My father's reply was that not all the old men were as tottery—besides, ailing people should be looked after and given peace; they had already done enough work in their lifetimes. "Don't you forget that you yourself will soon be getting on in years," my father said, "you too will not earn your keep, and when that time comes, you will want to have rest." Mironych's reply was: "Very well, sir, your orders shall be carried out, though this Vassily Terentiev of yours does not deserve kindly treatment. His grandson is a young rebel: only the other day he threatened to slit my throat." To this my father replied with a vigor and a tone of voice which I had never once heard from him before: "So you'd punish the old man for his grandson's faults, eh? Well, now you just tackle the man who's to blame, will you!" Mironych was quick to agree. "Don't you fear, Batiushka Alexey Stepanych, it shall all be exactly as you say."

Why, I do not know, but I began to feel shivery inside. Seeing that we had paused, Vassily Terentiev, who had meant to follow us, so now heard what was said, stood rooted to the spot, trembling all over and never stopping bowing. Even when we had got to the top of the hill and I looked back, the old man was still standing there, bowing to the ground.

As soon as we reached our apartments, I forgot all about the springs and the mill, but lost no time in telling my mother about the old man. Mother was very moved by my story, and if she had had her way, she would have sent for Mironych at once and dressed him down and suspended him from his duties, while she hurried to write and tell Aunt Praskovia all about it. . . . Indeed, my father had no easy task restraining her from such hasty action.

There followed a lengthy discussion—indeed, a dispute. There was a lot I did not understand and much that I have forgotten; all indeed that I recall clearly is my father saying: "My dear, don't meddle in what does not concern you, you'll spoil it all, you will be the ruin of the whole family. Now, Mironych will never touch them, he will be bound to be afraid lest I write to Auntie, though if it came to a plain demand for his dismissal, Mikhailushka would never let the man go, and then I would not be able to show my face at Parashino, and nothing at all would have been achieved, except, indeed, annoying Aunt Praskovia." My mother argued back a while, but in the end gave way.

Heavens! What a mish-mash of notions there was now in my mind! What was it that this poor, dear, ailing old man was made to suffer for? And what exactly was this nasty Mironych? What sorts of powers were Mikhailushka and Father's Aunt Praskovia? Why exactly would Father not let Mother dismiss Mironych at once? For did this not mean that my father could have done so? Then why did he not do so? For Father was kind, was he not?—he was never angry. These were the questions that seethed in my mind then. The solution I found for myself was that Mikhailushka and Grandmother Praskovia Kurolessov were bad people, and my father was afraid of them.

The "devil's fingers" I gave away to my darling sister, she had missed me so much. We added our new treasure to the precious things we already possessed—our "billets" and those stones that came from the river Bielaia, which I always called "ores" (I had adopted this word from old Anichkov). With enthusiasm I told my dear sister about all I had seen. I always kept her informed about everything that happened to me without her. But it began to dawn on me that my little sister did not always understand, so I now began to adopt the language Nurse used and talk in a tongue that a little child could really understand.

After dinner Father and I set off for the fields in a long, low farm wagon. The loathsome Mironych also came with us. This was the first time in my life I had ridden on *rospuski*, as they called the cart, and I liked it very much indeed. Sitting on a felt rug folded in four, I swayed about just as if I were in a cradle slung on the whippy branch of a tree. In the ruts of the road over the steppe this wagon went down so low that the tall-growing grass and flowers whipped at my legs and my arms, and I found that very great fun. I even managed to pick some wild flowers. But it struck me that grown-ups found sitting like that uncomfortable because they could not let their feet down, but had to keep pulling them in and holding them in the air, so they did not touch the ground, whereas I could go on sitting with my legs almost full length, yet the grass only reached to my shoes.

When we drove between the wheat fields up the broad headlands overgrown with sour cherry trees with their reddish fruit and dwarf almonds with fruits that were still green, I begged Father to stop a moment, and with my own hands gathered a whole handful of those wild morellos. They were tiny and hard, like large peas. Father would not let me eat them. He said they were sour because they were not ripe; as for the fruit of the wild peach, which the peasants call *bobovnik,* I gathered a whole pocketful of these. I was also going to stuff my other pocket, to take my darling mother some, but Father said: "Your mother won't care about that rubbish," they would squash in my pocket, and I had better throw them away. I was sorry to part from them so quickly, and held them in my hand a long time, but at last I was obliged to throw them away, though I remember neither how nor when.

Wherever the rye had not drooped—was not laid, as one says—it was so tall that we and our wagon and the horses were quite hidden from view, and this new sight also delighted me very much. We drove for a long time along headlands, then a strange faraway sound, mixed with men's voices, began to be audible. The nearer we came to it, the more audible it became, till at last through the unreaped rye we began to get glimpses of the glint of sickles and of handfuls of bunched ears of the cut-off rye swept up into the air by unseen hands. Soon the shoulders and backs of peasant men and women bending double could be seen.

The moment we drove out on to the *desiatina* [*2.7 acre strip*] on which about ten men were working, their talk at once ceased and the rasp of the sickle blades through the straw also increased and filled the whole field with those sounds that were unusual and that I had never heard before. We drew up and got down out of the wagon and walked across toward the reapers, men and women, and in a kindly sort of voice my father cried: "God aid ye all!"

At once they all left their work, turned to face us, and bowed very low, while some of the men, those who were older, greeted my father and me. Real delight was to be read on their sun-tanned faces. Some of them were breathing hard, others had their bare feet and their fingers bandaged with dirty rags, but they were all cheerful. My father asked how many men worked on a *desiatina*, if they found the work hard, and for answer got the statement: "'Tis a bit hard-like, but how can you help it? 'Tis powerful rye, but we'll manage by nightfall." Father said: "Then carry on, and God be wi' ye!" In

a moment the sickles all flashed, handfuls of rye flashed over the workers' heads, and the sound of cutting through the tough straw was louder and spread more vigorously over the whole field. I stood lost in wonder.

All at once the whimpering of a baby attracted my attention, and then I saw that in various places cradles were dangling from three sticks planted in the ground and tied together at the top. A young woman now stuck her sickle in the sheaf she had just tied, unhurriedly went to her baby, who was crying, took him in her arms, sat down under a stook, and, kissing and fondling him, gave the babe her breast. The babe was soon soothed and fell asleep, when his mother put him in the cradle, took up her sickle, and set to work reaping with extra vigor, so as to catch up with the other women and not be left behind them.

Father had been talking to Mironych, and I had had time to take a good look at everything all about me. My heart was seized with an inexpressible sense of sympathy for these people working at such strain under the scorching sun, and many a time after that, when I found myself in the harvest field, I would recall that first impression.

From this *desiatina* we drove on to another, then yet another, and still another. At first we would get out of the wagon and go over to the reapers, but afterward we would merely drive up close to them and halt a while. Father would say: "God aid ye!" It was the same performance everywhere, the same bows, the same kindly, delighted faces, and the same simple words of thanks to their "dear master Alexey Stepanych." It was impossible to make a stop everywhere. There would not have been enough time. We drove through all the spring wheat fields that were also beginning to ripen, about which my father and Mironych talked with alarm, as they did not know where to find the labor or how they were to get the corn in. "There you have the trouble, and a real trouble it is, Master," said the chief foreman. "The rye ripened late and now, as you see, here's the spring wheat's coming on, even the late oats are coming into the picture, and it's already time to start sowings. Yesterday Providence granted a shower big enough to break the crust, now the soil's nice and moist, so tomorrow I'm going to get 'em all on to sowing. So you can just see for yourself, can't you—we're not going to get a lot harvested with only the womenfolk, yet there's half the rye still unreaped. I wondered if you wouldn't think of ordering them all to turn out on a free day?"

My father replied that Mironych ought to know well enough that the folk needed to get in their own corn, too, and it was not at all right to take a day of their own time in the height of August heat—far better to have a round robin for labor and call on the neighboring estates to help out. The foreman was beginning to spread word about how any neighbors they had were a long distance away and not very used to the idea of helping out, but at this point we had reached the pea fields and the poppy fields, and these took our attention.

Father told Mironych to break off a few poppy heads, which were still quite green, and pluck out a handful of peas, root and all, with their young stalks and fresh green, still unplimped pods. All this he gave into my care, and even let me eat one pod, and the flat little peas seemed very sweet and tasty to me. At any other time this would have occupied my attention more strongly, but just now it was the rye fields with all the reapers, men and women, which occupied my imagination, and I just held those dozen poppy heads with their slender stems and the handful of green peas in my hand and did not take much interest in them.

On the way back we went around by the fallow lands. They were overgrown with green sow-thistle and goat's beard, about which my father remarked to Mironych, but he made the excuse that these fields were so far out that there was no possibility of pasturing either the manor or the peasants' herds on them, and he made out that the peasants' plows would cut under all those weeds and they wouldn't "belch" any more—that is, would not spring up again. In spite of all this talk, my father was not particularly pleased with the fallows. He said the feed was very poor in places and the furrows were far apart and that was why there was such a lot of weed growth.

The sun was sinking now, and we hardly had time at all to inspect the two herds of the manor horses, which had been specially turned out close to the fallow lands. One consisted of a great number of fillies

and mares of all ages and of mares with foals, and these to some extent took my mind off the harvest fields and cheered me up with their prancing and nuzzling their mothers. The other herd, to which we were told we should be very cautious about going near, only my father looked at, walking across to it with the herdsmen. In it were a number of unbroken, bad-tempered horses, which were liable to attack strangers. It was getting quite dark when we got back, and Mother was beginning to get alarmed and regret having let me go. It was quite true; I was far too tired, and fell asleep without even waiting for tea.

I got up rather late because nobody awakened me, and then saw that there was a great deal of excitement going on all around, a lot of fuss and packing. A great many peasants had come to see Father, with all sorts of requests, things Mironych could not take it on himself to do—so he said—or, most likely, things he did not want to do. All this I found out afterward, from the discussions between Father and Mother. However, my father would not assume any authority at all, and his answer to them all was that his aunt had told him only to inspect the estate and report to her about everything, but she had not told him to interfere in any arrangements made by the steward.

All the same, when he had Mironych alone, I did hear Father say that Mironych might do so-and-so for such-and-such a peasant, and something else for another. To any such observation the steward's usual reply was: "Yes, sir, it shall be done," although my father would repeat several times: "My dear man, I am not giving any orders, I am only asking you if you don't think yourself that that is what should be done. But I shall make a point of it to my aunt that I have given no instructions, so don't you refer her back to me about anything."

Still more peasant women came to see my mother than peasants came to see Father. Some of them had requests about poll tax that was due, others about all sorts of ailments. Mother would not even listen to the healthy women's tales, but she did give the ailing ones her advice and even some medicines out of her traveling medicine chest. The evening before, while I was asleep, my father had had a meeting with the older men whom he had had sent to him, and clearly they had not had anything particularly bad to say about Mironych, because Father was nicer to him than he had been yesterday and even praised him for his good work.

The priest and his wife also came to bid us farewell and they, too, spoke well of Mironych. One of the things that the priest said was that the steward was a yes-man, he did whatever he was told to do, and, with a smile, the priest added that it was only God who was faultless; the only thing he himself regretted was that Mironych had so many kinsfolk in the village and favored them. I did not understand at all what that could mean—indeed, it seemed to me that the more kinsfolk Mironych had and the more he favored them, the better.

Why our packing took so long I do not know, but we did not start out till about midday. Mironych and some of the older men, with a crowd of peasant boys and girls, accompanied us to the boundary. We now had forty-five versts to go, to spend a night on the river "Ik," which, so my father said, was at least as good as the Djoma and full of fish, so pleasant thoughts stirred again in my head.

— READING 49 —

A Life Under Russian Serfdom

Savva Purlevskii

Born into a serf family in central Russia, where nonagricultural pursuits such as weaving had already supplanted farming, Savva Purlevskii provides the other side of the picture to Aksakov's recollections. Of interest is that Purlevskii does not exaggerate the peasants' good qualities or the nobles' bad ones. Everyone is evaluated objectively. Purlevskii also reminds us that not all peasants supported themselves by agriculture.

Around this time our communal management became more and more chaotic. The peasants' complaints about the bailiff annoyed the landlords to such a degree that they finally ordered the estate management office to appoint me as a bailiff. I was to take charge of all forthcoming communal affairs and to ask the former bailiff for detailed reports about all previous activities in village life.

Although this prestigious assignment certainly pleased my self-esteem, it hardly made me happy. Indeed, it scared me, because I had no experience in village governance. In light of my objective view of this matter, I repeatedly implored the landlords to spare me from the new responsibility they had imposed on me. They disagreed and kindly confirmed my appointment. They suggested that I find a responsible knowledgeable assistant so that I could sustain my own commercial activity without restraint.

This solution soothed my concerns and allowed me to undertake the new tasks in addition to my existing ones. I began to dig into communal matters. When I studied the commune's outstanding affairs, various abuses came to the surface. They were so serious that the former bailiff even voluntarily returned some of the communal money he had spent. To my misfortune, under the cover of submissiveness to his lot he became very hostile

toward me, which I noticed but to which I hardly paid any attention. For my part, I tried to finish the initial inspection in a quite lenient, everyday way without spreading gossip or initiating any scandals.

Having finished with the outstanding business, I moved on to establish my own routine. Although I had become a public person without any desire on my part, I still faced the task of dealing with communal needs in a fair way. For instance, I was one of the first to notice that our important commercial village did not even have a school. Nobody had ever taken care of this.

I immediately told the commune that we needed a school and it enthusiastically supported my opinion. I drew up a plan. Of course, the landlords' agreement was needed. They did not put any objections and indeed commissioned me to take care of all educational matters.

Everything was approved! The archpriest of our church became the theology teacher. The local authorities sent a teacher to our staff to teach grammar, calculus and orthography. . . . By the day of the grand opening, seventy boys who wished to study had come forward. During the first year, this number increased to one hundred. On the exams, in the presence of the principal, many pupils did excellently. In general, all were able to read and write, whereas in my childhood a boy, even a gifted one, having spent the same amount of time with a priest, could merely mumble the syllables of the Psalter. Even then, he would mostly rely on memory, what I had experienced myself.

From: Savva Purlevskii, "Memoirs of a Serf, 1800–1868," *Russkii Vestnik* 130 (July 1877), 321–347, translated by Boris Gorshkov.

Because this success appealed to me so much, I decided to suggest a trade school in addition to our regular school. This was necessary in Velikoe because we never engaged in agriculture but already for generations dealt in trade and commerce. Unfortunately, I had no success with this idea. The landlords refused to donate five thousand rubles in cash and the village communal assembly denied approval and even openly resisted my intention, viewing it as a king of corvee. . . .

Then I noticed that the area of our residence, which already had three thousand souls of both sexes, did not have any local medical facility. Ill people could have the benefit of only occasional visits by a district physician and even that was only for the prosperous in exceptional cases. All others either perished without medical care, or resorted to a quack-woman's drugs. I was very upset with this situation. However, I did not dare to suggest my idea to the village commune, because I knew about their deeply rooted superstitions. Instead, I presented the idea directly to the landlords.

They approved it immediately and, in addition, themselves arranged for the arrival of a physician in private practice by the name of Mikhail Loginovich. They set doctor's salary, which they agreed to fund, and made arrangements for an appropriate living place, servants, and firewood. This kind man rendered us great service or one might even say goodness. He set up a small village pharmacy and taught several boys pharmaceutics and nursing arts—all that, thanks to the landlords, without the slightest burden to the commune. The commune, after a while, realized the usefulness of what had been done and appreciated our doctor, who also valued the simple openness of our peasants. I was very pleased by this mutual respect. Mikhail Loginovich was always an admired guest in my house.

Finally, the idea of improving our cottage industry and village crafts occurred to me. All commerce and trades must be carried out on the basis of clear honesty. In truth, one needs to have patience to make commerce fair; but in return, when your reputation for fairness has reinforced your business reputation, everyone will gladly do business with you and even allow your trade to predominate with them. Besides honesty, trade must not confine itself to old-fashioned production methods, but must follow the needs of the times. Profit should come not from the use of cheap, low-quality or spurious materials for the manufacturing of goods but from skillful mastery and the durability of the products.

Now I need to reiterate what I have already said in part. From time immemorial, in my motherland, in Velikoe, females developed high skills in producing fine linen cloth, which was famous everywhere for its quality. This women's labor was fully rewarded until foreign technical innovations developed cheaper and improved modes of production. In the face of competition, our women now should have taken advantage of previous profits to develop new methods. But instead of doing everything they could to readjust their work to the new conditions, they tried to serve their self-interest by adding cotton threads in the weft. At first they gained big profits from doing this way because even a skilled dealer could not notice the fraud.

But, of course, the admixture became clear during the product's use. We began to lose our reputation for fine linen cloth to such an extent that people stopped buying it! Therefore, I made a plan and suggested to the commune that it forbid this evil fraud. At first, no one seemed to understand me; they could not figure where their real advantage lay. I brought my concerns to the consideration of the village's chief management. They not only paid no attention to the issue, but returned my papers to me with a reprimand and prohibited me in the future to bother them with "ideas of this kind that can disturb the collection of rent. . . ."

The Mayor of Casterbridge

Thomas Hardy

Susan Henchard and her daughter return to the Casterbridge area after many years abroad. Elizabeth-Jane believes her father died in her infancy, whereas in reality, in a fit of drunkenness, he had literally sold wife and infant daughter to the highest bidder at a fair. To Susan's surprise, her husband, a completely reformed character and prosperous businessman in the wheat trade, is mayor of Casterbridge.

Henchard's wife acted for the best, but she had involved herself in difficulties. A hundred times she had been upon the point of telling her daughter Elizabeth-Jane the true story of her life, the tragical crisis of which had been the transaction at Weydon Fair, when she was not much older than the girl now beside her. But she had refrained. An innocent maiden had thus grown up in the belief that the relations between the genial sailor and her mother were the ordinary ones that they had always appeared to be. The risk of endangering a child's strong affection by disturbing ideas which had grown with her growth was to Mrs. Henchard too fearful a thing to contemplate. It had seemed, indeed, folly to think of making Elizabeth-Jane wise.

But Susan Henchard's fear of losing her dearly loved daughter's heart by a revelation had little to do with any sense of wrong-doing on her own part. Her simplicity—the original ground of Henchard's contempt for her—had allowed her to live on in the conviction that Newson had acquired a morally real and justifiable right to her by his purchase—though the exact bearings and legal limits of that right were vague. It may seem strange to sophisticated minds that a sane young matron could believe in the seriousness of such a transfer, and were there not numerous other instances of the same belief the thing might scarcely be credited. But she was by no means the first or last peasant woman who had religiously adhered to her purchaser, as too many rural records show.

The history of Susan Henchard's adventures in the interim can be told in two or three sentences. Absolutely helpless she had been taken off to Canada, where they had lived several years without any great worldly success, though she worked as hard as any woman could to keep their cottage cheerful and well-provided. When Elizabeth-Jane was about twelve years old the three returned to England and settled at Falmouth, where Newson made a living for a few years as boatman and general handy shoreman.

He then engaged in the Newfoundland trade, and it was during this period that Susan had an awakening. A friend to whom she confided her history ridiculed her grave acceptance of her position; and all was over with her peace of mind. When Newson came home at the end of one winter he saw that the delusion he had so carefully sustained had vanished for ever.

There was then a time of sadness, in which she told him her doubts if she could live with him longer. Newson left home again on the Newfoundland trade when the season came round. The vague news of his loss at sea a little later on solved a problem which had become torture to her meek conscience. She saw him no more.

Of Henchard they heard nothing. To the liege subjects of Labour, the England of those days was a continent, and a mile a geographical degree.

From: Thomas Hardy, *The Mayor of Casterbridge* (New York: Signet, 1984), pp. 32–38.

Elizabeth-Jane developed early into womanliness. One day, a month or so after receiving intelligence of Newson's death off the Bank of Newfoundland, when the girl was about eighteen, she was sitting on a willow chair in the cottage they still occupied, working twine nets for the fishermen. Her mother was in a back corner of the same room, engaged in the same labour; and dropping the heavy wood needle she was filling she surveyed her daughter thoughtfully. The sun shone in at the door upon the young woman's head and hair, which was worn loose, so that the rays streamed into its depths as into a hazel copse. Her face, though somewhat wan and incomplete, possessed the raw materials of beauty in a promising degree. There was an under-handsomeness in it, struggling to reveal itself through the provisional curves of immaturity, and the casual disfigurements that resulted from the straitened circumstances of their lives. She was handsome in the bone, hardly as yet handsome in the flesh. She possibly might never be fully handsome, unless the carking accidents of her daily existence could be evaded before the mobile parts of her countenance had settled to their final mould.

The sight of the girl made her mother sad—not vaguely, but by logical inference. They both were still in that strait-waistcoat of poverty from which she had tried so many times to be delivered for the girl's sake. The woman had long perceived how zealously and constantly the young mind of her companion was struggling for enlargement; and yet now, in her eighteenth year, it still remained but little unfolded. The desire—sober and repressed—of Elizabeth-Jane's heart was indeed to see, to hear, and to understand. How could she become a woman of wider knowledge, higher repute—"better," as she termed it—this was her constant inquiry of her mother. She sought further into things than other girls in her position ever did, and her mother groaned as she felt she could not aid in the search.

The sailor, drowned or no, was probably now lost to them; and Susan's staunch, religious adherence to him as her husband in principle, till her views had been disturbed by enlightenment, was demanded no more. She asked herself whether the present moment, now that she was a free woman again, were not as opportune a one as she would find in a world where anything had been so inopportune, for making a desperate effort to advance Elizabeth. To pocket her pride and search for the first husband seemed, wisely or not, the best initiatory step. He had possibly drunk himself into his tomb. But he might, on the other hand, have had too much sense to do so; for in her time with him he had been given to bouts only, and was not a habitual drunkard.

At any rate, the propriety of returning to him, if he lived, was unquestionable. The awkwardness of searching for him lay in enlightening Elizabeth, a proceeding which her mother could not endure to contemplate. She finally resolved to undertake the search without confiding to the girl her former relations with Henchard, leaving it to him if they found him to take what steps he might choose to that end. This will account for their conversation at the fair and the half-informed state in which Elizabeth was led onward.

In this attitude they proceeded on their journey, trusting solely to the dim light afforded of Henchard's whereabouts by the furmity woman. The strictest economy was indispensable. Sometimes they might have been seen on foot, sometimes on farmers' waggons, sometimes in carriers' vans; and thus they drew near to Casterbridge. Elizabeth-Jane discovered to her alarm that her mother's health was not what it once had been, and there was ever and anon in her talk that renunciatory tone which showed that, but for the girl, she would not be very sorry to quit a life she was growing thoroughly weary of.

It was on a Friday evening, near the middle of September, and just before dusk, that they reached the summit of a hill within a mile of the place they sought. There were high-banked hedges to the coach-road here, and they mounted upon the green turf within, and sat down. The spot commanded a full view of the town and its environs.

"What an old-fashioned place it seems to be!" said Elizabeth-Jane, while her silent mother mused on other things than topography. "It is huddled all together; and it is shut in by a square wall of trees, like a plot of garden ground by a box-edging."

Its squareness was, indeed, the characteristic which most struck the eye in this antiquated borough, the borough of Casterbridge—at that time, recent as it was, untouched by the faintest sprinkle of modernism. It was compact as a box of dominoes.

It had no suburbs—in the ordinary sense. Country and town met at a mathematical line.

To birds of the more soaring kind Casterbridge must have appeared on this fine evening as a mosaic-work of subdued reds, browns, greys, and crystals, held together by a rectangular frame of deep green. To the level eye of humanity it stood as an indistinct mass behind a dense stockade of limes and chestnuts, set in the midst of miles of rotund down and concave field. The mass became gradually dissected by the vision into towers, gables, chimneys, and casements, the highest glazings shining bleared and bloodshot with the coppery fire they caught from the belt of sunlit cloud in the west.

From the centre of each side of this tree-bound square ran avenues east, west, and south into the wide expanse of corn-land and coomb to the distance of a mile or so. It was by one of these avenues that the pedestrians were about to enter. Before they had risen to proceed two men passed outside the hedge, engaged in argumentative conversation.

"Why, surely," said Elizabeth, as they receded, "those men mentioned the name of Henchard in their talk—the name of our relative?"

"I thought so too," said Mrs. Newson.

"That seems a hint to us that he is still here."

"Yes."

"Shall I run after them, and ask them about him—"

"No, no, no! Not for the world just yet. He may be in the workhouse, or in the stocks, for all we know."

"Dear me—why should you think that, Mother?"

"'Twas just something to say—that's all! But we must make private inquiries."

Having sufficiently rested they proceeded on their way at evenfall. The dense trees of the avenue rendered the road dark as a tunnel, though the open land on each side was still under a faint daylight; in other words, they passed down a midnight between two gloamings. The features of the town had a keen interest for Elizabeth's mother, now that the human side came to the fore. As soon as they had wandered about they could see that the stockade of gnarled trees which framed in Casterbridge was itself an avenue, standing on a low green bank or escarpment, with a ditch yet visible without. Within the avenue and bank was a wall more or less discontin-

uous, and within the wall were packed the abodes of the burghers.

Though the two women did not know it these external features were but the ancient defences of the town, planted as a promenade.

The lamplights now glimmered through the engirdling trees, conveying a sense of great snugness and comfort inside, and rendering at the same time the unlighted country without strangely solitary and vacant in aspect, considering its nearness to life. The difference between burgh and champaign was increased, too, by sounds which now reached them above others—the notes of a brass band. The travellers returned into the High Street, where there were timber houses with overhanging stories, whose small-paned lattices were screened by dimity curtains on a drawing-string, and under whose barge-boards old cobwebs waved in the breeze. There were houses of brick-nogging, which derived their chief support from those adjoining. There were slate roofs patched with tiles, and tile roofs patched with slate, with occasionally a roof of thatch.

The agricultural and pastoral character of the people upon whom the town depended for its existence was shown by the class of objects displayed in the shop windows. Scythes, reap-hooks, sheep-shears, bill-hooks, spades, mattocks, and hoes at the iron-monger's; beehives, butter-firkins, churns, milking stools and pails, hay-rakes, field-flagons, and seed-lips at the cooper's; cart-ropes and plough-harness at the saddler's; carts, wheelbarrows, and mill-gear at the wheelwright's and machinist's; horse-embrocations at the chemists's; at the glover's and leather-cutter's, hedging-gloves, thatchers' knee-caps, ploughmen's leggings, villagers' patterns and clogs.

They came to a grizzled church, whose massive square tower rose unbroken into the darkening sky, the lower parts being illuminated by the nearest lamps sufficiently to show how completely the mortar from the joints of the stonework had been nibbled out by time and weather, which had planted in the crevices thus made little tufts of stonecrop and grass almost as far up as the very battlements. From this tower the clock struck eight, and thereupon a bell began to toll with a peremptory clang. The curfew was still rung in Casterbridge, and it was utilized by the inhabitants as a signal for shutting their shops. No sooner did the deep notes of the bell throb between the housefronts than a clatter of shutters arose through the whole length of the High Street. In a few minutes business at Casterbridge was ended for the day.

Other clocks struck eight from time to time—one gloomily from the gaol, another from the gable of an almshouse, with a preparative creak of machinery, more audible than the note of the bell; a row of tall, varnished case-clocks from the interior of a clock-maker's shop joined in one after another just as the shutters were enclosing them, like a row of actors delivering their final speeches before the fall of the curtain; then chimes were heard stammering out the Sicilian Mariners' Hymn; so that chronologists of the advanced school were appreciably on their way to the next hour before the whole business of the old one was satisfactorily wound up.

In an open space before the church walked a woman with her gown-sleeves rolled up so high that the edge of her underlinen was visible and her skirt tucked up through her pocket hole. She carried a loaf under her arm from which she was pulling pieces of bread, and handing them to some other women who walked with her; which pieces they nibbled critically. The sight reminded Mrs. Henchard-Newson and her daughter that they had an appetite; and they inquired of the woman for the nearest baker's.

"Ye may as well look for manna-food as good bread in Casterbridge just now," she said, after directing them. "They can blare their trumpets and thump their drums, and have their roaring dinners"—waving her hand towards a point further along the street, where the brass band could be seen standing in front of an illuminated building—"but we must needs be put-to for want of a wholesome crust. There's less good bread than good beer in Casterbridge now."

"And less good beer than swipes," said a man with his hands in his pockets.

"How does it happen there's no good bread?" asked Mrs. Henchard.

"Oh, 'tis the corn-factor—he's the man that our millers and bakers all deal wi', and he has sold 'em growed wheat, which they didn't know was growed, so they *say,* till the dough ran all over the ovens like quicksilver, so that the loaves be as flat as toads, and like suet pudden inside. I've been a wife, and I've been a mother, and I never see such unprincipled bread in Casterbridge as this before.—But you must be a real stranger here not to know what's made all the poor volks' insides plim like blowed bladders this week?"

"I am," said Elizabeth's mother shyly.

Not wishing to be observed further till she knew more of her future in this place, she withdrew with her daughter from the speaker's side. Getting a couple of biscuits at the shop indicated as a temporary substitute for a meal, they next bent their steps instinctively to where the music was playing.

Reeds in the Wind
Grazia Deledda

Deledda's topic is the intersection of the lives and outlooks of elites and former elites with those at the bottom of Sardinian society. Both segments of society are beset with customs and understandings that represent a world before science, industry, and mass education.

Tied to the past, the servant Efix, of local peasant stock, tends to the needs of his mistresses, impoverished sisters of noble birth. They live out their lives in a decaying grand house on a tiny farm, all that remains of vast estates.

Efix, the Pintor sisters' servant, had worked all day to shore up the primitive river embankment that he had slowly and laboriously built over the years. At nightfall he was contemplating his work from where he was sitting in front of his hut halfway up white Doves' Hill. A blue-green fringe of reeds rustled behind him.

Silently stretching out before him down to the river sparkling in the twilight was the little farm that Efix considers more his than the owners': thirty years of possession and work had certainly made it his, and the two hedgerows of prickly pear that enclose it like two gray walls meandering from terrace to terrace, from the hill to the river, are like the boundaries of the world to him.

In his survey the servant ignored the land on either side of the farm because it had once been Pintor property. Why dredge up the past? Useless regret. Better to think about the future and hope in God's help.

And God promised a good year, or at least He had covered all the almond and peach trees in the valley with blossoms; and this valley, between two rows of white hills covered with spring vegetation, water, scrub, flowers, together with the distant blue

mountains to the west and the blue sea to the east, gave the impression of a cradle billowing with green veils and blue ribbons, with the river murmuring monotonously like a sleepy child.

But the days were already too hot and Efix was also thinking about the torrential rains that swell the bankless river and make it leap like an all-destroying monster. One could hope, but had to be watchful, like the reeds along the riverbank beating their leaves together with every breath of wind as though warning of danger.

That was why he had worked all day and now, waiting for night, he wove a reed mat so as not to waste time and prayed that God make his work worthwhile. What good is a little embankment if God's will doesn't make it as formidable as a mountain?

Seven reeds across a willow twig, and seven prayers to the Lord and to Our Lady of Rimedio, bless her. In the intense twilight blue her little church and the quiet circle of cabins around it down below lay like a centuries-old abandoned prehistoric village. At this hour, as the moon bloomed like a big rose in the bushes on the hill and euphorbia spread its perfume along the river, Efix's mistresses were also praying. Donna Ester, the oldest, bless her, was certainly remembering him, the sinner. This was enough to make him feel happy, compensated for his efforts.

From: Grazia Deledda, *Reeds in the Wind* (New York: Ithaca Press, 1999), 1–10.

Footsteps in the distance made him look up. They sounded familiar. It was the light, swift stride of a boy, the stride of an angel hurrying with some happy or sad announcement. God's will be done. It's He who sends good and bad news; but Efix's heart began to pound, and his black cracked fingers trembled on the silvery reeds shining in the moonlight like threads of water.

The footsteps were no longer heard. Nevertheless, Efix remained motionless, waiting.

The moon rose before him, and evening voices told him the day had ended: a cuckoo's rhythmical cry, the early crickets' chirping, a bird calling; the reeds sighing and the ever more distinct voice of the river; but most of all a breathing, a mysterious panting that seemed to come from the earth itself. Yes, man's working day was done, but the fantastic life of elves, fairies, wandering spirits was beginning. Ghosts of the ancient Barons came down from the Castle ruins above Galte on Efix's left and ran along the river hunting wild boar and fox. Their guns gleamed in the short alder trees along the riverbed, and the faint sound of barking dogs in the distance was a sign of their passing.

Efix could hear the sound that the *panas*—women who died in childbirth—made while washing their clothes down by the river, beating them with a dead man's shin bone, and he believed he saw the *ammattadore* (the elf with seven caps where he hid his treasure) jumping about under the almond woods, followed by vampires with steel tails.

It was the elf that caused the branches and rocks to glitter under the moon. And along with the evil spirits were spirits of unbaptized babies—white spirits that flew through the air changing themselves into little silvery clouds behind the moon. And dwarfs and *janas*—the little fairies who stay in their small rock houses during the day weaving gold cloth on their golden looms—were dancing in the large phillyrea bushes, while giants looked out from the rocks on the moonstruck mountains, holding the bridles of enormous horses that only they can mount, squinting to see if down there within the expanse of evil euphorbia a dragon was lurking. Or if the legendary *cananèa*, living from the time of Christ, was slithering around on the sandy marshland.

During moonlit nights especially this entire mysterious population animates the hills and valleys. Man has no right to disturb it with his presence, just as the spirits have respected him during the sun's course; therefore it's time to retire and close one's eyes under the protection of guardian angels.

Efix made the sign of the cross and stood up, but he was still waiting for someone. Nevertheless he shoved the plank that served as a door across the entry way and leaned a big reed cross against it to keep spirits and temptation from entering his hut.

Through the cracks the moonlight illuminated the corners of the low, narrow room—but a room large enough for someone like him who was as small and scrawny as a young boy. From the conical cane and reed roof over the dry stone walls, with a hole in the middle for the smoke to escape, hung bunches of onions and dry herbs, palm crosses and blessed olive branches, a painted candle, a scythe for keeping vampires away, and a little sack of barley for protection against the *panas*. With every breath of air everything quivered and spider webs shone in the moonlight. On the floor a two-handled pitcher lay on its side, and a pan rested upside down next to it.

Efix unrolled his mat but didn't lie down. He thought he kept hearing the sound of a boy's footsteps. Someone was certainly coming, and in fact dogs on nearby farms suddenly began to bark, and the whole countryside, which a few moments earlier seemed to sleep amid prayers murmured by nocturnal voices, was full of echoes and rustling almost as though it had suddenly jerked awake.

Efix pushed the plank aside. A black figure was coming over the rise where the low bean plants grew silvery under the moonlight, and he, to whom even human shapes seemed mysterious at night, made the sign of the cross again. But a voice he recognized called out to him. It was the clear but slightly breathless voice of the boy who lived next door to the Pintor sisters.

"Zio Efisè, Zio Efisè!"

"What's happened, Zuannantò? Are the women all right?"

"They seem all right to me. They sent me to tell you to go to town early tomorrow, because they need to talk to you. Maybe it's because of the yellow letter I saw in Donna Noemi's hand."

"A letter? Do you know who it's from?"

"I don't know. I don't know how to read. But grandmother says maybe it's from their nephew, Giacinto."

Yes, Efix felt it had to be. Nevertheless, head down, he thoughtfully rubbed his cheek, and hoped and feared he was wrong.

The tired boy sat down on a rock in front of the hut and unlaced his boots, asking if there was something to eat.

"I ran like a deer. I was afraid of the spirits. . . ."

Efix raised his olive-colored face, hard as a bronze mask, and gazed at the boy with his little bluish eyes, deep set and surrounded by wrinkles. Those lively, shining eyes were full of childish anxiety.

"They said for me to go to town tomorrow or tonight?"

"Tomorrow, I told you! I'll stay here to guard the farm while you're in town."

The servant was accustomed to obeying the women without asking questions. He pulled an onion from the bunch, a piece of bread from his bag, and while the boy ate, laughing and crying from the sharp onion, they began to talk. The town's most important people entered their conversation. First came the Rector, then the Rector's sister, then Milese who had married a daughter of the Rector and had gone from hawking oranges and amphoras to being the richest merchant in the village. The mayor, Don Predu, came next, the Pintor sisters' cousin. Don Predu was also rich, but not like Milese. Then came Kallina the usurer, she also rich, but in a mysterious way.

"Thieves tried to break down her wall. Impossible. It's bewitched. And she was laughing this morning in her courtyard, saying: even if they get in they'll only find ashes and nails, poor as Christ. But my grandmother says that Zia Kallina has a little sack of gold hidden in the wall."

These stories were really of little interest to Efix. Lying on his mat, with one hand tucked under his arm and the other on his cheek, he felt his heart beating, and the reeds rustling on the riverbank sounded like an evil spirit sighing.

A yellow letter! An ugly color, yellow. Who knows what had happened to those women. For twenty years whenever some event broke the monotonous life at the Pintor house it was inevitably a disaster.

The boy also lay down, but he didn't feel like sleeping.

"Zio Efix, just today my grandmother said that the Pintors were once as rich as Don Predu. Is that true?"

"It's true," the servant said with a sigh. "But now's not the time to be thinking about these things. Go to sleep."

The boy yawned. "But my grandmother said that after saintly old Donna Maria Cristina died she walked around her house like an excommunicated soul. Is that true or not?"

"Go to sleep, I say. Now's not the time. . . ."

"Let me talk! Why did Donna Lia run away? My grandmother says you knew about it and you helped her, you went to the bridge with Donna Lia where she hid until a cart came by that would take her to the sea to get on a boat. And that her father Don Zame looked for her till he died. He died there, by the bridge. Who killed him? My grandmother says you know. . . ."

"Your grandmother is a witch! She and you, both of you, should leave the dead in peace!" shouted Efix; but his voice was hoarse and the boy laughed insolently.

"Don't get mad 'cause it's not good for you, Zio Efix! My grandmother says a goblin killed Don Zame. Is that true or not?"

Efix didn't answer. He closed his eyes and put his hand over his ear, but the boy's voice buzzed in the dark and it sounded to him the voice of spirits from the past.

Little by little they all gathered around him, entering through the cracks like moonbeams: Donna Maria Cristina, beautiful and calm as a saint; Don Zame, red and violent as the devil; their four daughters whose pale faces have the serenity of their mother and their father's flame in the depths of their eyes; maidservants and menservants, relatives, friends—everyone who invades the rich house of the Barons' descendants. But once the wind of misfortune blows, people disperse like little clouds around the moon when the wind blows off the mountains.

Donna Cristina dies; her daughters' pale faces lose some of their serenity, and the deep flame in their eyes grows. It grows to such a degree that after his wife's death, Don Zame becomes as domineering as his Baron ancestors, and like them keeps his four daughters shut up in the house like slaves while they wait for husbands worthy of them. And like slaves they had to work, make bread, weave, sew, cook, know how to take care of their things. But above all they couldn't raise their eyes to men, or even allow themselves to think about anyone not destined to become a husband. But the years went by and the husbands didn't come along. And the older his daughters became the more Don Zame expected them to adhere to a strict manner of comportment. If he saw them at the windows overlooking the lane behind the house or if they went out without his permission, he would slap them and shout insults, while threatening death to the young men who passed by on the lane more than twice in succession.

Don Zame spent his days roaming around town or sitting on the stone bench in front of the shop belonging to the Rector's sister. When people saw him they would slink away, afraid as they were of his tongue. He quarreled with everyone, and was so envious of others that when he passed by a nice farm he would say, "may lawsuits devour you." But lawsuits ended up devouring his land, and an unspeakable catastrophe struck him suddenly like punishment from God for his pride and his prejudices. His third daughter, Donna Lia, disappeared one night from the paternal house and nothing more was known about her for a long time. A deathly shadow fell over the house. Never had the town known such a scandal; never had such a noble and well-brought up young woman like Lia run away like that. Don Zame seemed to go mad; he ran around here and there searching for Lia all over the Baronia district and along the Coast; but no one could give him any information. At last she wrote her sisters saying she was safe and happy to have broken her chains. However, her sisters didn't forgive her or answer her. Don Zame became even more tyrannical. He sold what was left of his inheritance, mistreated the servant, annoyed half the world with lawsuits, kept traveling in the hopes of tracking down his daughter and bringing her back home. The shadow of dishonor over him and his entire family because of Lia's flight weighed on him like a cloak of the damned. One morning they found him dead on the bridge outside town. A stroke must have killed him, because there was not a sign of violence—only a small green mark on the back of his neck.

People said that maybe Don Zame had quarreled with someone who had struck him with a walking stick. But in time this rumor faded and the certainty prevailed that he had died of a broken heart over his daughter's leaving.

While her sisters, dishonored by her escape, were unable to find husbands, Lia wrote announcing her marriage. Her husband was a cattle dealer that she had met by chance. They lived at Civitavecchia, were comfortably well off, and would soon have a child.

Her sisters did not forgive her this new wrong: marriage with a common man met in such a sorry manner. They did not reply.

Some time later Lia wrote announcing Giacinto's birth. They sent a present to their little nephew, but didn't write his mother.

The years went by. Giacinto grew up, and every year he wrote his aunts at Easter time and Christmas, and his aunts sent him a present. Once he wrote that he was studying, another time that he wanted to join the navy, and still another time that he had found a job; then he wrote about his father's death, then his mother's, and finally he expressed the desire to visit them and settle down if he could find work in town. He didn't like his job with the Customs Office: it was menial and tiresome, a waste of his youth. Of course he loved to work, but out in the open. Everyone advised him to go to his mother's island and try his luck with an honest job.

His aunts began to talk it over, and the more they talked the less they agreed.

"Work?" said Ruth, the calmest sister. "If the little town can't provide work even for those who were born here?"

Ester, on the other hand, was sympathetic with their nephew's plans; while the youngest, Noemi, smiled coldly and scornfully.

"Perhaps he thinks to come here to play the gentleman. Come right ahead! He can go fishing in the river. . . ."

"He says he wants to work, Noemi! Then he'll work: he might be a trader like his father."

"He needs experience first. Our family has never dealt with cattle."

"In the past, dear Noemi! Nowadays gentlemen are merchants. See Milese? He says he's the Baron of Galte now."

Noemi laughed with an evil look deep in her eyes, and her laugh was more discouraging to Ester than all her other sister's arguments.

Everyday it was the same story: Giacinto's name resounded throughout the house, and even when the three sisters were silent he was in their midst, as he had always been anyway from the day he was born, his unknown shape filling the decaying house with life.

Efix didn't remember ever taking part directly in their discussions. He didn't dare. First of all because they didn't consult him, and then not to have qualms of conscience. But he wanted the boy to come.

He loved him. He had always loved him like a member of the family.

After Don Zame's death, Efix had remained with the three women to help them settle their tangled affairs. Their relatives didn't care about them, they even held them in contempt and spurned them. The sisters were only capable of domestic tasks and knew nothing about the little farm, their last remaining inheritance.

"I'll stay another year in their service," Efix had said, moved to pity by their helplessness. And he had stayed twenty years.

The three women lived on the income from the farm he cultivated. In lean years, Donna Ester would say to Efix when the moment came to pay him (thirty scudi a year and a pair of boots): "Be patient, for the love of God. You'll get what's coming to you."

He was patient, and their debt to him grew year after year, so much that Donna Ester, half joking, half serious, promised to leave him the farm and house, although he was older than they. Old now, and weak, but he was still a man, and his shadow was still enough to protect the three women.

Now it was he who dreamed about good fortune for them. At least that Noemi might find a husband! What if the yellow letter brought good news, after all? What if it was about an inheritance? What if it was a marriage request for Noemi? The Pintor sisters still had rich relatives living in Sassari and Nuoro. Why couldn't one of them marry Noemi? Don Predu himself could have written the yellow letter. . . .

And there in the servant's tired imagination things have suddenly changed as from night to day; everything is light, sweetness. His noble mistresses have become young again, they rise on wings like eagles taking flight; their house rises up from ruin and all around everything blooms again like the valley in spring.

And for him, the poor servant, there's nothing left to do but retire to the little farm for the remainder of his life, to spread out his mat and rest with God, while in the silence of the night the reeds whisper the prayer of the sleeping earth.

Effi Briest

Theodor Fontane

This novel highlights problems for middle-class and elite women in Germany toward the end of the nine-teenth century. Its setting is Berlin and the semirural location of her husband's family estate. Social mores, scandal, a duel, and a fall in status are the subjects. The author's approach is nonjudgmental toward the heroine and clear-eyed toward the society whose foibles are under examination.

Effi Briest, daughter of a middle-class family, marries into the titled nobility. After the birth of her daughter, her friendship with a local man leads to scandal and her expulsion from her home and the loss of her daughter. In this selection, she picks of the threads of a new simpler life in Berlin.

Three years had passed and for almost that length of time Effi had been living in a small apartment on Königgrätz Street—a front room and back room, behind which was the kitchen with a servant's bed-room, everything as ordinary and commonplace as possible. And yet it was an unusually pretty apart-ment, that made an agreeable impression on every-body who saw it, the most agreeable perhaps on old Dr. Rummschüttel, who called now and then and had long ago forgiven the poor young wife, not only for the rheumatism and neuralgia farce of bygone years, but also for everything else that had happened in the meantime—if there was any need of forgiveness on his part, considering the very dif-ferent cases he knew about. He was now far along in the seventies, but whenever Effi, who had been ailing considerably for some time, wrote a letter asking him to call, he came the following forenoon and would not listen to any excuses for the number of steps he had to climb. "No excuse, please, dear, most gracious Lady; for in the first place it is my calling, and in the second I am happy and almost proud that I am still able to climb the three flights

so well. If I were not afraid of inconveniencing you,—since, after all, I come as a physician and not as a friend of nature or a landscape enthusiast,—I should probably come oftener, merely to see you and sit down for a few minutes at your back win-dow. I don't believe you fully appreciate the view."

"Oh, yes I do," said Effi; but Rummschüttel, not allowing himself to be interrupted, continued: "Please, most gracious Lady, step here just for a moment, or allow me to escort you to the window. Simply magnificent again today! Just see the various railroad embankments, three, no, four, and how the trains glide back and forth continually, and now that train yonder disappears again behind a group of trees. Really magnificent! And how the sun shines through the white smoke! If St. Matthew's Church-yard were not immediately behind it it would be ideal."

"I like to look at churchyards."

"Yes, you dare say that. But how about us? We physicians are unavoidably confronted with the question, might there, perhaps, not have been some fewer graves here? However, most gracious Lady, I am satisfied with you and my only complaint is that you will not listen to anything about Ems. For your catarrhal affections—"

Effi remained silent.

From: Theodor Fontane, *Effi Briest*, translated by William A. Cooper (New York: Frederick Ungar, 1975), pp. 196–206.

"Ems would work miracles. But as you don't care to go there—and I understand your reasons—drink the water here. In three minutes you can be in the Prince Albrecht Garden, and even if the music and the costumes and all the diversions of a regular watering-place promenade are lacking, the water itself, you know, is the important thing."

Effi was agreed, and Rummschüttel took his hat and cane, but stepped once more to the window. "I hear people talking about a plan to terrace the Hill of the Holy Cross. God bless the city government! Once that bare spot yonder is greener—A charming apartment! I could almost envy you—By the way, gracious Lady, I have been wanting for a long time to say to you, you always write me such a lovely letter. Well, who wouldn't enjoy that? But it requires an effort each time. Just send Roswitha for me."

"Just send Roswitha for me," Rummschüttel had said. Why, was Roswitha at Effi's? Instead of being on Keith Street was she on Königgrätz Street? Certainly she was, and had been for a long time, just as long as Effi herself had been living on Königgrätz Street. Three days before they moved Roswitha had gone to see her dear mistress and that was a great day for both of them, so great that we must go back and tell about it.

The day that the letter of renunciation came from Hohen-Cremmen and Effi returned from Ems to Berlin she did not take a separate apartment at once, but tried living in a boarding house, which suited her tolerably well. The two women who kept the boarding house were educated and considerate and had long ago ceased to be inquisitive. Such a variety of people met there that it would have been too much of an undertaking to pry into the secrets of each individual. Such things only interfered with business. Effi, who still remembered the cross-questionings to which the eyes of Mrs. Zwicker had subjected her, was very agreeably impressed with the reserve of the boarding house keepers. But after two weeks had passed she felt plainly that she could not well endure the prevailing atmosphere of the place, either the physical or the moral. There were usually seven persons at the table. Beside Effi and one of the landladies—the other looked after the kitchen—there were two Englishwomen, who were attending the university, a noblewoman from Saxony, a very pretty Galician Jewess, whose real occupation nobody knew, and a precentor's daughter from Polzin in Pomerania, who wished to become a painter. That was a bad combination, and the attempts of each to show her superiority to the others were unrefreshing. Remarkable to relate, the Englishwomen were not absolutely the worst offenders, but competed for the palm with the girl from Polzin, who was filled with the highest regard for her mission as a painter. Nevertheless Effi, who assumed a passive attitude, could have withstood the pressure of this intellectual atmosphere if it had not been combined with the air of the boarding house, speaking from a purely physical and objective point of view. What this air was actually composed of was perhaps beyond the possibility of determination, but that it took away sensitive Effi's breath was only too certain, and she saw herself compelled for this external reason to go out in search of other rooms, which she found comparatively near by, in the above-described apartment on Königgrätz St. She was to move in at the beginning of the autumn quarter, had made the necessary purchases, and during the last days of September counted the hours till her liberation from the boarding house. On one of these last days, a quarter of an hour after she had retired from the dining room, planning to enjoy a rest on a sea grass sofa covered with some large-figured woolen material, there was a gentle rap at her door.

"Come in!"

One of the housemaids, a sickly looking person in the middle thirties, who by virtue of always being in the hall of the boarding house carried the atmosphere stored there with her everywhere, in her wrinkles, entered the room and said: "I beg your pardon, gracious Lady, but somebody wishes to speak to you."

"Who?"

"A woman."

"Did she tell you her name?"

"Yes. Roswitha."

Before Effi had hardly heard this name she shook off her drowsiness, sprang up, ran out into the corridor, grasped Roswitha by both hands and drew her into her room.

"Roswitha! You! Oh, what joy! What do you bring! Something good, of course. Such a good old face can bring only good things. Oh, how happy I am! I could give you a kiss. I should not have thought such joy could ever come to me again. You good old soul, how are you anyhow? Do you still remember how the ghost of the Chinaman used to stalk about! Those were happy times. I thought then they were unhappy, because I did not yet know the hardness of life. Since then I have come to know it. Oh, there are far worse things than ghosts. Come, my good Roswitha, come, sit down by me and tell me—Oh, I have such a longing. How is Annie?"

Roswitha was unable to speak, and so she let her eyes wander around the strange room, whose gray and dusty-looking walls were bordered with narrow gilt molding. Finally she found herself and said that his Lordship was back from Glatz. That the old Emperor had said, "six weeks were quite sufficient (imprisonment) in such a case," and she had only waited for his Lordship's return, on Annie's account, who had to have some supervision. Johanna was no doubt a proper person, but she was still too pretty and too much occupied with herself, and God only knows what all she was thinking about. But now that his Lordship could again keep an eye on Annie and see that everything was right, she herself wanted to try to find out how her Ladyship was getting on.

"That is right, Roswitha."

"And I wanted to see whether your Ladyship lacked anything, and whether you might need me. If so I would stay right here and pitch in and do everything and see to it that your Ladyship was getting on well again."

Effi had been leaning back in the corner of the sofa with her eyes closed, but suddenly she sat up and said: "Yes, Roswitha, what you were saying there is an idea, there is something in it. For I must tell you that I am not going to stay in this boarding house. I have rented an apartment farther down the street and have bought furniture, and in three more days I shall move in. And if, when I arrive there, I could say to you: 'No, Roswitha, not there, the wardrobe must stand here and the mirror there,' why, that would be worth while, and I should like it. Then when we got tired of all the drudgery I should say: 'Now, Roswitha, go over there and get us a decanter of Munich beer, for when one has been working one is thirsty for a drink, and, if you can, bring us also something good from the Habsburg Restaurant. You can

return the dishes later.' Yes, Roswitha, when I think of that it makes my heart feel a great deal lighter. But I must ask you whether you have thought it all over? I will not speak of Annie, to whom you are so attached, for she is almost your own child; nevertheless Annie will be provided for, and Johanna is also attached to her, you know. So leave her out of the consideration. But if you want to come to me remember how everything has changed. I am no longer as I used to be. I have now taken a very small apartment, and the porter will doubtless pay but little attention to you and me. We shall have to be very economical, always have what we used to call our Thursday meal, because that was cleaning day. Do you remember? And do you remember how good Mr. Gieshübler once came in and was urged to sit down with us, and how he said he had never eaten such a delicate dish! You probably remember he was always so frightfully polite, but really he was the only human being in the city who was a connoisseur in matters of eating. The others called everything fine."

Roswitha was enjoying every word and could already see everything running smoothly, when Effi again said: "Have you considered all this? For, while it is my own household, I must not overlook the fact that you have been spoiled these many years, and formerly no questions were ever asked, for we did not need to be saving; but now I must be saving, for I am poor and have only what is given me, you know, remittances from Hohen-Cremmen. My parents are very good to me, so far as they are able, but they are not rich. And now tell me what you think."

"That I shall come marching along with my trunk next Saturday, not in the evening, but early in the morning, and that I shall be there when the settling process begins. For I can take hold quite differently from your Ladyship."

"Don't say that, Roswitha. I can work too. One can do anything when obliged to."

"And then your Ladyship doesn't need to worry about me, as though I might think: 'that is not good enough for Roswitha.' For Roswitha anything is good that she has to share with your Ladyship, and most to her liking would be something sad. Yes, I look forward to that with real pleasure. Your

Ladyship shall see I know what sadness is. Even if I didn't know, I should soon find out. I have not forgotten how I was sitting there in the churchyard, all alone in the world, thinking to myself it would probably be better if I were lying there in a row with the others. Who came along? Who saved my life? Oh, I have had so much to endure. That day when my father came at me with the red-hot tongs—"

"I remember, Roswitha."

"Well, that was bad enough. But when I sat there in the churchyard, so completely poverty stricken and forsaken, that was worse still. Then your Ladyship came. I hope I shall never go to heaven if I forget that."

As she said this she arose and went toward the window. "Oh, your Ladyship must see *him* too."

Effi stepped to the window. Over on the other side of the street sat Rollo, looking up at the windows of the boarding house.

A few days later Effi, with the aid of Roswitha, moved into the apartment on Königgrätz St., and liked it there from the beginning. To be sure, there was no society, but during her boarding house days she had derived so little pleasure from intercourse with people that it was not hard for her to be alone, at least not in the beginning. With Roswitha it was impossible, of course, to carry on an esthetic conversation, or even to discuss what was in the paper, but when it was simply a question of things human and Effi began her sentence with, "Oh, Roswitha, I am again afraid," then the faithful soul always had a good answer ready, always comfort and usually advice.

Until Christmas they got on excellently, but Christmas eve was rather sad and when New Year's Day came Effi began to grow quite melancholy. It was not cold, only grizzly and rainy, and if the days were short, the evenings were so much the longer. What was she to do! She read, she embroidered, she played solitaire, she played Chopin, but nocturnes were not calculated to bring much light into her life, and when Roswitha came with the tea tray and placed on the table, beside the tea service, two small plates with an egg and a Vienna cutlet carved in small slices, Effi said, as she closed the piano: "Move up, Roswitha. Keep me company."

Roswitha joined her. "I know, your Ladyship has been playing too much again. Your Ladyship always

looks like that and has red spots. The doctor forbade it, didn't he?"

"Ah, Roswitha, it is easy for the doctor to forbid, and also easy for you to repeat everything he says. But what shall I do? I can't sit all day long at the window and look over toward Christ's Church. Sundays, during the evening service, when the windows are lighted up, I always look over that way; but it does me no good, it always makes my heart feel heavier."

"Well, then, your Ladyship ought to go to church. Your Ladyship has been there once."

"Oh, many a time. But I have derived little benefit from it. He preaches quite well and is a very wise man, and I should be happy if I knew the hundredth part of it all. But it seems as though I were merely reading a book. Then when he speaks so loud and saws the air and shakes his long black locks I am drawn entirely out of my attitude of worship."

"Out of?"

Effi laughed. "You think I hadn't yet got into such an attitude. That is probably true. But whose fault is it? Certainly not mine. He always talks so much about the Old Testament. Even if that is very good it doesn't edify me. Anyhow, this everlasting listening is not the right thing. You see, I ought to have so much to do that I should not know whither to turn. That would suit me. Now there are societies where young girls learn housekeeping, or sewing, or to be kindergarten teachers. Have you ever heard of these?"

"Yes, I once heard of them. Once upon a time little Annie was to go to a kindergarten."

"Now you see, you know better than I do. I should like to join some such society where I can make myself useful. But it is not to be thought of. The women in charge wouldn't take me, they couldn't. That is the most terrible thing of all, that the world is so closed to one, that it even forbids one to take a part in charitable work. I can't even give poor children a lesson after hours to help them catch up."

"That would not do for your Ladyship. The children always have such greasy shoes on, and in wet weather there is so much steam and smoke, your Ladyship could never stand it."

Effi smiled. "You are probably right, Roswitha, but it is a bad sign that you should be right, and it shows me that I still have too much of the old Effi in me and that I am still too well off."

Roswitha would not agree to that. "Anybody as good as your Ladyship can't be too well off. Now you must not always play such sad music. Sometimes I think all will be well yet, something will surely turn up."

And something did turn up. Effi desired to become a painter, in spite of the precentor's daughter from Polzin, whose conceit as an artist she still remembered as exceedingly disagreeable. Although she laughed about the plan herself, because she was conscious she could never rise above the lowest grade of dilettantism, nevertheless she went at her work with zest, because she at last had an occupation and that, too, one after her own heart, because it was quiet and peaceful. She applied for instruction to a very old professor of painting, who was well-informed concerning the Brandenburgian aristocracy, and was, at the same time, very pious, so that Effi seemed to be his heart's delight from the outset. He probably thought, here was a soul to be saved, and so he received her with extraordinary friendliness, as though she had been his daughter. This made Effi very happy, and the day of her first painting lesson marked for her a turning point toward the good. Her poor life was now no longer so poor, and Roswitha was triumphant when she saw that she had been right and something had turned up after all.

Thus things went on for considerably over a year. Coming again in contact with people made Effi happy, but it also created within her the desire to renew and extend associations. Longing for Hohen-Cremmen came over her at times with the force of a true passion, and she longed still more passionately to see Annie. After all she was her child, and when she began to turn this thought over in her mind and, at the same time, recalled what Miss Trippelli had once said, to wit: "The world is so small that one could be certain of coming suddenly upon some old acquaintance in Central Africa," she had a reason for being surprised that she had never met Annie. But the time finally arrived when a change was to occur. She was coming from her painting lesson, close by the Zoological Garden, and near the station stepped into a horse car. It was very hot and it did her good to see the lowered curtains blown out and back by the strong current of air passing through

the car. She leaned back in the corner toward the front platform and was studying several pictures of blue tufted and tasseled sofas on a stained window pane, when the car began to move more slowly and she saw three school children spring up with school bags on their backs and little pointed hats on their heads. Two of them were blonde and merry, the third brunette and serious. This one was Annie. Effi was badly startled, and the thought of a meeting with the child, for which she had so often longed, filled her now with deadly fright. What was to be done? With quick determination she opened the door to the front platform, on which nobody was standing but the driver, whom she asked to let her get off in front at the next station. "It is forbidden, young lady," said the driver. But she gave him a coin and looked at him so appealingly that the good-natured man changed his mind and mumbled to himself: "I really am not supposed to, but perhaps once will not matter." When the car stopped he took out the lattice and Effi sprang off.

She was still greatly excited when she reached the house.

"Just think, Roswitha, I have seen Annie." Then she told of the meeting in the tram car. Roswitha was displeased that the mother and daughter had not been rejoiced to see each other again, and was very hard to convince that it would not have looked well in the presence of so many people. Then Effi had to tell how Annie looked and when she had done so with motherly pride Roswitha said: "Yes, she is what one might call half and half. Her pretty features and, if I may be permitted to say it, her strange look she gets from her mother, but her seriousness is exactly her father. When I come to think about it, she is more like his Lordship."

"Thank God!" said Effi.

"Now, your Ladyship, there is some question about that. No doubt there is many a person who would take the side of the mother."

"Do you think so, Roswitha? I don't."

"Oh, oh, I am not so easily fooled, and I think your Ladyship knows very well, too, how matters really stand and what the men like best."

"Oh, don't speak of that, Roswitha."

The conversation ended here and was never afterward resumed. . . .

Chadwick's Report on Sanitary Conditions

This 1842 report reflected the British Poor Law Commissioners' findings about how laborers lived in industrial environments. The report notes that, despite the workers' superior wages and access to foodstuffs as compared to their former lives in rural areas, disease and premature death threaten their existence and cause widespread orphanage and destitution of families. The recommended solution is public drainage, increased water supplies, and waste removal, improvements that did not really occur until the late nineteenth or early twentieth centuries.

After as careful an examination of the evidence collected as I have been enabled to make, I beg leave to recapitulate the chief conclusions which that evidence appears to me to establish.

First, as to the extent and operation of the evils which are the subject of this inquiry:—

That the various forms of epidemic, endemic, and other disease caused, or aggravated, or propagated chiefly amongst the labouring classes by atmospheric impurities produced by decomposing animal and vegetable substances, by damp and filth, and close and overcrowded dwellings prevail amongst the population in every part of the kingdom, whether dwelling in separate houses, in rural villages, in small towns, in the larger towns—as they have been found to prevail in the lowest districts of the metropolis.

That such disease, wherever its attacks are frequent, is always found in connexion with the physical circumstances above specified, and that where those circumstances are removed by drainage, proper cleansing, better ventilation, and other means of diminishing atmospheric impurity, the frequency and intensity of such disease is abated; and where the removal of the noxious agencies appears to be complete, such disease almost entirely disappears.

That high prosperity in respect to employment and wages, and various and abundant food, have afforded to the labouring classes no exemptions

from attacks of epidemic disease, which have been as frequent and as fatal in periods of commercial and manufacturing prosperity as in any others.

That the formation of all habits of cleanliness is obstructed by defective supplies of water.

That the annual loss of life from filth and bad ventilation are greater than the loss from death or wounds in any wars in which the country has been engaged in modern times.

That of the 43,000 cases of widowhood, and 112,000 cases of destitute orphanage relieved from the poor's rates in England and Wales alone, it appears that the greatest proportion of deaths of the heads of families occurred from the above specified and other removable causes; that their ages were under 45 years; that is to say, 13 years below the natural probabilities of life as shown by the experience of the whole population of Sweden.

That the public loss from the premature deaths of the heads of families is greater than can be represented by any enumeration of the pecuniary burdens consequent upon their sickness and death.

That, measuring the loss of working ability amongst large classes by the instances of gain, even from incomplete arrangements for the removal of noxious influences from places of work or from abodes, that this loss cannot be less than eight or ten years.

That the ravages of epidemics and other diseases do not diminish but tend to increase the pressure of population.

From: Chadwick's Report on Sanitary Conditions, http://www.geocities.com/couple_colour/Worker/index2.html?200513

That in the districts where the mortality is greatest the births are not only sufficient to replace the numbers removed by death, but to add to the population.

That the younger population, bred up under noxious physical agencies, is inferior in physical organization and general health to a population preserved from the presence of such agencies.

That the population so exposed is less susceptible of moral influences, and the effects of education are more transient than with a healthy population.

That these adverse circumstances tend to produce an adult population short-lived, improvident, reckless, and intemperate, and with habitual avidity for sensual gratifications.

That these habits lead to the abandonment of all the conveniences and decencies of life, and especially lead to the overcrowding of their homes, which is destructive to the morality as well as the health of large classes of both sexes.

That defective town cleansing fosters habits of the most abject degradation and tends to the demoralization of large numbers of human beings, who subsist by means of what they find amidst the noxious filth accumulated in neglected streets and bye-places.

That the expenses of local public works are in general unequally and unfairly assessed, oppressively and uneconomically collected, by separate collections, wastefully expended in separate and inefficient operations by unskilled and practically irresponsible officers.

That the existing law for the protection of the public health and the constititional machinery for reclaiming its execution, such as the Courts Leet, have fallen into desuetude, and are in the state indicated by the prevalence of the evils they were intended to prevent.

Secondly. As to the means by which the present sanitary condition of the labouring classes may be improved:—

The primary and most important measures, and at the same time the most practicable, and within the recognized province of public administration, are drainage, the removal of all refuse of habitations, streets, and roads, and the improvement of the supplies of water.

That the chief obstacles to the immediate removal of decomposing refuse of towns and habitations have been the expense and annoyance of the hand labour and cartage requisite for the purpose.

That this expense may be reduced to one-twentieth or to one-thirtieth, or rendered inconsiderable, by the use of water and self-acting means of removal by improved and cheaper sewers and drains.

That the expense of public drainage, of supplies of water laid on in houses, and of means of improved cleansing would be a pecuniary gain, by diminishing the existing charges attendant on sickness and premature mortality.

That for the protection of the labouring classes and of the ratepayers against inefficiency and waste in all new structural arrangements for the protection of the public health, and to ensure public confidence that the expenditure will be beneficial, securities should be taken that all new local public works are devised and conducted by responsible officers qualified by the possession of the science and skill of civil engineers.

That the oppressiveness and injustice of levies for the whole immediate outlay on such works upon persons who have only short interests in the benefits may be avoided by care in spreading the expense over periods coincident with the benefits.

That by appropriate arrangements, 10 or 15 per cent. on the ordinary outlay for drainage might be saved, which on an estimate of the expense of the necessary structural alterations of one-third only of the existing tenements would be a saving of one million and a half sterling, besides the reduction of the future expenses of management.

That for the prevention of the disease occasioned by defective ventilation and other causes of impurity in places of work and other places where large numbers are assembled, and for the general promotion of the means necessary to prevent disease, that it would be good economy to appoint a district medical officer independent of private practice, and with the securities of special qualifications and responsibilities to initiate sanitary measures and reclaim the execution of the law.

That by the combinations of all these arrangements, it is probable that the full ensurable period of life indicated by the Swedish tables; that is, an increase of 13 years at least, may be extended to the whole of the labouring classes.

That the attainment of these and the other collateral advantages of reducing existing charges and expenditure are within the power of the legislature, and are dependent mainly on the securities taken for the application of practical science, skill, and economy in the direction of local public works.

And that the removal of noxious physical circumstances, and the promotion of civic, household, and personal cleanliness, are necessary to the improvement of the moral condition of the population; for that sound morality and refinement in manners and health are not long found co-existent with filthy habits amongst any class of the community.

That refuse when thus held in suspension in water may be most cheaply and innoxiously conveyed to any distance out of towns, and also in the best form for productive use, and that the loss and injury by the pollution of natural streams may be avoided.

That for all these purposes, as well as for domestic use, better supplies of water are absolutely necessary.

That for successful and economical drainage the adoption of geological areas as the basis of operations is requisite.

That appropriate scientific arrangements for public drainage would afford important facilities for private land-drainage, which is important for the health as well as sustenance of the labouring classes.

PART TWELVE

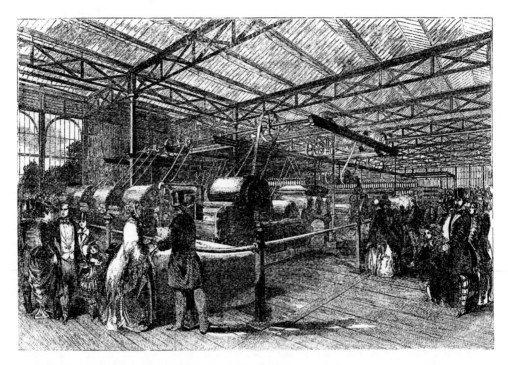

Print of Moving Machinery Hall at the Crystal Palace
The power and beauty of the massive machinery displayed in the special machinery hall at London's Crystal Palace Exposition of 1851 tell an important story. These machines often produced cheap and not always beautiful goods, which were, however, affordable to persons without great means. The image also reminds us, as did Monet's painting of the railroad engine at a station, that the era's aesthetic impulses to some degree had transferred to machines, bridges, and other projects made possible by the industrial revolution.

Material Culture

Commercial and industrial achievements altered Europe's social and economic landscapes. Machine-made goods poured onto the market and found eager purchasers among prosperous populations. Although mass production bankrupted many artisans and craftsmen who could not compete, on the whole the process led to unparalleled prosperity for middle classes that stamped their politics and culture on whole societies. Middle-class women were not expected to work and instead turned their attention to their homes, domestic staffs, and children. Although comfort, richness, and even display were desirable, the new styles in furniture, architecture, and clothing did not equal the opulence of the Old Regime's monarchies and high aristocracy. By mid-century, Victorian luxury wares sacrificed refined elegance in favor of heaviness and excess, whereas cheaper manufactured items created an impression of dull sameness. Both lacked artistry. A surfeit of goods did not guarantee happiness or fulfillment.

In post-Napoleanic Germany, bourgeois aspirations found a reflection in the Biedermeier style of architecture and interior décor. Photographs and text from Sigrid Sangl's *Biedermeier to Bauhaus* (2000) illustrate this Restoration style, which retained a classical elegance. In *The Ladies' Paradise* (1883), Emile Zola (1840–1902) describes the phenomenon of shopping, a form of self-expression for middle- and upper-class women. The rise of department stores with their extravagant, even vulgar displays of merchandise reflected in part the economic growth and pretensions of Napoleon III's Second Empire. The heroine of the novel is, however, not a shopper but an employee. Department stores and the production of the goods in them provided working- and lower-middle class women with occupation, even as they provided prosperous women with preoccupation. The print of machinery at the Crystal Palace Exposition in London (1851) suggests the vast productive potential of industry by mid-century. William Morris (1834–1896), who promoted and practiced handicrafts, became a leader of the Arts and Crafts Movement that espoused a return to artistic values in everyday material life. In *The Revival of Handicraft* (1888), he outlined the case for hand-made versus machine-produced goods. Regardless, the industrial age's array of practical, if not beautiful, manufactured goods remained a boon for working and lower-middle-class families. For better or worse, the age of mass production and consumption had begun.

Study Questions

1. What stage of production does the Biedermeier style represent?
2. How does the Industrial Revolution affect peoples' everyday home lives?
3. What is consumerism and how does it originate?
4. In terms of quality and availability, what is the relationship between machine-produced and hand-produced goods?
5. What does Morris object to in the material culture of the Industrial Revolution?
6. Image: What does the machinery at the Crystal Palace Exposition tell us about the place of manufactured goods by the mid-1800s?

Biedermeier to Bauhaus

Sigrid Sangl

The images of interior décor during the Biedermeier period, that is, the early decades of the nineteenth century in Germany, clearly demarcate a transitional period. The furnishings suggest the past more than the future. Machine-made goods are not in evidence. Perceptions of classical Greece and Rome and of the Enlightenment seem to predominate. Within a few years, middle- and upper-class interiors would be filled with objects of a quite different nature.

Whereas the princely interiors of the decade between 1800 and 1830 made full use of the international design repertoire, the members of the educated middle classes, unhampered by the nobility's need for pomp and circumstance, preferred to furnish their houses with simplicity and functionality. The outcome was often highly aesthetic, and in its later guise, labeled Biedermeier, came to have a profound and lasting influence on the history of interior decoration. This style of living can be seen at its best in the houses of Weimar's two literary giants, Johann Wolfgang von Goethe and Friedrich Schiller. Even before the end of the nineteenth century the homes of these two poets had already become places of pilgrimage for devotees of German Neo-Classicism. As a result the interiors have been well preserved and—after some late-twentieth-century restoration and the removal of many dubious devotionals from the previous century—provide us with a true testimony to German domestic culture of the time.

Goethe's Garden House where, from the time he moved to Weimar in 1776 to his death in 1832, he would go to write poetry away from the stresses of the world, is proof of his theory that a comfortable and tastefully furnished environment, while it may lull one into a state of comfort, also induces passivity and elevates the mind. The sparing nature which distinguishes both this little house in the park by the River Ilm and the work rooms of his town house on

the Frauenplan is the result of a deliberate scheme, which the poet was to sum up in 1829: 'Sumptuous buildings and rooms are for princes and the rich. Whoever lives there feels at ease; one is contented and wants for nothing. But that goes completely against my nature. In such an ostentatious dwelling I immediately become lazy and listless. A simple house on the other hand . . . like this meagre room where we are now, in a sort of ordered disarray, a little gypsy-like, is the right environment for me; it allows my spirit complete freedom to be busy and to create.

One might be tempted to see the grand old poet's declaration as part of an elaborate self-deception, for the truth is that his house on the Frauenplan was thoroughly sumptuous, with reception rooms furnished with the singular purpose of impressing the ladies who came to tea as well as all his other numerous learned and noble visitors. There is nevertheless an almost spartan simplicity to the work rooms, both in the house on the Frauenplan and in the Garden House. Goethe had an aversion to carpets, believing that they often 'embarrassed' the other furnishings with their overpowering designs. So there were no carpets on the plain wooden floorboards just as there were no curtains at the windows. The poet employed local Weimar joiners to make simple wooden chairs, glass-fronted specimen cabinets and functional desks, 'without excess fuss or frills'. He made do with a simple camp bed with cross-straps and a straw mattress. Throughout his house there was not a single Rococo flourish, no

From: Sigrid Sangl, *From Biedermeier to Bauhaus* (New York: Harry Abrams Inc., 2000), pp. 94–95.

ornamental columns or capitals, no lions' feet or bronze mounts, in fact nothing from the vocabulary of ornament which was otherwise current at the turn of the nineteenth century.

As far as the decoration of the walls was concerned, there is evidence that the poet did not stick to his first choice of colours which had been governed by the rigid categorizations set out in his *Theory of Colour* of 1810. He began by painting his garden house in a cool green throughout, only to redecorate later with a strong yellow set off by red ceilings. The subject of colours, their inherent significance and their effect on the human body and spirit, was one of the greatest issues of the time. Even such a complex philosopher as Kant wrote an article on the subject in the *Zeitung für die elegante Welt* (*Newspaper for the Elegant World*) in 1804. Entitled 'On the Meaning of Colours,' the piece endowed each colour with a specific virtue: for example, yellow for candidness, green for friendliness or dark blue for steadfastness. In the sixth section of his *Theory of Colour* Goethe had argued for a 'sensual and moral effect of colours'. He recommended green wallpapers for rooms in which one spent a lot of time, whereas 'rooms papered purely in blue may appear larger, but in fact come across as empty and cold'. But the poet hardly practised what he preached: his bedroom in town changed from pistachio green to rose pink with grey-blue borders, only to be painted over again in apple green with a pink ceiling. Goethe loved nothing better than to rearrange his rooms. One reason for this was his ever-growing collection of art works—ranging from ancient Egyptian sculptures of Isis to contemporary oil paintings—which he always liked to display against an appropriate background.

Interiors in the Biedermeier Style.

The Ladies' Paradise

Emile Zola

Zola's novel may be the first literary description of a new phenomenon, the department store. Whereas previously shopping had occurred in small shops dedicated to one or another kind of goods produced by artisans or masters, now goods of all kinds from all over the world, produced by hand and by machine, filled the shelves of large stores with masses of employees to serve droves of customers. The department store was the equivalent of today's malls and reflected the enormous prosperity created by the Industrial Revolution. Poorer people could hardly afford to shop in such stores but they did provide employment for lower-middle and working-class people.

After the death of her parents, Denise arrives from the provinces with her young brothers to live in Paris with her uncle, who has commercial connections. Mesmerized by the extravagant Paris department stores, she arranges for a position in one of them, The Ladies' Paradise.

The following Monday, the 10th of October, a clear, victorious sun pierced the grey clouds which had darkened Paris during the previous week. It had drizzled all the previous night, a sort of watery mist, the humidity of which dirtied the streets; but in the early morning, thanks to the sharp wind which was driving the clouds away, the pavement had become drier, and the blue sky had a limpid, spring-like gaiety.

Thus The Ladies' Paradise, after eight o'clock, blazed forth beneath the clear rays of the sun, in all the glory of its great sale of winter novelties. Flags were flying at the door, and pieces of woollens were flapping about in the fresh morning air, animating the Place Gaillon with the bustle of a country fair; whilst in both streets the windows developed symphonies of displays, the clearness of the glass showing up still further the brilliant tones. It was like a debauch of colour, a street pleasure which burst forth there, a wealth of goods publicly displayed, where everybody could go and feast their eyes.

But at this hour very few people entered, only a few rare customers, housewives of the neighbourhood, women desirous of avoiding the afternoon crush. Behind the stuffs which decorated it, one could feel the shop to be empty, under arms and waiting for customers, with its waxed floors and counters overflowing with goods.

The busy morning crowd barely glanced at the windows, without lingering a moment. In the Rue Neuve-Saint-Augustin and in the Place Gaillon, where the carriages were to take their stand, there were only two cabs at nine o'clock. The inhabitants of the district, especially the small traders, stirred up by such a show of streamers and decorations, formed little groups in the doorways, at the corners of the streets, gazing at the shop, making bitter remarks. What most filled them with indignation was the sight of one of the four delivery vans just introduced by Mouret, which was standing in the Rue de la Michodière, in front of the delivery office. They were green, picked out with yellow and red, their brilliantly varnished panels sparkling in the sun with the brightness of purple and gold. This van, with its brand-new medley of colours, the

From: Emile Zola, *The Ladies' Paradise* (Berkeley: University of California Press, 1992), pp. 77–82.

name of the house painted on each side, and surmounted with an advertisement of the day's sale, finished by going off at a trot, drawn by a splendid horse, after being filled up with the previous night's parcels; and Baudu, who was standing on the threshold of The Old Elbeuf, watched it as far as the boulevard, where it disappeared, to spread all over Paris in a starry radiance the hated name of The Ladies' Paradise.

However, a few cabs were arriving and forming a line. Every time a customer entered, there was a movement amongst the shop messengers, who were drawn up under the lofty doorway, dressed in livery consisting of a light green coat and trousers, and striped red and yellow waistcoat. Jouve, the inspector and retired captain, was also there, in a frockcoat and white tie, wearing his decoration like a sign of respectability and probity, receiving the ladies with a gravely polite air, bending over them to point out the departments. Then they disappeared in the vestibule, which was transformed into an oriental saloon.

From the very threshold it was a marvel, a surprise, which enchanted all of them. It was Mouret who had been struck with this idea. He was the first to buy, in the Levant, at very advantageous rates, a collection of old and new carpets, articles which up to the present had only been sold at curiosity shops, at high prices; and he intended to flood the market with these goods, selling them at a little over cost price, simply drawing from them a splendid decoration destined to attract the best class of art customers to his establishment. From the centre of the Place Gaillon could be seen this oriental saloon, composed solely of carpets and door curtains which had been hung under his orders. The ceiling was covered with a quantity of Smyrna carpets, the complicated designs of which stood out boldly on a red ground. Then from each side there hung Syrian and Karamanian door-curtains, speckled with green, yellow, and vermilion; Diarbekir door-curtains of a commoner type, rough to the touch, like shepherds' cloaks; besides these there were carpets which could be used as door-curtains and hangings—long Ispahan, Teheran, and Kermancha rugs, the larger Schoumaka and Madras carpets, a strange florescence of peonies and palms, the fancy let loose in a garden of dreams. On the floor were more carpets, a heap of greasy

fleeces: in the centre was an Agra carpet, an extraordinary article with a white ground and a broad delicate blue border, through which ran violet-coloured ornaments of exquisite design. Everywhere there was an immense display of marvellous fabrics; Mecca carpets with a velvety reflection, prayer carpets from Daghestan with a symbolic point, Kurdistan carpets covered with blossoming flowers; and finally, piled up in a corner, a heap of Gherdes, Koula, and Kirchur rugs from fifteen francs a piece.

This sumptuous pacha's tent was furnished with divans and arm-chairs, made with camel sacks, some ornamented with many-coloured lozenges, others with primitive roses. Turkey, Arabia, and the Indies were all there. They had emptied the palaces, plundered the mosques and bazaars. A barbarous gold tone prevailed in the weft of the old carpets, the faded tints of which still preserved a sombre warmth, as of an extinguished furnace, a beautiful burnt hue suggestive of the old masters. Visions of the East floated beneath the luxury of this barbarous art, amid the strong odour which the old wools had retained of the country of vermin and of the rising sun.

In the morning at eight o'clock, when Denise, who was to commence on that very Monday, had crossed the oriental saloon, she stood there, lost in astonishment, unable to recognise the shop entrance, entirely overcome by this harem-like decoration planted at the door. A messenger having shown her to the top of the house, and handed her over to Madame Cabin, who cleaned and looked after the rooms, this person installed her in No. 7, where her box had already been put. It was a narrow cell, opening on the roof by a skylight, furnished with a small bed, a walnut-wood wardrobe, a toilet-table, and two chairs. Twenty similar rooms ran along the convent-like corridor, painted yellow; and, out of the thirty-five young ladies in the house, the twenty who had no friends in Paris slept there, whilst the remaining fifteen lodged outside, a few with borrowed aunts and cousins. Denise at once took off her shabby woollen dress, worn thin by brushing and mended at the sleeves, the only one she had brought from Valognes; she then put on the uniform of her department, a black silk dress which had been altered for her and which she found ready on the bed. This dress was still too large, too wide across the shoulders; but she was so hurried in her emotion that she paid no heed to these details of coquetry. She had never worn silk before. When she went downstairs again, dressed up, uncomfortable, she looked at the shining skirt, feeling ashamed of the noisy rustling of the silk.

Down below, as she was entering her department, a quarrel burst out. She heard Clara say, in a shrill voice:

"Madame, I came in before her."

"It isn't true," replied Marguerite. "She pushed past me at the door, but I had already one foot in the room."

It was for the inscription on the list of turns, which regulated the sales. The saleswomen wrote their names on a slate in the order of their arrival, and whenever one of them had served a customer, she re-wrote her name beneath the others. Madame Aurélie finished by deciding in Marguerite's favour.

"Always some injustice here!" muttered Clara, furiously.

But Denise's entry reconciled these young ladies. They looked at her, then smiled to each other. How could a person truss herself up in that way! The young girl went and awkwardly wrote her name on the list, where she found herself last. Meanwhile, Madame Aurélie was examining her with an anxious face. She could not help saying:

"My dear, two like you could get into your dress; you must have it taken in. Besides, you don't know how to dress yourself. Come here and let me arrange you a bit."

And she placed herself before one of the tall glasses alternating with the doors of the cupboards containing the dresses. The vast apartment, surrounded by these glasses and the wood-work in carved oak, the floor covered with red Wilton carpet of a large pattern, resembled the commonplace drawing-room of an hotel, traversed by a continual stream of travellers. The young ladies completed the resemblance, dressed in the regulation silk, promenading their commercial charms about, without ever sitting down on the dozen chairs reserved for the customers. All wore between two buttonholes of the body of their dresses, as if stuck in their bosoms, a long pencil, with its point in the air; and half out of their pockets, could be seen the white cover of the book of debit-notes. Several risked wearing jewellery—rings, brooches, chains; but their great coquetry, the luxury they all struggled for in the forced uniformity of their dress, was their bare hair, quantities of it, augmented by plaits and chignons when their own did not suffice, combed, curled, and decked out in every way.

Victorian styles were ornate to the point of excess, as suggested by these objects created for domestic use and exhibited at the Crystal Palace Exposition.

The Revival of Handicraft

William Morris

The flood of cheap, machine-produced goods brought about a reaction. Moved by aesthetic concerns, William Morris suggested reviving handicrafts in order to produce goods of greater beauty and lasting value. The values of the Biedermeier and earlier periods appealed to him more than those of the high Victorian era. He also felt that persons chained to the drudgery of machinery in factories would be better off making beautiful objects by hand on the basis of skills. Well-intentioned as it was, Morris's outlook represented an elite reaction to a phenomenon, the industrial revolution, that inexorably transformed human life.

The Revival of Handicraft, an Article in the "Fortnightly Review," November 1888

For some time past there has been a good deal of interest shown in what is called in our modern slang Art Workmanship, and quite recently there has been a growing feeling that this art workmanship to be of any value must have some of the workman's individuality imparted to it beside whatever of art it may have got from the design of the artist who has planned, but not executed the work. This feeling has gone so far that there is growing up a fashion for demanding handmade goods even when they are not ornamented in any way, as, for instance, woollen and linen cloth spun by hand and woven without power, hand-knitted hosiery, and the like. Nay, it is not uncommon to hear regrets for the hand-labour in the fields, now fast disappearing from even backward districts of civilized countries. The scythe, the sickle, and even the flail are lamented over, and many are looking forward with drooping spirits to the time when the hand-plough will be as completely extinct as the quern, and the rattle of the steam-engine will take the place of the whistle of the curly-headed ploughboy through all the length and breadth of the land. People interested, or who suppose that they are interested, in the details of the arts of life feel a desire to revert to methods of handicraft for production in general; and it may therefore be worth considering how far this is a mere reactionary sentiment incapable of realization, and how far it may foreshadow a real coming change in our habits of life as irresistible as the former change which has produced the system of machine-production, the system against which revolt is now attempted.

In this paper I propose to confine the aforesaid consideration as much as I can to the effect of machinery *versus* handicraft upon the arts; using that latter word as widely as possible, so as to include all products of labour which have any claims to be considered beautiful. I say as far as possible: for as all roads lead to Rome, so the life, habits, and aspirations of all groups and classes of the community are founded on the economical conditions under which the mass of the people live, and it is impossible to exclude socio-political questions from the consideration of aesthetics. Also, although I must avow myself a sharer in the above-mentioned reactionary regrets, I must at the outset disclaim the mere aesthetic point of view which looks upon the ploughman and his bullocks and his plough, the reaper, his work, his wife, and his dinner, as so many elements which compose a pretty tapestry hanging, fit to adorn the study of a contemplative

From: William Morris, *The Collected Works of William Morris*, vol. 22 (London: Longmans Green & Co., 1914), pp. 331–341.

person of cultivation, but which it is not worth while differentiating from each other except in so far as they are related to the beauty and interest of the picture. On the contrary, what I wish for is that the reaper and his wife should have themselves a due share in all the fullness of life; and I can, without any great effort, perceive the justice of their forcing me to bear part of the burden of its deficiencies, so that we may together be forced to attempt to remedy them, and have no very heavy burden to carry between us.

To return to our aesthetics: though a certain part of the cultivated classes of to-day regret the disappearance of handicraft from production, they are quite vague as to how and why it is disappearing, and as to how and why it may reappear. For to begin with the general public is grossly ignorant of all the methods and processes of manufacture. This is of course one result of the machine-system we are considering. Almost all goods are made apart from the life of those who use them; we are not responsible for them, our will has had no part in their production, except so far as we form a part of the market on which they can be forced for the profit of the capitalist whose money is employed in producing them. The market assumes that certain wares are wanted, it produces such wares, indeed, but their kind and quality are only adapted to the needs of the public in a very rough fashion, because the public needs are subordinated to the interest of the capitalist masters of the market, and they can force the public to put up with the less desirable article, if they choose, as they generally do. The result is that in this direction our boasted individuality is a sham; and persons who wish for anything that deviates ever so little from the beaten path have either to wear away their lives in a wearisome and mostly futile contest with a stupendous organization which disregards their wishes, or to allow those wishes to be crushed out for the sake of a quiet life.

Let us take a few trivial but undeniable examples. You want a hat, say, like that you wore last year; you go to the hatter's, and find you cannot get it there, and you have no resource but in submission. Money by itself won't buy you the hat you want; it will cost you three months' hard labour and twenty pounds to have an inch added to the brim of your wideawake; for you will have to get hold of a small capitalist (of whom but few are left), and by a series of intrigues and resolute actions which would make material for a three-volume novel, get him to allow you to turn one of his hands into a handicraftsman for the occasion; and a very poor handicraftsman he will be, when all is said. Again, I carry a walking-stick, and like all sensible persons like it to have a good heavy end that will swing out well before me. A year or two ago it became the fashion to pare away all walking-sticks to the shape of attenuated carrots, and I really believe I shortened my life in my attempts at getting a reasonable staff of the kind I was used to, so difficult it was. Again, you want a piece of furniture, which the trade (mark the word, Trade, not Craft!) turns out blotched over with idiotic sham ornament; you wish to dispense with this degradation, and propose it to your upholsterer, who grudgingly assents to it; and you find that you have to pay the price of two pieces of furniture for the privilege of indulging your whim of leaving out the trade finish (I decline to call it ornament) on the one you have got made for you. And this is because it has been made by handicraft instead of machinery. For most people, therefore, there is a prohibitive price put upon the acquirement of the knowledge of methods and processes. We do not know how a piece of goods is made, what the difficulties are that beset its manufacture, what it ought to look like, feel like, smell like, or what it ought to cost apart from the profit of the middleman. We have lost the art of marketing, and with it the due sympathy with the life of the workshop, which would, if it existed, be such a wholesome check on the humbug of party politics.

It is a natural consequence of this ignorance of the methods of making wares, that even those who are in revolt against the tyranny of the excess of division of labour in the occupations of life, and who wish to recur more or less to handicraft, should also be ignorant of what that life of handicraft was when all wares were made by handicraft. If their revolt is to carry any hope with it, it is necessary that they should know something of this. I must assume that many or perhaps most of my readers are not acquainted with Socialist literature, and that few of them have read the admirable account of the

different epochs of production given in Karl Marx'
great work entitled "Capital." I must ask to be
excused, therefore, for stating very briefly what,
chiefly owing to Marx, has become a common-place
of Socialism, but is not generally known outside it.
There have been three great epochs of production
since the beginning of the Middle Ages. During the
first or mediæval period all production was individ-
ualistic in method; for though the workmen were
combined into great associations for protection and
the organization of labour, they were so associated
as citizens, not as mere workmen. There was little
or no division of labour, and what machinery was
used was simply of the nature of a multiplied tool,
a help to the workman's hand-labour and not a
supplanter of it. The workman worked for himself
and not for any capitalistic employer, and he was
accordingly master of his work and his time; this
was the period of pure handicraft. When in the latter half of the sixteenth century the capitalist
employer and the so-called free workman began to
appear, the workmen were collected into workshops, the old tool-machines were improved, and at
last a new invention, the division of labour, found
its way into the workshops. The division of labour
went on growing throughout the seventeenth century, and was perfected in the eighteenth, when the
unit of labour became a group and not a single man;
or in other words the workman became a mere part
of a machine composed sometimes wholly of human
beings and sometimes of human beings plus labour-
saving machines, which towards the end of this
period were being copiously invented; the fly-shuttle
may be taken for an example of these. The latter
half of the eighteenth century saw the beginning of
the last epoch of production that the world has
known, that of the automatic machine which super-
sedes hand-labour, and turns the workman who was
once a handicraftsman helped by tools, and next a
part of a machine, into a tender of machines. And as
far as we can see, the revolution in this direction as
to kind is complete, though as to degree, as pointed
out by Mr. David A. Wells last year (1887), the tendency is towards the displacement of ever more and
more "muscular" labour, as Mr. Wells calls it.

This is very briefly the history of the evolution of
industry during the last five hundred years; and the
question now comes: Are we justified in wishing that
handicraft may in its turn supplant machinery? Or it
would perhaps be better to put the question in
another way: Will the period of machinery evolve
itself into a fresh period of machinery more independent of human labour than anything we can conceive of now, or will it develop its contradictory in
the shape of a new and improved period of production by handicraft? The second form of the question
is the preferable one, because it helps us to give a reasonable answer to what people who have any interest in external beauty will certainly ask: Is the change
from handicraft to machinery good or bad? And the
answer to that question is to my mind that, as my
friend Belfort Bax has put it, statically it is bad,
dynamically it is good. As a condition of life, production by machinery is altogether an evil; as an instrument for forcing on us better conditions of life it has
been, and for some time yet will be, indispensable.

Having thus tried to clear myself of mere reactionary pessimism, let me attempt to show why statically handicraft is to my mind desirable, and its
destruction a degradation of life. Well, first I shall
not shrink from saying bluntly that production by
machinery necessarily results in utilitarian ugliness
in everything which the labour of man deals with,
and that this is a serious evil and a degradation of
human life. So clearly is this the fact that though
few people will venture to deny the latter part of the
proposition, yet in their hearts the greater part of
cultivated civilized persons do not regard it as an
evil, because their degradation has already gone so
far that they cannot, in what concerns the sense of
seeing, discriminate between beauty and ugliness:
their languid assent to the desirableness of beauty is
with them only a convention, a superstitious survival from the times when beauty was a necessity to
all men. The first part of the proposition (that
machine-industry produces ugliness) I cannot argue
with these persons, because they neither know, nor
care for, the difference between beauty and ugliness;
and with those who do understand what beauty
means I need not argue it, as they are but too familiar with the fact that the produce of all modern
industrialism is ugly, and that whenever anything
which is old disappears, its place is taken by something inferior to it in beauty; and that even out in

the very fields and open country. The art of making beautifully all kinds of ordinary things, carts, gates, fences, boats, bowls, and so forth, let alone houses and public buildings, unconsciously and without effort, has gone; when anything has to be renewed among these simple things the only question asked is how little it can be done for, so as to tide us over our responsibility and shift its mending on to the next generation.

It may be said, and indeed I have heard it said, that since there is some beauty still left in the world and some people who admire it, there is a certain gain in the acknowledged eclecticism of the present day, since the ugliness which is so common affords a contrast whereby the beauty, which is so rare, may be appreciated. This I suspect to be only another form of the maxim which is the sheet-anchor of the laziest and most cowardly group of our cultivated classes, that it is good for the many to suffer for the few; but if any one puts forward in good faith the fear that we may be too happy in the possession of pleasant surroundings, so that we shall not be able to enjoy them, I must answer that this seems to me a very remote terror. Even when the tide at last turns in the direction of sweeping away modern squalor and vulgarity, we shall have, I doubt, many generations of effort in perfecting the transformation, and when it is at last complete, there will be first the triumph of our success to exalt us, and next the history of the long wade through the putrid sea of ugliness which we shall have at last escaped from. But furthermore, the proper answer to this objection lies deeper than this. It is to my mind that very consciousness of the production of beauty for beauty's sake which we want to avoid; it is just what is apt to produce affectation and effeminacy amongst the artists and their following. In the great times of art conscious effort was used to produce great works for the glory of the City, the triumph of the Church, the exaltation of the citizens, the quickening of the devotion of the faithful; even in the higher art, the record of history, the instruction of men alive and to live hereafter, was the aim rather than beauty; and the lesser art was unconscious and spontaneous, and did not in any way interfere with the rougher business of life, while it enabled men in general to understand and sympathize with the

nobler forms of art. But unconscious as these producers of ordinary beauty may be, they will not and cannot fail to receive pleasure from the exercise of their work under these conditions, and this above all things is that which influences me most in my hope for the recovery of handicraft. I have said it often enough, but I must say it once again, since it is so much a part of my case for handicraft, that so long as man allows his daily work to be mere unrelieved drudgery he will seek happiness in vain. I say further that the worst tyrants of the days of violence were but feeble tormentors compared with those Captains of Industry who have taken the pleasure of work away from the workmen. Furthermore I feel absolutely certain that handicraft joined to certain other conditions, of which more presently, would produce the beauty and the pleasure in work above mentioned; and if that be so, and this double pleasure of lovely surroundings and happy work could take the place of the double torment of squalid surroundings and wretched drudgery, have we not good reason for wishing, if it might be, that handicraft should once more step into the place of machine-production?

I am not blind to the tremendous change which this revolution would mean. The maxim of modern civilization to a well-to-do man is, Avoid taking trouble! Get as many of the functions of your life as you can performed by others for you! Vicarious life is the watchword of our civilization, and we well-to-do and cultivated people live smoothly enough while it lasts. But, in the first place, how about the vicars, who do more for us than the singing of mass for our behoof for a scanty stipend? Will they go on with it for ever? For indeed the shuffling off of responsibilities from one to the other has to stop at last, and somebody has to bear the burden in the end. But let that pass, since I am not writing politics, and let us consider another aspect of the matter. What wretched lop-sided creatures we are being made by the excess of the division of labour in the occupations of life! What on earth are we going to do with our time when we have brought the art of vicarious life to perfection, having first complicated the question by the ceaseless creation of artificial wants which we refuse to supply for ourselves? Are all of us (we of the great middle class I mean) going to turn philosophers, poets, essayists—men of genius, in a word, when we have come to look down on the ordinary functions of life with the same kind of contempt wherewith persons of good breeding look down upon a good dinner, eating it sedulously however? I shudder when I think of how we shall bore each other when we have reached that perfection. Nay, I think we have already got in all branches of culture rather more geniuses than we can comfortably bear, and that we lack, so to say, audiences rather than preachers. I must ask pardon of my readers; but our case is at once so grievous and so absurd that one can scarcely help laughing out of bitterness of soul. In the very midst of our pessimism we are boastful of our wisdom, yet we are helpless in the face of the necessities we have created, and which, in spite of our anxiety about art, are at present driving us into luxury unredeemed by beauty on the one hand, and squalor unrelieved by incident or romance on the other, and will one day drive us into mere ruin.

Yes, we do sorely need a system of production which will give us beautiful surroundings and pleasant occupation, and which will tend to make us good human animals, able to do something for ourselves, so that we may be generally intelligent instead of dividing ourselves into dull drudges or duller pleasure-seekers according to our class, on the one hand, or hapless pessimistic intellectual personages, and pretenders to that dignity, on the other. We do most certainly need happiness in our daily work, content in our daily rest; and all this cannot be if we hand over the whole responsibility of the details of our daily life to machines and their drivers. We are right to long for intelligent handicraft to come back to the world which it once made tolerable amidst war and turmoil and uncertainty of life, and which it should, one would think, make happy now we have grown so peaceful, so considerate of each other's temporal welfare.

Then comes the question, How can the change be made? And here at once we are met by the difficulty that the sickness and death of handicraft is, it seems, a natural expression of the tendency of the age. We willed the end, and therefore the means also. Since the last days of the Middle Ages the creation of an intellectual aristocracy has been, so to say, the spiritual purpose of civilization side by side

with its material purpose of supplanting the aristocracy of status by the aristocracy of wealth. Part of the price it has had to pay for its success in that purpose (and some would say it is comparatively an insignificant part) is that this new aristocracy of intellect has been compelled to forgo the lively interest in the beauty and romance of life, which was once the portion of every artificer at least, if not of every workman, and to live surrounded by an ugly vulgarity which the world amidst all its changes has not known till modern times. It is not strange that until recently it has not been conscious of this degradation; but it may seem strange to many that it has now grown partially conscious of it. It is common now to hear people say of such and such a piece of country or suburb: "Ah! it was so beautiful a year or so ago, but it has been quite spoilt by the building." Forty years back the building would have been looked on as a vast improvement; now we have grown conscious of the hideousness we are creating, and we go on creating it. We see the price we have paid for our aristocracy of intellect, and even that aristocracy itself is more than half regretful of the bargain, and would be glad if it could keep the gain and not pay the full price for it. Hence not only the empty grumbling about the continuous march of machinery over dying handicraft, but also various elegant little schemes for trying to withdraw ourselves, some of us, from the consequences (in this direction) of our being superior persons; none of which can have more than a temporary and very limited success. The great wave of commercial necessity will sweep away all these well-meant attempts to stem it, and think little of what it has done, or whither it is going.

Yet after all even these feeble manifestations of discontent with the tyranny of commerce are tokens of a revolutionary epoch, and to me it is inconceivable that machine-production will develop into mere infinity of machinery, or life wholly lapse into a disregard of life as it passes. It is true indeed that powerful as the cultivated middle class is, it has not the power of re-creating the beauty and romance of life; but that will be the work of the new society which the blind progress of commercialism will create, nay, is creating. The cultivated middle class is a class of slave-holders, and its power of living according to its choice is limited by the necessity of finding constant livelihood and employment for the slaves who keep it alive. It is only a society of equals which can choose the life it will live, which can choose to forgo gross luxury and base utilitarianism in return for the unwearying pleasure of tasting the fullness of life. It is my firm belief that we shall in the end realize this society of equals, and also that when it is realized it will not endure a vicarious life by means of machinery; that it will in short be the master of its machinery and not the servant, as our age is.

Meantime, since we shall have to go through a long series of social and political events before we shall be free to choose how we shall live, we should welcome even the feeble protest which is now being made against the vulgarization of all life: first because it is one token amongst others of the sickness of modern civilization; and next, because it may help to keep alive memories of the past which are necessary elements of the life of the future, and methods of work which no society could afford to lose. In short, it may be said that though the movement towards the revival of handicraft is contemptible on the surface in face of the gigantic fabric of commercialism; yet, taken in conjunction with the general movement towards freedom of life for all, on which we are now surely embarked, as a protest against intellectual tyranny, and a token of the change which is transforming civilization into socialism, it is both noteworthy and encouraging.

PART THIRTEEN

Photo of Dreyfus Passing Through the "Guard of Dishonor"

The new emphasis on nationality tended to stimulate hostility toward other peoples. Anti-Semitism, an undercurrent in European culture, increased heavily in central and eastern Europe, where Jewish populations were very large, and also in Western Europe, as revealed by France's infamous Dreyfus Affair during the 1890s. Falsely charged with spying by military authorities who knew the truth, Dreyfus was drummed out of the army in a ceremony shown in this photograph and sent to imprisonment, until he was finally cleared. For years controversy and scandal surrounded the affair, which split France into two camps and induced Herzl to found the Zionist movement. The incident suggests the interplay between public opinion and politics during a new age of mass media and also reminds us that Europe's Jewish populations viewed themselves as loyal citizens of their respective countries.

Mass Politics and Society, 1850–1900

Despite failure, the 1848 revolutions altered Europe's path. Bad conscience and the wish to avoid future revolutions motivated governments to intervene on behalf of workers and the poor. European nations extended voting rights toward universal male suffrage and offered health insurance, pensions, and education to laboring people, thus compromising *laissez faire* and initiating the welfare state. Paid for by rapid industrialization, these programs softened the feared worker-bourgeois clashes. By the end of the century, most European states rested firmly on their entire populations. Still, perfected democracy was a mixed blessing. Governments utilized newspapers, accessible to literate populations, to stir mass opinion for various causes, not all good. Likewise, under mass suffrage, public opinion, with all its variability and unreliability, heavily influenced everyday politics. With full mass support, governments pursued policies of militarism, imperialism, and chauvinism.

In his Open Letter to Michelet (1851), the Russian socialist Alexander Herzen (1812–1870) underscored the awesome uncertainties of the post-1848 era. Couched in alarming terms, Herzen's analysis implies a positive European future, possibly under the influence of a revived and innovative Russia. *The Belleville Manifesto* (1869), with its call for universal manhood suffrage, and *Educating the Peasantry* (1873), both by future French president Leon Gambetta (1838–1882), and the papal encyclical *Rerum Novarum* (1891) by Pope Leo XIII (1810–1903) outlined the case for state intervention in favor of laborers. Gambetta and other European politicians utilized social programs to strengthen their nation states, a tactic that in fact persuaded many workers and their leaders to reject Marx's violent vision. In his 1898 *Evolutionary Socialism,* the German Social Democrat Eduard Bernstein (1850–1932) proposed a revisionist socialist program of gradual reform within the capitalist state. Regardless, chauvinism and anti-Semitism plagued even European countries normally viewed as havens of freedom and equality. The Dreyfus Affair, as suggested by the photograph of Alfred Dreyfus (1859–1935) being drummed out of the French Army, reflected overt anti-Semitism and fractured French society along liberal-conservative lines. In defense of Dreyfus, Emile Zola (1840–1902) made his famous speech, "J'accuse" (1898), in which he condemned the government and military for falsely blaming the Jewish officer Dreyfus for the treasonous activities of a well-connected non-Jewish officer.

Study Questions

1. How do Herzen's ideas compare to those of Gambetta and Leo XIII?
2. How do Gambetta and Leo XIII agree in their views of social problems?
3. How do Bernstein's ideas of socialism differ from those of Marx and Lenin?
4. Why do anti-Semitism and chauvinism bring class compromise in mass politics?
5. Why did some people fear mass politics in the late nineteenth century?
6. Image: Why is Dreyfus doing what he is doing in the photo of a military ritual?

Letter to Michelet

Alexander Herzen

Alexander Herzen, known as the father of Russian socialism, helped create the atmosphere in Russia that led to the emancipation of the serfs in 1861. He traveled widely throughout Europe and was well versed in European affairs. In his letter to the French historian Jules Michelet (1798–1874), Herzen argues against certain derogatory comments made by Michelet concerning the Russian people. This excerpt contains an unfavorable picture of mid-century Europe.

Europe is approaching a terrible cataclysm. The world of the Middle Ages has come to an end. The world of feudalism is expiring. The religious and political revolutions are petering out under the weight of their own complete impotence. They have great achievements to their credit, but they have failed to complete their tasks. They have stripped Throne and Altar of the prestige they once enjoyed, but they have not established the era of freedom. They have lit new desires in the hearts of men but they have not provided ways of satisfying them. Parliamentarianism, Protestantism—these are mere prevarications, temporary measures, attempts to stave off the flood, which can arrest only for a short while the process of death and rebirth. The time for them has passed. Since 1848 it has become apparent that no amount of delving into Roman law, of barren casuistry, of thin philosophic deism, of sterile religious rationalism can hold back society from fulfilling its destiny.

The storm draws near. There can no longer be doubt about it; on this point revolutionaries and reactionaries agree. Men's minds are unbalanced: a serious question, a question of life and death, lies heavy on their hearts. Men grow worried, disturbed. They ask themselves, is it still possible for Europe, that hoary Proteus, that decaying organism, to find within itself the strength to bring about its own recovery? And having asked the question, they dread the answer. They tremble with suspense.

It *is* a grave question.

Will old Europe find the means to rid itself of its sluggish blood, so that it may plunge headlong into the limitless future—the future, that passionate, fatal creature who draws us all towards her with irresistible force, towards whom we fling ourselves with utter recklessness, not caring whether our path is driven across the ruins of our ancestral homes, whether we have to squander the treasure of ancient civilizations and the material wealth of modern culture?

On both sides the position is fully understood. Europe has slipped back into the grim, unbroken darkness that must come before the dawn of the final struggle. It is not life but mere suspense, anxiety. Everything is upside down. There is no regard for law, no justice, not even a semblance of liberty. A secular and irreligious inquisition reigns supreme: civil rights have been suspended, and in their stead martial law and a state of siege proclaimed. There is only one moral force that still has any authority over men, that still demands and receives their obedience: and that is Fear, which is universal. All other issues have to give way before the over-riding interest of Reaction. Governments that to all appearances are sharply divided on questions of principle, come together affectionately to form a single œcumenical police force. The Emperor of Russia, without troubling to conceal his loathing

From: Alexander Herzen, *From the Other Shore and The Russian People under Socialism* (Cleveland: The World Publishing Co., 1963), pp. 167–169.

for the French, rewards the Prefect of the Paris police: the King of Naples confers a decoration on the President of the Republic with his own hand—the hand of a turnkey: the King of Prussia muffles himself up in his Russian uniform and hurries off to Warsaw to embrace his old enemy the Emperor of Austria and receive the blessing of Nicholas—Nicholas, the heretical Emperor, who, to complete the picture, lends out his soldiers to protect the Roman Pontiff. On this witches' Sabbath, on this Walpurgis night of reaction, all personal security vanishes: safeguards that exist even in the most backward societies, in China, in Persia, are no longer respected in the capitals of what was once the civilized world.

We can no longer believe our eyes. Is this really the Europe that we once knew and loved?

Indeed if there were no longer an England, free and proud, if that diamond set in the silver sea, as Shakespeare called it, no longer shone bright: if Switzerland were to deny its principles time and time again, like St Peter in fear of Caesar: if Piedmont, the one free, strong element in Italy, the last refuge of civilization which, expelled from the North, shelters south of the Alps but without daring to cross the Appenines, were suddenly to grow insensible to all human feelings—if in a word, these three countries were to fall victims to that pestilential air which blows from Paris and Vienna, then we should have to say that the dissolution of the old world was complete, that the parricidal hands of the conservatives had done their worst and that barbarism was already upon us in France and Germany.

The Belleville Manifesto and Educating the Peasantry
Leon Gambetta

Leon Gambetta was elected to the French legislature in 1869 based on the radical program of the Belleville Manifesto, which called for the abolition of standing armies, the disestablishment of the church, and freedom of the press, assembly, and of association. Later Gambetta also espoused free elementary education for workers and peasants, as suggested by the second essay. While striving to protect the opponents of Napoleon III's regime, he became one of the leaders of the republican minority. Although he often criticized the foreign policy of Napoleon III, Gambetta remained a devout French patriot. His ideas about voting and education aimed at strengthening the French nation.

The Belleville Manifesto

Citizen Electors—I accept this mandate.

On these conditions I shall be especially proud to represent you because this election will have been conducted in conformity with the true principles of universal suffrage. The electors will have freely chosen their candidate. The electors will have determined the political programme of their delegate. The method seems to me at once right and in line with the traditions of the early days of the French Revolution.

I therefore in my turn adhere freely to the declaration of principles and the rightful claims which you commission me to press at the tribune.

With you, I think that there is no other sovereign but the people, and that universal suffrage, the instrument of this sovereignty, has no value and basis and carries no obligation, unless it is radically free.

The most urgent reform must therefore be to free universal suffrage from every tutelage, every shackle, every pressure, every corruption.

With you, I think that universal suffrage, once made the master, would suffice to sweep away all the things which your programme demands, and to establish all the freedoms, all the institutions which we are seeking to bring about.

With you, I think that France, the home of indestructible democracy, will know liberty, peace, order, justice, material prosperity and moral greatness only through the triumph of the principles of the French Revolution.

With you, I think that a legal and loyal democracy is the political system *par excellence* which achieves most promptly and certainly the moral and material emancipation of the greatest number, and best ensures social equality in laws, actions and customs.

But—with you also—I consider that the progressive achievement of these reforms depends absolutely on the political regime and on political reforms, and it is for me axiomatic in these matters that the form involves and determines the substance.

It is, furthermore, this sequence and order of priority which our fathers have indicated and fixed in the profound and comprehensive slogan beyond which there is no safety: Liberty, Equality, Fraternity. We are thus in mutual agreement. Our contact is completed. I am at once your delegate and your trustee.

I go further than signifying agreement. I give you my vow: I swear obedience to this present contract and fidelity to the Sovereign people.

From: *Democracy in France: the Third and Fourth Republics,* comp. by David Thompson (London: Oxford University Press, 1952), pp. 270–271.

Educating the Peasantry

The peasantry is intellectually several centuries behind the enlightened and educated classes in this country. The distance between them and us is immense. We have received a classical or scientific education—even the imperfect one of our day. We have learned to read our history, to speak our language, while (a cruel thing to say) so many of our countrymen can only babble! Ah! that peasant, bound as he is to the tillage of the soil, who bravely carries the burden of his day, with no other consolation than that of leaving to his children the paternal fields, perhaps increased an acre in extent; all his passions, joys, and fears concentrated in the fate of his patrimony. Of the external world, of the society in which he lives, he apprehends only legends and rumors. He is the prey of the cunning and fraudulent. He strikes, without knowing it, the bosom of the revolution, his benefactress; he gives loyally his taxes and his blood to a society for which he feels fear as much as respect. But there his role ends, and if you speak to him of principles, he knows nothing of them.

It is to the peasantry, then, that we must address ourselves. We must raise and instruct them.... Enlightened and free peasants who are able to represent themselves ... should be a tribute rendered to the progress of the civilization of the masses. This new social force should be utilized for the general welfare.

Unfortunately we have not yet reached that point. Progress will be denied us as long as the French democracy fail to demonstrate that if we would remake our country, if we would bring back her grandeur, her power, and her genius it is of vital interest to her superior classes to elevate and emancipate this people of workers, who hold in reserve a force still virgin but able to develop inexhaustible treasures of activity and aptitude. We must learn and then teach the peasant what he owes to Society and what he has the right to ask of her.

On the day when it shall be well understood that we have no grander or more pressing work; that we should put aside and postpone all other reforms: that we have but one task—the Instruction of the people, the diffusion of education, the encouragement of science—on that day a great step will have been taken in your regeneration. But our action needs to be a double one, that it may bear upon the body as well as the wind. To be exact, each man should be intelligent, trained not only to think, read, and reason, but made able to act and fight. Everywhere beside the teacher we should place the gymnast and the soldier, to the end that our children, our soldiers, our fellow citizens, may be able to hold a sword, to carry a gun on a long march, to sleep under the canopy of the stars, to support valiantly all the hardships demanded of a patriot. We must push to the front education. Otherwise we only make a success of letters, but do not create a bulwark of patriots ...

If it need ten years, if it need twenty years, then we must devote to it ten or twenty years. But we must begin at once, that each year may see the advancing life of a new generation, strong, intelligent, as much in love with science as with the Fatherland, having in their hearts the double sentiment that he serves his country well only when he serves it with his reason and his arm.

We have been educated in a rough school. We must therefore cure ourselves of the vanity which has caused us so many disasters. We must realize conscientiously where our responsibility exists, and, seeing the remedy, sacrifice all to the object to be attained—to remake and reconstitute France! ...

From: *The World's Famous Orations*. William Jennings Bryan, editor-in-chief, 10 vols. (New York and London: Funk and Wagnalls Co., 1906), vol. 4, 32–33.

Evolutionary Socialism

Eduard Bernstein

During the late nineteenth century, socialist and working-class movements had gained ground in many countries. Divisions arose among socialists about how best to interpret Marx and serve the interests of the proletariat. Some Marxists and other socialists continued to support a revolutionary overthrow of the capitalist order, whereas others, such as the German Eduard Bernstein began to argue in favor of evolutionary socialism. Bernstein and others believed that socialism could be achieved through reform, not revolution, which was no longer needed in states that were carrying out important reforms.

Ultimate Aim and Tendency

Reference has already been made in different passages of this book to the great influence which tradition exercises, even amongst socialists, upon judgments regarding facts and ideas. I say expressly "even amongst socialists" because this power of tradition is a very widespread phenomenon from which no party, no literary or artistic line of thought, is free, and which penetrates deeply even into most of the sciences. It will probably never be quite rooted out. A certain interval of time must always pass before men so far recognise the inconsistency of tradition with what exists as to put the former on the shelf. Until this happens tradition usually forms the most powerful means of linking those together whom no strong, constant, effective interest or external pressure knits together. Hence the intuitive preference of all men of action, however revolutionary they may be in their aims, for tradition. "Never swap horses whilst crossing a stream." This motto of old Lincoln is rooted in the same thought as Lassalle's well-known anathema against the "nagging spirit of liberalism, the complaint of individual opining and wanting to know better." Whilst tradition is essentially conservative, criticism is almost always destructive. At the moment of important action, therefore, criticism,

even when most justified by facts, can be an evil, and therefore be reprehensible.

To recognise this is, of course, not to call tradition sacred and to forbid criticism. Parties are not always in the midst of rapids when attention is paid to one task only.

For a party which has to keep up with a real evolution, criticism is indispensable and tradition can become an oppressive burden, a restraining fetter.

But men in very few cases willingly and fully account for the importance of the changes which take place in their traditional assumptions. Usually they prefer to take into account only such changes as are concerned with undeniable facts and to bring them into unison as far as can be with the traditional catchwords. The method is called pettifogging, and the apologies and explanations for it are called cant.

Cant—the word is English, and is said to have been first used in the sixteenth century as a description of the saintly sing-song of the Puritans. In its more general meaning it denotes an unreal manner of speech, thoughtlessly imitative, or used with the consciousness of its untruth, to attain any kind of object, whether it be in religion, politics, or be concerned with theory or actuality. In this wider meaning cant is very ancient—there were no worse "canters," for example, than the Greeks of the past classic period—and it permeates in countless forms the whole of our civilised life. Every nation, every class and every group united by theory or interest

From: Eduard Bernstein, *Evolutionary Socialism* (New York: Schocken Books, 1970), pp. 200–224.

has its own cant. It has partly become such a mere matter of convention, of pure form, that no one is any longer deceived by its emptiness, and a fight against it would be shooting idly at sparrows. But this does not apply to the cant that appears in the guise of science and the cant which has become a political battle cry.

My proposition, "To me that which is generally called the ultimate aim of socialism is nothing, but the movement is everything," has often been conceived as a denial of every definite aim of the socialist movement, and Mr. George Plechanow has even discovered that I have quoted this "famous sentence" from the book *To Social Peace*, by Gerhard von Schulze-Gävernitz. There, indeed, a passage reads that it is certainly indispensable for revolutionary socialism to take as its ultimate aim the nationalisation of all the means of production, but not for practical political socialism which places near aims in front of distant ones. Because an ultimate aim is here regarded as being dispensable for practical objects, and as I also have professed but little interest for ultimate aims, I am an "indiscriminating follower" of Schulze-Gävernitz. One must confess that such demonstration bears witness to a striking wealth of thought.

When eight years ago I reviewed the Schulze-Gävernitz book in *Neue Zeit*, although my criticism was strongly influenced by assumptions which I now no longer hold, yet I put on one side as immaterial that opposition of ultimate aim and practical activity in reform, and admitted—without encountering a protest—that for England a further peaceful development, such as Schulze-Gävernitz places in prospect before her was not improbable. I expressed the conviction that with the continuance of free development, the English working classes would certainly increase their demands, but would desire nothing that could not be shown each time to be necessary and attainable beyond all doubt. That is at the bottom nothing else than what I say to-day. And if anyone wishes to bring up against me the advances in social democracy made since then in England, I answer that with this extension a development of the English social democracy has gone hand in hand from the Utopian, revolutionary sect, as Engels repeatedly represented it to be, to the party of political reform which we now know. No socialist capable of thinking, dreams to-day in Eng-

land of an imminent victory for socialism by means of a violent revolution—none dreams of a quick conquest of Parliament by a revolutionary proletariat. But they rely more and more on work in the municipalities and other self-governing bodies. The early contempt for the trade union movement has been given up; a closer sympathy has been won for it and, here and there also, for the co-operative movement.

And the ultimate aim? Well, that just remains an ultimate aim. "The working classes have no fixed and perfect Utopias to introduce by means of a vote of the nation. They know that in order to work out their own emancipation—and with it that higher form of life which the present form of society irresistibly makes for by its own economic development—they, the working classes, have to pass through long struggles, a whole series of historical processes, by means of which men and circumstances will be completely transformed. They have no ideals to realise, they have only to set at liberty the elements of the new society which have already been developed in the womb of the collapsing bourgeois society." So writes Marx in *Civil War in France*. I was thinking of this utterance, not in every point, but in its fundamental thought in writing down the sentence about the ultimate aim. For after all what does it say but that the movement, the series of processes, is everything, whilst every aim fixed beforehand in its details is immaterial to it. I have declared already that I willingly abandon the form of the sentence about the ultimate aim as far as it admits the interpretation that every general aim of the working class movement formulated as a principle should be declared valueless. But the preconceived theories about the drift of the movement which go beyond such a generally expressed aim, which try to determine the direction of the movement and its character without an ever-vigilant eye upon facts and experience, must necessarily always pass into Utopianism, and at some time or other stand in the way, and hinder the real theoretical and practical progress of the movement.

Whoever knows even but a little of the history of German social democracy also knows that the party has become important by continued action in contravention of such theories and of infringing resolutions founded on them. What Engels says in the preface to the new edition of *Civil War* with regard to the Blanquists and Proudhonists in the Paris Commune of 1871, namely that they both had been obliged in practice to act against their own theory, has often been repeated in another form. A theory or declaration of principle which does not allow attention being paid at every stage of development to the actual interests of the working classes, will always be set aside just as all foreswearing of reforming detail work and of the support of neighbouring middle class parties has again and again been forgotten; and again and again at the congresses of the party will the complaint be heard that here and there in the electoral contest the ultimate aim of socialism has not been put sufficiently in the foreground.

In the quotation from Schulze-Gävernitz which Plechanow flings at me, it runs that by giving up the dictum that the condition of the worker in modern society is hopeless, socialism would lose its revolutionary point and would be absorbed in carrying out legislative demands. From this contrast it is clearly inferred that Schulze-Gävernitz always used the concept "revolutionary" in the sense of a struggle having revolution by violence in view. Plechanow turns the thing round, and because I have not maintained the condition of the worker to be hopeless, because I acknowledge its capability of improvement and many other facts which bourgeois economists have upheld, he carts me over to the "opponents of scientific socialism."

Unfortunately for the scientific socialism of Plechanow, the Marxist propositions on the hopelessness of the position of the worker have been upset in a book which bears the title, *Capital: A Criticism of Political Economy*. There we read of the "physical and moral regeneration" of the textile workers in Lancashire through the Factory Law of 1847, which "struck the feeblest eye." A bourgeois republic was not even necessary to bring about a certain improvement in the situation of a large section of workers! In the same book we read that the society of to-day is no firm crystal, but an organism capable of change and constantly engaged in a process of change, that also in the treatment of economic questions on the part of the official representatives of this society an "improvement was unmistakable." Further that the author had devoted

so large a space in his book to the results of the English Factory Laws in order to spur the Continent to imitate them and thus to work so that the process of transforming society may be accomplished in ever more humane forms. All of which signifies not hopelessness but capability of improvement in the condition of the worker. And, as since 1866, when this was written, the legislation depicted has not grown weaker but has been improved, made more general, and has been supplemented by laws and organisations working in the same direction, there can be no more doubt to-day than formerly of the hopefulness of the position of the worker. If to state such facts means following the "immortal Bastiat," then among the first ranks of these followers is— Karl Marx.

Now, it can be asserted against me that Marx certainly recognised those improvements, but that the chapter on the historical tendency of capitalist accumulation at the end of the first volume of *Capital* shows how little these details influenced his fundamental mode of viewing things. To which I answer that as far as that is correct it speaks against that chapter and not against me.

One can interpret this chapter in very different kinds of ways. I believe I was the first to point out, and indeed repeatedly, that it was a summary characterisation of the tendency of a development which is found in capitalist accumulation, but which in practice is not carried out completely and which therefore need not be driven to the critical point of the antagonism there depicted. Engels has never expressed himself against this interpretation of mine, never, either verbally or in print, declared it to be wrong. Nor did he say a word against me when I wrote, in 1891, in an essay on a work of Schulze-Gävernitz on the questions referred to: "It is clear that where legislation, this systematic and conscious action of society, interferes in an appropriate way, the working of the tendencies of economic development is thwarted, under some circumstances can even be annihilated. Marx and Engels have not only never denied this, but, on the contrary, have always emphasised it." If one reads the chapter mentioned with this idea, one will also, in a few sentences, silently place the word "tendency" and thus be spared the need of bringing this chapter into accord with reality by distorting arts of interpretation. But then the chapter itself would become of less value the more progress is made in actual evolution. For its theoretic importance does not lie in the argument of the general tendency to capitalistic centralisation and accumulation which had been affirmed long before Marx by bourgeois economists and socialists, but in the presentation, peculiar to Marx, of circumstances and forms under which it would work at a more advanced stage of evolution, and of the results to which it would lead. But in this respect actual evolution is really always bringing forth new arrangements, forces, facts, in face of which that presentation seems insufficient and loses to a corresponding extent the capability of serving as a sketch of the coming evolution. That is how I understand it.

One can, however, understand this chapter differently. One can conceive it in this way, that all the improvements mentioned there, and some possibly ensuing, only create temporary remedies against the oppressive tendencies of capitalism, that they signify unimportant modifications which cannot in the long run effect anything substantially against the critical point of antagonisms laid down by Marx, that this will finally appear—if not literally yet substantially—in the manner depicted, and will lead to catastrophic change by violence. This interpretation can be founded on the categoric wording of the last sentences of the chapter, and receives a certain confirmation because at the end reference is again made to the *Communist Manifesto*, whilst Hegel also appeared shortly before with his negation of the negation—the restoration on a new foundation of individual property negatived by the capitalist manner of production.

According to my view, it is impossible simply to declare the one conception right and the other absolutely wrong. To me the chapter illustrates a dualism which runs through the whole monumental work of Marx, and which also finds expression in a less pregnant fashion in other passages—a dualism which consists in this, that the work aims at being a scientific inquiry and also at proving a theory laid down long before its drafting; a formula lies at the basis of it in which the result to which the exposition should lead is fixed beforehand. The return to

the *Communist Manifesto* points here to a real residue of Utopianism in the Marxist system. Marx had accepted the solution of the Utopians in essentials, but had recognised their means and proofs as inadequate. He therefore undertook a revision of them, and this with the zeal, the critical acuteness, and love of truth of a scientific genius. He suppressed no important fact, he also forebore belittling artificially the importance of these facts as long as the object of the inquiry had no immediate reference to the final aim of the formula to be proved. To that point his work is free of every tendency necessarily interfering with the scientific method.

For the general sympathy with the strivings for emancipation of the working classes does not in itself stand in the way of the scientific method. But, as Marx approaches a point when that final aim enters seriously into the question, he becomes uncertain and unreliable. Such contradictions then appear as were shown in the book under consideration, for instance, in the section on the movement of incomes in modern society. It thus appears that this great scientific spirit was, in the end, a slave to a doctrine. To express it figuratively, he has raised a mighty building within the framework of a scaffolding he found existing, and in its erection he kept strictly to the laws of scientific architecture as long as they did not collide with the conditions which the construction of the scaffolding prescribed, but he neglected or evaded them when the scaffolding did not allow of their observance. Where the scaffolding put limits in the way of the building, instead of destroying the scaffolding, he changed the building itself at the cost of its right proportions and so made it all the more dependent on the scaffolding. Was it the consciousness of this irrational relation which caused him continually to pass from completing his work to amending special parts of it? However that may be, my conviction is that wherever that dualism shows itself the scaffolding must fall if the building is to grow in its right proportions. In the latter, and not in the former, is found what is worthy to live in Marx.

Nothing confirms me more in this conception than the anxiety with which some persons seek to maintain certain statements in *Capital*, which are falsified by facts. It is just some of the more deeply devoted followers of Marx who have not been able to separate themselves from the dialectical form of the work—that is the scaffolding alluded to—who do this. At least, that is only how I can explain the words of a man, otherwise so amenable to facts as Kautsky, who, when I observed in Stuttgart that the number of wealthy people for many years had increased, not decreased, answered: "If that were true then the date of our victory would not only be very long postponed, but we should never attain our goal. If it be capitalists who increase and not those with no possessions, then we are going ever further from our goal the more evolution progresses, then capitalism grows stronger, not socialism."

That the number of the wealthy increases and does not diminish is not an invention of bourgeois "harmony economists," but a fact established by the boards of assessment for taxes, often to the chagrin of those concerned, a fact which can no longer be disputed. But what is the significance of this fact as regards the victory of socialism? Why should the realisation of socialism depend on its refutation? Well, simply for this reason: because the dialectical scheme seems so to prescribe it; because a post threatens to fall out of the scaffolding if one admits that the social surplus product is appropriated by an increasing instead of a decreasing number of possessors. But it is only the speculative theory that is affected by this matter; it does not at all affect the actual movement. Neither the struggle of the workers for democracy in politics nor their struggle for democracy in industry is touched by it. The prospects of this struggle do not depend on the theory of concentration of capital in the hands of a diminishing number of magnates, nor on the whole dialectical scaffolding of which this is a plank, but on the growth of social wealth and of the social productive forces, in conjunction with general social progress, and, particularly, in conjunction with the intellectual and moral advance of the working classes themselves.

Suppose the victory of socialism depended on the constant shrinkage in the number of capitalist magnates, social democracy, if it wanted to act logically, either would have to support the heaping up of capital in ever fewer hands, or at least to give no support to anything that would stop this shrinkage. As a matter of fact it often enough does neither the one nor the other. These considerations, for instance, do not govern its votes on questions of taxation. From the standpoint of the catastrophic theory a great part of this practical activity of the working classes is an undoing of work that ought to be allowed to be done. It is not social democracy which is wrong in this respect. The fault lies in the doctrine which assumes that progress depends on the deterioration of social conditions.

In his preface to the *Agrarian Question*, Kautsky turns upon those who speak of the necessity of a triumph over Marxism. He says that he sees doubt and hesitation expressed, but that these alone indicate no development. That is so far correct in that doubt and hesitation are no positive refutation. They can, however, be the first step towards it. But is it altogether a matter of triumphing over Marxism, or is it not rather a rejection of certain remains of Utopianism which adhere to Marxism, and which are the cause of the contradictions in theory and practice which have been pointed out in Marxism by its critics? This treatise has become already more voluminous than it ought to have been, and I must therefore abstain from going into all the details of this subject. But all the more I consider it my duty to declare that I hold a whole series of objections raised by opponents against certain items in Marx's theory as unrefuted, some as irrefutable. And I can do this all the more easily as these objections are quite irrelevant to the strivings of social democracy.

We ought to be less susceptible in this respect. It has repeatedly happened that conclusions by followers of Marx, who believed that they contradicted the theories of Marx, have been disputed with great zeal, and, in the end, the supposed contradictions were proved for the most part not to exist. Amongst others I have in my mind the controversy concerning the investigations of the late Dr. Stiebling on the effect of the concentration of capital on the rate of exploitation. In his manner of expression, as well as in separate items of his calculations, Stiebling made some great blunders, which it is the merit of Kautsky to have discovered. But on the other hand the third volume of *Capital* has shown that the fundamental thought of Stiebling's works—the decrease of the rate of exploitation with the increasing concentration of capital did not stand in such opposition to Marx's doctrine as then appeared to most of us, although his proof of the phenomenon is different from that of Marx. Yet in his time Stiebling had to hear (from Kautsky) that if what he inferred was correct, the theoretical foundation of the working class movement, the theory of Marx, was false. And as a matter of fact those who spoke thus could refer to various passages from Marx. An analysis of the controversy which was entered into over the essays of Stiebling could very well serve as an illustration of some of the contradictions of the Marxist theory of value.

Similar conflicts exist with regard to the estimate of the relation of economics and force in history, and they find their counterpart in the criticism on the practical tasks and possibilities of the working class movement which has already been discussed in another place. This is, however, a point to which it is necessary to recur. But the question to be investigated is not how far originally, and in the further course of history, force determined economy and *vice versa*, but what is the creative power of force in a given society.

Now it would be absurd to go back to the prejudices of former generations with regard to the capabilities of political power, for such a thing would mean that we would have to go still further back to explain those prejudices. The prejudices which the Utopians, for example, cherished rested on good grounds; indeed, one can scarcely say that they were prejudices, for they rested on the real immaturity of the working classes of the period as a result of which, only a transitory mob rule on the one side or a return to the class oligarchy on the other was the only possible outcome of the political power of the masses. Under these circumstances a reference to politics could appear only to be a turning aside from more pressing duties. To-day these conditions have been to some extent removed, and therefore no person capable of reflecting will think of criticising political action with the arguments of that period.

Marxism first turned the thing round, as we have seen, and preached (in view of the potential capacity of the industrial proletariat) political action as the most important duty of the movement. But it was thereby involved in great contradictions. It also recognised, and separated itself thereby from the demagogic parties, that the working classes had not yet attained the required maturity for their emancipation, and also that the economic preliminary conditions for such were not present. But in spite of that it turned again and again to tactics which supposed both preliminary conditions as almost fulfilled. We come across passages in its publications where the immaturity of the workers is emphasised with an acuteness which differs very little from the doctrinairism of the early Utopian socialists, and soon afterwards we come across passages according to which we should assume that all culture, all intelligence, all virtue, is only to be found among the working classes—passages which make it incomprehensible why the most extreme social revolutionaries and physical force anarchists should not be right. Corresponding with that, political action is ever directed towards a revolutionary convulsion expected in an imminent future, in the face of which legislative work for a long time appears only as a *pis aller*—a merely temporary device. And we look in vain for any systematic investigation of the question of what can be expected from legal, and what from revolutionary action.

It is evident at the first glance that great differences exist in the latter respect. But they are usually found to be this: that law, or the path of legislative reform, is the slower way, and revolutionary force the quicker and more radical. But that only is true in a restricted sense. Whether the legislative or the revolutionary method is the more promising depends entirely on the nature of the measures and on their relation to different classes and customs of the people.

In general, one may say here that the revolutionary way (always in the sense of revolution by violence) does quicker work as far as it deals with removal of obstacles which a privileged minority places in the path of social progress: that its strength lies on its negative side.

Constitutional legislation works more slowly in this respect as a rule. Its path is usually that of compromise, not the prohibition, but the buying out of acquired rights. But it is stronger than the revolution scheme where prejudice and the limited horizon of the great mass of the people appear as hindrances to social progress, and it offers greater advantages where it is a question of the creation of permanent economic arrangements capable of lasting; in other words, it is best adapted to positive social-political work.

In legislation, intellect dominates over emotion in quiet times; during a revolution emotion dominates over intellect. But if emotion is often an imperfect leader, the intellect is a slow motive force. Where a revolution sins by over haste, the every-day legislator sins by procrastination. Legislation works as a systematic force, revolution as an elementary force.

As soon as a nation has attained a position where the rights of the propertied minority have ceased to be a serious obstacle to social progress, where the negative tasks of political action are less pressing than the positive, then the appeal to a revolution by force becomes a meaningless phrase. One can overturn a government or a privileged minority, but not a nation. When the working classes do not possess very strong economic organisations of their own, and have not attained, by means of education on self-governing bodies, a high degree of mental independence, the dictatorship of the proletariat means the dictatorship of club orators and writers. I would not wish that those who see in the oppression and tricking of the working men's organisations and in the exclusion of working men from the legislature and government the highest point of the art of political policy should experience their error in practice. Just as little would I desire it for the working class movement itself.

One has not overcome Utopianism if one assumes that there is in the present, or ascribes to the present, what is to be in the future. We have to take working men as they are. And they are neither so universally pauperised as was set out in the *Communist Manifesto*, nor so free from prejudices and weaknesses as their courtiers wish to make us believe. They have the virtues and failings of the economic and social conditions under which they live. And neither these conditions nor their effects can be put on one side from one day to another.

Have we attained the required degree of development of the productive forces for the abolition of classes? In face of the fantastic figures which were formerly set up in proof of this and which rested on generalisations based on the development of particularly favoured industries, socialist writers in modern times have endeavoured to reach by carefully detailed calculations, appropriate estimates of the possibilities of production in a socialist society, and their results are very different from those figures. Of a general reduction of hours of labour to five, four, or even three or two hours, such as was formerly accepted, there can be no hope at any time within sight, unless the general standard of life is much reduced. Even under a collective organisation of work, labour must begin very young and only cease at a rather advanced age, if it is to be reduced considerably below an eight-hours' day. Those persons ought to understand this first of all who indulge in the most extreme exaggerations regarding the ratio of the number of the non-propertied classes to that of the propertied. But he who thinks irrationally on one point does so usually on another. And, therefore, I am not surprised if the same Plechanow, who is angered to see the position of working men represented as not hopeless, has only the annihilating verdict, "Philistine," for my conclusions on the impossibility at any period within sight of abandoning the principle of the economic self-responsibility of those capable of working. It is not for nothing that one is the philosopher of irresponsibility.

But he who surveys the actual workers' movement will also find that the freedom from those qualities which appeared Philistine to a person born in the bourgeoisie, is very little valued by the workers, that they in no way support the morale of proletarianism, but, on the contrary, tend to make a "Philistine" out of a proletarian. With the roving proletarian without a family and home, no lasting, firm trade union movement would be possible. It is no bourgeois prejudice, but a conviction gained through decades of labour organisation, which has made so many of the English labour leaders—socialists and non-socialists—into zealous adherents of the temperance movement. The working class socialists know the faults of their class, and the most conscientious among them, far from glorifying these faults, seek to overcome them with all their power.

We cannot demand from a class, the great majority of whose members live under crowded conditions, are badly educated, and have an uncertain and insufficient income, the high intellectual and moral standard which the organisation and existence of a socialist community presupposes. We will, therefore, not ascribe it to them by way of fiction.

Let us rejoice at the great stock of intelligence, renunciation, and energy which the modern working class movement has partly revealed, partly produced; but we must not assign, without discrimination to the masses, the millions, what holds good, say, of hundreds of thousands. I will not repeat the declarations which have been made to me on this point by working men verbally and in writing; I do not need to defend myself before reasonable persons against the suspicion of Pharisaism and the conceit of pedantry. But I confess willingly that I measure here with two kinds of measures. Just because I expect much of the working classes I censure much more everything that tends to corrupt their moral judgment than I do similar habits of the higher classes, and I see with the greatest regret that a tone of literary decadence is spreading here and there in the working class press which can only have a confusing and corrupting effect. A class which is aspiring needs a sound morale and must suffer no deterioration. Whether it sets out for itself an ideal ultimate aim is of secondary importance if it pursues with energy its proximate aims. The important point is that these aims are inspired by a definite principle which expresses a higher degree of economy and of social life, that they are an embodiment of a social conception which means in the evolution of civilisation a higher view of morals and of legal rights.

From this point of view I cannot subscribe to the proposition: "The working class has no ideas to realise." I see in it rather a self-deception, if it is not a mere play upon words on the part of its author.

And in this mind, I, at the time, resorted to the spirit of the great Königsberg philosopher, the critic of pure reason, against the cant which sought to get a hold on the working class movement and to which the Hegelian dialectic offers a comfortable refuge. I did this in the conviction that social democracy required a Kant who should judge the received opinion and examine it critically with deep acuteness, who should show where its apparent materialism is the highest—and is therefore the most easily misleading—ideology, and warn it that the contempt of the ideal, the magnifying of material factors until they become omnipotent forces of evolution, is a self-deception, which has been and will be exposed as such at every opportunity by the

action of those who proclaim it. Such a thinker, who with convincing exactness could show what is worthy and destined to live in the work of our great champions, and what must and can perish, would also make it possible for us to hold a more unbiased judgment on those works which, although not starting from premises which to-day appear to us as decisive, yet are devoted to the ends for which social democracy is fighting. No impartial thinker will deny that socialist criticism often fails in this and discloses all the dark sides of epigonism. I have myself done my share in this, and therefore cast a stone at no one. But just because I belong to the school, I believe I am justified in giving expression to the need for reform. If I did not fear that what I write should be misunderstood (I am, of course, prepared for its being misconstrued), I would translate *Back to Kant* by *Back to Lange*. For, just as the philosophers and investigators who stand by that motto are not concerned with going back to the letter of what the Königsberg philosopher wrote, but are only concerned with the fundamental principles of his criticism, so social democracy would just as little think of going back to all the social-political views of Frederick Albert Lange. What I have in mind is the distinguishing union in Lange of an upright and intrepid championship of the struggles of the working classes for emancipation with a large scientific freedom from prejudice which was always ready to acknowledge mistakes and recognise new truths. Perhaps such a great broad-mindedness as meets us in Lange's writings is only to be found in persons who are wanting in the penetrating acuteness which is the property of pioneer spirits like Marx. But it is not every epoch that produces a Marx, and even for a man of equal genius the working class movement of to-day is too great to enable him to occupy the position which Marx fills in its history. To-day it needs, in addition to the fighting spirit, the co-ordinating and constructive thinkers who are intellectually enough advanced to be able to separate the chaff from the wheat, who are great enough in their mode of thinking to recognise also the little plant that has grown on another soil than theirs, and who, perhaps, though not kings, are warm-hearted republicans in the domain of socialist thought.

Rerum Novarum

Leo XIII

During his papacy (1878-1903), Leo XIII worked to improve the relationship between the Church and the modern world, which had suffered under the previous pope's reactionary policies. To the dislike of French monarchists, Leo strongly supported the Third French Republic, even though he did not equate democracy with egalitarianism. He saw the flaws of both communism and capitalism. His encyclical, "Rerum Novarum," spelled out the rights and duties of both capital and labor. Leo supported the right to create unions but rejected socialism.

Once the passion for revolutionary change was aroused—a passion long disturbing governments—it was bound to follow sooner or later that eagerness for change would pass from the political sphere over into the related field of economics. In fact, new developments in industry, new techniques striking out on new paths, changed relations of employer and employee, abounding wealth among a very small number and destitution among the masses, increased self-reliance on the part of the workers as well as a closer bond of union with one another, and, in addition to all this, a decline in morals, have caused conflict to break forth.

The momentous nature of the questions involved in this conflict is evident from the fact that it keeps men's minds in anxious expectation, occupying the talents of the learned, the discussions of the wise and experienced, the assemblies of the people, the judgment of the lawmakers, and the deliberations of rulers, so that now no topic more strongly holds men's interests.

Therefore, Venerable Brethren, with the cause of the Church and the common welfare before Us, We have thought it advisable, following Our custom on other occasions when We issued to you the Encyclicals On Political Power, On Human Liberty, On the Christian Constitution of States, and others of simi-

From: *The Western Tradition: A Book of Readings from the Ancient World to the Atomic Age*, ed. by Eugen Weber (Boston: D.C. Heath and Co., 1965), pp. 688-697).

lar nature, which seemed opportune to refute erroneous opinions, that We ought to do the same now, and for the same reasons, On the Condition of Workers. We have on occasion touched more than once upon this subject. In this Encyclical, however, consciousness of Our Apostolic office admonishes Us to treat the entire question thoroughly, in order that the principles may stand out in clear light, and the conflict may thereby be brought to an end as required by truth and equity.

The problem is difficult to resolve and is not free from dangers. It is hard indeed to fix the boundaries of the rights and duties within which the rich and the proletariat—those who furnish material things and those who furnish work—ought to be restricted in relation to each other. The controversy is truly dangerous, for in various places it is being twisted by turbulent and crafty men to pervert judgment as to truth and seditiously to incite the masses.

In any event, We see clearly, and all are agreed that the poor must be speedily and fittingly cared for, since the great majority of them live undeservedly in miserable and wretched conditions.

After the old trade guilds had been destroyed in the last century, and no protection was substituted in their place, and when public institutions and legislation had cast off traditional religious teaching, it gradually came about that the present age handed over the workers, each alone and defenseless, to the inhumanity of employers and the unbridled greed of competitors. A devouring usury, although often condemned by the Church, but practiced nevertheless under another form by avaricious and grasping men, has increased the evil; and in addition the whole process of production as well as trade in every kind of goods has been brought almost entirely under the power of a few, so that a very few rich and exceedingly rich men have laid a yoke almost of slavery on the unnumbered masses of nonowning workers.

To cure this evil, the Socialists, exciting the envy of the poor toward the rich, contend that it is necessary to do away with private possession of goods, and in its place to make the goods of individuals common to all, and that the men who preside over a municipality or who direct the entire State should act as administrators of these goods. They hold that, by such a transfer of private goods from private individuals to the community, they can cure the present evil through dividing wealth and benefits equally among the citizens.

But their program is so unsuited for terminating the conflict that it actually injures the workers themselves. Moreover, it is highly unjust, because it violates the rights of lawful owners, perverts the functions of the State, and throws governments into utter confusion.

Clearly the essential reason why those who engage in any gainful occupation undertake labor, and at the same time the end to which workers immediately look, is to procure property for themselves and to retain it by individual right as theirs and as their very own. When the worker places his energy and his labor at the disposal of another, he does so for the purpose of getting the means necessary for livelihood. He seeks in return for the work done, accordingly, a true and full right not only to demand his wage but to dispose of it as he sees fit. Therefore, if he saves something by restricting expenditures and invests his savings in a piece of land in order to keep the fruit of his thrift more safe, a holding of this kind is certainly nothing else than his wage under a different form; and on this account land which the worker thus buys is necessarily under his full control as much as the wage which he earned by his labor. But, as is obvious, it is clearly in this that the ownership of movable and immovable goods

consists. Therefore, inasmuch as the Socialists seek to transfer the goods of private persons to the community at large, they make the lot of all wage earners worse, because in abolishing the freedom to dispose of wages they take away from them by this very act the hope and the opportunity of increasing their property and of securing advantages for themselves.

But, what is of more vital concern, they propose a remedy openly in conflict with justice, inasmuch as nature confers on man the right to possess things privately as his own. . . .

The fact that God gave the whole human race the earth to use and enjoy cannot indeed in any manner serve as an objection against private possessions. For God is said to have given the earth to mankind in common, not because He intended indiscriminate ownership of it by all, but because He assigned no part to anyone in ownership, leaving the limits of private possessions to be fixed by the industry of men and the institutions of peoples. Yet, however the earth may be apportioned among private owners, it does not cease to serve the common interest of all, inasmuch as no living being is sustained except by what the fields bring forth. Those who lack resources supply labor, so that it can be truly affirmed that the entire scheme of securing a livelihood consists in the labor which a person expends either on his own land or in some working occupation, the compensation for which is drawn ultimately from no other source than from the varied products of the earth and is exchanged for them.

For this reason it also follows that private possessions are clearly in accord with nature. The earth indeed produces in great abundance the things to preserve and, especially, to perfect life, but of itself it could not produce them without human cultivation and care. Moreover, since man expends his mental energy and his bodily strength in procuring the goods of nature, by this very act he appropriates that part of physical nature to himself which he has cultivated. On it he leaves impressed, as it were, a kind of image of his person, so that it must be altogether just that he should possess that part as his very own and that no one in any way should be permitted to violate his right. . . .

The fundamental principle of Socialism which would make all possessions public property is to be utterly rejected because it injures the very ones whom it seeks to help, contravenes the natural rights of individual persons, and throws the functions of the State and public peace into confusion. Let it be regarded, therefore, as established that in seeking help for the masses this principle before all is to be considered as basic, namely that private ownership must be preserved inviolate.

It is a capital evil with respect to the question we are discussing to take for granted that the one class of society is of itself hostile to the other, as if nature had set rich and poor against each other to fight fiercely in implacable war. This is so abhorrent to reason and truth that the exact opposite is true; for just as in the human body the different members harmonize with one another, whence arises that disposition of parts and proportion in the human figure rightly called symmetry, so likewise nature has commanded in the case of the State that the two classes mentioned should agree harmoniously and should properly form equally balanced counterparts to each other. Each needs the other completely: neither capital can do without labor, nor labor without capital. Concord begets beauty and order in things. Conversely, from perpetual strife there must arise disorder accompanied by bestial cruelty. But for putting an end to conflict and for cutting away its very roots, there is wondrous and multiple power in Christian institutions.

And first and foremost, the entire body of religious teaching and practice, of which the Church is the interpreter and guardian, can pre-eminently bring together and unite the rich by recalling the two classes of society to their mutual duties, and in particular to those duties which derive from justice.

Among these duties the following concern the poor and the workers: To perform entirely and conscientiously whatever work has been voluntarily and equitably agreed upon; not in any way to injure the property or to harm the person of employers; in protecting their own interests, to refrain from violence and never to engage in rioting; not to associate with vicious men who craftily hold out exaggerated hopes and make huge promises, a course usually ending in vain regrets and in the destruction of wealth.

The following duties, on the other hand, concern rich men and employers: Workers are not to be treated as slaves; justice demands that the dignity of human personality be respected in them, ennobled as it has been through what we call the Christian character. If we hearken to natural reason and to Christian philosophy, gainful occupations are not a mark of shame to man, but rather of respect, as they provide him with an honorable means of supporting life. It is shameful and inhuman, however, to use men as things for gain and to put no more value on them than what they are worth in muscle and energy. Likewise it is enjoined that the religious interests and the spiritual well-being of the workers receive proper consideration. Wherefore, it is the duty of employers to see that the worker is free for adequate periods to attend to his religious obligations; not to expose anyone to corrupting influences or the enticements of sin, and in no way to alienate him from care for his family and the practice of thrift. Likewise, more work is not to be imposed than strength can endure, nor that kind of work which is unsuited to a worker's age or sex.

Among the most important duties of employers the principal one is to give every worker what is justly due him. Assuredly, to establish a rule of pay in accord with justice, many factors must be taken into account. But, in general, the rich and employers should remember that no laws, either human or divine, permit them for their own profit to oppress the needy and the wretched or to seek gain from another's want. To defraud anyone of the wage due him is a great crime that calls down avenging wrath from Heaven. "Behold, the wages of the laborers . . . which have been kept back by you unjustly, cry out: and their cry has entered into the ears of the Lord of Hosts." Finally, the rich must religiously avoid harming in any way the savings of the workers either by coercion, or by fraud, or by the arts of usury; and the more for this reason, that the workers are not sufficiently protected against injustices and violence, and their property, being so meager, ought to be regarded as all the more sacred. Could not the observance alone of the foregoing laws remove the bitterness and the causes of conflict? . . .

Those who lack fortune's goods are taught by the Church that, before God as Judge, poverty is no disgrace, and that no one should be ashamed because he makes his living by toil. And Jesus Christ has confirmed this by fact and by deed, Who for the salvation of men, "being rich, became poor"; and although He was the Son of God and God Himself, yet He willed to seem and to be thought the son of a carpenter; nay, He even did not disdain to spend a great part of his life at the work of a carpenter. "Is not this the carpenter, the Son of Mary?" Those who contemplate this Divine example will more easily understand these truths: True dignity and excellence in men resides in moral living, that is, in virtue; virtue is the common inheritance of man, attainable equally by the humblest and the mightiest, by the rich and the poor; and the reward of eternal happiness will follow upon virtue and merit alone, regardless of the person in whom they may be found. Nay, rather the favor of God Himself seems to incline more toward the unfortunate as a class; for Jesus Christ calls the poor blessed, and He invites most lovingly all who are in labor or sorrow to come to Him for solace, embracing with special love the lowly and those harassed by injustice. At the realization of these things the proud spirit of the rich is easily brought down, and the downcast heart of the afflicted is lifted up; the former are moved toward kindness, the latter, toward reasonableness in their demands. Thus the distance between the classes which pride seeks is reduced, and it will easily be brought to pass that the two classes, with hands clasped in friendship, will be united in heart.

Such is the economy of duties and rights according to Christian philosophy. Would it not seem that all conflict would soon cease wherever this economy were to prevail in civil society?

*   *   *

But it is now in order to inquire what portion of the remedy should be expected from the State. By State here We understand not the form of government which this or that people has, but rather that form which right reason in accordance with nature required and the teachings of Divine wisdom approve. . .

Therefore those governing the State ought primarily to devote themselves to the service of individual groups and of the whole commonwealth, and through the entire scheme of laws and institutions to cause both public and individual well-being to develop spontaneously out of the very structure and administration of the State. For this is the duty of wise statesmanship and the essential office of those in charge of the State. Now, States are made prosperous especially by wholesome morality, properly ordered family life, protection of religion and justice, moderate imposition and equitable distribution of public burdens, progressive development of industry and trade, thriving agriculture, and by all other things of this nature, which the more actively they are promoted, the better and happier the life of the citizens is destined to be. Therefore, by virtue of these things, it is within the competence of the rulers of the State that, as they benefit other groups, they also improve in particular the condition of the workers. Furthermore, they do this with full right and without laying themselves open to any charge of unwarranted interference. For the State is bound by the very law of its office to serve the common interest. And the richer the benefits which come from this general providence on the part of the State, the less necessary it will be to experiment with other measures for the well-being of workers.

This ought to be considered, as it touches the question more deeply, namely, that the State has one basic purpose for existence, which embraces in common the highest and the lowest of its members. Non-owning workers are unquestionably citizens by nature in virtue of the same right as the rich, that is, true and vital parts whence, through the medium of families, the body of the State is constituted; and it hardly need be added that they are by far the greatest number in every urban area. Since it would be quite absurd to look out for one portion of the citizens and to neglect another, it follows that public authority ought to exercise due care in safeguarding the well-being and the interests of non-owning workers. Unless this is done, justice, which commands that everyone be given his own, will be violated. Wherefore St. Thomas says wisely: "Even as part and whole are in a certain way the same, so too that which pertains to the whole pertains in a certain way to the part also." Consequently, among the numerous and weighty duties of rulers who would serve their people well, this is first and foremost, namely, that they protect equitably each and every class of citizens, maintaining inviolate that justice especially which is called distributive.

Although all citizens, without exception, are obliged to contribute something to the sum-total of common goods, some share of which naturally goes back to each individual, yet all can by no means contribute the same amount and in equal degree.

Whatever the vicissitudes that occur in the forms of government, there will always be those differences in the condition of citizens without which society could neither exist nor be conceived. It is altogether necessary that there be some who dedicate themselves to the service of the State, who make laws, who dispense justice, and finally, by whose counsel and authority civil and military affairs are administered. These men, as is clear, play the chief role in the State, and among every people are to be regarded as occupying first place, because they work for the common good most directly and preeminently. On the other hand, those engaged in some calling benefit the State, but not in the same way as the men just mentioned, nor by performing the same duties; yet they, too, in a high degree, although less directly, serve the public weal. Assuredly, since social good must be of such a character that men through its acquisition are made better, it must necessarily be founded chiefly on virtue.

Nevertheless, an abundance of corporeal and external goods is likewise a characteristic of a well constituted State, "the use of which goods is necessary for the practice of virtue." To produce these goods the labor of the workers, whether they expend their skill and strength on farms or in factories, is most efficacious and necessary. Nay, in this respect, their energy and effectiveness are so important that it is incontestable that the wealth of nations originates from no other source than from the labor of workers. Equity therefore commands that public authority show proper concern for the worker so that from what he contributes to the common good he may receive what will enable him, housed, clothed, and secure, to live his life without hardship. Whence, it follows that all those measures ought to be favored which seem in any way capable of benefiting the condition of workers. Such solicitude is so far from injuring anyone, that it is destined rather to benefit all, because it is of absolute interest to the State that those citizens should not be miserable in every respect from whom such necessary goods proceed.

It is not right, as We have said, for either the citizen or the family to be absorbed by the State; it is proper that the individual and the family should be permitted to retain their freedom of action, so far as this is possible without jeopardizing the common good and without injuring anyone. Nevertheless, those who govern must see to it that they protect the community and its constituent parts: the community, because nature has entrusted its safeguarding to the sovereign power in the State to such an extent that the protection of the public welfare is not only the supreme law, but is the entire cause and reason for sovereignty; and the constituent parts, because philosophy and Christian faith agree that the administration of the State has from nature as its purpose, not the benefit of those to whom it has been entrusted, but the benefit of those who have been entrusted to it. And since the power of governing comes from God and is a participation, as it were, in His supreme sovereignty, it ought to be administered according to the example of the Divine power, which looks with paternal care to the welfare of individual creatures as well as to that of all creation. If, therefore, any injury has been done to or threatens either the common good or the interests of individual groups, which injury cannot in any other way be repaired or prevented, it is necessary for public authority to intervene.

It is vitally important to public as well as to private welfare that there be peace and good order; likewise, that the whole regime of family life be directed according to the ordinances of God and the principles of nature, that religion be observed and cultivated, that sound morals flourish in private and public life, that justice be kept sacred and that no one be wronged with impunity by another, and that strong citizens grow up, capable of supporting, and if necessary, of protecting the State. Wherefore, if at any time disorder should threaten because of strikes or concerted stoppages of work, if the natural bonds of family life should be relaxed among the poor, if religion among the workers should be outraged by failure to provide sufficient opportunity for performing religious duties, if in factories danger should assail the integrity of morals through the mixing of the sexes or other pernicious incitements to sin, or if the employer class should oppress the working class with unjust burdens or should degrade them with conditions inimical to human personality or to human dignity, if health should be injured by immoderate work and such as is not suited to sex or age—in all these cases, the power and authority of the law, but of course within certain limits, manifestly ought to be employed. And these limits are determined by the same reason which demands the aid of the law, that is, the law ought not undertake more, nor go farther, than the remedy of evils or the removal of danger requires.

Rights indeed, by whomsoever possessed, must be religiously protected; and public authority, in warding off injuries and punishing wrongs, ought to see to it that individuals may have and hold what belongs to them. In protecting the rights of private individuals, however, special consideration must be given to the weak and the poor. For the nation, as it were, of the rich, is guarded by its own defenses and is in less need of governmental protection, whereas the suffering multitude, without the means to protect itself, relies especially on the protection of the State. Wherefore, since wage workers are numbered among the great mass of the needy, the State must include them under its special care and foresight.

But it will be well to touch here expressly on certain matters of special importance. The capital point is this, that private property ought to be safeguarded by the sovereign power of the State and through the bulwark of its laws. And especially, in view of such a great flaming up of passion at the present time, the masses ought to be kept within the bounds of their moral obligations. For while justice does not oppose our striving for better things, on the other hand, it does forbid anyone to take from another what is his and, in the name of a certain absurd equality, to seize forcibly the property of others; nor does the interest of the common good itself permit this. Certainly, the great majority of working people prefer to secure better conditions by honest toil, without doing wrong to anyone. Nevertheless, not a few individuals are found who, imbued with evil ideas and eager for revolution, use every means to stir up disorder and incite to violence. The authority of the State, therefore, should intervene and, by putting restraint upon such disturbers, protect the morals of workers from their corrupting arts and lawful owners from the danger of spoliation.

Labor which is too long and too hard and the belief that pay is inadequate not infrequently give workers cause to strike and become voluntarily idle. This evil, which is frequent and serious, ought to be remedied by public authority, because such interruption of work inflicts damage not only upon employers and upon the workers themselves, but also injures trade and commerce and the general interest of the State; and, since it is usually not far removed from violence and rioting, it very frequently jeopardizes public peace. In this matter it is more effective and salutary that the authority of the law anticipate and completely prevent the evil from breaking out by removing early the causes from which it would seem that conflict between employers and workers is bound to arise.

*   *   *

Now as concerns the protection of corporeal and physical goods, the oppressed workers above all, ought to be liberated from the savagery of greedy men, who inordinately use human beings as things of gain. Assuredly, neither justice nor humanity can countenance the exaction of so much work that the spirit is dulled from excessive toil and that along with it the body sinks crushed from exhaustion. The working energy of a man, like his entire nature, is circumscribed by definite limits beyond which it cannot go. It is developed indeed by exercise and use, but only on condition that a man cease from work at regular intervals and rest. With respect to daily work, therefore, care ought to be taken not to extend it beyond the hours that human strength warrants. The length of rest intervals ought to be decided on the basis of the varying nature of the work, of the circumstances of time and place, and of the physical condition of the workers themselves. Since the labor of those who quarry stone from the earth, or who mine iron, copper, and other underground materials, is much more severe and harmful to health, the working period for such men ought to be correspondingly shortened. The seasons of the year also must be taken into account; for often a given kind of work is easy to endure in one season but cannot be endured at all in another, or not without the greatest difficulty.

Finally, it is not right to demand of a woman or a child what a strong adult man is capable of doing or would be willing to do. Nay, as regards children, special care ought to be taken that the factory does not get hold of them before age has sufficiently matured their physical, intellectual, and moral powers. For budding strength in childhood, like greening verdure in spring, is crushed by premature harsh treatment; and under such circumstances all education of the child must needs be foregone. Certain occupations likewise are less fitted for women, who are intended by nature for work of the home—work indeed which especially protects modesty in women and accords by nature with the education of children and the well-being of the family. Let it be the rule everywhere that workers be given as much leisure as will compensate for the energy consumed by toil, for rest from work is necessary to restore strength consumed by use. In every obligation which is mutually contracted between employers and workers, this condition, either written or tacit, is always present, that both kinds of rest be provided for; nor would it be equitable to make an agreement otherwise, because no one has the right to demand of, or to make an agreement with, anyone to neglect those duties which bind a man to God or to himself.

J'accuse!

Emile Zola

Among other accomplishments, Emile Zola became a strong critic of the French government when he felt it was at fault. In early 1898 he published "J'accuse" as an open letter to the French President on the front page of a Paris newspaper. The letter accused the French government of wrongly imprisoning Alfred Dreyfus. The Dreyfus Affair demonstrated the extent of anti-Semitism in large segments of French society. Positions for or against Dreyfus divided all of France into conservative and liberal camps and served as a kind of referendum on whether the country was to enter the modern world or preserve the old one.

Monsieur le Président,

Will you allow me, out of my gratitude for the gracious manner in which you once granted me an audience, to express my concern for your well-deserved glory? Will you allow me to tell you that although your star has been in the ascendant hitherto, it is now in danger of being dimmed by the most shameful and indelible of stains?

You have emerged unscathed from libellous slurs. You have won the people's hearts. You are the radiant centre of our apotheosis, for the Russian alliance has been indeed, for France, a patriotic celebration. And now you are about to preside over our World Fair. What a solemn triumph it will be, the crowning touch on our grand century of diligent labour, truth and liberty. But what a blot on your name (I was about to say, on your reign) this abominable Dreyfus Affair is! A court martial, acting on orders, has just dared to acquit such a man as Esterhazy. Truth itself and justice itself have been slapped in the face. And now it is too late, France's cheek has been sullied by that supreme insult, and History will record that it was during your Presidency that such a crime against society was committed.

They have dared to do this. Very well, then, I shall dare too. I shall tell the truth, for I pledged that I would tell it, if our judicial system, once the matter was brought before it through the normal channels, did not tell the truth, the whole truth. It is my duty to speak up: I will not be an accessory to the fact. If I were, my nights would be haunted by the spectre of that innocent man so far away, suffering the worst kind of torture as he pays for a crime he did not commit.

And it is to you, M. le Président, that I will shout out the truth with all the revulsion of a decent man. To your credit, I am convinced that you are unaware of the truth. And to whom should I denounce the evil machinations of those who are truly guilty if not to you, the First Magistrate in the land?

*   *   *

First of all, the truth about the trial and the verdict against Dreyfus.

One wicked man has led it all, done it all: Lt-Col du Paty de Clam. At the time he was only a Major. He is the entire Dreyfus Affair. Not until a fair inquiry has clearly established his actions and his responsibilities will we understand the Dreyfus Affair. He appears to have an unbelievably fuzzy and complicated mind, haunted by implausible plots and indulging in the methods that litter cheap novels—stolen papers, anonymous letters, rendez-vous in deserted places, mysterious women who flit about at night to peddle damaging proof. It was his idea to dictate the bordereau to Dreyfus; it was his idea to examine it in a room entirely lined with mirrors; it was du Paty de Clam, Major Forzinetti tells us, who went out with a dark lantern intending to slip into

From: Emile Zola, *The Dreyfus Affair*, ed. by Alain Pages (New Haven, CN: Yale University Press, 1996), pp. 43–53.

the cell where the accused man was sleeping and flash the light on his face all of a sudden so that he would be taken by surprise and blurt out a confession. And there is more to reveal, but it is not up to me to reveal it all; let them look, let them find what there is to be found. I shall simply say that Major du Paty de Clam, in charge of investigating the Dreyfus Affair, in his capacity as a criminal police officer bears the greatest burden of guilt—in terms of chronological order and rank—in the appalling miscarriage of justice that has been committed.

For some time already, the bordereau had been in the possession of Colonel Sandherr, head of the Intelligence Bureau, who has since died of total paralysis. There were 'leaks', papers disappeared, just as papers continue to disappear today; and efforts were being made to find out who had written the bordereau when a conviction slowly grew up that that person could only be an officer from the General Staff, and an artillery officer at that. This was a glaring double error, which shows how superficially the bordereau had been examined, since a close and rational scrutiny of it proves that it could only have been written by an infantry officer.

Accordingly, they searched throughout the premises; they examined handwriting samples as if it were a family matter: a traitor was to be caught by surprise in the offices themselves and expelled from them. Now, the story is partly familiar to us and I do not wish to repeat it all over again; but this is where Major du Paty de Clam comes into it, as soon as the first suspicion falls on Dreyfus. From that moment on, it was du Paty de Clam who invented Dreyfus. The Affair became *his* affair. He was sure that he could confound the traitor and wring a complete confession from him. Of course, there is the War Minister, General Mercier, whose intelligence seems to be on a mediocre level: and of course there is the Chief of the General Staff. General de Boisdeffre, who appears to have been swayed by his intense clericalism, and there is the Deputy Chief, General Gonse, whose conscience managed to make room for a good many things. But to begin with, there was really only Major du Paty de Clam. He led those men by the nose. He hypnotized them. Yes indeed, he also dabbles in spiritism and occultism: he converses with spirits. The experiments to which he subjected the unfortunate Dreyfus and the whole demented system of torture—the traps he attempted to make him fall into, the foolish investigations, the monstrous fabrications—are beyond belief.

Ah, for anyone who knows the true details of the first affair, what a nightmare it is! Major du Paty de Clam arrests Dreyfus and has him placed in solitary confinement. He rushes to the home of Madame Dreyfus and terrifies her, saying that if she speaks up, her husband is lost. Meanwhile the unfortunate man is tearing out his hair, clamouring his innocence. And that is how the investigation proceeded, as in some fifteenth-century chronicle, shrouded in mystery and a wealth of the wildest expedients, and all on the basis of a single, childish accusation, that idiotic bordereau, which was not only a very ordinary kind of treason but also the most impudent kind of swindle, since almost all of the so-called secrets that had supposedly been turned over to the enemy were of no value. I dwell on this point because this is the egg from which the real crime—the dreadful denial of justice which has laid France low—was later to hatch. I would like to make it perfectly clear how the miscarriage of justice came about, how it is the product of Major du Paty de Clam's machinations, how General Mercier and Generals de Boisdeffre and Gonse came to be taken in by it and gradually became responsible for this error and how it is that later they felt they had a duty to impose it as the sacred truth, a truth that will not admit of even the slightest discussion. At the beginning, all they contributed was negligence and lack of intelligence. The worst we can say is that they gave in to the religious passions of the circles they move in and the prejudices wrought by esprit de corps. They let stupidity have its way.

But now, here is Dreyfus summoned before the court martial. The most utter secrecy is demanded. They could not have imposed stricter silence and been more rigorous and mysterious if a traitor had actually opened our borders to the enemy and led the German Emperor straight to Notre Dame. The entire nation is flabbergasted. Terrible deeds are whispered about, monstrous betrayals that scandalize History itself, and of course the nation bows to these rumours. No punishment can be too severe; the nation will applaud the traitor's public humiliation; the nation is adamant: the guilty man shall remain on the remote rock where infamy has placed him and he shall be devoured by remorse. But then, those unspeakable accusations, those dangerous accusations that might inflame all of Europe and had to be so carefully concealed behind the closed doors of a secret session—are they true? No, they are not! There is nothing behind all that but the extravagant, demented flights of fancy of Major du Paty de Clam. It's all a smokescreen with just one purpose: to conceal a cheap novel of the most outlandish sort. And to be convinced of this, one need only examine the formal indictment that was read before the court martial.

How hollow that indictment is! Is it possible a man has been found guilty on the strength of it? Such iniquity is staggering. I challenge decent people to read it: their hearts will leap with indignation and rebellion when they think of the disproportionate price Dreyfus is paying so far away on Devil's Island. So Dreyfus speaks several languages, does he? This is a crime. Not one compromising paper was found in his home? A crime. He occasionally pays a visit to the region he hails from? A crime. He is a hard-working man, eager to know everything? A crime. He does not get flustered? A crime. He does get flustered? A crime. And how naively it is worded! How baseless its claims are! They told us he was indicted on fourteen different counts but in the end there is actually only one: that famous bordereau; and we even find out that the experts did not all agree, that one of them, M. Gobert, was subjected to some military pressure because he dared to come to a different conclusion from the one they wanted him to reach. We were also told that twenty-three officers had come and testified against Dreyfus. We still do not know how they were questioned, but what is certain is that not all of their testimony was negative. Besides, all of them, you will notice, came from the offices of the War Department. This trial is a family conclave; they all *belong*. We must not forget that. It is the General Staff who wanted this trial: it is they who judged Dreyfus; and they have just judged him for the second time.

So all that was left was the bordereau, on which the experts had not agreed. They say that in the council chambers, the judges were naturally leaning towards acquittal. And if that is the case then you can understand why, on the General Staff, they are so desperately insistent today on proclaiming, in order to justify the judgement, that there was a damning but secret document: they cannot reveal it but it makes everything legitimate and we must bow before it, as before an invisible and unknowable God! I deny the existence of any such document, I deny it with all my strength! Some ridiculous piece of paper, possibly; perhaps the one that talks about easy women and mentions a man named D. . . who is becoming too demanding: no doubt some husband or other who feels they're not paying him enough for the use of his wife. But a document that concerns the national defence, a document that would cause war to be declared immediately if ever it was produced? No! No! It's a lie! And what makes the whole business all the more odious and cynical is that they are lying with impunity and there is no way to convict them. They turn France inside out, they shelter behind the legitimate uproar they have caused, they seal mouths by making hearts quake and perverting minds. I know of no greater crime against society.

These, M. le Président, are the facts that explain how a miscarriage of justice has come to be committed. And the evidence as to Dreyfus's character, his financial situation, his lack of motives, the fact that he has never ceased to clamour his innocence—all these demonstrate that he has been a victim of Major du Paty de Clam's overheated imagination, and of the clericalism that prevails in the military circles in which he moves, and of the hysterical hunt for 'dirty Jews' that disgraces our times.

*   *   *

Now we come to the Esterhazy affair. Three years have passed. Many people's consciences are still profoundly uneasy; worried, they look further, and ultimately they become convinced that Dreyfus is innocent.

I will not retrace the story of M. Scheurer-Kestner's doubts and then of the certainty he came to feel. But while he was conducting his investigation, very serious events were taking place within the General Staff itself. Colonel Sandherr had died and Lt-Col Picquart had succeeded him at the head of the Intelligence Bureau. And it is in that capacity and in the exercise of his functions that Picquart one day held in his hands a special delivery letter addressed to

Major Esterhazy by an agent of a foreign power. It was Picquart's strictest duty to launch an investigation. It is clear that he never acted otherwise than with the consent of his superior officers. So he outlined his suspicions to his hierarchical superiors—General Gonse, then General de Boisdeffre, then General Billot, who had succeeded General Mercier as Minister of War. The famous Picquart file that has been talked about so much was never anything more nor less than the Billot file, by which I mean the file that a subaltern prepared for his Minister, the file that they must still have in the War Ministry. The inquiry lasted from May to September 1896, and two things must be stated in no uncertain terms: General Gonse was convinced that Esterhazy was guilty, and neither General de Boisdeffre nor General Billot questioned the fact that the bordereau was in Esterhazy's handwriting. Lt-Col Picquart's investigation had led to that indubitable conclusion. But feeling ran very high, for if Esterhazy was found guilty, then inevitably the Dreyfus verdict would have to be revised, and that was what the General Staff was determined to avoid at all costs.

At that point there must have been an instant of the most intense psychological anguish. Note that General Billot was not compromised in any way; he had just come on stage: it was within his power to reveal the truth. But he dared not do it—terrified of public opinion, no doubt, and certainly afraid as well of handing over the entire General Staff, including General de Boisdeffre and General Gonse, not to mention the subalterns. Then there was but one minute of struggle between his conscience and what he thought was in the best interests of the army. Once that minute was over, it was already too late. He had made his choice, he was compromised. And ever since then his share of responsibility has grown and grown; he has taken the others' crime upon himself; he is as guilty as the others; he is guiltier than the others, for he had the power to see that justice was done and he did nothing. Understand that if you can! For a year now, General Billot, General de Boisdeffre and General Gonse have known that Dreyfus is innocent, and they have kept this appalling knowledge to themselves! And people like that sleep soundly! And they have wives and children, and love them dearly!

Lt-Col Picquart had done his duty as a decent man. In the name of justice, he insisted to his superior officers. He even begged them: he told them how impolitic their dithering was, what a terrible storm was building up, how it was going to burst once the truth became known. Later on, M. Scheurer-Kestner used the same words to General Billot: out of patriotism, he implored him to get a grip on the Affair instead of letting it go from bad to worse until it became a public disaster. But no, the crime had been committed and the General Staff could no longer confess to it. And Lt-Col Picquart was sent away on mission; they sent him farther and farther away, all the way to Tunisia where one day they even tried to do his bravery the honour of assigning him to a mission that would assuredly have got him slaughtered, in the same region where the Marquis de Morès had been killed. Mind you, Picquart was not in disgrace: General Gonse had a friendly exchange of letters with him. Only, there are some secrets it is not wise to have discovered.

In Paris, the all-conquering truth was on the march, and we know how the predictable storm eventually burst. M. Mathieu Dreyfus denounced Major Esterhazy as the real author of the bordereau just as M. Scheurer-Kestner was about to place in the hands of the Minister of Justice a request for a revision of the Dreyfus trial. And this is where Major Esterhazy appears. Witnesses state that at first he panicked; he was on the verge of suicide or about to flee. Then suddenly he became boldness itself and grew so violent that all Paris was astonished. The reason is that help had suddenly materialized in the form of an anonymous letter warning him of his enemies' doings; a mysterious lady had even gone to the trouble one night of bringing him a document that had been stolen from the General Staff and was supposed to save him. And I cannot help suspecting Lt-Col du Paty de Clam, for I recognize the type of expedients in which his fertile imagination delights. His achievement—the decision that Dreyfus was guilty—was in danger, and no doubt he wished to defend his achievement. A revision of the verdict? Why, that would put an end to the far-fetched, tragic work of cheap fiction whose abominable last chapter is being written on Devil's Island! He could not allow that to happen. Henceforth, a duel was bound to take place between Lt-Col Picquart and Lt-Col du Paty de Clam. The one shows his face for all to see; the other is masked. Soon we will see them both in the civil courts. Behind it all is the General Staff, still defending itself, refusing to admit to its crime, which becomes more of an abomination with every passing hour.

In a daze, people wondered who Major Esterhazy's protectors could be. Behind the scenes there was Lt-Col du Paty de Clam, first of all; he cobbled it all together, led the whole thing. The means used were so preposterous that they give him away. Then, there are General de Boisdeffre and General Gonse and General Billot himself, who are obliged to get Esterhazy acquitted since they dare not let Dreyfus's innocence be acknowledged lest the War Office collapse as the public heaps scorn on it. It's a prodigious situation and the impressive result is that Lt-Col Picquart, the one decent man involved, the only one who has done his duty, is going to be the victim, the person they will ride rough-shod over and punish. Ah justice! what dreadful despair grips my heart! They are even claiming that Picquart is the forger, that he forged the letter-telegram purposely to cause Esterhazy's downfall. But in heaven's name, why? To what end? State one motive. Is he too paid by the Jews? The funniest thing about the whole story is that in fact he was anti-Semitic. Yes, we are witnessing an infamous sight: men heavily in debt and guilty of evil deeds but whose innocence is being proclaimed while the very honour of a man whose record is spotless is being dragged in the mud! When a society comes to that, it begins to rot away.

This, M. le Président, is the Esterhazy affair: a guilty man who had to be proved innocent. For almost two months now, we have been following every single episode of this pitiful business. I am simplifying, for by and large this is only a summary of the story, but one day every one of its turbulent pages will be written in full. So it is that we saw General de Pellieux, first of all, then Major Ravary, conduct a villainous investigation from which the scoundrels emerged transfigured while decent people were besmirched. Then, the court martial was convened.

*　　*　　*

Did anyone really hope that one court martial would undo what another court martial had done in the first place?

I am not even talking about the judges, who could have been chosen differently. Since these sol-diers have a lofty idea of discipline in their blood, isn't that enough to disqualify them from arriving at an equitable judgement? Discipline means obedience. Once the Minister of War, the supreme commander, has publicly established the authority of the original verdict, and has done so to the acclamations of the nation's representatives, how can you expect a court martial to override his judgement officially? In hierarchical terms, that is impossible. General Billot, in his statement, planted certain ideas in the judges' minds, and they proceeded to judge the case in the same way as they would proceed to go into battle, that is, without stopping to think. The preconceived idea that they brought with them to the judges' bench was of course as follows: 'Dreyfus was sentenced for treason by a court martial, therefore he is guilty; and we, as a court martial, cannot find him innocent. Now, we know that if we recognize Esterhazy's guilt we will be proclaiming Dreyfus's innocence.' And nothing could make them budge from that line.

They reached an iniquitous verdict which will forever weigh heavy on all our future courts martial and forever make their future decisions suspect. There may be room for doubt as to whether the first court martial was intelligent but there is no doubt that the second has been criminal. Its excuse, I repeat, is that the commander in chief had spoken and declared the previous verdict unattackable, holy and superior to mere mortals—and how could his subordinates dare to contradict him? They talk to us about the honour of the army; they want us to love the army, respect the army. Oh yes, indeed, if you mean an army that would rise up at the very first hint of danger, that would defend French soil; that army is the French people themselves, and we have nothing but affection and respect for it. But the army that is involved here is not the dignified army that our need for justice calls out for. What we are faced with here is the sabre, the master that may be imposed on us tomorrow. Should we kiss the hilt of that sabre, that god, with pious devotion? No, we should not!

As I have already shown, the Dreyfus Affair was the affair of the War Office: an officer from the General Staff denounced by his fellow officers on the General Staff, sentenced under pressure from the Chiefs of the General Staff. And I repeat, he cannot emerge from his trial innocent without all of the General Staff being guilty. Which is why the War Office employed every means imaginable— campaigns in the press, statements and innuendoes, every type of influence—to cover Esterhazy, in order to convict Dreyfus a second time. The republican government should take a broom to that nest of Jesuits (General Billot calls them that himself) and make a clean sweep! Where, oh where is a strong and wisely patriotic ministry that will be bold enough to overhaul the whole system and make a fresh start? I know many people who tremble with alarm at the thought of a possible war, knowing what hands our national defence is in! and what a den of sneaking intrigue, rumour-mongering and back-biting that sacred chapel has become—yet that is where the fate of our country is decided! People take fright at the appalling light that has just been shed on it all by the Dreyfus Affair, that tale of human sacrifice! Yes, an unfortunate, a 'dirty Jew' has been sacrificed. Yes, what an accumulation of madness, stupidity, unbridled imagination, low police tactics, inquisitorial and tyrannical methods this handful of officers have got away with! They have crushed the nation under their boots, stuffing its calls for truth and justice down its throat on the fallacious and sacrilegious pretext that they are act-ing for the good of the country!

And they have committed other crimes. They have based their action on the foul press and let themselves be defended by all the rogues in Paris— and now the rogues are triumphant and insolent while law and integrity go down in defeat. It is a crime to have accused individuals of rending France apart when all those individuals ask for is a gener-ous nation at the head of the procession of free, just nations—and all the while the people who commit-ted that crime were hatching an insolent plot to make the entire world swallow a fabrication. It is a crime to lead public opinion astray, to manipulate it for a death-dealing purpose and pervert it to the point of delirium. It is a crime to poison the minds of the humble, ordinary people, to whip reactionary and intolerant passions into a frenzy while shelter-ing behind the odious bastion of anti-Semitism. France, the great and liberal cradle of the rights of man, will die of anti-Semitism if it is not cured of it. It is a crime to play on patriotism to further the

aims of hatred. And it is a crime to worship the sabre as a modern god when all of human science is labouring to hasten the triumph of truth and justice.

Truth and justice—how ardently we have striven for them! And how distressing it is to see them slapped in the face, overlooked, forced to retreat! I can easily imagine the harrowing dismay that must be filling M. Scheurer-Kestner's soul, and one day, no doubt, he will wish that when he was questioned before the Senate he had taken the revolutionary step of revealing everything he knew, ripping away all pretence. He was your true good man, a man who could look back on an honest life. He assumed that truth alone would be enough—could not help but be enough, since it was plain as day to him. What was the point of upsetting everything, since the sun would soon be shining? He was serene and confident, and how cruelly he is being punished for that now! The same is true of Lt-Col Picquart: out of a lofty sense of dignity, he refrained from pub-lishing General Gonse's letters. His scruples do him honour, particularly since while he was being respectful of discipline, his superior officers were busy slinging mud at him, conducting the investiga-tion prior to his trial themselves, in the most outra-geous and unbelievable way. There are two victims, two decent, stout-hearted men, who stood back to let God have His way—and all the while the devil was doing his work. And where Lt-Col Picquart is concerned, we have even seen this ignoble thing: a French court first allowed the rapporteur to bring charges against a witness publicly, accuse him pub-licly of every wrong in the book, and then, when that witness was called to give an account of himself and speak in his own defence, that same court held its session behind closed doors. I say that that is still another crime, and I say that it will arouse the con-science of all mankind. Our military tribunals cer-tainly do have a peculiar idea of justice.

That, M. le Président, is the plain truth. It is appalling. It will remain an indelible blot on your term as President. Oh, I know that you are power-less to deal with it, that you are the prisoner of the Constitution and of the people nearest to you. But as a man, your duty is clear, and you will not overlook it, and you will do your duty. Not for one minute do I despair that truth will triumph. I am confident and

I repeat, more vehemently even than before, the truth is on the march and nothing shall stop it. The Affair is only just beginning, because only now have the positions become crystal clear: on the one hand, the guilty parties, who do not want the truth to be revealed; on the other, the defenders of justice, who will give their lives to see that justice is done. I have said it elsewhere and I repeat it here: if the truth is buried underground, it swells and grows and becomes so explosive that the day it bursts, it blows everything wide open along with it. Time will tell; we shall see whether we have not prepared, for some later date, the most resounding disaster.

*   *   *

But this letter has been a long one, M. le Président, and it is time to bring it to a close.

I accuse Lt-Col du Paty de Clam of having been the diabolical agent of a miscarriage of justice (though unwittingly, I am willing to believe) and then of having defended his evil deed for the past three years through the most preposterous and most blameworthy machinations.

I accuse General Mercier of having been an accomplice, at least by weak-mindedness, to one of the most iniquitous acts of this century.

I accuse General Billot of having had in his hands undeniable proof that Dreyfus was innocent and of having suppressed it, of having committed this crime against justice and against humanity for political purposes, so that the General Staff, which had been compromised, would not lose face.

I accuse Generals de Boisdeffre and Gonse of having been accomplices to this same crime, one out of intense clerical conviction, no doubt, and the other perhaps because of the esprit de corps which makes the War Office the Holy of Holies and hence unattackable.

I accuse General de Pellieux and Major Ravary of having led a villainous inquiry, by which I mean a most monstrously one-sided inquiry, the report on which, by Ravary, constitutes an imperishable monument of naive audacity.

I accuse the three handwriting experts, Messrs Belhomme, Varinard and Couard, of having submitted fraudulent and deceitful reports—unless a medical examination concludes that their eyesight and their judgement were impaired.

I accuse the War Office of having conducted an abominable campaign in the press (especially in *L'Eclair* and *L'Echo de Paris*) in order to cover up its misdeeds and lead public opinion astray.

Finally, I accuse the first court martial of having violated the law by sentencing a defendant on the basis of a document which remained secret, and I accuse the second court martial of having covered up that illegal action, on orders, by having, in its own turn, committed the judicial crime of knowingly acquitting a guilty man.

In making these accusations, I am fully aware that my action comes under Articles 30 and 31 of the law of 29 July 1881 on the press, which makes libel a punishable offence. I deliberately expose myself to that law.

As for the persons I have accused, I do not know them; I have never seen them; I feel no rancour or hatred towards them. To me, they are mere entities, mere embodiments of social malfeasance. And the action I am taking here is merely a revolutionary means to hasten the revelation of truth and justice.

I have but one goal: that light be shed, in the name of mankind which has suffered so much and has the right to happiness. My ardent protest is merely a cry from my very soul. Let them dare to summon me before a court of law! Let the inquiry be held in broad daylight!

I am waiting.

M. le Président, I beg you to accept the assurance of my most profound respect.

PART FOURTEEN

Print of The Assassination of Alexander II of Russia in 1881

Terrorists use directed violence to achieve goals that they cannot attain by normal political or military means. The assassins of Alexander II believed in justice for the downtrodden peasants and in democracy. They became convinced that the tsarist regime would never relinquish its hold on power and that, if only they could eliminate the person at the top, the entire edifice would collapse. For fanatical idealists of this kind, the high goal justified the horrible means. The young men and women who threw the grenades that killed the tsar made no attempt to escape, were arrested, and used their trials to indict the regime. Their executions turned them into heroes and martyrs in the eyes of many people.

Violence and Terrorism

Although during the second half of the nineteenth century Europe achieved high levels of prosperity and democracy, violent episodes and undercurrents disturbed the peace and quiet of everyday life. Society's willingness to tolerate and even encourage militarism, chauvinism, and anti-Semitism at home and racism and colonialism abroad found a reflection in the willingness to see force used against any internal group perceived as different or "other," especially if that "other" stepped too far out of line. Furthermore, compromises that dulled outright class conflict did not blot out all class resentment. Some radical personalities of various viewpoints regretted the glossing over of principle entailed in the great state compromises of the second half of the nineteenth and the early twentieth centuries. The violence and terrorism that arose out of these tendencies both shocked and titillated pre-World War I European societies as precursors of the shattering destruction of the war itself.

An example of internally directed violence arose out of France's humiliating defeat in the 1870 Franco-Prussian War. Paris's working classes seized on the surrender as an opportunity to proclaim a radical "Commune of Paris." Having failed against the Germans, the French generals led a militia from other parts of France to Paris, laid siege to the city, and mercilessly bombarded working-class areas, inflicting more casualties and damage than had the Germans. John Leighton, an obscure eyewitness, described some of the events in an 1871 essay, "One Day under the Paris Commune." Michael Bakunin (1814–1876), the Russian revolutionary who helped launch the anarchist movement and who once wrote that "the urge to destroy is a creative urge," described his anti-state theories in *Statism and Anarchy* (1873). Decades later, the French theorist Georges Sorel (1847–1922) bitterly condemned the retreat of the working class and its leaders from the stern revolutionism of an earlier era, as exemplified by Bakunin. His *Reflections on Violence* (1908) exposed what he saw as the hypocrisy of half-measures that left things essentially as they were. Others saw social compromise as the period's chief accomplishment. In the novel *The Secret Agent* (1907), Joseph Conrad (1857–1924) described the murky world of radical terrorism that haunted Europe from Russia to the continent's western shores and even the United States. In attempting to counter the threat, police sometimes resorted to methods hardly better than those of the terrorists.

Study Questions

1. What do these selections reveal about the role of violence in the new democratic societies?
2. Why does Bakunin urge the use of violence?
3. Are Sorel's ideas the same as Bakunin's?
4. What role did terrorism play in Europe at the turn of the twentieth century?
5. Does terrorism then differ from terrorism now or are they the same?
6. Image: What does the image of the assassination of Alexander II of Russia in 1881 tells us about the technologies of security in those days and now?

Reflections on Violence

Georges Sorel

In midlife, Sorel announced that he had had to read for decades to unlearn the false things he had been taught during his education. He joined the ranks of many radical thinkers who feel that they see through the ideologies and beliefs that hold societies together. Like earlier socialists and anarchists, Sorel yearned for a drastic restructuring of society. In his 1908 Reflections on Violence, *he regretted what he saw as the selling out of the cause of the working class by its leaders and by workers themselves. Violence was a necessity for change.*

The Ethics of Violence

I

There are so many legal precautions against violence, and our upbringing is directed towards so weakening our tendencies towards violence, that we are instinctively inclined to think that any act of violence is a manifestation of a return to barbarism. Peace has always been considered the greatest of blessings and the essential condition of all material progress, and it is for this reason that industrial societies have so often been contrasted favourably with military ones. This last point of view explains why, almost uninterruptedly since the eighteenth century, economists have been in favour of strong central authorities, and have troubled little about political liberties. Condorcet levels this reproach at the followers of Quesnay, and Napoleon III had probably no greater admirer than Michel Chevalier.

It may be questioned whether there is not a little stupidity in the admiration of our contemporaries for gentle methods. I see, in fact, that several authors, remarkable for their perspicacity and their interest in the ethical side of every question, do not seem to have the same fear of violence as our official professors.

P. Bureau was extremely surprised to find in Norway a rural population which had remained pro-

foundly Christian. The peasants, nevertheless, carried a dagger at their belt; when a quarrel ended in a stabbing affray, the police enquiry generally came to nothing for lack of witnesses ready to come forward and give evidence.

The author concludes thus: "In men, a soft and effeminate character is more to be feared than their feeling of independence, however exaggerated and brutal, and a stab given by a man who is virtuous in his morals, but violent, is a social evil less serious and more easily curable than the excessive profligacy of young men reputed to be more civilised."

I borrow a second example from P. de Rousiers, who, like P. Bureau, is a fervent Catholic and interested especially in the moral side of all questions. He narrates how, towards 1860, the country of Denver, the great mining centre of the Rocky Mountains, was cleared of the bandits who infested it; the American magistracy being impotent, courageous citizens undertook the work. "Lynch law was frequently put into operation; a man accused of murder or of theft might be arrested, condemned and hanged in less than a quarter of an hour, if an energetic Vigilance Committee could get hold of him. The American who happens to be honest has one excellent habit—he does not allow himself to be crushed on the pretext that he is virtuous. A law-abiding man is not necessarily a craven, as is often the case with us; on the contrary, he is convinced that his interests ought to be considered before those of an habitual criminal or of a gambler. Moreover, he possesses the necessary energy to resist, and the kind of life

From: Georges Sorel, *Reflections on Violence* (London: George Allen & Unwin, Ltd., 1925, reprint of 1915 edition), pp. 205–208, 212–228, 240–251.

which he leads makes him capable of resisting effectively, even of taking the initiative and the responsibility of a serious step when circumstances demand it. . . . Such a man, placed in a new country, full of natural resources, wishing to take advantage of the riches it contains and to acquire a superior situation in life by his labour, will not hesitate to suppress, in the name of the higher interests he represents, the bandits who compromise the future of this country. That is why, twenty-five years ago at Denver, so many corpses were dangling above the little wooden bridge thrown across Cherry Creek."

This is a considered opinion of P. de Rousiers, for he returns elsewhere to this question. "I know," he says, "that lynch law is generally considered in France as a symptom of barbarism. . .; but if honest virtuous people in Europe think thus, virtuous people in America think quite otherwise." He highly approved of the Vigilance Committee of New Orleans which, in 1890, "to the great satisfaction of all virtuous people," hanged *maffiosi* acquitted by the jury.

In Corsica, at the time when the *vendetta* was the regular means of supplying the deficiencies or correcting the action of a too halting justice, the people do not appear to have been less moral than to-day. Before the French conquest, Kabylie had no other means of punishment but private vengeance, yet the Kabyles were not a bad people.

It may be conceded to those in favour of mild methods that violence may hamper economic progress, and even, when it goes beyond a certain limit, that it is a danger to morality. This concession cannot be used as an argument against the doctrine set forth here, because I consider violence only from the point of view of its influence on social theories. It is, in fact, certain that a great development of brutality accompanied by much blood-letting is quite unnecessary in order to induce the workers to look upon economic conflicts as the reduced facsimiles of the great battle which will decide the future. If a capitalist class is energetic, it is constantly affirming its determination to defend itself; its frank and consistently reactionary attitude contributes at least as greatly as proletarian violence towards keeping distinct that cleavage between the classes which is the basis of all Socialism.

*   *   *

It is possible, therefore, to conceive Socialism as being perfectly revolutionary, although there may only be a few short conflicts, provided that these have strength enough to evoke the idea of the general strike: all the events of the conflict will then appear under a magnified form, and the idea of catastrophe being maintained, the cleavage will be perfect. Thus one objection often urged against revolutionary Socialism may be set aside—there is no danger of civilisation succumbing under the consequences of a development of brutality, since the idea of the general strike may foster the notion of the class war by means of incidents which would appear to middle-class historians as of small importance.

When the governing classes, no longer daring to govern, are ashamed of their privileged situation, are eager to make advances to their enemies, and proclaim their horror of all cleavage in society, it become much more difficult to maintain in the minds of the proletariat this idea of cleavage which without Socialism cannot fulfil its historical role. So much the better, declare the *worthy progressives*; we may then hope that the future of the world will not be left in the hands of brutes who do not even respect the State, who laugh at the lofty ideas of the middle class, and who have no more admiration for the professional expounders of lofty thought than for priests. Let us therefore do more and more every day for the disinherited, say these gentlemen; let us show ourselves more Christian, more philanthropic, or more democratic (according to the temperament of each); let us unite for the accomplishment of *social duty*. We shall thus get the better of these dreadful Socialists, who think it possible to destroy the prestige of the Intellectuals now that the Intellectuals have destroyed that of the Church. As a matter of fact, these cunning moral combinations have failed; it is not difficult to see why.

The specious reasoning of these gentlemen—the pontiffs of "social duty"—supposes that violence cannot increase, and may even diminish in proportion as the Intellectuals unbend to the masses and make platitudes and grimaces in honour of the union of the classes. Unfortunately for these great thinkers, things do not happen in this way; violence does not diminish in the proportion that it should diminish according to the principles of advanced sociology. There are, in fact, Socialist scoundrels, who, profiting by middle-class cowardice, entice the masses into a movement which every day becomes less like that which ought to result from the sacrifices consented to by the middle class in order to obtain peace. If they dared, the sociologists would declare that the Socialists cheat and use unfair methods, so little do the facts come up to their expectations.

However, it was only to be expected that the Socialists would not allow themselves to be beaten without having used all the resources which the situation offered them. People who have devoted their life to a cause which they identify with the regeneration of the world, could not hesitate to make use of any weapon which might serve to develop to a greater degree the spirit of the class war, seeing that greater efforts were being made to suppress it. Existing social conditions favour the production of an infinite number of acts of violence, and there has been no hesitation in urging the workers not to refrain from brutality when this might do them service. Philanthropic members of the middle class having given a kindly reception to members of the syndicates who were willing to come and discuss matters with them, in the hope that these workmen, proud of their aristocratic acquaintances, would give peaceful advice to their comrades, it is not to be wondered their fellow-workmen soon suspected them of treachery when they became upholders of "social reform." Finally, and this is the most remarkable fact in the whole business, anti-patriotism becomes an essential element of the Syndicalist programme.

The introduction of anti-patriotism into the working-class movement is all the more remarkable because it came just when the Government was about to put its theories about the solidarity of the classes into practice. It was in vain that Léon Bourgeois approached the proletariat with particularly amiable airs and graces; in vain that he assured the workers that capitalist society was one great family, and that the poor had a right to share in the general riches; he maintained that the whole of contemporary legislation was directed towards the application of the principles of solidarity; the proletariat replied to him by denying the social compact in the most brutal fashion—by denying the duty of patriotism. At the moment when it seemed that a means of suppressing the class war had been found, behold, it springs up again in a particular displeasing form.

Thus all the efforts of the *worthy progressives* only brought about results in flat contradiction with their aims; it is enough to make one despair of sociology! If they had any common sense, and if they really desired to protect society against an increase of brutality, they would not drive the Socialists into the necessity of adopting the tactics which are forced on them to-day; they would remain quiet instead of devoting themselves to "social duty"; they would bless the propagandists of the general strike, who, as a matter of fact, endeavour to *render the maintenance of Socialism compatible with the minimum of brutality*. But these *well-intentioned* people are not blessed with common sense; and they have yet to suffer many blows, many humiliations, and many losses of money, before they decide to allow Socialism to follow its own course.

II

We must now carry our investigations farther, and enquire what are the motives behind the great aversion felt by moralists for acts of violence; a very brief summary of a few very curious changes which have taken place in the manners of the working classes is first of all indispensable.

A. I observe, in the first place, that nothing is more remarkable than the change which has taken place in the methods of bringing up children; formerly it was believed that the rod was the most necessary instrument of the schoolmaster; nowadays corporal punishments have disappeared from our public elementary schools. I believe that the competition which the latter had to maintain against the Church schools played a very great part in this progress; the Brothers applied the old principles of clerical pedagogy with extreme severity; and these, as is well known, involve an excessive amount of corporal punishment inflicted for the purpose of taming the demon who prompted so many of the child's bad habits. The Government was intelligent enough to set up in opposition to this barbarous system a milder form of education which brought it a great deal of sympathy; it is not at all improbable that the severity of clerical punishments is largely responsible for the present tumult of hatred against which the Church is struggling with such difficulty. In 1901 I wrote: "If (the Church) were well advised, it would suppress entirely that part of its activities which is devoted to children; it would do away with its schools and workshops; it would thus do away with the principal sources of anti-clericalism: far from showing any desire to adopt this course, it seems to be its intention to develop these establishments still further, and thus it is laying up for itself still further opportunities for displays of popular hatred for the clergy." What has happened since 1901 surpasses my forecast.

In factories and workshops customs of great brutality formerly existed, especially in those where it was necessary to employ men of superior strength, to whom was given the name of "*grosses culottes*" (big breeches); in the end these men managed to get entrusted with the task of engaging other men, because "any individual taken on by others was subjected to an infinite number of humiliations and insults"; the man who wished to enter *their* workshop had to buy them drink, and on the following day to treat all his fellow-workers. "The notorious *When's it to be? (Quand est-ce?)* would be started; everybody gets tipsy....*When's it to be?* is the devourer of savings; in a workshop where *When's it to be?* is the custom, you must stand your turn or beware." Denis Poulot, from whom I borrow these details, observes that machinery did away with the prestige of the *grosses culottes*, who were scarcely more than a memory when he wrote in 1870.

The manners of the *compagnonnages* (a kind of trade union) were for a long time remarkable for their brutality. Before 1840 there were constant brawls, often ending in bloodshed, between groups with different rites. Martin Saint Léon, in his book on the *compagnonnage*, gives extracts from really barbarous songs. Initiation into the lodge was accompanied by the severest tests; young men were treated as if they were pariahs in the "*Devoirs de Jacques et de Subise*": "*Compagnons* (carpenters) have been known," says Perdiguier, "to call themselves the Scourge of the Foxes (candidates for admission), the Terror of the Foxes....In the provinces, a 'fox' rarely works in the towns; he is hunted back, as they say, into the brushwood." There were many secessions when the tyranny of the companions came into opposition with the more liberal habits which prevailed in society. When the workers were no longer in need of protection, especially for the purpose of finding work, they were no longer so willing to submit to the demands which had formerly seemed to be of little consequence in comparison with the advantages of the *compagnonnage*. The struggle for work more than once brought candidates into opposition with companions who wished to reserve certain privileges. We might find still other reasons to explain the decline of an institution which, while rendering many important services, had contributed very much to maintaining the idea of brutality.

Everybody agrees that the disappearance of these old brutalities is an excellent thing. From this opinion it was so easy to pass to the idea that all violence is an evil, that this step was bound to have been taken; and, in fact, the great mass of the people, who are not accustomed to thinking, have come to this conclusion, which is accepted nowadays as a dogma by the *bleating herd* of moralists. They have not asked themselves what there is in brutality which is reprehensible.

When we no longer remain content with current stupidity we discover that our ideas about the disappearance of violence depend much more on a very important transformation which has taken place in the criminal world than on ethical principles. I shall endeavour to prove this.

B. Middle-class scientists are very chary of touching on anything relating to the dangerous classes; that is one of the reasons why their observations on the history of morals always remain superficial; it is not very difficult to see that it is a knowledge of these classes which alone enables us to penetrate the mysteries of the moral thought of peoples.

The dangerous classes of past times practised the simplest form of offence, that which was nearest to hand, that which is nowadays left to groups of young scoundrels without experience and without judgment. Offences of brutality seem to us nowadays something abnormal; so much so, that when the brutality has been great we often ask ourselves whether the culprit is in possession of all his senses. This transformation has evidently not come about because criminals have become moral, but because they have changed their method of procedure to suit the new economic conditions, as we shall see farther on. This change has had the greatest influence on popular thought.

We all know that by using brutality, associations of criminals manage to maintain excellent discipline among themselves. When we see a child ill-treated we instinctively suppose that its parents have criminal habits. The methods used by the old schoolmasters,

360 Part Fourteen • Violence and Terrorism

which the ecclesiastical houses persist in preserving, are those of vagabonds who steal children to make clever acrobats or interesting beggars of them. Everything which reminds us of the habits of dangerous classes of former times is extremely odious to us.

There is a tendency for the old ferocity to be replaced by cunning, and many sociologists believe that this is a real progress. Some philosophers who are not in the habit of following the opinions of the herd, do not see exactly how this constitutes progress, from the point of view of morals: "If we are revolted by the cruelty, by the brutality of past times," says Hartmann, "it must not be forgotten that uprightness, sincerity, a lively sentiment of justice, pious respect before holiness of morals characterised the ancient peoples; while nowadays we see predominant lies, duplicity, treachery, the spirit of chicane, the contempt for property, disdain for instinctive probity and legitimate customs—the value of which is not even understood. Robbery, deceit, and fraud increase in spite of legal repression more rapidly than brutal and violent crimes, like pillage, murder, and rape, etc., decrease. Egoism of the basest kind shamelessly breaks the sacred bonds of the family and friendship in every case in which these oppose its desires."

At the present time money losses are generally looked upon as accidents to which we are constantly exposed and easily made good again, while bodily accidents are not so easily reparable. Fraud is therefore regarded as infinitely less serious than brutality; criminals benefit from this change which has come about in legal sentences.

Our penal code was drawn up at a time when the citizen was pictured as a rural proprietor occupied solely with the administration of his property, as a good family man, saving to secure an honourable position for his children; large fortunes made in business, in politics, or by speculation were rare and were looked on as real monstrosities; the defense of the savings of the middle classes was one of the first concerns of the legislator. The previous judicial system had been still more severe in the punishment of fraud, for a royal declaration of August 5, 1725, punished a fraudulent bankrupt with death; it would be difficult to imagine anything further removed from our customs. We are now inclined to consider that offences of this sort can, as a rule,

only be committed as the result of the imprudence of the victims, and that it is only exceptionally that they deserve severe penalties; we, on the contrary, content ourselves with light punishment.

In a rich community where business is on a very large scale, and in which everybody is wide awake in defence of his own interests, as in America, crimes of fraud never have the same consequences as in a community which is forced to practise rigid economy; as a matter of fact, these crimes seldom cause a serious and lasting disturbance in the economic system; it is for this reason that Americans put up with the excesses of their politicians and financiers with so little complaint. P. de Rousiers compares the American to the captain of a ship who, during a dangerous voyage, has no time to look after his thieving cook. "When you point out to Americans that they are being robbed by their politicians, they usually reply, 'Of course we are quite aware of that! But as long as business is good and politicians do not get in the way, it will not be very difficult for them to escape the punishment they deserve.'"

In Europe also, since it has become easy to gain money, ideas, analogous to those current in America, have spread among us. Great company promoters have been able to escape punishment because in their hour of success they were clever enough to make friends in all circles. We have finally come to believe that it would be extremely unjust to condemn bankrupt merchants and lawyers who retire ruined after moderate catastrophes, while the princes of financial swindling continue to lead gay lives. Gradually the new industrial system has created a new and extraordinary indulgence for all crimes of fraud in the great capitalist countries.

In those countries where the old parsimonious and nonspeculative family economy still prevails, the relative estimation of acts of fraud and acts of brutality has not followed the same evolution as in America, England, and France; this is why Germany has preserved so many of the customs of former times, and does not feel the same horror that we do for brutal punishments; these never seem to them, as they do to us, only suitable to the most dangerous classes.

Many philosophers have protested against this mitigation of sentences; after what we have related earlier about Hartmann, we shall expect to meet him among those who protest. "We are already," he says, "approaching the time when theft and lying condemned by law will be despised as vulgar errors, as gross clumsiness, by the clever cheats who know how to preserve the letter of the law while infringing the rights of other people. For my part, I would much rather live amongst the ancient Germans, at the risk of being killed on occasion, than be obliged, as I am in modern cities, to look on every man as a swindler or a rogue unless I have evident proofs of his honesty." Hartmann takes no account of economic conditions; he argues from an entirely personal point of view, and never looks at what goes on round him. Nobody today wants to run the risk of being slain by ancient Germans; fraud or a theft are very easily reparable.

C. Finally, in order to get to the heart of contemporary thought on this matter, it is necessary to examine the way in which the public judges the relations existing between the State and the criminal associations. Such relations have always existed; these associations, after having practised violence, have ended by employing craft alone, or at least their acts of violence have become somewhat exceptional.

Nowadays we should think it very strange if the magistrates were to put themselves at the head of armed bands, as they did in Rome during the last years of the Republic. In the course of the Zola trial, the Anti-Semites recruited bands of paid demonstrators, who were commissioned to manifest patriotic indignation; the Government of Méline protected these antics, which for some months had considerable success and helped considerably in hindering a fair revision of the sentence on Dreyfus.

I believe that I am not mistaken in saying that these tactics of the partisans of the Church have been the principal cause of all the measures directed against Catholicism since 1901; the middle-class liberals would never have accepted these measures if they had not still been under the influence of the fear they had felt during the Dreyfus affair. The chief argument which Clemenceau used to stir up his followers to fight against the Church was that of fear; he never ceased to denounce the danger which the Republic ran in the continued existence of the Romish faction; the laws about the congregations, about education and the administration of the churches were made with the object of preventing the Catholic party again taking up its former war-

like attitude, which Anatol France so often compared to that of the League; they were *laws inspired by fear*. Many Conservatives felt this so strongly that they regarded with displeasure the resistance recently opposed to the inventories of churches; they considered that the employment of bands of *pious apaches* would make the middle classes still more hostile to their cause. It was not a little surprising to see Brunetière, who had been one of the admirers of the anti-Dreyfus apaches, advise submission; this was because experience had enlightened him as to the consequences of violence.

Associations which work by craft provoke no such reactions in the public; in the time of the "clerical republic," the society of Saint Vincent de Paul was an excellent centre of surveillance over officials of every order and grade; it is not surprising, then, that freemasonry has been able to render services to the Radical Government of exactly the same kind as those which Catholic philanthropy was able to render to former Governments. The history of recent spying scandals has shown very plainly what the point of view of the country actually was.

When the nationalists obtained possession of the documents containing information about officers of the army, which had been compiled by the dignitaries of the masonic lodges, they believed that their opponents were lost; the panic which prevailed in the Radical camp for some time seemed to justify their hopes, but before long the democracy showed only derision for what they called the "petty virtue" of those who publicly denounced the methods of General André and his accomplices. In those difficult days Henry Bérenger showed that he understood admirably the ethical standards of his contemporaries; he did not hesitate to approve of what he called the "legitimate supervision of the governing classes exercised by the organisations of the vanguard"; he denounced the cowardice of the Government which had "allowed those who had undertaken the difficult task of opposing the military caste and the Roman Church, of examining and denouncing them, to be branded as informers" (*Action*, Oct. 31, 1904); he loaded with insults the few Dreyfusards who dared to show their indignation; the attitude of Joseph Reinach appeared particularly scandalous to him; in his opinion the latter should have felt himself extremely honoured by being tolerated in the "League of the

Rights of Man," which had decided at last to lead "the good fight for the defence of rights of the citizen, sacrificed too long to those of one man" (*Action*, Dec. 12, 1904). Finally, a law of amnesty was voted declaring that no one wanted to hear anything more of these trifles.

There was some opposition in the provinces, but was it very serious? I am inclined to think not, when I read the documents published by Peguy in the ninth number of the sixth series of his *Cahiers de la quinzaine*. Several people, accustomed to speaking a verbose, sonorous, and nonsensical language, doubtless found themselves a little uncomfortable under the smiles of the leading grocers and eminent chemists who constituted the élite of the learned and musical societies before which they had been accustomed to hold forth on Justice, Truth, and Light. They found it necessary to adopt a stoical attitude.

Could anything be finer than this passage from a letter of Professor Bougle, an eminent doctor of social science, which I find on page 13: "I am very happy to learn that at last the League is going to speak. *Its silence astonishes and frightens us.*" He must be a man who is easily astonished and frightened! Francis de Pressensé also suffered some anxiety of mind—he is a specialist in that kind of thing—but his feelings were of a very distinguished kind, as is only proper for an aristocratic Socialist; he was afraid that democracy was threatened with a new *guillotine sèche*, resembling that which had done so much harm to virtuous democrats during the Panama scandal. When he saw that the public quietly accepted the complicity of the Government with a philanthropic association which had turned into a criminal association, he hurled his avenging thunders against the protestors. Among the most comical of these protestors I pick out a political pastor of St-Etienne called L. Comte. He wrote, in the extraordinary language employed by the members of the League of the Rights of Man: "I had hoped that the [Dreyfus] affair would have definitely cured us of the moral malaria from which we suffer, and that it would have cleansed the republican conscience of the clerical virus with which it was impregnated. It has done nothing. We are more clerical than ever." Accordingly this austere man remained in the League! Protestant and middle-class logic! It is always possible, you see, that the League

might one of these days be able to render some small service to the deserving ministers of the Gospel.

I have insisted rather lengthily on these grotesque incidents because they seem to me to characterize very aptly the moral ideas of the people who claim to lead us. Henceforth it must be taken for granted that politico-criminal associations which work by craft have a recognised place in any democracy that has attained its maturity. P. de Rousiers believes that America will one day cure itself of the evils which result from the guilty manœuvres of its politicians. Ostrogorski, after making a long and minute inquiry into "Democracy, and the organisation of political parties," believes that he has found remedies which will enable modern states to free themselves from exploitation by political parties. These are platonic vows; no historical experience justifies the hope that a democracy can be made to work in a capitalist country, without the criminal abuses experienced everywhere nowadays. When Rousseau demanded that the democracy should not tolerate the existence in its midst of any private association, he reasoned from his knowledge of the republics of the Middle Ages; he knew that part of history better than his contemporaries did, and was struck with the enormous part played at that time by the politico-criminal associations; he asserted the impossibility of reconciling a rational democracy with the existence of such forces, but we ought to learn from experience that there is no way of bringing about their disappearance.

*   *   *

IV

The study we have just made has not led us to think that the theorists of "social peace" are on the way to an ethic worthy of acknowledgment. We now pass to a counterproof and enquire whether proletarian violence might not be capable of producing the effect in vain expected from tactics of moderation.

First of all, it must be noticed that modern philosophers seem to agree in demanding a kind of sublimity from the ethics of the future, which will distinguish it from the petty and insipid morality of the Catholics. The chief thing with which the theologians are reproached is that they make too great use of the conception of probabilism; nothing seems more absurd (not to say more scandalous) to contemporary philosophers than to count the opinions which have been emitted for and against a maxim, in order to find out whether we ought to shape our conduct by it or not.

Professor Durkheim said recently, at the *Société française de philosophie* (February 11, 1906), that it would be impossible to suppress the religious element in ethics, and that what characterized this element was its incommensurability with other human values. He recognised that his sociological researches led him to conclusions very near those of Kant; he asserted that utilitarian morality had misunderstood the problem of duty and obligation. I do not want to discuss these here; I simply cite them to show to what point the character of the sublime impresses itself on authors who, by the nature of their work, would seem the least inclined to accept it.

No writer has defined more forcibly than Proudhon the principles of that morality which modern times have in vain sought to realise. "To feel and to assert the dignity of man," he says, "first in everything in connection with ourselves, then in the person of our neighbour, and that without a shadow of egoism, without any consideration either of divine or communal sanction—therein lies Right. To be ready to defend that dignity in every circumstance with energy, and, if necessary, against oneself, that is Justice." Clemenceau, who doubtless can hardly be said to make a personal use of this morality, expresses the same thought when he writes: "Without the dignity of the human person, without independence, liberty, and justice, life is but a bestial state not worth the trouble of preserving" (*Aurore*, May 12, 1905).

One well-founded reproach has been brought against Proudhon, as well as against many others of the great moralists; it has been said that his maxims were admirable, but that they were doomed to remain ineffective. And, in fact, experience does prove, unfortunately, that those precepts which the historians of ideas call the most elevated precepts are, as a rule, entirely ineffective. This was evident in the case of the Stoics, it was no less remarkable in Kantism, and it does not seem as if the practical influence of Proudhon has been very noticeable. In order that a man may suppress the tendencies against which morality struggles, he must have in himself some source of conviction which must dominate his whole consciousness, and act before the calculations of reflection have time to enter his mind.

It may even be said that all the fine arguments by which authors hope to induce men to act morally are more likely to lead them down the slope of probabilism; as soon as we consider an act to be accomplished, we are led to ask ourselves if there is not some means of escaping the strict obligations of duty. A. Comte supposed that human nature would change in the future and that the cerebral organs which produce altruism (?) would destroy those which produce egoism; in saying this he very likely bore in mind the fact that moral decision is instantaneous, and, like instinct, comes from the depth of man's nature.

At times Proudhon is reduced, like Kant, to appeal to a kind of scholasticism for an explanation of the paradox of moral law. "To feel himself in others, to the point of sacrificing every other interest to this sentiment, to demand for others the same respect as for himself, and to be angry with the unworthy creature who suffers others to be lacking in respect for him, as if the care of his dignity did not concern himself alone, such a faculty at first sight seems a strange one. . . . There is a tendency in every man to develop and force the acceptance of that which is essentially himself—which is, in fact, his own dignity. It results from this that the essential in man being identical and one for all humanity, each of us is aware of himself at the same time as individual and as species; and that an insult is felt by a third party and by the offender himself as well as by the injured person, that in consequence the protest is common. This precisely is what is meant by Justice."

Religious ethics claim to possess this source of action which is wanting in lay ethics, but here it is necessary to make a distinction if an error, into which so many authors have fallen, is to be avoided. The great mass of Christians do not carry out the real Christian ethic, that which the philosopher considers as really peculiar to their religion; worldly people who profess Catholicism are chiefly preoccupied with probabilism, mechanical rites and proceedings more or less related to magic and which are calculated to assure their present and future happiness in spite of their sins.

Theoretical Christianity has never been a religion suited to worldly people; the doctors of the spiritual life have always reasoned about those people who were able to escape from the conditions of ordinary life. "When the Council of Gangres, in 325," said Renan, "declared that the Gospel maxims about poverty, the renunciation of the family and virginity, were not intended for the ordinary Christian, the perfectionists made places apart where the evangelical life, too lofty for the common run of men, could be practised in all its rigour." He remarks, moreover, very justly, that the "monastery took the place of martyrdom so that the precepts of Jesus might be carried out somewhere," but he does not push this comparison far enough; the lives of the great hermits were a material struggle against the infernal powers which pursue them even to the desert, and this struggle was to continue that which the martyrs had waged against their adversaries.

These facts show us the way to a right understanding of the nature of lofty moral convictions; these never depend on reasoning or on any education of the individual will, but on a state of war in which men voluntarily participate and which finds expression in well-defined myths. In Catholic countries the monks carry on the struggle against the prince of evil who triumphs in this world, and would subdue them to his will; in Protestant countries small fanatical sects take the place of the monasteries. These are the battle-fields which enable Christian morality to hold its own, with that character of sublimity which to-day still fascinates many minds and gives it sufficient luster to beget in the community a few pale imitations.

When one considers a less accentuated state of the Christian ethic, one is struck by seeing to what extent it depends on strife. Le Play, who was an excellent Catholic, often contrasted (to the great scandal of his co-religionists) the solidity of the religious convictions he met with in countries of mixed religions, with the spirit of inactivity which prevails in the countries exclusively submitted to the influence of Rome. Among the Protestant peoples, the more vigorously the Established Church is assailed by dissident sects the greater the moral fervour developed. We thus see that conviction is founded on the competition of communions, each of which regards itself as the army of truth fighting the armies of evil. In such conditions it is possible to find sublimity; but when religious warfare is much weakened, probabilism, mechanical rites having a certain resemblance to magic, take the first place.

We can point out quite similar phenomena in the history of modern Liberal ideas. For a long while our fathers regarded from an almost religious point of view the Declaration of the Rights of Man, which seems to us nowadays only a colourless collection of abstract and confused formulas, without any great practical bearing. This was due to the fact that formidable struggles had been undertaken on account of the institutions which originated in this document; the clerical party asserted that it would demonstrate the fundamental error of Liberalism; everywhere it organised fighting societies intended to enforce its authority on the people and on the Government; it boasted that it would be able to destroy the defenders of the Revolution before long. At the time when Proudhon wrote his book on Justice, the conflict was far from being ended; thus the whole book is written in a warlike tone astonishing to the reader of to-day: the author speaks as if he were a veteran in the wars of Liberty; he would be revenged on the temporary conquerors who threaten the acquisitions of the Revolution; he announces the dawn of the great revolt.

Proudhon hopes that the duel will be soon, that the forces will meet with their whole strength, and that there will be a Napoleonic battle, finally destroying the opponent. He often speaks in a language which would be appropriate to an epic. He did not perceive that when later on his belligerent ideas had disappeared, his abstract reasonings would seem weak. There is a ferment all through his soul which colours it and gives a hidden meaning to his thought, very far removed from the scholastic sense.

The savage fury with which the Church proceeded against Proudhon's book shows that the clerical camp had exactly the same conception of the nature and consequences of the conflict as he had.

As long as the "sublime" imposed itself in this way on the modern spirit, it seemed possible to create a lay and democratic ethic; but in our time such an enterprise would seem almost comic. Everything is changed now that the clericals no longer seem formidable; there are no longer any Liberal convictions, since the Liberals have ceased to be animated by their former warlike passions. Nowadays everything is in such confusion that the priests claim to be the best of democrats; they have adopted the *Marseillaise* as their party hymn, and if a little persuasion is exerted they will have illuminations on the anniversary of August 10, 1792. Sublimity has vanished from the ethics of both parties, giving place to a morality of extraordinary meanness.

Kautsky is evidently right when he asserts that in our time the advancement of the workers has depended on their revolutionary spirit. At the end of a study on social reform and revolution he says, "It is hopeless to try, by means of moral homilies, to inspire the English workman with a more exalted conception of life, a feeling of nobler effort. The ethics of the proletariat spring from its revolutionary aspirations, these are what give it the greatest force and elevation. It is the idea of revolution which has raised the proletariat from its degradation." It is clear that for Kautsky morality is always subordinate to the idea of sublimity.

The Socialist point of view is quite different from that of former democratic literature; our fathers believed that the nearer man approached Nature the better he was, and that a man of the people was a sort of savage; that consequently the lower we descend the more virtue we find. The democrats have many times, in support of this idea, called attention to the fact that during revolutions the poorest people have often given the finest examples of heroism; they explain this by taking for granted that these obscure heroes were true children of Nature. I explain it by saying that, these men being engaged in a war which was bound to end in their triumph or their enslavement, the sentiment of sublimity was bound to be engendered by the conditions of the struggle. As a rule, during a revolution the higher classes show themselves in a particularly unfavourable light, for this reason, that, belonging to a defeated army, they experience the feelings of conquered people, suppliant, or about to capitulate.

When working-class circles are *reasonable*, as the professional sociologists wish them to be, when conflicts are confined to disputes about material interests, there is no more opportunity for heroism than when agricultural syndicates discuss the subject of the price of guano with manure merchants. It has never been thought that discussions about prices could possibly exercise any ethical influence on men; the experience of sales of live stock would lead to the supposition that in such cases those interested are led to admire cunning rather than good faith; the *ethical values* recognised by horse-dealers have never passed for very elevated. Among the important things accomplished by agricultural syndicates, De Rocquigny reports that in 1896, "the municipality of Marmande having wanted to impose on beasts brought to the fair a tax which the cattle-breeders *considered iniquitous. . .* the breeders struck, and stopped supplying the market of Marmande, with such effect that the municipality found itself forced to give in." This was a very peaceful procedure which produced results profitable to the peasants; but it is quite clear that nothing ethical was involved in such a dispute.

When politicians intervene there is, almost necessarily, a noticeable lowering of ethical standards, because they do nothing for nothing and only act on condition that the favoured association becomes one of their customers. We are very far here from the path of sublimity, we are on that which leads to the practices of the political-criminal societies.

In the opinion of many well-informed people, the transition from violence to cunning which shows itself in contemporary strikes in England cannot be too much admired. The great object of the Trades Unions is to obtain a recognition of the right to employ threats disguised in diplomatic formulas; they desire that their delegates should not be interfered with when going the round of the workshops charged with the mission of bringing those workmen who wish to work to understand that it would be to their interests to follow the *directions* of the Trades Unions; they consent to express their desires in a form which will be perfectly clear to the listener, but which could be represented in a court of justice as a solidarist* sermon. I protest I cannot see what is so admirable in these tactics, which are worthy of Escobar. In the past the Catholics have often employed similar methods of intimidation against the Liberals; I understand thus perfectly well why so many *worthy progressives* admire the Trades Unions, but the morality of the *worthy-progressives* does not seem to me very much to be admired.

---

*[This is a reference to the "solidarista" doctrine, invented by Buisson; the interests of the classes are not opposed, and the more wealthy have their duties toward the poorer—*Trans. Note.*]

It is true that for a long time in England violence has been void of all revolutionary character. Whether corporative advantages are pursued by means of blows or by craft, there is not much difference between the two methods; yet the pacific tactics of the Trades Unions indicate an hypocrisy which would be better left to the *"well intentioned progressives."* In a country where the conception of the general strike exists, the blows exchanged between workmen and representatives of the middle classes have an entirely different import, their consequences are far reaching and they may beget heroism.

I am convinced that in order to understand part, at any rate, of the dislike that Bernstein's doctrines rouse in German social democracy we must bear in mind these conclusions about the nature of the sublime in ethics. The German has been brought up on sublimity to an extraordinary extent, first by the literature connected with the wars of independence, then by the revival of the taste for the old national songs which followed these wars, then by a philosophy which pursues aims very far removed from sordid considerations. It must also be remembered that the victory of 1871 has considerably contributed toward giving Germans of every class a feeling of confidence in their strength that is not to be found to the same degree in this country at the present time; compare, for instance, the German Catholic party with the chicken-hearted creatures who form the clientèle of the Church in France! Our clergy only think of humiliating themselves before their adversaries and are quite happy, provided that there are plenty of evening parties during the winter; they have no recollection of services which are rendered to them.

The German Socialist party drew its strength particularly from the catastrophic idea everywhere spread by its propagandists, and which was taken very seriously as long as the Bismarckian persecutions maintained a warlike spirit in the groups. This spirit was so strong in the masses that they have not yet succeeded in understanding thoroughly that their leaders are anything but revolutionaries.

When Bernstein (who was too intelligent not to know what was the real spirit of his friends on the directing committee) announced that the grandiose hopes which had been raised must be given up, there was a moment of stupefaction; very few people understood that Bernstein's declarations were courageous and honest actions, intended to make the language of Socialism accord more with the real facts. If hereafter it was necessary to be content with the policy of social reform, the parliamentary parties and the ministry would have to be negotiated with—that is, it would be necessary to behave exactly as the middle classes did. This appeared monstrous to men who had been brought up on a catastrophic theory of Socialism. Many times had the tricks of the middle class politicians been denounced, their astuteness contrasted with the candour and disinterestedness of the Socialists, and the large element of artificiality and expediency in their attitude of opposition pointed out. It could never have been imagined that the disciples of Marx might follow in the footsteps of the Liberals. With the new policy, heroic characters, sublimity, and convictions disappear! The Germans thought that the world was turned upside down.

It is plain that Bernstein was absolutely right in not wanting to keep up a revolutionary semblance which was in contradiction with the real state of mind of the party; he did not find in his own country the elements which existed in France and Italy; he saw no other way then of keeping Socialism on a basis of reality than that of suppressing all that was deceptive in a revolutionary programme which the leaders no longer believed in. Kautsky, on the contrary, wanted to preserve the veil which hid from the workmen the real activity of the Socialist party; in this way he achieved much success among the politicians, but more than any one else he has helped to intensify the Socialist crisis in Germany. The ideas of Socialism cannot be kept intact by diluting the phrases of Marx in verbose commentaries, but by continually adapting the spout of Marx to facts which are capable of assuming a revolutionary aspect. The general strike alone can produce this result at the present day.

One serious question must now be asked. "Why is it that in certain countries acts of violence grouping themselves round the idea of the general strike, produce a Socialist ideology capable of inspiring sublimity, and why in others do they seem not to have that power?" Here national traditions play a great part; the examination of this problem would perhaps help to throw a strong light on the genesis of ideas; but we will not deal with it here.

One Day Under the Paris Commune, 1871
John Leighton

An Englishman who happened to be in Paris during the events he described, John Leighton is otherwise unknown to historians. When Napoleon III's regime collapsed after his defeat at the hands of German armies, working-class districts of Paris rose up in revolt and established the Commune, which aimed at full economic equality on the basis of socialist ideas. Members of the bourgeoisie were arrested and shot. An army from the rest of France marched on Paris and reconquered the city by means reminiscent of and in some ways worse than those used by the invading Germans. Class conflict seemed to threaten Europe.

The roaring of cannon close at hand, the whizzing of shells, volleys of musketry. I hear this in my sleep, and awake with a start. I dress and go out. I am told the troops have come in. "How? Where? When?" I ask of the National Guards who come rushing down the street, crying out, "We are betrayed!" They, however, know but very little. They have come from the Trocadero, and have seen the red trousers of the soldiers in the distance. Fighting is going on near the viaduct of Auteuil, at the Champ de Mars. Did the assault take place last night or this morning? It is quite impossible to obtain any reliable information. Some talk of a civil engineer having made signals to the Versaillais; others say a captain in the navy was the first to enter Paris. Suddenly about thirty men rush into the streets, crying, "We must make a barricade." I turn back, fearing to be pressed into the service. The cannonading appears dreadfully near. A shell whistles over my head. I hear some one say, "The batteries of Montmartre are bombarding the Arc de Triomphe"; and strangely enough, in this moment of horror and uncertainty, the thought crosses my mind that now the side of the arch on which is the bas-relief of Rudé will be exposed to the shells. On the Boulevard there is only here and there a passenger hurry-

ing along. The shops are closed; even the cafes are shut up; the harsh screech of the mitrailleuse grows louder and nearer. The battle seems to be close at hand, all round me. A thousand contradictory suppositions rush through my brain and hurry me along, and here on the Boulevard there is no one that can tell me anything. I walk in the direction of the Madeleine, drawn there by a violent desire to know what is going on, which silences the voice of prudence. As I approach the Chaussee d'Antin, I perceive a multitude of men, women, and children running backwards and forwards, carrying paving-stones. A barricade is being thrown up; it is already more than three feet high. Suddenly I hear the offing of heavy wheels; I turn, and a strange sight is before me—a mass of women in rags, livid, horrible, and yet grand, with the Phrygian cap on their heads, and the skirts of their robes tied around their waists, were harnessed to a mitrailleuse, which they dragged along at full speed; other women pushing vigorously behind. The whole procession, in its somber colors, with dashes of red here and there, thunders past me; I follow it as fast as I can. The mitrailleuse draws up a little in front of the barricade, and is hailed with wild clamors by the insurgents. The Amazons are being unharnessed as I come up. "Now," said a young gamin, such as one used to see in the gallery of the Theatre Porte St.-Martin, "don't you be acting the spy here, or I will break your head open as if you were a Versaillais."— "Don't waste ammunition," cried an old man with a

From: *The World's Story: A History of the World in Story, Song and Art*, 14 vols. (Boston: Houghton Mifflin, 1914), vol. V: *Italy, France, Spain, and Portugal*, pp. 406–418.

long white beard—a patriarch of civil war—"don't waste ammunition; and as for the spy, let him help to carry paving-stones. Monsieur," said he, turning to me with much politeness, "will you be so kind as to go and fetch those stones from the corner there?"

I did as I was bid, although I thought, with anything but pleasure, that if at that moment the barricade were attacked and taken, I might be shot before I had the time to say, "Allow me to explain." But the scene which surrounds me interests me in spite of myself. Those grim hags, with their red head-dresses, passing the stones I give them rapidly from hand to hand, the men who are building them up only leaving off for a moment now and then to swallow a cup of coffee, which a young girl prepares over a small tin stove; the rifles symmetrically piled; the barricade, which rises higher and higher; the solitude in which we are working—only here and there a head appears at a window, and is quickly withdrawn; the ever-increasing noise of the battle; and, over all, the brightness of a dazzling morning sun—all this has something sinister, and yet horribly fascinating about it. While we are at work they talk; I listen. The Versaillais have been coming in all night. The Porte de la Muette and the Porte Dauphine have been surrendered by the 13th and the 113th battalions of the first arrondissement. "Those two numbers 13 will bring them ill luck," says a woman. Vinoy is established at the Trocadero, and Douai at the Point du Jour: they continue to advance. The Champ de Mars has been taken from the Federals after two hours' fighting. A battery is erected at the Arc de Triomphe, which sweeps the Champs Elysees and bombards the Tuileries. A shell has fallen in the Rue du Marche Saint-Honore. In the Cours-la-Reine the 138th battalion stood bravely. The Tuileries is armed with guns, and shells the Arc de Triomphe. In the Avenue de Marigny the gendarmes have shot twelve Federals who had surrendered; their bodies are still lying on the pavement in front of the tobacconist's. Rue de Sevres, the *Vengeurs de Flourens* have put to flight a whole regiment of the line: the *Vengeurs* have sworn to resist to a man. They are fighting in the Champs Elysees, around the Ministere de la Guerre, and on the Boulevard Haussmann. Dombrowski has been killed at the Chateau de la Muette. The Versaillais

have attacked the Western Saint-Lazare Station, and are marching towards the Pepiniere barracks. "We have been sold, betrayed, and surprised; but what does it matter, we will triumph. We want no more chiefs or generals; behind the barricades every man is a marshal!"

Close to Saint-Germain l'Auxerrois women are busy pulling down the wooden seats; children are rolling empty wine-barrels and carrying sacks of earth. As one nears the Hotel de Ville the barricades are higher, better armed, and better manned. All the Nationals here look ardent, resolved, and fierce. They say little, and do not shout at all. Two guards, seated on the pavement, are playing at picquet. I push on, and am allowed to pass. The barricades are terminated here, and I have nothing to fear from paving-stones. Looking up, I see that all the windows are closed, with the exception of one, where two old women are busy putting a mattress between the window and the shutter. A sentinel, mounting guard in front of the Cafe de la Compagnie du Gaz, cries out to me, "You can't pass here!"

I therefore seat myself at a table in front of the cafe, which has doubtless been left open by order, and where several officers are talking in a most animated manner.

One of them rises and advances towards me. He asks me rudely what I am doing there. I will not allow myself to be abashed by his tone, but draw out my pass from my pocket and show it to him, without saying a word. "All right," says he; and then seats himself by my side, and tells me, "I know it already, that a part of the left bank of the river is occupied by the troops of the Assembly, that fighting is going on everywhere, and that the army on this side is gradually retreating—Street fighting is our affair, you see," he continues. "In such battles as that, the merest gamin from Belleville knows more about it than MacMahon. . . It will be terrible. The enemy shoots the prisoners." (For the last two months the Commune had been saying the same thing.) "We shall give no quarter."—I ask him, "Is it Delescluze who is determined to resist?"—"Yes," he answers. "Lean forward a little. Look at those three windows to the left of the trophy. That is the Salle de l'Etat-Major. Delescluze is there giving orders, signing commissions. He has not slept for three days. Just now I scarcely knew him, he was so worn out with fatigue. The Committee of Public Safety sits permanently in a room adjoining, making out proclamations and decrees."—"Ha, ha!" said I, "decrees!"—"Yes, citizen, he has just decreed hero-ism!" The officer gives me several other bits of information: tells me that "Lullier this very morning has had thirty *réfractaires* shot, and that Rigault has gone to Mazas to look after the hostages."

While he is talking, I try to see what is going on in the Place de l'Hôtel de Ville. Two or three thousand Federals are there, some seated, some lying on the ground. A lively discussion is going on. Several little barrels are standing about on chairs; the men are con-tinually getting up and crowding round the barrels, some have no glasses, but drink in the palms of their hands. Women walk up and down in bands, gesticu-lating wildly. The men shout, the women shriek. Mounted expresses gallop out of the Hotel, some in the direction of the Bastille, some towards the Place de la Concorde. The latter fly past us crying out, "All's well!" A man comes out on the balcony of the Hôtel de Ville and addresses the crowd. All the Federals start to their feet enthusiastically.—"That's Valles," says my neighbor to me. I had already recognized him. I frequently saw him in the students' quarter in a little *crémerie* in the Rue Serpente. He was given to making verses, rather bad ones by the bye; I remember one in particular, a panegyric on a green coat. They used to say he had a situation as a professional mourner. His face even then wore a bitter and violent expression. He left poetry for journalism, and then journalism for politics. Today he is spouting forth at a window of the Hôtel de Ville. I cannot catch a word of what he says; but as he retires he is wildly applauded. Such applause pains me sadly. I feel that these men and these women are mad for blood, and will know how to die. Alas! how many dead and dying already! Neither the can-nonading nor the musketry has ceased an instant.

I now see a number of women walk out of the Hôtel, the crowd makes room for them to pass. They come our way. They are dressed in black, and have black crape tied round their arms and a red cockade in their bonnets. My friend the officer tells me that they are the governesses who have taken the places of the nuns. Then he walks up to them and says, "Have you succeeded?"—"Yes," answers one of

them, "here is our commission. The school-children are to be employed in making sacks and filling them with earth, the eldest ones are to load the rifles behind the barricades. They will receive rations like National Guards, and a pension will be given to the mothers of those who die for the republic. They are mad to fight, I assure you. We have made them work hard during the last month; this will be their holiday!" The woman who says this is young and pretty, and speaks with a sweet smile on her lips. I shudder. Suddenly two staff officers appear and ride furiously up to the Hôtel de Ville; they have come from the Place Vendôme. An instant later and the trumpets sound. The companies form in the Place, and great agitation reigns in the Hôtel. Men rush in and out. The officers who are in the cafe where I am get up instantly, and go to take their places at the head of their men. A rumor spreads that the Versail-lais have taken the barricades on the Place de la Concorde.—"By Jove! I think you had better go home," says my neighbor to me, as he clasps his sword-belt; "we shall have hot work here, and that shortly." I think it prudent to follow this advice.

One glance at the Place before I go. The compa-nies of Federals have just started off by the Rue de Rivoli and the quays at a quick march, crying, "*Vive la Commune!*" a ferocious joy beaming in their faces. A young man, almost a lad, lags a little behind; a woman rushes up to him, and lays hold of his collar, screaming, "Well, and you! are you not going to get yourself killed with the others?"

I reach the Rue Vieille-du-Temple, where another barricade is being built up. I place a paving-stone upon it and pass on. Soon I see open shops and pas-sengers in the streets. This tradesmen's quarter seems to have outlived the riot of Paris. Here one might almost forget the frightful civil war which wages so near, if the conversation of those around did not betray the anguish of the speakers, and if you did not hear the cannon roaring out unceasingly, "People of Paris, listen to me! I am ruining your houses. Listen to me! I am killing your children."

On the Boulevards more barricades; some nearly finished, others scarcely commenced. One con-structed near the Porte Saint-Martin looks formida-ble. That spot seems destined to be the theater of bloody scenes, of riot and revolution. In 1852, corpses lay piled up behind the railing, and all the pavement was tinged with blood. I return home profoundly sad; I can scarcely think—I feel in a dream, and am tired to death; my eyelids droop of themselves; I am like one of those houses there with closed shutters.

Near the Gymnase I meet a friend who I thought was at Versailles. We shake hands sadly. "When did you come back?" I ask.—"Today; I followed the troops."—Then turning back with me he tells me what he has seen. He had a pass, and walked into Paris behind the artillery and the line, as far as the Trocadero, where the soldiers halted to take up their line of battle. Not a single man was visible along the whole length of the quays. At the Champ de Mars he did not see any insurgents. The musketry seemed very violent near Vaugirard on the Pont Royal and around the Palais de l'Industrie. Shells from Montmartre repeatedly fell on the quays. He could not see much, however, only the smoke in the distance. Not a soul did he meet. Such frightful noise in such solitude was fearful. He continued his way under the shelter of the parapet. On one place he saw some gamins cutting huge pieces of flesh off the dead body of a horse that was lying in the path. There must have been fighting there. Down by the water a man fishing while two shells fell in the river, a little higher up, a yard or two from the shore. Then he thought it prudent to get nearer to the Palais de l'Industrie. The fighting was nearly over then, but not quite. The Champs Elysees was melancholy in the extreme; not a soul was there. This was only too literally true, for several corpses lay on the ground. He saw a soldier of the line lying beneath a tree, his forehead covered with blood. The man opened his mouth as if to speak as he heard the sound of footsteps, the eyelids quivered and then there was a shiver, and all was over.

My friend walked slowly away. He saw trees thrown down and bronze lamp-posts broken; glass crackled under his feet as he passed near the ruined kiosques. Every now and then turning his head he saw shells from Montmartre fall on the Arc de Triomphe and break off large fragments of stone. Near the Tuileries was a confused mass of soldiery against a background of smoke. Suddenly he heard the whizzing of a ball and saw the branch of a tree fall.

From one end of the avenue to the other, no one; the stones glistened white in the sun. Many dead were to be seen lying about as he crossed the Champs Élysées. All the streets to the left were full of soldiery; there had been fighting there, but it was over now. The insurgents had retreated in the direction of the Madeleine. In many places tricolor flags were hanging from the windows, and women were smiling and waving their handkerchiefs to the troops. The presence of the soldiery seemed to reassure everybody. The concierges were seated before their doors with pipes in their mouths, recounting to attentive listeners the perils from which they had escaped; how balls pierced the mattresses put up at the windows, and how the Federals had got into the houses to hide. One said, "I found three of them in my court; I told a lieutenant they were there, and he had them shot. But I wish they would take them away; I cannot keep dead bodies in my house." Another was talking with some soldiers, and pointing out a house to them. Four men and a corporal went into the place indicated, and an instant afterwards my friend heard the cracking of rifles. The concierge rubbed his hands and winked at the bystanders, while another was saying, "They respect nothing, those Federals; during the battle they came in to steal. They wanted to take away my clothes, my linen, everything I have; but I told them to leave that, that it was not good enough for them, that they ought to go up to the first floor, where they would find clocks and plate, and I gave them the key. Well, messieurs, you would never believe what they have done, the rascals! They took the key and went and pillaged everything on the first floor!" My friend had heard enough, and passed on. The agitation everywhere was very great. The soldiers went hither and thither, rang the bells, went into the houses and brought out with them pale-faced prisoners. The inhabitants continued to smile politely but grimly. Here and there dead bodies were lying in the road. A man who was pushing a truck allowed one of the wheels to pass over a corpse that was lying with its head on the curbstone. "Bah!" said he, "it won't do him any harm." The dead and wounded were, however, being carried away as quickly as possible.

The cannon had now ceased roaring, and the fight was still going on close at hand—at the Tuileries doubtless. The townspeople were tranquil and the soldiery disdainful. A strange contrast; all these good citizens smiling and chatting, and the soldiers, who had come to save them at the peril of their lives, looking down upon them with the most careless indifference. My friend reached the Boulevard Haussmann; there the corpses were in large numbers. He counted thirty in less than a hundred yards. Some were lying under the door-ways; a dead woman was seated on the bottom stair of one of the houses. Near the church of "La Trinité" were two guns, the reports from which were deafening; several of the shells fell in a bathing establishment in the Rue Taitbout opposite the Boulevard. On the Boulevard itself, not a person was to be seen. Here and there dark masses, corpses doubtless. However, the moment the noise of the report of a gun had died away, and while the gunners were reloading, heads were thrust out from doors to see what damage had been done—to count the number of trees broken, benches torn up, and kiosques overturned. From some of the win-dows rifles were fired. My friend then reached the street he lived in and went home. He was told dur-ing the morning they had violently bombarded the College Chaptal, where the Zouaves of the Com-mune had fortified themselves; but the engagement was not a long one, they made several prisoners and shot the rest.

My friend shut himself up at home, determined not to go out. But his impatience to see and hear what was going on forced him into the streets again. The Pepiniere barracks were occupied by troops of the line; he was able to get to the New Opera without trouble, leaving the Madeleine, where dreadful fighting was going on, to the right. On the way were to be seen piled muskets, soldiers sitting and lying about, and corpses everywhere. He then managed, without incurring too much danger, to reach the Boulevards, where the insurgents, who were then very numerous, had not yet been attacked. He worked for some little time at the bar-ricade, and then was allowed to pass on. It was thus that we had met. Just as we were about to turn up the Faubourg Montmartre a man rushed up saying that three hundred Federals had taken refuge in the church of the Madeleine, followed by gendarmes, and had gone on fighting for more than an hour. "Now," he finished up by saying, "if the curé were to return, he would find plenty of people to bury!"

I am now at home. Evening has come at last; I am jotting down these notes just as they come into my head. I am too much fatigued both in mind and body to attempt to put my thoughts into order. The cannonading is incessant, and the fusil-lade also. I pity those that died, and those that kill! Oh! poor Paris, when will experience make you wiser?

Statism and Anarchy

Michael Bakunin

Bakunin, an associate of his fellow nobleman Alexander Herzen, was one of the creators of the Russian revolutionary tradition. In the name of the oppressed peasantry, the revolutionaries wished to overthrow the ruling regime and establish freedom and equality. After escaping exile in Siberia, Bakunin became one of the founders of the anarchist movement in Europe. He felt that existing states and laws had the goal of protecting economic elites and caused the very problems they seemed to control. Governments, in this view, not only needed to be overthrown but states needed to be destroyed. Human societies without governments, harsh laws, police, and armies would thrive in harmony.

I

In science the living, concretely rational method of procedure is to go from the actual fact to the thought that embraces it, expresses it, and thereby explains it. In the practical world it is the movement from social life to the most rational possible organization of it in accordance with the indications, conditions, needs, and more or less passionate demands of life itself.

That is the broad popular way, the way of real and total liberation, open to anyone and therefore truly popular. It is the way of the *anarchistic* social revolution which arises of itself among the people and destroys everything that obstructs the broad flow of popular life, in order then to create new forms of free social existence from the very depths of the people's being.

The way of the metaphysicians is quite different. The people we call metaphysicians are not just the followers of Hegel's doctrines, who are no longer very numerous, but also the positivists and all the contemporary devotees of the goddess science; all those who, by one means or another, such as a meticulous but necessarily always imperfect study of the past and present, have devised an ideal of social organization to which, like a new

Procrustes, they want to make the life of future generations conform whatever the cost; in a word, all those who, instead of regarding thought or science as one of the necessary manifestations of natural and social life, regard this poor life as a practical manifestation of their own thought and their own science, which, of course, is always imperfect.

Thus the imaginary tsar-father, the guardian and benefactor of the people, is raised high, high above us, almost to the heavens, while the real tsar, the tsar-knout, the tsar-thief, the tsar-destroyer—the state—takes his place. A natural result is the strange fact that our people at one and the same time venerate an imaginary, fantastic tsar and hate the real tsar who is manifested in the state.

Our people deeply and passionately hate the state and all its representatives, whatever form they take. Not long ago their hatred was still divided between the nobles and the officials, and sometimes they even seemed to hate the former more than the latter, although in fact they hated them equally. But when the nobility, as a result of the abolition of serfdom, began visibly to decay, to disappear, and to revert to its original role as a class exclusively devoted to state service, the people included it in their general hatred for the whole caste of officials. Need we prove how legitimate that hatred is!

The state crushed and completed the corruption of the Russian commune, which was already cor-

From: *The Essential Works of Anarchism*, ed. by Marshall S. Shatz (Bantam Books: New York, 1971), pp. 177–183.

rupted enough by its patriarchal foundations. Under the yoke of the state, communal elections became a fraud and the temporary representatives elected by the people themselves, the chiefs, elders, tithingmen, and foremen, turned into tools of the government, on the one hand, and bribed servants of the rich peasants on the other. Under these conditions the last vestiges of justice, truth, and plain humanity finally disappeared from the communes, which in addition were ravaged by state taxes and dues and thoroughly downtrodden by the arbitrariness of the authorities. More than ever, banditry remained the sole recourse for the individual, and for the people as a whole a universal insurrection, a revolution.

Under these circumstances, what can our intellectual proletariat do, our social-revolutionary Russian youth, honest, sincere, and totally dedicated? Without doubt they must go to the people because nowhere today, and least of all in Russia, is there life or a cause or a future outside of the people, outside of the multimillion-strong laboring masses. But how, and why, should they go to the people?

At the moment, after the unfortunate outcome of the Nechayev affair,* opinions on this score seem to be very much divided. But out of the general confusion of thought two main opposing tendencies are now crystallizing. One is of a more pacific and preparatory character; the other is insurrectionary and aims directly at the organization of the people's defense.

The advocates of the first tendency do not believe that the revolution is a real possibility. But since they do not want to remain, and cannot remain, passive spectators of the people's misfortunes, they are resolving to go to the people and share these misfortunes fraternally with them while at the same time teaching and preparing them, not theoretically but practically, by their own living example. Some will go among the fac-

tory workers, to work beside them as equals and try to spread the spirit of association among them.

Others will try to establish agrarian colonies where, besides the principle of common use of the land, which is so well known to our peasants, they will pursue and apply a principle which is still totally unfamiliar but economically indispensable to them. That is the principle of collective cultivation of the common land and the equal division of its products, or the value of its products, in accordance with the strictest rules of justice—not juridical justice but human justice, which demands more work from the capable and strong, and less from the incapable and weak, and distributes earnings not according to each one's work but according to his needs.

They hope to entice the peasants by their example and particularly by the advantages which they hope to derive from the organization of collective labor. It is the same hope that Cabet nursed after the unsuccessful revolution of 1848, when he set out for America with his Icarians and founded New Icaria. The colony lasted only a very short while, and American soil, it should be noted, was more favorable than Russian for such an experiment. In America the fullest freedom reigns, while in our blessed Russia the tsar reigns.

But the hopes of those who want to prepare the people and influence them by peaceful persuasion go further. By organizing their own domestic life on a foundation of complete freedom of person, they want to counteract the vile patriarchalism that lies at the basis of our Russian slavery. That is, they want to strike our principal social evil at its very root and thereby contribute directly to the correction of the people's ideal and the dissemination among them of practical notions of justice, freedom, and the means of liberation.

All this is beautiful, extremely magnanimous and noble, but scarcely realizable. Even if they do succeed somewhere it will be a drop in the ocean, and a drop is far from sufficient to prepare, rouse, and liberate our people; it will take many resources and a great deal of vital energy, and the results will be negligible.

Those who draw up such plans and sincerely intend to carry them out doubtlessly do so with their eyes closed so as not to see our Russian reality in all its ugliness. We can predict in advance all the

---

*Sergei Nechayev was a bizarre individual who claimed to be the head of a network of revolutionary cells across Russia. His organization proved to be largely imaginary, but for a time he won the support and collaboration of Bakunin himself. Nechayev was extradited to Russia by the Swiss as a common criminal, in connection with the murder of a student who had belonged to his group in Moscow. He was convicted and died in prison.

terrible, painful disappointments that will befall them right at the start, for except in a few, a very few fortunate cases the majority of them will get no further than the initial stages and will not have the strength to go on.

Let them try it if they see no alternative, but at the same time let them recognize that this is too little, much too little to liberate and save our poor martyred people. The other path is the militant one of insurrection. That is the one we believe in, and it is the only one from which we expect salvation.

Our people are in obvious need of help. They are in such desperate straits that a revolt can be raised in any village without difficulty. But although an uprising, even if unsuccessful, is always useful, sporadic outbursts are not enough. All the villages must rise at once. The vast popular movements led by Stenka Razin and Pugachev prove that this is possible. They prove that an ideal does in fact live in the consciousness of our people which they aspire to realize, while we conclude from the failure of these movements that this ideal has fundamental defects which have obstructed it and are continuing to obstruct it.

We have identified those defects and voiced our conviction that the immediate obligation of our revolutionary youth is to counteract them and to exert all their forces to overcome them in the popular consciousness. In order to demonstrate the possibility of such a struggle we showed that it began long ago among the people themselves.

The war against patriarchalism is being waged today in nearly every village and every family. The commune, the *mir,* have turned into instruments of the detested state and bureaucracy to such a degree that an uprising against the latter becomes at the same time an uprising against the despotism of the commune and the *mir.*

Veneration of the tsar remains, but we believe that it has palled and grown considerably weaker in the popular consciousness over the last ten or twelve years, thanks to Emperor Alexander the Benevolent's* wisdom and love of the people. The noble serfowner is no more, and he used to serve as the

---

*An ironic reference to Alexander II, who emancipated the serfs in 1861 but failed to satisfy all of their demands. He was assassinated by revolutionaries in 1881.

main lighting rod for the thunder bolts of popular hatred. The noble or bourgeois land owner has remained, the rich peasant, and particularly the official, the angel or archangel of the tsar. But the official executes the tsar's will. Befogged though our peasant may be by his insane historical faith in the tsar he is finally beginning to understand this. And how can he not help understanding it! For ten years, from all corners of Russia, he has been sending his deputies to petition the tsar, and they all hear from the tsar's own lips just one answer: *"You will get no other freedom!"!*

No, the Russian peasant may very well be ignorant but he is no fool. And in view of the facts staring him in the face and the many proofs carried out on his own hide, he would have to be a perfect fool not to begin to understand at last that he has no worse enemy than the tsar. This must be explained to him, he must be made to feel it by every possible means. All the lamentable and tragic incidents that fill the daily life of the people must be used to show him how the actions of the officials, landowners, priests, and rich peasants, the violence, robbery, and pillaging that make life impossible for him, emanate directly from the tsar's authority, rely upon it, and are possible only because of it. In a word, he must be shown that the state which is so hateful to him is the tsar himself and nothing but the tsar. That is the immediate and at the moment the chief duty of revolutionary propaganda.

But that is not all. The main defect which paralyzes a general insurrection of the people in Russia and has hitherto made it impossible is the self-containment of the communes, the isolation and separation of the local peasant communities. At all costs this self-containment must be breached and a living current of revolutionary thought, will, and deed created between the separate communes. The best peasants of all the villages, counties, and districts (if possible), the forward-looking individuals, the natural revolutionaries of the Russian peasant world, must be linked together, and wherever possible the same living link must be created between the factory workers and the peasantry. This link can only be a personal one. While observing the utmost circumspection, the best or most advanced peasants of each village, each county, and each district must get to know their counterparts in every other village, county, and district.

The first task is to convince these forward-looking individuals, and through them, if not all the people then at least a sizable segment of them, the most energetic segment, that the people as a whole, all the villages, counties, and districts throughout Russia, and outside of Russia as well, suffer from a common misfortune and therefore have a common cause. They must be convinced that an invincible force lives in the people which nothing and no one can withstand; and that if this force has not yet emancipated the people it is because it is powerful only when unified and acting everywhere at the same time, in concert, with one aim, and until now it has not been unified. In order to unify it the villages, counties, and districts must be linked together and organized according to a common plan and with the single goal of liberating the entire people. In order to create in our people a feeling and consciousness of real unity, some kind of popular newspaper must be started—printed, lithographed, handwritten, or even oral—that would immediately publicize throughout Russia every local popular uprising, of peasants or of factory workers, breaking out now in one place, now in another, as well as the major revolutionary movements of the West European proletariat. Then our peasant and our worker would no longer feel himself to be alone but would know that behind him, laboring under the same yoke but with the same passion and will to liberate itself, stands a vast innumerable world of laboring masses preparing a universal explosion.

That is the task and, frankly speaking, the sole object of revolutionary propaganda. It is inconvenient to put in writing just how this object is to be achieved by our young people.

Let us say one thing only: the Russian people will acknowledge our educated youth as their own only when they see them taking part in their lives, their misfortunes, their cause, and their desperate revolt. From now on the youth must be present not as witnesses but as activists who are ready to sacrifice themselves and participate in all popular disturbances and uprisings, big ones and small ones, wherever and whenever they break out. By acting according to a rigorously conceived and prescribed plan and subjecting all their actions to the strictest discipline in order to create the unanimity without which victory is impossible, they must learn for themselves and must teach the people not only how to resist desperately but how to attack boldly.

In conclusion let us say one word more. The class which we call our intellectual proletariat and which in Russia is already in a social-revolutionary situation, a situation that is simply desperate and impossible, must now become imbued with conscious passion for the social-revolutionary cause if it does not want to perish shamefully and futilely. This is the class that today is called upon to prepare, that is, to organize the popular revolution. It has no alternative. To be sure, it could try to use the education it has received to win a more or less advantageous place for itself in the already overcrowded and extremely inhospitable ranks of the robbers, exploiters, and oppressors of the people. But such places are becoming fewer and fewer, accessible only to a very small minority. The majority will be left only with the shame of treason and will die in want, mediocrity, and baseness. We are addressing ourselves, however, only to those for whom treason is unthinkable and impossible.

Once they have irrevocably broken all their ties with the world of the exploiters, destroyers, and enemies of the Russian people, they must consider themselves a precious capital that belongs exclusively to the cause of the people's liberation, a capital that must be expended only on popular propaganda and on gradually arousing and organizing a universal uprising.

The Secret Agent
Joseph Conrad

British novelist Joseph Conrad is known for his penetrating analyses of some of the sharpest problems of the early twentieth century, including European attitudes toward other races and, in this case, terrorism. Conrad uses this novel to explore the dark world of spies and secret organizations willing to utilize the most brutal methods to accomplish their goals.

IV

Most of the thirty or so little tables covered by red cloths with a white design stood ranged at right angles to the deep brown wainscoting of the underground hall. Bronze chandeliers with many globes depended from the low, slightly vaulted ceiling, and the fresco paintings ran flat and dull all round the walls without windows, representing scenes of the chase and of outdoor revelry in mediæval costumes. Varlets in green jerkins brandished hunting knives and raised on high tankards of foaming beer.

"Unless I am very much mistaken, you are the man who would know the inside of this confounded affair," said the robust Ossipon, leaning over, his elbows far out on the table and his feet tucked back completely under his chair. His eyes stared with wild eagerness.

An upright semi-grand piano near the door, flanked by two palms in pots, executed suddenly all by itself a valse tune with aggressive virtuosity. The din it raised was deafening. When it ceased, as abruptly as it had started, the bespectacled, dingy little man who faced Ossipon behind a heavy glass mug full of beer emitted calmly what had the sound of a general proposition.

"In principle what one of us may or may not know as to any given fact can't be a matter for inquiry to the others."

"Certainly not," Comrade Ossipon agreed in a quiet undertone. "In principle."

With his big florid face held between his hands he continued to stare hard, while the dingy little man in spectacles coolly took a drink of beer and stood the glass mug back on the table. His flat, large ears departed widely from the sides of his skull, which looked frail enough for Ossipon to crush between thumb and forefinger; the dome of the forehead seemed to rest on the rim of the spectacles; the flat cheeks, of a greasy, unhealthy complexion, were merely smudged by the miserable poverty of a thin dark whisker. The lamentable inferiority of the whole physique was made ludicrous by the supremely self-confident bearing of the individual. His speech was curt, and he had a particularly impressive manner of keeping silent.

Ossipon spoke again from between his hands in a mutter.

"Have you been out much to-day?"

"No. I stayed in bed all the morning," answered the other. "Why?"

"Oh! Nothing," said Ossipon, gazing earnestly and quivering inwardly with the desire to find out something, but obviously intimidated by the little man's overwhelming air of unconcern. When talking with this comrade—which happened but rarely—the big Ossipon suffered from a sense of moral and even physical insignificance. However, he ventured another question. "Did you walk down here?"

"No; omnibus," the little man answered, readily enough. He lived far away in Islington, in a small house down a shabby street, littered with straw and

From: Joseph Conrad, *The Secret Agent* (New York: Doubleday & Company, 1953), pp. 61–76.

dirty paper, where out of school hours a troop of assorted children ran and squabbled with a shrill, joyless, rowdy clamour. His single back room, remarkable for having an extremely large cupboard, he rented furnished from two elderly spinsters, dressmakers in a humble way with a clientele of servant girls mostly. He had a heavy padlock put on the cupboard, but otherwise he was a model lodger, giving no trouble, and requiring practically no attendance. His oddities were that he insisted on being present when his room was being swept, and that when he went out he locked his door, and took the key away with him.

Ossipon had a vision of these round black-rimmed spectacles progressing along the streets on the top of an omnibus, their self-confident glitter falling here and there on the walls of houses or lowered upon the heads of the unconscious stream of people on the pavements. The ghost of a sickly smile altered the set of Ossipon's thick lips at the thought of the walls nodding, of people running for life at the sight of those spectacles. If they had only known! What a panic! He murmured interrogatively: "Been sitting long here?"

"An hour or more," answered the other, negligently, and took a pull at the dark beer. All his movements—the way he grasped the mug, the act of drinking, the way he set the heavy glass down and folded his arms—had a firmness, an assured precision which made the big and muscular Ossipon, leaning forward with staring eyes and protruding lips, look the picture of eager indecision.

"An hour," he said. "Then it may be you haven't heard yet the news I've heard just now—in the street. Have you?"

The little man shook his head negatively the least bit. But as he gave no indication of curiosity Ossipon ventured to add that he had heard it just outside the place. A newspaper boy had yelled the thing under his very nose, and not being prepared for anything of that sort, he was very much startled and upset. He had to come in there with a dry mouth. "I never thought of finding you here," he added, murmuring steadily, with his elbows planted on the table.

"I come here sometimes," said the other, preserving his provoking coolness of demeanour.

"It's wonderful that you of all people should have heard nothing of it," the big Ossipon continued. His eyelids snapped nervously upon the shining eyes. "You of all people," he repeated, tentatively. This obvious restraint argued an incredible and inexplicable timidity of the big fellow before the calm little man, who again lifted the glass mug, drank, and put it down with brusque and assured movements. And that was all.

Ossipon, after waiting for something, word or sign, that did not come, made an effort to assume a sort of indifference.

"Do you," he said, deadening his voice still more, "give your stuff to anybody who's up to asking you for it?"

"My absolute rule is never to refuse anybody—as long as I have a pinch by me," answered the little man with decision.

"That's a principle?" commented Ossipon.

"It's a principle."

"And you think it's sound?"

The large round spectacles, which gave a look of staring self-confidence to the sallow face, confronted Ossipon like sleepless, unwinking orbs flashing a cold fire.

"Perfectly. Always. Under every circumstance. What could stop me? Why should I not? Why should I think twice about it?"

Ossipon gasped, as it were, discreetly.

"Do you mean to say you would hand it over to a 'tec' if one came to ask you for your wares?"

The other smiled faintly.

"Let them come and try it on, and you will see," he said. "They know me, but I know also every one of them. They won't come near me—not they."

His thin, livid lips snapped together firmly. Ossipon began to argue.

"But they could send someone—rig a plant on you. Don't you see? Get the stuff from you in that way, and then arrest you with the proof in their hands."

"Proof of what? Dealing in explosives without a licence perhaps." This was meant for a contemptuous jeer, though the expression of the thin, sickly face remained unchanged, and the utterance was negligent. "I don't think there's one of them anxious to make that arrest. I don't think they could get one of them to apply for a warrant. I mean one of the best. Not one."

"Why?" Ossipon asked.

"Because they know very well I take care never to part with the last handful of my wares. I've it always by me." He touched the breast of his coat lightly. "In a thick glass flask," he added.

"So I have been told," said Ossipon, with a shade of wonder in his voice. "But I didn't know if—"

"They know," interrupted the little man, crisply, leaning against the straight chair back, which rose higher than his fragile head. "I shall never be arrested. The game isn't good enough for any policeman of them all. To deal with a man like me you require sheer, naked, inglorious heroism."

Again his lips closed with a self-confident snap. Ossipon repressed a movement of impatience.

"Or recklessness—or simply ignorance," he retorted. "They've only to get somebody for the job who does not know you carry enough stuff in your pocket to blow yourself and everything within sixty yards of you to pieces."

"I never affirmed I could not be eliminated," rejoined the other. "But that wouldn't be an arrest. Moreover, it's not so easy as it looks."

"Bah!" Ossipon contradicted. "Don't be too sure of that. What's to prevent half-a-dozen of them jumping upon you from behind in the street? With your arms pinned to your sides you could do nothing—could you?"

"Yes; I could. I am seldom out in the streets after dark," said the little man, impassively, "and never very late. I walk always with my left hand closed round the india-rubber ball which I have in my trouser pocket. The pressing of this ball actuates a detonator inside the flask I carry in my pocket. It's the principle of the pneumatic instantaneous shutter for a camera lens. The tube leads up—"

With a swift, disclosing gesture he gave Ossipon a glimpse of an india-rubber tube, resembling a slender brown worm, issuing from the armhole of his waistcoat and plunging into the inner breast pocket of his jacket. His clothes, of a nondescript brown mixture, were threadbare and marked with stains, dusty in the folds, with ragged button-holes. "The detonator is partly mechanical, partly chemical," he explained, with casual condescension.

"It is instantaneous, of course?" murmured Ossipon, with a slight shudder.

"Far from it," confessed the other, with a reluctance which seemed to twist his mouth dolorously. "A full twenty seconds must elapse from the moment I press the ball till the explosion takes place."

"Phew!" whistled Ossipon, completely appalled. "Twenty seconds! Horrors! You mean to say that you could face that? I should go crazy—"

"Wouldn't matter if you did. Of course, it's the weak point of this special system, which is only for my own use. The worst is that the manner of exploding is always the weak point with us. I am trying to invent a detonator that would adjust itself to all conditions of action, and even to unexpected changes of conditions. A variable and yet perfectly precise mechanism. A really intelligent detonator."

"Twenty seconds," muttered Ossipon again. "Ough! And then—"

With a slight turn of the head the glitter of the spectacles seemed to gauge the size of the beer saloon in the basement of the renowned Silenus Restaurant.

"Nobody in this room could hope to escape," was the verdict of that survey. "Nor yet this couple going up the stairs now."

The piano at the foot of the staircase clanged through a mazurka with brazen impetuosity, as though a vulgar and impudent ghost were showing off. The keys sank and rose mysteriously. Then all became still. For a moment Ossipon imagined the overlighted place changed into a dreadful black hole belching horrible fumes choked with ghastly rubbish of smashed brickwork and mutilated corpses. He had such a distinct perception of ruin and death that he shuddered again. The other observed, with an air of calm sufficiency:

"In the last instance it is character alone that makes for one's safety. There are very few people in the world whose character is as well established as mine."

"I wonder how you managed it," growled Ossipon.

"Force of personality," said the other, without raising his voice; and coming from the mouth of that obviously miserable organism the assertion caused the robust Ossipon to bite his lower lip. "Force of personality," he repeated, with ostentatious calm.

"I have the means to make myself deadly, but that by itself, you understand, is absolutely nothing in the way of protection. What is effective is the belief those people have in my will to use the means. That's their impression. It is absolute. Therefore I am deadly."

"There are individuals of character amongst that lot, too," muttered Ossipon ominously.

"Possibly. But it is a matter of degree obviously, since, for instance, I am not impressed by them. Therefore they are inferior. They cannot be otherwise. Their character is built upon conventional morality. It leans on the social order. Mine stands free from everything artificial. They are bound in all sorts of conventions. They depend on life, which, in this connection, is a historical fact surrounded by all sorts of restraints and considerations, a complex, organized fact open to attack at every point; whereas I depend on death, which knows no restraint and cannot be attacked. My superiority is evident."

"This is a transcendental way of putting it," said Ossipon, watching the cold glitter of the round spectacles. "I've heard Karl Yundt say much the same thing not very long ago."

"Karl Yundt," mumbled the other, contemptuously, "the delegate of the International Red Committee, has been a posturing shadow all his life. There are three of you delegates, aren't there? I won't define the other two, as you are one of them. But what you say means nothing. You are the worthy delegates for revolutionary propaganda, but the trouble is not only that you are as unable to think independently as any respectable grocer or journalist of them all, but that you have no character whatever."

Ossipon could not restrain a start of indignation.

"But what do you want from us?" he exclaimed in a deadened voice. "What is it you are after yourself?"

"A perfect detonator," was the peremptory answer. "What are you making that face for? You see, you can't even bear the mention of something conclusive."

"I am not making a face," growled the annoyed Ossipon, bearishly.

"You revolutionists," the other continued, with leisurely self-confidence, "are the slaves of the social convention, which is afraid of you; slaves of it as much as the very police that stands up in the defence of that convention. Clearly you are, since you want to revolutionize it. It governs your thought, of course, and your action, too, and thus neither your thought nor your action can ever be conclusive." He paused, tranquil, with that air of close, endless silence, then almost immediately went on: "You are not a bit better than the forces arrayed against you—than the police, for instance. The other day I came suddenly upon Chief Inspector Heat at the corner of Tottenham Court Road. He looked at me very

steadily. But I did not look at him. Why should I give him more than a glance? He was thinking of many things—of his superiors, of his reputation, of the law courts, of his salary, of newspapers—of a hundred things. But I was thinking of my perfect detonator only. He meant nothing to me. He was as insignificant as—I can't call to mind anything insignificant enough to compare him with—except Karl Yundt perhaps. Like to like. The terrorist and the policeman both come from the same basket. Revolution, legality—counter moves in the same game; forms of idleness at bottom identical. He plays his little game—so do you propagandists. But I don't play; I work fourteen hours a day, and go hungry sometimes. My experiments cost money now and again, and then I must do without food for a day or two. You're looking at my beer. Yes. I have had two glasses already, and shall have another presently. This is a little holiday, and I celebrate it alone. Why not? I've the grit to work alone, quite alone, absolutely alone. I've worked alone for years."

Ossipon's face had turned dusky red.

"At the perfect detonator—eh?" he sneered, very low.

"Yes," retorted the other. "It is a good definition. You couldn't find anything half so precise to define the nature of your activity with all your committees and delegations. It is I who am the true propagandist."

"We won't discuss that point," said Ossipon, with an air of rising above personal considerations. "I am afraid I'll have to spoil your holiday for you, though. There's a man blown up in Greenwich Park this morning."

"How do you know?"

"They have been yelling the news in the streets since two o'clock. I bought the paper, and just ran in here. Then I saw you sitting at this table. I've got it in my pocket now."

He pulled the newspaper out. It was a good-sized, rosy sheet, as if flushed by the warmth of its own convictions, which were optimistic. He scanned the pages rapidly.

"Ah! Here it is. Bomb in Greenwich Park. There isn't much so far. Half-past eleven. Foggy morning. Effects of explosion felt as far as Romney Road and Park Place. Enormous hole in the ground under a tree filled with smashed roots and broken branches. All round fragments of a man's body blown to pieces. That's all. The rest's mere newspaper gup. No doubt a wicked attempt to blow up the Observatory, they say. H'm. That's hardly credible."

He looked at the paper for a while longer in silence then passed it to the other, who after gazing abstractedly at the print laid it down without comment.

It was Ossipon who spoke first—still resentful.

"The fragments of only *one* man, you note. Ergo: blew *himself* up. That spoils your day off for you—don't it? Were you expecting that sort of move? I hadn't the slightest idea—not the ghost of a notion of anything of the sort being planned to come off here—in this country. Under the present circumstances it's nothing short of criminal."

The little man lifted his thin black eyebrows with dispassionate scorn.

"Criminal! What is that? What *is* crime? What can be the meaning of such an assertion?"

"How am I to express myself? One must use the current words," said Ossipon, impatiently. "The meaning of this assertion is that this business may affect our position very adversely in this country. Isn't that crime enough for you? I am convinced you have been giving away some of your stuff lately."

Ossipon stared hard. The other, without flinching, lowered and raised his head slowly.

"You have!" burst out the editor of the F. P. leaflets in an intense whisper. "No! And are you really handing it over at large like this, for the asking, to the first fool that comes along?"

"Just so! The condemned social order has not been built up on paper and ink, and I don't fancy that a combination of paper and ink will ever put an end to it, whatever you may think. Yes, I would give the stuff with both hands to every man, woman, or fool that likes to come along. I know what you are thinking about. But I am not taking my cue from the Red Committee. I would see you all hounded out of here, or arrested—or beheaded for that matter—without turning a hair. What happens to us as individuals is not of the least consequence."

He spoke carelessly, without heat, almost without feeling, and Ossipon, secretly much affected, tried to copy this detachment.

"If the police here knew their business they would shoot you full of holes with revolvers, or else try to sandbag you from behind in broad daylight."

The little man seemed already to have considered that point of view in his dispassionate, self-confident manner.

"Yes," he assented with the utmost readiness. "But for that they would have to face their own institutions. Do you see? That requires uncommon grit. Grit of a special kind."

Ossipon blinked.

"I fancy that's exactly what would happen to you if you were to set up your laboratory in the States. They don't stand on ceremony with their institutions there."

"I am not likely to go and see. Otherwise your remark is just," admitted the other. "They have more character over there, and their character is essentially anarchistic. Fertile ground for us, the States—very good ground. The great Republic has the root of the destructive matter in her. The collective temperament is lawless. Excellent. They may shoot us down, but—"

"You are too transcendental for me," growled Ossipon, with moody concern.

"Logical," protested the other. "There are several kinds of logic. This is the enlightened kind. America is all right. It is this country that is dangerous, with her idealistic conception of legality. The social spirit of this people is wrapped up in scrupulous prejudices, and that is fatal to our work. You talk of England being our only refuge! So much the worse. Capua! What do we want with refuges? Here you talk print, plot, and do nothing. I daresay it's very convenient for such Karl Yundts."

He shrugged his shoulders slightly, then added with the same leisurely assurance: "To break up the superstition and worship of legality should be our aim. Nothing would please me more than to see Inspector Heat and his likes take to shooting us down in broad daylight with the approval of the public. Half our battle would be won then; the disintegration of the old morality would have set in in its very temple. That is what you ought to aim at. But you revolutionists will never understand that. You plan the future, you lose yourselves in reveries of economical systems derived from what is; whereas what's wanted is a clean sweep and a clear start for a new conception of life. That sort of future will take care of itself if you will only make room for it. Therefore I would shovel my stuff in heaps at the corners of the streets if I had enough for that; and as I haven't, I do my best by perfecting a really dependable detonator."

Ossipon, who had been mentally swimming in deep waters, seized upon the last word as if it were a saving plank.

"Yes. Your detonators. I shouldn't wonder if it weren't one of your detonators that made a clean sweep of the man in the park."

A shade of vexation darkened the determined, sallow face confronting Ossipon.

"My difficulty consists precisely in experimenting practically with the various kinds. They must be tried, after all. Besides—"

Ossipon interrupted.

"Who could that fellow be? I assure you that we in London had no knowledge— Couldn't you describe the person you gave the stuff to?"

The other turned his spectacles upon Ossipon like a pair of searchlights.

"Describe him," he repeated, slowly. "I don't think there can be the slightest objection now. I will describe him to you in one word—Verloc."

Ossipon, whom curiosity had lifted a few inches off his seat, dropped back, as if hit in the face.

"Verloc! Impossible."

The self-possessed little man nodded slightly once.

"Yes. He's the person. You can't say that in this case I was giving my stuff to the first fool that came along. He was a prominent member of the group as far as I understand."

"Yes," said Ossipon. "Prominent. No, not exactly. He was the centre for general intelligence, and usually received comrades coming over here. More useful than important. Man of no ideas. Years ago he used to speak at meetings—in France, I believe. Not very well, though. He was trusted by such men as Latorre, Moser, and all that old lot. The only talent he showed really was his ability to elude the attentions of the police somehow. Here, for instance, he did not seem to be looked after very closely. He was regularly married, you know. I suppose it's with her money that he started that shop. Seemed to make it pay, too."

Ossipon paused abruptly, muttered to himself "I wonder what that woman will do now?" and fell into thought.

The other waited with ostentatious indifference. His parentage was obscure, and he was generally known only by his nickname of Professor. His title to that designation consisted in his having been once assistant demonstrator in chemistry at some technical institute. He quarrelled with the authorities upon a question of unfair treatment. Afterwards he obtained a post in the laboratory of a manufactory of dyes. There, too, he had been treated with revolting injustice. His struggles, his privations, his hard work to raise himself in the social scale, had filled him with such an exalted conviction of his merits that it was extremely difficult for the world to treat him with justice—the standard of that notion depending so much upon the patience of the individual. The Professor had genius, but lacked the great social virtue of resignation.

"Intellectually a nonentity," Ossipon pronounced aloud, abandoning suddenly the inward contemplation of Mrs. Verloc's bereaved person and business. "Quite an ordinary personality. You are wrong in not keeping more in touch with the comrades, Professor," he added in a reproving tone. "Did he say anything to you—give you some idea of his intentions? I hadn't seen him for a month. It seems impossible that he should be gone."

"He told me it was going to be a demonstration against a building," said the Professor. "I had to know that much to prepare the missile. I pointed out to him that I had hardly a sufficient quantity for a completely destructive result, but he pressed me very earnestly to do my best. As he wanted something that could be carried openly in the hand, I proposed to make use of an old one-gallon copal varnish can I happened to have by me. He was pleased at the idea. It gave me some trouble, because I had to cut out the bottom first and solder it on again afterwards. When prepared for use, the can enclosed a wide-mouthed, well-corked jar of thick glass packed around with some wet clay and containing sixteen ounces of X_2 green powder. The detonator was connected with the screw top of the can. It was ingenious—a combination of time and shock. I explained the system to him. It was a thin tube of tin enclosing a—"

Ossipon's attention had wandered.

"What do you think has happened?" he interrupted.

"Can't tell. Screwed the top on tight, which would make the connection, and then forgot the time. It was set for twenty minutes. On the other hand, the time contact being made, a sharp shock would bring about the explosion at once. He either ran the time too close, or simply let the thing fall. The contact was made all right—that's clear to me at any rate. The system's worked perfectly. And yet you would think that a common fool in a hurry would be much more likely to forget to make the contact altogether. I was worrying myself about that sort of failure mostly. But there are more kinds of fools than one can guard against. You can't expect a detonator to be absolutely foolproof."

He beckoned to a waiter. Ossipon sat rigid, with the abstracted gaze of mental travail. After the man had gone away with the money he roused himself, with an air of profound dissatisfaction.

"It's extremely unpleasant for me," he mused. "Karl has been in bed with bronchitis for a week. There's an even chance that he will never get up again. Michaelis is luxuriating in the country somewhere. A fashionable publisher has offered him five hundred pounds for a book. It will be a ghastly failure. He has lost the habit of consecutive thinking in prison, you know."

The Professor on his feet, now buttoning his coat, looked about him with perfect indifference.

"What are you going to do?" asked Ossipon, wearily. He dreaded the blame of the Central Red Committee, a body which had no permanent place of abode, and of whose membership he was not exactly informed. If this affair eventuated in the stoppage of the modest subsidy allotted to the publication of the F. P. pamphlets, then indeed he would have to regret Verloc's inexplicable folly.

"Solidarity with the extremest form of action is one thing, and silly recklessness is another," he said, with a sort of moody brutality. "I don't know what came to Verloc. There's some mystery there. However, he's gone. You may take it as you like, but under the circumstances the only policy for the militant revolutionary group is to disclaim all connection with this damned freak of yours. How to make the disclaimer convincing enough is what bothers me."

The little man on his feet, buttoned up and ready to go, was no taller than the seated Ossipon. He leveled his spectacles at the latter's face point-blank.

"You might ask the police for a testimonial of good conduct. They know where every one of you slept last night. Perhaps if you asked them they would consent to publish some sort of official statement."

"No doubt they are aware well enough that we had nothing to do with this," mumbled Ossipon, bitterly. "What they will say is another thing." He remained thoughtful, disregarding the short, owlish, shabby figure standing by his side. "I must lay hands on Michaelis at once, and get him to speak from his heart at one of our gatherings. The public has a sort of sentimental regard for that fellow. His name is known. And I am in touch with a few reporters on the big dailies. What he would say would be utter bosh, but he has a turn of talk that makes it go down all the same."

"Like treacle," interjected the Professor, rather low, keeping an impassive expression.

The perplexed Ossipon went on communing with himself half audibly, after the manner of a man reflecting in perfect solitude.

"Confounded ass! To leave such an imbecile business on my hands. And I don't even know if—"

He sat with compressed lips. The idea of going for news straight to the shop lacked charm. His notion was that Verloc's shop might have been turned already into a police trap. They will be bound to make some arrests, he thought, with something resembling virtuous indignation, for the even tenor of his revolutionary life was menaced by no fault of his. And yet unless he went there he ran the risk of remaining in ignorance of what perhaps it would be very material for him to know. Then he reflected that, if the man in the park had been so very much blown to pieces as the evening papers said, he could not have been identified. And if so, the police could have no special reason for watching Verloc's shop more closely than any other place known to be frequented by marked anarchists—no more reason, in fact, than for watching the doors of the Silenus. There would be a lot of watching all round, no matter where he went. Still—

"I wonder what I had better do now?" he muttered, taking counsel with himself.

A rasping voice at his elbow said, with sedate scorn:

"Fasten yourself upon the woman for all she's worth."

After uttering these words the Professor walked away from the table. Ossipon, whom that piece of insight had taken unawares, gave one ineffectual start, and remained still, with a helpless gaze, as though nailed fast to the seat of his chair. The lonely piano, without as much as a music stool to help it, struck a few chords courageously, and beginning a selection of national airs, played him out at last to the tune of "The Blue-bells of Scotland." The painfully detached notes grew faint behind his back while he went slowly upstairs, across the hall, and into the street.

In front of the great doorway a dismal row of newspaper sellers standing clear of the pavement dealt out their wares from the gutter. It was a raw, gloomy day of the early spring; and the grimy sky, the mud of the streets, the rags of the dirty men harmonized excellently with the eruption of the damp, rubbishy sheets of paper soiled with printers' ink. The posters, maculated with filth, garnished like tapestry the sweep of the curb-stone. The trade in afternoon papers was brisk, yet, in comparison with the swift, constant march of foot traffic, the effect was of indifference, of a disregarded distribution. Ossipon looked hurriedly both ways before stepping out into the cross-currents, but the Professor was already out of sight.

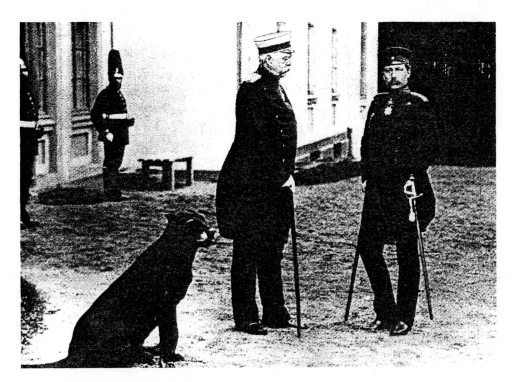

PART FIFTEEN

Photo of Meeting of Bismarck and Wilhelm II, 1888

The photograph of an 1888 meeting between Bismarck and the young Kaiser captures many of the problems of the late nineteenth and early twentieth century leading to World War I. The image's themes are the troubled relationship between the two leaders and the militarized atmosphere (note the uniforms both are wearing). Two years after this meeting, the inexperienced and headstrong Wilhelm forced Bismarck to resign by refusing to endorse his German-Russian alliance. Wilhelm believed that German military power was sufficient and the German nation great enough on its own to forgo help from Russia. The Franco-Russian alliance of 1894, a direct result of Wilhelm's policy, divided Europe in a way disadvantageous for Germany and headed the continent toward war. The postures of the two figures almost seem to suggest the problems that led to a fundamental realignment of European diplomacy from Bismarck's cynical but sound structures aimed at avoiding war to reliance on military force.

Pre-War Politics and Society

Historians often describe the early twentieth century as part of a long nineteenth century from 1789 to 1914. In this view, the French Revolution and Great War, rather than 1800 and 1900, were watersheds in European history. Of course, much changed after 1914, but the new world was already underway. The desire for national self-determination, a catch-phrase of the 1919 Paris peace conference, already appeared in nineteenth-century struggles for national independence. Although no European-wide conflicts broke out after the final defeat of Napoleon in 1815, war had hardly disappeared from the scene only to reappear in 1914. Europe had witnessed the Crimean War (1854–1856), the Franco-Prussian War (1870–1871), and other conflicts. Furthermore, as the photograph of Bismarck and Wilhelm II (1859–1941) reminds us, great European nations were forming military alliances aimed at conflict. They also engaged in huge military build-ups. By 1900, the British were fighting the Boers of South Africa and European armed forces were struggling against the "Boxers" in China. A few years later, the First and Second Balkan Wars broke out (1912 and 1913). World War I set in motion great changes but continuity still played a role. Pre-1914 politics, society, and culture thoroughly intertwined the old and the new.

As the twentieth century dawned, the Russian Empire remained an autocracy. Even as social discontent grew, Nicholas II (1868–1919) refused concessions. Yet when revolution broke out in 1905, the beleaguered emperor issued the October Manifesto that promised civil liberties and a Duma to be elected by all citizens. Unfortunately, once the revolutionary turmoil had quieted, Nicholas reneged on many of the manifesto's promises, thus setting the stage for the 1917 revolutions. Britain witnessed a different kind of struggle early in the new century. Beginning in 1908, Chancellor of the Exchequer (later Prime Minister) David Lloyd George (1863–1945) waged war on poverty. His 1909 People's Budget proposed progressive income and inheritance taxes that burdened the wealthy to pay for social programs and the Royal Navy. When the House of Lords rejected the budget, a new law weakened its power, after which the program went into effect. The movement toward national self-determination faltered in 1908 when Austro-Hungarian Emperor Francis-Joseph (1830–1918) annexed Bosnia and Herzegovina, former Ottoman territories under Austro-Hungarian administration. In the cultural realm, Marcel Proust (1871–1922) encapsulated the new century's characteristic blending of the old and new by exploring memory and sensation against the backdrop of wealthy, aristocratic French society in his novel, *Swann's Way* (1913).

Study Questions

1. What do Nicholas II's and Lloyd George's policies tell us about their nations?
2. In light of the October Manifesto, how does Russia compare to Western Europe?
3. What was so serious about Austria-Hungary's annexation of Bosnia?
4. What is modern about Proust's focus on memory and sensation?
5. Do these selections better serve to end one era or begin another?
6. Image: What does this photo suggest about Wilhelm's relationship to Bismarck?

October Manifesto, 1905

Nicholas II

In the midst of the 1905 revolution, Emperor Nicholas reluctantly endorsed the October Manifesto's guarantees, although he and his wife Alexandra still believed in autocracy. When conditions improved, the government infringed upon many of the new rights granted to society, placing the tsarist government in conflict with much of the Russian Empire's population. An emperor who hated the very idea of a constitution presided over a modernizing economy and a population that wanted to participate in the nation's governance. These contradictions did not promise good results when Russia was drawn into world conflict in 1914.

On the Improvement of Order in the State

The disturbances and unrest in St. Petersburg, Moscow and in many other parts of our Empire have filled Our heart with great and profound sorrow. The welfare of the Russian Sovereign and His people is inseparable and national sorrow is His too. The present disturbances could give rise to national instability and present a threat to the unity of Our State. The oath which We took as Tsar compels Us to use all Our strength, intelligence and power to put a speedy end to this unrest which is so dangerous for the State. The relevant authorities have been ordered to take measures to deal with direct outbreaks of disorder and violence and to protect people who only want to go about their daily business in peace. However, in view of the need to speedily implement earlier measures to pacify the country, we have decided that the work of the government must be unified. We have therefore ordered the government to take the following measures in fulfillment of our unbending will:

1. Fundamental civil freedoms will be granted to the population, including real personal inviolability, freedom of conscience, speech, assembly and association.

2. Participation in the Duma will be granted to those classes of the population which are at present deprived of voting powers, insofar as is possible in the short period before the convocation of the Duma, and this will lead to the development of a universal franchise. There will be no delay to the Duma elect already been organized.

3. It is established as an unshakeable rule that no law can come into force without its approval by the State Duma and representatives of the people will be given the opportunity to take real part in the supervision of the legality of government bodies.

We call on all true sons of Russia to remember the homeland, to help put a stop to this unprecedented unrest and, together with this, to devote all their strength to the restoration of peace to their native land.

From: *Polnoe sobranie zakonov Rossiiskoi Imperii*, 3rd series, vol. XXV/I, no. 26803. www.dur.ac.uk/~dm10www/octmannif.html

People's Budget

David Lloyd George

Born to a middle-class religious family, Lloyd George became a star orator and defender of the common folk in the Parliament. As Chancellor of the Exchequer (Finance Minister), during 1909 he pushed the People's Budget, a graduated income tax to finance old age pensions. After overcoming opposition from the conservative House of Lords, he further expanded coverage to include health and unemployment insurance and in 1911 passed a bill that reduced the House of Lords' traditional powers. Great Britain joined other European countries in extending protection to the population, a development that ensured popular support when World War I broke out.

Extract from Mr. Lloyd George's speech at Limehouse 30 July 1909 as reported in *The Times* 31 July 1909

Under the auspices of the Budget League Mr Lloyd-George, Chancellor of the Exchequer, addressed a very large meeting in the Edinburgh Castle, Limehouse, last night. The building was crowded with an audience which numbered about 4,000.

A large body of police was on duty outside the building. The suffragists mustered in considerable strength and endeavoured to get admission to the hall. They were, however, repulsed by the officers who were charged with the duty of keeping the doors. Mr Lloyd-George, who was accompanied by Mrs Lloyd-George, had an enthusiastic reception on reaching the platform.

Whilst the cheers which greeted him were in progress a man who wore the suffragist colours climbed up the pillar supporting the roof and tied himself to it. He was soon followed by half-a-dozen stewards. One climbed up to him, and, pulling out a knife, cut the straps and ropes by which the individual had fastened himself. They then hauled the man down among the great crowd of stewards collected around the base of the pillar. It was soon apparent that several

From: J. H. Bettey, *English Historical Documents 1906–1939* (London: Routledge & Kegan Paul, 1967), pp. 15–19.

sympathizers with the suffragists had ranged themselves in the particular quarter of the hall, and six of them were promptly removed. Though the stewards apparently used no more violence than was necessary, each man received a rough handling at the hands of the members of the audience whom he passed, and one, it was stated, had to be taken to hospital.

Mr Lloyd-George, who on rising had an enthusiastic reception, said, 'A few months ago a meeting was held not far from this hall, in the heart of the City of London, demanding that the Government should launch out and run into enormous expenditure on the Navy. That meeting ended up with a resolution promising that those who passed that resolution would give financial support to the Government in their undertaking. There have been two or three meetings held in the City of London since (laughter and cheers), attended by the same class of people, but not ending up with a resolution promising to pay. (Laughter.) On the contrary, we are spending the money, but they won't pay. (Laughter.) What has happened since to alter their tone? Simply that we have sent in the bill. (Laughter and cheers.) We started our four Dreadnoughts. They cost eight millions of money. We promised them four more; they cost another eight millions. Somebody has got to pay, and these gentlemen say, "Perfectly true; somebody has got to pay, but we would rather that somebody were somebody else." (Laughter.) We started building; we wanted money to pay for the building; so we sent the hat round. (Laughter.) We sent it round amongst the workmen (hear, hear), and the miners of Derbyshire (loud cheers) and Yorkshire, the weavers of High Peak (cheers) and the Scotchmen of Dumfries (cheers), who, like all their countrymen, know the value of money. (Laughter.) They all brought in their coppers. We went round Belgravia, but there has been such a howl ever since that it has completely deafened us.'

Old Age Pensions

'But they say "It is not so much the Dreadnoughts we object to, it is the pensions." (Hear, hear.) If they object to pensions, why did they promise them? (Cheers.) They won elections on the strength of their promises. It is true they never carried them out. (Laughter.) Deception is always a pretty contemptible vice, but to deceive the poor is the meanest of all crimes. (Cheers.) But they say, "When we promised pensions we meant pensions at the expense of the people for whom they were provided. We simply meant to bring in a Bill to compel workmen to contribute to their own pensions." (Laughter.) If that is what they meant, why did they not say so? (Cheers.) The Budget, as your chairman has already so well reminded you, is introduced not merely for the purpose of raising barren taxes, but taxes that are fertile taxes, taxes that will bring forth fruit—the security of the country which is paramount in the minds of all. The provision for the aged and deserving poor— it was time it was done. (Cheers.) It is rather a shame for a rich country like ours—probably the richest country in the world, if not the richest the world has ever seen—that it should allow those who have toiled all their days to end in penury and possibly starvation. (Hear, hear.) It is rather hard that an old workman should have to find his way to the gates of the tomb, bleeding and footsore, through the brambles and thorns of poverty. (Cheers.) We cut a new path through it (cheers) an easier one, a pleasanter one, through fields of waving corn. We are raising money to pay for the new road (cheers), aye, and to widen it so that 200,000 paupers shall be

able to join in the march. (Cheers.) There are many in the country blessed by Providence with great wealth, and if there are amongst them men who grudge out of their riches a fair contribution towards the less fortunate of their fellow-countrymen they are shabby rich men. (Cheers.) We propose to do more by means of the Budget. We are raising money to provide against the evils and the sufferings that follow from unemployment. (Cheers.) We are raising money for the purpose of assisting our great friendly societies to provide for the sick and the widows and orphans. We are providing money to enable us to develop the resources of our own land. (Cheers.) I do not believe any fair-minded man would challenge the justice and the fairness of the objects which we have in view in raising this money.'

*   *   *

'The other day, at the great Tory meeting held at the Cannon-street Hotel, they had blazoned on the walls, "We protest against the Budget in the name of democracy—(loud laughter)—liberty, and justice." Where does the democracy come in in this landed system? Where is the justice in all these transactions? We claim that the tax we impose on land is fair, just, and moderate. (Cheers.) They go on threatening that if we proceed they will cut down their benefactions and discharge labour. What kind of labour? (A voice, "Hard labour," and laughter.) What is the labour they are going to choose for dismissal? Are they going to threaten to devastate rural England while feeding themselves, and dressing themselves? Are they going to reduce their gamekeepers? That would be sad! (Laughter.) The agricultural labourer and the farmer might then have some part of the game which they fatten with their labour. But what would happen to you in the season? No week-end shooting with the Duke of Norfolk for any of us! (Laughter.) But that is not the kind of labour that they are going to cut down. They are going to cut down productive labour— builders and gardeners—and they are going to ruin their property so that it shall not be taxed. All I can say is this—the ownership of land is not merely an enjoyment, it is a stewardship. (Cheers.) It has been reckoned as such in the past, and if they cease to discharge their functions, the security and defence of the country, looking after the broken in their villages and neighbourhoods—then those functions which are part of the traditional duties attached to the ownership of land and which have given to it its title—if they cease to discharge those functions, the time will come to reconsider the conditions under which land is held in this country. (Loud cheers.) No country, however rich, can permanently afford to have quartered upon its revenue a class which declines to do the duty which it was called upon to perform. (Hear, hear.) And, therefore, it is one of the prime duties of statesmanship to investigate those conditions. But I do not believe it. They have threatened and menaced like that before. They have seen it is not to their interest to carry out these futile menaces. They are now protesting against paying their fair share of the taxation of the land, and they are doing so by saying: "You are burdening the community; you are putting burdens upon the people which they cannot bear." Ah! they are not thinking of themselves. (Laughter.) Noble souls! (Laughter.) It is not the great dukes they are feeling for, it is the market gardener (laughter), it is the builder, and it was, until recently, the small holder. (Hear, hear.) In every debate in the House of Commons they said: "We are not worrying for ourselves. We can afford it with our broad acres; but just think of the little man who has only got a few acres"; and we were so very

impressed with this tearful appeal that at last we said, "We will leave him out." (Cheers.) And I almost expected to see Mr Pretyman jump over the table and say: "Fall on my neck and embrace me." (Loud laughter.) Instead of that, he stiffened up, his face wreathed with anger, and he said, "The Budget is more unjust than ever." (Laughter and cheers.) Oh! no. We are placing the burdens on the broad shoulders. (Cheers.) Why should I put burdens on the people? I am one of the children of the people. (Loud and prolonged cheering, and a voice, "Bravo, David; stand by the people and they will stand by you.") I was brought up amongst them. I know their trials; and God forbid that I should add one grain of trouble to the anxiety which they bear with such patience and fortitude. (Cheers.) When the Prime Minister did me the honour of inviting me to take charge of the National Exchquer (A voice, "He knew what he was about," and laughter) at a time of great difficulty, I made up my mind, in framing the Budget which was in front of me, that at any rate no cupboard should be bared (loud cheers), no lot would be harder to bear. (Cheers.) By that test, I challenge them to judge the Budget.' (Loud and long-continued cheers, during which the right hon. gentleman resumed his seat.) Afterwards the audience rose and sang, *For he's a jolly good fellow.*

A resolution was carried in favour of the Budget.

On the Annexation of Bosnia and Herzegovina

Francis-Joseph

Austria-Hungary wished to compensate for its lack of a global empire by expanding into the Balkans. In 1908 Francis-Joseph annexed Bosnia and Herzegovina, former Ottoman territories under temporary Austro-Hungarian administration. The territories' intermixed Catholic, Orthodox, and Muslim populations (ethnically Croatians, Serbs, and Bosnian Muslims) offered daunting problems, unresolved even a century later. The annexation, a power play not hidden by Francis-Joseph's rhetoric of freedom and security, frustrated the national sentiments of Serbs and insulted a Russian Empire publicly committed to protecting their fellow Orthodox brothers.

We, Francis-Joseph, Emperor of Austria, King of Bohemia, and Apostolic King of Hungary, to the inhabitants of Bosnia and Herzegovina:

When a generation ago our troops crossed the borders of your lands, you were assured that they came not as foes, but as friends, with the firm determination to remedy the evils from which your fatherland had suffered so grievously for many years. This promise given at a serious moment has been honestly kept. It has been the constant endeavor of our government to guide the country by patient and systematic activity to a happier future.

To our great joy we can say that the seed then scattered in the furrows of a troubled soil has richly thrived. You yourselves must feel it a boon that order and security have replaced violence and oppression, that trade and traffic are constantly extending, that the elevating influence of education has been brought to bear in your country, and that under the shield of an orderly administration every man may enjoy the fruits of his labors.

It is the duty of us all to advance steadily along this path. With this goal before our eyes, we deem the moment come to give the inhabitants of the two

From: James Harvey Robinson and Charles A. Beard, eds. *Readings in Modern European History*, vol. II (Boston: Ginn & Company, 1909), pp. 401–403.

lands a new proof of our trust in their political maturity. In order to raise Bosnia and Herzegovina to a higher level of political life we have resolved to grant both of those lands constitutional governments that are suited to the prevailing conditions and general interests, so as to create a legal basis for the representation of their wishes and needs. You shall henceforth have a voice when decisions are made concerning your domestic affairs, which, as hitherto, will have a separate administration. But the necessary premise for the introduction of this provincial constitution is the creation of a clear and unambiguous legal status for the two lands.

For this reason, and also remembering the ties that existed of yore between our glorious ancestors on the Hungarian throne and these lands, we extend our suzerainty over Bosnia and Herzegovina, and it is our will that the order of succession of our House be extended to these lands also. The inhabitants of the two lands thus share all the benefits which a lasting confirmation of the present relation can offer. The new order of things will be a guarantee that civilization and prosperity will find a sure footing in your home.

Inhabitants of Bosnia and Herzegovina:

Among the many cares of our throne, solicitude for your material and spiritual welfare shall not be the last. The exalted idea of equal rights for all before the law, a share in the legislation and administration of the provincial affairs, equal protection for all religious creeds, languages, and racial differences, all these high possessions you shall enjoy in full measure. The freedom of the individual and the welfare of the whole will be the aim of our government in the two lands. You will surely show yourselves worthy of the trust placed in you, by attachment and loyalty to us and to our House. And thus we hope that the noble harmony between the prince and the people, that dearest pledge of all social progress, will ever accompany us on our common path.

FRANCIS-JOSEPH

Swann's Way

Marcel Proust

Swann's Way, the opening novel of Proust's masterwork, Remembrance of Things Past, *sets the stage for a lengthy unfolding of memories of an unnamed novelistic hero. Beset by chronic illnesses and allergies, Proust himself gradually withdrew from the outside world, which he replaced with a rich inner life, as suggested by this selection's childhood reminiscence of a natural world almost magical in its beauty. The literary withdrawal from present-day life was one of the hallmarks of modernism. The world of art and literature mirrored the new uncertainties of science, religion, and politics.*

For there were, in the environs of Combray, two 'ways' which we used to take for our walks, and so diametrically opposed that we would actually leave the house by a different door, according to the way we had chosen: the way towards Méséglise-la-Vineuse, which we called also 'Swann's way,' because, to get there, one had to pass along the boundary of M. Swann's estate, and the 'Guermantes way.' Of Méséglise-la-Vineuse, to tell the truth, I never knew anything more than the way there, and the strange people who would come over on Sundays to take the air in Combray, people whom, this time, neither my aunt nor any of us would 'know at all,' and whom we would therefore assume to be 'people who must have come over from Méséglise.' As for Guermantes, I was to know it well enough one day, but that day had still to come; and, during the whole of my boyhood, if Méséglise was to me something as inaccessible as the horizon, which remained hidden from sight, however far one went, by the folds of a country which no longer bore the least resemblance to the country round Combray; Guermantes, on the other hand, meant no more than the ultimate goal, ideal rather than real, of the 'Guermantes way,' a sort of abstract geographical term like the North Pole or the Equator. And so to 'take the Guermantes way' in order to get to Méséglise, or *vice versa*, would

have seemed to me as nonsensical a proceeding as to turn to the east in order to reach the west. Since my father used always to speak of the 'Méséglise way' as comprising the finest view of a plain that he knew anywhere, and of the 'Guermantes way' as typical of river scenery, I had invested each of them, by conceiving them in this way as two distinct entities, with that cohesion, that unity which belongs only to the figments of the mind; the smallest detail of either of them appeared to me as a precious thing, which exhibited the special excellence of the whole, while, immediately beside them, in the first stages of our walk, before we had reached the sacred soil of one or the other, the purely material roads, at definite points on which they were set down as the ideal view over a plain and the ideal scenery of a river, were no more worth the trouble of looking at them than, to a keen playgoer and lover of dramatic art, are the little streets which may happen to run past the walls of a theatre. But, above all, I set between them, far more distinctly than the mere distance in miles and yards and inches which separated one from the other, the distance that there was between the two parts of my brain in which I used to think of them, one of those distances of the mind which time serves only to lengthen, which separate things irremediably from one another, keeping them for ever upon different planes. And this distinction was rendered still more absolute because the habit we had of never going both ways on the same day, or in the course of the same walk, but the 'Méséglise way'

From: Marcel Proust, *Swann's Way*, trans. C.K. Scott Moncrieff (New York: Vintage Books, 1928). Pp. 103–106.

one time and the 'Guermantes way' another, shut them up, so to speak, far apart and unaware of each other's existence, in the sealed vessels—between which there could be no communication—of separate afternoons.

When we had decided to go the 'Méséglise way' we would start (without undue haste, and even if the sky were clouded over, since the walk was not very long, and did not take us too far from home), as though we were not going anywhere in particular, by the front-door of my aunt's house, which opened on to the Rue du Saint-Esprit. We would be greeted by the gunsmith, we would drop our letters into the box, we would tell Théodore, from Françoise, as we passed, that she had run out of oil or coffee, and we would leave the town by the road which ran along the white fence of M. Swann's park. Before reaching it we would be met on our way by the scent of his lilac-trees, come out to welcome strangers. Out of the fresh little green hearts of their foliage the lilacs raised inquisitively over the fence of the park their plumes of white or purple blossom, which glowed, even in the shade, with the sunlight in which they had been bathed. Some of them, half-concealed by the little tiled house, called the Archers' Lodge, in which Swann's keeper lived, overtopped its gothic gable with their rosy minaret. The nymphs of spring would have seemed coarse and vulgar in comparison with these young houris, who retained, in this French garden, the pure and vivid colouring of a Persian miniature. Despite my desire to throw my arms about their pliant forms and to draw down towards me the starry locks that crowned their fragrant heads, we would pass them by without stopping, for my parents had ceased to visit Tansonville since Swann's marriage, and, so as not to appear to be looking into his park, we would, instead of taking the road which ran beside its boundary and then climbed straight up to the open fields, choose another way, which led in the same direction, but circuitously, and brought us out rather too far from home.

One day my grandfather said to my father: "Don't you remember Swann's telling us yesterday that his wife and daughter had gone off to Rheims and that he was taking the opportunity of spending a day or two in Paris? We might go along by the park, since the ladies are not at home; that will make it a little shorter."

We stopped for a moment by the fence. Lilac-time was nearly over; some of the trees still thrust aloft, in tall purple chandeliers, their tiny balls of blossom, but in many places among their foliage where, only a week before, they had still been breaking in waves of fragrant foam, these were now spent and shriveled and discoloured, a hollow scum, dry and scentless. My grandfather pointed out to my father in what respects the appearance of the place was still the same, and how far it had altered since the walk that he had taken with old M. Swann, on the day of his wife's death; and he seized the opportunity to tell us, once again, the story of that walk.

In front of us a path bordered with nasturtiums rose in the full glare of the sun towards the house. But to our right the park stretched away into the distance, on level ground. Overshadowed by the tall trees which stood close around it, an 'ornamental water' had been constructed by Swann's parents but, even in his most artificial creations, nature is the material upon which man has to work; certain spots will persist in remaining surrounded by the vassals of their own especial sovereignty, and will raise their immemorial standards among all the 'laid-out' scenery of a park, just as they would have done far from any human interference, in a solitude which must everywhere return to engulf them, springing up out of the necessities of their exposed position, and superimposing itself upon the work of man's hands. And so it was that, at the foot of the path which led down to this artificial lake, there might be seen, in its two tiers woven of trailing forget-me-nots below and of periwinkle flowers above, the natural, delicate, blue garland which binds the luminous, shadowed brows of water-nymphs; while the iris, its swords sweeping every way in regal profusion, stretched out over agrimony and water-growing king-cups the lilied scepters, tattered glories of yellow and purple, of the kingdom of the lake.

The absence of Mlle. Swann, which—since it preserved me from the terrible risk of seeing her appear on one of the paths, and of being identified and scorned by this so privileged little girl who had Bergotte for a friend and used to go with him to visit cathedrals—made the exploration of Tansonville, now for the first time permitted me, a matter of indifference to myself, seemed however to invest the property, in my grandfather's and father's eyes, with a fresh and transient charm, and (like an entirely cloudless sky when one is going mountaineering) to make the day extraordinarily propitious for a walk in this direction; I should have liked to see their reckoning proved false, to see, by a miracle, Mlle. Swann appear, with her father, so close to us that we should not have time to escape, and should therefore be obliged to make her acquaintance. And so, when I suddenly noticed a straw basket lying forgotten on the grass by the side of a line whose float was bobbing in the water, I made a great effort to keep my father and grandfather looking in another direction, away from this sign that she might, after all, be in residence. Still, as Swann had told us that he ought not, really, to go away just then, as he had some people staying in the house, the line might equally belong to one of these guests. Not a footstep was to be heard on any of the paths. Somewhere in one of the tall trees, making a stage in its height, an invisible bird, desperately attempting to make the day seem shorter, was exploring with a long, continuous note the solitude that pressed it on every side, but it received at once so unanimous an answer, so powerful a repercussion of silence and of immobility that, one would have said, it had arrested for all eternity the moment which it had been trying to make pass more quickly. The sunlight fell so implacably from a fixed sky that one was naturally inclined to slip away out of the reach of its attentions, and even the slumbering water, whose repose was perpetually being invaded by the insects that swarmed above its surface, while it dreamed, no doubt, of some imaginary maelstrom, intensified the uneasiness which the sight of that floating cork had wrought in me, by appearing to draw it at full speed across the silent reaches of a mirrored firmament; now almost vertical, it seemed on the point of plunging down out of sight, and I had begun to ask myself whether, setting aside the longing and the terror that I had of making her acquaintance, it was not actually my duty to warn Mlle. Swann that the fish was biting—when I was obliged to run after my father and grandfather, who were calling me, and were surprised that I had not followed them along the little path, climbing up hill towards the open fields, into which they had already turned. I found the whole path throbbing with the fragrance of hawthorn-blossom. The hedge resembled a series of chapels, whose walls were no longer visible under the mountains of flowers that were heaped upon their altars; while underneath, the sun cast a square of light upon the ground, as though it had shone in upon them through a window; the scent that swept out over me from them was as rich, and as circumscribed in its range, as though I had been standing before the Lady-altar, and the flowers, themselves adorned also, held out each its little bunch of glittering stamens with an air of inattention, fine, radiating 'nerves' in the flamboyant style of architecture, like those which, in church, framed the stair to the rood-loft or closed the perpendicular tracery of the windows, but here spread out into pools of fleshy white, like strawberry-beds in spring. How simple and rustic, in comparison with these, would seem the dog-roses which, in a few weeks' time, would be climbing the same hillside path in the heat of the sun, dressed in the smooth silk of their blushing pink bodices, which would be undone and scattered by the first breath of wind.

—ACKNOWLEDGMENTS—

Text acknowledgments

Declaration of the Rights of Woman: From *The French Revolution and Human Rights*, edited and translated by Lynn Hunt. Copyright © 1996 by Bedford/St. Martin's. Reproduced by permission of Bedford/St. Martin's.

Speech on Terror: Translated by Marguerite Greene from *Reimpression de l'ancien moniteur* (Paris), XIX.

Writings and Sayings: From *The Mind of Napoleon: A Selection From His Written and Spoken Words*, edited and translated by J. Christopher Herold. Copyright 1955 Columbia University Press. Reprinted with permission of the publisher.

A Harlot High and Low: From *A Harlot High and Low* by Honoré de Balzac, translated with an introduction by Rayner Heppenstall, London: Penguin Books, Ltd., 1970. Translation and Introduction copyright © Rayner Heppenstall, 1970. Reproduced by permission of Penguin Books Ltd.

The Sorrows of Young Werther: From *The Sorrows of Young Werther* by Johann Wolfgang von Goethe, translated by Burton Pike, copyright © 2004 by Random House, Inc. Used by permission of Modern Library, a division of Random House, Inc.

The Poor Fiddler: From *The Poor Fiddler*, translated from the German by Alexander and Elizabeth Henderson. Copyright © 1967 by Frederick Ungar. Reprinted with the permission of the publisher, The Continuum International Publishing Group.

Two Essays: *Factory Workers* and *How to Constitute a Working Class*: From *Flora Tristan, Utopian Feminist: Her Travel Diaries and Personal Crusade,* selected, translated and edited by Doris and Paul Beik, Bloomington, IN: Indiana University Press, 1993. Reprinted by permission of the publisher.

Three Essays: *Germany, England,* and *Russia: From On Politics, Literature, and National Character* by Germaine de Staël, translated and edited by Morroe Berger. Copyright © 2000 by Transaction Publishers. Reprinted by permission of the publisher.

Why I Mention Women: From *The Workers' Union* by Flora Tristan, translated by Beverly Livingston, (University of Illinois Press, 1983). Reprinted by permission of Beverly Livingston.

Anna Karenina: From *Anna Karenina* by Leo Tolstoy, edited by Leonard Kent & Nina Berberova, translated by Constance Garnett, copyright © 1965 by Random House, Inc. Used by permission of Random House, Inc.

A Doll's House: From *A Doll's House and Other Plays* by Henrik Ibsen, translated by Peter Watts, London: Penguin Books, Ltd, 1965. Copyright © Peter Watts, 1965. Reproduced by permission of Penguin Books, Ltd.

Photo Acknowledgments

Page 2: Reunion des Musees Internationaux/Art Resource, NY

Page 26: Culver Pictures

Page 50: Reunion des Musees Internationaux/Art Resource, NY

Page 82: Fogg Museum, Harvard University

Page 126: AKG London

Page 158: Jimmy Sime/Getty Images

Page 186: Culver Pictures

Page 218: Hulton Archive/Getty Images

Page 246: American Heritage/Carousel

Page 262: Bildarchiv Preussischer Kulturbesitz/Art Resource, NY

Page 284: National Gallery, London

Page 312: Mary Evans Picture Library/The Image Works

Page 315: Barbara and Rene Stoeltie

Page 319: From *The Crystal Palace Illustrated Catalogue*, by Dover Publications

Page 326: Hulton Archive/Getty Images

Page 354: The Granger Collection

Page 384: Keystone/Getty Images